What Others

"Frank Dixon, an accomplished writer on these topics, not only provides substantive evidence that needs widespread attention. He also describes the linkages between food, climate change and other societal challenges within a whole system perspective that, sadly, is too often missing. It's like Aristotle once told us two millennia ago, "The whole is greater than the sum of its parts."

—**T. Colin Campbell, PhD, Jacob Gould Schurman Professor Emeritus of Nutritional Biochemistry, Cornell University, Best-selling author of** *The China Study* **(2005, 2016),** *Whole* **(2013), and** *The Future of Nutrition* **(2020)**

"Frank Dixon has produced a monumentally sobering look at a modern food system that has done more to make people unwell than all the classic plagues of the ages. What we're seeing in our maniacal output of "products" purporting to be food is blow-back from over-investments in complexity with diminishing returns. What is mostly diminishing is the human species' ability to thrive and survive over time. But now we're moving into a whole new set of circumstances as techno-industrialism winds down due to energy and resource scarcity. The future will require us to live differently and Mr. Dixon's book is an excellent road-map for that journey."

—**James Howard Kunstler, Best-selling author of** *The Long Emergency* **and the** *World Made by Hand* **novels**

"Frank has a rare combination of being a detective, (like Michael Connolly), a magician and a wise sage, lifting the lid on the topic of Food, dispelling some of its mysteries and myths, revealing fascinating and enlightening truths. I changed my diet after reading the Food book, giving up eating meat which led to a better diet, enhancing good health. Do step into this fabulous book and improve the health of yourself and your family!

—**Ros Morley, B.A.Hons. Fine Art, MA Printmaking**

Everyone can benefit from reading Sustainable Food Production and Diet. Frank's food book has been life-changing for me.

His extensive research into industrial agriculture has sensitized me to the cruelty animals endure, what is in the food I eat and how it gets from the field and farm to my table.

Since reading this book, I have strived to eat more of a whole plant food diet and encourage others to do so. I now understand the extent to which it can help us improve our health, protect from chronic diseases, improve the environment and benefit all creatures on earth.

Although the content is at times upsetting, Frank remains optimistic. He manages to explain how this has happened to well-intentioned people and companies by flawed systems and advises on how we can improve our systems through specific strategies and advice. In addition, he helps us see the absurdities of our current systems with his great sense of humor throughout the book.

It energizes you immediately to take action by simply making changes in the food you eat and becoming part of the solution!

— Carol Anne Cushing, Executive Recruiter

Approximately 50 years ago, human civilization began to overstep earth's biological carrying capacity. Since then we have entered a period of accelerating ecosystem degradation and climate change, whose costs today overwhelm our economies and threaten our public health. One of the most overlooked elements of this threshold period is the destruction created by our industrial food systems, which have disrupted the capacities of the earth's arable land and seas to feed us. Frank Dixon walks us through this dilemma with devastating insight and clarity. In so doing, he presents us with two fundamental options: either continue with business as usual (an ego-centric lose-lose proposition) or work in harmony with life and each other in sustaining our shared resources (the eco-centric win-win alternative).

Jay Bragdon, Author of *Economies That Mimic Life*,
Director, Academy for Systems Change

SUSTAINABLE
FOOD
PRODUCTION & DIET

Sustainable Food Production and Diet
Global System Change Book Series, Volume 4 of 7

First Edition, published May 2022

Copyright © 2022 by Frank Dixon

Cover Design and Interior Layout by Reprospace, LLC

Paperback ISBN-13: 978-1-95268534-7

20220126

KITSAP
PUBLISHING

Published by Kitsap Publishing
P.O. Box 572
Poulsbo, WA 98370
www.KitsapPublishing.com

Dedication

Current and Future Generations. Adopting the suggestions in this book will greatly enhance the long-term well-being of humanity.

Animals. Honoring and protecting the innate rights of conscious beings on Earth increases our humanity and greatly benefits society.

Acknowledgment

Rosalind Morley, my dear friend who provided extensive editing and inspirational support for all of the Global System Change books.

Francis J. Dixon and Carol J. Dixon, my wonderful parents.

William B. Dixon and Kathleen Gavigan, my wise and supportive uncle and aunt.

Evelyn Brandin, my lifelong friend.

Contents

Foreword

by T. Colin Campell

Within the pages of this book, *Sustainable Food Production and Diet*, you will find a complete description of the effect of food choice on the environmental, health, hunger, animal cruelty and pandemic crises. Frank Dixon, an accomplished writer on these topics, not only provides substantive evidence that needs widespread attention. He also describes the linkages between food, climate change and other societal challenges within a whole system perspective that, sadly, is too often missing. It's like Aristotle once told us two millennia ago, "The whole is greater than the sum of its parts."

Understanding details of complex systems is critical information to help us solve problems. But that understanding is likely to mean little if we fail to consider their larger domain. It is absolutely essential to consider complex problems from Dixon's whole system perspective because, on the environmental and other crises, we don't have time to do otherwise.

This book places food production in the context of larger environmental, economic and political systems. It describes the root causes and systemic solutions to major challenges related to food production and diet. In doing so, the book empowers individuals to improve their lives and drive systemic change.

I particularly applaud his effort to bring into this whole system discussion the matter of food choice. A growing body of evidence now shows it to be THE KEY component to consider. Here again, within discussions on the biology of food choice, the Aristotelian philosophy looms large. That is, our choice of which food to eat ought to consider what it does to our health and how it is used by our body during consumption, digestion, metabolism, storage and excretion of its nutrient parts. That perspective is called 'nutrition'.

Unfortunately, most of the research effort on food and nutrition has been focused, almost exclusively, on the nutrient parts of food, rather than whole foods. But it is the whole interaction of nutrients where we see the huge impact on health. What Dixon describes for his 'global' perspective on sustainable food production and utilization dovetails beautifully with the same perspective concerning the biological utilization of food itself. Indeed, his Aristotelian argument extends throughout Nature.

—T. Colin Campbell, PhD

Jacob Gould Schurman Professor Emeritus of Nutritional Biochemistry, Cornell University, Author of *The China Study* (2005, 2016), *Whole* (2013), and *The Future of Nutrition* (2020)

Introduction

Transforming food production and diet represents a huge, literally life-saving, potentially society-saving opportunity for humanity. Industrial agriculture and the foods it provides strongly degrade human health and environmental life support systems. They also are a main cause of global hunger and create vast pain and suffering among our fellow creatures on Earth. In addition, industrial animal operations provide a nearly perfect environment for the evolution of highly virulent and transmissible viruses that could decimate humanity.

Most people in developed countries have eaten industrial food their entire lives. They live under these systems, often unaware of the tremendous problems they cause. This book illuminates the extensive harm caused by industrial agriculture. A main theme is, darkness cannot survive in the light.

The book has two general purposes. First, it empowers individuals to strongly benefit themselves, their families and society. Second, the book facilitates system change by illuminating the characteristics of sustainable food production and diet and the actions needed to achieve them.

For individuals, switching to whole plant food diets usually is the single most powerful action they can take to improve their health, extend their lives, lose weight, protect the environment, relieve world hunger, reduce animal cruelty and prevent a pandemic that is far worse than COVID-19. About 75 percent of people in the US die of chronic diseases, including heart disease, cancer and diabetes. These diseases are rare among people who eat whole plant foods.

Producing animal products is one of the two most environmentally destructive activities on Earth (along with burning fossil fuels). It is grossly inefficient compared to producing plant products. Substantially reducing animal product production would create a large surplus of food and greatly reduce global hunger.

H5N1 influenza (60 percent lethality) and several other harmful viruses almost certainly evolved in industrial animal operations. Many experts believe it is only a matter of time before they spawn a deadly pandemic that shuts down much of human society. Billions of animals raised for food are being tortured and slaughtered each year in industrial operations. The extensive pain and suffering we impose on them reflects a profound lack of humanity.

Industrial agriculture provides a good example of the tragedy of the commons. It increases short-term food production at the expense of long-term production. To feed ourselves, we greatly reduce the ability of future generations to feed themselves. Consuming animal products and refined carbohydrates causes widespread chronic disease and greatly increases healthcare costs (by literally trillions of dollars over several years in the US). Growing animal product consumption, driven by rising incomes in several regions, is making the situation worse. We cannot feed a growing population increasing amounts of animal products. It will drive vast environmental destruction, hunger and chronic disease, and then cause system collapse.

Nearly all large food companies have implemented sustainability strategies. Many of them are substantially reducing their negative environmental and social impacts and providing healthier food products. But in spite of this good work, the negative impacts of industrial animal and plant product production are growing rapidly.

As the head of research for the largest corporate sustainability research firm in the world, I saw that companies could profitably mitigate about 20 percent of their short-term and long-term, tangible and intangible, negative environmental and social impacts. Beyond this point, costs usually went up. If they continued to voluntarily reduce impacts, they would put themselves out of business long before reaching full impact mitigation. Flawed economic and political systems unintentionally create a situation where companies must degrade the environment and society to survive. System change is at least 80 percent of the sustainability solution. But it gets relatively little attention in the financial and corporate sectors.

There are many system flaws that force companies to cause harm. One of the most important is the focus on shareholder returns. Corporate charters generally do not require companies to maximize financial returns to shareholders. Instead, this is a defacto requirement of the capital markets.

When companies fail to put shareholder returns ahead of human health, environmental protection and all other factors, managers frequently gets fired, companies get taken over or they go out of business. The primary system flaw is the failure to hold companies fully responsible for negative impacts. In competitive markets, this makes it impossible for them to stop harming society and remain in business.

Reductionism is the root cause of the major environmental, social and economic challenges facing humanity. It involves focusing on parts without adequately considering the whole system that contains them. This myopia produced flawed economic and political systems. They unintentionally put business in conflict with society and humanity in conflict with nature.

As Einstein famously said, we must think at a higher level to solve our most complex challenges. That higher level is whole system thinking. It recognizes that all major parts of human society, including food production, are interconnected, and therefore cannot be effectively addressed in isolation.

This book is part of the *Global System Change* book series. The books use whole system thinking to provide systemic solutions for all major areas of society. Many of the root causes and optimal solutions to food problems lie outside the food sector. As a result, *Sustainable Food Production and Diet* often refers to other *Global System Change* book sections.

System change is getting increased attention in the sustainability movement. Many approaches advocate incremental improvements to current systems, such as incorporating external costs into prices. But time is limited. We almost certainly do not have enough time for incremental approaches. Current systems violate the laws of nature. Throughout human history, all systems that did this changed, usually by collapsing. This high-level system change nearly always happens quickly (i.e. American and French revolutions, end US of slavery and USSR communism).

Humanity is near or beyond many environmental and social tipping points. Growing political turmoil, vitriol between conservatives and liberals, and many other factors show that human systems have entered the phase of rapid transformation. Keeping food and other systems the same is not an option for very much longer. If we do not voluntarily change them, nature and reality will impose involuntary change, almost certainly in a highly traumatic manner. *Global System Change* empowers business and society to change systems in a beneficial, minimally disruptive way.

This book applies whole system thinking to sustainable food production and diet. All major aspects are taken into account and integrated with larger environmental, economic, political and social systems. Humanity is still dealing with the worst pandemic in over 100 years. As a result, *Sustainable Food Production and Diet* starts by discussing far worse potential pandemics and their strong links to industrial animal product production. Then the book discusses environmental problems caused by industrial agriculture, food contamination, harmful production processes, and human health impacts.

Many people understand that overeating unhealthy foods often causes obesity, extensive health problems and premature death. But they continue to overeat anyway. To address this, the book discusses the psychological causes of overeating and several strategies for overcoming food addiction and adopting healthier lifestyles.

Sustainable Food Production and Diet also discusses the causes and solutions to global hunger, the vast cruelty of industrial animal operations, and how this harms humanity. Public deceptions used to perpetuate industrial agriculture and unhealthy diets are discussed. Then the book concludes by discussing many systemic and specific solutions needed to achieve sustainable food production and diet.

The number one suggestion of this book is to greatly reduce or nearly eliminate the consumption of animal products. As discussed extensively in the Health sections, humans anatomically are herbivores, not omnivores. Whole plant foods are the optimal foods for us. Overwhelming evidence shows that they consistently provide long, healthy, vital lives.

Culture is a main barrier to sustainable food production and diet. Eating animal products is a foundational part of culture, especially in developed countries. Greatly reducing this consumption can seem difficult or impossible, as ending slavery did 200 years ago. But the motivation and power to change will arise as the huge negative impacts of eating animals are illuminated.

Humanity is making the same mistakes we made in the past. To illustrate, 200 years ago in the Southern US, slave owners, community leaders and others made passionate, supposedly logical arguments about why it would be impossible to end slavery. Instead, they sometimes sought to improve the system, for example, by treating slaves better.

Today we look back at these arguments as being absolutely insane. The solution was not to improve destructive systems. It was to end them. A whole system perspective would have shown that slavery grossly violated the implied natural law of equality. It was inevitable that this system would end, as all other systems that violate this and other natural laws end. Had they seen the big picture, slave societies could have voluntarily ended their grossly destructive systems in a less disruptive manner, rather than waiting for nature and reality to end them in a highly traumatic, often life-ending way.

We are doing the exact same thing today. Flawed economic and political systems compel companies to massively degrade the environment and society. This occurs because these systems do not hold companies fully responsible for the harm they cause. Instead of changing systems by requiring responsible behavior, we encourage companies to voluntarily stop harming the environment and society. Over the past 20 plus years, nearly the entire responsible investing, corporate responsibility and general sustainability movements have been focusing on improving performance under current systems that compel harm, instead of changing these systems. Advocates make the business case for sustainability. They help companies to see how they often could make more money by reducing the harm they impose on society.

People in the future will look back on these arguments as being insane, just like we view slavery. To illustrate the irrationality and destructive nature of current systems, voluntary corporate responsibility is like voluntary individual responsibility. Under this system, there might be no murder laws or penalties for murder. Instead, we would encourage citizens to voluntarily not murder anyone, and explain how this would make them happier and more successful. In other words, we would make the business case for voluntarily not murdering people. This position is ridiculous. But that is exactly what we are doing with corporate responsibility.

People in the future will incredulously ask, why didn't you prohibit companies from harming the environment and society, in the same way that you prohibited murder and other individual crimes? Companies must be held fully responsible for harm, instead of allowed to cause it without penalty. The current system will be seen as insane in the future. Informed citizens in a democracy would tell business, you are a tool meant to serve society. You can only exist if you benefit and do not harm us. Why do we not do this? In large part, because citizens are not fully informed and we do not live in a democracy.

The voluntary corporate responsibility system has produced some benefits. When cost-effective alternatives are available, companies sometimes can fully eliminate certain types of negative impacts. But as noted, they generally only can mitigate about 20 percent of total negative impacts in a profitable manner. Full impact mitigation (i.e. ending environmental and social destruction) essentially always is impossible under a voluntary system, even for companies that are the most proactive and committed to sustainability.

Voluntary responsibility (i.e. no consequences for causing harm) is irrational. This system probably would work better for individuals. For example, if there were no murder laws, most people would voluntarily not murder anyone. But if companies try to voluntarily stop harming society under current systems, they will put themselves out of business. Beyond a certain point, voluntary corporate responsibility equals voluntary corporate suicide. The purpose here obviously is not to suggest that individual responsibility laws be removed. Instead, it is to show the far greater importance of holding companies, rather than individuals, responsible. But we irrationally and suicidally do the opposite.

There are many apparently logical reasons why we do not hold companies fully responsible, in the same way that there appeared to be logical reasons for perpetuating slavery. For example, it often is difficult to quantify intangible, long-term impacts and attribute them to particular companies. But a reality-based, whole system perspective shows that there are no rational reasons for allowing destruction of the environment and society. Suicide is not rational.

We have the ability to overcome all barriers to holding companies fully responsible. For example, expert panels could estimate total negative impacts. Then companies could be held responsible for the harm and burdens they impose on society through taxes, fees and other mechanism. Prices might rise in some cases. But taxes and other externalized business costs would decline by much more. Total costs to individuals and society would substantially decline because citizens would be paying to prevent problems rather than remediate them.

Purpose-driven business is an increasingly popular sustainability approach. The work involves helping companies to expand their goals or purpose from primarily benefiting shareholders to benefiting all stakeholders and society. It is a well-intentioned approach that improves companies and society.

But it often is out of context. The context is that companies are human-created, nonliving structures that essentially are systemically required to put shareholder returns before all else. Asking them to voluntarily do something they were not designed or incentivized to do would be like asking your washing machine to drive you to the store to pick up groceries.

The key question with purpose-driven business is, why are companies not required to focus primarily on maximizing the well-being of society? This should not be voluntary. Purpose-driven business is based on voluntary corporate responsibility, which ultimately cannot work. However, companies can collaboratively work for system changes that mandate a society-enhancing purpose for business.

When I was getting an MBA at the Harvard Business School and learning about corporate strategy, they neglected to teach us an essential component. We were not taught that companies must integrate harming the environment and society into their business strategies. Without exception, if they fail to do this, they will harm or kill themselves. Managers effectively are given a choice – destroy society or destroy your company. Of course destroying society ultimately destroys the company. But in the short-term, more money often is made, and that is the primary goal.

Obviously, no one intended that economic and political systems would force companies to destroy life support systems and society. That outcome is an unintended consequence of reductionism. Business students and leaders are good people who intend to benefit society. They obviously are not taught to harm it. Harm is the inevitable outcome of our flawed systems.

Slave owners long ago also often meant well. They usually believed they were doing the right thing. They frequently were good parents, spouses and community leaders. They went to church and sometimes treated slaves well. But we look back on their actions with horror. In the same way, people in the future might look back with horror at the massive harm caused by current leaders.

People are products of their time. We live under systems where companies are allowed to cause harm. In competitive markets, allowing harm often compels it. Instead of changing flawed systems, we encourage companies to voluntarily stop harming the environment and society. It is impossible for this system to work. But people usually do not see this because we view society through prevailing mindsets.

Pain is the great teacher. Our suicidally flawed systems will change one way or another. If we continue voluntary corporate responsibility instead of mandating it, conditions will rapidly deteriorate and we will be forced to change. Over the past 100 years, this type of system change could be put off without system collapse. We recovered from depressions and recessions without substantial system changes. But nature and reality ultimately always win.

We are in the end times of current systems. We almost certainly do not have generations or decades to change them. We probably only have five to ten years before they change themselves through collapse and great disruption of humanity. In the end, we are no different than any other species on Earth. We will comply with the laws of nature and reality, or we will cease to exist. Fortunately, self-reflective consciousness gives us the ability to choose our destiny or fate. We do not need to ignorantly destroy ourselves by failing to change our systems.

The primary concern of the US Founders about democracy was the ease with which non-expert citizens could be misled. For all of US history, vested interests took advantage of tribalistic tendencies and divided citizens into debating factions, such as conservatives and liberals. When this occurs, emotions often trump logic. Citizens become unable to work together on their many common interests. They are misled into focusing on false enemies (each other) and ignoring major problems, including lack of democracy, unfair concentration of wealth and destruction of life support systems.

The United States is a product of the Age of Enlightenment and Reason. Following the Dark and Middle Ages, science and rational thinking triumphed over superstition and blind faith in dogma. The irrational, counterproductive fighting between conservatives and liberals shows that we have descended into a new Dark Age. We need a Second Enlightenment. Science and rational thinking must once again triumph over destructive, anti-science irrationality.

Global System Change seeks to model and promote a Second Enlightenment. The books are based on science, extensive expert citations, logic and rational, whole system thinking. Readers are encouraged to consider the logic, facts and science presented. They show that the systemic changes advocated here are essential for establishing sustainable food production and diet and maximizing the well-being of society.

Global System Change uses the laws of nature to provide a system change roadmap for humanity. The map has three parts. First, the laws of nature define the most important aspects of sustainable society. These laws are objective, observable requirements for living system survival at all levels. They include equitable resource distribution, producing no waste, seeking balance not growth, widespread cooperation, and decentralized governance and production.

Second, with the end state clear at a high-level, systemic changes needed to achieve it are illuminated. The rule of law is a foundational system change principle. *Global System Change* uses it to frame up system change in the corporate and financial sectors. This principle says that individuals and companies should be free to do what they want, provided that they do not harm others. Current systems allow massive harm, and thereby grossly violate the rule of law. They inevitably will collapse, unless they are brought into alignment with this principle.

Third, once the end state and necessary systemic changes are clear at a high level, actions required in all major areas of society to bring about the changes are identified. System Change Investing (SCI) represents the single most powerful short-term strategy available to humanity for driving system change and achieving the UN Sustainable Development Goals (SDGs).

The $40 trillion global responsible investing market is almost completely focused on addressing symptoms (e.g. climate change), instead of root causes (e.g. flawed systems that compel companies to burn fossil fuels). Responsible investing also is essentially entirely focused on changing companies rather than the economic and political systems that largely control corporate behavior.

SCI is a new paradigm responsible investing approach. It largely switches the focus of corporate sustainability analysis and investment from symptoms and company change to root causes and system change. The best that current approaches can do is slow the rate of environmental and social descent because they focus on symptoms instead of root causes. SCI is the first investment approach that has the potential to resolve climate change and other SDG problems. It uses the capital markets to strongly incentivize companies to engage in system change.

(The *Global System Change books* were originally published as one integrated, whole system volume entitled *Global System Change: A Whole System Approach to Achieving Sustainability and Real Prosperity*. The last part of the whole system book also was published as a separate book called *Global System Change: We the People Achieving True Democracy, Sustainable Economy and Total Corporate Responsibility*. Both books are available at www.GlobalSystemChange.com. *Global System Change* is being republished in a seven volume series. *Sustainable Food Production and Diet* is Volume Four.)

Global System Change lays out the path to human survival and prosperity. The food book is an important part of this integrated, whole system path. It illuminates the extensive harm caused by companies and flawed systems. Darkness cannot survive in the light. This book is intended to illuminate the darkness of our unintentionally destructive food systems. This light will create public demand for sustainable food systems and diets.

Business can and should play a major role in system change. It is a tool meant to serve humanity. Sectors should be regularly expanding or contracting based solely on what maximizes the well-being of society. Business and the economy have transitioned to new technologies, processes and products many times. A major transition is needed in the food area.

This book discusses many problems caused by food companies. But they are not the enemy. The purpose here is to help improve the flawed systems that force well-intentioned companies to degrade life support systems and society. The corporate and financial sectors are powerful. In collaboration with others, they can drive the systemic changes needed to establish sustainable food production and diet.

Vested interests might argue that system change is the job of government, not business. But enlightened self-interest shows that companies ultimately cannot prosper under systems that compel them to degrade the environment and society. These larger systems enable business existence. Systemic changes that require total corporate responsibility are essential for the well-being of business and society.

The technology, sophistication and coordination of nature are essentially infinitely greater than those of humanity. But we are parts of nature. We can be nearly infinitely more sustainable and prosperous than we are now. A main part of reaching our fullest potential individually and collectively is eating the foods that nature intended for us – whole plant foods. This is the foundation of sustainable food production and diet.

Our progeny will be looking back at us. They would want us to change our systems to ones that prohibit harm instead of compel it. This is a huge challenge, perhaps the greatest of our time. But we are highly creative and resourceful. Survival is a great motivator. The survival of our children and future generations depends on system change. Let's make them proud and do what needs to be done.

Influenza Pandemic

An influenza (i.e. flu) pandemic potentially represents the single greatest threat to humanity. As discussed below, flu pandemics are strongly linked to the industrial production of animal products. Flu viruses are among the few known pathogens capable of rapidly infecting a large percentage of the global population. Highly lethal forms of the flu have evolved. For example, H5N1 influenza kills about 60 percent of victims.[1] (The global COVID-19 mortality rate is about two percent.)

H5N1 and similar virulent viruses have not developed the ability to move easily between humans. However, many experts believe that the viruses are only a few mutations away from gaining this ability. Prior to COVID-19, the director of the US Centers for Disease Control and Prevention (CDC) described a flu pandemic as the number-one health threat in the world. The head of the UN World Health Organization (WHO) in Asia said that the world is in the gravest possible danger of a pandemic. And the US National Intelligence Council called a pandemic the single greatest threat to the global economy.[2]

Industrial animal production, especially of chicken, provides a nearly perfect environment for the evolution of highly pathogenic flu viruses that could be easily transmitted between humans. The WHO and UN Food and Agriculture Organization (FAO) identified industrial animal production as a main factor driving the rapid emergence of virulent influenza and other diseases.[3]

In the past, experts have warned us about impending disasters, for example, related to September 11th and the vulnerability of New Orleans to hurricanes. Unfortunately, we did not adequately respond to this expert advice, and thereby suffered the consequences. However, the consequences of failing to prevent an H5N1 or similar pandemic while we have the opportunity to do so could be devastating. A flu pandemic might kill well over one billion people in 12 to 18 months. It would be like a Katrina type disaster hitting every city in the US at once. Much of society would collapse. Chaos would be widespread.

If this disaster occurs, it will not be a natural disaster. It will be a disaster of our own making. In other words, it will be a human-created disaster resulting from our failure to think and act from a whole system perspective. In this case, it is absolutely essential that we not ignore the experts. We have the ability to greatly reduce the risk of a pandemic by limiting or eliminating the industrial animal production practices that promote it. If we fail to act now while we have the opportunity to do so, it may be the greatest mistake and disgrace of humanity.

This section summarizes the evolution of influenza, the role of industrial animal production in promoting it, the consequences of an H5N1 or similar pandemic, how the public is misled about pandemic risks, and how flu pandemics can be avoided. The section focuses mainly on H5N1 influenza. However, other forms could be deadly to humans. For example, the 1918 influenza pandemic that killed millions of people around the world was caused by H1N1 influenza. More recently, H7N9 influenza infected over 200 people in China and killed more than 20 percent of them.[4]

Besides H5N1, the industrial animal operations discussed in this book promote the development of many forms of influenza and other viruses that could severely harm humanity. This section draws heavily on an outstanding book by Dr. Michael Greger, called *Bird Flu: A Virus of Our Own Hatching*.[5]

1918 Pandemic

The 1918 influenza pandemic was the worst known plague in human history. As much as half the world became infected. About 50 million to 100 million people died. (As of November 2021, COVID-19 has killed about five million people.) The 1918 pandemic killed more people in one year than the Middle Ages bubonic plague killed in 100 years. The pandemic killed more people in 25 weeks than AIDS killed in 25 years.[6]

Like all influenza viruses with pandemic potential, the 1918 virus originated in waterfowl, such as ducks. It is unknown how the virus moved from waterfowl to humans and became so virulent. Some experts believe that the virus became virulent while evolving in the trenches of World War I. Soldiers were forced to remain in close quarters with sick solders in unsanitary conditions. Toxic gases often weakened soldiers' lungs. This could have provided an ideal environment for the evolution of a highly pathogenic virus.[7]

The 1918 pandemic caused great suffering among humanity. Victims often bled from nostrils, ears and eye sockets. They vomited and coughed up blood. They often turned a deep indigo blue from lack of oxygen. Fingers and genitals frequently turned black. Victims sometimes could smell their flesh rotting as they died. Autopsies often showed lungs swollen with bodily fluids up to six times their normal weight and looking like melted red jelly.[8]

The regular seasonal flu tends to kill only the elderly or infirm. But the 1918 flu killed mostly young people. In effect, the flu caused the stronger immune systems of young people to attack and kill the body. Mortality rates were highest in the 20-34 year old age group.[9] Cities around the world were overwhelmed with the dead. In the US, carpenters often could not make coffins fast enough. Bodies sometimes were taken away in garbage trucks and buried in mass graves. Homeless children wandered the streets. In New York City, about 21,000 children lost both parents. Many farms, factories, schools and churches were closed for extended periods of time.[10]

The 1918 pandemic was so traumatic, disruptive and painful that it seems we shut it out of our collective memory and history in some ways. Many people probably know more about the Middle Ages plague than the 1918 pandemic. The pandemic was quickly followed by the Roaring Twenties in the US and some parts of Europe, perhaps at least in part to suppress painful memories.

Infectious Diseases

Most of the infectious (i.e. communicable) diseases plaguing humanity over the past 10,000 years came from domesticated animals. Many scientists say that there have been three eras of epidemic diseases in human history. The first era began about 10,000 years ago with the domestication of animals. Nomadic groups rarely suffered contagious diseases. With the advent of agriculture, people and groups of domesticated animals began to congregate in fixed locations. This facilitated the evolution and maintenance of animal diseases that often were transmitted to humans.[11]

For example, humans are thought to have acquired tuberculosis from domesticated goats. The disease killed about 100 million people in the 20th Century. Measles is thought to have come from domesticated cattle. It killed about 200 million people over the past 150 years. Smallpox is thought to have come from cattle, typhoid fever from chicken, whooping cough from pigs, leprosy from water buffalo, the common cold from cattle or horses, and influenza from domesticated ducks.[12]

The second era of epidemic disease began with the Industrial Revolution in the 18th and 19th Centuries. These diseases sometimes are called diseases of civilization or affluence. They include cancer, heart disease, stroke and diabetes. As discussed in the Health section below, chronic diseases such as these result in large part from eating animal products. Chronic diseases cause about 75 percent of deaths in the US and the majority of deaths in developed countries.[13]

The Third era of epidemic diseases began in the 1970s. It often is referred to as the age of emerging plagues or zoonotic diseases (i.e. infection diseases transmitted from animals to humans). Since the 1970s, more new diseases have emerged in a shorter period of time than any in human history. From about 1975 to 2005, 30 new diseases emerged, most of them newly discovered viruses.[14]

The main factor driving the rapid emergence of new diseases transmitted from animals to humans is environmental degradation, such as forest clearing. As discussed in the Land section of *Global System Change*, since 1950, more than half of the world's tropical forests have been cleared. As humans intrude into wild areas, we often become exposed to diseases that formerly were isolated from humans.

For example, clearing forests in South America led to the evolution of Venezuelan hemorrhagic fever and Argentine hemorrhagic fever, which kills about one-third of those infected. Clearing African tropical forests exposed humans to the Lassa virus, Rift Valley Fever and Ebola. Ebola is an extremely lethal virus with mortality rates ranging from 50-90 percent. Ebola has been traced to exposure to infected great apes hunted for food. Genetically, humans are 95 percent the same as great apes. When we cannibalize our fellow primates, we expose ourselves to pathogens that are well adjusted to human physiology. Many experts believe that the HIV virus arose from butchering and eating chimpanzees in the forests of west equatorial Africa.[15]

Some experts estimate that each mammal and fish probably has about 30 to 40 major diseases. The vast majority of viruses that could infect humans are unknown. For each identified virus, there probably are hundreds of unidentified ones.[16] Like plants and animals, viruses try to adapt to new environments to survive. If forests are cleared and new hosts appear, such as humans, viruses will try to adapt to the new hosts. As we continue to rapidly convert natural area to human uses, we expose ourselves to potentially thousand of new diseases.

This once again illustrates how religious, economic and other ideas that place humans above nature are unintentionally suicidal. From the perspective of reality and nature, humans are no more important than other creatures. We are part of one interdependent system. Nature demands and always ultimately establishes balance. If humans throw nature off balance by pushing other creatures aside and seeking to dominate the Earth, nature has ways of culling back humans and restoring balance.

Infectious diseases from the animal kingdom are one way of restoring balance in nature. As discussed throughout *Global System Change*, we do not have the ability to dominate or control nature. Believing that we do is a suicidal fantasy. We must voluntarily live in balance with nature. If we do not, nature absolutely will impose balance, possibly by using rapidly emerging plagues to vastly cull back or eliminate humanity.

Beyond environmental degradation, as discussed below, the growing industrialization and concentration of animal production also supports the rapid emergence of highly pathogenic, zoonotic diseases, such as H5N1 influenza.

Influenza Evolution

Influenza has existed as an intestinal virus in ducks for possibly as long as 100 million years. Influenza has survived for so long because it reached a balance where it does not harm ducks. Healthy ducks fly to new ponds, excrete the virus in water and pass it on to other ducks that drink the water. If influenza killed ducks, the virus would be less able to spread to new hosts and survive. Prior to the domestication of ducks, influenza probably never infected humans because humans and ducks are substantially different.

The influenza link to humans probably began when ducks were domesticated in China about 4,500 years ago. This brought ducks into year-round contact with farmyard birds and animals, which in turn served as bridges to humans. For example, ducks were raised in flooded rice fields in China. This brought avian influenza viruses into close year-round contact with humans and farm animals. In addition, pig-hen-aquaculture greatly facilitated the evolution of influenza viruses that could infect humans. Under this system, chicken cages are placed directly over pig feeding troughs. Pigs eat chicken feces then excrete into water used to grow fish. The water is then used as drinking water for the pigs and chickens. Wild or domestic ducks sometimes excrete into the water. In this way, influenza cycles through pigs and chickens and can adapt to mammals.

When viruses such as influenza enter a new environment, they try to adapt and survive. To illustrate, influenza spreads between ducks mainly via the fecal-oral route in water. But pigs and chickens do not live in water. Fecal-oral contamination plays a major role in pig and chicken influenza infection. But to further facilitate survival, influenza adapted by becoming a respiratory virus.[17] This enabled it to move more easily among pigs and chickens. Ducks and humans have different viral linkages. As a result, influenza generally does not move directly from ducks to humans (although humans can get influenza by handling infected ducks). But pigs and chicken have both duck and human type viral receptors. As a result, influenza can move from ducks to pigs or chicken, and then mutate into forms that can infect humans.[18] As a result of the domestication of ducks, influenza probably has been infecting humans for over 2,000 years. Human forms of influenza spread independently of animals. Humans sometimes infect animals, such as pigs, with influenza.

Influenza viruses have hemagglutinin (H) and neuraminidase (N) type spikes protruding from the virus. Under the WHO-naming scheme, there are 16 known H spikes (H1 – H16) and nine known N spikes (N1 – N9). The H and N spikes enable influenza viruses to penetrate the cells of mammals. Once inside, the virus takes over the cells and converts them to virus-producing factories.[19]

The human immune system can build up immunity to influenza viruses. A pandemic can occur when human influenza viruses acquire avian H or N combinations to which the present human generation has not been exposed. For example, the 1918 virus was an H1N1 type that humans had not encountered. As a result, it often was highly virulent. Those who survived the 1918 pandemic usually gained immunity to this type of H1N1 virus. As a result, future infections of this type were far less harmful.

Besides the 1918 pandemic, there were two other influenza pandemics in the 20th Century – the 1957 "Asian Flu" pandemic (an H2N2 virus) and the 1968 "Hong Kong Flu" pandemic (an H3N2 virus). Both pandemics infected many people around the world. For example, about 50 percent of US school children were infected in 1957 and about 40 percent were infected in 1968. Fortunately, humans apparently had some immunity to the 1957 and 1968 viruses. As a result, mortality rates were relatively low.[20]

Humans have no exposure and therefore no immunity to the H5N1 virus circulating in bird populations. As a result, the virus can be highly lethal to humans. As noted, if H5N1 mutates into a form that is easily transmitted between humans, one billion or more people around the world might die. But those who survive might gain immunity to this type of virus. Viruses frequently evolve and mutate as they seek to survive and prosper in new hosts, such as humans. As a result, there can be different types of a particular virus such as H5N1. This frequent mutation of influenza viruses is a main reason why it can be difficult to develop effective influenza vaccines.

Prior to 1997, bird flu (i.e. avian influenza) was rare in poultry. H5 and H7 types of influenza can evolve into forms that are highly lethal to poultry.

One of the largest bird flu outbreaks in the US occurred in 1983 among commercial chicken operations in Pennsylvania. An H5N2 virus spread quickly in concentrated chicken operations. As a result, 17 million chickens died or were culled to prevent further spread of the virus. The outbreak cost taxpayers about $400 million, primarily to reimburse chicken companies for culled birds.[21] H5N2 emerged again in US poultry operations in 2014. As a result, more than 39 million chickens and turkeys died or were slaughtered in 14 states.[22]

In 1997, thousand of chickens began dying from H5N1 bird flu in Hong Kong. Eighteen people became infected with H5N1, mostly from handling chicken, and six people died. To prevent the spread of H5N1, about one million chickens were culled in Hong Kong. After killing the chickens, human infections ended. There was evidence that H5N1 was rapidly adapting to humans. As a result, culling the entire chicken population of Hong Kong may have prevented a pandemic.[23]

But it did not stop the spread of H5N1. The domestic duck of southern China is considered to be the principle host of all influenza viruses with pandemic potential. China is the world's largest producer of chicken, duck and goose meat for human consumption. Widespread production of waterfowl provides an extensive reservoir from which influenza viruses can arise. The 1997 H5N1 outbreak was traced to a 1996 goose farm outbreak of H5N1 in China. After the Hong Kong outbreak, H5N1 continued to appear initially in Asia and then in other parts of the world.[24]

H5N1 and other bird flu viruses are spread through various mechanisms. Live poultry markets are one of the most important mechanisms. In live markets, poultry sometimes is slaughtered on site. This can spread viruses, bacteria and other pathogens to live and dead birds. Live birds sometimes are transported back to flocks. In this and other ways, live markets and live transport can quickly spread contamination over a wide area. The 1983 Pennsylvania outbreak was traced to live poultry markets in the northeastern US. Live markets also played a major role in the 1997 Hong Kong outbreak.

Beyond live markets, legal and illegal trade of wild birds and poultry can spread H5N1 and other viruses. For example, in 2006, 14 random US inspections of duck meat from China found that 13 of the 14 lots contained H5N1.[25] Viruses also can be spread by importing live animals, as is done extensively in the US, and through international smuggling for cock fighting. Migratory and other wild birds also can spread H5N1 and other viruses.

These factors combined with the intensification of industrial poultry production are causing bird flu outbreaks in poultry to expand rapidly. There were more serious outbreaks in the first few years of the 21st Century than in all of the 20th Century. As bird flu increases in poultry, chicken viruses are increasingly infecting humans. For example, H9N2 infected children in China in 1999 and 2003. H7N2 infected people in New York and Virginia in 2002 and 2003. H7N7 infected over 1,000 people in the Netherlands in 2003. H7N3 infected poultry workers in Canada in 2004.[26] And as noted, N7N9 infected over 200 people in China in 2013, with a lethality rate of over 20 percent.

H5N1 re-appeared in chicken in China in 2001 and 2002. Then in 2003, H5N1 spread from China to eight other Asian countries and began killing humans again. Within a few months, more than 100 million chickens were killed by H5N1 or culled.[27] Beyond Asia, migratory waterfowl and possibly the poultry trade and other mechanisms were spreading H5N1 to other parts of the world, including the Middle East, Europe and Africa.

H5N1 has evolved to become by far the most virulent and lethal form of influenza ever seen. It is capable of quickly killing whole flocks of chickens, often turning their bodies into a bloody jello. The virus also is rapidly adapting to become more lethal to mammals. In China, it has killed cats, tigers and leopards. Influenza viruses typically do not kill mammals, such as mice. But H5N1 is 100 percent lethal to mice. It nearly dissolves their lungs.[28]

H5N1 also is evolving to become more lethal to humans. Very few human pathogens approach 50 percent mortality. As noted, H5N1 kills about 60 percent of infected humans. Only Ebola and untreated HIV are more lethal than H5N1. But Ebola and HIV do not spread easily among humans. H5N1 has the potential to quickly infect more than half the world. The 1918 virus primarily attacked the lungs. But H5N1 attacks the whole body. This appears to be why the virus is more than ten times as lethal as the 1918 virus. H5N1 often causes multiple organ failure. In some victims, lungs were filled with blood, livers and kidneys were clogged with dead tissue, blood was curdled, and brains were swollen with fluid. H5N1 frequently attacks the central nervous system and places people in rapidly progressing fatal comas.[29] Like the 1918 virus, H5N1 seems to trigger an over-response from the immune system. However, with H5N1 the immune system can destroy multiple organs, rather than focusing mainly on the lungs. The immune system over-response can make H5N1 more lethal to younger people with stronger immune systems.

H5N1 has infected mostly chicken. Humans have been infected mostly by handling chicken. However, pigs also could facilitate the evolution of an H5N1 virus that is easily transmitted between humans. Since 1918, an H1N1 swine flu has been circulating in US and other pig populations. But in 1998, at an industrial pig farm in North Carolina, an aggressive H3N2 virus infected thousands of pigs. The virus contained elements of human, pig and bird influenza viruses. Within one year, the virus had spread across the US to other pig farms, largely due to live animal transportation. Ten years later, this virus combined with a Eurasian swine flu virus and caused the flu pandemic of 2009.[30]

This virus sickened millions of people around the world. But fortunately, it was not nearly as harmful as H5N1. Pigs can be infected with human and avian influenza. As a result, pigs can serve as mixing vessels for more virulent human influenza viruses. Some pigs were infected with H5N1 in China and Indonesia. If pigs become co-infected with H5N1 and the 2009 H1N1 pandemic virus, a hybrid virus could evolve in pigs that had the human transmissibility of swine flu and the lethality of bird flu.[31]

The longer that H5N1 circulates in poultry and wild bird populations, the greater the likelihood that an H5N1 virus will evolve that moves easily between humans. Each time a human is infected with H5N1, the probability that H5N1 will evolve and gain easy human transmissibility increases. There are more than 13 billion chickens and 500 million pigs in China, mostly grown in concentrated conditions. US populations are nearly as large. As discussed below, concentrated poultry operations provide an ideal environment for the rapid evolution of highly pathogenic H5N1 and other viruses. H5N1 has gained the ability to quickly kill millions of chickens. Given similarities between chicken and human respiratory systems, only a few mutations are needed for H5N1 to gain the ability to kill millions or billions of humans.

Evidence suggests that the 1918 virus was evolving for several years before it mutated into pandemic form.[32] H5N1 also is continuing to mutate and evolve. It is difficult to know when or if H5N1 will mutate into pandemic form and plague humanity. As Yogi Berra once said, "It's tough to make predictions, especially about the future."[33] However, to ensure the well-being of humanity, we probably should act as if an H5N1 pandemic will happen tomorrow, because it might.

Industrial Chicken Production

If an H5N1 pandemic occurs, it will not be a natural phenomenon. It almost certainly will be caused by the concentrated, industrial production of animal products, primarily chicken.[34] All bird flu viruses originate from the perpetual, stable reservoir of essentially harmless waterfowl influenza. They start out as mild, low-pathogenicity avian influenza (LPAI). However, H5 and H7 viruses can mutate into highly pathogenic avian influenza (HPAI). HPAI viruses have no natural reservoir. They arise when a wild bird introduces an LPAI virus into poultry. Once in poultry, the virus can mutate into a highly virulent (harmful) and pathogenic (disease causing) form. The evolution of LPAI into HPAI is extremely rare among wild birds or outdoor, free-range barnyard poultry flocks. Highly pathogenic bird flu nearly always arises in concentrated, industrial, usually indoor flocks.[35]

Outdoor flocks are exposed to LPAI from duck droppings and other sources. But there are several natural barriers that nearly always prevent LPAI from evolving to HPAI in outdoor, free-range flocks. For example, H5N1 and many other viruses are primarily transmitted among poultry via the fecal-oral route. In outdoor settings, sunlight and fresh air quickly dry feces, which can kill viruses and other pathogens in it. Sunlight also often directly kills viruses. In addition, birds raised outside nearly always have healthier, stronger immune systems because they are under less stress, have room to move and engage in natural behavior, can breathe fresh air, and are less exposed to fecal contamination. As a result, they are better able to resist infections.

Perhaps most importantly, HPAI viruses rarely evolve in outdoor, less concentrated settings because it would be suboptimal for the virus. As noted, viruses strive to survive by adapting to their environment. To survive, viruses must be able to move from bird to bird. In outdoor settings, viruses must find a balance between being too weak or too strong. If the virus is too weak, the immune systems of birds might defeat it. Then the virus would not spread and survive. If the virus is too strong and kills birds too quickly, birds will be less able to spread the virus to other birds. In other words, if a flu virus evolves to a highly pathogenic form, it often will not survive in outdoor flocks. In outdoor natural settings, viruses often maximize longevity by remaining in a less pathogenic form.

Concentrated poultry operations, especially indoor chicken operations, on the other hand, are extremely well-suited for the evolution of HPAI viruses. In these settings, viruses often maximize their ability to spread quickly by becoming as lethal and pathogenic as possible. There are many factors that promote the rapid evolution of HPAI viruses in concentrated, indoor chicken production facilities. For example, high stress often substantially weakens chickens' immune systems. This makes it easier for viruses to spread and mutate.[36]

Industrial chicken operations create high stress in many ways. Birds are packed together with little room to move. In broiler chicken operations (i.e. chicken raised for meat), 20,000 to 30,000 day-old chicks often are placed on wood shavings or other litter material in a barren shed. As the chickens grow, the space between them decreases until there is little to no room to move. Egg-laying hen operations sometimes confine over 100,000 hens per shed. Hens often are placed in battery cages (up to ten hens per cage). Then, the cages are stacked on top of each other. Hens need 291 square inches to flap wings, 197 square inches to turn around, and 72 square inches to stand freely. US commercial battery facilities provide an average of 64 square inches of space per hen.[37] Living conditions create great stress in part by preventing birds from engaging in natural behavior. Hens often beat off half of their feathers by flapping their wings against cages.

Chickens often fight when crowded together. To minimize injury, beaks and toes often are cut off. This causes pain and stress. Cattle and chicken remains often are fed to chickens, which are not naturally carnivores. This can facilitate the spread of viruses and other pathogens. Industrial chicken operations have widespread fecal contamination. One gram of chicken manure can contain enough virus to infect one million birds. A 20,000-bird broiler flock produces more than one ton of feces per day.[38] Feces often is not removed until chickens are slaughtered. As a result, growing birds live among an increasing amount of their own feces. Broiler sheds sometimes are not cleaned out between flocks. When this occurs, new chicks are placed directly on tons of feces from previous flocks. Living in feces greatly facilitates virus transmission and mutation.

Broiler chickens are bred to grow larger more quickly. Ancestor chickens grew to about two pounds in four months. Broiler chickens now grow to about five pounds in 45 days. Birds bred for size often cannot support their own weight. The stress on their hips and legs often is so great that they spend more than three-quarters of their time lying in their own feces.[39] Ancestor hens laid about 25 eggs per year. Industrial hens are bred to lay over 250 eggs per year. Breeding chickens to have more breast meat or egg-laying ability diverts resources from other body parts and systems, including the immune system. Chickens often outgrow their hearts and lungs. About one to four percent of broilers die of heart failure. Breeding for size and egg-laying ability produces birds with weaker immune systems. This further facilitates virus transmission and mutation.

Industrial broiler chicken sheds usually do not have windows. The sheds usually are nearly constantly lit at low light levels (about five percent of normal office lighting). Nearly constant light accelerates growth, while dim light minimizes activity. Brighter light makes chickens more active. As a result, they burn energy by moving instead of growing. Keeping broiler chickens in near darkness results in more efficient conversion of feed to meat or eggs. Sunlight makes birds healthier, dries out feces and kills pathogens. Keeping sunlight out of broiler chicken sheds allows feces to remain moist for extended periods of time. H5N1 and other pathogens can survive for weeks in moist feces. As a result, keeping sheds nearly dark facilitates virus transmission and mutation. Egg-laying hen sheds, on the other hand, usually are kept constantly lit at higher light levels because this maximizes egg production.

Large amounts of putrefying feces in chicken sheds generate irritating chemicals, such as hydrogen sulfide, methane and ammonia. Lying in ammonia-producing feces often causes chickens to develop sores or ammonia burns. Ammonia also burns chickens' eyes and lungs. This weakens lungs and makes birds more susceptible to viral infections. Ammonia also enters the bloodstream and directly weakens immune systems.[40] The air in industrial chicken sheds often is thick with fecal dust. The dust frequently contains viruses, bacteria and other pathogens. Fecal dust often clogs chickens' lungs and makes them more vulnerable to infections.[41]

Intensive breeding greatly reduces genetic diversity in industrial chicken operations. Five broiler breeding companies provide more than 95 percent of the world's breeding stock. Five egg-laying hen breeding companies also provide over 95 percent of the world's breeding stock. Homogenizing poultry stock greatly increases the ability of viruses to quickly move through entire flocks.[42]

Crowded, unsanitary conditions facilitate infections with immunosuppressive viruses in chicken. This can further weaken already compromised immune systems. Indicating the link between these viruses and H5N1, outbreaks of immunodeficiency virus occurred at some Hong Kong chicken farms about six months before the first outbreak of H5N1 in 1997.[43]

Another requirement for the evolution of HPAI viruses appears to be the size of viral doses. As viruses attempt to adapt to new environments, they produce many mutations. If chickens get a small dose or viral exposure, it is less likely that viral mutations will cause infections. However, if chickens are exposed to large viral doses containing many different mutations, it is much more likely that they will become infected. Large viral doses generally do not occur in natural or outdoor settings, in part because viruses often are diffused before coming into contact with other birds. Large doses usually only occur in unnatural settings, such as laboratories or industrial chicken sheds where birds are intensively confined in their own waste.[44]

Creating HPAI viruses essentially is a numbers game. The risk of highly pathogenic viruses evolving increases as more birds are quickly exposed to large viral doses. This often is what happens in industrial chicken operations. Tens of thousands of immune-compromised birds are crammed together in dark, feces-laden sheds. Outside of a laboratory, it probably would be difficult to develop a more efficient and effective means of promoting the rapid evolution of highly pathogenic viruses.

As noted, natural barriers nearly always prevent HPAI viruses from evolving in outdoor, less crowded flocks. If a virus becomes too virulent, it usually will not survive because it is more difficult to spread to other birds. However, these barriers often do not apply in intensive confinement settings. Birds are constantly close to other birds and their feces. As a result, sick, dying or dead birds often can easily pass viruses to other birds. In this setting, there are few limits on pathogenicity. As a result, viruses can evolve to highly pathogenic forms.

Many experts around the world say that highly pathogenic bird flu viruses are the product of industrial animal product production. The WHO blames the emergence of H5N1 on intensive poultry production.[45] In other words, HPAI viruses nearly always are not natural phenomena. They are unintentionally created by humans through our failure to see the big picture and adequately consider the consequences of our actions.

Influenza has been infecting poultry and humans in China for thousands of years. But HPAI viruses rarely appeared before industrial poultry production. The expansion of highly pathogenic bird flu coincides with the expansion of industrial poultry production. Concentrated poultry production began in the 1950s. There was one outbreak of HPAI in the 1950s, two in the 1960s, three in the 1970s, three in the 1980s, and nine in the 1990s. HPAI, including H5N1, has continued to expand rapidly in the 21st Century. There were more outbreaks of HPAI in the first few years of the 21st Century than in all of the 20th Century. About 20 million birds were infected with HPAI in the last 50 years of the 20th Century. More than 200 million birds were infected in the first few years of 21st Century.[46]

As one might suspect, given the barriers to HPAI in outdoor flocks and the strong promotion of HPAI in concentrated indoor flocks, the vast majority of HPAI outbreaks have occurred in industrial poultry operations. Thailand and Vietnam, for example, industrialized poultry production to a much greater degree than nearby Cambodia and Laos. Largely as a result, they experienced substantially more HPAI outbreaks and human H5N1 infections. As of 2011, Thailand and Vietnam had 144 human cases of H5N1and 76 deaths. Cambodia and Laos had 15 cases and 13 deaths. A Johns Hopkins University study found that industrial-scale chicken and egg operations in Thailand had four times more HPAI outbreaks than outdoor flocks. Among the few outbreaks in Laos, 90 percent occurred in commercial poultry operations.[47]

While there are many free-range flocks in Europe and Africa, the first HPAI outbreaks in these regions occurred in concentrated industrial poultry operations. The first HPAI outbreaks in the UK also occurred in an industrial poultry operation. The 1999 HPAI outbreak in Italy occurred among industrial poultry operations. The 2003 H7N7 outbreak in the Netherlands that resulted in the deaths of 30 million birds spread quickly through industrial poultry operations and affected few free-range flocks. During the 2004 HPAI outbreak in Canada that resulted in the deaths of 19 million chickens, the virus jumped from broiler shed to broiler shed, and largely skipped free-range flocks. Industrial indoor flocks were nearly six times more likely to be infected than outdoor flocks.[48] In Mexico in the 1990s and Chile in 2002, low-grade viruses entered industrial poultry operations and evolved into highly pathogenic bird flu. Further reflecting the link between industrial poultry operations and bird flu, the US pioneered industrial poultry production. It has reported more bird flu than any other country.[49]

Minnesota is the largest brooding area for wild ducks in the US. It also is a central flyway for migratory waterfowl. One duck can drop billions of infectious viral doses per day. Minnesota is the largest turkey producer in the US. Since the 1970s, outdoor turkey flocks have been infected with LPAI over 100 times. Yet even in concentrated outdoor flocks as large as 100,000 birds, LPAI never has evolved into HPAI in an outdoor turkey flock. In general, LPAI viruses never have been known to evolve into highly pathogenic forms in outdoor chicken or turkey flocks.[50]

While low-path viruses rarely, if ever, evolve to high-path forms in outdoor flocks, they can lower meat and egg production. To minimize economic losses, many companies moved turkey flocks indoors in Minnesota. This substantially lowered LPAI infections in part because turkeys were more separated from duck droppings and other sources. However, moving flocks indoors did not eliminate the risk of LPAI infections and it greatly increased the risk of HPAI evolving. In the three years after moving most free-range flocks indoors, more than 25 indoor flocks tested positive for bird flu.[51]

Poultry companies implement biosecurity measures in an effort to keep bird flu and other viruses out of production facilities. But regular outbreaks of low-path and high-path bird flu at industrial poultry operations show that biosecurity is routinely breached around the world. There are many ways that bird flu viruses can enter supposedly biosecure poultry facilities. One of the most common means of contamination is employees and equipment tracking or carrying in viruses. Rats and mice frequently infest poultry operations. They can carry H5N1 and other viruses. Extensive fecal contamination attracts many flies to poultry operations. Flies also can carry H5N1 and other viruses. Skunks, ground squirrels, raccoons and wild birds periodically enter poultry facilities through foundation cracks and other openings. They also can carry H5N1 and other viruses. Rodents, birds and small mammals are attracted to the food in poultry sheds in the same way that bank robbers are attracted to the money in banks.

H5N1 and other viruses also can enter poultry facilities through contaminated feed and drinking water as well as through ventilation systems. Indicating the ease with which biosecurity is routinely breached at industrial poultry facilities, during the 1983 Pennsylvania bird flu outbreak, many infected wild birds and rodents were found in the area around contaminated facilities.

Probably the only way to ensure that industrial poultry operations are not contaminated with LPAI viruses would be to implement the same biosecurity measures used in laboratories. These might include filtered air and water, purified feed, airtight seals, solid rodent/bird/bug-proof construction, and rigorous employee and equipment decontamination procedures. However, measures such as these would greatly increase costs, and thereby probably make concentrated indoor poultry production uneconomic.

In the same way that LPAI viruses easily and regularly enter industrial poultry facilities, HPAI viruses also can exit. As noted, low-path viruses often enter industrial poultry facilities through many means, including bugs, birds, rodents, small mammals, air, water, feed, humans and equipment. Once inside, low-path viruses can evolve into high-path forms. Then, using nearly all the same entrance vectors, HPAI viruses can exit industrial facilities and infect wild waterfowl and other creatures, including humans.

This is exactly what happened. Initially, H5N1 viruses emerging from industrial poultry operations in China were lethal to waterfowl. But H5N1 evolved so that it often became harmless to wild waterfowl, but retained its lethality to poultry and humans. Now the highly lethal virus is being carried around the world by wild migratory birds. Again, this lethal virus is not a natural phenomenon. It did not evolve in nature. It almost certainly evolved from low-path to high-path form in industrial poultry operations, and then was re-introduced to wild birds.

(Some might argue that humans are part of nature. Therefore anything that we do is natural and part of nature's activities. Technically, this is true. But the implied intelligence and sophistication of nature are vastly greater than conscious human intelligence. As a result, human activities often are put into a separate category and labeled unnatural. As humans access the wisdom of nature through the intuitive function, begin to emulate the intelligence and sophistication of nature, and learn to live in balance with it, perhaps we could call our actions natural. At present, the vast, suicidal stupidity of humanity does not warrant use of the natural label.)

Humanity's great stupidity (or failure to think systemically and consider the consequences of our actions) is reflected in the fact that we unintentionally created a lethal virus with the potential to kill billions of people and greatly disrupt human society. Then we placed it into wild bird populations where it is being transported around the world. Now that H5N1 has moved into wild bird populations, it probably is impossible to eradicate the virus. Fortunately, H5N1 has not yet mutated into a form that moves easily between humans, like the common flu. However, it is vastly more likely that these final few mutations will occur in industrial poultry operations, rather than in outdoor flocks.[52]

Influenza from wild waterfowl rarely infects humans. Poultry serves as the primary bridge between waterfowl and humans. As noted, chickens and humans have similar respiratory systems. As H5N1 becomes more effective at killing chickens, it also often becomes more effective at killing humans. Industrial chicken operations are like giant petri dishes for promoting the formation of HPAI viruses. Humans are in regular contact with these facilities. As a result, there are many opportunities for H5N1 and other viruses to jump to humans. In industrial poultry operations, H5N1 might evolve to a form that moves easily between humans and then jump to humans. Or it might jump to humans first, and then evolve into more transmissible forms. Or it might do both.

As discussed below, the consequences of an H5N1 pandemic could be extremely severe. As a result, some experts recommend that the entire global chicken population be eliminated. Eliminating all of the chickens in Hong Kong in 1997 ended human H5N1 infections there and possibly prevented a pandemic. Eliminating the global chicken population would not eliminate H5N1 because it remains in wild waterfowl. However, it would vastly lower the risk of a pandemic by eliminating the primary bridge between waterfowl and humans and greatly reducing the risk that H5N1 evolves into pandemic form.

Eliminating the global chicken population is not as drastic as it sounds. Boiler and egg-laying hens have short lives. As noted, broiler chickens grow to full size in about six weeks and then are slaughtered. As a result, nearly all of the global chicken population is killed on a regular basis. If we stopped birthing new chickens, the chicken population would quickly disappear. At a minimum, we should end or reduce industrial chicken production and return to lower risk, less concentrated methods. Poultry provides one percent of humanity's calories and three percent of our protein. Poultry is not needed for human survival. As discussed in the Health section below, plants provide the healthiest protein for humans. Production of poultry, especially chicken, represents the largest driver of H5N1 pandemic risk. We should not be placing the lives of hundreds of millions, possibly billions, of people at risk so that we can eat cheap chicken.

But unfortunately, this is exactly what we are doing. Rather than reducing industrial chicken production, it is growing rapidly. Chicken is the fastest growing meat sector in the world. Rising population and living standards are driving rapid growth in meat consumption. Global meat consumption was projected to double by 2020 from 2005 levels.[53] The most slaughtered animals in the world are pigs, ducks and chickens. In 2003, about one billion pigs, two billion ducks and 45 billion chickens were slaughtered. As discussed, industrial production of these animals greatly increases the risk of an H5N1 pandemic.

Industrial chicken production is increasing in the US and many other countries. In the US, about one out of every 9,000 chickens is tested for bird flu. While this number is low, it probably is one of the highest monitoring rates in the world. The US poultry industry argues that biosecurity measures limit pandemic risk. But biosecurity is a deceptive word in this case. Biosecure usually refers to laboratories and other facilities that effectively prevent pathogens from entering and leaving.

Industrial poultry operations in the US and other countries do not do this. As a result, they are not biosecure. At best, they provide a speed bump or minor deterrent to viruses. For example, virus-laden duck droppings might not fall directly onto chickens in a broiler shed, as they might fall on an outdoor flock. But the droppings might fall next to the shed. Then humans, equipment, bugs, rodents, birds, small mammals, water and air can carry the virus into the shed. After evolving into high-path forms, these vectors can carry the virus back out. Industrial chicken production facilities often are as effective at blocking and containing viruses as sieves are at containing water.

It is inappropriate to use the term biosecure with industrial poultry operations. It probably is not possible to make these operations biosecure (i.e. reliably prevent viruses from entering and exiting) at a reasonable cost. As noted, implementing construction, systems and procedures that actually make industrial poultry facilities biosecure probably would cause the operations to become uneconomic.

The situation in developing countries is even worse than in the US. From the late 1980s to 2005, poultry production in Thailand, Vietnam and Indonesia tripled, while doubling in China. Outdoor flocks are being rapidly replaced by industrial production facilities. Poultry facilities in China confine up to five million chickens. Pig facilities confine up to 250,000 pigs. US companies are establishing industrial production facilities in China and often putting smaller local producers out of business.[54]

Industrial animal production in developing countries combines the worst of both worlds – the intensive confinement of the West with the impoverished infrastructure of the East and global South. Developing countries often have limited resources to implement biosecurity measures, monitor bird flu outbreaks and contain them if outbreaks occur. In China and other developing countries, billions of chickens and ducks are intensively confined in unsanitary, unsecure conditions near millions of people. This creates high risks that an H5N1 virus which moves easily between humans will arise and spread around the world.

Pandemic Strategies

Influenza pandemics essentially are inevitable. They have occurred on average about every 30 years for the past 300 years.[55] The key question is, what is the likelihood of a lethal H5N1 or similar pandemic occurring? The longer H5N1 circulates in industrial poultry operations, the higher the likelihood of additional human exposure and evolution of the virus into an easily transmissible form. Tens of billions of chickens intensively confined in unsanitary, unsecure conditions around the world provide trillions or more opportunities for H5N1 to mutate into pandemic form. A Harvard epidemiologist said, it is not possible to predict exactly when an H5N1 pandemic will occur, but "we are in a period where the risk is growing and where it's higher than we've ever seen it before."[56]

Many influenza experts report suffering sleepless nights. They say that an H5N1 or similar pandemic could happen at any time. The CDC pandemic plan states, "no other infectious disease, whether natural or engineered, poses the same current threat for causing increases in infections, illnesses, and deaths so quickly in the United States and worldwide." A WHO spokesperson said, "All the indicators are that we are living on borrowed time... The lethality of the virus is unprecedented for influenza... The change that needs to happen to create a pandemic is such a small change – it could literally happen any day."[57]

Even if an H5N1 or similar pandemic were only a remote possibility, the consequences are so severe that we must act aggressively to prevent it. However, this type of pandemic is not a remote possibility. It is highly possible and perhaps highly likely. In other words, based on expert concerns, research and knowledge, the probability of an H5N1 or similar pandemic occurring might be in the range of 20 percent up to nearly 100 percent. As a result, we absolutely must do everything within our power as quickly as possible to prevent these types of pandemics.

Due in large part to the flawed ideas and systems discussed in *Global System Change*, such as the failure to think systemically and the over-emphasis on economic growth and shareholder returns, not nearly enough is being done to prevent and prepare for an H5N1-type pandemic. Pandemic strategies could be segmented into two areas – prevention and response (which includes preparation).

Some actions are being taken in the prevention area, such as improving monitoring and biosecurity measures in developed countries. Similar actions are occurring in developing countries, but often to a lesser degree due to limited resources and weaker regulations. Overall, actions being taken to prevent an H5N1 or similar pandemic are grossly inadequate and irresponsible.

The most important prevention action by far is eliminating the activities that created and perpetuate H5N1 and similar viruses. As discussed, H5N1 and other HPAI viruses nearly always are the product of the industrial production of animal products, primarily chicken. The H5N1 virus circulating in wild bird populations almost certainly was produced in these operations. Even if H5N1 was eradicated from wild bird populations, it is virtually certain that similar highly pathogenic viruses would arise in industrial chicken operations and be re-introduced to nature. In addition, the remaining few mutations needed to evolve H5N1 into an easily transmissible form most likely will occur in industrial chicken operations. Some European countries are taking actions to reduce concentrated animal operations, such as restricting the use of battery cages for egg-laying hens. But overall, concentrated production of chicken and other animals is growing rapidly in many areas around the world.

The need to provide ever-increasing shareholder returns often creates nearly constant pressure to further reduce costs in industrial chicken operations. This can lead to weaker biosecurity, more overcrowding, and other practices that increase H5N1-type pandemic risk. Now that H5N1 is in wild bird populations, chicken producers sometimes have greater incentives to move birds into concentrated indoor facilities. As noted, low-path viruses can reduce meat and egg production. But high-path viruses such as H5N1 being dropped by waterfowl can quickly kill many birds, and thereby cause much greater economic losses. Moving birds indoors may lower H5N1 poultry infections. But it will not eliminate infections because no industrial poultry facilities are biosecure. Instead, moving birds indoors will greatly increase the risk that H5N1 will evolve into pandemic form.

The pandemic strategies of nearly all countries, especially the US, are far more focused on responding to an H5N1 or similar pandemic once it arises, rather than preventing it in the first place. Given the severe consequences of these types of pandemics, the obviously superior strategy is to emphasize reducing the likelihood of occurrence, most importantly by eliminating the industrial animal operations that spawned H5N1 and will likely evolve it into pandemic form.

Many actions are being taken in the H5N1-type pandemic preparation and response areas. But these actions are woefully inadequate in many ways. Vaccination and the use of antiviral drugs are critical elements of pandemic response strategies. As noted, HPAI viruses mutate rapidly. This makes it difficult to develop effective vaccines. The most effective vaccines cannot be made until the pandemic begins and the specific form of pandemic HPAI becomes clear. It can take six to eight months to produce a vaccine. By this time many people probably would have died from H5N1 or similar infection.[58]

Global vaccine production capacity is limited. Depending on the amount of vaccine required per person, current capacity might only be able to produce enough vaccine for one to fifteen percent of the global population within one year of a pandemic outbreak.[59] In other words, effective vaccines would arrive too late or not be available for the vast majority of people around the world.

Vaccines based on current forms of H5N1 are being developed. However, since H5N1 mutates so rapidly, there is a significant possibility that these pre-pandemic vaccines will have little or no impact on preventing H5N1 infections. Nevertheless, many countries are stockpiling vaccines based on current H5N1 viruses in the hope that pre-pandemic vaccines will confer at least some immunity to pandemic H5N1, and thereby slow the progression of a pandemic. Australia and Ireland, for example, have announced plans to stockpile enough pre-pandemic H5N1 vaccine to inoculate their entire populations.

The US Department of Health and Human Services plans to stockpile enough pre-pandemic H5N1 vaccine to immunize 20 million people (seven percent of the US population).[60] Vaccines are being made for different versions of H5N1. Some of these might be less effective against pandemic H5N1. As noted, there is a significant possibility that none of the pre-pandemic vaccines will work against pandemic H5N1. Pre-pandemic vaccines have a shelf life of about two years. Due to expirations and varying effectiveness of different vaccine versions, there may only be enough pre-pandemic vaccine to inoculate substantially fewer than 20 million US citizens.[61]

Pre-pandemic vaccines (again, that potentially will not work) would be available for emergency workers, politicians and perhaps wealthy people who give money to politicians. But pre-pandemic vaccination would not be available for the vast majority of US citizens. The situation would be even worse in developing countries. Very few people would have access to these vaccines.

Several factors limit global vaccine production capacity. Most flu vaccine viruses are grown in live chicken eggs. As noted, this process takes about six to eight months to produce vaccine. During a bird flu outbreak that kills many chickens, there may be insufficient egg supply to produce large quantities of vaccine. An H5N1 pandemic that kills many humans also might limit egg supply and vaccine production because workers might not be available to manage egg production.

Vaccines often are not as profitable for drug companies as repeat-use drugs because they frequently only require one or two doses. Drug companies frequently can make substantially more money, for example, by selling antidepressants and erectile dysfunction drugs. Lower profit potential often limits the development of vaccines and other drugs needed to treat infectious diseases.

Prompted partly by pandemic concerns, much research is being done to improve the scale, timeliness and effectiveness of vaccine production. For example, newer production methods grow influenza vaccines in mammalian cell cultures, instead of chicken eggs. This has the potential to substantially increase production capacity. But it probably would not significantly reduce the amount of time needed to produce vaccines. Research also is being conducted on using vaccines in combination with other drugs (adjuvants) that increase immune system response. This could lower required vaccine doses and thereby increase the number of people who could be vaccinated.

Newer production methods also use genetic engineering instead of chicken eggs or mammalian cell cultures to produce vaccines. Genetic engineering potentially could substantially speed up vaccine production. In addition, work is being done to develop a universal vaccine that provides long-lasting immunity for multiple influenza strains, possibly including H5N1.[62]

Antiviral drugs can be used to treat and in some cases prevent H5N1 and other influenza infections. The drugs generally do not kill influenza viruses. But they can block or slow the spread of them in the body. Tamiflu and Relenza are common antiviral drugs used to treat H5N1. Relenza is taken as an inhaled powder. Little of the drug is absorbed from the lungs into the bloodstream. This can work well for regular flu which often focuses on the lungs. But it is less effective against H5N1 which can infect many organs and systems in the body.[63]

Tamiflu often is taken in capsule form and is considered to be more effective against H5N1. However, H5N1 has shown resistance to Tamiflu in some human cases.[64] In addition, rare side effects of Tamiflu include liver damage, seizures, confusion and hallucinations sometimes leading to suicide.[65] Nevertheless, many countries are preparing for a pandemic by stockpiling Tamiflu and other antiviral drugs.

Two antiviral drugs, amantadine and rimantadine, were highly effective at treating influenza viruses with pandemic potential, including H5N1. However, chicken companies in the US and China gave large amounts of the drugs to chickens to prevent bird flu outbreaks. This caused H5N1 to become resistant to these drugs. As a result, they no longer are effective at treating human H5N1 infections.

This is unfortunate because amantadine is a highly stable, low-cost, widely available antiviral drug. Tamiflu often costs more than $10 per 75 mg capsule. Amantadine costs as little as $10 per pound.[66] In other words, the drugs needed to produce over 6,000 75 mg amantadine capsules cost the same as one Tamiflu capsule. Tamiflu expires in three to five years. As a result, countries must regularly replace stockpiles. But amantadine remains effective for decades. Countries could have stockpiled amantadine to treat an H5N1 pandemic for at least one generation with no loss of effectiveness.[67] This illustrates why antivirals, antibiotics and other drugs potentially needed for human health and survival generally should not be given to animals raised for food.

One strategy for preventing pandemics is to quickly identify H5N1 outbreaks and then treat everyone in the area with Tamiflu or other antiviral drugs. In theory, this might halt the spread of pandemic H5N1. But the strategy probably will not work. An H5N1 pandemic most likely would start in Asia due to the existence of large concentrated chicken, duck and pig populations near large human populations. Weak biosecurity along with limited monitoring and public health resources further increase the likelihood of a pandemic starting in Asia.

People can be infected with influenza for several days before showing symptoms. This combined with limited monitoring resources means that H5N1 outbreaks often would not be identified quickly enough to contain them. Even if they were, developing countries usually cannot afford to stockpile large amounts of antiviral drugs. As a result, limited stockpiles would greatly restrict the ability to treat everyone in the area and halt a pandemic. The WHO and other agencies and countries probably would attempt to provide antiviral drugs. But they probably often would not arrive in time to prevent an H5N1 pandemic. The desire to avoid negative economic impacts sometimes makes developing countries reluctant to admit outbreaks. This further lowers the probability that an H5N1 outbreak would be contained.

New antiviral drugs, including Rapivab and Xofluza, have been introduced. Research indicates that they could effectively treat H5N1 and other

HPAI viruses, sometimes including those with Tamiflu resistance. Many formulas for new, inexpensive influenza drugs have been identified. Preliminary testing shows one potential drug to be hundreds of times more potent than drugs currently in use. However, these potential drugs often are not being developed, primarily due to lack of commercial interest.[68]

Companies often face great pressure to sell infectious disease drugs at low prices. As a result, it often is more profitable to develop lifestyle and other multiple-dose drugs. Once again, this shows the destructive, even suicidal nature of our myopic economic systems. The requirement to maximize shareholder returns often compels companies to focus drug development efforts on lifestyle drugs rather than on drugs that help to ensure the health and survival of humanity.

Probably no country is well prepared for an H5N1 pandemic in terms of being able to avoid widespread loss of life and great economic and social disruption. The US in particular is poorly prepared compared to many other developed countries, in part because it has smaller stockpiles of vaccines and antiviral drugs.[69] As a result, loss of life in the US probably would be substantially higher.

There are several other weak aspects of the US pandemic strategy. For example, during an H5N1 or similar pandemic, state and local public health agencies will be required to provide many prevention and treatment services. But funding for state and local public health has been severely reduced since the 1980s. As a result, these agencies often will not have the resources needed to protect communities during a pandemic.[70] Funding for public health training and research, for example focused on developing new antiviral drugs, also has been substantially reduced. Conflicting goals within the US government also restrict pandemic preparedness. For example, the US Department of Agriculture (USDA) is largely focused on promoting and protecting the economic interests of agriculture. This potentially puts them in conflict with government agencies that might suggest limiting industrial animal production activities which increase pandemic risk.

The US government also is doing a poor job of making citizens aware of the risks of an H5N1-type pandemic, perhaps to avoid alarming the public. Several polls have shown that citizens are apathetic about an H5N1 or similar pandemic.[71] People must be made aware of the grave risks facing them. This will create public demand for effective action, such as reducing industrial production of chicken and other animal products, providing adequate state and local funding, and increased stockpiling of drugs.

Unfortunately, countries often do not adequately focus on potential disasters until they occur. But if we wait for an H5N1-type pandemic to occur, it will be too late. Raising public awareness about the grave dangers of this type of pandemic will greatly increase our ability to take effective action and prevent it.

One of the most important weaknesses of pandemic strategies in the US and several other developed countries is the failure to adequately help developing countries prepare for pandemics. An H5N1 pandemic could start in the US or other countries with extensive industrial chicken operations. But it most likely will start in Southeast Asia for the reasons given above. Limited monitoring resources and drug stockpiles make it unlikely that an H5N1 pandemic could be contained in Asia. Rather than waiting for a pandemic to hit the US, we should do all that we can to help contain or at least slow it where it starts. This includes providing substantially more resources and other assistance to developing countries so that they are better able to contain or slow outbreaks.

Pandemic Consequences

If H5N1 becomes easily transmissible between humans, we almost certainly will not be able to stop the spread of the virus in developing and developed countries.[72] As noted, it is highly unlikely that developing countries will be able to contain H5N1 once it evolves to pandemic (i.e. easily transmissible) form. In addition, if Tamiflu or other antiviral drugs are used incorrectly (i.e. if citizens are not given enough antivirals to complete the full treatment), H5N1 may develop further resistance to them.

Due to extensive global travel and shipping, an H5N1 pandemic almost certainly will spread much faster than the 1918 pandemic virus. The 1918 virus took several weeks to spread around the world. Some experts believe that an H5N1 pandemic begun in Asia could reach the US, for example, in less than 24 hours. Based on past pandemics, an H5N1 pandemic is expected to occur in several waves. Two to three waves have been predicted, each lasting six to eight weeks and occurring several months apart. The second wave could be deadlier than the first as the virus hones its ability to kill humans. In total, the H5N1 pandemic could last one to two years.[73]

In 2005, President Bush authorized the use of quarantines in the US to contain a pandemic. But many experts say that quarantines will be impractical and ineffective.[74] To illustrate, during the SARS epidemic, people usually developed symptoms before becoming infectious. As a result, thermal imaging and other methods could be used to identify and restrict potentially infected people before they could spread the virus. But influenza works in the opposite way. Adults can be infected and spreading the virus for up to four days before showing symptoms. Children can be infected for up to six days before showing symptoms. As a result, before a quarantine could be implemented in an area with H5N1, people with the disease probably would have left and spread the disease to other regions.

In addition, using the military to impose quarantines in the US could create many problems. An 1878 law bars the military from playing a policing role in the US.[75] Soldiers are not trained to be police officers. During the SARS outbreak in Toronto in 2003, teenagers and healthcare workers were the main violators of quarantines. Would US soldiers shoot healthcare workers and teenagers if they tried to leave quarantine areas?

Even if soldiers were used in a policing role, there would not be enough soldiers and police officers to impose quarantines or maintain civil order. An H5N1 pandemic would affect nearly every city and town in the US. Potentially hundreds of Katrina-level disasters could be occurring simultaneously and lasting a year or more. Federal resources would be quickly overwhelmed.

As noted, the vast majority of US citizens would not have access to vaccines or antiviral drugs. Also, many US citizens would not have access to healthcare services during a pandemic. As discussed in the Healthcare section, the US is the only developed country in the world with a for-profit healthcare system. Every other developed country uses a not-for-profit system. These systems focus on maximizing public health. But the primary goal and focus of a for-profit healthcare system is to maximize shareholder returns. To achieve this, the US healthcare system has been eliminating excess capacity for decades. Hundreds of hospitals have been closed. From 1995 to 2005, the number of emergency departments declined by about 14 percent.[76]

When the goal of a healthcare system is to maximize investor returns instead of public health, it makes sense to maximize capacity utilization by eliminating excess capacity. However, this leaves the US healthcare system with little surge capacity to handle disasters, such as an H5N1 pandemic. The US ranks 55th in the world in acute care beds per capita.[77] This is closer to Third World healthcare performance. European countries have about twice as many acute care beds per capita on average. European countries often can provide twice the acute care capacity for two to three times lower overall healthcare costs because the goal of a not-for-profit healthcare system is to maximize public health instead of providing ever-increasing shareholder returns.

Ventilators often will be needed to keep people with H5N1 influenza alive. Prior to COVID-19, the US had about 100,000 ventilators. About 75,000 were in regular use. While capacity has increased recently, among the millions of people who might need ventilators during an H5N1-type pandemic, few people would have access to them. A survey by the American College of Emergency Physicians found that 90 percent of the country's 4,000 emergency departments are severely understaffed and overcrowded. Emergency departments in major metropolitan areas often close their doors and turn people away because they are so crowded.[78] During an H5N1 pandemic, hospitals and emergency departments would be quickly filled to capacity. Sick and dying people might be waiting in corridors. Gymnasiums, community centers and other facilities would be used to treat the sick and dying. But this still probably would not provide nearly enough capacity.

A John Hopkins survey found that nearly half of local healthcare department workers would not report for duty during a pandemic, in part because of concerns about bringing infections home to their families. The American Medical Association code of ethics used to require that doctors report for work, even when they face danger. This obligation remains in Canada, but was eliminated in the US.[79]

The Department of Homeland Security (DHS) has responsibility for overseeing H5N1-type pandemic response in the US. But many experts are concerned that the DHS does not have the infrastructure or technical expertise needed to adequately manage this type of pandemic. The DHS would not have time to get up to speed during a pandemic. Traditionally, health emergencies were handled by the US Public Health Service, CDC and other health agencies. Some experts contend that pandemic response should be managed by healthcare professionals, not bureaucrats or other leaders who lack expertise in this area.[80]

The 1918 pandemic shows some of the actions that probably would be taken during an H5N1 pandemic. For example, laws were passed that prohibited coughing or sneezing in public, shaking hands and not wearing masks. People who coughed or sneezed in public in New York City faced up to a year in jail. In some cities, people who did not wear masks in public were put in jail for up to 30 days. In some states, public gatherings of any type, including funerals, were prohibited. As noted, businesses, schools and churches often were closed. Family members sometimes stopped feeding and caring for each other because they were afraid of catching the pandemic flu. Neighbors rarely took in children who had lost their parents.[81]

These actions were taken in response to a pandemic flu with a five percent mortality rate. As of 2011, there had been 543 cases of H5N1 avian influenza in humans, all in developing countries. Of these, 318 people died, a nearly 60 percent mortality rate. Many developing countries have limited healthcare capacity. Bird flu cases have been low so far. As a result, people infected with H5N1 often received the best available medical care and antiviral drugs, equivalent to top-quality care in the US. Nevertheless, in spite of often receiving the best available healthcare, more than half of the people infected with H5N1 bird flu died.

As noted, during a pandemic, nearly all people in developing countries and the large majority of people in the US and many other developed countries will not have access to healthcare and flu drugs. As a result, the H5N1 mortality rate could be substantially higher than 60 percent, perhaps as high as 80 to 90 percent. In addition, in 1918, people in developed countries were far more self-sufficient than we are today. Many people lived on or near farms. People often produced their own clothes and other basic goods. Today, people in developed countries, especially in urban areas, often are highly dependent on a far-flung supply system that probably would be shut down in a few days. In other words, the disruption, trauma and mortality of an H5N1 pandemic could be vastly worse than the 1918 and COVID-19 pandemics.

Many economic and policy experts predict that an H5N1 pandemic could cause a catastrophic collapse of the global economy.[82] A WHO spokesperson said that during an H5N1 pandemic, billions of people would get sick, and billions more probably would be too afraid to go to work.[83] The flu virus can last for up to 48 hours on hard surfaces, such as doorknobs and railings. As shown during COVID-19, fear of infection would cause many people to avoid public transportation and public places. Utilities, including electricity, gas, water, wastewater treatment, phone and Internet, often would be shut down in a few days. To prevent contamination, many countries would close or restrict their borders. Global trade would be greatly reduced. Widespread use of just-in-time supply systems would cause the shutdown of many manufacturers that could not get supplies. Many stores quickly would be emptied and closed. Some UN simulations suggest that more lives could be saved by focusing on meeting the basic needs of healthy people (i.e. food, water, power), rather than focusing on treating the sick.[84]

Rationing antiviral drugs during an H5N1 pandemic could cause many problems. US antiviral stockpiles are limited. In 2009, the US had stockpiled enough Tamiflu to treat 12 percent of the population. The US military has long claimed first access to the antiviral stockpile. First responders, such as police, emergency workers and healthcare workers, also would be given early access. In addition, politicians and perhaps those who give large amounts of money to politicians often probably would have access. Many corporations have been stockpiling Tamiflu and other antiviral drugs for employees. And many doctors and public health officials also have stockpiled these drugs for their families and themselves.

Given claims on antiviral stockpiles, most average citizens probably will not have access to the drugs. Allocation of healthcare services and life-saving drugs during a pandemic would be like access to lifeboats on the Titanic. Wealthy citizens and politicians often would have access to healthcare and antiviral drugs. But little would be available for low and middle-income citizens. This could cause riots and other social disruption. Low and middle-income citizens will not stand by and watch their children die while wealthy citizens, politicians, soldiers and others receive life-saving drugs.

Disasters often bring out the best and worst in people. During an H5N1 pandemic, there undoubtedly would be many acts of heroism, as there were in 1918. However, people filled with fear seeking to survive also would engage in many negative, even barbaric acts. Based on actions taken during the 1918 pandemic, the likely much higher mortality rate of an H5N1 pandemic and the vastly lower self-sufficiency of modern society, many experts predict that civil society would quickly disintegrate during a H5N1-type pandemic.[85] With the low mortality rate of COVID-19, essential services largely remained available and society was able to function. This almost certainly would not be the case with an H5N1 or similar pandemic.

Panic and rioting might occur as people attempt to flee contaminated areas and possibly violate quarantines en masse. It is unclear if soldiers would be ordered to shoot thousands of citizens fleeing quarantined areas or if they would let the citizens leave. Mass looting probably would occur. Price gouging might be rampant. Black markets would form. And currency might be worth little or nothing. All levels of government probably would be severely crippled. Public services would be greatly reduced or not available. Communities could expect little or no assistance from the federal government. They largely would be on their own.

During the 1918 pandemic, dead bodies sometimes accumulated for months before they were buried. With a larger population and higher mortality rate, the problem of managing dead bodies probably would be much greater during an H5N1-type pandemic. Caskets would be sold out quickly, crematoria would be rapidly overwhelmed, and there might be fewer people available to collect and dispose of dead bodies. In preparing for a pandemic, the UK and several other countries have identified sites that potentially could be used for mass graves.[86]

Also based on 1918 actions, a *Lord of the Flies* social pathology of hate probably would develop in some areas. A pandemic would create widespread fear and distrust in many people. Minorities and other groups might be persecuted and irrationally blamed for the pandemic, as they were in 1918.[87] Mental illness and stress would occur, especially among victims of the pandemic. As occurred in 1918, victims probably often would display hysteria or melancholy, and sometimes insanity with suicidal intent.[88]

According to the WHO, children probably would be the primary vectors for spreading pandemic influenza.[89] As noted, children can shed the virus for up to six days before showing any flu symptoms. During the 1918 pandemic, social service agencies begged neighbors to take in children whose parents were dead or dying. But almost no one did.[90] People probably were afraid that taking in a child from a pandemic home might be equivalent to imposing a death sentence on their own family. As occurred in 1918, we can expect that many children who lost their parents would be left to wander the streets and die.

As noted, many polls have shown that the public remains apathetic about the threat of an H5N1 or similar pandemic. A poll in Europe showed that the majority of people felt that government would be able to protect them during a pandemic. Given European not-for-profit healthcare systems focused on protecting public health instead of shareholder returns and superior pandemic preparation relative to the US and many other countries, European governments probably would be able to provide relatively more pandemic protection. However, even in Europe, governments and healthcare systems often would be overwhelmed during an H5N1-type pandemic. In the US and most developing countries, the large majority of citizens probably would have little or no access to healthcare services and life-saving drugs.

One public health expert predicted that citizens could expect 12 to 18 months of watching their loved ones die, potentially not going to work, and wondering if food, water, and other life-sustaining resources and services would be available.[91] Many people in urban and suburban areas probably would wander into rural areas seeking food, water and a better chance for survival. During the 1918 pandemic, some communities around the world minimized infections by stationing men with guns on roads into town. No one was allowed to enter. Similar activity, especially in rural areas, could be expected during an H5N1 or similar pandemic.

An H5N1 pandemic with high mortality would be the worst disaster ever to hit humanity. With mortality rates possibly ranging as high as 80 to 90 percent, potentially half of humanity could be killed. An H5N1 pandemic could bring about an end to civilization as we know it.[92] The pandemic largely would shut down the economy and society. It probably would take years for humanity to recover.

Perhaps the best description of pandemic consequences could be found in horror or science fiction novels. But an H5N1 pandemic is not fiction. Probably only global nuclear war could kill more people. While nuclear weapons might be used by terrorists, widespread nuclear war is extremely unlikely. An H5N1 pandemic, on the other hand, has a high probability of occurring. Humanity is walking along the edge of a cliff. Probably the only way to step back from the cliff is to end the industrial poultry production that almost certainly spawned H5N1 and probably will evolve it or similar HPAI viruses into pandemic form.

Individual Actions

The bad news about the 1918 pandemic is that half the world got infected. But the good news is that half the world did not. This indicates that it will be possible to avoid becoming infected with H5N1 or a similar virus during a pandemic if people take certain precautions. Dr. Greger's Bird Flu book provides extensive information about how individuals and communities can prepare for and minimize H5N1-type infections. Several other websites, such as www.PandemicFlu.gov, also provide useful information about preparing for pandemics. This section summarizes a few key suggestions for avoiding H5N1 and similar infections.

Influenza virus mainly is transmitted by coughed or exhaled respiratory droplets of virus-laden mucus and saliva. Conventional speech can produce thousands of very small droplets that settle out of the air within a few feet of an infected person's immediate environment. Smaller virus-laden droplets potentially can be carried much farther, for example, if they attach to particles of dust in the wind. Infections occur when virus-laden respiratory droplets land in another person's eyes, nose or mouth, or get planted there by contaminated hands. Infection also can occur through the fecal-oral route. As a result, proper bathroom hygiene is essential.[93]

Many of the H5N1 infections so far resulted from handling contaminated poultry. People can get H5N1 and other infections from handling chicken. As a result, proper handling of chicken, for example by decontaminating all surfaces touched by chicken 'juice', is important. However, H5N1-type infections from handling chicken are less likely in the US and other developed countries. During a pandemic, the primary means of transmission would be respiratory droplets.[94]

As a result, social distancing is one of the most important means of avoiding H5N1 and similar infections. If a person is not in the vicinity of infected people, it is much less likely that they will become infected. Therefore, as was seen during COVID-19, it is important to avoid public places, especially indoors, to the greatest extent possible. If people have the option to move from more populated to less populated areas, it generally would be advisable to do so. Isolation often is difficult. But it can be effective. During the 1918 pandemic, the island of American Samoa was completely cut off from the outside world. Even mail service was discontinued. As a result, it was the only region in the world that suffered no pandemic deaths.

In the remote mining town of Gunnison, Colorado, armed men blockaded the two mountain passes into town. As a result, Gunnison had one of the lowest infection rates in the US. Some countries are considering a total blockade during a pandemic. Even citizens who are away from home would not be allowed to return.[95]

Total isolation is not possible for nearly everyone in society. Therefore, other actions are needed to avoid H5N1-type infection. For example, surgical or N95 masks that effectively block the H5N1 virus should be worn in public.[96] As noted, influenza viruses can survive on hard surfaces, such as doorknobs, for up to 48 hours, and on soft surfaces, such as cloth, paper or tissues, for up to 12 hours.[97] As a result, people should not touch their eyes, nose or mouth in public until they wash their hands. Regular, thorough hand washing with soap and water is critical. Washing hands with alcohol-based sanitizing rubs or gels also is effective at killing or washing away the virus.[98] Surfaces should be washed with chlorine bleach solution. Clothes and bedding also should be washed in chlorine bleach, not color-safe bleach.[99]

Another important, but controversial, suggestion is that citizens should have a supply of Tamiflu or other antiviral drugs in their homes. Some public health experts claim that citizens should not have personal antiviral supplies. They argue that using the drugs without the advice of a doctor could cause H5N1 and similar viruses to become resistant to antivirals. This is partly deceptive. For example, if people take Tamiflu by mistake thinking that they are infected with H5N1 when they are not, Tamiflu resistance will not develop because H5N1 is not coming into contact with Tamiflu. However, if people who are infected with H5N1 do not take the full treatment, H5N1 resistance to Tamiflu could develop. Citizens might not be able to tell if they are infected with H5N1 or the regular flu. If they use Tamiflu when they do not need it, they might not have the drugs when they need them. Therefore, people with personal antiviral supplies might not take the drugs unless they have symptoms and the pandemic virus is known to be in their area.[100]

Experts who say that citizens should not have personal antiviral supplies sometimes suggest that the drugs will be available from doctors, pharmacies and public health agencies during a pandemic. But this often will not be the case. Tamiflu and Relenza must be taken within 36 to 48 hours of initial symptoms. Otherwise, the drugs often will not work.[101] Even with the regular flu, it frequently is difficult to go to a doctor and get drugs within 48 hours. During a pandemic, it often will be impossible to get antiviral drugs, especially within 48 hours of initial H5N1 symptoms.

First responders and other critical personnel would quickly claim much of the limited US antiviral stockpile. As noted, average citizens would have little chance of getting the drugs. Many experts claim that the federal government is not well prepared for a pandemic. As indicted by the federal government's response to hurricane Katrina, the government might be unable to adequately and effectively distribute drugs during a pandemic.

Taking drugs without a doctor's prescription is suboptimal. But doctor-supervised antiviral drug use probably will not be an option for the vast majority of citizens in the US and many other countries during an H5N1-type pandemic. The only options might be unsupervised use of antiviral drugs or no drugs at all. For those with antiviral supplies, doing research and speaking with doctors beforehand can greatly lower the risk of drug misuse. Many of the public health experts who suggest that citizens should not have personal antiviral supplies probably have their own supplies at home to protect their families and themselves.

Dr. Greger points out that public health experts might want to conserve antivirals for vulnerable people during the regular flu season. But the mortality rate for seasonal influenza is about 0.1 percent. In other words, seasonal flu kills one out of every 1,000 people infected. H5N1 kills about 600 out of every 1,000 people infected, and might be even more lethal during a pandemic. As a result, some experts claim that antivirals should not be used to treat seasonal influenza, but rather should be conserved for an H5N1-typle pandemic.[102]

Beyond having antiviral supplies, many experts suggest that each family should develop a pandemic plan and pandemic preparedness kit. Some experts suggest that people should have enough food and water in their homes to survive for four to five weeks. Food ideally should be ready-to-eat. It should not require refrigeration or cooking because utilities might not be available.[103] Many experts also suggest that each community prepare their own pandemic plans and strategies. As noted, during a pandemic, federal and possibly state assistance might not be available. Each community often will be on its own.

Pandemic Deceptions

Business deceptions about industrial chicken production may be the most dangerous public deceptions discussed in *Global System Change*. Publicly traded companies are structurally required to protect shareholder returns. If reducing negative impacts hurts returns and if negative impacts are not immediate and obvious, companies often essentially are required to oppose lowering impacts. Dr. Greger's book provides over 3,000 references and cites many public health and other experts who say that industrial chicken production promotes H5N1, and that continuing this practice puts society at grave risk of an H5N1 pandemic. But the risks are not immediate and obvious to many citizens because an H5N1 pandemic has not occurred yet. The vast majority of people probably do not understand what happens in industrial chicken facilities, how these operations almost certainly spawned H5N1, and how they are the most likely place where H5N1 or similar viruses will evolve into pandemic form.

The priority of human society should be to ensure the survival and prosperity of humanity over the long-term. But as discussed, while this may be the stated and intended goal of economic, political and other systems, it is not the measured and managed goal. As a result, it is not the actual goal that we implement in society. We myopically and suicidally often believe that putting economic growth and shareholder returns before everything else will maximize the well-being of society. The situation with H5N1 shows how insanely suicidal this myopic belief is.

As shown by many expert citations in Dr. Greger's book, there is overwhelming evidence that industrial chicken production places society at grave risk. From a whole system perspective, it becomes clear that the well-being of society demands that we end the current form of industrial chicken production.

Under true democracy (where the people control government instead of business) and fair, sustainable capitalism, business sectors would be constantly expanding, contracting or adapting based completely on what is best for society. But our grossly flawed, myopic systems do not demand this. Instead, we allow business sectors to expand, even when they harm society or place us at great risk. Our suicidal systems often require business managers and politicians who accept money from business to oppose actions that threaten shareholder returns. Managers of chicken companies, politicians who accept money from them, and judges appointed by politicians who took money from business probably often would vigorously oppose the reduction or elimination of industrial chicken production.

In addition to being allowed to legally bribe politicians and influence the appointment of radical, myopic, pro-business judges, business also is allowed to mislead the public. To protect shareholder returns, companies often essentially are compelled to deceive the public into believing that industrial chicken production poses no significant risk to society.

Once again this illustrates how flawed systems often compel good people to do bad things. No chicken company manager or politician who accepted money from them wants to harm society. Their sincere desire as human beings almost certainly is to enhance society. But as agents of corporations (both directly in the case of managers and indirectly in the case of financially-influenced politicians), business managers and politicians often must subvert their human goals whenever they conflict with the paramount goal of maximizing shareholder returns. Managers essentially are not allowed to potentially kill their companies by acknowledging the grave risk that industrial chicken production poses to society.

If it is a choice between killing the company or killing human society, business managers and politicians who take money from business (i.e. nearly all Republican and Democratic politicians) essentially are required to choose killing or severely harming society. Obviously, this is not the intention. But it often is the actual outcome of our grossly flawed systems. As discussed, if the choice is lie or die, business managers and their paid (i.e. legally bribed) political servants often will choose to lie.

The following public deceptions illustrate some of the ways in which citizens are misled about the strong links between H5N1-type pandemics and industrial poultry production.

Blame wild birds and outdoor flocks

One of the most common strategies for turning the public's attention away from the grave pandemic risks posed by industrial poultry production is to say or imply that wild birds and outdoor flocks pose a greater H5N1-

type pandemic risk. As discussed in the Industrial Chicken Production section, HPAI viruses such as H5N1 rarely evolve in wild bird populations or outdoor poultry flocks. However, indoor industrial poultry operations provide a nearly perfect environment for the evolution of HPAI viruses. Intensively confining genetically-similar, immune-compromised birds in their own waste with little sunlight and fresh air strongly promotes the development of HPAI viruses. While some HPAI outbreaks have occurred in outdoor flocks, the large majority of outbreaks occurred in industrial poultry operations.

The FAO said, "We are wasting valuable time pointing fingers at wild birds when we should be focusing on the root causes of the epidemic spread which... [include] farming methods that crowd huge numbers of animals into small spaces." The WHO blames the emergence of H5N1 on "intensive poultry production."[104] The National Manager of Disease Control of Canada's Food Inspection Agency said, "it is high-density chicken farming that gives rise to highly-virulent influenza viruses."[105] The director of the Consortium of Conservation Medicine said, "The global poultry industry is clearly linked to avian influenza [H5N1]. It would not have happened without it."[106]

Also as noted, it is difficult for influenza to move from wild birds to humans. Chicken serves as the main bridge. The US geological survey said, "Currently there is no evidence that humans have been infected with influenza viruses through contact with wild birds. All reported human infections have been associated with contact with domestic poultry."[107]

Indoor flocks are easier to cull

Culling (i.e. killing) infected or potentially infected birds has been the primary means of preventing the spread of H5N1 and other HPAI viruses in poultry. Chicken companies sometimes point out that it is easier to quickly cull many birds when they are intensively confined indoors. This generally is true. But concentrated indoor poultry production produces the

HPAI viruses that require culling. In other words, culling rarely would be required if industrial poultry operations did not exist.

Confining birds indoors is safe

Chicken companies and their allies often argue that keeping chickens indoors lowers exposure to influenza viruses carried by wild birds. This is true. But as noted, keeping birds indoors lowers but does not eliminate bird flu infections. Probably no industrial chicken production facility in the world is biosecure in the sense of being able to fully prevent pathogens from entering and exiting. Biosecure laboratories do this. Industrial chicken facilities do not. Calling industrial chicken production facilities biosecure would be like saying that sieves are secure containers for water.

Outdoor flocks are more exposed to LPAI viruses. But these viruses rarely evolve to highly pathogenic forms outdoors. Indoor flocks have less LPAI exposure. But once it occurs, as it frequently does, indoor facilities strongly promote the evolution into high-path forms. Also, indoor facilities are more likely to promote the evolution of HPAI viruses into pandemic form.

Highly pathogenic H5N1 evolved in industrial chicken operations. Then it was released into the environment where it infected wild waterfowl. Now, thanks to concentrated, indoor poultry production, it is possible for wild birds to infect outdoor flocks with H5N1. The greater risk of poultry deaths increases the incentive to move flocks indoors. This pits the economic interests of chicken companies against the survival interests of humanity. As noted, moving flocks indoors greatly increases the risk that H5N1 will evolve into pandemic form. In other words, keeping birds outdoors may increase H5N1 bird deaths. But moving birds indoors may increase H5N1 human deaths. From the industry's shareholder-focused perspective, it is better to lower potential bird deaths by greatly increasing potential human deaths.

Cheap chicken benefits humanity

Cost reduction is one of the main arguments used to defend industrial chicken production. Less expensive food, including chicken, obviously benefits people in developed and developing countries. But as discussed in the Misleading the Public section of *Global System Change*, the primary reason chicken companies or any publicly traded company takes particular actions is not to lower prices or feed hungry people. Reasons such as these may be part of marketing or public deception strategies. But the foundational reason for nearly all corporate action is maximizing shareholder returns.

Chicken companies must compete with other animal and non-animal food products. Keeping prices low facilitates ongoing growth in sales and shareholder returns. But in reality, industrial chicken is not cheap. This is an illusion created by our grossly flawed economic and political systems. Many of the real, actual costs and risks of industrial chicken production are not included in prices. Fixing this problem is discussed in the Pandemic Solutions section below.

Technology can prevent pandemics

Industrial chicken companies seek to avoid death in the same way that individuals do. Ending the industrial chicken practices that spawned H5N1 and likely will evolve it into pandemic form will shrink and probably eliminate some chicken companies. To avoid sales reductions or death, companies sometimes seek technological solutions that potentially can lower pandemic risks. Technological solutions can enable companies to continue growing chickens in crowded, unsanitary conditions, and thereby provide ongoing growth in shareholder returns.

For example, vaccination could keep birds superficially healthy, but not stop the replication and excretion of H5N1 and other influenza viruses. This could help profitability. But chicken sheds may remain breeding grounds for HPAI viruses. Many experts say that vaccination could stimulate the evolution of more virulent viruses when animals are intensively confined together.[108] In other words, vaccination could protect chicken company profits, but increase pandemic risk.

Some chicken companies are funding the development of genetically-engineered chickens that would not be able to pass the H5N1 virus to other birds.[109] This also potentially would enable companies to continue growing chickens in crowded, filthy conditions, and thereby protect shareholder returns. But as discussed in the Genetic Engineering section of *Global System Change*, there are many problems and risks associated with genetic engineering. It often is difficult or impossible to anticipate how GE chickens would interact with other lifeforms or how eating GE chicken might impact human health. Extensive independent research would be needed before GE chickens were grown to ensure that they posed no environmental or human health risks.

In addition, influenza viruses mutate rapidly. It is possible that H5N1 could mutate in ways that allow it to bypass defenses built into GE chicken. As a result, there is no guarantee that H5N1 and other influenza viruses would not be able to spread among GE chickens, and thereby promote the growth of pandemic H5N1. Furthermore, bringing GE chicken to market would take many years. But we must lower pandemic risks quickly. We should not delay protecting the lives of potentially one billion or more people so that the shareholder returns of chicken companies can continue to grow.

Technological solutions can protect shareholder returns. But the priority is protecting society, not business. As discussed in *Global System Change*, businesses have no innate right to exist. They are tools that should be used only to the extent that they benefit and do not harm humanity. However, humans do have a right to exist. The best way to protect society is to end the industrial chicken operations that promote H5N1 and similar HPAI viruses.

Biased/Illogical Characterization

As discussed in the Misleading the Public section, when companies have no logical means of opposing suggestions that benefit society but threaten shareholder returns, they often use illogical means. This frequently involves characterizing positions in distorted, illogical ways and hoping that non-expert citizens will be deceived. For example, to defend the intensive confinement of animals and protect shareholder returns, a meat industry representative said, "Confinement rearing has its precedence. Schools are examples of confinement rearing of children which, if handled properly, are effective."[110]

Comparing the intensive confinement of food animals to schools might be logical and valid if school activities included the following. Thousands of newborn children would be placed on a sawdust covered floor in a large shed. The children would be fed human remains, animal remains, feces, antibiotics and some grain. Children would spend their whole lives in the shed. They would have little room to move and live among a growing amount of their own feces. They would be engineered to grow faster and larger. Their legs and hips would not support their larger bodies well. As a result, they would spend about 75 percent of their time lying in their own feces. Hands and teeth would be removed without anesthesia so that children could not hurt each other while fighting. Ammonia would burn their lungs and bodies. They would have no sunlight or fresh air. They would never see parents or teachers. Of course, they would never learn anything (except that life is extremely painful). And they would be slaughtered painfully once they reach full size.

Fortunately, we do not treat our children this way. Therefore, it is absolutely absurd to compare schools to industrial animal production facilities. But most people probably do not understand how animals are raised in these facilities. As a result, some non-expert citizens might be misled into believing that industrial animal production is like confining children in schools.

There is little evidence of H5N1 human transmissibility

In defending industrial chicken production, a meat industry official said, "We care about a pandemic. We do care. But so far, there is no scientific evidence of human-to-human transmission."[111] This may be the most dangerous and outrageous public deception discussed in *Global System Change*. This perfectly illustrates the Wrong Reference Point deception technique discussed in the Misleading the Public section. Wrong Reference Point involves suggesting or implying that potentially dangerous activities should be continued until we are highly certain that they are harmful. It would be like parents not putting seatbelts on their children until they were at least 90 percent certain that they would have an accident.

In this case, the implication is that we should continue industrial chicken production until H5N1 or similar viruses nearly evolve or evolve into pandemic form. But then it would be too late. As discussed, we probably would not be able to stop the spread of H5N1 in developed or developing countries once it reaches pandemic form. The virus could kill billions of people, perhaps half of humanity. It would take years for the economy and society to recover. It could be the worst disaster in human history by far.

As a result, we absolutely must do all that we can to prevent H5N1-type viruses from reaching pandemic form. This includes ending the industrial chicken practices that create HPAI viruses and likely will evolve them into pandemic form. As noted, many experts are concerned that H5N1 is on the verge of reaching pandemic form. We know how influenza viruses evolve and adapt to new hosts. Based on this knowledge, many experts say that there already is a high probability that H5N1 will reach pandemic form.

H5N1 and similar viruses will not announce that they are about to go pandemic. The transition to pandemic form could happen unexpectedly any day. Billions of intensively confined chickens around the world provide trillions or more potential opportunities for the virus to evolve. Delaying action until we are more certain that HPAI viruses will reach pandemic form would help chicken company shareholders. But it may be the worst mistake that humanity ever makes.

Government Deception

When politicians accept money and other inappropriate influence from business, they often become primarily focused on protecting shareholder returns. As a result, they could be compelled to participate in public deceptions about pandemic risks. Government officials often argue that they do not want to alarm citizens. This helps to protect the shareholder returns of companies that gave money to politicians.

As discussed, several polls have found that the public is apathetic about an H5N1-type pandemic. This indicates that the government has not adequately informed the public about pandemic risks. If it had, citizens would demand more effective action to prevent an H5N1-type pandemic.

A 2002 bird flu outbreak in Virginia, West Virginia and North Carolina indicates the bias of the US government toward protecting chicken company shareholder returns instead of public health. The outbreak caused the culling of millions of infected and potentially infected birds. The FAO recommends that, "[Culled] poultry from infected flocks should be disposed of by environmentally sound methods and should not be processed for animal and human consumption." But landfilling or incinerating infected, culled chickens is expensive. As a result, some USDA officials suggested that chicken companies could recoup culling costs by selling infected birds for human consumption.[112]

Pandemic Solutions

Protecting human society from an H5N1 or other severe pandemic requires a whole system approach. Many system changes and other actions must be taken simultaneously. As discussed extensively in *Global System Change*, the root cause of virtually all major economic, political, environmental and social problems facing humanity is the same – our flawed ideas and systems. As a result, the foundational solution to virtually all major problems facing humanity also is the same – improving ideas and systems. Many of the system change actions discussed in *Global System Change*, such as returning control of government to the people and holding companies fully responsible for negative impacts, are major components of effectively addressing pandemic risk. This section discusses systemic changes and other actions needed to protect human society from an H5N1 or similar pandemic.

Zero Tolerance

Viruses from animals can be extremely dangerous to humans because we are animals too. Eleven of the twelve most dangerous bioterrorism agents are pathogens from animals.[113] H5N1 probably is the most dangerous virus in terms of mortality rate and ability to quickly infect millions or billions of people. An H5N1 pandemic could be the worst disaster to hit humanity by far. The 1918 pandemic killed nearly 700,000 people in the US.[114] It was the worst disaster in US history. It killed more people than any natural disaster or war, including the Civil War. An H5N1 pandemic could infect half of the US with a lethality rate of 60 percent or more. In other words, while the 1918 pandemic killed nearly 700,000, an H5N1 pandemic could kill 90 million people or more in the US. Many people who did not die from H5N1 could die from starvation, exposure and other factors due to the loss of utilities, shutting down of supply chains, and general collapse of society.

In statistics, the expected value of an event can be measured by multiplying the positive or negative impact by the probability that the event will occur. Probably only global nuclear war could kill more people and devastate humanity more than an H5N1 pandemic. But the probability of global nuclear war is extremely low. Many experts say that the probability of an H5N1 pandemic is very high. Combining potential negative impact with probability of occurrence, an H5N1-type pandemic probably poses the greatest threat to humanity by far.

In cases where an event could cause extremely high and unacceptable negative impacts, society generally must have zero tolerance for the event. The negative consequences of an H5N1 pandemic are so severe that we must do everything we can to ensure that it does not happen. As discussed in the Well-Being of Society section of *Global System Change*, the first priority of humanity should be the survival of current generations (because future generations will not survive if we do not). The second priority should be the survival of future generations. The third priority should be the comfort and well-being of future generations. And finally, the lowest priority is our own comfort and well-being. The Founders of the US risked and sometimes gave their lives so that current and future citizens could survive and be free. We also must be willing to make sacrifices for future generations if necessary so that they can survive and prosper.

Chicken represents the main H5N1/HPAI bridge to humans. Eliminating the global chicken population would vastly lower the risk of an H5N1-type pandemic. Humanity does not need meat and eggs from chicken to survive. As discussed in the Health section below, plant-based proteins are healthier, less expensive and less environmentally destructive. Giving up the ability to eat chicken meat and eggs is a small price to pay to vastly reduce potentially the greatest threat facing humanity.

Many people enjoy eating chicken. But as discussed below, tastes often are a matter of habit. There are many other delicious foods. People can learn to enjoy other foods in a few weeks or months. Most importantly, as noted, our comfort and convenience should be the lowest priority. Our Founders sometimes sacrificed their lives for us. The least we can do is sacrifice our ability to eat a particular food to protect our children and ourselves.

Adequately protecting people from an H5N1-type pandemic requires far greater prevention efforts. Pandemic preparation is important. But preparation probably will only slow the progress of a pandemic by a small degree. As noted, there is a good chance that vaccines based on current strains of H5N1 will not work. The virus might develop further resistance to Tamiflu and other antiviral drugs, thereby rendering them ineffective. Even if vaccines and antivirals do work, the vast majority of people, even in developed countries like the US, probably will not have access to the drugs.

In addition, citizens probably cannot count on the federal government to help during an H5N1 pandemic. It took the federal government five days to get water to the Superdome during Hurricane Katrina. It did a poor job of handling one disaster in one city. It would be foolish to assume that the federal government could adequately respond to disasters occurring simultaneously in virtually every city and town in the country.

The inability of government to help citizens is part of the grave consequences of an H5N1-type pandemic. It further shows why zero tolerance for an HPAI pandemic is critical. Zero tolerance means that prevention efforts must be increased. The most important aspect of prevention is eliminating or greatly improving the main driver of H5N1-type pandemics – industrial chicken production.

Global society largely has been using a firefighting approach to HPAI pandemic risk. We expand the main factor driving H5N1-type viruses (i.e. industrial chicken production), and then seek to stamp out bird flu outbreaks with culling and other actions once they occur. This pandemic firefighting strategy probably will not work. If we continue to fan the flames of H5N1 and similar viruses with industrial chicken production, there is a strong chance that they will evolve into pandemic form. Then it will be too late. We will not be able to put out the pandemic fire.

People often have difficulty focusing on potential threats. They are busy living their lives and providing for their families. They frequently do not have time to think about something that might happen. Also, they often assume that government will protect them. It frequently is difficult to balance an obvious cost with a non-obvious benefit. Giving up chicken will be difficult for some people who enjoy it. This obvious cost must be balanced against a nebulous benefit (i.e. preventing a pandemic that has not yet occurred). But in this case in particular, we must find the courage to deal with uncertainty. Individuals buy home, car and other insurance to protect from uncertain risks. Collectively, we must do the same with H5N1-type pandemics. In other words, we must do all we can to ensure that the impacts of an HPAI pandemic do not become immediate and obvious. If we wait for certainty, billions might die. In this case, we must act in the face of uncertainty.

To protect shareholder returns, some chicken companies, politicians who accept money from them and other allies probably will attempt to mislead the public about H5N1-type pandemic risks. They might suggest that we wait for more evidence that a pandemic will occur before taking action that eliminates or significantly modifies their operations. But we already have more than enough evidence. Many experts say that the risk of an H5N1 pandemic is very high. We must not ignore the experts in this case. Some companies almost certainly will seek to discredit experts who threaten shareholder returns or business survival. But the survival of humanity is more important than the survival of chicken companies. To protect our children and ourselves, we must do a better job of seeing through business deceptions intended to protect shareholder returns.

We must work much harder to lower pandemic risks. We should act as if an H5N1-type pandemic will happen tomorrow because there is a significant chance that it will. Even at a low risk of occurrence, the grave potential consequences of an HPAI pandemic warrant, even demand, a zero tolerance approach. But we are well beyond low risk of occurrence. Therefore, zero tolerance for an H5N1-type pandemic is mandatory.

Hold Companies Fully Responsible

Failing to hold companies fully responsible for all negative environmental and social impacts is one of the most important economic and political system flaws discussed in *Global System Change*. In competitive markets, failing to hold publicly traded companies fully responsible puts them in fundamental, structurally-mandated conflict with society. If companies attempt to voluntarily mitigate all negative impacts, they will put themselves out of business. Our myopic systems unintentionally compel companies to degrade the environment and society that supports business, which ultimately degrades business. Our systems are unintentionally suicidal.

Private enterprise is incompatible with the survival and prosperity of humanity when businesses are not held fully responsible. The obvious solution is to hold companies fully responsible for all negative impacts. This eliminates structurally-mandated conflicts between business and society. It makes acting in a fully responsible manner the profit-maximizing strategy.

In the chicken area, this means that industrial chicken companies must be held fully responsible for all actual and potential negative impacts. In terms of liability, industrial chicken production is similar to nuclear power production. As discussed in the Nuclear section of *Global System Change*, the potential negative impacts of nuclear power are so great that they cannot be insured by the private sector. The only way that nuclear power can exist is if taxpayers and government agree to act as the owners of nuclear power plants on the downside by paying for or assuming responsibility for many of the potential negative impacts and risks of nuclear power. Nuclear power would not exist if citizens were not compelled to act as owners. This is not capitalism. It is a grossly unfair form of socialism. Taxpayer/citizens are forced to act as the owners of business by covering the downside. But they receive none of the financial upside.

The same situation exists with industrial chicken production. As discussed, the current form of highly virulent H5N1 almost certainly was created in industrial chicken operations. In addition, these operations are the most likely place where H5N1 will evolve into pandemic form. In other words, probably the largest source of H5N1 pandemic risk results from industrial chicken production. The potential consequences of an H5N1 pandemic are extremely severe. It is not possible for the private sector to insure the potential deaths of millions or billions of people as well as insure the potential collapse of human society. The only way that industrial chicken production can exist is if taxpayers/citizens are forced to cover the downside. But again, this is grossly unfair socialism, not capitalism.

In this situation probably more than any other, it is absolutely essential that chicken companies be held fully responsible. For example, taxpayers should not reimburse companies for culled birds. This removes the incentive to raise chickens safely. If companies wish to increase profits by raising chicken in crowded, filthy conditions, they must bear full responsibility for the consequences. Investors in chicken companies or any other company never should have the expectation that taxpayers will cover the downside. If investors do not do adequate due diligence and anticipate risks, they should and even must lose their investments. Failing to hold investors and their companies fully responsible compels them to maximize profits by engaging in risky activities, such as industrial chicken production.

In addition, taxpayers should not be paying for most pandemic preparation costs. This once again removes the incentive to act responsibly. If industrial chicken companies put society at risk of an H5N1-type pandemic, they should be paying to stockpile vaccines and antiviral drugs, as well as bear any other costs and risks they are imposing on society.

In addition, there should be no limited liability, especially in the industrial chicken area. As discussed in Limited Liability and Corporations section of *Global System Change*, limited liability and capitalism are mutually exclusive. Limited liability is a grossly unfair form of socialism because taxpayers/citizens are compelled to act as the owners of business on the downside, while receiving none of the financial upside. Therefore, limited liability cannot exist under a true capitalist system. When limited liability exists widely, the economic system largely is socialist.

Limited liability and private enterprise also are mutually exclusive because taxpayers and government are compelled to act as the owners of business on the downside. Limited liability is a misleading term. The far more accurate name is taxpayer liability corporation. No limited liability corporation is a private enterprise. It is a grossly unfair quasi-public organization. Obviously, if industrial chicken companies and their investors were held fully responsible for all negative impacts, industrial chicken production would quickly disappear. The current form of industrial chicken production cannot exist under true, fair capitalism. The existence of industrial chicken production requires a grossly unfair, suicidal form of socialism.

Human society, health and environmental life support systems take priority over everything else. There never should be any trade-offs between these critical factors and anything else. Business is tremendously creative. If companies are held fully responsible for all negative impacts and risks, they will figure out how to achieve full responsibility, or they will cease to exist. Society's demand for products and services, and the economy that this demand creates and drives, will not disappear. More competent companies will replace those that could not figure out how to act responsibly.

Charge Accurate Prices

Accurate pricing is critical in all areas, especially industrial chicken production. As discussed in Externalities section of *Global System Change*, under our myopic economic and political systems, nearly all prices are distorted, often grossly distorted, by the failure to include all real, relevant, actual costs and risks in prices. This causes our market system to be a major driver of environmental and social decline. Under sustainable, fair capitalism, all real costs and risks would be included in prices.

Industrial chicken production potentially poses the largest risk to the economy and society. In reality, it is not possible to place a value on the loss of millions, potentially billions, of lives and the near shutdown of the economy and society for years. Human life is priceless. In this sense, the potential cost of an H5N1-type pandemic is infinite. If this risk and all other externalized chicken production costs were included in prices, industrial chicken probably would be the most expensive product on Earth, far more expensive than gold for example.

Our current grossly flawed pricing system is suicidal. We must implement sustainable capitalism and charge accurate prices. Once this occurs, the current form of industrial chicken production will quickly disappear. Our suicidal economic and political systems create the illusion that industrial chicken is cheap. But in reality, the cost essentially is infinite.

Separate Business and Government

As discussed throughout *Global System Change*, only government can hold businesses fully responsible for all negative impacts. Government is the only entity which can ensure that all real, relevant costs and risks are included in prices. But government cannot hold companies fully responsible, ensure accurate prices or adequately protect the public when it is strongly influenced or controlled by business. In a democracy, government is supposed to be the agent and protector of the people. But when politicians accept money and other inappropriate influence from companies and their owners, they often primarily become the agents and protectors of business.

Government probably will not be able to effectively prevent and prepare for an H5N1-type pandemic until it becomes truly and completely the agent of the people. Returning control of government to the people in the US requires taking the many actions discussed in *Global System Change*, including publicly funding political campaigns, imposing term limits on Congress and the Judicial branch, implementing popular election of the President, and redefining corporations as artificial persons.

Implement Effective Regulations

Holding chicken and other companies fully responsible requires implementation of effective regulations. This includes implementing regulations that hold companies fully responsible for all negative environmental, social and economic impacts. It also includes ensuring that regulators have adequate resources and authority to effectively enforce regulations. In addition, especially in the pandemic area, severe penalties must be imposed to ensure regulatory compliance. Failing to minimize pandemic risks puts human lives at risk. Failing to comply with regulations intended to lower pandemic risks could be equivalent to murder. As a result, managers and employees who violate regulations should receive long jail sentences in some cases. This will maximize the likelihood that companies comply with regulations.

Severe penalties particularly should be imposed for failing to disclose bird flu outbreaks. For example, in 2002, an H6N2 bird flu outbreak in California infected millions of birds. To protect economic interests, chicken companies did not disclose the outbreak to regulators or neighboring chicken farms. A National Institute of Medicine report stated that the bird flu outbreak was kept quiet "by corporate decision-makers who feared that consumer demand would plummet if the public knew they were buying infected meat and eggs."[115]

This perfectly illustrates the grossly flawed, suicidal nature of our economic and political systems. Companies are required to put shareholder returns before all else, including public health and survival. Failing to disclose this and other outbreaks puts citizens' lives and health at risk. Companies, managers, employees and even investors must be held responsible for actions such as these.

In the US, the USDA represents a major barrier to effective pandemic regulation and protection. The USDA has the dual, conflicting goals of promoting and regulating the agricultural sector. This can put the agency in conflict with other government agencies that are more focused on protecting public health. Allowing the USDA to be the promoter and regulator of agriculture would be like allowing a person to simultaneously be a defendant's prosecuting and defense attorney or allowing a judge to oversee the trial of a defendant with whom the judge had a close business relationship.

Obviously, the USDA cannot effectively regulate chicken and other companies if it is simultaneously tasked with promoting the business of those companies. Regulation of companies must be done by separate government agencies that are not conflicted in this or other ways. For example, in the Netherlands, meat inspection is overseen by the Ministry of Health, rather than the Ministry of Agriculture. An editor of a US meat and poultry trade journal said that the Netherlands meat safety inspection program "makes the USDA's look like quality control at the 'Laverne and Shirley' brewery."[116]

In the pandemic area, improved regulation at the international level is critical. Under international law, countries generally are seen as absolutely sovereign states that cannot be ordered to take actions within their borders. During past outbreaks, countries sometimes gave priority to economic and trade issues, rather than public health. To protect economic interests, they sometimes failed to disclose outbreaks. An H5N1-type pandemic arising in one country could spread to the rest the world in a few days. This puts all of humanity at risk. As a result, this type of pandemic is a global, not national issue. Currently, the WHO only can recommend that countries take certain actions to protect humanity. It does not have the power to issue binding obligations.[117]

The survival of humanity takes priority over national sovereignty and all else. As a result, the WHO or other international organizations should be given the power to compel countries to take actions needed to protect humanity. This means that the US and all other countries must sacrifice national sovereignty in this area for the good of all humans, including US citizens.

End or Vastly Improve Industrial Chicken Production

As noted, domesticated chickens were raised in Asia in outdoor flocks for thousands of years. But H5N1 did not show up until humans began intensively confining chickens in their own waste. The main action needed to greatly reduce the risk of an H5N1-type pandemic is to end or vastly improve the industrial production of chicken, ducks, pigs and turkey. Industrial production of all these animals increases H5N1-type pandemic risk. However, industrial chicken production is by far the largest driver, due in part to similarities between the human and chicken respiratory systems and the much greater number of chickens produced around the world each year.

As shown by H5N1 human infections, the virus can be contracted by handling infected chicken. However, the much greater risk relates to the industrial chicken production process itself. This process of raising chicken in crowded, unsanitary conditions already almost certainly produced highly virulent H5N1. It also is the most likely place where H5N1 will evolve into pandemic form. Once the virus reaches this stage, chickens become irrelevant. The virus will move easily between humans, possibly killing billions of people.

Dr. Greger's Bird Flu book provides extensive detail about improving industrial chicken production. Important improvements include raising poultry in smaller, less crowded and less stressful flocks, providing abundant sunlight and fresh air, maintaining hygienic conditions that minimize exposure to other birds' feces, not feeding feces and animal remains to chickens, and breeding for increased immunity instead of increased meat and egg production. As discussed, chickens probably should not be vaccinated because this could promote the development of more virulent viruses. Also, antiviral and other drugs that might be used by humans should not be given to chickens. In addition, live animal transport and live poultry markets should be minimized or eliminated.

These actions would make indoor chicken production much safer. But the safest option, in terms of lowering pandemic risk, probably is to return to the outdoor, free-range chicken production that worked for thousands of years. Unfortunately, even this is not a risk-free option. Industrial chicken production unintentionally developed virulent H5N1, and then essentially placed it in wild birds. As a result, outdoor flocks now can become infected with the highly virulent virus. While the virus is much less likely to reach pandemic form in outdoor flocks, it still is possible. Alternatively, H5N1 could jump to humans from outdoor flocks, and then evolve to pandemic form. As a result, biosecurity measures are needed to minimize risks in outdoor flocks as well.

To reduce the risk of H5N1 and other diseases that could arise in industrial chicken operations, many experts recommend that industrial chicken production be eliminated or greatly reduced. Meriel Watts, a safety advisor to the poultry industry, stated, "Governments should take heed of this latest food crisis and outlaw the rearing of chickens in overcrowded factory farms. Chickens can be sustainably reared in free-range, organic systems that dramatically improve the health of the birds, and consequently also dramatically reduces the risk to human health... Cramming tens of thousands of birds into cramped sheds is a human health disaster in waiting."[118]

Europe is taking the lead in scaling back the industrial production of animal products. The vice president of the European Parliament's Environmental Committee said, "Factory farming and global transportation are behind the breeding and spreading of diseases like avian influenza. The EU must act now to prevent further outbreaks of such diseases. Measures must be taken to regionalize production, reduce transport distances, and impose animal welfare standards so that European factory farming is phased out in the coming years."[119]

The Chancellor of Germany called for an end to factory farming and implementation of "a new politics that stands for consumer protection, improved food safety, and natural, environmentally-friendly farming."[120] Many experts recommend that the focus of industrial animal operations should be switched from increased production to factors such as protection of human health and environmental sustainability.[121]

Several of the changes discussed above could be implemented for relatively low cost. For example, one study found that transitioning to slower-growing breeds of broiler chickens with improved immunity probably would cost consumers less than two dollars per year.[122] But publicly traded chicken companies essentially are structurally required to focus on protecting shareholder returns, rather than human health or anything else. Until businesses are held fully responsible for all negative impacts, chicken companies often will resist efforts that lower H5N1-type pandemic risks, but threaten shareholder returns. Once chicken companies are held fully responsible, taking the actions discussed above often will be the low-cost, profit-maximizing strategies.

Increase Pandemic Preparation

Prevention obviously should be the most important component of pandemic strategies. As noted, prevention mainly involves eliminating or greatly improving industrial animal production, especially chicken. Chicken and other companies often will resist modifications to their operations if shareholder returns are threatened. This can be rectified once citizens regain control of government and demand that businesses not harm human health or life support systems. But since pandemic risks are high, we must act in advance of establishing democracy in the US and other countries where business largely controls government. Increased pandemic preparation is especially important in the US because we are poorly prepared compared to many European and other countries.

Increased preparation requires increased funding. In the US, we spend far more on nuclear weapons, for example, than we do on pandemic preparation. But an H5N1-type pandemic poses a far greater threat to society than nuclear war. Pandemic funding should reflect this greater risk. If the US had a capitalist economic system, businesses would pay for risks that they impose on society. Business owners would assume the financial risks of their operations as well as get the financial rewards. But under the grossly unfair socialist economic system in the US, taxpayers assume much of the financial risks of business, while business owners get the financial rewards. If true, fair, sustainable capitalism existed in the US, chicken companies would pay for a large percentage of pandemic preparation costs because they are the primary factor creating pandemic risks.

Once again, when the people regain control of government, we can implement capitalism and require companies to bear full responsibility for negative impacts on society. Unfortunately, since democracy and capitalism largely do not exist in the US, taxpayers often must pay to protect themselves from risks created by business.

Increased pandemic funding and preparation are needed in several areas in the US and many other countries. A critical requirement is to develop more effective and less expensive vaccines and antiviral drugs. Development of these drugs has been severely restricted by patents and the need to maximize shareholder returns. But as discussed in the Property Rights section of *Global System Change*, humanity's collective right to survive takes priority over individual property rights. The ability of humanity to protect itself should not be hindered by property rights or shareholder return requirements.

This is another example of how philosophies often interfere with maximizing the well-being of society. For example, many people have a philosophical bias towards the private sector and against government. They often assume that government-based actions are socialist. They do not realize that what they call capitalism actually is a grossly unfair form of socialism. As discussed in the Misleading the Public section, philosophies often are used to mislead the public and protect shareholder returns.

Philosophies often cloud issues and block objective assessment of what actually is the best strategy for maximizing the well-being of society. At least among non-experts, philosophies, such as biases for or against the private sector or government, should be placed in the garbage can. Analysis should be completely focused on which options provide the highest quality service or outcomes, at the lowest possible cost, through the most efficient and effective means possible, measured in an accurate and objective manner. In other words, decisions should be based completely on logical, fact-based, objective assessments of reality, rather than on biases, opinions or philosophies.

As noted, many high potential antiviral drugs have not been developed because they do not provide the same profit potential as multiple use drugs. More effective, lower-cost antiviral drugs and vaccines are needed to protect people from what may be the greatest threat facing humanity. In this case, it probably does not make sense to count on a profit-focused (so-called) private sector to develop these drugs. Instead, government probably should fund substantial research and then place the results in the public domain. In this way, many countries could produce low-cost essential drugs. Once the drugs are developed, competitive bidding could be used to engage the private sector in manufacturing the drugs for the lowest possible cost.

In advance of developing more effective, lower-cost drugs, government should increase stockpiles of Tamiflu, other antiviral drugs and pre-pandemic vaccines. In addition to stockpiling drugs, as shown during COVID-19, masks and other supplies needed during pandemics should be stockpiled. Funding for state and local public health agencies should be significantly increased because these agencies often will be the main line of defense during a pandemic. Developed countries should substantially increase funding and other assistance to developing countries, the likely source of an H5N1-type pandemic.

Also, governments probably should consider providing antiviral drugs to citizens before a pandemic, along with clear instructions about how and when to use them. As noted, using drugs without doctor supervision is suboptimal. But the vast majority of citizens in the US and nearly all other countries probably will not have access to doctor-supervised drugs during a pandemic. Their only options may be to get the drugs before a pandemic or have no drugs at all.

Another critical action in the US involves doing what every other developed country has proven to be more effective – implement a not-for-profit government-owned or government-managed healthcare system. Once the focus of the US healthcare system is switched from maximizing shareholder returns to maximizing public health, greater disaster surge capacity can be developed while total healthcare costs are greatly reduced. As noted, every other developed country provides adequate healthcare to all citizens often for about half the cost of the US, frequently with nearly twice the surge capacity.

Limit Deceptive Business Communications

As discussed in the Misleading the Public section, flawed systems often compel companies to use all legal means available to protect shareholder returns. Modifying industrial chicken operations in ways that lower H5N1-type pandemic risks probably often would lower shareholder returns. In these cases, companies often essentially are structurally required to oppose significant changes to their operations. Admitting the real reason for opposing changes (i.e. protecting shareholder returns, even if it increases risks to society) frequently would not work. Citizens rightly would say, human life and the stability of human society take priority over shareholder returns. Honesty often would not protect shareholder returns in this case. As a result, dishonesty or deception is required.

Some companies probably will use the deceptions discussed above, such as blaming wild birds or outdoor flocks for H5N1 or similar viruses. In addition, as frequently occurs in other sectors, some chicken companies might hire scientists and other experts who, not surprisingly, say that industrial chicken production does not increase H5N1-type risks. They might even go on the offensive and argue that industrial chicken production lowers pandemic risk by reducing infections from wild birds. Companies also might seek to discredit scientists and public health experts who suggest eliminating or reducing industrial chicken production. These deceptions confuse or mislead the public about pandemic risk, lower public demand for change, and thereby protect shareholder returns.

This once again shows why non-human entities must not be allowed to participate in conversations about what is best for society. As man-made entities designed to put shareholder returns before all else, we know that publicly traded companies will seek to maximize shareholder returns, even if their actions degrade society in ways that are not immediate and obvious. Companies usually will not voluntarily shrink or die. If the choice is lie or die, they often will choose to lie.

Unfortunately, since businesses and their owners are allowed to give money to politicians, not only will politicians frequently fail to prevent businesses from misleading the public, they often probably will work with businesses to mislead the public about H5N1-type pandemic risks. This is not said as a criticism of business or political leaders. Flawed systems frequently compel these deceptive, destructive actions.

Business-influenced politicians often will support rather than prevent public deception. As a result, people freqently are on their own. They must strive to see beyond deception. The evidence and information in Dr. Greger's Bird Flu book show the strong links between industrial chicken production and H5N1-type pandemic risk. This evidence is logical, compelling, clear and overwhelming. No rational person considering the breadth of the evidence could conclude that industrial chicken production does not significantly increase pandemic risk.

Citizens must think for themselves more, even in the face of extensive business deception. The lives of millions, perhaps billions, of people are at stake. We must not allow ourselves to be deceived by businesses and their paid political servants who are trying to protect shareholder returns. Once the people regain control of government, we can prohibit deceptive and destructive business communications intended to protect shareholder returns

Raise Public Awareness

Raising public awareness is one of the most important actions needed to prevent, prepare for and manage an H5N1-type pandemic. Politicians might not adequately inform citizens about pandemic risks to protect chicken company shareholder returns and avoid alarming the public. But the priority is not avoiding alarm. It is avoiding death. The level of apathy about an

H5N1-type pandemic in the US and many other countries shows that citizens have not been sufficiently informed about the grave risks facing them.

People often will not take action if they do not have some level of concern or alarm. As discussed, individual preparation and action will be critical to surviving a pandemic. If citizens are not advised to take actions, such as those discussed in the Individual Actions section above, many more people could die. In other words, failing to adequately inform people could substantially increase pandemic deaths.

Raising public awareness will encourage citizens to be better prepared. This will lower panic and chaos during a pandemic because people will know what to do. Government should tell the truth to citizens, even if it causes some alarm. If people believe that politicians are being dishonest or deceptive, they will not trust government. This could increase panic during a pandemic.

Citizens should be told in advance what might happen during a pandemic. For example, as we partly saw during COVID-19, people should know that openly coughing, sneezing or not wearing masks in public could be illegal. Schools, churches, businesses and other public places might be closed for extended periods of time. Utilities might not be available. Drugs and healthcare services also often would not be available. If the public learns about government's probable inability to protect many citizens during a pandemic, it will greatly increase public demand for more effective pandemic prevention and preparation efforts. Failing to stimulate this demand by raising public awareness also could significantly increase pandemic deaths.

Government must balance raising awareness and some alarm with avoiding panic. But citizens in the US are familiar with warnings, such as terrorism alerts. An H5N1-type pandemic represents a far larger threat than terrorism. A pandemic could strike nearly every city and town, while terrorism might affect one or a few areas. Also, an HPAI pandemic might be more likely than large-scale terrorist attacks. An H5N1-type pandemic almost certainly will cause far more deaths than terrorism. It essentially would be criminal to not adequately inform citizens of pandemic risks and give them an opportunity to prepare and protect their families and themselves.

People also should be made aware of the risks of industrial chicken production. Helping them to understand how industrial chickens are raised in crowded, unsanitary conditions would clarify why these operations strongly promote the development and spread of diseases. This awareness would cause citizens to demand improvements to industrial chicken production. To protect shareholder returns, chicken companies and their allies often seem to aggressively work to prevent people from learning the truth about industrial chicken operations.

An animal agriculture textbook states, "If most urban meat-eaters were to visit an industrial broiler house, to see how the birds are raised, and could see the birds being "harvested" and then being "processed" in a poultry processing plant, some, perhaps many of them, would swear off eating chicken and perhaps all meat. For modern animal agriculture, the less the consumer knows about what's happening before the meat hits the plate, the better."[123]

Raising public awareness about crowded, unsanitary industrial chicken production would increase demand for change and lower pandemic risk. But chicken companies often aggressively oppose raising awareness. Once again, when the people regain control of government, they can demand that government adequately inform citizens about H5N1 and other grave risks facing society.

Do Not Eat Chicken

Politicians who accept money from chicken companies and their owners cannot be trusted to put public safety ahead of shareholder returns, even though industrial chicken production probably represents the greatest threat to humanity. As awareness of industrial production risk grows, politicians might discuss the need for some improvement and take some token actions. But they probably will not bite the hand that feeds them until H5N1-type pandemic impacts become immediate and obvious. But once this occurs, it probably will be too late to avoid mass deaths and the collapse of society.

Citizens probably cannot trust that government will protect them from the H5N1-type risks related to industrial chicken production. Shutting down or vastly improving this production is critical to lowering pandemic risks. But governments that are heavily influenced by business, such as the US government, probably will not do it. As a result, people mostly are on their own.

Citizens collectively are the most powerful force in human society. They create and control the economy through their purchases of products and services. In the absence of government and business protections, people might have to protect themselves by not buying chicken. If they stop buying chicken, industrial chicken production would be shut down quickly.

As discussed in the Animal Welfare section below, the vast majority free-range and organic chicken is raised in crowded, unsanitary, industrial operations. Therefore, buying free-range or organic chicken usually would do little to lower the risk of an H5N1 or similar pandemic. Probably only chicken produced on local, truly free-range farms could lower pandemic risks. But since H5N1 is in wild birds, even buying truly free-range chicken increases the risk of an H5N1 pandemic. As a result, the safest option probably is to not buy chicken.

Food risks often are born mainly by the people eating the food. However, people who eat chicken place all humans at risk, even those who do not eat chicken. H5N1 and similar viruses make eating chicken a global problem. The negative consequences of an H5N1-type pandemic are so severe that it probably does not make sense to continue chicken production. Some activities provide benefits to humanity. But if the costs and potential risks are vastly greater than the benefits, humanity probably should not engage in them. The potential negative consequences of eating chicken, especially industrial chicken, essentially are infinitely greater than the benefits. Therefore, we probably should not eat it.

Viruses have existed on Earth for over two billion years. They often rapidly adapt to new hosts and environments. Humans, on the other hand, only have been on Earth for about two million years and we adapt relatively slowly. In a battle with viruses, humans probably will lose. We cannot be certain of this. But that is irrelevant. Waiting for certainty is suicidal. It would be like a parent saying, I will not protect my child unless I am 99 percent certain that he or she is at risk. We have more than enough evidence to end chicken production. Many experts have warned us of the grave threat that chicken poses to humans.

If industrial chicken production had never been implemented, H5N1 probably would not have evolved and we could have continued to raise chicken as we did for thousands of years. But industrial chicken production made all chicken potentially risky by creating H5N1. Killing all of the chickens in Hong Kong stopped human H5N1 infections in 1997. But H5N1 began killing humans again possibly because wild birds infected other chicken flocks. As noted, chicken is the primary H5N1 bridge to humans. If we burn this bridge by ending chicken production, we will vastly lower pandemic risks.

As long as poultry production continues, especially industrial poultry production, H5N1-type pandemic risks will remain high. When it comes to chickens versus humans, it may be us or them. We must not wait for certainty on this issue. Certainty might mean death. We must act in the face of uncertainty. Humans can survive without chicken. But we might not be able to survive with it. The pandemic risk of chicken production, especially industrial chicken production, is too high. It is a bet that we should not make. We should not play chicken with industrial chicken.

Whole System Strategy

The main suggestion of this Influenza Pandemic section is to end chicken production and consumption on Earth, or at the very least, vastly improve or eliminate industrial chicken production. Some people might argue that it would be impractical to end all chicken production and consumption. The implication is that humanity is too weak-minded to do whatever it takes to protect our children. But we are not weak-minded. Humanity has done amazing things. And we will continue to do them. We are smart enough to figure out how to survive, prosper and protect our children.

The history of humanity often has been one of struggle and sacrifice. The priority is not to continue eating one of our favorite foods. It is to do whatever it takes to ensure that humanity survives and prospers, even if it means making some sacrifices. We know how to vastly lower H5N1-type pandemic risks. As discussed throughout *Global System Change*, success requires a whole system approach. Many system change actions will be needed, such as charging accurate prices, holding businesses fully responsible and returning control of government to the people.

Another important action needed in the US is to rebuild the social safety net that was substantially dismantled under deregulation since the 1980s. As businesses gave money to politicians and asked them to remove impediments to shareholder returns, the social safety net was greatly weakened. At the same time, a very strong investor safety net was put in place. Through public deception, we often have been misled into believing that the Christian principle of helping the needy is bad. We have become less willing to help parents striving to feed their children or elderly people struggling to meet basic needs. We often seem to be deceived into believing that these actions are un-American, anti-capitalist or unchristian.

At the same time, we are tricked into believing that transferring literally trillions of dollars of taxpayer wealth to the small group that gives the most money to politicians is somehow consistent with the American way or living up to some type of capitalistic ideal. As discussed in the Corporate Welfare section of *Global System Change*, in the US, at least several trillion dollars of public wealth are transferred to the top of society each year through many forms of corporate welfare, including limited liability, externalities, private sector money creation, and unfair taxation. Through one form of corporate welfare (allowing banks to create the money supply), taxpayers are forced to give hundreds of billions of dollars every year to bank owners and other investors in government securities.

Helping a parent to feed their children, build a home or send a child to college seems to have become un-American. However, requiring low-income and middle-income citizens to help a billionaire to build another mansion is somehow consistent with the American way. But it is not. Wealthy people do not need welfare. Those who prosper financially should help those who enabled them to prosper, such as consumers and employees. Rather than forcing low and middle-income citizens to provide welfare to wealthy people, these citizens have an obligation to pay to support the society that made them wealthy. That is the American way. Allowing a small group of wealthy people who control government to steal wealth from average citizens is the way of corrupt dictators.

The investor safety net in the US is a travesty. It must be dismantled quickly. Taxpayers covering the downside of business is grossly unfair socialism. Allowing citizens to be dependent on business for healthcare, retirement security and other basic needs perpetuates socialism because taxpayers are compelled to bailout and provide welfare to companies. The US should do what nearly every other developed country does – provide a strong social safety net. This will greatly facilitate the transition to true, fair, sustainable capitalism. In addition, dismantling the investor safety net and ending corporate welfare is the most important action needed to end deficit spending and quickly pay down the national debt.

It does not matter if a non-human entity, such as a chicken company, dies. It was not alive in the first place. However, all of the people associated with the chicken company do matter. With a strong social safety net, chicken company employees can be transitioned to sustainable business sectors with minimal disruption. Employees will not become destitute when chicken companies shrink or disappear. If investors in chicken companies lose their money, that is a risk they take with equity investing. Taxpayers should not protect business investments. This removes incentives to act responsibly and minimize total costs to society. If investors lose everything and cannot feed their children, they can be supported by the same social safety net that protects their employees and other citizens.

Beyond industrial chicken production, many people, especially in developing countries, survive by raising small flocks of chicken. Obviously, they must be protected too. Through a whole system approach, small-scale chicken farmers often could be transitioned to other means of livelihood. Alternatively, some chicken production might continue if experts find that limited production in small, outdoor flocks does not pose H5N1-type pandemic risks.

Humans have the ability to end chicken production or any other activity that threatens the ability of current and future generations to survive and prosper. Achieving this transition to sustainability through collaborative efforts is discussed throughout *Global System Change*.

People often seem to sit around, acting as if we have no power to change things. How could we completely eliminate the chicken industry, one might say. It seems impossible, others might say. But that is the mistake of the narrowly-focused human mind. Humanity has made vastly greater changes than eliminating a particular food. We must not be afraid of business and political leaders who are structurally required to put shareholder returns ahead of human life. They are good people being forced to do bad things by suicidally flawed systems. In this situation probably more than any other, we must act in advance of disaster. We must find the courage to stand up and protect ourselves and future generations.

Environmental Impacts

Industrial agriculture is one of the most environmentally-destructive activities in human society. In particular, the production of animal products (meat, poultry, dairy, eggs, fish) imposes extremely large negative impacts on environmental life support systems. This section summarizes the negative environmental impacts of industrial crop and animal product production.

Climate Change

As discussed in the Climate Change section of *Global System Change*, the production of animal products is one of the largest drivers of human-induced global warming. A World Watch Institute report found that livestock production accounts for about 51 percent of global greenhouse gas emissions.[124] By comparison, the combustion of fossil fuels in the transportation sector, including all cars, trucks, ships, airplanes and trains, only produces about 13 percent of emissions.[125]

Animal product production is highly energy intensive compared to plant product production. Producing one pound of beef generates 30 pounds of greenhouse gases, whereas producing one pound of carrots, potatoes and rice generates 0.42, 0.45 and 1.3 pounds, respectively. About 25 kilocalories of fossil fuel energy are required to produce one kilocalorie of meat-based protein. But only 2.2 kilocalories of fossil fuels are needed to produce one kilocalorie of grain-based protein.[126]

In addition to high carbon dioxide emissions, livestock production causes about 37 percent of human-induced methane emissions. Methane is about 23 times more potent than carbon dioxide at causing global warming. Livestock production also accounts for about 65 percent of human-induced nitrous oxide emissions. Nitrous oxide is nearly 300 times more potent at causing global warming than carbon dioxide.[127]

Chemicals

Industrial agriculture often involves extensive use of chemicals, including insecticides, herbicides and other pesticides. Pesticides are designed to damage or kill certain lifeforms. Some organophosphate pesticides are derived from nerve gas and can be highly toxic to humans. Like many other chemicals, pesticides often tend to spread out in the land, air and water, and then accumulate in animals and humans. As discussed in the Chemicals section of *Global System Change*, all people in the US and many other countries are exposed to pesticides on a daily basis.

Numerous peer-reviewed, independent studies have linked pesticides to a wide range of health problems, including cancer and nervous system disorders. Many pesticides are thought to be potential endocrine disrupting chemicals (EDC's). The endocrine system is extremely sensitive. It sometimes functions at hormone concentrations as low as a few parts per trillion. Nearly all people in the US have potential EDC pesticides in their bodies at these concentrations or higher. EDC's potentially can cause many human health problems, including breast cancer, early puberty in females, genital deformities and breast development in males, infertility and erectile dysfunction. EDC's may be more harmful at low doses that at high doses. In addition, people virtually always are exposed to multiple pesticides, EDC's and other chemicals at once. Exposure to multiple chemicals can greatly increase harm. However, very few threshold or safety levels have been set for exposure to multiple pesticides, EDC's and other chemicals.

Due at least in part to strong business influence of government, many toxic pesticides and other chemicals that are banned in other countries are allowed in the US. For example, the pesticide Atrazine is banned in Europe, but allowed in the US. Atrazine has been linked to cancer, hormonal and reproductive problems, and birth defects. Millions of US citizens, including pregnant women, are exposed to Atrazine in drinking water at levels that are linked to birth defects and other health problems.[128]

One of the most effective ways to lower pesticide exposure is to buy organic fruits, vegetables, grains and animal products. (Most synthetic pesticides are prohibited on organic crops and produce.) A study published in the journal Environmental Health Perspectives, found that pesticides in children's bodies dropped to zero in a few days after switching from conventional to organic food, including organic produce. Pesticide levels in the children quickly went back up when they switched back to eating conventional food. The study was prompted by an earlier study of pesticide levels in 110 children. Only one child was found to be pesticide-free – a child who regularly ate organic food.[129]

Bioaccumulation is another food issue related to chemicals and the environment. As discussed in the Chemicals section, toxic chemicals often bioaccumulate as they move up the food chain. To illustrate, small fish might regularly absorb toxic chemicals from surrounding water. When larger fish eat smaller fish, they often get high doses of toxic chemicals. Humans are at the top of the food chain. As a result, people who eat animal products often have the highest concentration of toxic chemicals in their bodies.

Persistent organic pollutants (POP's) are chemicals that can remain in the environment without breaking down for decades. POP's include highly toxic substances, such as DDT, other organochlorine pesticides, PCB's and dioxins. POP's tend to accumulate in the fat of animals and humans. To illustrate, a study of 31 types of food found DDT and its byproduct DDE to be the most common POP in US food, even though DDT was banned in the US in 1972.[130]

Dioxins are among the most toxic chemical substances. Dioxin was the primary toxic component of Agent Orange. It was one of the most toxic substances found at the Love Canal Superfund site in Niagara Falls. And it caused evacuations in Times Beach, Missouri and Seveso, Italy.[131] Dioxin has been linked to cancer, birth defects, reproductive problems, endocrine disruption and many other human health problems. Many dioxins are thought to be toxic in the parts per trillion range. Any exposure can be harmful. As POP's, dioxins can remain in the human body for many years. Their half-life in the body is estimated to be seven to eleven years.[132] Men have limited ability to eliminate dioxin from the body. However, dioxins can exit women's bodies, for example, in breast milk and through the placenta to developing children.[133] Fetuses and newborn children often are more sensitive to dioxin because they are developing rapidly.[134]

In the US, about 93 percent of dioxin exposure results from eating animal products, including meat, poultry, dairy, eggs and fish. Dioxin is hydrophobic (water-fearing) and lipophilic (fat-loving). As a result, dioxin in water will rapidly accumulate in fish rather than remain in water. Dioxin levels in fish can be 100,000 times higher than in the surrounding water.[135]

As discussed in the Chemicals section, animal products have the highest concentration of dioxin and other POP's. The most effective way to minimize or eliminate exposure to dioxin and many other toxic chemicals often is to adopt a vegan diet (i.e. avoid animal products, eat only plant-based foods). This particularly applies to pesticides. Animals are regularly fed pesticide-treated crops. Many of these pesticides accumulate in animals. About 80 to 90 percent of dietary pesticide exposure results from eating animal products.[136] As a result, switching to a vegan diet can substantially lower pesticide exposure, frequently by more than switching from conventional to organic produce.

As discussed in the Food Deceptions section below, food companies and their allies often argue that animal products are safe. Admitting that their products are harmful might be the equivalent of committing voluntary corporate suicide. Food companies, for example, might argue that their research shows that their products are safe. Alternatively, they might argue that there is not enough research to show that animal products are unsafe. As discussed extensively, both of these statements are deceptive.

Company research about the safety of their products is inherently untrustworthy due to the financial bias. Also, the statement that there is inadequate research to show that animal products are unsafe is the wrong perspective. The implication is that we should continue to consume potentially unsafe products until we are virtually certain that the products are unsafe. This is the equivalent of using humans as laboratory test animals. In rational food and other product safety systems, the standard would be that we do not consume or use any product until there is overwhelming independent research and evidence showing that it is safe.

Genetic Engineering

As discussed in the Genetic Engineering (GE) section of *Global System Change*, crops that are genetically modified to resist herbicides or pests are widely used in the US and some other countries. Over 90 percent of the corn, soybeans, canola, sugar beets and cotton grown in the US are genetically modified.[137] GE involves manipulating genetic material in ways that produce new lifeforms. These lifeforms bypass evolutionary screens. They generally would not be produced by the nearly infinitely greater intelligence of nature. It often is impossible to predict how GE crops will interact, interfere or breed with non-GE crops or wild plants. Given the nearly infinite number of potential interactions in nature, it is virtually guaranteed that there will be at least some negative impacts in nature.

This already is occurring. One study found that 80 percent of wild canola in North Dakota were integrating various GE traits from different GE crops.[138] Many experts are concerned that GE crops could cause human health problems, including allergic reactions, other illnesses and nutritional problems.[139] Little independent research and safety testing of GE crops has been done, in part because GE companies often suppress or control independent research through patents. Several of the few independent studies done on GE foods found that they can cause health problems in animals including infertility and immune system problems.[140] As a result, GE foods could and might already be causing these and other health problems in humans.

In spite of potentially large environmental and human health risks, heavy business influence of government and public deceptions about the risks, costs and benefits of GE crops have enabled widespread use of GE foods. About 70 percent of processed food sold in the US contains GE ingredients.[141] Virtually every GE labeling poll has found strong to overwhelming support for labeling.[142] GE foods provide no more nutritional benefit to consumers than conventional crops, and they may cause harm. As a result, labeling GE foods almost certainly would cause large reductions in the sales of GE crops, ingredients and foods. To protect shareholder returns, GE companies, politicians paid by them, and other business allies have aggressively and successfully opposed GE labeling. Nearly every other developed country requires labeling of GE foods or does not allow them. The failure to label GE foods in the business-dominated US often removes citizens' ability to choose whether or not they will eat them. In effect, citizens are being forced to eat GE foods.

GE crops usually are designed to benefit farmers, not consumers. GE companies often claim that GE crops will increase yields and reduce pesticide use and soil erosion. However, as discussed in the GE section, these benefits frequently are not materializing. A report by the Union of Concerned Scientists found that extensive use of GE crops did not significantly increase yields in the US.[143] In addition, herbicide-resistant superweeds have infested millions of acres of farmland.[144] Controlling these weeds often requires increased herbicide use and soil tilling, which increases soil erosion.

It frequently is impossible to predict the consequences of releasing unnatural GE lifeforms into the environment and human body. Use of GE is likely to have unintended and uncontrollable consequences, including making the environment less hospitable to humanity. The highest priority is the survival and health of citizens. As a result, adequate independent safety testing must be done before GE crops are used. But the business-dominated US government does not require this. Instead, it appears to place the financial well-being of companies that give money to politicians ahead of public safety. Once the people regain control of government, we can demand that our servant put public survival and health ahead of shareholder returns and all else.

As discussed in the GE section, many studies have shown that organic and other natural farming methods can increase yields and control pests more effectively than using GE crops. These natural farming methods often have little or no extra cost, or even cost less. As a result, GE companies frequently would not make money on them. To protect shareholder returns, GE companies sometimes apparently inappropriately influence government and mislead the public in an effort to maintain GE seed sales. As discussed, businesses have no innate right to earn a profit or exist. Under healthy, fair capitalism, companies and business sectors would be continuously expanding or contracting based on what maximizes the well-being of society. If replacing GE industrial agriculture with sustainable organic farming benefits society, as numerous studies and common sense shows that it does, we must ensure that this transition occurs.

Another large food risk related to GE involves GE fish and animals. As discussed in the GE section, in 2015, the the US Food and Drug Administration (FDA) approved the production and sale of GE salmon based largely on safety testing done by the company making the salmon. It often will be difficult or impossible to project the environmental and human health impacts of producing, consuming and releasing unnatural fish and animals into the environment. Potential risks are catastrophic. Human survival and health take priority over everything else. Only independent research can ensure that these most important factors are protected. Once democracy is restored in the US, we can demand that government stops putting the financial well-being of companies that give money to politicians ahead of human health and survival.

Also as discussed in the GE section, GE companies often promote rapid implementation of GE crops. Once these crops are in the ground, it frequently is impossible to prevent or reverse GE contamination of non-GE crops and wild areas. The difficulty or impossibility of reversing GE crop contamination makes it less likely that GE crops will be discontinued. By working aggressively to get GE crops planted quickly before adequate independent research is conducted, GE companies can ensure a steady stream of revenues, and thereby protect shareholder returns.

In spite of strong opposition from many farmers and citizens, the USDA approved unregulated cultivation of GE alfalfa. Alfalfa is a main feed crop. As a result, this almost certainly will increase GE contamination of organic meat and dairy products. Organic certification prohibits the use of GE ingredients. But widespread use of GE crops is causing GE contamination to become ubiquitous, especially in the US. Food labeled organic is allowed to have up to five percent non-organic ingredients. This makes some GE contamination of organic food legal. As GE contamination expands, as it inevitably will if GE crops are used, it might become impossible to buy truly GE-free foods.

Inadequate independent safety testing was done prior to the use of GE crops and foods. They already are causing negative environmental impacts. At some point, we might find that they also are causing negative human health impacts. It probably will be impossible to remove GE contamination from the environment and food supply. As a result, we might be compelled to suffer the consequences of myopic GE use. Given widespread GE contamination, it already might be too late to prevent this. However, we can lower the risk of catastrophic and other negative outcomes by prohibiting future GE use until GE is incontrovertibly proven to be safe by truly independent research.

Nanotechnology

As discussed in the Nanotechnology (NT) section of *Global System Change*, engineered nanomaterials (ENM's) are used in thousands of food, beverage and other products that directly or indirectly come into contact with humans, including food containers, cosmetics, sunscreens, other personal care products, clothing, drugs and pesticides. ENM's are extremely small, human-created or manipulated materials. They usually range in size from one to 100 nanometers (a human hair is about 80,000 nm thick). The unusual properties of ENM's enable them to enhance the performance of many products. However, they also pose very large, potentially catastrophic risks.

The small size of ENM's enables them to pass through organs, blood vessels and cell walls as well as bypass the blood-brain barrier. As human-created materials, ENM's were not present when humans and other lifeforms were evolving. As a result, when they penetrate the brain and other organs, our bodies might not know how to deal with them.

ENM's are so small that it often is difficult to detect them in the environment or humans. It also frequently would be impossible to remove them, even if they could be detected. As a result, to protect the health and well-being of humans and environmental life support systems, it is imperative that these substances be thoroughly and independently safety tested before they are used. But unfortunately, the business-dominated US government does not require independent testing. In many cases, no safety testing is required before these new materials, never seen before on Earth, are used in or on the human body. Nearly all ENM's are unregulated. This is a gross violation of public safety and environmental protection. As noted, the survival and health of humanity take priority over everything else. We must be virtually certain that anything which threatens these most important factors is safe before it is used.

With limited liability and other forms of corporate welfare, taxpayers often are required to cover most of the downside of ENM use, while investors receive nearly all of the upside. This is grossly unfair. Companies and their investors must be held fully responsible for all potential and actual negative environmental and human health impacts of ENM's. When this occurs, they will be highly motivated to develop safe products and services. Once democracy is restored in the US, we the people can direct politicians, regulators and judges to abide by the Constitution and place the general welfare of society ahead of the financial welfare of the small group that largely controls government.

Oceans

As discussed in the Oceans section of *Global System Change*, there are many environmental problems related to food and the oceans. Rising demand for fish is driving overfishing and depletion of ocean fish stocks. The global seafood catch has been declining since the late 1980s. A UN report found that 80 percent of the world's seafood stocks are significantly to fully exploited. About 29 percent of fish and seafood species have collapsed, meaning that their catch has fallen by 90 percent or more. If current overfishing trends continue, all fish and seafood species are projected to collapse by 2048.[145]

As ocean catches decline, aquaculture (i.e. fish farming) has increased rapidly. Aquaculture causes many negative impacts on ocean environments. For example, mangrove wetlands serve as buffers between oceans and land. They are among the most productive and diverse ecosystems on Earth. Shrimp farming has destroyed about 38 percent of the world's mangrove wetlands.[146] In addition, farmed fish often escape from open water net pens and contaminate wild fish. Also, as discussed in the Chemicals section, farmed fish frequently have much higher levels of PCB's and other toxins than wild fish.

Unsustainable fishing practices, such as bottom trawling, often destroy ocean environments and waste or deplete fish stocks. For example, bottom trawling, and trawling in general, frequently produces large amounts of by-catch (i.e. unwanted species scooped up and often thrown back into the water dead or dying).

Runoff of fertilizer and animal waste from industrial agriculture is causing a growing number of oxygen-depleted dead zones around the world. These zones frequently occur in prime fishing areas, such as the Gulf of Mexico. Other than lower lifeforms such as jellyfish, most marine species cannot survive in dead zones. Currently, it is more profitable for industrial agriculture companies to pollute and cause dead zones and other environmental problems. If these companies were held fully responsible for all negative impacts, they would maximize profits by acting responsibly and not polluting.

Water

Water is critical for food production. As discussed in the Freshwater section of *Global System Change*, rising meat consumption, energy use and other factors are causing demand for water to double about every 20 years, growing about twice as fast as the human population. At the same time, aquifer depletion, wetland destruction, pollution and other factors are causing the supply of freshwater to decline rapidly. By 2025, it is estimated that worldwide demand for water will exceed supply by about 50 percent.[147] In less than 20 years, water scarcity could reduce the world grain harvest by an amount equivalent to the grain harvests of India and the US.[148] While grain supply is falling, demand for grain is projected to grow rapidly. Water and food shortages are projected to be among the most important challenges facing humanity in the 21st Century.

Irrigation of crops represents about 70 percent of worldwide freshwater use.[149] As a result, improving water use efficiency in the agricultural area is critical for addressing projected water shortages. Producing protein from animal products uses far more water than producing protein from plant sources. It takes about 100,000 liters of water to produce a kilogram of beef, but only about 900 liters of water to produce a kilogram of wheat.[150] In other words, wheat production is over 100 times more water efficient than beef production. In addition, it takes nearly 1,000 liters of water to produce one liter of milk.[151] Given the gross water inefficiency of animal production versus plant production, greatly lowering the consumption of animal products is one of the most important actions needed to successfully address water shortages.

As discussed in the Freshwater section, charging accurate prices for water also is critical. Water prices are hugely subsidized in the US and many other countries. This drives vast water waste and overconsumption. It also makes animal products appear to be far less expensive than they actually are. One study found that beef prices would be about six times higher if water were priced accurately.[152]

As discussed throughout *Global System Change*, the market system can be a major driver of sustainability, but only if it is used correctly. This means that all real, actual costs of water use must be included in water prices. This will drive substantial improvements in water use efficiency, in large part by encouraging a shift to more water-efficient plant-based diets.

Beyond gross water use inefficiency, the livestock sector also is the largest sectoral source of water pollution in the world.[153] Livestock grazing and growing feed crops for animals causes about 55 percent of the soil erosion in the US.[154] Erosion causes sedimentation in streams, rivers and coastal areas. Animal production also is responsible for about one third of nitrogen and phosphorus nutrient pollution, which contributes to algae blooms and dead zones. In addition, the production of animal products causes about one-third of water pollution from pesticides and about one-half of water pollution from antibiotics.[155]

Regions facing water shortages, such as California, Israel and Spain, increasingly are using treated wastewater to irrigate crops. Pharmaceutical drugs often pass through humans or are dumped down the toilet. Wastewater treatment usually does not remove drugs. Many US studies found drugs in drinking water. A University of Jerusalem study found that produce irrigated with wastewater contained higher levels of pharmaceutical drugs than produce irrigated with fresh water. While drug levels in the produce were low, researchers said that they potentially could cause negative effects in people with a genetic sensitivity to the drugs, pregnant women, children and those who eat large amounts of produce, such as vegetarians and vegans. Improving agricultural water use efficiency can reduce the need to irrigate crops with wastewater, and thereby reduce drug contamination of produce.[156]

Air

As discussed in the Air section of *Global System Change*, food issues related to air pollution include mercury contamination of fish. The largest human source of mercury contamination is emissions from coal-fired power plants.[157] Mercury is highly toxic, especially to fetuses, infants and children. About half of freshwater fish in the US is contaminated with levels of mercury that are unsafe for children and women of childbearing age.[158] Eating contaminated fish contributes to about 23 percent of women of childbearing age having unsafe levels of mercury in their bodies.[159] As many as 640,000 unborn children per year in the US are exposed to unsafe levels of mercury in utero. This often causes reduced IQ's and other cognitive and developmental problems.[160]

As noted, the production of animal products causes substantial methane and nitrous oxide air pollution. It also is responsible for about two-thirds of human-related ammonia emissions, which contribute to acid rain and acidification of ecosystems.[161]

Land

As discussed in the Land section of *Global System Change*, industrial crop and livestock production are driving widespread degradation of the Earth's land areas. Industrial agriculture provides a perfect example of myopia. For more than 50 years, increased chemical use, farm mechanization, crop breeding, irrigation and other factors drove rising crop yields. This supported an expanding human population. However, industrial agriculture causes many problems, such as high soil erosion and aquifer depletion. These problems are slowing or reversing agricultural productivity gains in many areas. To illustrate, from 1950 to 1990, world grain yield per hectare increased by 2.1 percent per year. However, from 1990 to 2008, it rose by only 1.3 percent annually.[162]

From a whole system perspective, one sees that industrial agriculture is becoming counterproductive. By degrading soil, water and other life support systems, industrial agriculture increased short-term food production. But this was done at the expense of long-term production. Attempting to overcome or defeat nature in the short-term is degrading the environment and reducing the ability to feed future generations.

Industrial crop and livestock production degrade life support systems in many ways. Industrial agriculture often involves tilling the soil. This makes topsoil highly vulnerable to erosion. Over the past 150 years, about half of all agricultural topsoil around the world has been lost due to unsustainable farming practices.[163] Overall, about 85 percent of agricultural land has been degraded by erosion, salinization, soil compression, nutrient depletion, biological degradation and/or pollution.[164]

Healthy, natural topsoil often is a rich, diverse biological community containing billions of beneficial microbes, nitrogen-fixing fungi, nutrients, earthworms and other lifeforms.[165] Pesticides and other chemicals degrade or destroy life the soil. The dead or nearly dead soil of industrial agriculture farms often produces fruits and vegetables with substantially lower vitamins, minerals, antioxidants and other nutrients than produce from farms using organic or more natural farming methods.[166]

Crop and livestock production also are the primary drivers of grassland loss and desertification. As a result of human activities, about half of the world's grasslands have been cleared or degraded.[167] Agriculture and other activities have transformed about 10 percent of the Earth's forests and grasslands to deserts. This destruction of life support systems is continuing. Unsustainable agricultural practices cause about 120,000 square kilometers of land to become desert each year.[168] Crop and livestock production also are major drivers of wetland loss and conversion. Since 1900, more than half of the world's coastal and inland wetlands have been lost due to unsustainable agriculture and other human activities.[169]

Widespread forest loss also is driven mainly by agricultural conversion and livestock production. Forests once covered about half of the Earth's land areas. Agriculture and other activities have reduced this to about 30 percent. Since 1950, about half of the world's tropical forests have been cleared.[170] Since 1970, livestock production has driven more than 90 percent of the deforestation in the Amazon. About 70 percent of previously forested land in the Amazon is used for livestock grazing. A large portion of the remainder is used to grow feed crops.[171]

Rising population, meat consumption and other factors are rapidly increasing demand for food, biofuel and wood. As discussed in the Land section, without significant increases in agricultural productivity, an additional five million square kilometers of land will be needed by 2030 to meet demand for food and other products. Probably at least three million square kilometers of this would come from clearing tropical forests. If current plateaus in agricultural productivity continue, an additional 30 million square kilometers of land would be needed by 2050 to meet global food demand.[172]

It seems more likely that agricultural productivity will decrease rather than increase due to ongoing desertification, topsoil erosion, aquifer depletion and other degradation. This will create great pressure to convert much of the Earth's remaining forests and grasslands to agriculture. It is grossly unfair to future generations to try to convert much of the Earth's remaining wild areas to agriculture, especially industrial agriculture. This form of food production degrades the environment and human health.

To provide food security, countries in the Middle East, Asia and Europe are buying or leasing large amounts of land in Africa. This will drive widespread conversion of African forests and grasslands to agricultural uses. Many foreign buyers of African land plan to increase food production through the use of industrial agriculture. This often will lower the productive capacity of the land over the longer-term by creating the same types of degradation seen in other areas. These include soil erosion, pesticide contamination, fertilizer runoff and algae blooms, unsustainable water use, desertification, monoculture degradation and GMO contamination.

Land sales are creating many problems in Africa. Indigenous people often are being displaced from their land and hunger is increasing as food is sent offshore. Through corruption and lack of democracy, land frequently is being sold or leased at deeply discounted prices.[173] In effect, much of the African people's wealth is being stolen while their land is being degraded.

Livestock production is the most unsustainable aspect of humanity's food production system. About 30 percent of the Earth's land is used for livestock grazing. An additional 13 percent is used for growing crops.[174] About 35 percent of the world's grain harvest is fed to animals.[175] Combining grazing and crop production for animals, livestock production represents the largest human land use on Earth by far.

Beyond being the largest land user, livestock production, especially industrial livestock production, is one of the most environmentally destructive activities in human society. The Earth cannot and will not sustain a growing human population eating increasing amounts of animal products. Greatly reducing the consumption of animals is essential for reducing environmental degradation, feeding future generations, and, as discussed below, improving human health.

Waste

The livestock sector produces huge amounts of waste. As noted, it is the largest sectoral source of water pollution in the world. Cattle, chickens, pigs and other farmed animals produce 17 billion tons of excrement per year worldwide. This is 60 times more than the human population produces.[176] Producing animal products is far less grain and water efficient than producing plant products. It takes far more grain and water to feed a meat-eater than a vegan. Much of the grain and water fed to animals is turned into waste that often pollutes water supplies. For example, producing one pound of beef in the US creates 53 pounds of animal urine and feces.[177]

Packaging is another food-related waste issue. Food packaging often is extremely wasteful. It frequently contains various types of materials that make it difficult to recycle or process. The growing use of individually packaged servings also increases packaging waste. Food packaging waste once again illustrates the failure of our myopic, unintentionally destructive economic system to integrate full, actual costs in prices. If all of the negative impacts of packaging were included in prices, food manufacturers would be highly motivated to develop more efficient packaging or sell products from bulk containers. Citizens also would be less inclined to buy individually packaged items because they would be too expensive.

Another waste issue related to food involves food itself. As discussed in the Waste section of *Global System Change*, about one-third of the food produced in the US is discarded. This represents a huge waste of water (about 10 trillion gallons per year) and other resources.[178] In addition, about 40 to 50 percent of fruit and vegetables ready for harvest never get eaten. The produce often is left in the field or plowed under.[179] This waste of food is especially tragic because many people suffer from hunger, malnutrition and starvation around the world.

Biodiversity

A UN report found that livestock production might be the largest driver of biodiversity loss.[180] As noted, livestock production is by far the largest land use on Earth. As a result, it has driven the greatest habitat loss and species displacement. A report by Conservation International found that 23 of 35 critical areas threatened with biodiversity loss are affected by livestock production.[181] In addition to habitat loss, livestock production is a major driver of climate change, water pollution and other environmental problems that cause biodiversity loss.

An important biodiversity issue related to food involves the rapid loss of honeybees in the US and some European countries. Honeybees are critical to food production. They pollinate many fruits, vegetables, feed crops and other important plants. As discussed in the Biodiversity section of *Global System Change*, many experts believe that neonicotinoid pesticides are a main driver of honeybee losses in the US and Europe. As a result, several European countries have banned them. But the business-dominated US government still allows the use of neonicotinoid pesticides. It appears that politicians who accept money from businesses are putting shareholder returns ahead of the safety and security of the US food supply.

Contamination and Production

The large majority of food in the US and many other developed countries is produced through industrial agriculture. This sector can be divided into industrial crop production and industrial animal product production. Many problems related to industrial crop production were discussed in the environmental sections, including climate change, pesticide contamination, GE contamination, soil erosion and salination, air and water pollution, monoculture risks, aquifer depletion, contamination of produce with pharmaceutical drugs, and slowing or declining crop yields. This section focuses mainly on industrial animal product production and food contamination in general.

Industrial Farm Animal Production

About 99 percent of the meat, dairy and eggs sold in the US are produced in industrial farm animal production facilities (IFAP's).[182] A main goal of these facilities is to maximize the output of animal products while achieving the lowest possible cost. To achieve this, IFAP's regularly confine many animals in small spaces, use pesticides and antibiotics to minimize illness, promote rapid growth with hormones and antibiotics, physically restrain animals to prevent fighting and other undesirable behavior, and use breeding programs to produce animals that are better suited for confined living and provide a consistent food product.

Large IFAP's often are referred to as concentrated animal feeding operations (CAFO's). Animals grown in CAFO's usually are sent to industrial-scale slaughterhouses, where they are killed and processed. About 10 billion cattle, pigs, sheep, chickens and turkeys are slaughtered for food each year in the US.[183]

Raising many animals in confined conditions generates large amounts of excrement. About one billion tons of manure are produced each year in the US – the weight of 10,000 Nimitz-class aircraft carriers.[184] Industrial animal operations produce over 100 times more excrement than all people in the US.[185] A dairy farm with 2,500 cows, for example, can produce as much excrement as a city of 400,000 people.[186] Large amounts of manure produced in confined areas often cause widespread fecal contamination of CAFO animals. Fecal contamination frequently causes contamination of meat with harmful bacteria, such as E. coli, Salmonella and Campylobacter.

To illustrate how meat can be contaminated, beef cattle often are kept in feedlots where they stand ankle deep in their own manure.[187] As a result, cattle often arrive at slaughterhouses with feedlot feces on their bodies. Workers try to remove feces from cattle, for example, by carefully removing animals' hides. However, the need to provide ever-increasing financial returns often creates pressure to increase slaughterhouse processing speeds. As a result, workers frequently are under pressure to rapidly kill and process animals. Working rapidly to cut the hides off of animals can cause feces on the hide to spread into the meat. Carcasses often are washed with hot water and lactic acid to remove feces before being sent to the cutting floor. But these processes are not foolproof.[188]

At some slaughterhouses, one half of a cattle carcass arrives in the meat-cutting side of the slaughterhouse every five seconds. As a result, workers often do not have enough time to remove feces from meat, assuming that they even see it. Meat also can get contaminated with feces and harmful bacteria at the gutting station where intestines are removed.[189] Each animal is different. They are processed partly by humans. Humans can become distracted or overwhelmed. They also can slightly vary cutting and other activities from animal to animal. As a result, nearly every piece of meat potentially could have fecal contamination. In spite of slaughterhouse efforts to remove feces from meat, high processing speeds and the close proximity of feces to meat cause frequent fecal contamination. A University of Minnesota study of over 1,000 food samples from multiple retail outlets in the US found fecal contamination on 69 percent of beef.[190]

As discussed in the Influenza Pandemic section, industrial chicken operations often confine many birds in areas that leave little room to move. Egg-laying hens frequently are kept in battery cages that crowd birds together for their whole lives. Cages usually are stacked on top of each other. As a result, feces often drops on birds below. Larger operations frequently have over 100,000 birds per chicken shed. Extensive feces and fecal dust in industrial chicken operations cause widespread fecal contamination of chicken. Workers try to remove feces from birds in processing facilities. But high processing speeds often make this difficult. As a result, processed chicken meat often is contaminated with feces. The University of Minnesota study mentioned above found that 92 percent of chicken had fecal contamination.

Pig CAFO's also often have widespread fecal contamination. In the US, pregnant sows frequently are kept in gestation crates – metal crates barely larger than pigs' bodies. These and other concentrated living conditions promote and facilitate fecal contamination. Pig slaughter and processing operations try to remove feces from pigs. But the frequent demand for faster processing speeds often makes this difficult. The study noted above found that 69 percent of pork had fecal contamination.

Over time, large companies have come to dominate the US food sector, as they have in many other sectors. Large companies generally give more money to politicians and inappropriately influence government more than smaller companies. As a result, they can influence or compel politicians to implement policies that favor and subsidize larger companies. Inappropriate government influence probably has contributed to high concentration in the US food sector. In the 1930s, 24 percent of the US population worked in agriculture. By 2002, this had fallen to 1.5 percent.[191] Four companies process over 80 percent of the beef in the US. Three of these companies plus a fourth company process over 60 percent of the country's pork. In the chicken area, four companies produce over half of the output.[192] In the 1970s, there were thousands of slaughterhouses in the US. By 2008, 13 large slaughterhouses processed the majority of beef in the US.[193]

Industrial meat production appears to have benefited US citizens in some ways. For example, in 1970, US citizens spent 4.2 percent of their income to buy 194 pounds of red meat and poultry on average. By 2005, citizens were spending 2.1 percent of their income to buy 221 pounds of meat and poultry per year.[194]   It appears that industrial animal product production lowered costs. But this is an illusion resulting from myopia and grossly flawed economic and political systems. The industrial production of animal products imposes many real, relevant costs on society that are not included in prices. This creates the illusion that industrial animal products are much cheaper than they actually are. As with fossil fuels, much of the cost of industrial animal products is paid through higher taxes, lower quality of life and other factors.

A report by the Pew Charitable Trusts described the hidden costs of industrial animal product production. These costs include extensive contamination of water bodies and water supplies. For example, billions of pounds of manure have flowed into the Chesapeake Bay from chicken CAFO's over the past few decades. This has substantially degraded water quality and marine life in the Chesapeake.[195]

Manure runoff has contaminated many drinking wells near CAFO's with parasites and bacteria.[196]   CAFO's and slaughterhouses also disturb neighbors by producing extremely vile smells, fecal dust contamination and swarms of flies. In addition, as discussed below, industrial animal product production causes widespread negative human health impacts, for example, through the spread of viruses and bacteria. Extensive taxpayer subsidies of corn and other animal feed artificially lowers the cost of animal products, and in effect hides the real cost in higher taxes. If all of the real, actual, relevant costs of industrial animal product production were included in prices (i.e. if we used the market system correctly), locally-produced, sustainable animal products probably nearly always would be the lowest cost options.

E. Coli

E. coli is a bacterium commonly found in the lower intestines of warm-blooded animals. Some strains of E. coli, such as O157:H7, can cause severe health problems or death. Beef and dairy cows are primary reservoirs of E. coli. However, E. coli also can contaminate chicken and other animals as well as spinach and other plants. E. coli and nearly all other food poisoning comes from animals.[197] Therefore, when spinach and other plants are contaminated with E. coli, the source of contamination usually is animal feces. As noted, vast amounts of excrement are produced by farm animals. This frequently contaminates water supplies. When manure contaminates irrigation water, spinach and other crops can become contaminated with E. coli. Crops also can become contaminated when manure is spread on fields as fertilizer.

CAFO's often promote the spread of E. coli not only by causing widespread fecal contamination, but also by feeding animals unnatural food. For example, cattle in CAFO's often are fed corn, in part because it is highly subsidized, and therefore cheaper, and it makes animals grow faster. But corn is not a natural food for cattle. They naturally eat grass. E. coli often is killed by stomach acid in humans. Corn acidifies the digestive tracts of cattle. This promotes the development of acid-resistant E. coli that might not be killed in the human stomach. In addition, feeding corn to cattle also appears to promote the development of dangerous E. coli O157: H7. A Cornell University study found that grain-fed cattle had at least five times more E. coli O157:H7 in their digestive tracts than grass-fed cattle.[198]

In the US, E. coli O157: H7 infects about 50,000 people per year. Complications include end-stage kidney disease, permanent brain damage, insulin-dependent diabetes and death. Children are more vulnerable because their immune systems are not fully developed. E. coli O157:H7 is the leading cause of acute kidney failure in US children.[199]

E. coli also is responsible for about 90 percent of urinary tract infections (UTI's). UTI's kill about 36,000 people per year in the US.[200] People get E. coli mainly from eating contaminated meat and poultry. After bowel movements, E. coli bacteria can enter the urinary tract and cause infections. The anatomy of women make them 14 times more likely to suffer E. coli related UTI's than men.[201] An article by Dr. Michael Greger, called *Superbugs: Chicken Out of Urinary Tract Infections*, discusses how women can avoid UTI's. One of the most important suggestions is to reduce or eliminate the consumption of meat and poultry because these are the primary sources of E. coli that causes UTI's.[202]

The USDA regulates all meat production and sales in the US. Following an outbreak of E. coli O157:H7 in 1994 that killed four children, the USDA prohibited food companies from selling ground beef that is contaminated with the bacteria. However, strong business influence of government drives weak USDA regulations. This enables or drives frequent E. coli contamination, especially of ground beef. As discussed throughout *Global System Change*, the requirement to place shareholder returns before everything else often compels companies to oppose food safety and other regulations that protect society, but restrict shareholder returns. Food safety regulations have been weakened or not enforced in many cases because businesses are allowed to give money to politicians and inappropriately influence government in other ways.

As noted, the USDA has the conflicting goals of ensuring the safety of animal products while also promoting animal product markets. The need to balance economic and safety concerns often results in compromises on food safety that sicken and kill citizens. To illustrate weak food safety regulations, the USDA relies on a largely voluntary approach to meat safety. The agency suggests that meat companies develop and implement voluntary food safety programs. In other words, meat safety in the US frequently is voluntary rather than mandatory. When safety interferes with providing ever-increasing shareholder returns, meat safety and public health often suffer.

The USDA has inspectors at meat processing plants. However, following an E. coli outbreak in 2007, the USDA conducted spot checks at 224 meat processing plants. In spite of USDA inspectors being on site, the agency found serious violations at 55 plants. Companies were putting the public at risk by not following their own safety plans. But the USDA imposed no fines or sanctions.[203]

The USDA has no power to order recalls if it discovers contaminated meat. Instead, it can suggest that companies voluntarily recall meat. The USDA also does not have the power to shut down meat processing plants, even when it discovers ongoing sanitary violations. USDA inspectors can shut down processing lines, but they are strongly discouraged from doing so.

One USDA memorandum stated that inspectors would be held responsible for halting production unless there was absolute evidence of meat contamination.[204]

Failing to give regulators the authority to enforce regulations and protect public safety would be like failing to give police officers the authority to enforce laws. For example, police officers might be stationed in downtown areas. When they saw people committing crimes, police could inform criminals that the activities are illegal and suggest that they voluntarily stop committing crimes. However, criminals would be free to ignore police officers and continue committing crimes, usually without receiving any penalty or punishment.

The production of ground beef illustrates weak food safety regulations that put the public at risk. Companies that grind ground beef often use meat from different parts of cattle and from different slaughterhouses. Combining meat from different sources can substantially increase the risk of contamination with E. coli, Salmonella and other pathogens. In addition, ground beef often is made from lower quality cuts and slaughterhouse scraps that are more likely to be contaminated with feces.[205]

To reduce costs, about 70 percent of ground beef in the US contained an ingredient called lean finely textured beef (LFTB) in 2009.[206] LFTB is made from beef trimmings that average 50 to 75 percent fat and are more likely to have fecal contamination. To make LFTB, fatty meat trimmings are mixed and spun in a centrifuge to remove fat. Then the product is treated with ammonia to kill E. coli and other harmful bacteria. Some customers complained about the ammonia smell of LFTB. As a result, the manufacturer lowered ammonia content. This apparently contributed to greater E. coli and Salmonella contamination of LFTB. The USDA allowed the producer of LFTB to classify ammonia as a processing agent. As a result, ground beef labels are not required to show ammonia as an ingredient, even when the meat contains ammonia.

In 2009, the federal school lunch program used about 5.5 million pounds of LFTB. The program found E. coli and Salmonella in the beef product dozens of times.[207] In describing LFTB, a USDA microbiologist referred to it as "pink slime" and said, "I do not consider the stuff to be ground beef, and I consider allowing it in ground beef to be a form of fraudulent labeling."[208] Increased public awareness about LFTB reduced demand. But some companies and state school lunch programs still use it.[209]

Beyond ammonia, the USDA allows many other chemicals to be used in the production or disinfection of meat, poultry and egg products without disclosing the presence of these chemicals in food.[210] Chemicals for which disclosure is not required include sulfuric acid, hydrochloric acid, chlorine gas, chlorine dioxide (used to bleach wood pulp), propylene glycol (used in antifreeze), calcium hypochlorite (used to clean swimming pools), hypobromous acid (used to disinfect hot tubs), 1,3-dibromo-5,5-dimethylhydantoin (used in water treatment), and trisodium phosphate.[211] However, food companies are required to disclose more natural substances that are used to treat animal products, including salt, sugar, egg whites, spices and lemon extract. Requiring disclosure of natural substances but not chemicals in food once again indicates inappropriate business influence of government.

A New York Times article, called *Trail of E. Coli Shows Flaws in Inspection of Ground Beef,* discusses weak safety regulations.[212] For example, after several E. coli outbreaks, the USDA suggested that grinders test beef supplies before grinding. This would facilitate tracking of contaminated meat back to the source. However, many companies opposed this suggestion. Some grinders stated that slaughterhouses would not supply them unless they agreed to not test meat for E. coli and other pathogens. Beef suppliers were concerned that a positive test would lead to recalls from several customers, which would hurt profitability. As a result, most ground beef grinders do not test meat before it is ground. A USDA survey of over 2,000 plants found that about half of grinders do not test finished ground beef for E. coli. Only six percent tested incoming ingredients at least four times per year. When testing is done, it often is flawed. An analysis of independent laboratories used by food companies found that some labs missed E. coli in as many as 80 percent of samples.[213]

Reflecting weak regulations, even though selling beef contaminated with E. coli O157: H7 is prohibited, about 50,000 people are infected with this potentially lethal bacteria every year. Apparently to compensate for weak regulations that enable widespread fecal contamination of meat, the

USDA recommends that consumers cook meat thoroughly and wash down surfaces used to prepare meat. However, several studies have shown that these precautions are inadequate. For example, E. coli can remain on cutting boards, even after the boards have been washed with soap and water. As a result, some experts suggest that cutting boards should be sterilized with bleach to remove E. coli. The bacteria is dangerous in part because only a few cells can make someone sick. In a warm kitchen, E. coli cells can double every 45 minutes.[214] A University of Arizona study found that fecal contamination in the kitchens of meat-eaters, for example on sponges, towels and dish drains, often is higher than fecal contamination found in toilets.[215]

As noted, 92 percent of chicken and 69 percent of beef and pork were found to have fecal contamination. In an article called *How Factory Farms are Pumping Americans Full of Deadly Bacteria and Pathogens*, Dr. Michael Greger refers to the juice or liquid in packaged chicken as "raw fecal soup". This soup contaminates not only kitchens, but also supermarkets and other public places. For example, liquid or fecal soup sometimes leaks out of chicken and other packaged meat onto conveyor belts at supermarket checkout aisles. When customers set fruit, vegetables and other products on conveyor belts, the products can become contaminated with E. coli and other pathogens. Supermarket cashiers often clean liquid that leaked from meat packages off of conveyor belts (and possibly infect themselves in the process). But as noted, soap and water sometimes do not remove E. coli from cutting boards. Quickly wiping conveyor belts with paper towels probably will not remove fecal contamination in some cases.

A study published in the Journal of Food Protection examined packaged meat sold in grocery stores. The study found fecal contamination, E. coli and other pathogens on the outside of many meat packages. As a result, just picking up packaged meat can expose people to contamination. The CDC warns people to not touch their eyes, nose or mouth after handling meat, even packaged meat.[216]

Citizens are placed at substantial risk by the need to provide ever-increasing shareholder returns, inappropriate business influence of government and weak regulations. Some regulators argue that they must balance food safety with economic concerns. This illustrates our grossly flawed economic and political systems. The implication is that eliminating exposure to potentially lethal pathogens sometimes is too expensive. Food companies frequently take this position because they usually are not held responsible for the illnesses and premature deaths caused by their products. If they were held responsible, they often would slow down processing lines and take other actions to reduce fecal contamination of meat because this would be the profit-maximizing strategy.

Salmonella and Other Foodborne Illnesses

Foodborne illnesses often result from eating food that is contaminated with harmful bacteria, viruses or parasites. Bacterial contamination is one of the largest causes of foodborne illness. Besides E. coli O157:H7, harmful bacteria often found in food include Salmonella, Campylobacter, Listeria and Clostridium perfringens. These and other potentially harmful bacteria frequently are found in the intestinal tracts of animals raised for food. As a result, when animal feces comes into contact with animal or plant-based foods, food can become contaminated. Obviously, animal feces is in much closer proximity to animal products. As a result, most bacterial food contamination occurs in animal products.

However as noted, animal feces from CAFO's and other industrial animal product operations often contaminates water. This can cause bacterial contamination of fruit and vegetables. Humans do not get plant diseases. We get animal diseases.[217] Fruits and vegetables never are the source of contamination with intestinal bacterial such as E. coli and Salmonella. Plants do not have intestines. E. coli can live in soil. But the source virtually always is animal feces. If fruits and vegetables are contaminated with feces in irrigation water or manure spread on fields, they can become the vehicles for transmitting feces to humans. Nearly all foodborne illnesses result from food coming into contact with animal feces.[218]

Salmonella kills more people in the US than any other foodborne illness. It frequently is found in chicken, beef and eggs. Fecal contamination is widespread in chicken CAFO's. This can cause Salmonella contamination of chicken meat and eggs. In addition, dead egg-laying hens often are ground up and fed to live hens. This also facilitates the spread of Salmonella and other diseases.

There are many points in chicken processing where Salmonella and other pathogens can contaminate meat. For example, at the end of processing lines, chickens frequently are soaked together in chilled water tanks. This adds water weight to chicken, which increases profitability. But it also adds contamination. Water in the tank often is like a chilled fecal soup. A former USDA microbiologist said, "At the end of the processing line, the birds are no cleaner than if they had been dipped in a toilet." Collective chicken soaking increases fecal contamination by as much as 25 percent.[219]

Salmonella can infect the ovaries of hens. As a result, infected birds can lay eggs with Salmonella inside. This bacteria can survive in eggs that are cooked sunny side up, over-easy or scrambled. Buying eggs from cage-free hens can lower Salmonella risk. A large European study found that eggs from cage-free hens had 40 percent lower risk of containing Salmonella.[220]

As the food production industry becomes more concentrated, long-distance transportation of live animals from CAFO's to slaughterhouses is increasing. Live animal transport can greatly increase the spread of diseases because animals from different herds often are combined together for long periods of time in crowded, stressful, poorly ventilated conditions. A Texas Tech study found that the average presence of Salmonella in cattle feces was 18 percent before transport and 46 percent after transport. Salmonella presence on the hides of cattle was six percent before transport and 89 percent after transport.[221]

Salmonella infection usually causes several days of fever, diarrhea and abdominal cramps. But the bacteria also can pass through the intestine and infect the brain, bones, heart and other organs. Salmonella infection can cause persistent irritable bowel syndrome and reactive arthritis, which can become a debilitating lifelong condition of painful, swollen joints.[222]

As noted, it is illegal to sell meat that is contaminated with E. coli O157: H7 (although weak regulations enable frequent E. coli contamination). However, it is not illegal to sell meat that is contaminated with Salmonella.[223] Once again, our business-dominated government apparently is putting shareholder returns ahead of public safety. To compensate for the failure to prohibit the sale of contaminated meat, the USDA suggests that citizens cook meat thoroughly and wash down surfaces that come into contact with meat. Thorough cooking kills most of the pathogens that result from fecal contamination. If the government served the people instead of business, it probably would prohibit fecal contamination of meat, rather than placing the burden on citizens to protect themselves by cooking meat thoroughly and washing down surfaces.

Campylobacter is the most common cause of bacterial food poisoning in the US. The bacteria are commonly found in animal feces. Chicken frequently is contaminated with Campylobacter. Buying organic chicken does little to lower the risk of contamination. A Consumer Reports study found that 59 percent of conventional factory-farmed store-brand chicken and 57 percent of organically-raised store-brand chicken were contaminated with Campylobacter. Campylobacter can cause gastroenteritis, heart and blood infections, and Guillain-Barre syndrome, a condition that can leave people permanently disabled and paralyzed. With the near elimination of polio, eating chicken has become the most common cause of neuromuscular paralysis in the US.[224]

Listeria monocytogenes is a harmful bacterium sometimes found in the intestines of cattle. As a result, Listeria contamination can result from fecal contamination of meat. This type of contamination mostly occurs in foods such as hot dogs, deli meat, soft cheeses, ice cream and poultry. It can cause Listeriosis, a rare but potentially lethal foodborne infection. The disease primarily affects pregnant women, newborn children and adults with weakened immune systems. In pregnant women, eating Listeria-contaminated foods can cause miscarriages, fetal death or severe illness or death of newborn infants.[225]

Clostridium perfringens bacteria are one of the most common causes of foodborne illness in the US.[226] It is most often found in poorly prepared meat and poultry. C. perfringens infection can cause diarrhea and severe abdominal pain. The bacteria produce heat-resistant spores that can reproduce if food is allowed to cool slowly. Meat and poultry cooked slowly and allowed to stand for a long time at room temperature, for example in buffets, are most likely to contain C. perfringens.[227]

About 48 million people get food poisoning in the US each year.[228] Approximately 5,000 people die annually from these infections.[229] Salmonella causes about 30 percent of the deaths. Most people who get food poisoning do not seek medical care. Many of those who do are not screened for foodborne infections. A Consumer Reports study using CDC data found that Salmonella and Campylobacter infect about 3.4 million people in the US each year, send 25,000 people to hospitals and kill about 500 people annually. However, the study found that actual infections probably are higher than 3.4 million (as indicated by the 48 million infections noted above) because most people do not seek medical treatment for food poisoning. As part of the study, Consumer Reports tested chicken from over 100 supermarkets, mass merchandisers, and gourmet and natural food stores in 22 states. The analysis found that 62 percent of chickens were contaminated with Campylobacter and 14 percent were contaminated with Salmonella.[230]

Animal Feed

The need to provide ever-increasing shareholder returns creates frequent pressure to lower costs in the industrial animal production sector. Feed usually is the largest expense. To lower feed costs, the livestock industry has experimented with feeding newspaper, cardboard, cement dust and sewage sludge to farm animals.[231] Different aspects of animal feed are discussed in sections below, including antibiotics, hormones and contaminated meat. This section focuses on some of the riskier ingredients in animal feed, such as slaughterhouse waste, blood and excrement.

Cattle, pigs and chicken primarily are herbivores (although chickens and pigs sometimes eat rodents). But partly to lower feed costs, animal remains from slaughterhouses regularly are fed to farm animals in some countries. The World Health Organization (WHO) estimates that about 11 million tons of slaughterhouse waste are fed to livestock annually. In line with WHO guidelines, the EU prohibits feeding slaughterhouse waste to livestock. However, the practice is widely used in the US. Cattle remains often are fed to pigs, chicken and cattle. Pig remains sometimes are fed to cattle. Protein concentrates, frequently referred to as meat and bone meal, regularly are fed to most livestock. This feed often contains trimmings from the killing floor, inedible parts and organs, cleaned entrails and fetuses.[232]

Forcing herbivores to eat animal remains can create several problems. For example, mad cow disease (also known as BSE) probably originally resulted from feeding diseased sheep to cattle. The disease then spread by putting infected cattle remains in cattle feed. Unlike most other foodborne pathogens, mad cow disease is transmitted by heat-resistant prions that are not killed by cooking. Humans can get mad cow disease by eating contaminated meat. The human form of mad cow disease, Creutzfeldt-Jacob disease (CJD), always results in death. Victims' brains become riddled with holes. People often become blind, mute and paralyzed before dying.[233]

Mad cow prions usually are found in certain parts of cattle, such as brains and spinal cords. As a result, in the US, the brains and spinal cords of cattle older than 2.5 years are prohibited in animal feed. However, several studies have found that prions could reside in other parts of cattle that are regularly put in animal feed, such as blood.[234] Cattle that have tested positive for mad cow disease cannot be used in animal feed. The WHO recommends that all downed cattle (i.e. cattle too sick or crippled to walk) be tested for this disease. But the US government only tests a small fraction of downed cattle. People in the US could get mad cow disease from eating beef because prions can reside in untested downed cattle and body parts that are regularly used in animal feed. Some experts believe that pigs and poultry can harbor mad cow disease and pass it to humans because cattle remains often are fed to these animals.[235]

After eating infected meat, it can take decades before CJD symptoms appear. As a result, some people, perhaps many, already might be infected with this always-lethal disease. It is difficult to diagnose CJD when patients are alive. CJD sometimes is misdiagnosed as Alzheimer's disease. In one study, postmortem examinations of 46 patients diagnosed with Alzheimer's disease found that 13 percent had CJD. With four million cases of Alzheimer's in the US, some experts believe that many people could have CJD.[236] Cattle infected with BSE periodically are found in the US and Canada.[237] This potentially indicates that the deadly pathogen remains in the US food supply and that regulations intended to eliminate mad cow disease are inadequate.

In some countries, animal feed often contains blood collected at slaughterhouses. In the US, calves born to dairy cows usually are separated from their mothers immediately or within one day so that cow's milk can be sold to humans. The majority of dairy calves in the US are fed milk replacer, which usually contains cattle blood. An industry spokesperson said that the brown milk replacer does not look like milk, but the "calves don't care". Dairy calves in the US drink about three cups of blood protein concentrate per day. The majority of pigs in the US also are raised on feed that contains blood. Young pigs often do not like the blood-containing feed. But they eventually get used to it.[238] As noted, the WHO recommends that cattle remains not be fed to cattle. Cattle blood potentially could be infected with mad cow prions and other pathogens, possibly as a result of the slaughtering process. The EU prohibits suckling calves on cow's blood instead of cow's milk. But large amounts of slaughterhouse blood regularly are fed to farm animals in the US.

One of the most surprising and disturbing ingredients in animal feed is feces. In nature and natural systems, there is no waste. Every output is an input to another process. Animal waste becomes food for plants. Plants then become food for animals. However, industrial animal production generates huge amounts of animal excrement. For example, a two kg hen produces about 0.8 kg of feces per week. A 650 kg cow produces about 150 kg per week and an 80 kg pig produces about 40 kg of feces per week.[239] Animal waste often is spread on land as fertilizer. But the industry produces far more waste than can be used this way. As a result, managing animal waste often is expensive. Feeding feces to farm animals lowers feed and waste disposal costs. This in turn can substantially increase profitability. Animal feces frequently contains high levels of protein, vitamins and other nutrients. Recycling nutrient-rich feces back to animals minimizes costs.

Feeding feces to animals can cause many problems. As noted, cattle are completely herbivores. Pigs and poultry mainly are herbivores. They did not evolve to eat other animals or feces. Some animals, such as pigs, occasionally eat feces if it contains undigested food. But herbivores mostly eat plants. Feces often contains pathogens. As a result, eating feces can recycle pathogens back to farm animals. The WHO recommends that feces not be fed to animals. The EU prohibits this practice. But in the US, feces is widely fed to farm animals. Cattle manure sometimes is fed to cattle and pigs. Pig manure sometimes is fed to pigs, poultry and sheep.[240]

The largest volume of feces fed to animals results from feeding poultry feces/litter to cattle. Poultry litter is bedding material, such as sawdust or straw, used in poultry operations. After it is used, poultry litter consists mostly of poultry feces. But it also contains bedding material, feathers and spilled feed. In addition, it often contains pathogens, antibiotics, heavy metals, dead rodents, dirt and rocks.[241] As noted, poultry feed often contains cattle remains. As a result, feeding chicken feces and spilled chicken feed back to cattle potentially could cause mad cow disease and other problems. Poultry feces/litter often contains about 25 percent protein. It also can be as much as eight times cheaper than alfalfa and other animal feed. Given these nutritional and financial benefits, about one to two million tons of poultry feces/litter (mostly chicken) are fed to cattle in the US each year.[242]

One cow can eat as much as three tons of poultry feces/litter per year. One thousand chickens can produce enough feces to feed a growing calf year-round.[243] Feeding chicken feces to cattle does not appear to affect the taste of milk or meat. Taste panels found little difference in the tenderness, juiciness and flavor of beef fed up to 50 percent poultry feces/litter. Feeding chicken feces to cattle actually might make beef more tender and juicy.[244] However, cattle usually are not given feed that contains more than 80 percent poultry feces/litter because they often do not like the taste, and therefore eat less of it. Also, feed containing more than 80 percent feces might not provide adequate nutrition.[245]

In 1967, the FDA banned feeding poultry feces/litter to cattle in the US. However in 1980, at the beginning of deregulation, the FDA made it legal again. The situation with feeding feces to farm animals illustrates what happens when businesses are allowed to strongly influence government. Feeding chicken feces to cattle is prohibited in the EU and Canada. But in the US, businesses and their owners are allowed to indirectly give unlimited amounts of money to politicians and inappropriately influence government in other ways. As a result, the primary focus of politicians and regulators who work for them often becomes maximizing shareholder returns, rather than protecting public safety.

Feeding feces to farm animals increases shareholder returns. As a result, the business-dominated US government allows this practice. When businesses control the entity regulating business (i.e. government), self-regulation affectively exists. As discussed in *Global System Change*, self-regulation essentially equals no regulation. In competitive markets, businesses often cannot voluntarily constrain themselves when they are structurally required to put shareholder returns before all else. Voluntarily doing this frequently would put them out of business. Companies without regulations are like children without parents. They often cannot voluntarily modulate their behavior. Altering their primary focus on shareholder returns might cause business death. Lack of regulation inevitably produces *Lord of the Flies*-type behavior, such as feeding feces to food animals.

This is a violation of the public trust. Probably the large majority of citizens do not know that they are eating meat and drinking milk from animals that were fed feces. But they have a right to know this. Many people probably would not eat meat and dairy products that were produced this way. Raising public awareness about feeding feces to food animals could reduce sales and shareholder returns. As a result, food companies and politicians who accept money from them often aggressively oppose raising awareness. Failing to inform citizens essentially forces them to eat feces-fed animals. People have no choice. They become like the farm animals that are forced to eat feces.

Antibiotics

In 1951, the FDA approved the use of penicillin and tetracycline in chicken feed because it was discovered that antibiotics could make animals grow faster. But this only applies to industrial animal production. As discussed in the Influenza Pandemic section, industrial animal operations strongly promote the spread of disease among animals because the operations usually are crowded, stressful and feces-laden. Animals raised in these conditions spend much of their metabolic energy trying to avoid disease rather than growing. Giving the animals antibiotics minimizes disease and thereby facilitates growth. Animals raised in less crowded, less stressful and more hygienic conditions do not grow faster when given antibiotics.[246]

Reducing overcrowding and filth in industrial animal operations would lower disease and thereby reduce the need for antibiotics. But this also might lower profits. Antibiotics enable industrial animal companies to maximize shareholder returns by intensively confining animals in their own waste.

In the US, the large majority of chicken, cattle and pigs in industrial operations are given antibiotics on a regular basis. About 29 million pounds of many different types of antibiotics were administered to farm animals in 2009.[247] In the US, about 80 percent of antibiotics are given to farm animals while 20 percent are given to humans.[248] More than 90 percent of the antibiotics given to farm animals are used to promote growth and prevent disease, rather than to treat sick animals.[249] In non-therapeutic antibiotic applications (i.e. using antibiotics to promote growth instead of treat illness), animals usually are given regular low doses of antibiotics. This strongly promotes the development of antibiotic-resistant bacteria in farm animals. Antibiotics kill weaker bacteria. But stronger germs often survive and become resistant to antibiotics.

These antibiotic-resistant bacteria often are transferred to humans through several mechanisms. As discussed, millions of people are infected each year with E. coli, Salmonella, Campylobacter and other bacteria from animals. Many of these pathogens are resistant to various antibiotics because they came from animals that were being treated with antibiotics.

Antibiotic-resistant bacteria also can be transmitted to humans through feces-contaminated crops, flies, cockroaches and other mechanisms.[250]

Farm animals often are given many of the same antibiotics that are used to treat humans. As a result, bacteria in animals often develop resistance to human antibiotics. When people are infected with antibiotic-resistant bacteria from animals, human antibiotics frequently are ineffective at treating the disease.

Since the 1960s, many doctors and public health experts have strongly recommended that antibiotics used for humans should not be given to farm animals, especially for non-therapeutic applications.[251] Antibiotic-resistant infections kill about 90,000 people per year in the US and increase healthcare costs by about $30 billion.[252] Much antibiotic resistance results from doctors overprescribing antibiotics and from patients not completing full antibiotic treatments. However, there is extensive genetic and other evidence which shows that substantial antibiotic resistance in the US and other countries also results from giving human antibiotics to farm animals.[253]

To illustrate, E. coli contamination of meat causes millions of urinary tract infections (UTI's) in the US each year. About 30 percent of these infections are resistant to the main antibiotic treatments. Resistance to newer antibiotics also is emerging.[254] Another foodborne pathogen, Campylobacter, was effectively treated with quinolone antibiotics, such as Cipro. However, quinolone use in chicken was allowed in the early 1990s. Widespread quinolone-resistant Campylobacter emerged shortly afterwards.[255]

A study of chicken, turkey, pork and ground beef sold in grocery stores found that 47 percent of the samples contained Staphylococcus aureus, a bacteria that can cause serious infection or death. Ninety-six percent of the contaminated meat contained staph bacteria that were resistant to one antibiotic and about half contained staph bacteria that were resistant to three or more.[256]

One type of staph bacteria (MRSA) is resistant to several antibiotics. In 2005, there were nearly 100,000 cases of MRSA infection in the US. These caused about 19,000 deaths.[257] MRSA originally mostly infected people in hospitals and nursing homes. However, in the 1990s, healthy people who had not been near hospitals began getting MRSA infections.

Many studies have linked MRSA to industrial pig operations in Europe and North America. One study found MRSA at 81 percent of pig farms in the Netherlands. Another study found MRSA at 45 percent of pig farms in Canada. In the US, an Iowa study found MRSA in 49 percent of pigs and 45 percent of swine workers.[258] Further indicating the link between industrial animal operations and antibiotic resistance, retail chicken samples from chicken factories that use antibiotics were 450 times more likely to have antibiotic-resistant bacteria.[259]

Antibiotics are critical to modern medicine. They are used to treat and cure many illnesses. Extensive research shows that feeding human antibiotics to farm animals increases antibiotic resistance in humans. Growing antibiotic resistance severely restricts the ability to treat many diseases. It threatens large parts of modern medicine. For example, it may become difficult or impossible to treat infections during surgery, intensive care or cancer treatments such as chemotherapy if no effective antibiotics are available.

New bacteria are emerging with even more antibiotic resistance than MRSA. For example, bacteria with a gene called NDM1 are spreading around the world. NDM1 bacteria are resistant to nearly all antibiotics, including the most powerful.[260] NDM1 has been found in many pathogens, including E. coli. As noted, E. coli causes millions of UTI's in the US, which in turn kill about 36,000 people per year. If E. coli that is resistant to nearly all antibiotics expands, the UTI death rate could grow much higher.

In 2015, bacteria that are resistant to the most powerful antibiotic (colistin) were found in over 24 countries. Colistin was approved in the 1950s. But its use has declined since the 1970s due to high toxicity. Doctors use colistin as a last resort when nothing else works. The first case of colistin-resistant bacteria in the US was found in 2015 in a woman with a UTI caused by colistin-resistant E. coli bacteria.[261] As discussed in the E. coli section, to avoid antibiotic-resistant and possibly life-threatening UTIs, Dr. Michael Greger suggested that people, especially women, reduce or eliminate the consumption of meat and poultry, the primary source of E. coli that causes 90 percent of UTIs.

The director-general of the WHO said rapidly expanding antibiotic resistance is threatening to "send the world back to a pre-antibiotic age."[262]

It can take up to 17 years to develop a new antibiotic. But bacteria can develop antibiotic resistance in minutes. Antibiotic resistance is advancing faster than humanity's ability to control it. To maintain the ability to effectively fight disease, we must do all that we can to accelerate the development of new antibiotics and slow the growth of antibiotic resistance.

Most drug companies have stopped developing antibiotics because the drugs are not highly profitable. People usually only take antibiotics for a few days or weeks. It often is more profitable to develop antidepressants and other types of regular use drugs.[263] As corporate welfare is ended in the US, we can use the public wealth to develop antibiotics and other drugs that are essential for the well-being of humanity, but do not provide large profits for drug companies.

One of the most important actions needed to slow the growth of antibiotic resistance is ending the non-therapeutic use of human antibiotics in industrial animal operations. Numerous medical and public health organizations have recommended banning the non-therapeutic use of human antibiotics in farm animals, including the WHO, CDC, American Medical Association, American Public Health Association and the Infectious Diseases Society of America.[264] The director of the CDC said that, "there is strong scientific evidence of a link between antibiotic use in food animals and antibiotic resistance in humans."[265]

Even the FDA and USDA have expressed concern that antibiotic use in farm animals could be exposing humans to antibiotic-resistant bacteria.[266] Several examples have been given in *Global System Change* of how the FDA and USDA often give shareholder returns higher priority than public health, in large part because the agencies are overseen by politicians who accept money and other inappropriate influence from food and other companies. The usually shareholder-friendly FDA and USDA publicly discussing the risks of antibiotic use in farm animals strongly indicates the danger of this practice. Politicians and regulators usually do not bite the business hands that feed them, unless negative business impacts are immediate and obvious. The fact that regulators are biting indicates this is occurring.

In 1998, the EU banned using antibiotics that are important for human health to promote animal growth. In 2006, the EU banned all drugs used to promote growth in animals. In the US, the pharmaceutical and meat industries have aggressively opposed bans on the non-therapeutic use of antibiotics in farm animals. As is so often the case, the main strategies for blocking actions that benefit society but threaten shareholder returns are influencing government and misleading the public. By giving money to politicians and inappropriately influencing government in other ways, businesses can shift the focus of government from protecting public health to protecting shareholder returns. This inappropriate influence probably is the main reason why the business-influenced US government has not ended the non-therapeutic use of antibiotics in farm animals.

As discussed in the Misleading the Public section of *Global System Change*, if businesses have no logical way of protecting shareholder returns, they often essentially are compelled to use illogical means. There is overwhelming genetic and other evidence linking human antibiotic resistance to antibiotic use in farm animals. As noted, many doctors and public health experts have opposed this practice for decades. Nevertheless, a meat industry trade group said, "there is no conclusive scientific evidence that antibiotics used in farm animals have a significant impact on the effectiveness of antibiotics in people."[267]

This illustrates the Wrong Reference Point deception technique. The implication is that society should not end a potentially harmful practice until we are certain that the practice is dangerous. In this case, there is overwhelming evidence that antibiotic use in farm animals is harmful. Yet flawed systems compel companies to press for absolute certainty of harm before ending activities that threaten shareholder returns. The priority is protecting human lives and health, not shareholder returns. When these critical factors are threatened, we should not wait for 90 percent certainty of harm. The appropriate trigger point for action may be in the 10 to 20 percent certainty range. This level of certainty probably was achieved in the 1960s. The fact that human antibiotics are still given to farm animals illustrates the degree to which business controls government and misleads the public in the US.

Several studies have shown that ending non-therapeutic antibiotic use in farm animals would raise meat prices by less than five percent.[268] In 1994,

Denmark banned the use of antibiotics to promote growth in pigs. The ban had no significant impact on productivity.[269] Instead of using antibiotics to prevent disease in crowded, filthy conditions, pigs were kept in less crowded, more sanitary conditions with improved ventilation and given higher quality feed. Ending non-therapeutic antibiotic use substantially lowered the presence of antibiotic-resistant bacteria in pigs that could be passed to humans.

US meat companies could adopt similar practices. But our flawed systems often compel companies to oppose anything that threatens shareholder returns. This once again shows the suicidal nature of our economic and political systems. Genetics can be used to track antibiotic-resistant bacteria that sicken and kill people back to farm animals. In this case, antibiotic use in farm animals literally is killing people and raising health care costs by billions of dollars per year. But companies are not being held responsible for these real, actual costs that they are imposing on society. If they were, ending non-therapeutic antibiotic use in farm animals would be the vastly lower cost strategy. Meat raised with antibiotics is not cheap. But our grossly flawed market system creates the illusion that it is. Once democracy and capitalism are implemented in the US, citizens will demand that businesses be held fully responsible for all negative impacts.

Hormones

In the US, about two-thirds of cattle are treated with hormones, including the female hormones estrogen and progesterone.[270] Using hormones increases profitability by increasing the weight of cattle. In 1987, the EU banned the use of hormones in cattle based on potential risks to human health. Hormone-treated beef can have higher than normal levels of hormones. As discussed in the Chemicals section of *Global System Change*, the human endocrine system is extremely sensitive. Even small amounts of natural or synthetic hormones contained in meat can cause significant harm. Many experts say that adding feminine hormones to meat can increase the risk of breast cancer and other types of cancer.[271] Feminine hormones in meat also have been linked to early puberty in girls[272] and breast development in boys.[273]

As discussed in the Genetic Engineering section, recombinant Bovine Growth Hormone (BGH) is still used in the US dairy industry. BGH contains high levels of the cancer-causing hormone IGF-1. Milk from BGH-treated cows often contains high levels of IGF-1, which can be absorbed into the blood. Many studies have linked increased IGF-1 levels to increased rates of breast, colon and prostate cancer.[274] The US is the only country in the world that allows its citizens to consume BGH milk and milk products.

The use of hormones in US beef and dairy products once again illustrates inappropriate government influence and public deception. Giving money to politicians and inappropriately influencing government in other ways can shift the focus of the FDA, USDA and other regulators from protecting public health to protecting shareholder returns. A Congressional report found that, "the FDA has consistently disregarded its responsibility – has repeatedly put what it perceives are interests of veterinarians and the livestock industry ahead of its legal obligation to protect consumers – jeopardizing the health and safety of consumers' meat, milk and poultry."[275]

Based largely on industry information, the FDA and USDA found that hormone levels in hormone-treated meat were safe. As a result, the agencies waived any requirements for monitoring or testing of hormones in meat. An unpublished USDA study found that hormones were administered illegally in about half of cattle. This could result in high levels in certain cuts of meat.[276] But this probably would not be detected because the FDA and USDA do not monitor the levels of hormones in US meat.[277] Hormonal cancers in the US have been rising rapidly while hormones are used in meat and dairy products. For example, from 1975 to 2010, prostate and testicular cancer rates rose by 60 percent.[278]

Meat companies, politicians paid by them and other business allies often argue that there is not enough evidence of human harm to warrant banning hormones in US meat and dairy products. This once again illustrates Wrong Reference Point thinking. Meat companies and their allies imply that we should wait for a high level of certainty of harm before banning potentially harmful activities. But this is the wrong reference point. The priority is human health, not shareholder returns. With a greater focus on protecting public health, Europe banned hormones in meat and dairy products many years ago. But the shareholder-focused US government continues to allow hormone use in food animals.

Public deception in the hormone area largely occurs through the lack of labeling. Inappropriate government influence by food companies and their allies has blocked the mandatory labeling of hormone-treated meat and dairy products. Other countries have banned hormone use based on expert advice and evidence of harm. Citizens in the US at least should be given the choice to avoid hormone-treated meat and dairy products. But the failure to label takes this choice away. It essentially forces people to eat hormone-treated meat and dairy products.

Contaminated Meat and Seafood

Meat and seafood in the US and some other countries often is contaminated with a wide variety of toxic and potentially toxic substances. Several contaminants have been discussed. US meat often is contaminated with pathogens such as E. coli, Salmonella and Campylobacter. Animals frequently are treated with antibiotics and hormones, which can contaminate meat. Many toxins accumulate in the fat of animals, such as pesticides and POP's, including dioxin. In the US, 80 to 90 percent of pesticide exposure and 93 percent of dioxin exposure results from eating animal products. Beyond these substances, many other contaminants frequently are found in US meat, including veterinary drugs and heavy metals, such as arsenic and copper.

Veterinary drugs can contaminate meat in various ways. For example, sick dairy cows often are given drugs to help them recover. However, if it appears that an animal will die, it often is rushed to a slaughterhouse so that it can be killed before it dies. Selling the meat of sick, medicated animals helps to recover the costs of raising animals, and thereby protects shareholder returns. But it also can expose people to animal drugs because they often still are in the meat at the time of slaughter. Taking animal drugs not intended for humans can cause many problems, including kidney damage, allergic reactions and neurological damage.[279] People also can be exposed to veterinary drugs by eating veal. Milk from medicated cows cannot be sold to humans. But this waste milk often is fed to veal calves. As a result, veal sometimes contains animal drugs.[280]

Meat in the US also can be contaminated with ractopamine, a drug that is banned in 160 countries including China. In the US, ractopamine is given to many cattle, pigs and turkeys shortly before slaughter to promote muscle growth. As much as 20 percent of the drug remains in meat after slaughter.[281] Ractopamine is banned in many countries due to negative impacts on animals, including death. Also, many people have been sickened by ractopamine-contaminated meat.[282] While ractopamine sickens and kills some animals, increased growth frequently more than makes up for losses, and thereby enables enhanced profitability.

Heavy metals, such as copper and arsenic, often contaminate US meat and poultry. For example, in 2008, a shipment of US beef was rejected in Mexico because it exceeded regulatory threshold levels for copper. The US has no threshold levels for copper in meat. As a result, the contaminated meat that was considered to be unfit for human consumption in Mexico was returned to the US and sold to US consumers.[283]

The use of arsenic in animal feed never has been permitted in Europe. But in the US, arsenic has been added to animal feed to promote growth since the 1940s. Arsenic is used in turkey, pig and chicken feed.[284] It is added in organic form, which is not immediately toxic. But it often converts to inorganic form, which is highly toxic. One study of chicken sold in US supermarkets and fast food restaurants found that over half contained arsenic and 55 percent of it was in inorganic (i.e. toxic) form.[285]

USDA research found that eating two ounces of chicken per day exposes people to about four micrograms of inorganic arsenic on average. Daily exposure to low doses of arsenic can greatly increase the risk of cancer, dementia, neurological damage and other health problems.[286] Industrial chicken operations produce large amounts of waste. Arsenic in chicken manure quickly turns to inorganic form. As a result, runoff from chicken farms can contaminate water supplies with arsenic. Chicken feces also can contaminate beef with arsenic because large amounts of it are fed to cattle in the US.[287]

The USDA has programs for monitoring chemical residues and other contamination in meat. But the programs often are woefully inadequate. For example, no threshold levels have been set for many dangerous substances in meat, such as copper and dioxin.[288] Testing programs often are limited and underfunded. From 2000 to 2008, one out of every 12 million US chickens was tested for arsenic.[289] The USDA is supposed to test for 23 classes of pesticides in meat. But it only tests for one, due mainly to limited resources.[290] In addition, it allows many potentially harmful practices, such as permitting sick, medicated cattle to be slaughtered and sold for human consumption. Developing countries such as China and Mexico sometimes have more stringent meat safety standards than the US. Once again, this reflects how inappropriate business influence of government often compels regulators to focus more on protecting shareholder returns than public health.

While the US has among the most contaminated meat in the developed and even developing world, other countries also have meat contamination problems. For example, a European study examined meat, dairy and other foods that typically would be fed to a 10-year-old child in one day. The study found 128 chemical residues in the food. Many of the substances were probable or known carcinogens or endocrine disruptors.[291]

Regarding seafood, contamination is rising as chemicals and other pollution increase in the oceans and freshwater bodies. Following the BP oil spill in the Gulf of Mexico, many experts questioned the FDA's safety standards for shellfish and other seafood. A study published in the journal Environmental Health Perspectives found that the FDA allows 100 to 10,000 times more carcinogenic polycyclic aromatic hydrocarbons (PAHs) in seafood than is safe.[292] (PAH's are found in oil, coal and tar deposits.) The study also found that the FDA ignored FDA and EPA staff members who said that more stringent safety standards should be set for PAHs in seafood.

Reflecting possible business influence, the FDA defended its position by arguing that allowing lower levels of carcinogenic PAHs would increase harm. The FDA did not mean that reducing toxic chemicals in food would harm public health. It defined harm as making less food available (i.e. low-ering business revenues). The FDA in effect was arguing that allowing more carcinogenic toxic chemicals in seafood was justified because it would make more food available. The agency appeared to be trading off public health with protecting business interests. In addition, allowing lower levels of chemicals from the BP oil spill in seafood would have increased harm to fishermen. As a result, BP and other companies that gave money to politi-cians could have been required to pay out greater damages.

The study found that the FDA uses outdated PAH safety standards that do not take early-life exposure into account. When this exposure was considered, it found that 53 percent of shrimp from the Gulf of Mexico had PAH levels that were unsafe for pregnant women. Specific safety standards for PAHs are set in Europe. But the FDA develops PAH standards on a case-by-case basis following each oil spill. The toxicity of the same chemical does not vary. But varying safety standards on a case-by-case basis enables the FDA to balance business interests and public health. If the government served the people instead of business, there would be no trade offs with public health.

Cloned Meat

Meat and dairy products from cloned beef cattle, dairy cows, pigs, goats and their offspring have been sold in the US for several years.[293] It is difficult to determine the volume of cloned animal products sold because the government does not require that these products be labeled. It also does not track or disclose sales volume. There is widespread scientific concern that meat and dairy products from cloned animals and their offspring might be harmful to human health. No long-term studies and few independent studies have been done on cloned food safety.[294]

In 2008, the FDA released a report prepared in collaboration with two animal cloning companies. In spite of widespread scientific concerns about safety, the FDA said that cloned meat and dairy products were as safe as non-cloned products. As a result, no labeling or additional safety testing of cloned food was required. The FDA's position once again indicates how inappropriate influence of government often compels regulators to focus more on protecting shareholder returns than public health.

Animal cloning involves mixing genetic material from a cloned animal with a donor egg, and then inserting it into a surrogate mother. As many as 90 percent of cloning attempts fail. Clones often are born with birth defects, heart and intestine problems, and/or Large Offspring Syndrome, which sometimes kills the clone and surrogate mother.[295] Cloned animals also sometimes have different mineral, glucose and fatty acid levels than normal animals. Genetic defects can be passed on to the offspring of cloned animals. Rats fed cloned meat and dairy products have exhibited abnormal behavior and other problems. Some experts argue that the standards used by the FDA to determine the safety of cloned animal products are extremely weak. A veterinarian and microbiologist said that, using the same FDA standards, eating cancerous tissue or pus also would be considered safe.[296]

Many scientists are concerned that genetic defects and other abnormalities in meat and dairy products from cloned animals and their offspring could harm human health. As a result, many experts recommend that much more research should be done before cloned animal products are consumed.[297]

The FDA's approval of cloned meat and dairy products in the US well illustrates Wrong Perspective logic and deception. As discussed in the Misleading the Public section, the Wrong Perspective deception technique involves assuming that activities or products that potentially threaten human health and survival are safe until they are proven otherwise. But this is the wrong perspective. Human survival and health take priority over all other issues. Therefore, anything that threatens these critical factors should be considered to be unsafe until it is proven to be safe with a high degree of certainty, probably over 99 percent. This level of safety and certainty only can be achieved through rigorous, independent research. But this largely was not done in the cloned animal product area. Using mainly industry information, the FDA found that cloned animal products were safe, in spite of many experts saying that they might not be. This strongly indicates inappropriate business influence of government.

Public deception is used to protect shareholder returns in the cloned animal product area. For example, meat companies, the FDA and other business allies sometimes argue that cloning is no worse than in vitro fertilization and other assisted reproductive techniques used in industrial animal production. But this is highly misleading. In vitro fertilization involves combining normal male and female cells, as regularly occurs in nature. Cloning involves using genetic manipulation to create altered eggs in ways that never would occur in nature. It is difficult, and perhaps impossible, to predict the negative impacts of cloning on animal and human health, especially over the long-term. As discussed in the Genetic Engineering section, the potential negative impacts of genetic manipulation can be vastly greater than the benefits. Therefore, these types of activities should not be done unless there is overwhelming independent evidence showing that they are safe.

The most important form of public deception in the cloned meat and dairy area involves the failure to label. Several polls have found that the majority of people in the US do not want to eat cloned meat and dairy products and that they are opposed to cloning on moral and ethical grounds.[298] Prior to issuing its safety ruling, the FDA received comments from about 150,000 people who opposed the approval of cloned meat and dairy products. Nevertheless, the FDA approved them and did not require labeling. The failure to label takes away consumer choice. People essentially are being forced to eat cloned meat and dairy products in the US. Those who oppose cloning on moral and ethical grounds are being forced to feed these potentially harmful foods to their families.

European governments generally focus more strongly on the well-being of society than the US government, due largely to greater restrictions on inappropriate business influence of government. However, businesses apparently inappropriately influence governments in Europe as well. European citizens are strongly opposed to eating cloned meat and dairy products. One European poll found that 83 percent believed cloned meat should be labeled and 63 percent said that they probably would not buy it.[299] But in spite of strong opposition, meat and dairy products from cloned animals and their offspring are not labeled in Europe.

As in the US, people have no choice. They essentially are being forced to eat cloned animal products. Once citizens regain control of government in the US and other countries, they can compel government to implement the will of the people, label or ban cloned meat and dairy products, and put public health before shareholder returns and all else.

Irradiated Food

Irradiation is used to kill bacteria, viruses, parasites, insects and mold on many different types of food in the US and some other countries. The US allows three types of ionizing radiation to be used on food: Gamma rays, x-rays and high-energy electrons. The maximum dose of radiation allowed on food is 450,000 rads (equivalent to about 150 million chest x-rays).[300] Radioactive waste from nuclear power plants often is used to irradiate food. Radiation works by breaking apart molecules, inducing ionization and damaging DNA beyond its ability to repair itself. This process can kill pathogens in food, such as E. coli. It also can delay ripening, extend shelf life and allow food to be transported longer distances. Irradiation facilitates industrial, centralized food production. It particularly facilitates industrial animal production because irradiation kills many of the pathogens resulting from widespread fecal contamination of meat and poultry products. These benefits help large food companies to maximize shareholder returns.

The FDA allows most food in the US to be irradiated. Foods exposed to radiation include beef, poultry, pork, lamb, potatoes, wheat, wheat flour, vegetables, fruits, shell eggs, seeds for sprouting, spices and herb teas.[301] (Dairy products usually are pasteurized. Therefore, irradiation is not needed.) Weak labeling requirements often make it difficult for consumers to determine which foods have been irradiated. For example, labeling only is required to the first purchaser, who often is not the consumer. As a result, labeling is not required for irradiated food sold in restaurants, hotels, hospitals, salad bars, delis and similar locations. If some but not all ingredients in a product are irradiated, labeling usually is not required. When labeling is required, the type can be as small as the type on ingredients labels and the radura symbol must be used.[302] This symbol looks like a flower in a circle with sun shining on it. To those not familiar with it, the symbol provides little indication that food was irradiated.

Labeling food as irradiated can lower sales. As a result, companies are seeking approval to replace the word radiation with electronic or cold pasteurization. But this is highly deceptive. Pasteurization and irradiation are very different. Pasteurization is a safe process that involves heating food to kill pathogens. Irradiation involves bombarding food with high doses of ionizing radiation.

The approval of food irradiation by the FDA once again reflects strong business influence of the US government. Many scientists and other experts believe that the FDA's decision was irresponsible and biased toward protecting shareholder returns instead of public health. The agency reviewed over 400 studies, but based its decision on only five. It appeared to ignore many studies which found that eating irradiated food increases the risk of cancer, genetic damage and other health problems. It also ignored its own expert committees who expressed concerns about the human health risks of eating irradiated food.[303]

High doses of ionizing radiation not only damage and genetically alter pathogens in food, they also can damage and genetically alter food. Irradiation creates free radicals that can combine with pesticides and other chemicals in food to create unique radiolytic products (URP's). Some URP's in food are known toxins, such as benzene and formaldehyde. Other URP's are uniquely created in irradiated food. No long-term safety studies of these new chemicals have been conducted.[304]

In the same way that irradiation destroys pathogens, it also can damage or destroy fatty acids, digestive enzymes and other nutrients. Irradiation can destroy up to 80 percent of the vitamins in food. For example, it destroys about 80 percent of vitamin A in eggs.[305] Irradiated fruits and vegetables can look fresh, but be nutritionally equivalent to cooked food because they have degraded or reduced vitamins, enzymes and other nutrients.[306] Irradiation also can negatively affect the flavor, odor and texture of food.

Irradiation often does not kill all bacteria in food. As a result, it sometimes can grow back in a few hours to levels present before irradiation. In addition, radiation does not kill some viruses and prions, such as those that cause mad cow disease. Some bacteria can become radiation-resistant and spread in industrial animal operations. Also, when high levels of radiation are used, trace amounts of radioactivity can be created in food.[307]

Many animal studies have shown that eating irradiated food can cause increased tumors, cancer, reproductive failure, genetic damage, liver and kidney damage, vitamin deficiencies and premature death. The largest human studies of eating irradiated food lasted 15 weeks. No long-term human health studies have been conducted.[308] As a result, the long-term health effects of eating irradiated food are unknown. Due to weak labeling, nearly everyone in the US eats irradiated food. This means there is no irradiated food-free control group to use as a baseline for assessing long-term health impacts.

Irradiation kills pathogens. But it does not remove the feces, urine, pus and vomit that often contaminate beef, pork and chicken produced in industrial animal operations.[309] As noted, a University of Minnesota study found evidence of fecal contamination on 92 percent of chicken and 69 percent of beef and pork sold in retail outlets. Irradiation can make feces on meat and poultry safer to eat. However, rather than eating purified or sanitized feces, the obviously superior strategy is to not put feces on meat in the first place.

Irradiation helped to put many small farmers out of business by facilitating centralized, industrial animal production and long-distance food transportation. Our flawed economic and political systems create the illusion that irradiated food is cheap. But many of the real, actual costs of irradiation are not included in prices. These costs include potential negative human health impacts and the negative economic and community impacts of centralized, industrial animal production facilitated by irradiation.

Once citizens regain control of government in the US, they can demand that the FDA and other regulators put public health ahead of shareholder returns and all other factors. Extensive, independent, long-term safety studies should have been conducted before food irradiation was allowed. If the US government were democratic, citizens could demand that food irradiation be halted until independent research shows it to be safe. In the meantime, weak, deceptive labeling requirements should be replaced with strong, clear labeling. The failure to adequately label effectively forces people to eat irradiated food. They should be given the choice to avoid these potentially harmful products.

Food Additives

More than 3,000 and possibly as many as 14,000 synthetic chemicals and other substances are added to US food products.[310] Food additives include many types of artificial and natural flavors, artificial dyes, flavor enhancers, preservatives, fungicides, fruit and vegetable coatings, sweeteners, stabilizers, solvents, dispersing agents and nutrients. Additives can extend shelf life, improve the appearance and taste of food, and provide several other benefits.

However, synthetic chemicals and other substances added to food can cause many negative human health impacts. In Europe, food additives must be shown to be safe before they are used in food. But this frequently is not the case in the US. As discussed in the Chemicals section, the vast majority of synthetic chemicals were not independently safety tested and many are not tested at all. US chemical regulations are based on Wrong Perspective logic. Chemicals often are assumed to be safe until there is overwhelming evidence that they are unsafe. But the correct perspective is to assume that chemicals, or anything else that threatens human health and survival, are unsafe until there is overwhelming evidence that they are safe.

A 2010 report by the US government Accountability Office (GAO) analyzed several ways in which the FDA's food additive regulations fail to adequately protect public health.[311] Under FDA regulations, food companies are allowed to unilaterally assign "generally recognized as safe" (GRAS) status to many types of additives. Once a company decides that its additives are safe, it can use them freely without regulation. Companies often are not required to inform the FDA that they developed new food additives and assigned GRAS status to them.[312]

The FDA does not monitor whether companies are appropriately assigning GRAS status. It is supposed to amend or revoke the status if emerging science shows that additives are harmful. But this is difficult to do when companies do not inform the FDA that new food additives are being used. In addition, the GAO report noted that the FDA has not used new scientific information to systematically reconsider GRAS status since the beginning of deregulation in the 1980s.

Engineered nanomaterials (ENM's) once again illustrate how FDA regulations seem to be more focused on protecting shareholder returns than public health. As discussed in the Nanotechnology section, ENM's are new materials created by humans. Little independent research has been done to determine the impacts of ENM's on human health. In Europe and Canada, ENM's must have regulatory approval before they can be used in food. But in the US, food companies often are allowed to unilaterally assign GRAS status to ENM's, and then use them in food without informing regulators or consumers. For example, nano titanium dioxide is used in many vitamin, food supplement and food products. A UCLA study found that it causes genetic damage and cancer in mice. Weak GRAS regulations make it difficult to determine the volume of nano titanium dioxide and other potentially harmful ENM's used in the US food supply.

The situation with food additive regulations once again shows the great extent to which business controls government in the US. Many citizens probably would find it unbelievable that companies are allowed to unilaterally declare food additives to be safe with no regulatory oversight. This would be like implementing self-regulation of traffic laws. For example, if a citizen noticed that they were speeding, they could pull over, write themselves a ticket, send in a check and request that points be added to their driver's license. Obviously, not many speeding tickets would be written under such a system.

Even when safety testing of food additives is required, the FDA often relies on testing that was conducted, funded or influenced by the companies that made the additives. As discussed in *Global System Change*, this type of testing should not be used to determine public safety or use. A company's research of its own products is not trustworthy. It is inherently biased because companies have large financial incentives to find their products safe when there are no immediate and obvious negative impacts and no cost-effective alternatives available.

Beyond relying on biased company testing, food additive safety testing fails to protect public safety in several other ways. For example, additives often are not tested for allergic reactions, hormone disruption and impacts on children. Perhaps most importantly, food additives virtually always are tested in isolation. But citizens rarely are exposed to only one food additive at a time. Several studies have shown that food additives which cause little or no harm in isolation can cause substantial harm when combined with other additives.[313] The typical US diet can expose people to 40 or more food additives per day in many different combinations. Virtually none of these combinations have been safety tested. In effect, US citizens are being used as laboratory test animals to determine the harmful effects of thousands of additives.

A few harmful, but nevertheless widely used food additives are summarized below.

Aspartame. Aspartame is a widely used artificial sweetener sold under names including NutraSweet, Equal and Canderel. It is used in over 6,000 products, including soft drinks, chewing gum and diet foods. The approval of aspartame once again illustrates inappropriate business influence of government. During the 1970s, the FDA did not approve aspartame because many studies showed that it caused seizures and brain tumors in laboratory animals.[314] In 1980, a public board of inquiry appointed by the FDA concluded that aspartame could cause brain tumors, and therefore should not be approved. In 1981, a new FDA Commissioner overrode FDA experts and approved aspartame. The Commissioner left the FDA shortly afterwards and took a job with the main public relations firm servicing the manufacturer of aspartame.

Over the past 30 years, there have been many studies that link aspartame to cancer, neurological disorders and numerous other health problems. Aspartame accounts for more adverse health reactions reported to the FDA than all other food additives combined.[315] A book called *Sweet Deception* describes extensive research showing many negative health impacts of aspartame. The sweetener mainly is comprised of amino acids that are harmless when eaten as bound components of food. However, when the amino acids are separated from food prior to ingestion and then eaten in abundance, they often become toxic.[316]

The aspartic acid in aspartame is an excitotoxin. It can overstimulate brain cells to the point of damage or death. Several studies have linked aspartame to neurological and other disorders, including Alzheimer's disease, Parkinson's disease, multiple sclerosis and lupus. Many patients with multiple sclerosis, lupus, fibromyalgia or vision impairment lost their symptoms when they stopped drinking diet sodas that contained aspartame. Thousands of children diagnosed with ADD and ADHD lost their symptoms and no longer needed prescription drugs once they stopped consuming foods and beverages containing aspartame.[317] Aspartame breaks down into methanol and formaldehyde, a known carcinogen, especially when heated above 86°F. This is a primary factor causing the link between aspartame and cancer shown in many studies.[318]

Not surprisingly, research conducted or influenced by food companies nearly always finds aspartame to be safe. In spite of thousands of reports of adverse reactions and extensive independent research showing that aspartame is harmful, the business-dominated FDA continues to rely on biased company research and allow widespread, unrestricted use of aspartame.

High Fructose Corn Syrup (HFCS). HFCS is a widely used food additive and sweetener. Beyond sweet foods such as cookies and sodas, it is used in many other foods, including breads, condiments and pasta sauces. US citizens consume an average of about 45 to 60 pounds of HFCS per person per year.[319] HFCS is a highly processed, unnatural food. Many chemicals are used to process it, often including caustic soda and hydrochloric acid. These frequently contain traces of mercury, a highly toxic substance. A peer-reviewed study published in the journal Environmental Health found mercury in 31 percent of HFCS-containing food products tested.[320]

Several studies have found that HFCS contributes substantially more to obesity and type 2 diabetes than regular sugar, which is about 50 percent fructose and 50 percent glucose. HFCS can be as much as 65 percent fructose.[321] Fructose and glucose are metabolized differently by the body. A University of California study found that volunteers who ate a high fructose diet had substantially more fat accumulation around the heart, liver and digestive organs than those who ate a high glucose diet. As a highly processed, unnatural food, HFCS can cause metabolic changes that prevent the body from burning fat normally.[322]

Sodium Nitrate. Sodium nitrate is added to most packaged meat products in the US, including bacon, ham, pepperoni, hot dogs and lunch meats. Meat often turns gray quickly. Sodium nitrate adds red color. It can keep packaged meats looking fresh and appetizing for months. When sodium nitrate is mixed with saliva and digestive enzymes in the human body, cancer-causing compounds called nitrosamines are formed. These sometimes are used to cause cancer in laboratory rats. In humans, sodium nitrate consumption has been strongly linked to brain tumors, leukemia and digestive tract cancers.[323]

Preservatives. Preservatives, such as BHA (Butylated Hydroxyanisole), are used to preserve foods such as meats, fats, nuts, dehydrated foods, flavorings, desserts, beer and beverages. Preservatives inhibit mold and other organisms that result from the natural breakdown of food. They are toxic to many lifeforms, sometimes including humans. For example, the US Department of Health and Human Services classifies BHA as a probable human carcinogen.[324] Many customers avoid foods containing preservatives. As a result, companies frequently use alternative means of preserving food, such as adding vitamin E or using more effective packaging.

Natural and Artificial Flavors. Processed food represents about 90 percent of food expenditures in the US.[325] Food processing, for example through dehydration, freezing and canning, often destroys much of the natural flavor of food. As a result, chemicals frequently are used to add flavor. Much of the 'taste' of food results from the sense of smell. Natural and artificial flavors frequently combine volatile (i.e. off-gassing) chemicals in ways that mimic the natural taste and smell of food.

Natural and artificial flavors usually use the same chemicals to produce a certain flavor. But they are derived from different sources. Chemicals in natural flavors must be derived from bacteria, plants or animals. Those in artificial flavors are synthetically created from other sources.

The terms natural flavors and natural flavoring are highly deceptive. For example, a strawberry flavored product might contain the ingredient "natural flavors". This might lead many customers to believe that the product actually was flavored with strawberries and contained strawberries. However, this often would not be the case. Instead, off-gassing chemicals would mimic the flavor of strawberries. As Eric Schlosser said in his excellent book *Fast Food Nation*, processed foods might taste like shredded cardboard without natural and artificial flavoring.

The word natural also can deceptively imply that the ingredient natural flavors is safe. There are many types of "natural flavors" made from a wide variety of natural chemicals. But just because a chemical is derived from a natural plant or animal source does not mean it is safe. Many natural substances, such as arsenic, are toxic. The aspartic acid in aspartame and glutamic acid in MSG (discussed below) are natural chemicals. But they can be highly toxic when consumed excessively.

Beyond ingredients and additives listed on food labels, there are many other chemicals and potentially harmful substances in food that are not required to be shown on food labels. For example, titanium dioxide often is used in skim milk, cottage cheese, ice cream and other dairy products to provide white color. Without titanium dioxide, skim milk frequently would be pale blue and cottage cheese would be light yellow. Titanium dioxide contained in dairy products does not have to be listed as an ingredient because a labeling loophole allows it to classified as a manufacturing aid.[326] The International Agency for Research on Cancer classifies nano titanium dioxide as a possible human carcinogen. It is unclear how much of this material is being used in US dairy and other food products because the US government does not require disclosure.

As discussed above, chemicals often are used to process ingredients and foods. Residues of these chemicals as well as pesticides and other residues frequently are contained in processed foods, but not shown on food labels. Also, heating food can create harmful byproducts and chemicals. As noted, heating aspartame produces formaldehyde. As a result, baked goods sweetened with aspartame can contain this known carcinogen. In general, the business-influenced US government allows many harmful or potentially harmful additives, chemicals and other substances in food products, often without disclosure.

Business influence of US food regulators is further indicated in a book called *Rich Food, Poor Food*. The book lists many food ingredients that are banned in other countries but allowed in the US. About 80 percent of all convenience foods sold in the US (i.e. packaged foods that can be quickly prepared) contain ingredients that are banned in other countries.[327] For example, brominated vegetable oil is banned in over 100 countries. It is strongly linked to many thyroid diseases, including cancer and autoimmune diseases. But brominated vegetable oil is used in many sodas and sports drinks in the US.[328]

Olestra is banned in the UK and Canada. It can cause severe gastro-intestinal problems. But it is used in many low or no fat snack foods and other products in the US. Azodicarbonamide can induce asthma and cause other health problems. It is banned in most European countries. But it is included in many frozen food products in the US. The food dyes yellow #5 and yellow #6 are made from coal tar. They are linked to allergies, ADHD and cancer. As discussed in the Chemicals section, these dyes are banned in much of Europe. But they are widely used in packaged macaroni and cheese and many other products in the US. As noted, the preservative BHA is a probable carcinogen. Another preservative, BHT, also is a known or probable carcinogen. BHA and BHT are made from petroleum. They are banned in England and Japan. But the preservatives are widely used in cereals and many other products in the US.[329]

MSG

MSG is included as a separate section because it is one of the most important, harmful and widely used food additives. As discussed in the Advertising, Media and Culture section of *Global System Change*, obesity has grown rapidly in the US and many other countries over the past 40 years. Several factors drive this epidemic. MSG is one of them. It probably is obvious to most people over 50 years old and younger people looking at old films and photos that there are many more overweight and obese people today than there were 40 years ago. Some people probably wonder if chemicals are being added to food that cause people to overeat and gain weight.

This is exactly what is happening. MSG affects the appetite control function of the brain. It often causes people to eat more food than they normally would. Through deceptive labeling practices, MSG is included in most processed, packaged, prepared and restaurant food.

The situation with MSG once again shows the myopic and destructive nature of our economic and political systems. Adding MSG to food provides large financial benefits to food companies. But it also imposes large negative impacts on society, including strongly promoting obesity. Companies are not held responsible for many of these negative impacts. As a result, the requirement to maximize shareholder returns essentially compels them to use MSG.

Scientists long thought that the human tongue could sense only four tastes – sweet, salty, sour and bitter. However, it was discovered that the tongue can sense a fifth taste, called unami. Unami makes food taste more savory. MSG creates the unami taste. It is an excitotoxin. MSG overstimulates taste buds and the brain, and thereby changes the perception of how food tastes. It intensifies and enhances the flavor and smell of food, including bland tasting, low-fat foods.

MSG allows food companies to increase profits by using lower quality, less tasteful ingredients. But the main financial benefit results from suppressing the appetite control function of the brain. As discussed below, MSG can suppress the sense of fullness and satisfaction that comes from eating, and thereby create an ongoing desire to eat.[330] Chemically inducing people to eat much more food than they physically need can substantially increase food company sales and shareholder returns.

Many of the negative impacts of MSG have been known for decades. About 30 percent of people have short-term adverse reactions, including nausea, headaches, chest pain and drowsiness.[331] As a result, customers often avoid foods that list MSG as an ingredient. Food companies know this. But removing MSG frequently would raise costs. Companies would have to use higher quality, more tasteful ingredients to create appealing products. In addition, even if foods tasted better naturally, people frequently would eat less because their appetite regulation ability would not be suppressed.

Flawed systems often compel publicly traded companies to put shareholder returns before public health, honesty and all other factors. As a result, deceptive labeling is used to put MSG in most foods, including many organic foods. Several websites, such as www.TruthInLabeling.org and www.MSGmyth.com, provide extensive information about deceptive MSG labeling practices, human health impacts and MSG production.

MSG stands for monosodium glutamate. The ingredient MSG usually is comprised of 78 percent processed glutamic acid, 12 percent sodium, 10 percent water and less than one percent contaminants.[332] Processed glutamic acid is the substance that enhances flavor, affects appetite and produces negative health impacts. Natural glutamic acid is a nonessential amino acid, meaning that the human body can produce it. Glutamic acid is an important neurotransmitter that supports many brain functions.[333] Natural glutamic acid in plant and animal-based foods is known as L-glutamic acid. Digestion separates L-glutamic acid bound in food. It then is delivered to glutamate receptors in the brain and body. Glutamic acid separated from food by digestion in the body usually is harmless.

However, manufactured glutamic acid that is separated from food before entering the body can be harmful. During manufacturing, bound glutamic acid in foods such as corn, molasses, wheat and yeast is separated or made free through various processes. Common processes include hydrolyzation and fermentation using chemicals or bacteria. Manufactured or processed free glutamic acid always contains contaminants, such as D-glutamic acid, a substance that never is found in natural food. It also sometimes contains carcinogens, such as propanols and heterocyclic amines.[334]

FDA regulations require that food ingredients be called by their common and usual names. MSG is the common and usual name for processed free glutamic acid (also known as free glutamate). Any ingredient that contains 78 percent or more free glutamate must be labeled MSG. However, the FDA does not require that the components of ingredients be identified. Therefore, if an ingredient contains less than 78 percent free glutamate, showing MSG content on food labels is not required.

To facilitate widespread use of MSG, many food ingredients have been developed that contain processed free glutamic acid. There are over 40 ingredients that always or often contain MSG. Ones that always contain it include yeast extract, autolysed yeast, yeast food, yeast nutrient, textured protein, whey protein, casein protein, soy protein, anything else labeled "protein", anything "hydrolyzed", and gelatin. Ingredients that often contain MSG include carrageenan, natural and artificial flavors and flavoring, maltodextrin, barley malt, malted barley, malt extract, brewer's yeast, citric acid, pectin, boulion, seasonings, spices, anything "ultra-pasteurized", beef/pork/chicken flavoring, and any other type of flavor or flavoring.[335]

Product labels sometimes deceptively state that foods contain "no MSG" or "no added MSG". But they often contain large amounts of it. MSG is not added. Instead, it is created through processing as glutamates resident in food are freed or separated. For example, processing yeast into yeast extract or autolysed yeast creates free glutamate (i.e. MSG) in the processed yeast products. Yeast derivatives and other MSG-containing ingredients are widely used as substitutes for MSG in processed foods.

For example, through the use of carrageenan, MSG often is added to ice cream, yogurt and other dairy products. It is included in nearly all fast food and restaurant food. MSG makes the restaurant experience more appealing.[336] Infant formulas, baby foods and processed children's food also often contain MSG. Ingredients containing MSG are not prohibited under the National Organic Program in the US. As a result, many organic and so-called healthy or natural foods contain it.[337] MSG even is sprayed on fruit, vegetables and nuts. A growth enhancer called AuxiGro contains about 30 percent MSG. Introduced in 1997, the product has been approved for use on nearly all produce in the US.[338]

Many processed foods include several MSG-containing ingredients. If people print out the list of ingredients that always or often contain MSG on the website www.truthinlabeling.org/hiddensources.html and take it to a supermarket, they will see that nearly all processed foods contain MSG in its many different deceptively labeled forms.

The regulation of MSG in the US once again illustrates business domination of government. In 1959, the FDA assigned "generally recognized as safe" status to MSG. About 10 years later, a condition now known as "MSG Symptom Complex" was recognized. According to the FDA, ingesting MSG causes many people to experience adverse effects, including headaches, nausea, burning sensations, chest pain, weakness, numbness, heart palpitations and drowsiness.[339] The fact that the FDA calls MSG safe while simultaneously acknowledging widespread adverse impacts indicates the agency's focus on protecting the shareholder returns of food companies rather than public health.

Glutamic acid is a natural and necessary chemical in the human body. However, high levels of excess glutamic acid are toxic to everyone. Eating MSG-containing foods can cause high concentrations of glutamic acid that cannot be utilized by the body. In addition, the contaminants always contained in MSG can cause adverse reactions. The amount of MSG in food varies based on the number and type of MSG-containing ingredients used.

Excess glutamate resulting from MSG ingestion can overstimulate or damage glutamate receptors in the brain and body. This can make the receptors more sensitive to subsequent MSG ingestion. In addition to short-term adverse reactions, MSG can cause longer-term negative impacts. Many studies indicate that MSG acts as a slow neurotoxin, producing damage such as dementia that only becomes apparent many years later.[340] A book written by George Schwartz, M.D., called *In Bad Taste: The MSG Symptom Complex*, describes the widespread toxicity caused by MSG in food. Through extensive case studies and research, Dr. Schwartz identifies 65 symptoms and conditions caused by MSG consumption.[341]

A book by neurosurgeon Dr. Russell Blaylock, called *Excitotoxins: The Taste That Kills*, describes extensive research showing links between MSG and many neurological disorders, including Alzheimer's, Parkinson's, Huntington's and Lou Gehrig's diseases.[342] Dr. Blaylock explains that MSG is an excitotoxin that can overstimulate brain and other cells to the point of damage or death. Numerous studies have shown that MSG damages the hypothalamus, the region of the brain that controls appetite. MSG can bypass the blood-brain barrier through the hypothalamus and contribute to neurological disorders.[343]

As awareness grows that MSG contributes to neurological problems, drugs are being developed that block the effects of glutamic acid on the brain and nervous system. Neuroscientist Dr. Richard Henneberry said, "I consider it ironic that the pharmaceutical industry is investing vast resources in the development of glutamate receptor blockers to protect central nervous system neurons against glutamate neurotoxicity in common neurological disorders, while at the same time the food industry, with the blessing of the FDA, continues to add great quantities of glutamate to the food supply."[344]

Extensive research shows that several types of cancer have glutamate receptors, including colon, breast, skin (melanoma), lung and thyroid. As a result, much cancer research is focused on blocking glutamate receptors. Dr. Blaylock stated, "If you're consuming a diet with glutamate in it, particularly high levels, you're making your cancer grow very rapidly. I refer to it as cancer fertilizer."[345]

Beyond neurological disorders and cancer, MSG has been linked to many other health problems. These include liver inflammation, type 2 diabetes, asthma, arthritis, epilepsy, mitrial valve prolapse, gastroesophageal reflux disease, stroke, autism, multiple sclerosis, ADHD, depression, and violent and aggressive behavior.[346 347]

Children are particularly vulnerable because they are more sensitive to MSG than adults. It can pass through the placenta to children in utero. MSG also can be delivered through breast milk to nursing children. Young children can be exposed through infant formulas that contain casein (cow's milk protein) or soy protein, both of which contain MSG.[348] The blood-brain barrier is not fully formed until children are about two years old. As a result, MSG can more easily access children's brains and cause neurological problems.[349] In utero and early childhood exposure to MSG has been linked to permanent hormone disruption, stunted growth and obesity.[350]

Obesity is one of the most important negative health impacts caused by MSG. Many studies have shown that it causes or contributes to overeating and obesity in all age groups.[351] Researchers regularly use MSG to fatten up laboratory rats for experiments. As noted, extensive research shows that it can damage the weight control center of the brain known as the hypothalamus. The damage includes causing resistance to leptin, the hormone that controls how much a person feels like eating. Leptin resistance blocks the sense of satisfaction that occurs from eating. As a result, the urge to eat continues.[352]

One study found that MSG increases appetite by 40 percent. Another study found that people who eat the most MSG are three times more likely to be overweight than those who do not consume MSG. The brain damage caused by MSG can be cumulative. As a result, the more processed and other MSG-containing foods that people eat, the more likely they could be to overeat over the long-term.[353] As an excitotoxin, MSG overstimulates the brain and can cause excessive production of dopamine. This produces a highly addictive, drug-like rush of well-being. The MSG rush causes people to continue eating MSG-laden foods, which can cause further brain damage.[354]

MSG acts like a drug in the body. It produces metabolic reactions that affect hormones, interfere with appetite regulation and increase dopamine levels. Overweight people often seem to be addicted to food. In a sense, they are addicted to the MSG in food. Eating MSG-laden food can produce a similar addictive sense of well-being as taking legal and illegal mind-altering drugs. This is one reason why ending the consumption of unhealthy, MSG-containing foods can be difficult. It is similar to quitting drugs, tobacco or any other physically addictive substance.

Obesity strongly contributes to many health problems, including diabetes, stroke, heart disease and cancer. People probably often wonder why obese people overeat and damage their health. Some believe that overeating reflects a lack of willpower. The implication is that it results from character flaws. But the situation with MSG shows that these characterizations are unfair and inaccurate. Probably no person would voluntarily choose to become morbidly obese, incur extensive health problems, restrict their ability engage in joyful activities, and possibly shorten their lives. But MSG can severely restrict the ability to voluntarily eat a healthy, non-excessive amount of food.

As discussed in the Animal Feed section, cattle in the US regularly are given feed that contains chicken feces. They generally would not eat feces. As a result, chemicals and other substances are added to make it more palatable. Processed food often is made from bland, low-quality ingredients that have little or no nutritional value. People frequently would not eat this food. However, by adding MSG and other chemicals, consumers can be tricked into eating bland, low-quality foods, in the same way that cattle are tricked into eating feces.

Many consumer advocates say that food companies should be held responsible for the obesity and other health problems caused by fattening, unhealthy foods. But companies, politicians paid by them and other allies often argue that people are freely choosing to overeat unhealthy food. Therefore, they cannot be held responsible for consumers' choices. If people were freely choosing to eat delicious, fattening foods, this might be true. But MSG often severely weakens people's ability to choose. Consumers essentially are being compelled to eat bland, unhealthy foods that they frequently would not freely choose to eat.

In addition, they often are compelled to eat more food than their bodies want and need. MSG frequently creates a conflict between the mind and body. When appetite control mechanisms are functioning normally, senses of satisfaction and fullness signal that no more food is needed. But MSG can trick the mind into wanting food, when the body does not want it. Forcing the body to eat more than it wants causes obesity and many other problems. Especially in this case, companies must be held responsible for negative impacts. If they chemically force consumers to overeat, they must be held accountable for resulting obesity and other health problems.

MSG provides a good example of negative business impacts that are not immediate and obvious. While many people have short-term adverse reactions to MSG, the major negative impacts, such as obesity and neurological disorders, occur over the longer-term. Our flawed systems often compel publicly traded companies to put shareholder returns before all else, when negative impacts are not immediate and obvious. Producing food that contains MSG frequently increases shareholder returns. As a result, companies essentially are compelled to argue for continued MSG use.

The two main strategies for protecting shareholder returns have been discussed extensively throughout *Global System Change* – inappropriately influencing government and misleading the public. Food companies often give large amounts of money to politicians and inappropriately influence government in other ways. As a result, the FDA and other regulators can be compelled to put shareholder returns before public health and argue that MSG is safe, when extensive evidence shows that it is not.

Food companies and their allies often mislead the public by using the Wrong Reference Point deception technique. They frequently fund or influence research which, not surprisingly, shows that MSG is safe. This can create confusion and uncertainty about the safety of MSG. This in turn enables companies to argue that there is no conclusive proof that MSG is harmful. But it is grossly irresponsible to take this position. The implication is that we should be nearly 100 percent certain that MSG and other additives are harmful before prohibiting their use. This is an outrageous and absurd position. We should have demanded nearly 100 percent certainty that MSG and other additives were safe before they were allowed in food.

Extensive evidence shows that MSG strongly contributes to widespread obesity, neurological disorders and other health problems. MSG-related problems probably have increased healthcare costs by hundreds of billions of dollars or more, as well as caused extensive pain, suffering and reduced quality of life. Many families were severely harmed when MSG in food caused family members to become morbidly obese or develop Alzheimer's, Parkinson's or other diseases.

Putting MSG in food imposes large financial costs and quality of life degradations on society. But these costs are externalized. They are not included in food prices. If companies were held responsible for negative impacts, they would quickly remove MSG from food because this would be the profit-maximizing strategy.

Once again, this shows the critical importance of ending business domination of government. When businesses control government, they essentially are unregulated. Few or no restrictions are placed on maximizing shareholder returns. Companies are allowed to add MSG and other harmful chemicals to food. Once citizens regain control of government, businesses will be compelled to benefit and not harm society. Food companies will earn reasonable profits by producing healthy, naturally tasteful foods. They will not be allowed to chemically compel citizens to eat bland, fattening, unhealthy foods.

Many customers care about ingredients. They seek to avoid fattening and harmful ones by regularly reading food labels. But this often will not help them to avoid harmful ingredients. Weak regulations and deceptive labeling frequently fail to disclose them. Processing residues, such as mercury and ammonia, are not disclosed. Byproducts of heating, such as methanol and formaldehyde, are not shown. And components of ingredients, in particular MSG, are not disclosed

Some companies are producing new additives that make it even more difficult to determine what chemicals are being added to food. For example, one company, Senomyx, makes chemicals intended to reduce the use of sugar, salt and MSG in processed food. But long-term independent safety studies generally have not been done to determine if these new chemicals are safe for human use. In one case, a new chemical never used in humans before was given "generally recognized as safe" status based on a three-month study of rats.[355] These new chemicals often will be included under the vague and misleading term artificial flavors. As noted, artificial and natural flavors are highly deceptive terms. For example, both ingredients could contain up to 77 percent MSG. But consumers never would know this by reading food labels.

The business-focused US government makes it nearly impossible to know all of the chemicals and additives in processed and prepared foods. Many of the undisclosed chemicals are harmful. It is particularly important to avoid MSG because it so strongly promotes obesity and neurological disorders. Once citizens regain control of government and establish democracy in the US, full disclosure of all chemicals and other ingredients will be required. This transparency will compel food companies to rapidly remove harmful chemicals and other ingredients.

In the short-term, people should demand that their servant government require disclosure of glutamates, in the same way that cholesterol and trans fats are disclosed on food labels. As people better understand how MSG drives obesity, neurological disorders and many other health problems, they will avoid foods with high glutamate (i.e. MSG) levels. Once labeling

FRANK DIXON

is required, food companies often would quickly lower glutamate content to avoid sales reductions. However, citizens should expect that some food companies and politicians paid by them will vigorously oppose glutamate disclosure because this would greatly reduce the ability to use large amounts of MSG in food. Taking away the ability of food companies to chemically force people to overeat could substantially lower shareholder returns.

Prior to the establishment of democracy in the US, probably the only safe way to avoid MSG and thousands of other disclosed and undisclosed chemicals and additives is to avoid processed and prepared food to the greatest extent possible. Even many organic processed foods contain MSG and other undisclosed harmful ingredients. In general, probably the safest food is that which is prepared at home using whole (i.e. not processed), truly natural ingredients. To save time, people can prepare large batches of food. Then for most days of the week, eating home-prepared foods will be easier and faster than preparing processed food or buying fast food. As discussed in the Health section below, eating home-prepared foods also often is substantially less expensive.

At first, ending the consumption of processed foods may be difficult because home-prepared foods do not contain the chemicals that trick people into thinking that bland, unhealthy foods taste good. However, as people wean themselves off of MSG and other chemical taste enhancers in processed food, they will come to enjoy the taste of real, truly natural foods that are honestly delicious and healthy.

Health

The large majority of people in the US and most other economically developed regions die of diseases of affluence. These chronic diseases include heart disease, cancer and diabetes. The vast majority of people in less developed, rural agricultural areas die of diseases of poverty. These include digestive and parasitic diseases, pneumonia, tuberculosis and diseases of pregnancy.[356] Diseases of affluence are caused mainly by diet. As regions develop economically, the consumption of animal products nearly always increases. This inevitably is accompanied by a rise in chronic diseases.

There is overwhelming scientific evidence showing strong correlations between eating animal products and the diseases that sicken and kill the large majority of people in the developed world. As discussed in previous sections, the consumption of animal products greatly harms human health through widespread contamination. Pesticides and other chemicals accumulate in the fat of animals and deliver doses to humans that frequently are harmful over the longer-term. However, the greater harm often is caused by the animal products themselves. Even the purest organic animal products substantially contribute to heart disease, cancer, diabetes and other chronic diseases.

This section discusses the dietary drivers of diseases of affluence and other health problems such as obesity. It also discusses switching to healthier diets and lifestyles. There are many excellent books in the field of diet and nutrition. This section relies strongly on an outstanding book by T. Colin Campbell, Ph.D., called *The China Study*.[357] Dr. Campbell has written over 300 research papers. He was a leader or member of several national panels and programs on diet and nutrition. He served as the Senior Science Advisor to the American Institute for Cancer Research and several other organizations. He received numerous research awards and participated in the development of national and international nutrition policies. He has been referred to as the "Einstein of Nutrition".[358]

139

Dr. Campbell also oversaw the most comprehensive study of health and nutrition ever conducted – The China Study. It is the culmination of a 20-year partnership between Cornell University, Oxford University and the Chinese Academy of Preventive Medicine. Begun in 1983, The China Study analyzed relationships between diet and many diseases among 6,500 people who consumed varying levels of animal products in China and Taiwan. The study gathered data on 367 variables and produced over 8,000 statistically significant associations between various dietary and lifestyle factors and disease.

The study consistently found that the people who ate the most animal products got the most chronic diseases. Those who ate the most plant-based foods were the healthiest and tended to avoid chronic disease.[359] The book *The China Study* cites many other peer-reviewed studies that find strong associations between the consumption of animal products and chronic diseases. Using unbiased, rigorous science, the studies control for age, lifestyle and other factors that could influence results.

With high levels of confidence, the China Study and many studies cited in the book strongly indicate that eating animal products is the largest cause of chronic disease. This makes it the largest killer of humans in the developed world. The research also consistently shows that eating a whole food, plant-based diet can prevent and often reverse health problems including cancer, heart disease, diabetes, autoimmune diseases, cognitive and neurological diseases such as Alzheimer's disease, and bone, kidney and vision disorders.[360]

Publicly traded food companies are systemically required to protect shareholder returns. This creates pressure to mislead the public about links between animal products and disease. Food companies often directly or indirectly fund or influence studies which, not surprisingly, show that eating animal products does not increase chronic disease risk. But these studies usually are highly biased or flawed.

To illustrate, a well-known US study (i.e. the Nurses' Health Study) analyzed links between diet, disease and several other factors among thousands of nurses over many years. The study found that eating meat and dairy products did not increase breast cancer risk. But virtually all of the nurses in the study were eating above-average amounts of meat and dairy products.[361] As a result, this study generally cannot be used to draw valid conclusions about the benefits of eating a plant-based diet. It often is difficult to accurately assess the benefits of plant-based diets by studying the US population because nearly everyone eats animal products. Only about five percent of adults in the US are vegetarians (i.e. people who eat eggs and dairy products, but no meat, poultry or fish) and 2.5 percent are vegans (i.e. people who eat no animal products).[362]

Assessing the benefits and risks of eating animal and plant products generally requires comparing groups of people who eat animal products to those who eat mainly or only plant-based diets. The China Study and many other studies cited in the book draw their conclusions from this type of valid research.

People are especially vulnerable to deception in the food area. For many, eating is one of the greatest joys of life. There often is strong resistance to the idea that favorite foods are harmful. But survival and health should take priority over eating pleasure. Treating chronic disease is a main cause of high and rapidly rising healthcare costs in the US and many other developed countries. Reducing the consumption of animal products is one of the most important actions needed to lower healthcare costs. But this often would reduce the sales of food, drug and healthcare companies (because far fewer people would get sick and die prematurely). To protect shareholder returns, these companies frequently engage in public deception.

It is critical that people apply rational thought and logic. They must be aware of vested interest bias and focus on the facts and unbiased science. The lives of their loved ones and themselves literally often will depend on it. People must not allow their preferences for animal products to block clear, honest, rational thinking. As discussed below, food tastes, especially for unhealthy foods, largely are a function of habit. Habits and tastes frequently can be changed in two to three months. There is no need to give up the joy of eating. There are thousands of delicious plant-based foods and meals. They strongly promote a clear mind, light body and long, healthy life.

Plant Versus Animal Products

Clarifying the differences between plant and animal products illustrates why eating plant products promotes long, healthy lives, while eating animal products often promotes chronic disease and premature death. Plant products contain several important nutrients that are not found in animal products or are contained in much smaller amounts. For example, fruits, vegetables, beans and nuts often have high levels of antioxidants. Sunshine, chemicals and poor diets can produce free radicals in the human body. These promote premature aging, cancer, heart disease, cognitive disorders and many other health problems. Antioxidants protect people from free radical damage. They act like a fountain of youth. Only plants produce antioxidants. Animal products sometimes contain small amounts as a result of animals eating plants. But antioxidant levels nearly always are much higher in plant products.[363]

Plant products also often have high levels of fiber. Fiber is highly beneficial. It lowers the risk of heart disease, several types of cancer, and many other health problems. It also creates a sense of fullness and satisfaction, which inhibits overeating. Animal products have no fiber. Plant products also often have higher levels of minerals and many types of vitamins.[364]

While animal products lack many essential nutrients, they also contain harmful substances that are not found in plants or usually are contained in much smaller amounts, such as cholesterol and saturated fat. Cholesterol is a necessary substance that is produced by the human body. Humans do not need to get cholesterol from food. High blood cholesterol is a primary cause of heart disease and many other health problems. Animal products often have high levels of cholesterol. Eating high cholesterol foods increases blood cholesterol in about 30 percent of people.[365] Plant products have no cholesterol. Instead, through mechanisms discussed in *The China Study*, plant products frequently reduce cholesterol in the body.

High levels of fat in food are strongly associated with many types of chronic diseases. With few exceptions, animal products contain substantially more fat than plant products. Plant products with high levels of fat, such as nuts and seeds, generally have healthier types of fat. They also contain other beneficial nutrients not found in animal products, such as antioxidants.[366]

There are wide variations in animal products. For example, fish and beef are substantially different. However, from a nutritional perspective, fish is much closer to beef than to rice or other plant products. Fish and chicken have high levels of cholesterol, like beef. But as noted, rice and other plant products have no cholesterol. Many factors other than diet influence health and disease levels. As discussed in *The China Study*, when these factors are controlled through rigorous science, extensive research shows that plant products produce substantially better health and disease prevention than animal products, including so-called healthier types of animal products such as fish.

Protein represents an important area of public misunderstanding and deception. Protein is an essential nutrient. Much of the human body is made of it. Human protein is comprised of about 20 amino acids. Twelve are made by the body. Eight essential amino acids must be provided in food. Animal products usually contain high levels of all eight essential amino acids. As a result, animal products can promote rapid growth. Due to this and the presence of essential amino acids, animal protein often is referred to as high-quality protein. But this designation is deceptive because it implies that animal protein is healthier than plant protein. Rapid growth often does not equal optimal health. As discussed in *The China Study* and summarized below, plant products are far more effective at preventing disease and promoting good health than animal products. In this most important sense, plant proteins are much higher quality than animal proteins.

All vegetables, beans, grains, nuts and seeds contain protein and essential amino acids. Many types of plant products contain all eight essential amino acids. However some plant proteins have lower levels of one or two essential amino acids. As a result, these types of plant proteins sometimes are called lower-quality. The implication is that plant products do not provide adequate protein. But this is deceptive. Protein in plant and animal products is not directly converted to human protein. Instead, the body breaks plant and animal proteins down into constituent amino acids and reformulates them into human protein.

A common misunderstanding about plant products is that complex and difficult food combining is needed to get adequate protein (i.e. all eight essential amino acids). But this misconception has been refuted by extensive research. As discussed in *The China Study*, through complex metabolic reactions, the human body can derive all essential amino acids from the natural variety of plant products consumed over one or two days. Meticulous meal planning or getting all eight essential amino acids in every meal is not required.[367]

Many simple plant-based meals provide all eight essential amino acids. For example, nearly all bean and whole rice combinations provide perfect protein, in the sense of providing abundant levels of all eight essential amino acids. Beans and rice also provide high levels of fiber and other nutrients not found in animal products. Unlike animal products, beans and rice have no cholesterol and very low fat. While animal products can promote fast growth, plant products also enable people to reach their full genetic potential size. As discussed below, there are many world-class athletes who only eat plant products.

Some groups of people in developing countries who eat mainly plant products do not grow as large as people in developed countries who eat animal products. But this largely does not result from the failure to eat animal products. It usually results from not eating enough food in general, not eating well-balanced plant-based diets, illness and other factors.

Humans require air, water and nutrition to survive. As Dr. Campbell discusses in *The China Study*, virtually all necessary nutrients, including protein, are better provided by plant products.[368] The optimal mix of plant-based foods for each person might vary based on individual characteristics. But in general, a plant-based diet would work for everyone. Due to various life circumstances, some people might need to eat meat to survive, for example because adequate plant products are not available. But from a nutritional perspective, no human needs to eat animal products.

Some people say that they tried a plant-based diet, but felt better when they switched back to eating animal products. This nearly always results from the failure to eat a well-balanced plant-based diet. There are thousands of plant-based foods and diets. Many plant products contain simple, refined carbohydrates and high levels of fat, salt and/or sugar. These types of plant-based foods strongly promote obesity and poor health.

Dr. Campbell and many other nutrition scientists and experts discuss the importance of whole food, plant-based diets. Whole foods include complex, unrefined carbohydrates, such as brown rice. People who did not thrive on plant-based diets probably were not eating important nutrients, virtually all of which are available in plant-based foods. Well-balanced whole food, plant-based diets would work for everyone. Saying that eating a healthy whole food, plant-based diet would not work, would be like saying that drinking clean water or breathing clean air would not work.

People who lived their whole lives breathing polluted air and drinking polluted water might experience some discomfort if they suddenly were placed in an environment with clean air and water. In the same way, people who ate animal products their whole lives, especially those contaminated with chemicals and other substances, might feel some discomfort if they suddenly switched to healthy whole food, plant-based diets. This does not mean that the diets would not vastly improve health, vitality and longevity. However, it does indicate that the transition to healthy eating, especially for people with health problems, should be done carefully and often with the advice and guidance of medical or nutrition experts.

Anatomy

Examining the anatomical differences between carnivores, omnivores, herbivores and humans shows that humans anatomically are herbivores, not omnivores or carnivores. We evolved to eat whole plant foods. As a result, these are the optimal, natural foods for humans. An article by Dr. Milton Mills, called *The Comparative Anatomy of Eating*, shows that humans are herbivores by comparing the anatomical features of carnivores, omnivores, herbivores and humans.[369]

Carnivores evolved to capture, kill, tear and digest animals. Herbivores evolved to consume and digest plants. Omnivores eat plants and animals. But to eat animals, they must retain their ability to capture, kill and digest prey. As a result, omnivores, such as bears and raccoons, anatomically are almost completely carnivores, with a few minor adaptations for eating plants.

Carnivores and omnivores have wide mouth openings relative to head size and jaw joints on the same plane as the teeth. The lower jaw cannot move forward or backwards and has very limited side-to-side motion. This provides the strong, stable jaws needed to capture, kill and dismember prey. Herbivores and humans have relatively small mouth openings and jaw joints above the plane of the teeth. This makes jaws much weaker. They would not be effective for capturing and killing prey. But they provide the front-to-back and side-to-side mobility needed to crush and grind fibrous plants.

Carnivores and omnivores have sharp, pointed, short front teeth for tearing flesh. Herbivores and humans have flat, long, shovel-like front teeth for cutting plants. Carnivores and omnivores have long, curved, sharp canines for capturing, killing and tearing prey. Canines vary in herbivores. Some have no canine teeth. Other herbivores, such as hippos and some primates, have longer canines that are thought to be for defense. Human canines are short and blunt. They function like incisors (i.e. front teeth). Carnivores have triangular molars for cutting flesh. Some omnivores have flat molars, like herbivores and humans, for crushing plants.

Carnivores and omnivores swallow food whole or simply crush it and have no digestive enzymes in their mouths. Herbivores and humans require extensive chewing and have digestive enzymes in their mouths. Carnivores and omnivores have a wide esophagus that can handle whole chucks of meat. Herbivores and humans have narrow esophagi that are best suited for swallowing small, soft, thoroughly chewed balls of food. Swallowing large chunks of meat is a common cause of choking in humans.

Carnivores and omnivores have large stomach capacities (60 to 70 percent of the digestive system). Herbivores and humans have smaller stomach capacities (less than 30 percent of the digestive system). Meat, especially decaying flesh, often has abundant pathogens. Carnivores and omnivores have high acid stomachs (about 1 pH) that kill pathogens. Herbivores and humans have low acid stomachs (4 to 5 pH). No animal cooks food, except humans. Cooking can kill pathogens in meat. It substitutes for the lack of a high acid carnivorous stomach and makes meat safer for humans to eat. But it also can degrade or destroy nutrients in food. However, minimal cooking or steaming of vegetables can make them easier to digest with little degradation of nutrients.

Carnivores and omnivores have relatively short, smooth small intestines (3 to 6 times body length). Herbivores and humans have relatively long, pouched small intestines that are about 10 to 12 times body length (the body length of humans is measured from the top of the head to the base of the spine). The long intestines of herbivores and humans are evolved to slowly digest fibrous plant material. Fatty, non-fibrous animal products and refined carbohydrates can accumulate in the many turns and pouches of the human digestive tract, putrefy and cause illness.

Carnivores and omnivores can eat high fat foods with high cholesterol (i.e. animal products) with no negative health impacts. However, as discussed in the Heart Disease section below, high fat foods often cause heart disease and other health problems in humans. Carnivores and omnivores have sharp claws for catching and tearing prey. Herbivores and humans have flat nails or hooves. Carnivores and omnivores cool themselves through hyperventilation. Humans and many herbivores cool themselves through perspiration. Also, humans are not instinctual carnivores. A child might pick an apple from a tree and eat it. But they would not chase down a small animal, kill it by biting it, and eat the flesh off its bones, as carnivores and omnivores would do.

Focusing on the anatomical features that differentiate carnivores and herbivores, humans have virtually no similarities to carnivores and virtually no differences from herbivores. The only similarities that humans have to omnivores are to the parts that are adapted to eating plants, such as flat molars. Humans are not omnivores because we are not evolved to eat meat. Our mouths, jaws, teeth, throats and digestive systems are not evolved to capture, kill, tear, swallow and digest animals. Observing our closest living relatives, gorillas, indicates our natural, optimal foods. Gorillas eat 97-100 percent plants.[370] Chimpanzees sometimes eat meat. But mostly they eat plants.[371]

The human ability to think, rather than anatomical features, enabled us to capture, cook and eat meat. But anatomy, not tradition or intellectual capacity, indicates the optimal diet. Based on anatomy, humans are raw food herbivores. All herbivores can digest and utilize some animal protein because all protein is biochemically related. All animal tissue ultimately is derived from broken down plant tissues. But the fact that herbivores and humans can digest some animal protein does not mean it is the optimal food for us. We evolved to eat raw plant foods. Significant variations from these optimal foods often will produce suboptimal health or illness.

Some Chinese and Ayurveda dietary philosophies say that humans are biochemically unique. Therefore, optimal diets should vary based on individual characteristics. But this is misleading. There are minor biochemical differences and other factors such as food allergies that indicate optimal diets should vary between individuals. But we mostly are the same. We all have essentially the same teeth, mouths and digestive systems. None of these anatomical features are evolved to eat animal products.

In the same way that there are minor differences between humans, there might be minor biochemical and other differences between tigers. But this does not mean that some tigers are better off eating plants while others are better off eating meat. All tigers prosper by eating what they evolved to eat – meat. All humans prosper by eating what we evolved to eat – plants. Our teeth are not evolved or designed to eat raw meat off the bones of animals. Cooking makes meat soft enough for our herbivorous teeth, mouths, throats and digestive systems.

To rationalize the consumption of animal products, some people support the opportunistic feeder theory. This circular (i.e. not logical) logic says that meat must be an optimal, healthy food for humans because humans frequently ate it in the past.[372] This would be like saying that, if many people regularly eat brownies and cheesecake, these foods must be optimal, healthy foods for humans.

There are several reasons why humans would eat animal products when they are not optimal foods for us. These include survival, convenience, acquired taste and intelligence. As we migrated north, humans often ate animal products to survive because adequate plant products were not available.

Also, animal products frequently are more nutritionally dense than plant products. This could make eating them more convenient. An equivalent amount of nutrition could be acquired with less time and effort by hunting animals rather than gathering plants. In addition, as we ate animal products, we often acquired a taste for them. Furthermore, our intelligence gave us the ability to make the weapons and tools needed to capture, kill, cook and eat animals.

As intelligent, higher life forms, humans have the ability to vary our behavior and diets. But just because we can survive by eating animal products, or enjoy eating them, does not mean that they are optimal, healthy foods for humans. As shown in the following sections, eating animal products often strongly promotes chronic diseases and other health problems.

Heart Disease

Heart disease is the number one killer of men and women in the US, and has been for nearly 100 years.[373] It kills more than 600,000 people per year.[374] About half of men and one-third of women will get heart disease. It kills eight times more women than breast cancer.[375]

Heart disease, also known as cardiovascular disease, usually is caused by the buildup of fatty material called plaque on the inner walls of blood vessels that supply the heart. This can cause narrowing and hardening of arteries (i.e. atherosclerosis), which can slow or stop blood flow to the heart. This in turn can cause chest pain (angina), shortness of breath, heart attacks and death. As discussed in the Blood Pressure section below, high blood pressure strongly contributes to plaque accumulation and narrowing and hardening of arteries. It is a major risk factor for heart disease. (In addition to plaque accumulation, heart infections and conditions that affect heart muscles, valves and beating rhythm are considered to be forms of heart disease.)

Since the 1940s, many studies have shown correlations between heart disease and consumption of saturated fat and cholesterol. But some recent studies found low or no correlation. These studies can be deceptive for several reasons. Food companies conduct, influence and fund many food studies. This research is inherently biased. As noted, all cholesterol and nearly all saturated fat comes from animal products. Showing low or no correlation between these fats and heart disease protects animal product sales.

Some studies had methodological flaws that distorted results. For example, a meta study that found no correlation between saturated fat and heart disease did not consider how saturated fat was reduced. Many food companies created low fat products by replacing saturated fat with sugar. Substituting one unhealthy food for another did not lower heart disease.[376] However, studies that compare high saturated fat animal products to low-fat whole plant foods nearly always find strong correlations to heart disease.

As discussed in more detail below, Dr. Campbell points out that studying food components, such as fat, is deceptive because people do not eat components. They eat complete foods. Focusing on fat protects animal product sales by distracting attention from high correlations between animal products and heart disease, cancer and other chronic diseases. In addition, Dr. Campbell notes that many studies since the early 1900's found much stronger correlations between animal protein and heart disease than fat and heart disease.[377] Fat often can be removed from animal products. Protein frequently cannot. The alternative is plant products. Focusing on fat instead of the foods that people actually eat protects animal product sales.

The idea that eating foods with high saturated fat and cholesterol will not increase the accumulation of fatty material in blood vessels and other parts of the body seems counter-intuitive and illogical. When people eat foods with high sugar, protein or other food components, it usually increases their concentration in the body. The human body is highly complex. It sometimes can eliminate excess materials. But the assertion that eating high-fat animal products will not increase body fat accumulation violates common sense. As discussed in the Diet section below, when people lose weight on high-fat diets, it usually is due to calorie restriction, not the irrational idea that eating more fat will lower fat in the body. Weight lost through these diets virtually always returns. High animal fat diets are not a healthy or sustainable form of eating for humans and other herbivores.

The components of food interact with each other and the human body in highly complex ways. From a human health perspective, it often is more useful to study the foods that people actually eat, rather than components of them. Nevertheless, focusing on fat helps to illuminate the disease promoting qualities of animal products. Many studies found correlations between consumption of harmful fats and heart disease. The most harmful fats in terms of promoting heart disease are cholesterol, saturated fat and trans fats. As noted, cholesterol is an important material made by the human body. The body does not need to get it from foods. All dietary cholesterol comes from animal products. As discussed in *The China Study*, for more than 50 years, many studies have shown that high blood cholesterol levels are strongly associated with greater risk of heart disease.

Two important types of cholesterol are low-density lipoproteins (LDL) and high-density lipoproteins (HDL). High levels of LDL increase plaque accumulation and heart disease. As a result, LDL often is called bad cholesterol. HDL removes cholesterol from the bloodstream, and thereby lowers plaque accumulation and heart disease risk. As a result, HDL frequently is called good cholesterol.

Important fats include saturated, unsaturated and trans fats. Like cholesterol, the human body makes all the saturated fat it needs. We do not need to get saturated fat from food.[378] Saturated fats contribute to heart disease and often are called bad fats. They increase the levels of bad cholesterol and are solid at room temperature. Nearly all saturated fat comes from animal products. However, all plant oils have some saturated fat. Palm and coconut oils have high levels of it.

Unsaturated fats often are called good fat because they can lower bad cholesterol and raise good cholesterol. Unsaturated fats nearly always come from plants. However, fish often have some unsaturated fat. Essential fatty acids are an important type of unsaturated fat that cannot be made by the human body, and therefore must be acquired from food. Fish and many types of plant products, such as flax, soy and walnuts, provide essential fatty acids.

Trans fats are the worst types of fats. They strongly contribute to heart disease by raising bad cholesterol and lowering good cholesterol. Partially hydrogenated oils are a main source of trans fat. These oils are stable and less likely to spoil. As a result, they were widely used in the fast food industry and products such as peanut butter. Partially hydrogenated oils were generally regarded as safe for many years. However, this status was removed in 2018. As a result, the oils and trans fats in them largely have been removed from US food products.

With all dietary cholesterol and nearly all saturated fat coming from animal products, it should not be surprising that heart disease consistently increases when animal product consumption rises. As discussed, studies in the US sometimes do not show this relationship between heart disease and animal product consumption because nearly everyone in the US eats animal products. *The China Study* cites many international studies that compare groups of people who eat all or nearly all plant products to those who eat animal products. They consistently find that societies which eat mainly plant products have low blood cholesterol and low heart disease. More than two-thirds of the world eats mainly plant-based diets. Heart disease is rare in these regions.[379] Societies that eat large amounts of animal products virtually always have higher blood cholesterol and higher heart disease rates.

As noted, the studies cited in *The China Study* control for age, lifestyle and other factors that might influence results. This isolates the relationship between heart disease and diet. Ethnicity and race have little impact on these international studies. When groups of people who formerly ate mainly plant products adopt Western, high-animal product diets, heart disease rates virtually always increase.[380] The link between dietary fat and heart disease has been confirmed in many animal studies. In one study for example, when monkeys were fed high-fat diets, heart disease progressed. When fat was reduced, heart disease reversed.[381]

The march towards heart disease and early death begins at a young age when people consume more fat than the body needs, especially harmful animal product fats. A study of 12-year-old children in the US found that 70 percent had fatty deposits in their arteries, a precursor to heart disease.[382] Another study examined the hearts of 300 US soldiers killed in the Korean War. At an average age of 22, none of the soldiers had been diagnosed with heart disease. They were in top condition in the prime of their physical lives.

Nevertheless, in line with the animal product intensive US diet, nearly 80 percent of the soldiers had gross evidence of heart disease (i.e. large fatty deposits in their arteries).[383] In line with Asian plant-based diets, autopsies of Asian soldiers found that their arteries largely were clean and free of fatty deposits.

The treatment of heart disease costs more than $250 billion per year in the US. Treatments often are expensive, risky, disfiguring, life-threatening and ineffective. In addition, they do nothing to address the cause of heart disease. Treatments for heart disease include angioplasty, inserting stents, bypass surgery and heart transplant.

Angioplasty involves inserting a balloon into a clogged artery, inflating it, and squishing plaque back against the artery wall. About 40 percent of arteries squished open with balloons close up again within four months.[384] A stent is a wire mesh tube inserted during angioplasty. When the balloon is inflated, the stent expands, locks into place and holds the artery open. About one million stent operations are performed in the US each year. About four percent of patients have heart attacks during the procedure and one percent die.[385]

Bypass surgery involves splitting the patient's chest open and diverting blood flow with pumps and clamps. A piece of blood vessel from another part of the body is used to bypass clogged coronary arteries. About 400,000 bypass surgeries are done in the US each year. During the procedure, about five percent of patients have a stroke or heart attack, and more than two percent die.[386] Clamping blood vessels during bypass surgery often causes plaque to break off, travel to the brain and cause mini strokes. One study found that 79 percent of patients showed some cognitive impairment seven days after the operation.[387] Many drugs also are used to treat heart disease. Heart disease treatment generates substantial revenue for the pharmaceutical and healthcare industries. With less than five percent of the world's population, over 50 percent of angioplasties and bypass surgeries are done in the US.[388]

As discussed in *The China Study*, several studies have shown that angioplasties and bypass surgeries do not lower heart attack rates, do not extend the lives of any but the sickest patients, and do not address the cause of heart disease. The heart attack death rate in the US has fallen by nearly 60 percent since 1950, in large part due to better emergency room treatments for heart attack victims. However, the incidence of heart disease is about the same as in the early 1970s. In other words, some emergency and other heart disease treatments have postponed heart disease deaths. But heart disease treatments in general have done little to address the rate at which hearts become diseased.[389]

The medical community has long recognized the link between heart disease and diet. In 1961, the well-known Framingham Heart Study found a strong correlation between high blood cholesterol and heart disease. Since then, many doctors and health organizations have advised people to lower heart disease and heart attack risk by consuming a low-fat, low-cholesterol diet.

Possibly the most successful heart disease treatment of any type was implemented by Dr. Caldwell B. Esselstyn, Jr. Dr. Esselstyn was an Olympic gold medalist in rowing, a decorated Army surgeon during the Vietnam War, and a leading surgeon at the prestigious Cleveland Clinic. He has published over 100 research papers and was named one of the best doctors in America in 1994-1995.[390] Dr. Esselstyn describes his successful heart disease prevention and treatment strategy in an outstanding book called *Prevent and Reverse Heart Disease*.[391]

In 1985, Dr. Esselstyn began his study with 24 patients. His goal was to reduce patients' blood cholesterol to below 150 mg/dL through diet and cholesterol-reducing drugs when necessary. Patients were encouraged to avoid added oils and all animal products except for skim milk and nonfat yogurt. After five years, Dr. Esselstyn recommended that patients avoid all dairy products due to the tumor-promoting properties of cow's milk protein (discussed under Cancer below) and the heart disease promoting properties of animal protein.[392] Instead, patients were encouraged to eat whole grains, beans, fruit and vegetables, and keep total calories from fat to about ten percent.[393] Five patients dropped out of the study within two years. One left the study and returned.

The 18 patients who remained in the study had 49 coronary events prior to the study, including angina, stroke, heart attack, angioplasty and bypass surgery. They reduced average cholesterol from 246 mg/dL to 137 mg/dL and had no further coronary events over the 12 year course of the study. Clogged arteries were opened in 70 percent of the patients. A patient who stopped the diet for two years experienced chest pain. When they resumed a plant-based diet, the chest pain ended. The five patients who left the study experienced ten new coronary events within ten years.[394]

Dr. Dean Ornish also had high levels of success in treating heart disease with plant-based diets. In one study, he treated two groups of heart disease patients. One group received standard treatments. Another group was put on a low-fat, plant-based diet for one year. The diet group also was encouraged to exercise regularly and practice various forms of stress management, such as meditation. In the diet group, chest pain was reduced by an average of 91 percent and heart disease regressed in 82 percent of patients within one year. Among the patients receiving standard heart disease treatments, chest pain increase by 165 percent and blockages of arteries became worse.[395]

In *Prevent and Reverse Heart Disease* and *The China Study*, Doctors Esselstyn and Campbell say that dietary guidelines for fat and blood cholesterol are set too high in the US. *The China Study* found that people in rural China get about 15 percent of calories from fat and have average blood cholesterol of 127 mg/dL.[396] At these levels, heart disease is rare. People in the US get about 37 percent of calories from fat and have average blood cholesterol of 215 mg/dL. At these levels, heart disease is the number one killer in the US. The heart disease death rate is 17 times higher among US men than rural Chinese men.[397]

US dietary guidelines recommend that people get up to 35 percent of calories from fat and less than 10 percent of calories from saturated fat. In addition, leading medical organizations in the US generally suggest that it is desirable to keep total blood cholesterol below 200 mg/dL. But 35 percent of heart attacks occur among people with cholesterol levels between 150 and 200 mg/dL.[398] These fat and cholesterol guidelines virtually guarantee that over 1.2 million people will have heart attacks each year in the US and millions more will experience advancing heart disease.[399]

Dr. Esselstyn explains that, when people use plant-based diets to lower total cholesterol to less than 150 mg/dL and bad cholesterol (LDL) to less than 80 mg/dL, fat and cholesterol cannot be deposited on coronary arteries. This makes people virtually immune to the number one killer in the US.[400] The key is using plant-based diets, and cholesterol-reducing drugs if necessary, to achieve the 150 mg/dL goal. Continuing to eat animal products and using drugs to lower cholesterol reduces heart disease but often does not eliminate it. In a study published in the New England Journal of Medicine, heart disease patients were given large doses of cholesterol-reducing drugs to get cholesterol below 150 mg/dL. No dietary changes were required. Heart disease improved in 75 percent of the patients. But 25 percent had a new coronary event or died within 2.5 years. These patients had high levels of a type of protein that indicated they were eating animal products.[401]

Dr. Esselstyn discusses how animal protein can cause inflammation of coronary arteries. This can enable heart disease to advance even when cholesterol levels are low. Plant products, on the other hand, improve the health of blood vessels in several ways. This combined with low cholesterol levels can prevent and reverse heart disease.[402]

In parts of the world where total cholesterol is consistently below 150 mg/dL, heart disease is rare. Blood cholesterol is low in these regions because people are eating mainly plant-based diets, not because they are taking cholesterol-reducing drugs. Drugs often have significant negative side effects. Whole food, plant-based diets, on the other hand, have overwhelmingly positive impacts. They provide vitality, longevity and optimal health. There are no negative impacts from a well-balanced whole food, plant-based diet that is adjusted to individual needs. *The China Study* provides extensive evidence which shows that plants are the optimal food for humans. Dr. Esselstyn helps to prove this by achieving essentially perfect results in halting and often reversing heart disease with plant-based diets.

An important element of the diet suggested by Dr. Esselstyn is avoiding added fats and oils. Humans did not evolve to eat concentrated, refined oils. For example, gorillas do not pour oil over vegetables before eating them, as humans often do with oily salad dressings. Patients on Dr. Esselstyn's diet get all the fat they need from whole plant foods, as gorillas and other herbivores do.

As noted, animal products have bad, artery-clogging saturated fats. Plant products provide healthier unsaturated fats. But unsaturated fats can become unhealthy if eaten excessively. In *Prevent and Reverse Heart Disease*, Dr. Esselstyn explains that the term "heart-healthy oil" is deceptive. The unsaturated fats in plant oils, such as olive oil, can slow the progression of heart disease relative to saturated fats. But they do not halt or reverse it.

The term heart-healthy oil often is linked to the Mediterranean diet, which largely is based on the Lyon Diet Heart Study.[403] Under the study, 605 people who had survived first heart attacks were divided into two groups. One group ate the typical US diet and got about 34 percent of calories from fat (12 percent from saturated fat). The diet group was instructed to eat larger amounts of fruit, vegetables, grains and beans, and lower amounts of fish, poultry and dairy products. Olive oil also was allowed. They got about 30 percent of calories from fat (eight percent from saturated fat).

Over the four-year period of the study, the diet group had 50 to 70 percent fewer heart problems of all types. These results were used to show the benefits of the Mediterranean diet. However, one-quarter of people on the Mediterranean diet died or had a new coronary event within four years. In other words, the diet slowed, but did not halt the progression of heart disease.

As noted, all plant oils contain some saturated fat. Olive oil, for example, contains about 15 percent artery-clogging saturated fat. *Prevent and Reverse Heart Disease* cites several human and animal studies which show that excess unsaturated fat contributes to heart disease nearly as much is saturated fat. For example, in one study, monkeys fed unsaturated fat had higher good cholesterol and lower bad cholesterol. But heart disease progressed as much as in monkeys fed saturated fat.[404] Dr. Esselstyn explains that there are no heart-healthy oils. All oils are heart unhealthy to varying degrees. As noted, concentrated oils are not a natural food for humans. We did not evolve to eat them. Therefore, it should not be surprising that all concentrated, refined oils can contribute to heart disease.

The US government dietary guidelines have a significant impact on the US diet and chronic disease levels. Dietary guidelines are issued every five years by the USDA and US Department of Health and Human Services (HHS). The guidelines are based on advice from a committee of experts established by the two departments, called the Dietary Guidelines Advisory Committee. The 2010 guidelines said that it was healthy to eat up to 35 percent of calories as total fat, 10 percent as saturated fat, 35 percent as protein and 25 percent as added sugars. They also suggested limiting cholesterol intake to 300 milligrams per day and implied that it was healthy to eat up to 50 percent of grains in refined form.

The 2015 dietary guidelines shifted the focus from nutrient restrictions (i.e. percentage of calories from fat and protein) to eating patterns. However, implied nutrient levels for fat, protein and refined grains were the same. Suggested sugar limits were reduced to 10 percent of calories.

The 2020 dietary guidelines continued the eating pattern focus of the 2015 guidelines and added recommendations for stages of life as well as pregnant and lactating women. But the implied nutrient levels are the same. Daily nutritional goals listed in Appendix 1 suggest that it is healthy to eat up to 35 percent of calories as total fat, 10 percent as saturated fat, 35 percent as protein, and 10 percent as sugar. The guidelines also continue to suggest that it is healthy to eat up to 50 percent of grains in refined form.[405] In other words, the guidelines say that it is healthy to eat large amounts of fat, animal protein and refined carbohydrates.

As discussed below, many studies show that eating high animal fat diets contributes to the buildup of fatty material in arteries (heart disease). As discussed in the Cancer section, extensive research shows that high animal protein diets strongly contribute to cancer. A key question is, why are fat and protein guidelines set at levels that are guaranteed to sicken and kill millions of people and increase healthcare costs by trillions of dollars over many years? Business influence of government and the conflicting goals of the USDA are main parts of the answer. Since the guidelines were first issued in 1980, dietary guidelines advisory committee members often had ties to the food industry. For example, over half of the members of the 2020 committee had ties.[406] Reflecting this influence, the committees frequently relied heavily on research that was conducted, influenced or funded by food companies.

A primary goal and responsibility of the USDA is to promote the sale of animal products. Implied dietary fat and protein guidelines are set at levels that allow high consumption of these foods. This once again shows the destructive nature of our economic and political systems that place shareholder returns before all else. In this case, implied fat and protein guidelines are set at levels that protect the shareholder returns of food companies, but literally kill people.

Food company influence and USDA promotion of animal products create strong bias toward protecting sales of these products in the guidelines. Several factors indicate this. As discussed in the Environmental Impacts section, industrial animal product production strongly contributes to climate change and other environmental problems. For the first time, the 2015 dietary guidelines discussed the impact of US eating habits on climate change and the environment. But pressure from the livestock industry contributed to this information being omitted from the 2020 guidelines.[407]

The guidelines also do not emphasize how replacing animal products with whole plant foods strongly prevents and often reverses chronic disease, as well as provides the most effective strategy for achieving long-term weight loss (discussed in the Diet section below). Instead, the 2020 guidelines emphasize eating nutrient-dense foods, which include many animal products.

Regarding cholesterol, the 2015 dietary guidelines removed the 300 milligram per day limit stated in the 2010 guidelines, based in part on research showing a lower correlation between dietary and blood cholesterol. However, the guidelines still suggested limiting dietary cholesterol because high cholesterol foods (i.e. animal products) often contain high levels of saturated fat, which is more strongly correlated to heart disease. The 2020 guidelines do not suggest dietary cholesterol limits. But they are implied. The guidelines state "The USDA Dietary Patterns are limited in *trans* fats and low in dietary cholesterol."[408]

The revised approach of the 2015 and 2020 dietary guidelines indicates food company influence of the USDA. Recommending healthy nutrient levels as a percentage of calories makes it fairly easy for citizens to calculate the composition of their diets and make adjustments when necessary. But this approach potentially threatens the sales and shareholder returns of food companies. Independent research increasingly shows the chronic disease-promoting qualities of animal products and refined carbohydrates. This creates growing pressure to lower the recommended percentage of calories from fat, protein and added sugars, which could reduce food company sales.

As noted, the 2010 dietary guidelines implied that eating up to 25 percent of calories as added sugars was healthy. But the World Health Organization said that added sugars should be limited to 10 percent of calories. As it became obvious that high-sugar diets strongly promoted the obesity and diabetes epidemics in the US, the USDA reduced its percentage of calories recommendation for added sugars.

Shifting the focus of the dietary guidelines from nutrient percentage of calories to eating patterns enabled the USDA to avoid reducing the recommended percentage of calories from fat and protein, as it was compelled to do for added sugars. This protected the shareholder returns of the food companies that heavily influence the USDA. Emphasizing eating patterns made the dietary guidelines more vague and confusing. It enabled them to discuss the increasingly obvious importance of eating whole plant foods, while simultaneously recommending diets that allow high consumption of animal products and refined carbohydrates.

To protect profits generated by high-fat diets, food companies and their allies often argued or implied that high-fat animal and other products did not cause the obesity epidemic in the US. Obesity has risen since the 1980s, in spite of a strong emphasis on low-fat diets. As discussed in the Obesity section, arguing that high-fat diets do not cause obesity is deceptive. To maintain sales, food companies often replaced fat in food products with sugar and other unhealthy flavor enhancers. Replacing high-fat foods with high-sugar foods did not slow the obesity epidemic. It might have accelerated it. In other words, replacing one type of unhealthy food with another did not benefit society. But replacing high-fat, animal product-intense diets with low-fat, whole plant food diets would have slammed the brakes on the obesity and chronic disease epidemics in the US and many other developed countries.

Instead of allowing the food company-influenced USDA to issue dietary guidelines, they should be issued by an organization that is completely focused on protecting public health, such as the HHS. Suggesting that people get 10 to 15 percent of calories from fat, avoid saturated and trans fats, and keep total cholesterol below 150 mg/dL would greatly reduce heart disease in the US. Some officials say that it is not practical to suggest that 10 to 15 percent of calories come from fat because people would not follow these guidelines. But this is ridiculous. It would be like saying that speed limits should not be set at safe levels because people will want to drive faster. People must be given correct information. Dietary guidelines should be set at levels that prevent heart disease, rather than kill people. If people choose to exceed the guidelines, that is their choice. But many people will strive to protect their families and themselves by following the guidelines.

Some experts have said that cholesterol levels below 150 mg/dL might be unhealthy. One study found that low cholesterol caused by using cholesterol-reducing drugs might increase accidental death, suicide risk or cancer. But subsequent studies showed this to be false. In a more recent study, a low-fat, cholesterol-reducing diet lowered depression and aggressive behavior. In another study, those on cholesterol-reducing drugs instead of a placebo experienced substantially fewer deaths, heart attacks, angioplasties and bypass surgeries, while also experiencing no increase in deaths from accidents, suicides or cancer.[409] As Dr. Campbell said, if total cholesterol levels below 150 mg/dL were unhealthy, nearly everyone in rural China would be in trouble. As Dr. Esselstyn's treatment showed, total cholesterol below 150 mg/dL is the opposite of unhealthy. It is life enhancing, and in many cases, life saving.

Suggesting that people get less than 15 percent of calories from fat and keep total cholesterol below 150 mg/dL could greatly reduce the sale of animal products. As noted, animal products often contain high levels of harmful fat and cholesterol. It often would be difficult or impossible to achieve these dietary and health goals if people were eating more than small amounts of animal products.

Flawed systems often compel publicly traded companies to protect shareholder returns, even when doing so degrades society in ways that are not immediate and obvious. Food companies sometimes directly or indirectly fund or influence studies that question links between heart disease, animal products, dietary cholesterol and fat. However, even publicly-funded, independent studies can suffer from methodological problems that produce misleading and dangerous results.

For example, in *Prevent and Reverse Heart Disease*, Dr. Esselstyn discusses the Women's Health Initiative. The study followed about 49,000 women over eight years. It found that eating a 'low-fat' diet did not lower the rates of heart attacks, strokes, or breast or colon cancer. But the woman on the low-fat diets were getting 29 percent of calories from fat compared to 38 percent in the usual diet group. Dr. Esselstyn points out that 29 percent of calories from fat is not a low-fat diet. It is nearly three times the level he recommended to successfully halt and often reverse heart disease.

Dr. Esselstyn used the analogy of a car crash test to illustrate the flaws of the Women's Health Initiative. For example, crashing a car into a wall at 90 mph kills all occupants. Reducing the speed to 70 mph still kills all occupants. Conclusion: reducing speed does not save lives. But the study fails to mention that when the car is crashed into a wall at 10 mph no one dies. This is like the Women's Health Initiative failing to analyze the impact of an actual low-fat diet. The supposedly low-fat diet used in the Women's Health Initiative allows continued high consumption of animal products. This indicates possible influence of the study by food companies. There are other indications that the Women's Health Initiative was flawed. For example, significant reductions in dietary fat usually cause reduced HDL and increased triglycerides (another type of fat). But HDL and triglycerides levels were the same in the low-fat and usual diet groups. This indicates that women in the low-fat group did not reduce fat consumption as much as they reported.[410]

The Nurses' Health Study is another well-known study that examines the impact of low-fat diets. The study enrolled over 120,000 nurses and gathered data for more than 20 years. It found that low-fat diets did not reduce breast cancer, colon cancer or heart disease. In *The China Study*, Dr. Campbell discussed the problem of reductionistic science in the food area and described how the Nurses' Health Study suffers from this methodological flaw. Reductionism, as Dr. Campbell describes it, involves studying specific components of food, such as fat, rather than studying complete foods, such as various plant and animal products. Like the human body, food is highly complex. It often is comprised of thousands of chemicals that interact with each other and the human body in ways that humans do not come close to understanding. While we know a lot about how food interacts with the body and promotes disease, compared to all there is to know, we know little.

In the Nurses' Health Study, nurses who ate the least fat got 20 to 25 percent of calories from fat. Nurses who ate the most got 50 to 55 percent of calories from fat. But virtually all of the nurses were consuming above average amounts of animal products.[411] Nurses in the low-fat group mainly lowered fat consumption by eating low-fat animal products. Nurses in the high and low-fat groups were eating few of the whole plant foods shown in international studies to reduce heart disease, cancer and other health problems.

Dr. Campbell explained that it could be misleading to break food into specific components and blame problems on one, such as saturated fat. The components of animal products work together to negatively impact health in several ways. For example, beyond the negative impacts of saturated fat, other negative impacts could result from the cholesterol exclusively found in animal products and the inflammatory properties of animal protein.

Blood cholesterol is highly correlated with heart disease risk. As discussed in *The China Study*, many human and animal studies show that consuming animal products is strongly associated with increased blood cholesterol and heart disease risk. Consuming saturated fat and dietary cholesterol also are associated, but not as strongly as animal product consumption. The lower correlation might result from focusing on specific components of food, rather than the whole food. Focusing on specific components creates an unrealistic situation because people do not eat components, such as saturated fat, in isolation. As noted, food components interact with each other and the body in complex ways. It is virtually impossible to control for all of these interactions. As a result, studies that focus on specific components of food can produce misleading results. Studying the complete foods that people actually eat can produce more accurate and useful results.

However, studying complete animal and plant products would illuminate the negative health impacts of animal products. Businesses strongly influence government, academic research and other areas in the US. As a result, this type of research can be discouraged. Focusing on the specific components of food provides many opportunities to mix and match ingredients, create new products such as low-fat animal products, and increase shareholder returns.

The Nurses' Health Study shows the dangers of reductionism in the food area. It provides misleading and dangerous information to the public by shifting attention from animal products to fat and by implying that animal products do not cause heart disease, cancer and other health problems. Dr. Campbell said, "The Nurses' Health Study suffers from flaws that seriously doom its results. It is the premier example of how reductionism in science can create massive amounts of confusion and misinformation, even when the scientists involved are honest, well intentioned and positioned at the top institutions in the world. Hardly any study has done more damage to the nutritional landscape than the Nurses' Health Study. It should serve as a warning for the rest of science about what not to do."[412]

Dr. Campbell also points out that some meta-studies in the US pooled many studies and found that eating animal products does not increase the risk of heart disease, cancer and other diseases. But all of the studies suffer from the same flaw as the Nurses' Health Study – nearly everyone was eating animal products. Pooling flawed studies still produces flawed results. These studies, in isolation or combination, generally cannot be used to draw valid conclusions about the relative effects of plant and animal products in promoting heart disease, cancer and other diseases of affluence because nearly no one in the studies was eating mainly or completely plant-based diets.[413]

As noted, food and other companies often seek to protect shareholder returns by directly or indirectly funding or influencing research which, not surprisingly, shows that their products are safe. For example, several studies found a weak link between dietary and blood cholesterol. The implication is that consuming high levels of cholesterol, which only comes from animal products, will not increase blood cholesterol and heart disease risk. This illustrates the danger of focusing on only one component of food. People do not eat pure cholesterol. As discussed in the 2015 dietary guidelines, high cholesterol foods often contain high levels of saturated fat, which is more strongly correlated with high blood cholesterol and heart disease.

Food industry influenced studies frequently find weak links between dietary and blood cholesterol. But many other studies find strong links.[414] Common sense also links the two. Several factors affect blood cholesterol levels, including diet and exercise. However, if people consume large amounts of cholesterol in food, it seems more likely that blood cholesterol will go up rather than down. Studies that find a weak link between dietary and blood cholesterol create confusion, delay action and protect the shareholder returns of food companies.

This delay of action might be legitimate if the trigger point for action to protect society were 90 percent certainty that harm exists. But it is not. As noted, the appropriate trigger point for action to protect society may be in the range of 10 to 20 percent certainty that harm exists. Once several credible studies show that eating cholesterol-laden foods (i.e. animal products) raises blood cholesterol and heart disease risk, the 10 to 20 percent certainty range probably has been reached and action should begin, for example by suggesting that people reduce consumption of animal products. The fact that some studies do not show a link between dietary and blood cholesterol is irrelevant when the trigger point for action is 10 to 20 percent certainty.

Like virtually everything else about the human body, heart disease is highly complex. Many factors influence it. We do not fully understand all of these factors. But lack of full understanding should not unnecessarily delay action. We do not need to fully understand all of the mechanisms of heart disease before taking action to prevent it. We know from international studies that eating animal products is highly correlated with heart disease risk. Heart disease is rare in regions where people eat mainly plant products. Animal products strongly promote heart disease by hardening and damaging coronary arteries and increasing blood cholesterol. Plant products, on the other hand, strongly protect from heart disease, for example by keeping coronary arteries flexible and healthy and lowering blood cholesterol. These are main reasons why plant-based diets are so effective at preventing and often reversing heart disease.

By switching to whole food, plant-based diets, people can make themselves nearly immune to the number one killer in the US and many other developed countries. The American Heart Association estimates that 80 percent of heart disease cases can be prevented with exercise and healthy diets.[415] The second half of *Prevent and Reverse Heart Disease* provides many recipes for delicious whole food, plant-based meals, snacks, soups, desserts and dressings with no added oils.

Cancer

Cancer may be the most feared disease of affluence. Death often occurs slowly and painfully over many months, or even years. The US has among the highest cancer rates in the world. About 47 percent of men and 38 percent of women get cancer.[416] Cancer is the number two killer in the US. It kills over 500,000 people per year.[417] Billions of dollars have been spent since the war on cancer was announced in 1971. But little progress has been made. Death rates for most cancers have not declined substantially.[418] Cancer treatments often are painful, debilitating and expensive. While some treatments are effective at delaying death, many others only extend life for short periods of time.

The China Study discusses cancer extensively. Dr. Campbell explains that it often is not a natural event. The majority of cancers in the US can be prevented with healthy diets and lifestyles.[419] Like heart disease and other chronic diseases, many types of cancer are strongly associated with the Western, animal product intensive diet. For example, numerous studies have show that people who eat red meat (i.e. beef, pork, lamb) or processed meat (i.e. ham, sausages, bacon, hot dogs) have a higher risk of getting several types of cancer, especially colon and breast cancer. In 2015, the WHO categorized processed meat as a carcinogen and red meat as a probable carcinogen.[420]

The China Study and many international studies show that cancer rates are low in regions with mainly plant-based diets, and much higher in regions where people eat large amounts of animal products. For example, the death rate from breast cancer is five times higher among US women than rural Chinese women.[421]

The international studies cited in *The China Study* isolate the relationship between diet and cancer by controlling for other factors that might influence results. As with heart disease, when groups of people who formerly ate mainly plant-based diets adopt the more animal product intensive Western diet, cancers considered to be diseases of affluence, such as breast, prostate and colorectal cancer, nearly always increase.[422] As noted, US studies, such as the Nurses' Health Study and Women's Health Initiative, generally cannot be used to draw valid conclusions about links between animal product consumption and cancer because nearly everyone in these studies was eating animal products.

The China Study describes many animal studies that show virtually perfect correlations between the consumption of animal protein and cancer. Many of the studies were done on rats. They are highly relevant for humans because humans and rats have a nearly identical need for protein, protein operates in virtually the same way in rats and humans, and the level of protein causing tumor growth in rats is the same level that humans consume.[423]

In some of the studies overseen by Dr. Campbell, rats were exposed to aflatoxin, a highly potent carcinogen that is sometimes found on peanuts. Many researchers consider aflatoxin to be a main cause of liver cancer.[424] Rats were put on low-protein diets (five percent of calories from protein) or high-protein diets (20 percent of calories from protein). The protein used in the diets was casein, which comprises about 80 percent of cow's milk protein.

The China Study describes the three stages of cancer – initiation, promotion and progression. During initiation, carcinogens such as aflatoxin often are transformed by enzymes into active form. These can bind to DNA. The body repairs most DNA. But if activated carcinogens remain bound to DNA while cells are dividing, genetically-damaged cancer-prone daughter cells can be formed. Then genetic damage becomes permanent. All progeny of these cells will be genetically-damaged and cancer-prone. The process of cancer initiation nearly always is irreversible.

During the promotion phase of cancer, cancer-prone cells grow and multiply until they become visibly detectable cancer. During the third phase of cancer, progression, advanced cancer cells invade neighboring tissues. Sometimes cancer metastasizes by breaking away from original sites and invading distant tissues. This final stage of cancer nearly always results in death.

Dr. Campbell used the analogy of planting a lawn to describe the three stages of cancer. During initiation, the cancer seeds are planted when carcinogens, radiation and other factors create permanently genetically-damaged, cancer-prone cells. During promotion, cancer cells begin to grow if they receive the right nutrients and other factors that promote growth, in the same way that grass seeds grow when they receive enough water, nutrients and sunlight. During progression, the lawn (i.e. cancer) spreads to everything around it.

During the initiation phase, the above rat studies found that cancer cell and tumor initiation were substantially lower in rats on the low-protein diet. Several mechanisms produce this effect. For example, on the low-protein diet, less aflatoxin was transformed into active form, less aflatoxin entered cells and attached to DNA, and cancer cells grew more slowly.[425] In other words, substantially fewer cancer cells were formed in rats on low-protein diets (i.e. fewer cancer seeds were planted).

Promotion probably is the most important stage of cancer because it potentially is reversible. Research by Dr. Campbell and others showed that promotion of cancer could be nearly perfectly controlled by diet. Promotion also is important because nearly everyone is exposed to carcinogens in our chemical-intensive society. As a result, virtually all people have cancer-prone cells in their bodies waiting to be promoted. However, there is wide variation in exposure to carcinogens, and therefore wide variations in potential cancer cells in people's bodies. Many substances enter the body through eating and drinking. Animal products are higher on the food chain. Through bioaccumulation, they often contain far more carcinogens and other toxic chemicals than plant products. As noted, 93 percent of dioxin exposure and more than 80 percent of pesticide exposure results from eating animal products. Therefore, people who eat all or nearly all plant products generally will have much lower exposure to carcinogens, and therefore far fewer cancer seeds planted in their bodies.

In the rat studies, Dr. Campbell found that, during the promotion phase, cancer essentially could be turned on and off by varying the level of animal protein in diets. Under the right conditions, cancer will grow in the human body. Animal protein appears to create ideal conditions for cancer growth. In the studies, rats fed high levels of casein had high cancer formation. Those on low-protein diets had low cancer formation. Cancer growth was almost completely dependent on how much casein was consumed. Rats given high aflatoxin doses and put on low-protein diets had very low cancer formation. Rats given low aflatoxin doses and put on high casein diets had high cancer formation. Rats on the low protein diet consistently had very low cancer formation, regardless of the level of aflatoxin exposure. However, among rats on the high casein diet, cancer formation increased as aflatoxin exposure increased. In addition, when rats on a high casein diet were switched to a low-protein diet, cancer formation decreased dramatically. When the high casein diet was a resumed, cancer growth also resumed. In other words, cancer was being turned on and off by varying the level of animal protein in diets.

The key issue appeared to be exceeding the amount of protein needed by the body. Rats and humans utilize protein in virtually the same ways at the same levels. Both species nearly always need only five to ten percent of calories from protein. Rats fed less than ten percent protein had very low cancer formation. But as protein levels exceeded ten percent, cancer growth increased. In other words, as rats were fed more protein than their bodies needed, cancer grew.

Rats generally live for about two years. After 100 weeks, all of the rats exposed to aflatoxin and fed 20 percent casein diets were dead or nearly dead from liver tumors. Rats exposed to the same level of aflatoxin, but fed five percent casein diets were all alive and thriving after 100 weeks. Rats on the low-protein diets were healthier on every measure. In addition, they voluntarily exercised twice as much as rats on the high casein diet.[426] These types of virtually perfect results are rare in research. All of the carcinogen exposed rats on the low-protein diet survived and thrived. All of the rats on the high casein diet died or were on the verge of death.

Perhaps the most important findings in the study were that these results only applied to animal protein. When rats were fed high wheat protein (i.e. wheat gluten) or high soy protein and exposed to aflatoxin, cancer formation was very low. As discussed in *The China Study* and following sections, there are several mechanisms by which animal products promote cancer growth and plant products suppress it.

The findings in the rat studies were confirmed in many other studies. For example, the hepatitis B virus (HBV) is thought to be a major risk factor for liver cancer. People with HBV have 20 to 40 times the risk of getting it. In one study, HBV transgenic mice (i.e. mice with liver cancer initiated with HBV) were placed on diets that provided six percent, 14 percent or 22 percent of calories from casein. As with the rat studies, there was virtually no cancer formation in the mice fed six percent casein. Cancer formation was high in the 14 percent group and very high in the 22 percent group.[427]

In another study of breast cancer in rats exposed to different carcinogens, researchers found that rats placed on higher casein diets had higher levels of breast cancer. Higher casein promoted breast cancer through the same female hormone system that operates in humans.[428] Similar studies examined the impact of fish protein and carotenoid antioxidants on cancer. Once again, the studies found that animal products increased cancer during the initiation and promotion phases, while nutrients from plant-based foods decreased or suppressed cancer during both phases.[429]

In *The China Study*, Dr. Campbell discusses the impact of genetics on cancer. Some people are genetically predisposed to get certain types of cancer. But cancer-prone genes do not have an effect unless they are activated or expressed. If the genes remain dormant, they have no impact on health. Nearly everyone has cancer-prone genes in their bodies, for example, due to genetic predisposition or exposure to carcinogens or radiation. But these genes will not grow or be expressed unless they have the proper environment.

Nutrition is the main environmental factor that determines the activity of genes in the body.[430] As Dr. Campbell's research showed, cancer genes essentially can be turned on and off by varying the level of animal protein in diets. Some dietary factors, called promoters, feed cancer growth. Other dietary factors, called anti-promoters, slow cancer growth.[431] Animal products are cancer promoters. Healthy, whole plant products are cancer anti-promoters. (This does not include highly refined sugar, fat and salt-laden plant products.)

A major analysis submitted to the US Congress of many cancer studies estimated that genetics only determine about two to three percent of total cancer risk.[432] Creating a cancer-promoting environment in the human body usually is far more important than genetics in determining cancer risk. Based on his extensive research and that of many other experts, Dr. Campbell found that casein, and very likely all animal proteins, may be the most cancer-causing substance that humans consume.[433]

It should not be surprising that casein strongly promotes cancer. No other mammal drinks milk or eats dairy products after it is weaned. They especially do not drink the milk of other mammals. Cow's milk is intended to help calves grow from 100 to 2,000 pounds in two years. Cow's milk is very different from human milk. For example, it has more fat and different proteins. Many people cannot digest it well. Cow's milk often produces mucus, which can promote colds and allergies. Humans did not evolve to drink cow's milk or eat dairy products. They are not natural foods for us. As a result, these unnatural foods can strongly promote disease.

Milk from industrial dairy operations can be even more harmful than pre-industrial cow's milk. In addition to the synthetic hormones sometimes added to milk, such as BGH, milk from industrial dairy operations frequently has high levels of natural hormones, such as estrogen and progesterone. A study of hormone levels compared milk from free range cattle in Mongolia to milk from industrial dairy operations in Japan. After World War II, US cows and dairy production techniques were exported to Japan. As a result, milk from Japanese industrial dairy operations is similar to US cow's milk. The study found that Japanese cow's milk had 67 percent more estrogen and 650 percent more progesterone than Mongolian cow's milk.[434]

As discussed in the Animal Welfare section below, the main reason for higher hormone levels is that cows in industrial dairy operations are kept in a nearly constant state of pregnancy and lactation. In Mongolia, cows are milked for about five to six months after giving birth. But in US and

Japanese industrial dairy operations, cows are milked for about ten months per year. Milk from pregnant cows has about five to 33 times more estrogen than milk from nonpregnant cows. This indicates one possible reason why prostate and breast cancer rates are much higher in Japan than Mongolia. Higher levels of estrogen in the blood have been linked to prostate, breast and other cancers. One study found strong correlations between milk consumption and rates of breast, ovarian and uterine cancer in 40 countries.[435]

As discussed extensively in *The China Study*, whole plant food diets can minimize the risk of all cancers. These are the natural, optimal foods for humans. As a result, we thrive the most on them. In addition to preventing cancer, many human and animal studies have shown that plant-based diets can be used to effectively treat several types of already diagnosed cancer.[436]

As a percentage of calories, only five to six percent dietary protein is needed to replace amino acids excreted by the body. In *the China Study*, Dr. Campbell points out that the recommended daily allowance (RDA) for protein has been about 10 percent of calories for 50 years. In rural China, people get about 10 percent of calories from protein, with only 10 percent coming from animal products. At this level, cancer rates are very low. In the US, people get about 11 to 21 percent of calories from protein (15 to 16 percent average), with about 80 percent of protein coming from animal products.[437] As shown in the above animal studies, as animal protein consumption rises above 10 percent of calories, cancer rates also rise. This is reflected in the high cancer rates in the US. As noted, nearly half of men and more than one-third of women in the US get cancer.

With an historical RDA of about 10 percent of calories, the USDA dietary guidelines imply that it is acceptable to get up to 35 percent of calories from protein. This level is unbelievable, especially given the extensive research linking animal protein levels above 10 percent to cancer. The 35 percent protein guideline once again shows what happens when vested interests are allowed to set standards in their area of interest. Allowing 35 percent protein helps the shareholder returns of food companies, for example, by implying that high-protein diets, such as the Atkins and South Beach diets, are healthy. As shown in *The China Study*, eating high levels of animal protein, saturated fat and dietary cholesterol is anything but healthy. These diets could be referred to as heart attack diets or make-yourself-sick diets.

Setting the protein RDA at 10 percent of calories but saying that up to 35 percent is acceptable and healthy would be like saying that 50 mph is the safe, recommended speed on a particular road. But it also is safe to drive as fast as 175 mph. Like the USDA fat guidelines, implying that it is safe to consume up to 35 percent of calories as protein literally kills people. This once again indicates how giving money to politicians and inappropriately influencing government in other ways often compels regulators to put shareholder returns ahead of the health and survival of citizens.

As noted, in spite of spending billions of dollars, there has been little progress in the war on cancer. It is an extremely complex disease. In many areas, we still know relatively little about it, as indicated by the failure to significantly lower most cancer death rates. Rather than using drugs and mechanical procedures, such as surgery and radiation, to win the war on cancer, it probably would be far more effective to use natural, biological approaches to prevent cancer. The war on cancer probably will be won more by preventing it rather than by curing it. Many human and animal studies show that switching to whole food, plant-based diets can greatly lower cancer rates. As shown in *The China Study*, even small amounts of animal-based foods raise the risk of cancer and other diseases of affluence.

The China Study and many other studies indicate that eating animal products often is the main factor promoting cancer growth. Rather than eating unnatural foods for humans that make us sick (i.e. animal products), and then trying to cure the disease, it would be vastly more effective and life-enhancing to avoid getting sick in the first place by not eating animal products. Switching to plant-based diets would vastly lower healthcare costs, while greatly improving quality of life. But switching to plant-based diets also would lower the sales of food, drug and healthcare companies, because far fewer people would be eating animal products, getting sick and dying prematurely.

Flawed systems probably will compel many companies to protect shareholder returns by aggressively opposing the transition to plant-based diets. Companies may directly or indirectly fund or influence studies that refute The China Study and other international studies. They might hope that conflicting research will create uncertainty and block change. But this approach is based on Wrong Reference Point logic. It assumes that high levels of certainty or conclusive proof are needed before we act to protect our children and ourselves. This is wrong. As discussed, the trigger point to protect our children and ourselves is not 90 percent certainty that harm exists. It may be in the 10 to 20 percent certainty range.

The China Study and many other studies show that we are well beyond 20 percent certainty that animal products strongly promote cancer, heart disease and other chronic diseases. It is well past the time for action. The priority is human survival and health, not protection of shareholder returns. Businesses have no innate right to exist. They will adapt to the needs of society by providing healthy products. Or they will cease to exist and be replaced by more competent and responsible companies.

In *The China Study*, Dr. Campbell notes that there is enough evidence to show that eating animal products is the largest cause of cancer in the US. As a result, doctors and health organization should be informing citizens that switching to whole food, plant-based diets could be a highly effective way to prevent and treat cancer.[438] This section discussed cancer in general. A few specific cancers are discussed below.

Breast Cancer

The US has among the highest breast cancer rates in the world. About one out of eight US women gets the disease.[439] *The China Study* book cites many studies, including The China Study itself, and other evidence that shows very strong links between the consumption of animal products and breast cancer.

Dr. Campbell discusses four of the most important breast cancer risk factors – early menstruation, late menopause, high levels of female hormones in the blood and high blood cholesterol. Each of these is strongly promoted by consuming animal products. Menstruation is triggered by growth rates. Animal products increase hormone levels and promote faster growth in young girls, which can trigger early menstruation and puberty. Feeding animal products to young girls often leads to greater adult height, weight and body fatness, all of which are associated with increased breast cancer risk.[440]

In rural China where few animal products are eaten, the average age of first menstruation is 17 years old. The animal product intensive US diet contributes to the average age of first menstruation being about 12 years old in the US.[441] A 2010 study of 3,000 girls found that those who ate eight portions of meat per week by age three and 12 portions of meat per week by age seven were more likely to start menstruation early. The study found that girls on high-meat diets when they were seven years old were 75 percent more likely to begin menstruation by age 12.[442]

There is overwhelming evidence that estrogen levels are a critical determinant of breast cancer risk.[443] Eating diets that are high in animal protein and fat and low in fiber causes increased levels of estrogen, progesterone and other female hormones in the body.[444] Cow's milk and other animal products often naturally contain female hormones. In addition, as discussed in the Hormone section, beef cattle in the US frequently are given female hormones to promote growth. This can further increase the level of female hormones in animal products. Also, as discussed in the Chemicals section, animal products often contain endocrine-disrupting chemicals that mimic estrogen.

As noted, cow's milk from industrial dairy operations often has substantially higher levels of estrogen and progesterone than traditional cow's milk. Higher hormone levels in industrial milk can increase the risk of breast cancer and other types of cancer. One study found that rats fed industrial cow's milk developed mammary tumors more often than those fed traditional cow's milk. Another study found that rats fed industrial milk had heavier uteruses than rats fed traditional milk or nondairy diets.[445]

Women who continue to eat animal products often maintain higher levels of estrogen and other female hormones throughout their reproductive years. Several studies have shown that higher hormone levels often defer menopause by three to four years.[446] In other words, eating animal products strongly contributes to early menstruation and later menopause. This can extend a woman's reproductive life by nine to ten years, and thereby greatly increase hormone exposure and breast cancer risk.

Estrogen levels among US women are about twice as high as rural Chinese women. In addition, the reproductive life of US women is more than 30 percent longer than Chinese women. Taken together, this causes lifetime estrogen exposure to be about 300 percent higher among US women than Chinese women. This is a primary reason why breast cancer rates are about 500 percent higher in the US than in rural China.[447]

Dr. Campbell discusses the relative importance of genetics to breast cancer. One study found that less than three percent of all breast cancer cases could be attributed to family history or genetics. Only about one out of every 500 women has the mutated forms of breast cancer genes BRCA–1 and BRCA–2. These women have about a 50 percent chance of getting breast cancer.[448] In other words, about half of women with BRCA genes do not get breast cancer. As discussed in *The China Study*, diet usually is far more important than genetics in determining who gets this disease. Animal products often create an ideal environment in the body for the formation and growth of breast cancer.

The same applies to carcinogenic chemicals. Nearly all women in the US and many other developed countries are exposed to chemicals that potentially promote breast cancer. But not all of these women get it. Once again, the key issue is diet. Eating animal products greatly increases women's exposure to carcinogenic chemicals, as well as creates an environment in the body that is conducive to breast cancer growth.

Toxins often accumulate more in breasts than in other organs, due in part to high fat content. This contributes to more tumors forming in breasts than in any other organ. Breast cancer is the most common malignancy in women worldwide.[449] Accumulation of toxins in breasts not only increases breast cancer risk, it also can harm nursing infants. Nursing mothers often transfer toxic chemicals to their children because toxins tend to accumulate in breasts. For example, women can transfer about three percent of PBDE's, eight percent of PCB's and 14 percent of dioxins in their bodies per month to nursing children.[450] As a result, nursing for a year can transfer much of the toxic chemicals in women to infants. These toxins can be far more harmful to infants due to their smaller size and rapidly developing bodies. As noted, many toxic chemicals tend to accumulate in animals. Therefore, people who eat animal products often have far high levels of toxins in their bodies. Greatly reducing or eliminating the consumption of animal products is one of the most important actions that women can take to protect nursing children from toxic chemicals.

In *The China Study*, Dr. Campbell discusses hormone replacement therapy (HRT). Many women use the treatment to alleviate the unpleasant effects of menopause, protect bone health and lower heart disease risk. However, some studies have shown that HRT may increase heart disease risk. It also appears to increase risks of breast cancer, stroke and pulmonary embolism, while lowering the risks of colorectal cancer and bone fractures.[451]

The uncomfortable symptoms of menopause largely are caused by an abrupt drop in hormone levels as women reach the end of their reproductive years. Women who eat all or nearly all plant products have lower female hormone levels. As a result, the drop in hormone levels, and accompanying symptoms, often is less severe for vegans. This indicates that switching to whole food, plant-based diets may be a more effective way to address menopause for many women. Not only could this potentially reduce the discomfort of menopause, as shown in *The China Study*, it also often would lower the risk of heart disease, breast cancer, other forms of cancer and many other health problems.

Women at high risk of breast cancer often are given three options – regular screening, mastectomy or taking drugs. Regular screening can increase the probability of early detection and longer-term survival. But screening does not treat or prevent breast cancer. Instead, it monitors whether the cancer has progressed to an observable state. Some women at high risk get preventative mastectomies (i.e. removal of breasts prior to getting cancer). Other women take drugs such as tamoxifen for many years to reduce breast cancer risk. But some studies have found that tamoxifen does not provide any significant risk reduction. In addition, the drug may increase the risk of uterine cancer, stroke, cataracts, deep vein thrombosis and pulmonary embolism.[452]

Tamoxifen and similar breast cancer drugs are anti-estrogen drugs. Dr. Campbell suggests that, rather than eating foods that increase estrogen levels (i.e. animal products), and then taking drugs that fight the effects of estrogen, women should be informed of a fourth breast cancer prevention option – avoiding foods that raise estrogen levels by eating whole food, plant-based diets. Extensive research shows that eating animal products substantially increases estrogen levels and breast cancer risk. Even eating small amounts of these foods increases risk.[453] By switching to whole food, plant-based diets, and continuing regular screening, especially for those at high risk, women can substantially lower breast cancer risk, or possibly nearly eliminate it.

The China Study cites a study that illustrates the benefits of plant-based diets for girls. Eight to ten-year-old girls were put on moderate low-fat, plant-based diets that allowed low amounts of animal products for seven years. Female hormone levels that increase with the onset of puberty were reduced by 20 to 50 percent. Dr. Campbell noted that if the girls had been placed at an earlier age on whole food, plant-based diets that allowed no animal products, even greater benefits probably would have been provided. These include an even lower risk of breast cancer later in life and delayed puberty. This in turn could provide further benefits, such as reduced teenage pregnancy.[454]

Prostate Cancer

Prostate cancer is the second most common cancer (after skin cancer) among men in the US. It also is the second leading cause of cancer death (after lung cancer) among US men. About one out of six men in the US gets prostate cancer. Approximately 240,000 new cases are diagnosed each year. Prostate cancer kills about 34,000 men per year in the US.[455]

Like heart disease and other diseases of affluence, prostate cancer rates are substantially higher in developed countries with high animal product consumption. As men in developing countries begin to eat more animal products, prostate cancer rates nearly always increase.[456] *The China Study* cites many studies that show a high correlation between the consumption of animal products and prostate cancer.

Dairy products in particular are highly correlated to increased prostate cancer rates. One meta-study found that men who consumed large amounts of dairy products had twice the risk of getting prostate cancer and four times the risk of dying from the disease, compared to men who consumed few dairy products.[457]

Like other cancers, there is no single mechanism that causes prostate cancer. Many factors or mechanisms combine to increase prostate cancer risk. In *The China Study*, Dr. Campbell explained some of the more important prostate cancer mechanisms, and how they are linked to animal product consumption. For example, eating animal products increases blood levels of the growth hormone IGF-1. High levels of this hormone promote the growth of cancer, including prostate cancer. Men with higher than normal blood levels of IGF-1 have five to ten times the risk of developing advanced-stage prostate cancer.[458]

Another mechanism involves vitamin D. The body produces vitamin D from sunlight, and then converts it to an active or supercharged form. Supercharged vitamin D provides many benefits, including helping to prevent cancer, autoimmune diseases and osteoporosis. Consuming animal products tends to block the production of supercharged vitamin D. Prostate cancer can result from consistently low levels of this vitamin. High calcium consumption also lowers supercharged vitamin D levels.

This helps to explain why consuming dairy products is so strongly correlated with prostate cancer. The animal protein in dairy products increases IGF-1 levels, which increases prostate cancer risk. In addition, the animal protein and calcium in dairy products suppresses supercharged vitamin D production, which further increases prostate cancer risk.[459]

As discussed in the Cancer section, milk from industrial dairy operations often has substantially higher levels of estrogen and other female hormones than traditional cow's milk. Several studies have shown that higher blood estrogen levels increase prostate cancer risk. The Japanese study mentioned above strongly linked milk consumption to prostate cancer. As noted, US cows and dairy production techniques were exported to Japan after

World War II. A 1954 Japanese law required that about one cup of milk to be served with each school lunch.

As milk consumption increased, prostate cancer rates in Japan increased 25-fold over the past 50 years. A review of 36 years of dietary data in Japan found that prostate cancer risk and mortality were most strongly correlated with milk consumption. Another Japanese study found that men's testosterone levels decreased when they drank industrial cow's milk, possibly due to the presence of female hormones in the milk.[460] As with other cancers, switching to a whole food, plant-based diet often may be the most important action that men can take to lower prostate cancer risk.

Colorectal Cancer

Colorectal cancer refers to cancers of the colon and rectum, both of which are part of the large bowel. This cancer is the second leading cause of cancer deaths among men and women combined in the US. About five percent of people in the US get this disease.[461] As with other diseases of affluence, colorectal cancer rates are much higher in developed countries with high animal product consumption. Many studies found a strong correlation between meat consumption and colon cancer.[462]

As discussed in the Cancer section, in 2015, the WHO categorized processed meat as a carcinogen and red meat as a probable carcinogen. The organization said that cancer risk increases as people consume more meat. The WHO found that eating a 50 gram portion of processed meat per day (i.e. two to three slices of bacon) increased colon cancer risk by 18 percent. Eating a 100 gram daily portion of red meat (i.e. quarter pound of steak) increased colon cancer risk by 17 percent.[463]

While meat consumption raises colorectal cancer risk, increased fiber consumption is strongly linked to reduced risk. A review of 60 studies found that people who consume the most fiber had a 43 percent lower risk of colon cancer than those who consumed the least fiber. People who ate the most vegetables had a 52 percent lower risk of colorectal cancer than those who ate the least vegetables. A European study of 520,000 people found that those who ate the most fiber had a 42 percent lower risk of colorectal cancer than those who ate the least fiber.[464]

These and many other studies that show the benefits of fiber consumption involve fiber consumed as a whole food, not as a dietary supplement. Fiber is a complex and varied substance that works through many mechanisms. These are not completely understood. It is highly unlikely that fiber supplements can provide the same high benefits as fiber consumed in whole foods. Our bodies evolved to eat whole foods, not supplements.

In *The China Study*, Dr. Campbell discusses the importance of eating whole, complex carbohydrates, instead of refined ones. Refined carbohydrates are starches and sugars obtained from plants by mechanically stripping off outer layers. These layers usually contain most of the plant's fiber, protein, vitamins and minerals.[465] As a result, refined carbohydrates usually have little nutritional value. The reduction in risk of colorectal cancer and other diseases of affluence results mainly from eating whole, not refined, plant products.

Some studies found that consuming dairy products lowered colorectal cancer risk. But Dr. Campbell questions these results. He points out that regions with the lowest dairy product consumption have the lowest colorectal cancer rates. Regions with high dairy product consumption, such as the US, have the highest colorectal cancer rates. The Nurses' Health Study found no link between colorectal cancer and fiber, fruit or vegetable consumption. But once again, studies such as these that do not assess people who eat all or nearly all plant products generally cannot be used to draw valid conclusions about the benefits of plant-based diets. As shown in *The China Study*, there is overwhelming evidence that whole food, plant-based diets can dramatically reduce colorectal cancer risk.

Dr. Campbell also discusses the importance of colorectal cancer screening and exercise. Screening via stool blood test, sigmoidoscopy or colonoscopy can substantially reduce the risk of colorectal cancer. As a result, regular screening is recommended.[466] In addition, many studies have shown that regular exercise substantially lowers the risk of colorectal cancer and many other diseases of affluence. As a result, regular exercise also is highly recommended.

Diabetes

In line with rapid growth in obesity, diabetes rates have tripled in the past 30 years in the US.[467] Type 2 diabetes represents 90 to 95 percent of cases. (Type 1 diabetes is discussed under Autoimmune Diseases below.) The US has among the highest diabetes rates in the world. About 10 percent of adults in the US have diabetes (24 million people). About six million of these people do not know that they have it.[468] An additional 75 million adults in the US have pre-diabetes (i.e. elevated glucose levels, but not high enough to be considered diabetes). Diabetes rates are substantially higher among African Americans, Native Americans and Hispanics.[469]

Excess weight is the main risk factor for type 2 diabetes. About 80 percent of people with this disease are overweight. Type 2 diabetes used to occur mostly among people over 40 years old. It therefore was called adult-onset diabetes. But poor diets, lack of exercise and rising obesity are contributing to teenagers and children as young as 10 years old getting type 2 diabetes more frequently. As a result, the disease no longer is called adult-onset diabetes.

By 2050, the CDC projects that one-third of adults in the US will have diabetes. Increasing diabetes rates are a major driver of rising healthcare costs. Treating diabetes costs about $174 billion per year in the US. The average type 2 diabetic incurs about $6,500 of diabetes-specific healthcare costs per year.[470]

Diabetes is a metabolic disorder. Most food is broken down through digestion partly into glucose, the main fuel of the body. The pancreas produces insulin, which enables the body to use glucose. People with type 2 diabetes develop insulin resistance. For unknown reasons, the body does not utilize insulin effectively. As a result, glucose cannot be utilized effectively. Instead, it builds up in the body. After several years of insulin resistance, insulin production often decreases.[471]

Diabetes negatively impacts almost every part of the body. It is the leading cause of lower limb amputations, end-stage kidney disease and blindness in adults. Nervous system damage occurs in 60 to 70 percent of diabetics. Diabetes also increases the risk of heart disease and stroke by two to four times.[472] It is the seventh leading cause of death in the US. However, diabetes affects many other health problems. As a result, it probably is under-reported as the underlying cause of death in many cases.[473]

Dr. Campbell and many other experts point out that type 2 diabetes largely is preventable and often reversible. It essentially is a voluntary disease. People give themselves diabetes mainly by eating unhealthy foods, not exercising and gaining weight. Many studies show strong correlations between the consumption of animal products and/or refined carbohydrates and diabetes. *The China Study* summarizes several of these studies.

For example, countries with mainly high carbohydrate, low-fat diets (i.e. plant-based diets) had up to five times lower diabetes rates than countries that consumed higher fat, animal product diets. Among Seventh-day Adventists, meat eaters had twice the diabetes rates of vegetarians. Japanese men in the US who ate the Western, animal product intensive diet had four times the diabetes rates of men in Japan who ate fewer animal products.[474] Another study found a strong correlation between persistent organic pollutants (POP's) such as PCB's and diabetes. As noted, POP's tend to accumulate in the fat of animals and fish. This reflects another way that eating animal products increases diabetes risk.[475]

In another study, 25 people with type 2 diabetes were put on a whole plant foods diet that allowed a small amount of meat. None of the patients were overweight. All were taking insulin shots to control blood sugar levels. Within three weeks, glucose levels dropped and 24 of the patients were able to discontinue taking insulin medication.[476] A review of eleven studies found that high-fiber, high or moderate carbohydrate (i.e. plant-based) diets resulted in improved blood sugar and cholesterol levels.[477] In another study, eleven diabetic patients were given meal replacement shakes and three servings of non-starchy vegetables per day. Within one week, glucose levels returned to normal and diabetes went into remission. Patients lost an average of 33 pounds on the diet. Those who retained most of their weight loss remained diabetes free after ending the diet.[478]

Many studies found that refined carbohydrates increase diabetes risk, while complex carbohydrates, such as whole grains, lower it. As noted, refined carbohydrates have most of their protein, fiber, vitamins and minerals stripped off. These unhealthy foods cause rapid rise and then decline of blood sugar levels. Complex carbohydrates are absorbed more slowly into the bloodstream and have a more gradual effect on blood sugar levels.[479]

The editors of the medical journal The Lancet called diabetes a "public health humiliation" because it largely is preventable, but the disease has been allowed to reach epidemic proportions.[480] Diabetes illustrates our flawed systems. In the US, we subsidize foods that contribute to diabetes, such as animal products and refined carbohydrates, including high-fructose corn syrup. Then we spend nearly $200 billion to treat the disease. It would be vastly more cost-effective to end the subsidization of unhealthy, disease-causing foods, and instead support foods that prevent diabetes and other chronic diseases, such as fruits and vegetables. This could substantially lower healthcare costs and disease, while greatly improving quality of life.

As Dr. Campbell discusses in The China Study, a whole food, plant-based diet can be used to prevent and often reverse diabetes. For example, the 75 million people in the US with pre-diabetes are at higher risk of becoming diabetic and requiring medication. By switching to whole food, plant-based diets, probably the large majority, if not nearly all, of pre-diabetics could avoid diabetes and the complications that go along with it, such as amputations, blindness, dementia and early death.

As shown in the studies noted above and many others, people with type 2 diabetes often can reverse their disease and stop taking medication by switching to whole food, plant-based diets and exercising more. However, over time the pancreas often loses its ability to produce insulin in type 2 diabetics. As a result, the sooner diabetics adopt whole plant food diets, the greater their chances of putting their disease into remission and ending medication use.

Weight loss is one of the main reasons why whole plant food diets help to prevent and reverse diabetes. As discussed below, adopting a whole food, plant-based diet (i.e. the natural and optimal foods for humans) is the most effective way to lose weight and keep it off over the long-term. Fad diets, such as high-protein, low carbohydrate diets, often lower weight in the short-term, partly due to calorie restriction. But these diets rarely result in long-term weight loss. Severe calorie restriction is not a good strategy for weight loss. The body needs a certain level of calories to survive, and it will find ways to get them.

Severe calorie restriction is not needed for long-term weight loss. People in rural China consume about 30 percent more calories than people in the US.[481] But they have far lower rates of obesity and chronic disease. This is because rural Chinese people get calories mainly from healthy whole plant-based foods. People in the US get calories mainly from animal products and refined, sugary, unhealthy carbohydrates. These foods strongly promote diabetes, obesity, heart disease, cancer and many other chronic diseases.

Autoimmune Diseases

There are about 40 autoimmune diseases. Common ones include type 1 diabetes, multiple sclerosis, Graves' disease, rheumatoid arthritis and lupus. About three percent of people in the US (9 million people) have one or more autoimmune diseases. Women are about three times more likely than men to be afflicted.[482]

Like the various types of cancer, autoimmune diseases share several common characteristics. The most important one is that the immune system attacks various parts of the body. For example, with type 1 diabetes, the immune system attacks insulin-producing cells in the pancreas. With multiple sclerosis, it attacks the insulating cover or sheath of nerve fibers. In spite of extensive research, the causes and mechanisms of action of autoimmune diseases largely are not well understood. However, many studies have found strong links between the consumption of animal products, especially cow's milk, and the diseases.

Dr. Campbell discusses several of these studies in *The China Study*. For example, there is strong evidence of a link between dairy products and type 1 diabetes. Dr. Campbell explains the possible mechanisms of the link. He notes that if a baby is switched too early from human milk to cow's milk, cow's milk protein that is not fully broken down into amino acids could pass through the small intestine to the bloodstream. The immune system attacks the invading cow's milk protein fragments. But some of them look like insulin-producing cells in the pancreas. As a result, the immune system also attacks and destroys the insulin-producing cells.

A study published in the New England Journal of Medicine examined 142 children with type 1 diabetes. All of them had high levels of antibodies to partly undigested cow's milk protein. This means that cow's milk protein had entered the bloodstream and been attacked by the immune system. The study also examined 79 children without type 1 diabetes. All of them had low levels of antibodies to cow's milk protein. This indicated a strong association between cow's milk protein and type 1 diabetes.[483] Another study found a nearly perfect correlation between cow's milk consumption by country and type 1 diabetes rates.[484] Yet another study found that cow's milk consumption increases the risk of type 1 diabetes by more than 500 percent.[485]

Genetics plays a role in type 1 diabetes. But as with cancer, genes do not act in isolation. They generally only can be expressed in a conducive environment. Dr. Campbell noted that genetics only could explain a small fraction of type 1 diabetes cases. To illustrate, if one identical twin gets type 1 diabetes, the other twin only has a 13 to 33 percent chance of getting it. If genetics were the main driver of the disease, the other twin would have close to a 100 percent chance of getting it.[486] Even the 13 to 33 percent probability could be explained by environmental factors because twins usually live in the same home and consume similar foods.

Further indicating the link between animal products and type 1 diabetes, another study placed 25 type 1 diabetics on a whole plant foods diet that only allowed a small amount of meat. Within three weeks, the patients were able to lower their insulin medication by an average of 40 percent. In addition, cholesterol levels declined by 30 percent, which lowered heart disease and stroke risk. This is important because diabetics have increased heart disease and stroke risk.[487]

Several studies also found strong links between the consumption of animal products and multiple sclerosis (MS). One study found a very high correlation between cow's milk consumption by country and MS.[488] In another study, 144 MS patients were placed on low saturated fat diets. (As noted, nearly all saturated fat comes from animal products.) About 95 percent of the patients who began the diet in the early stages of MS and maintained it experienced only mild disability for about 30 years. But about 80 percent of the early stage MS patients who did not stay on the diet (i.e. those who ate more saturated fat and animal products) died of MS.[489] As with type 1 diabetes, genetics plays a role in some MS cases. But genetics only can account for about one-fourth of the total disease risk.[490]

Beyond the immune system, autoimmune diseases share several other similar characteristics. For example, the autoimmune diseases that have been studied occur more frequently at higher geographic latitudes, where there is less constant sunshine. In addition, the consumption of animal products, especially cow's milk, is linked to increased disease risk. These factors relate to each other. For example, the consumption of animal products, especially cow's milk, usually increases with distance from the equator. Also, several animal experiments have shown that activated vitamin D helps to prevent some autoimmune diseases.[491] As discussed, cow's milk suppresses the production of activated or supercharged vitamin D. This could facilitate the development of autoimmune diseases.

The mechanisms of action of autoimmune diseases largely are unknown. Many factors probably contribute to them. For example, several studies indicate that viruses play a role in some autoimmune diseases. However, remaining uncertainty about the complex mechanics of the diseases does not invalidate the many studies that show high correlations to animal product consumption. Based on this research, the consumption of animal products, especially cow's milk, clearly plays a major role in autoimmune diseases.

In *The China Study*, Dr. Campbell extensively discusses how food companies and their allies mislead the public about links between animal product consumption and chronic diseases, including autoimmune diseases. One of the most common strategies for protecting shareholder returns and misleading the public is to create scientific uncertainty or take advantage of it. To illustrate, Dr. Campbell discussed a review of ten human studies that examined links between cow's milk consumption and type 1 diabetes. Five of the studies found statistically significant associations. Five others found no significant association. None of the studies found that cow's milk consumption lowered type 1 diabetes risk.[492]

Food companies and their allies argued that five studies finding no association indicated that considerable uncertainty remained about links between cow's milk consumption and type 1 diabetes. This enables food companies and their allies to protect shareholder returns by arguing that it would be premature to advise people to not feed cow's milk to babies. But there are many valid reasons why studies might find no association when one actually exists. In addition, the studies might have been influenced or biased by food companies. Dr. Campbell explains that there is less than a two percent probability that five studies would find statistically significant relationships between cow's milk and type 1 diabetes when no relationship actually exists (i.e. by mistake). In other words, the meta-study indicates that there is a greater than 98 percent probability that a link between cow's milk and type 1 diabetes exists.

The meta-review also examined other studies and found 20 statistically significant associations. Nineteen indicated a link between cow's milk and type 1 diabetes. Only one did not. Using studies like this to argue that uncertainty warrants taking no action reflects Wrong Reference Point logic. The trigger point for protecting children from type 1 diabetes and other threats is not 99 percent certainty that harm exists. It may be in the 10 to 20 percent certainty range.[493]

Dr. Campbell points out that, even though the mechanisms of type 1 diabetes are not fully understood, there is extensive evidence which shows that cow's milk consumption is a primary cause of the disease. Common sense supports this conclusion. Humans did not evolve to drink cow's milk. As a result, it should not be surprising that this unnatural food for humans sometimes creates problems in the human body, especially young, rapidly developing bodies. Dr. Campbell notes that human milk is the perfect food for infants. One of the most damaging and dangerous things a mother can do is to give her child cow's milk instead of human milk.[494]

Beyond dairy products, several animal studies have shown that high salt diets substantially increase the risk of getting MS as well as increase the severity of the disease.[495] As discussed below, salt is widely used in processed food to mask unpleasant tastes and increase sales. Increased MS risk provides another reason for avoiding processed foods, which often are comprised mainly of sugar, fat and salt-laded refined carbohydrates.

Osteoporosis

Osteoporosis is a bone disease that involves weakening of bones and increased risk of fractures. The disease most commonly occurs in women after menopause. About eight million women and two million men in the US have osteoporosis. Another 34 million people have low bone mass, which places them at increased risk of osteoporosis.[496]

Osteoporosis partly results from the loss of calcium from bones. Dairy products have high levels of calcium. As a result, some experts recommend that people consume dairy products to increase calcium levels and reduce osteoporosis risk. But many studies show that consuming dairy products increases rather than reduces osteoporosis risk. It has been known for over 100 years that consuming animal protein increases the acidity of the body. To neutralize acidity, the body often pulls calcium (a base) from bones. This can weaken bones and promote osteoporosis.

Numerous studies show that consuming animal protein increases calcium discharged in urine. This indicates that animal protein causes leaching of calcium from bones. One meta-study found that doubling protein intake (mostly animal protein) caused a 50 percent increase in urinary calcium. Another study found that calcium in urine increased by 50 percent after people had been on the high animal protein Atkins diet for six months.[497]

Bone mineral density (BMD) sometimes is used to measure osteoporosis risk. However, Dr. Campbell points out that there are many contradictory findings between BMD and osteoporosis. For example, some regions with low BMD also have low rates of bone fractures. Excessive fractures often are used as a reliable indicator of osteoporosis. Indicating that dairy product consumption raises, rather than lowers, osteoporosis risk, consumption of dairy products is higher in the US that most other countries. But women aged 50 and over in the US have among the highest rates of hip fractures in the world. The only countries with higher rates are those that consume more dairy products than the US (i.e. Australia, New Zealand and several European countries).[498]

Dr. Campbell points out that the ratio of animal to plant protein is a much better predictor of osteoporosis risk than BMD. A Yale University review of 34 studies found that 70 percent of the bone fracture rate in women over 50 years old was attributable to animal protein consumption.[499] A review done by the University of California at San Francisco of 87 studies found that, as the ratio of vegetable to animal protein increased, bone fractures decreased. People with the highest ratio had virtually no bone fractures. Another study found that women with the highest ratio of animal to vegetable protein had nearly four times more bone fractures than those with the lowest ratio.[500] The China Study found that people in rural China had fives times fewer fractures than people in the US. As noted, people in rural China get 10 percent of protein from animal products versus about 80 percent in the US.[501] Some studies found that high calcium consumption may reduce the body's ability to regulate calcium. This further indicates that excess calcium consumption may increase osteoporosis risk.[502]

Extensive public misconceptions and deceptions exist in the osteoporosis area. Dairy companies and their allies often strongly promote the idea that consumption of dairy products improves bone health. But extensive research shows that the opposite is true. Dairy consumption often degrades bone health and increases osteoporosis risk. Dr. Campbell suggests that people maintain bone health by eating whole plant foods, especially beans and leafy vegetables, which contain high levels of calcium. Humans evolved to get calcium from plants, not cow's milk.

Dr. Campbell also discusses the importance of exercise, especially weight-bearing exercise, to reducing osteoporosis risk. The human body evolved to do strenuous work. Lifting weights or stressing bones in other ways stimulates bones (as well as muscles, joints and tendons) to grow stronger.

Vision

Macular degeneration and cataracts are two common eye diseases. Both are promoted by eating animal products and suppressed by eating fruits and vegetables. Macular degeneration is the leading cause of irreversible blindness among people over 65 years old. Over 1.6 million people in the US have macular degeneration. Many of them go blind.[503]

Macular degeneration often results from free radicals damaging the macula, the central portion of the retina. Consuming animal products promotes excess free radicals in the body. Brightly colored fruits and vegetables have high levels of antioxidants that suppress or block free radical damage. Several studies have shown that carotenoids, a type of antioxidant, suppressed macular degeneration. One study found that people who consumed the most carotenoids had 43 percent less macular degeneration than those who consumed the least. Broccoli, carrots, spinach, collard greens, winter squash and sweet potato were associated with lower rates of macular degeneration. Spinach and collard greens provided the most protection. People who ate either vegetable five times per week had 88 percent less macular degeneration than those who ate them less than once per month.[504] In another study, people who had the highest levels of carotenoids in their blood had nearly 70 percent lower risk of macular degeneration than those with the lowest carotenoid levels.[505]

Cataracts involve clouding of the eye lens. The condition often is corrected through surgical replacement of the cloudy lens with an artificial one. About 20 million people over 40 years old have cataracts in the US. About half of people over 80 years old have them. The formation of cataracts is strongly associated with excess free radicals. One study of 1,300 people found that those who consumed the most lutein, a type of antioxidant, had 50 percent fewer cataracts than those who consumed the least. Spinach and other dark green leafy vegetables contain high levels of lutein.[506]

It is important to get antioxidants from fruits and vegetables, rather than supplements. These healthy foods contain hundreds, possibly thousands, of different antioxidants and other substances. Fruits and vegetables produce benefits by working together through complex mechanisms. It is highly unlikely that antioxidants extracted from plants and acting in isolation can produce the same benefits as whole plant foods. The benefits in the above studies largely were derived from eating fruits and vegetables, not supplements. In summary, free radicals resulting from animal consumption can promote eye disease. Eating fruits and vegetables, especially those with high levels of carotenoids and lutein, can strongly promote optimal vision.

Impotence

Male impotence, also known as erectile dysfunction (ED), is strongly linked to cardiovascular disease. In *Prevent and Reverse Heart Disease*, Dr. Esselstyn notes that several of his patients were able to reverse ED and heart disease by adopting whole food, plant-based diets.[507] ED often results from inadequate blood flow to the penis. Physical causes or risk factors for ED include cardiovascular disease, diabetes, high cholesterol, high blood pressure, stroke, obesity, hormone disorders, prostate cancer and surgery, kidney and liver disease, smoking, alcohol abuse, injury to the pelvic region, and medication side effects.

As discussed in previous sections, consuming animal products strongly promotes many of these conditions. Animal protein can cause inflammation of blood vessels. Animal products also often contain high levels of saturated fat and cholesterol. These frequently cause buildup of plaque and hardening of blood vessels. This can restrict blood flow to the heart and other parts of the body. Arteries supplying the penis are smaller than those supplying the heart. As a result, arteries clogged by animal products can cause ED before major heart problems. Through this mechanism, ED can be an indicator or early warning of heart disease. Dr. Esselstyn notes that ED predicts heart disease as reliably as high blood cholesterol. In *Prevent and Reverse Heart Disease*, he describes a major study that links ED and heart disease. The study of over 8,000 men found that those with ED were 45 percent more likely to experience a cardiovascular event than those without ED.

As discussed in the Chemicals section, ED is widely treated with drugs such as Viagra, Cialis and Levitra. These drugs work by inhibiting an enzyme called PDE5. This allows increased arterial expansion and blood flow.[508] Common side effects of PDE5 inhibitors include diarrhea, headache, upset stomach, flushing, dizziness and back pain. Less common, but more severe, side effects include allergic reactions, chest pain, fast or irregular heartbeat, fainting, swelling of face and mouth, numbness, ear ringing and memory loss.[509] In addition, some men have experienced seizures, fatal heart attacks, sudden drops in blood pressure, temporary or permanent hearing loss, and temporary or permanent blindness.[510]

Viagra and other PDE5 inhibitors do not cure ED. The drugs only allow temporary expansion of blood vessels, after which they return to their restricted and often clogged state. Instead of taking drugs to temporarily open clogged arteries, and possibly incurring severe side effects such as permanent blindness or deafness, a better strategy might be to avoid the foods that clogged arteries in the first place. As shown with Dr. Esselstyn's patients, switching to whole food, plant-based diets halted and often reversed plaque build up. This provided the life-saving benefit of halting and often reversing heart disease. It also reduced or eliminated ED.

Excess weight is another risk factor for ED. As discussed below, switching to a whole food, plant-based diet is the most effective way to achieve long-term weight loss, and thereby potentially alleviate ED. As discussed in the Chemicals section, animal products often contain endocrine-disrupting chemicals that mimic estrogen. In addition, animal products in the US often contain natural and added female hormones. Female hormones and chemicals that mimic them in animal products potentially could contribute to ED. This illustrates another way that avoiding animal products potentially could help to alleviate ED.

Taking ED drugs can cause insecurity and psychological dependence on the drugs. ED is strongly affected by psychological factors. After using ED drugs, some men might fear that they only can achieve erection by taking the drugs. Fear that this might occur can create a self-fulfilling prophecy. Switching to a whole food, plant-based diet potentially could cure the cause of ED and restore the body's natural ability to have sex without drugs. This can restore confidence and end psychological dependence on ED drugs. More importantly, switching to a whole food, plant-based diet greatly lowers the risk of heart disease, cancer and other life-threatening chronic diseases.

Brain Diseases

Having a clear, well functioning mind is an important component of achieving life success and satisfaction. Several of the brain conditions and diseases that degrade mental effectiveness are strongly promoted by eating animal products. Cognitive impairment and dementia are two main conditions that cause mental decline. Cognitive impairment refers to declining memory and ability to think clearly. Dementia refers to more serious and sometimes life-threatening conditions.

The two main types of dementia are vascular dementia and Alzheimer's disease. Vascular dementia mainly is caused by numerous mini strokes that result from clogged or broken blood vessels. Alzheimer's involves the accumulation of plaque called beta-amyloid in critical areas of the brain, in a similar way that cholesterol-laden plaque accumulates in blood vessels and causes cardiovascular disease.[511] About one percent of people over 65 years old have evidence of Alzheimer's. Once diagnosed with the disease, people live an average of seven years. People with cognitive impairment have about a ten times greater risk of progressing to more serious dementia than those without the condition.[512]

Global distribution of cognitive disorders is similar to other chronic, Western diseases. Alzheimer's rates, for example, are higher in developed countries that consume more fat and fewer grains.[513] The saturated fat and cholesterol in animal products that clog arteries supplying the heart also can clog arteries supplying the brain. Many studies have found that consuming saturated fat and cholesterol increases vascular dementia and Alzheimer's disease. For example, one study found that people who eat the most total fat and saturated fat had the highest risk of dementia due to vascular problems. Animal studies have shown that consuming high levels of dietary cholesterol (only found in animal products) promotes the production of the beta-amyloid plaque common to Alzheimer's. Many human studies have found that consuming higher levels of dietary fat and cholesterol increases the risk of Alzheimer's disease specifically and all dementia in general.[514]

Consuming plant products can promote improved brain health, while consuming animal products often degrades it. To illustrate, free radical damage to the brain strongly promotes cognitive impairment and dementia. As noted, animal products tend to promote free radical production, while the antioxidants found in plant products often prevent free radical damage. Several studies found that consuming antioxidants and other nutrients exclusively found in plants is associated with a lower risk of cognitive decline in old-age.[515]

The vascular problems that cause strokes and dementia are strongly affected by diet. One study found that each additional three servings of fruit and vegetables per day lowers the risk of stroke by 22 percent.[516] Other studies showed that cardiovascular disease, which is strongly promoted by eating animal products, reduces blood supply to the brain and causes people to do less well on mental acuity tests.[517]

Dr. Campbell points out that cognitive decline, memory loss, disorientation and confusion are not inevitable parts of aging. Many elderly people do not experience these conditions. Cognitive decline is strongly promoted by eating animal products. People's minds and memories can remain clear and sharp throughout their entire lives. Consuming a whole food, plant-based diet is one of the most important actions needed to maintain lifelong mental clarity and effectiveness.[518]

High Blood Pressure

High blood pressure is a major risk factor for heart disease. It causes blood to flow through arteries with too much force. This can overstretch and weaken arteries. This in turn can increase the risk of aneurysms, ruptures and strokes. Overstretching also can cause tiny tears in arteries. As these tears heal, scar tissue can form that traps white blood cells, plaque and cholesterol. This accumulation of plaque triggered by high blood pressure can cause narrowing and hardening of arteries (i.e. atherosclerosis).

It also can cause blood clots and blockages, which in turn can cause heart attacks, strokes and other problems.[519] People with high blood pressure are three times more likely to die of heart disease and four times more likely to die of stroke.[520] Left untreated, high blood pressure can quietly damage the body for years before symptoms appear. By damaging arteries and restricting blood flow, high blood pressure can cause or contribute to many problems, including dementia, kidney damage, vision problems and ED.[521]

About one-third of adults in the US have high blood pressure. Many do not know they have it.[522] The director of the CDC called high blood pressure a major public health problem and said that nothing would save more lives than getting blood pressure under control. High blood pressure causes or contributes to about 350,000 deaths per year in the US. The direct cost of this condition is about $130 billion per year.[523]

Many people take medication to control high blood pressure. However, like most other drugs, blood pressure medications often have negative side effects. Depending on the type of medication used, side effects can include erectile and other sexual dysfunction, depression, insomnia, irregular or rapid heartbeat, dizziness, headache, fever, constipation, joint pain, skin rash and loss of taste.[524]

To avoid side effects and medication, many people successfully lower blood pressure through lifestyle changes. Lifestyle is a major cause of high blood pressure. Therefore, changing it can and often should be a primary strategy for lowering blood pressure. Lifestyle factors related to high blood pressure include obesity, exercise, salt, stress, alcohol, tobacco and diet. Being overweight or obese is a main cause of high blood pressure. Overweight and obese people require more blood to supply their larger bodies. The higher volume of blood can increase blood pressure. Lack of exercise also can increase blood pressure. Inactive people tend to have higher heart rates, which can increase blood pressure. Consuming too much salt can cause the body to retain fluid to flush the excess salt from the body. This can increase blood pressure. High stress, tobacco use, and excessive alcohol consumption also can increase it.

Diet usually is the main lifestyle factor causing high blood pressure. Overeating unhealthy food often is the main cause of obesity, which in turn is a main cause of high blood pressure. The saturated fat, cholesterol and inflammatory properties of animal products strongly promote high blood pressure. Salt, fat and sugar-laden refined carbohydrates also strongly promote it.

Important lifestyle changes for reducing high blood pressure include weight loss, regular exercise, reducing stress, avoiding tobacco, limiting alcohol consumption, and reducing salt consumption. Overall, the most important action that people can take to reduce high blood pressure often is to adopt a whole plant food diet. Whole plant foods, including vegetables, grains, beans and fruits, strongly enhance blood vessel health and promote reduced, healthy blood pressure levels. As discussed in the following sections, adopting a whole plant food diet is the most effective way to achieve long-term weight loss, and thereby alleviate a main cause of high blood pressure.

Obesity

Widespread and growing obesity creates many health, quality of life, financial and other problems in the US and many other countries. The adult obesity rate in the US has risen from 13 percent in 1960 to 43 percent in 2018, with most of the increase occurring since 1980. About another third of adults are overweight. Taken together, nearly three-quarters of adults in the US are overweight.[525] More than half of adults in Europe are obese or overweight.[526] Obesity rates generally are higher among low-income and minority groups. For example, 50 percent of African Americans, 45 percent of Hispanics, and 42 percent of White adults are obese.[527] By 2030, nearly 50 percent of adults in the US are projected to be obese.[528]

Obesity strongly contributes to many health and psychological problems. For example, being obese or overweight can substantially increase the risk of diabetes, heart disease, high blood pressure, stroke, osteoarthritis (degeneration of joints), sleep apnea and other breathing problems, and breast, prostate, colorectal and kidney cancer. Obesity also can cause or contribute to pregnancy complications, menstrual irregularities, excess facial and body hair, urinary incontinence, social isolation, and psychological disorders, such as depression.[529] A study published in the journal Pediatrics found that women who are obese while pregnant have a 67 percent greater risk of giving birth to autistic children and a 100 percent greater risk of having children with other developmental delays.[530]

Obese people are nearly 300 percent more likely to develop dementia than people who are not overweight.[531] In addition, obese people have a substantially increased risk of death from all causes compared to healthy weight individuals. Obesity plays a major role in over 160,000 deaths per year in the US.[532] Being obese can greatly lower quality of life in many ways. For example, it often is difficult for obese people to walk long distances, play with children, participate in sports, have an active sex life, or find comfortable seats in movie theaters or on airplanes. For some obese people, even standing or sitting still causes back or joint pain.[533]

The direct medical costs of obesity in the US are about $190 billion per year, $90 billion more than is spent on cancer. Annual medical spending for an obese person is about $3,300 per year versus $500 for the non-obese.[534] Obesity accounts for about 21 percent of US healthcare costs.[535] The medical costs of obesity exceed those of smoking, in part because smokers tend to die more quickly. Drugs can keep obese people alive longer. Medical expenses for obese elderly people are much higher than expenses for non-overweight elderly people. Obesity increases medical costs in many ways. For example, some hospitals are buying mini-cranes to hoist obese patients out of bed.[536]

Obesity is a complex issue. Many factors promote it. As discussed in the Advertising, Media and Culture section, ubiquitous advertising and media messages create a pervasive sense of inadequacy and emptiness in society. To sell products, ads often strongly imply that people are inadequate without the advertised items. Media frequently conveys inaccurate messages about what it means to be a successful person. For example, advertising and media often emphasize looks, wealth and possessions, instead of the factors that actually produce a truly successful life, such as fulfilling relationships, rewarding work and being of service to others.

Many people futilely attempt to fill this media and advertising-induced void with overeating and other compulsive or addictive behaviors. Excessive TV watching, web surfing and other cyberworld activities promote sedentary lifestyles and obesity. Lack of exercise also promotes obesity. Only about 30 percent of adults in the US exercise regularly. About 40 percent do no exercise.[537] As discussed in the MSG section, MSG often suppresses the body's appetite regulation mechanism and promotes obesity.

Probably the main direct driver of obesity is the type and quantity of food consumed. As with Western chronic diseases, obesity usually increases substantially when people increase consumption of animal products. For example, obesity is virtually nonexistent in rural China. But when Chinese immigrants in Western countries adopt the local, animal product intensive diet, they often succumb to obesity.[538] In Thailand, as animal product consumption rose over the past 25 years, obesity, heart disease and other chronic diseases rose dramatically.[539]

With some exceptions, animal products contain substantially more fat than plant products. Consuming high-fat animal product diets often contributes to obesity. As discussed in the Heart Disease section, some people point out that, in spite of increased consumption of lower fat animal products, such as skim milk and chicken, obesity has grown rapidly since the 1980s. The implication is that high-fat diets do not cause obesity because reducing fat consumption did not lower obesity. But this position is misleading. Consuming more low-fat products reduced fat consumption as a percentage of total calories in the US. But it did not lower total fat consumption. To maintain palatability, many low-fat products replace fat with sugar. The reduction in fat consumption due to low-fat products was more than offset by increased calorie and total food consumption. As a result, annual fat consumption rose from 53 pounds per person in 1970 to 66 pounds in 1997.[540]

Many experts believe that refined carbohydrates, such as white flour and sugar, promote obesity as much or more then dietary fat consumption. As noted, refined carbohydrates often are stripped of fiber, vitamins, minerals and other nutrients. They have little or no nutritional value, beyond providing empty calories. Consuming refined carbohydrates causes glucose to rise rapidly. To metabolize sugar-laden, nutrient-empty foods, the body often must draw down nutrient reserves. Depleting these reserves inhibits the body's ability to metabolize fatty acids. This leads to increased fatty acid accumulation and obesity.[541] In effect, the body converts excess refined unhealthy carbohydrates into fat, which causes obesity.

Complex, unrefined carbohydrates, such as whole grains and vegetables, break down more slowly, are highly nutritious, and promote weight loss instead of weight gain. People in the US often eat large amounts of refined carbohydrates, but few complex carbohydrates. For example, 42 percent of people eat cookies, cakes, pastries or pies every day. But only 10 percent of people eat dark green vegetables daily.[542] Refined sugars, such as table sugar and high-fructose corn syrup, are among the simplest and most fattening carbohydrates. Many studies have shown that excess sugar consumption strongly promotes obesity. The American Heart Association recommends that women eat no more than six teaspoons of sugar per day and men eat no more than nine teaspoons daily. But people in the US eat an average of 32 teaspoons of sugar every day. (On food labels, four grams of sugar equals one teaspoon.) In 1830, people in the US ate an average of 11 pounds of sugar per year. This has risen to about 156 pounds annually, including 45 to 60 pounds of high-fructose corn syrup.[543]

Extensive research has led to a better understanding of the neurological and psychological aspects that drive overeating and obesity. Humans evolved in an environment of food scarcity and intense food competition. We evolved to get hungry when we see food, want high calorie foods with abundant sugar and fat, eat as much as possible when food is available, and store food as fat so that we can survive when food is not available.[544] These instinctual and psychological characteristics enabled humans to survive in nature. But they often do not work well in modern society.

In developed countries, people see food and images of food in advertising throughout the day. The cheapest, most widely available foods often are the least healthy. These foods frequently are comprised of refined carbohydrates with high levels of sugar, fat and/or salt. These so-called foods have little to no nutritional value. They do not satisfy. As a result, people often continue to eat. The foods frequently have little or no fiber, and thereby provide little sense of fullness. This can cause people to overeat.

An excellent book by Dr. David Kessler, called *The End of Overeating: Taking Control of the Insatiable American Appetite*, discusses how people often essentially become addicted to unhealthy processed food and how this drives obesity. Dr. Kessler formerly was the Commissioner of the FDA and Dean of the Yale Medical School. He explains that foods with large amounts of sugar and fat raise dopamine levels in the brain, as cocaine and amphetamines do.[545] Eating foods with high levels of sugar, fat and salt activates or develops reward circuits in the brain. Once people start eating these foods, higher dopamine levels and triggered reward circuits make it difficult to stop eating. Over time, the more sugar and fat-laden foods that people eat, the stronger the reward circuits become and the more difficult it becomes to avoid these foods.

Overeating often does not result from a lack of willpower. It results from physiological, neurological processes that essentially compel people to overeat. Dr. Kessler points out that obese and overweight people often display classic signs of addiction, such as loss of control, lack of satiation and preoccupation with food. In other words, people frequently are unable to resist their favorite foods, do not develop a sense of fullness or satisfaction when eating, and think about food frequently, even when they are not eating.

A study of rats illustrates how eating junk food (i.e. high sugar, fat and/or salt content, low nutritional value) can cause long-term or permanent damage to the brain's reward circuitry and drive addiction to junk food. The study found junk food addiction is similar to heroin addiction. During the study, a control group of rats were fed high nutrient, low-calorie food. Another group was fed junk food. The rats fed junk food developed compulsive eating habits, ate twice as many calories and became obese.

Junk food substantially reduced the sensitivity of the brain's pleasure centers. As a result, rats had to eat more junk food to get the same level of pleasure, in the same way that heroin addicts require more drugs over time to feel good. Illustrating the strength of junk food addiction, rats that had been constantly fed junk food continued to eat junk food even when they were shocked. Rats that were not addicted to junk food stopped eating it when they were shocked. When rats that had become addicted to junk food were given healthy food instead of junk food, they refused to eat. They chose to starve themselves instead of eating healthy food.[546] Another study of rats found that eating a high-fat diet similar to the average US diet not only caused obesity, it also damaged the hypothalamus, the region of the brain that controls appetite and body weight.[547]

The American Society of Addiction Medicine (ASAM) released a new definition of addiction that characterizes it as a distinct neurological disorder.[548] ASAM claims that addiction largely does not result from lack of willpower or psychological problems. It substantially results from a destructive imbalance in the brain's reward circuitry. ASAM further claims that essentially all addictions, including addiction to substances such as food, alcohol, tobacco and drugs as well as addictions to activities such as gambling, sex and shopping, result in large part from the same fundamental neurological disorder. Impairment of the pleasure centers strongly compels addicts to pursue the brain chemical highs caused by addictive substances and behaviors.

Genetics cause some people to be more susceptible to addiction. But eating sugar and fat-laden foods, taking drugs or engaging in other potential addictions often can promote addiction more strongly than genetics by permanently damaging reward circuits and pleasure centers. ASAM states that people cannot choose to not be addicts. Addiction largely is a physiological problem, not a choice. However, people can choose to not engage in addictive behavior. The process of overcoming addiction is discussed in the Changing Habits and other sections below.

Dr. Kessler points out that eating sugar and fat-laden junk food can be very damaging to children and teenagers because their brains are still developing. These foods can damage the neural circuitry of children's and teenagers' brains in ways that create a strong propensity to overeat and be obese throughout their adult lives. Childhood obesity is one of the strongest predictors of adult obesity.[549]

The obesity epidemic once again illustrates the destructive nature of our grossly flawed economic and political systems. Publicly traded food companies are structurally required to provide ever-increasing shareholder returns, even if it increases obesity, chronic disease, premature deaths and healthcare costs. In another excellent book about food, *The Omnivore's Dilemma*, Michael Pollan points out that food companies used to think that basic demand for food largely was fixed. In other words, people usually eat a fixed amount of food. As a result, companies could increase sales mainly by taking market share from competitors. However, in the 1960s, food companies began to realize that they could increase sales, profits and shareholder returns by getting customers to eat more food. Many strategies were employed to increase food consumption.

Dr. Kessler discusses how food experts analyzed which tastes and substances would compel people to eat more. They found that adding sugar, fat and/or salt, plus MSG and other chemicals, would compel people to continue eating, even when they no longer were physically hungry. Experts found that combining sweet and salty tastes, for example, would compel people to eat more. As a result, more processed foods contain sugar and salt. Companies also encouraged or compelled people to eat more by supersizing – providing larger portions of food at higher prices. Companies also learned that people often would eat more if individual pieces of food were smaller. As a result, companies began making more bite-size cookies, crackers and other products.[550]

In addition, companies studied how food feels and dissolves in the mouth. Dr. Kessler points out that, about 30 years ago, food used to require about 20 to 30 chews per bite-sized portion of food. To increase food sales, companies often made food easier to chew. Now only about half as many chews are required. Dr. Kessler says that many processed foods essentially are predigested adult baby foods. To further increase food sales, ubiquitous food advertisements were developed by experts in human psychology. Food ads often are designed to trigger food cravings and maximize food consumption.

Through strong government influence, food companies are able to protect their ability to maximize shareholder returns. For example, corn, wheat and crops fed to animals are heavily subsidized. These often are used to produce fattening refined carbohydrates and animal products. Subsidization makes these products appear to be much cheaper than they actually are.

People wind up paying for much of their food costs through higher income taxes and healthcare costs.

In addition, food companies and their allies strongly influence food guidelines in the US. As noted, the guidelines imply that it is acceptable and healthy for people to consume up to 35 percent of calories as fat, up to 35 percent as protein and up to 50 percent of grains in refined form. They also formerly implied that it was healthy to eat up to 25 percent of calories as added sugars. These guidelines are ridiculous. They show how strongly business controls the USDA. As discussed in the Heart Disease section, eating up to 35 percent of calories as fat strongly promotes heart disease, the number one killer in the US. As discussed in the Cancer section, eating up to 35 percent of calories as animal protein strongly promotes cancer, the number two killer in the US.

Dr. Campbell uses the added sugar component of the dietary guidelines to illustrate how business strongly influences government. Prior to the 2010 US dietary guidelines being issued, the World Health Organization (WHO) recommended that people get no more than 10 percent of calories from added sugars, such as those found in candy, soda, cookies and pastries. US food companies, politicians paid by them and other allies strongly pressured the WHO in an effort to discredit and block the release of the 10 percent guideline. This effort failed at the international level, but succeeded in the US. As noted, the 2010 dietary guidelines implied that eating up to 25 percent of calories as added sugars was healthy. The USDA panel that issued the 2010 guidelines received funding from candy and soda companies.[551] As it became increasingly obvious that high sugar diets strongly drive increased obesity and chronic diseases, the USDA was compelled to abide by the WHO recommendation and reduce its recommended percentage of calories from added sugars.

Sugar perfectly illustrates how business influence of government severely degrades society. A Credit Suisse report estimated that 30 to 40 percent of US healthcare expenditures are closely linked to excess consumption of sugar. This strongly promotes diabetes, heart disease, obesity, high blood pressure, high cholesterol, metabolic syndrome, gout, osteoarthritis, liver cancer, and many other health problems. As a result, excess sugar consumption increases US healthcare costs by potentially over $1 trillion per year.[552] Sugar crop producers spend substantial amounts on campaign contributions and lobbying. For example, they spent about $21 million on lobbying in 2009.[553] As a result, many Republican and Democrat politicians support large subsidies for the sugar industry. Strong business influence of government causes the US to heavily subsidize sugar, and then spend vastly more to treat health problems caused by it.

The strategies of food companies are similar to those of tobacco companies. Food companies apparently seek to get customers addicted to their products by manipulating sugar, fat and salt content, adding MSG and other chemicals, using psychologically compelling advertising, and influencing government to subsidize unhealthy foods and implement unhealthy dietary guidelines. Then, like tobacco companies, food companies and their allies work aggressively to mislead the public about the harmful nature of their products and block efforts to lower consumption. As always throughout this book, this is not said as a criticism of businesses or business and political leaders. Instead, it is said as a strong criticism of flawed economic and political systems that force good, well-intentioned leaders to take actions that severely harm society.

The food situation in the US illustrates one of the most tragic examples of the disruptive, even suicidal, nature of our flawed systems. Dr. Kessler points out that in the 1960s and 1970s, people gained about three pounds on average between the ages of 20 and 40 years old, and then lost the weight in their 60s and 70s. But today, most people continue to gain weight throughout their lives.

Unhealthy sugar and fat-laden foods are harming children. Dr. Kessler explains that average two-year-old children compensate for their eating. For example, if they are given more calories at lunch, they will eat fewer calories at dinner. However, by the time children reach four or five years old, the sugar, fat and salt-laden US diet often degrades or destroys their ability to compensate. Damaged brain reward circuits override children's ability to self-regulate and conditions them to a lifetime of overeating and obesity.[554]

Through the strategies discussed above, food companies are compelling citizens to eat large amounts of unhealthy food so that they can provide ever-increasing shareholder returns. Companies literally are massively degrading quality of life, driving vast chronic disease and premature deaths, and increasing healthcare costs by hundreds of billions of dollars per year. Businesses are not held fully responsible for these huge negative impacts mainly because they strongly control government and mislead the public. This once again illustrates why it is absolutely essential that businesses be held fully responsible for all negative environmental, social and economic impacts. When this occurs, companies will maximize shareholder returns by selling healthy, life-enhancing foods that maximize the well-being of society.

Children

Eating unhealthy food causes many problems for children and teenagers in the US and many other countries. As with adults, obesity rates have been growing rapidly among children and teenagers in the US. About one-third of children and teenagers are obese or overweight, three times the rate in 1963.[555] Obese young people face greatly increased risks of health and psychological problems. For example, obese children and teenagers have substantially increased risk of developing type 2 diabetes, high blood pressure, high blood cholesterol, bone problems, and sleep apnea and related neuro-cognitive problems.[556] Childhood obesity is one of the strongest predictors of adult obesity. This indicates that health problems will increase for obese children as they get older.

Children often lack the social skills, understanding and compassion of adults. As a result, life can be difficult for overweight and obese children and teenagers. They are more likely to be criticized and rejected by peers. They frequently are seen as being lazy and sloppy. Obese children and teenagers are more likely to have learning difficulties and psychological problems, such as depression and low self-esteem. The low self-esteem developed as an obese child can last a lifetime.[557]

Many factors drive childhood and teenage obesity. As discussed in the Obesity section, unhealthy foods, such as many types of animal products and refined, sugar and fat-laden carbohydrates, can damage reward circuits and pleasure centers in the brain. This can condition children and teenagers to a lifetime of overeating and obesity. Also, as discussed in the Chemicals section, many studies have shown that in utero and early childhood exposure to pesticides and other chemicals can increase the likelihood of becoming obese later in life. As noted, over 80 percent of pesticide exposure results from eating animal products. Additional exposure results from eating conventionally grown (i.e. industrial) fruits and vegetables.

Playing video games, watching television and other cyberworld activities also drive childhood and teenage obesity. A review of 123 studies found that TV watching is strongly correlated with childhood obesity.[558] In other words, the more TV that children watch, the more likely they are to become obese. While watching TV, children usually are inactive and often snacking. TV further promotes childhood obesity through advertising. About two-thirds of the 20,000 TV ads children see per year are for food. Most of these ads are for high calorie, high sugar, high-fat, low nutrient foods.[559] Food companies often use popular cartoon characters in food ads. These types of ads are highly effective at encouraging children to request and consume unhealthy, obesity-promoting foods.

Lack of exercise also strongly drives childhood and teenage obesity. Across the US, physical education programs often are being cut back or eliminated. This is an extremely unwise and myopic cost saving measure. Children in particular should be physically active for at least one hour every day.[560] This helps them to burn off their naturally high energy, maintain a healthy weight, and concentrate more effectively on their studies in school. In addition, habits developed in childhood often are maintained for life. Children who exercise regularly are much more likely to exercise as adults.

Parents often unintentionally promote childhood obesity. Children frequently adopt their parents' food and health-related beliefs and behaviors. If one parent is overweight or obese, a child has a 40 percent chance of also being overweight or obese. If both parents are overweight or obese, the risk increases to 80 percent. Overweight or obese parents are more likely to make disparaging remarks about themselves and their appearance in front of children. Modeling an unhealthy self-image can cause children to develop low self-esteem and a poor body image.[561]

In discussing the childhood obesity epidemic, the former Surgeon General of the US, Richard Carmona, said, "because of the increasing rates of obesity, unhealthy eating habits and physical inactivity, we may see the first generation that will be less healthy and have a shorter life expectancy than their parents."[562] A study by the American Heart Association found that 80 percent of teenagers in the US are eating unhealthy diets that promote heart disease. The diets include too much fat, salt and sugar and not enough fruits and vegetables. Only one percent of teenagers were eating what the Heart Association considers to be a healthy diet.[563]

Beyond obesity, eating unhealthy food causes many other problems for children. As discussed in the Air section, about half of the freshwater fish in the US is contaminated with mercury, mostly from coal-fired power plants. Eating mercury-contaminated fish contributes to 23 percent of women of childbearing age having unsafe levels of mercury in their bodies. As a result, about 640,000 children are exposed to unsafe mercury levels in utero each year. Many of them suffer reduced IQs and other cognitive problems.

Consumption of animal products by pregnant women can cause many other problems for children. Through bioaccumulation and other processes, animal products nearly always have higher levels of chemicals, hormones and other toxic contaminants than plant products. Beef in the US, for example, often is treated with the female hormones estrogen and progesterone. Exposing males developing in utero to female hormones can cause many negative impacts. To illustrate, the most important testicular development supporting sperm production occurs in utero. One study found that men born to women who ate large amounts of beef while pregnant had substantially lower sperm counts than those born to women who ate little or no beef while pregnant.[564]

Beef companies might argue that this research does not provide conclusive proof. But this reflects Wrong Reference Point and Wrong Perspective logic. We should not wait until we are 90 to 99 percent certain that beef treated with female hormones harms developing boys. Hormone treated beef never should have been allowed until we had independent, conclusive proof that it was safe.

Cow's milk can cause many problems for infants and children. As discussed in the Autoimmune Diseases section, many studies have shown that giving cow's milk to infants substantially increases the risk of type 1 diabetes. In addition, cow's milk is a leading cause of food allergies among infants and children. Cow's milk evolved in nature as food for calves that have four stomachs. It is substantially different from human milk. As a result, many people have difficulty digesting it. Millions of children and adults experience bloating, cramps, vomiting and headaches when they drink cow's milk because they are lactose intolerant. This includes about 90 percent of Asian Americans and 75 percent of African Americans and Native-Americans.[565]

Beyond damaging the brain in ways that cause overeating and obesity, unhealthy foods cause many other neurological, cognitive and behavior problems. For example, one study found that three-year-old children who ate processed food with high levels of sugar and fat had lower IQs at eight years of age than children who ate lower calorie, nutrient rich food.[566]

ADHD is one of the most important cognitive and behavioral problems related to unhealthy food. Since the 1970s, many studies have found that unhealthy foods, chemical food dyes and other food additives contribute to ADHD and hyperactivity in general.[567] For example, a study of 1,800 teenagers compared the prevalence of ADHD among those who consumed a Western diet (i.e. high amounts of refined carbohydrates, sugar, fat and animal products, and few fruits and vegetables) to those who ate a healthier diet (i.e. fruits, vegetables, whole grains and fish). The study found that teenagers who ate the Western diet had more than twice the rate of ADHD than those who ate healthier diets.[568]

Another study published in the journal The Lancet enrolled 100 children between the ages of four and eight who had been diagnosed with ADHD. Half of the children were placed on restrictive diets for five weeks. The diets eliminated processed foods that contained artificial dyes and other food additives. Instead, the children were fed whole foods including rice, turkey, carrots, lettuce, pears and water. Within five weeks, ADHD symptoms in 64 percent of the children essentially disappeared. They no longer were easily distracted or forgetful and they had no more temper-tantrums.[569]

Following this and other studies which indicated that artificial food dyes cause hyperactivity in children, the EU banned artificial dyes in foods intended for infants and small children. It also required a warning label on all other products that contain the dyes.[570] As discussed in the Chemicals section, many food companies are removing artificial dyes from European food products, but leaving them in US foods, in large part because the dyes are still allowed by the business-dominated US government.

More than six million school-age children (ages 4 to 17) have been diagnosed with ADHD in the US (about 11 percent of school-age children). Nearly three million children take Ritalin, Adderall or other stimulant drugs to treat their symptoms.[571] Common side effects of these drugs include headaches, stomachaches and sleeplessness. Less common side effects include feeling helpless, hopeless or worthless as well as developing new or worsening depression. These drugs also substantially increase the risk of sudden death from cardiac dysrhythmia or unexplained causes.[572]

Stimulants used to treat ADHD limit the childhood experience by suppressing some emotions. The long-term effects of these drugs are unknown. Exposing children's developing brains to powerful drugs for many years could cause permanent cognitive impairment or brain damage. Once children start taking one ADHD drug, doctors often recommend that they take additional drugs to manage side effects such as depression and sleeplessness. Children frequently are told that they might have to take the drugs for life.[573] Beyond harming the brain, stimulants also can negatively impact the body. A major study of Ritalin found that children who took the drug for three years were one inch shorter and four pounds lighter than their peers.[574]

Keeping millions of children, teenagers and adults on ADHD drugs is highly profitable for the pharmaceutical industry. To maximize shareholder returns, drug companies aggressively promote their drugs to doctors. In addition, they often directly or indirectly fund or influence research which shows that their drugs are safe and effective. To illustrate, following the above study which found that Ritalin stunted children's growth, a subsequent study disputed these findings. But all of the authors of the study had financial relationships with drug companies.[575]

As discussed in the Depression section of *Global System Change*, the business-friendly FDA often does not disclose research which shows that drugs are ineffective or harmful. As a result, doctors frequently develop inaccurate or biased perceptions of the safety and effectiveness of ADHD and other drugs. In addition, doctors sometimes are not informed about safer, more effective treatment options.

ADHD is a complex condition that is not fully understood. Several factors could contribute to or cause ADHD symptoms. However, it appears that possibly two-thirds of ADHD cases result in large part from eating unhealthy, processed foods. As a result, prior to placing children on powerful, potentially harmful drugs, the lead researcher of The Lancet study mentioned above suggests that children be placed on a restricted diet for five weeks. The diet should eliminate processed foods. Instead, children and teenagers should be fed whole foods, such as fruit, vegetables and whole grains. In many cases, perhaps the large majority, ADHD symptoms probably will decline or disappear when children are switched from unhealthy processed foods to healthy whole foods.[576]

However, it may be difficult to switch ADHD children to healthy foods if parents and other children continue to eat unhealthy animal products and sugar and fat-laden refined carbohydrates. As noted, nearly three-quarters of adults in the US are overweight or obese. Many parents probably would find it difficult to stop eating their favorite unhealthy foods. In these cases, it might be easier to drug disruptive ADHD children, while the whole family continues to eat unhealthy foods. But switching to healthy foods, such as whole plant-based foods, is worth the effort.

The smaller bodies and rapidly developing brains of children make them more vulnerable to the artificial dyes, MSG, other additives, sugar, fat, salt and refined carbohydrates in processed foods. These so-called foods could be thought of as anti-foods because they often deplete the body's nutrient reserves and strongly promote ADHD, obesity and other health problems. These anti-foods frequently cause adverse reactions in the body and mind. In effect, they are slow-acting poisons. Avoiding unhealthy animal products and refined carbohydrates not only will help children, it will help whole families by greatly lowering the risk of obesity, chronic disease and premature death.

ADHD is a large concern for many parents. Childhood obesity is an even larger one. It is the number one concern among US parents, ahead of drug abuse and smoking.[577] Switching to whole food, plant-based diets probably would end ADHD symptoms for many children and teenagers. As discussed below, it also is the most effective way to lose weight and maintain a healthy weight for life. Many studies have shown that children who eat healthy plant-based diets (i.e. with little or no refined carbohydrates) attain their full growth potential, have abundant energy and get all required nutrients.[578]

Healthcare Costs

As discussed in the Healthcare section of *Global System Change*, the US has the most expensive healthcare system in the world. Healthcare costs per person are two to three times higher in the US than in most other developed countries. At the same time, the US provides the worst healthcare coverage in the developed world by far, and achieves relatively poor healthcare outcomes. If one focused on facts such as these, instead of the deceptions promoted by vested interests, a strong argument could be made that the US has the worst healthcare system in the developed world by far. Providing excellent healthcare to wealthy people, but leaving 35 percent of citizens uninsured or under-insured does not qualify as good healthcare. No other developed country does this.

Healthcare costs in the US were about $3 trillion in 2014.[579] They are projected to rise from 18 percent of GDP to 33 percent by 2035. We cannot afford to continue paying two to three times more for healthcare than most other developed countries, while providing the worst coverage in the developed world and achieving inferior results. It is imperative that healthcare costs be vastly lowered, while adequate healthcare coverage is extended to all citizens, as occurs in every other developed country. One of the most important ways to achieve this is to implement what every other developed country has proven to be a more effective system – a government-owned or government-managed healthcare system.

Changing diets is another critical action needed to substantially lower healthcare costs. More than 75 percent of people in the US die of heart disease, cancer and other chronic diseases. Treating these diseases represents about 75 percent of healthcare expenditures.[580] As discussed in previous sections, most chronic diseases are caused mainly by eating animal products and refined carbohydrates.

In the US, we spend billions of dollars subsidizing unhealthy foods that cause chronic disease, and then spend trillions of dollars treating the diseases. Instead, we should subsidize healthy foods, such as fruits and vegetables, that will vastly lower healthcare costs. As Dr. Campbell and Dr. Esselstyn discuss extensively, switching to whole food, plant-based diets could prevent and often reverse many cases of heart disease, cancer, stroke, diabetes, brain diseases and other chronic diseases. It potentially could lower annual healthcare costs by hundreds of billions of dollars, while greatly improving quality of life and productivity for millions of citizens.

Nearly half of adults in the US have one or more preventable chronic diseases that are strongly linked to poor diets and physical inactivity.[581] Abundant evidence indicates that up to 75 percent of healthcare costs in the US could be eliminated if citizens were given sound dietary advice (i.e. eat whole plant food diets) as well as provided with encouragement and support in complying with the advice.[582]

However, there are several major barriers to changing diets and lowering healthcare costs, chronic disease and premature deaths. Probably the largest overall barriers are flawed economic and political systems that compel publicly traded companies to try to grow forever and allow businesses to inappropriately influence government and mislead the public. For example, food, pharmaceutical and other companies are required to protect shareholder returns, even if it degrades society in ways that are not immediate and obvious. To protect returns, food companies often give money to politicians, rotate employees in and out of regulatory roles, conduct biased research that shows their products to be safe, and engage in sophisticated public deception strategies.

Pharmaceutical companies in particular could be a major barrier to lowering healthcare costs. They strongly influence the healthcare sector and medical profession. For example, drug companies heavily influence research in the medical area. The vast majority of research is focused on developing new drugs, rather than on the causes of disease or non-drug interventions.[583] Drug companies often heavily control research by designing studies, collecting data and then deciding what data researchers are allowed to see. In addition, the companies often retain editorial and veto rights over research, which means that they can block the publication of unfavorable results.[584]

Drug companies frequently hire communications companies to write research articles and then find researchers who are willing to be listed as authors. Researchers often receive financial influence, such as serving as paid consultants or holding equity interests in drug companies, that causes their studies to be biased. Drug companies sometimes take actions that discredit or damage the careers and reputations of researchers who find their drugs to be ineffective or harmful.[585]

The companies also heavily influence medical journals, which frequently receive the majority of their income from drug advertising. Most of the research published in medical journals is funded by drug companies.[586] Taken together, these factors often cause doctors to receive biased information about the safety and effectiveness of drugs. To illustrate, as discussed in the Depression section, 51 percent of studies reviewed by the FDA found antidepressants to be effective. But 94 percent of published studies showed positive results.

Drug companies also heavily influence medical education. They frequently provide free gifts, meals, entertainment and travel to medical students. Drug companies also often pay up to 80 percent of doctors' continuing education costs.[587] Medical education is heavily focused on the treatment of disease, rather than prevention. Medical students and young doctors frequently learn that there is a pill for nearly every problem.[588]

Doctors usually receive little to no training in nutrition. One study found that doctors receive an average of 21 classroom hours of nutrition training during their four years of medical school. Most of this occurs as part of basic science classes and focuses on subjects such as how the body metabolizes nutrients. Meat, dairy and drug companies often provide 'educational' (i.e. promotional) materials to medical schools. This information almost certainly does not emphasize the role of animal products in promoting heart disease, cancer and other chronic diseases. Doctors usually receive little education about the links between chronic disease and diet.[589]

In *The China Study*, Dr. Campbell states, "You should not assume that your doctor has any more knowledge about food and its relation to health than your neighbors and coworkers. It's a tragic situation in which nutritionally untrained doctors prescribe milk and sugar-based meal-replacement shakes for overweight diabetics, high-meat, high-fat diets for patients who ask how to lose weight and extra milk for patients who have osteoporosis. The damage that results from doctors' ignorance of nutrition is astounding."[590]

Beyond doctors, citizens in the US also are taught that pills can solve many physical and mental health problems. The US and New Zealand are the only countries that allow television and other direct-to-consumer advertising of drugs. Heavy promotion of drugs and widespread chronic disease (largely due to eating unhealthy foods) contribute to about 70 percent of the people in the US taking at least one prescription drug. About half of citizens take two prescription drugs and one-quarter take five or more.[591] The drugs cost about $250 billion per year.[592]

An excellent book by Melody Peterson, called *Our Daily Meds*, describes how drug companies increase prescription drug use in the US.[593] For example, drug company representatives often encourage doctors to prescribe drugs for off-label uses (i.e. uses not approved by the FDA). Marketing drugs off-label is illegal. But drug companies often do it, in part because the benefits frequently outweigh the fines for off-label marketing.[594]

Selling drugs to children has become one of the highest growth areas for drug companies. Beyond the ADHD drugs described above, drug company representatives often encourage doctors to prescribe cholesterol-reducing drugs, antidepressants, antipsychotics and many other drugs to children.

Prescription drugs frequently have side effects, including severe ones such as death. The healthcare system is the number three killer in the US, behind heart disease and cancer. More than 200,000 people die each year due to causes including adverse drug effects and hospital errors and infections. Over 100,000 people die per year from correctly taking correctly prescribed drugs. Thousands more people die when doctors prescribe the wrong drugs or patients accidentally take too many.[595]

The US is the only developed country that does not control drug prices. As discussed in the Healthcare section, US citizens pay more for drugs than people in nearly all other countries. For example, US prescription drug prices are nearly twice as high as those in Canada. Restricting drug prices is critical because drug companies often can block competition by using patents, acquiring competitors and other means. In addition, citizens are highly vulnerable to price gouging in the drug area. People facing death or serious illness frequently would pay anything for potentially helpful drugs. Other countries do not allow drug companies to take advantage of limited competition and vulnerable citizens. But the business-influenced US government often appears to be more focused on protecting shareholder returns than the lives, health and wealth of citizens.

The healthcare system in the US well illustrates the grossly flawed nature of our economic and political systems that place economic growth and shareholder returns before the well-being of society and all other factors. Feeding people fattening, unhealthy foods, and then spending hundreds of billions of dollars to treat the resulting chronic diseases, often increases economic growth and shareholder returns. Therefore, according to our suicidally myopic systems, these actions benefit society.

If society were focused on what is best for society instead of business, we would not be subsidizing unhealthy foods, and then encouraging people to take drugs, for example, to lower cholesterol and blood pressure. Instead, we would encourage people to not eat the foods that caused these and other illnesses. MSG provides a similar example. Instead of taking drugs that treat neurological disorders by blocking the effects of glutamate on the brain, people would be encouraged to not eat foods that contain processed glutamates (i.e. MSG).

In *Prevent and Reverse Heart Disease*, Dr. Esselstyn explains that by-pass surgery, angioplasty and stenting often do not lower heart attack risk, because heavily clogged arteries that are the focus of these procedures often do not cause heart attacks. Less clogged arteries frequently are more likely to experience sudden blockages that cause heart attacks.[596] In addition, these procedures often are risky, disfiguring and expensive. Based on the virtually 100 percent success that Dr. Esselstyn had in halting or reversing heart disease with whole food, plant-based diets, he suggests that patients often should try 12 weeks of arrest-and-reverse plant-based nutrition therapy, and cholesterol-reducing drugs if necessary, before undergoing mechanical interventions.[597]

Bypass surgery and angioplasty cost about $110,000 and $60,000, respectively. But in *The China Study*, Dr. Campbell points out that the year-long diet and lifestyle intervention program used successfully by Dr. Ornish to halt and reverse heart disease only cost $7,000.[598] This illustrates another way that switching to whole food, plant-based diets would substantially lower healthcare costs, while greatly improving quality of life for many people.

Drug companies are structurally required to maximize profits and shareholder returns. They do this in part by heavily promoting drugs to doctors and citizens. Rather than making people sick with unhealthy foods and treating illness, the vastly superior strategy from a cost, quality of life and social well-being perspective is to prevent illness. But this often would lower the financial returns of drug company shareholders. As a result, through inappropriate government influence and public deception, drug companies, politicians paid by them and other allies often strongly and successfully oppose what clearly is the best option for society.

Only government can ensure that businesses do what is best for society. Unfortunately, as long as we allow business to control government, it may be difficult to refocus government on serving the people instead of the small group that gives the most money to politicians.

Prior to the implementation of democracy and capitalism in the US, citizens often will be on their own. They must protect themselves and their children, frequently without the support of government. In terms of vastly lowering or eliminating chronic disease risk, the most important action that citizens can take often is switching to whole food, plant-based diets.

Diet

Through visual images and other nonverbal messages, advertising and media often strongly promote the idea that thinner people are more attractive, successful and popular. At the same time, nearly three-quarters of adults and one-third of teenagers in the US are obese or overweight. As discussed in the Advertising, Media and Culture section, obese and overweight people often receive powerful reminders that their appearance is suboptimal. This helps to create a strong focus, even obsession, with dieting in the US and some other developed countries.

Annual diet industry sales are over $60 billion in the US. About 75 million people are estimated to be on diets. About 80 percent of them try to lose weight by themselves.[599] Dieting often increases the shareholder returns of pharmaceutical, food and other companies. But dieting largely does not work. About two-thirds of dieters regain all their lost weight within one year. About 97 percent regain the weight within five years.[600] A review of 31 long-term studies found that about half of dieters regain more weight than they lost within five years.[601] Diet drugs can produce temporary weight loss. But the drugs sometimes have severe side effects. In addition, lost weight nearly always returns once people stop taking diet drugs.[602]

The survival instinct is strong in humans. Various physiological and psychological processes related to survival contribute to diets nearly always failing. For example, the human body evolved to survive during lean times. Within 24 to 48 hours of sensing reduced food intake, the body's metabolism rate slows by 15 to 30 percent. This helps the body to conserve energy during famine or lean times.[603] Dieting often involves intentional self-deprivation. The body interprets this as famine and slows weight loss.

The body requires a certain level of calories to survive and remain healthy. As a result, excessive calorie restriction rarely produces long-term weight loss. Through physiological and psychological processes, people usually are compelled to end restricted food consumption and thereby often regain lost weight. Many fad diets, such is the high animal protein, low carbohydrate Atkins and South Beach diets, sometimes produce short-term weight loss, usually through calorie restriction. But these diets rarely achieve long-term weight loss. For example, no study has shown that the Atkins diet maintains weight loss for more than one year. Two studies found that weight loss stalls or reverses after six months.[604] In addition, as discussed in previous sections, high animal protein diets substantially increase the risk of heart disease, cancer and other chronic diseases. Dr. Campbell notes that high animal protein, low carbohydrate diets may be the single greatest threat to public health.[605]

The widespread failure of dieting causes many people to cycle between weight loss and weight gain. This cycling of weight often is worse than remaining overweight. Cycling weight substantially increases the risk of heart disease, type 2 diabetes and other health problems.[606] Calories are burned mostly by muscle. Virtually every dieting weight loss involves loss of muscle and fat. As a result, less muscle is available to burn calories. This makes it easier to regain weight. After dieting, weight often is regained mainly as fat. As a result, repeated dieting and weight cycling often substantially reduce muscle mass and increase the percentage of body fat.[607]

Beyond being ineffective and increasing chronic disease risk, dieting frequently causes many other problems. For example, dieters are eight times more likely to develop eating disorders. They often have higher levels of stress and depression than non-dieters. And dieters often feel shame about their appearance and repeated failure to maintain weight loss.[608]

Awareness that dieting rarely works and often increases health problems can cause some people to give up hope that weight loss is possible. Instead, they might resign themselves to being obese or overweight. But there is hope. The solution ultimately is simple – eat what we evolved to eat. Whole plant foods are the natural, optimal foods for humans. They minimize disease and maximize health, vitality and longevity.

In addition, plant-based diets are the only diets shown to consistently produce long-term weight loss. People can lose weight quickly by switching to whole food, plant-based diets and keep it off as long as they remain on the diet. Studies cited in *The China Study* show that vegetarians and vegans are 5 to 30 pounds lighter than meat eaters on average.[609] Meat eaters are three times more likely to be obese than vegetarians and nine times more likely than vegans.[610]

The China Study, Prevent and Reverse Heart Disease and many other books extensively discuss switching to whole food, plant-based diets. A main reason that these diets consistently provide long-term weight loss (when they are maintained) is that no calorie restriction is needed. Dieting usually involves restricting the consumption of unhealthy foods, such as animal products and refined carbohydrates. Rather than limiting the consumption of unhealthy foods, Drs. Campbell, Esselstyn and Ornish as well as many other nutrition experts suggest that people switch to healthy, whole plant foods and eat as much as they want. The body knows what to do when it gets the right food.

Some advocates of high-protein, animal product diets say that carbohydrates are unhealthy and fattening. The implication is that all carbohydrates are bad. This is highly deceptive. In the refined, processed form, carbohydrates often are stripped of nutrients and have high levels of fat, sugar and/or salt. As a result, refined carbohydrates usually are fattening and disease promoting. But whole, unprocessed, complex carbohydrates are highly nutritious. More than 99 percent of carbohydrates consumed by humans are derived from fruits, vegetables and grains.[611] These foods primarily are carbohydrates. However, in whole form, they contain many other important nutrients, such as fiber.

Fiber consumed in whole foods lowers heart disease, cancer and diabetes risk. It also can lower cholesterol levels, blood pressure, inflammation and blood sugar levels. Some experts believe that fiber can bind toxins and remove them from the body more quickly.[612] The Institute of Medicine suggests that men and women should eat 38 grams and 25 grams of fiber per day, respectively. However, the animal product and refined carbohydrate intensive US diet contributes to people eating only about 15 grams of fiber per day.[613]

Whole plant foods also often have high levels of vitamins, minerals, antioxidants and protein. In the whole, complex form, carbohydrates are the healthiest foods humans can eat. It would be difficult to be overweight, much less obese, while eating a whole food, plant-based diet. The fiber in whole plant foods makes people feel full and limits overeating. Fiber has virtually no calories. As a result, people often can eat more food, but consume fewer calories. The high levels of nutrients in whole plant foods produce satisfaction, which also limits overeating. Dr. Campbell notes that people should not feel hungry on a whole plant food diet. If they feel hungry, they are not eating enough or the right types of whole plant foods. People generally can eat as much whole plant food as they want without gaining weight.[614]

However, there are limits. If people ignore physical fullness and satiation signals, perhaps because they are eating to suppress emotions, and consistently consume more calories than their bodies burn, they could gain weight or remain overweight. But this is much less likely to occur if people are overeating whole plant foods with no added sugars or fats. As noted, these foods contain abundant fiber and other nutrients. They produce strong senses of fullness and satiation that would be difficult to ignore or consistently override.

People in rural China eat about 30 percent more calories than people in the US. But they weigh about 20 percent less when adjustments for body size, age, activity levels and other non-dietary factors are made. Dr. Campbell explains why people on whole plant food diets can eat more calories and food, but weigh less. People who consume high-fat, high animal protein diets tend to store more calories as body fat. People who consume plant-based diets have slightly higher resting metabolism rates.[615] Resting metabolism accounts for about 70 percent of calories burned by the body.[616] Rather than storing calories as fat, people on whole plant food diets tend to burn calories to keep the body warm, run metabolic processes and encourage physical activity.[617] As discussed in the Cancer section, rats fed less animal protein voluntarily exercised more.

Once again, the key is eating whole plant foods. It is possible to be a vegetarian or vegan and still consume an unhealthy, obesity-promoting diet. Dr. Campbell uses the term junk food vegetarian to describe such diets.[618] Junk food vegetarians might consume high levels of dairy products, such as ice cream and pizza, as well as sugar, fat and salt-laden refined carbohydrates. Junk food vegans might eat high levels of sugar, fat and salt-laden refined carbohydrates. Eating high-fat diets often causes the body to manufacture excess cholesterol. This helps to explain why vegetarians and vegans can have high cholesterol levels and get heart disease.[619] As discussed, Dr. Esselstyn suggests that people who wish to prevent or reverse heart disease get no more than 10 percent of calories from fat and avoid all added fats and oils. High-fat foods are calorie dense. Fat has nine calories per gram. Carbohydrates and proteins only have four calories per gram.[620] This further explains why high-fat refined carbohydrates and animal products strongly promote obesity.

A key element of healthy eating and maintaining a healthy weight is avoiding processed foods to the greatest extent possible. Instead, people should eat all or nearly all whole plant foods. The simplest of nature's creations essentially is infinitely more sophisticated and complex than the most advanced human creations and technologies. This applies to food. Anatomically we evolved to eat raw plant foods. Fruits, vegetables and other natural whole plant foods are highly complex. They are the perfect food for humans. Humans did not evolve to eat whole grains. But cooked whole grains essentially are rehydrated plant products. They are much more similar to our natural, evolved foods than animal products. In addition, extensive research shows that whole grains, along with fruits and vegetables, are the healthiest foods for humans.

Processed foods once again illustrate massive human myopia. These foods are not designed to exclusively maximize human health, as our evolved, natural foods implicitly are (because we evolved with and adapted to them). Processed foods are designed in large part to facilitate centralized production and distribution. Chemicals and other additives are used extensively to enhance the bland taste of processed foods and extend shelf lives. These foods usually are vastly different from those we evolved to eat. As a result, they often strongly promote disease, low energy levels, obesity and poor health.

Food production illustrates the flaws of our economic systems. Publicly traded food companies are structurally required to put maximizing shareholder returns before all other factors. They ultimately will die if they do not do this. Companies often maximize shareholder returns by creating many new processed food and supplement products.

The widespread sale of vitamins and other food supplements illustrates myopia in the food area. Humans evolved to get vitamins and other nutrients from whole foods. Vitamins operate with thousands of other natural chemicals in foods through essentially infinitely complex processes that provide maximal benefits to humans. It is extremely simplistic and myopic to think that isolating a particular vitamin or other nutrient and taking it in pill form would provide the same benefits as nutrients consumed in whole foods.

Many studies have shown that vitamins and other nutrient supplements frequently provide no health benefits.[621] Several studies have found that taking too many vitamins in supplement form can increase disease risk. For example, one study found that taking regular beta carotene supplements increased the risk of death from lung cancer by eight percent. Another found that vitamins C and E increased the risk of premature death among older women. Yet another found that vitamins A, C, E and beta carotene could increase bladder cancer risk by 50 percent. A different study found that vitamin E supplements increased prostate cancer risk by 17 percent.[622]

The National Institute of Health does not suggest that people take vitamins or supplements. Instead, it recommends speaking with a doctor before taking them. But extensive marketing has contributed to over half of adults in the US taking them, in spite of many studies showing that they are ineffective or harmful.[623] Many people take vitamins and other supplements to complement unhealthy diets. But Dr. Campbell notes that the dangers of the animal product intensive US diet cannot be overcome by consuming nutrient pills.[624]

Animal products and crops grown in dead industrial agriculture soil often lack vitamins and minerals. People who mainly eat animal products and refined carbohydrates might get some benefit from supplements. But the benefits are far greater from consuming whole plant foods. Dr. Campbell points out that vitamins A, D and B12 often are more available in animal products that in plant products. However, if people eat healthy whole plant foods and live healthy lifestyles, they can get adequate amounts of these vitamins.

The body makes vitamin A from beta-carotene, which is widely available in many vegetables. It makes enough vitamin D when people are in the sun for about 15 minutes every couple of days. And plants grown in healthy soil, such as organic vegetables, often have adequate levels of vitamin B12. However, Dr. Campbell suggests that vegans who do not get enough sunshine might need a low dose vitamin D supplement. Also, vegans who eat conventional (i.e. industrial) produce may need a vitamin B12 supplement.[625]

Vitamins and supplements can be beneficial when taken under the advice of a doctor or other health expert. However, citizens who are not health experts and are taking vitamins and other supplements without expert guidance (i.e. self-prescribing) could try weaning themselves off of supplements. If they are eating abundant organic whole plant foods, they probably often will not feel any difference, except in their wallets. Based on numerous studies showing potential adverse effects of supplements, they might feel better if they get nutrients from whole plant foods instead of pills.

The health risks of processed food apply to organic processed foods as well. As sales of organic food increased, many large food companies got into the organic food business. They often develop organic food products using similar processes to those used to make non-organic processed food. While processed organic food frequently might be marginally healthier than conventional processed food, it suffers from many of the same nutritional problems. For example, processed organic food often has high levels of fat, sugar and/or salt. It also often has high levels of MSG, which promotes overeating and obesity.

The widespread use of soy in conventional and organic processed food illustrates the risks of these foods. In the West, soybeans traditionally were grown mainly for producing soy oil, which is used in vegetable oil, margarine and shortenings. The soy protein left over from soy oil processing was used exclusively as animal feed. But feeding too much soy to animals causes serious reproductive and other health problems. To more fully utilize the byproducts from soy processing, the soy industry began marketing this material as a food for humans. But excess soy can cause reproductive and other health problems in humans, as it does in animals.

An excellent book by Dr. Kaayla Daniel, called *The Whole Soy Story*, describes extensive research showing health problems caused by soy. Dr. Daniel also discusses how processed soy was effectively marketed as a healthy food.[626] Small amounts of soy traditionally were eaten in many Asian countries in fermented forms, such as miso and tempeh. Fermentation limits the harmful effects of soy and can provide some health benefits. Much larger amounts of soy often are consumed in the US and many other developed countries in unfermented forms. For example, people in Asia consume an average of 9 to 36 grams of soy per day.[627] But one cup of soy milk or tofu contains over 200 grams of unfermented soy.

Consuming large amounts of unfermented soy can cause allergic reactions, digestive problems, reproductive problems and many other health problems. Soy left over from oil processing is not appetizing. Large amounts of sugar, salt and MSG often are used to make soy palatable for humans. In addition, the soy used in processed food usually is highly processed itself. Hexane and other toxic chemicals frequently are used to process soy. Also, most soy sold in the US is genetically-engineered. As discussed in the Genetic Engineering section, limited independent research has been conducted on GE soy. Some independent studies have shown that GE soy causes reproductive and other health problems. Soy left over from oil processing is inexpensive. This contributes to soy being included in about 75 percent of processed foods sold in the US. Soy often is contained in ingredients with names that do not indicate soy content, such as textured vegetable protein, hydrolyzed vegetable protein, lecithin, bouillon and vegetable oil.

Soy contains high levels of isoflavones, an antioxidant that can boost immunity. But isoflavones are phytoestrogens (plant estrogens). They often act like estrogen in the human body. As a result, women sometimes consume soy products to ease the symptoms of menopause. But consuming high levels of plant estrogens can cause many problems. For example, consuming soy while pregnant can increase estrogen levels and negatively impact the brain and reproductive development of children in utero.[628] Several studies have shown that soy formulas can harm infants. Infants consuming them can get the estrogen equivalent of taking three to five birth control pills per day.[629]

A study published in the journal The Lancet found that giving soy formula to girls could cause early puberty and increase the risk of obesity, breast cancer and other reproductive cancers. Feeding soy formula to infants could cause negative impacts that do not become obvious until puberty. For example, feeding high levels of the plant estrogens in soy formula to infant boys could delay puberty, increase the risk of testicular cancer and infertility,[630] and promote the development of breasts and smaller penises when boys reach puberty.[631] Animal and human studies have shown that the plant estrogens in soy can lower testosterone levels in males. This can cause reduced libido and sperm counts. In men and women, soy can affect the thyroid in ways that cause weight gain, reduced sex drive, lethargy and depression.[632]

The FDA claims that soy can provide health benefits, such as lowering cholesterol. But many experts claim that the FDA's endorsement of soy is heavily influenced by business. For example, the FDA based its position almost completely on industry-funded research, and appeared to ignore many studies which showed that soy caused allergic reactions, hormone disruption and other health problems. In addition, the FDA appeared to disregard concerns expressed by FDA scientists about the negative health impacts of soy.[633]

As more people switch to plant-based diets, many meat substitutes have been developed using soy ingredients such as textured vegetable protein. These soy-based meat substitutes eliminate many of the risks of animal product consumption. But they present their own set of health risks. Soy-based meat substitutes are highly processed, unnatural foods. Rather than eating processed fake meat products, it would be much healthier to eat whole plant foods.

Soy vested interests and their allies sometimes argue that there is no conclusive proof that soy causes reproductive and other health problems. But this is an irrelevant argument used to mislead the public and protect shareholder returns. The implication is that we should continue consuming large amounts of unfermented processed soy until we are nearly 100 percent certain that it is harmful. This illustrates Wrong Perspective and Wrong

Reference Point logic. Processed soy (and all other processed foods) should not have been approved until there was conclusive independent research showing that it was safe. But the business-dominated US government did not require this. We should not wait until we are 99 percent certain that processed soy feminizes boys and men or increases cancer risk in girls and women before banning or restricting it. As noted, the appropriate trigger point for protecting our children and ourselves may be 10 to 20 percent certainty that harm exists. Based on current research showing the harmful effects of processed soy, we probably are well past the 10 to 20 percent trigger point.

The term conventional produce and food is misleading. It implies a level of safety and healthiness that this food often does not deserve. Conventional produce frequently has high levels of pesticides and low levels of vitamins and minerals. Conventional processed foods often contain unhealthy ingredients such as MSG. It would be more accurate and honest to refer to this food as industrial produce and food.

For most of human history, conventional foods were whole foods that came from nature and farms. Over the past 60 years, industrial highly-processed foods have become conventional. But that does not mean that these foods are safe and healthy. Humans literally are what we eat. Our food becomes the substance of our bodies. If we eat unhealthy, processed, chemical-intensive industrial foods, we often will become sick and die prematurely. The selection of whole plant products with little or no processing often is limited. However, as more people switch to whole food, plant-based diets, food companies will develop and market healthier foods.

The USDA food guidelines are dangerous and misleading. They appear to represent a compromise between protecting public health and protecting the shareholder returns of food companies. But there should be no compromises with public health. The people's representative (government) should advise non-expert citizens about healthy diets. But the USDA guidelines encourage people to eat high levels of unhealthy food.

Beyond the harmful fat and protein guidelines discussed earlier, the guidelines say that it is acceptable to eat up to half of grains in refined form. But these grains are stripped of nutrients. They promote diabetes and other diseases. The guidelines also say that people should consume dairy products regularly. But as discussed extensively, dairy products are not natural foods for humans. They strongly promote cancer and many other chronic diseases.

In addition, the guidelines say that people should consume less than 10 percent of calories as saturated fat and formerly implied that cholesterol should be limited to 300 mg per day.[634] This implies that it is acceptable and healthy to get up 10 percent of calories from saturated fat and to eat up to 300 mg of cholesterol per day. But humans do not need to get any of these nutrients from food. The body makes all the saturated fat and cholesterol it needs. Consuming these fats in food strongly promotes heart disease and other chronic diseases.

Perhaps the USDA and some experts believe that people can tolerate some unhealthy food without getting sick. This often is true. Many people live long, healthy lives while eating animal products, refined carbohydrates and other unhealthy foods. But many other people get sick and die prematurely from eating them. Food guidelines should advise people to eat only healthy foods. If people wish to ignore the guidelines, that is their choice. But non-expert citizens should not be misled into believing that unhealthy foods are healthy.

People often use a restrictive diet to lose weight, and then switch to a less restricted diet when they reach their target weight. This usually does not work because people often want to get off the restricted diet and onto the more satisfying, less restricted diet. Dr. Campbell states that the diet used to lose weight should be the same as that used to maintain optimal weight over the long-term. Successful, long-term weight loss and maintenance of a healthy weight is greatly facilitated by eating healthy food. Dieting should not be seen as temporary, but rather as a lifestyle change. People generally can eat as much whole plant food as they want and still lose weight. Some people might lose weight more slowly due to genetics or slower metabolism rates. But essentially all overweight people can lose weight on a whole plant food diet, especially if they do some exercise.

Some people and vested interests say that a whole plant food diet is radical. But about two-thirds of people around the world consume mainly plant-based diets and have much lower levels of chronic disease and obesity.

Dr. Esselstyn notes that the radical diet is not a plant-based diet. It is the animal product intensive Western diet that sickens and kills more people in the developed world than any other factor by far.

Many people enjoy animal products because excellent chefs spent years developing new recipes and making animal products taste good. But good chefs often can make nearly any food tasty. Plant products can be made to taste as good as animal products. They frequently taste better because the body senses the health and vitality coming from the food.

By switching to whole plant food diets, people can lose weight, have more energy and often have clearer minds, while greatly enjoying the pleasure of eating. There are many excellent books that help people to transition to whole plant food diets. The second half of *Prevent and Reverse Heart Disease* provides many delicious whole plant food recipes. As people make the transition to whole plant foods, it often is helpful to experiment and find new favorite meals as well as find restaurants that serve delicious whole plant foods.

Eating raw vegetables is particularly healthy and important because humans anatomically are raw food herbivores. Eating salad is one of the best ways to consume raw vegetables. But salads often are mostly air. If people chopped up a normal salad they usually would have only a small amount of vegetables by weight. In the book *Fit For Life*, Harvey Diamond notes that humans are about 70 percent water. As a result, he suggests that at least 70 percent of our diet by weight should be high water content foods (i.e. vegetables and fruits). Raw vegetables are the healthiest foods for humans. Therefore, they should represent a large percentage by weight of healthy diets.

One way to conveniently consume a large amount of raw vegetables on a daily basis is to regularly make large chopped salads containing many different vegetables. Chopping vegetables removes the air and makes salads denser. This facilitates eating larger quantities of raw vegetables by weight. A chopped salad will stay fresh in an airtight container in a cold refrigerator for a week or more. Then on most days, people can quickly prepare a large chopped salad. Using organic or locally grown vegetables whenever possible is preferable. But even salads made with conventional (i.e. industrial) vegetables are much healthier than animal products and refined carbohydrates.

Lifestyle

Achieving optimal health and life satisfaction requires maintaining a healthy lifestyle. Many lifestyle suggestions have been made in previous sections. To bring these and other suggestions together in one place, this section summarizes important actions needed to minimize chronic disease risk, maintain a healthy weight and maximize life satisfaction.

Exercise. For nearly all of human history, survival required extensive, often strenuous physical activity. Our bodies evolved to function best when we are physically active on a regular basis. The conveniences of modern society frequently reduce the need for regular physical activity. As a result, sedentary lifestyles should be supplemented with regular aerobic and anaerobic exercise.

Aerobic exercise is any type of exercise or activity that builds cardiovascular endurance, usually by elevating the heart rate for at least 30 minutes several times per week. Anaerobic exercise, such as weight training, increases short-term muscle strength. It also strengthens bones, joints and tendons. Almost any type of physical activity or work, such as house cleaning or yard work, could be considered beneficial exercise. One study found that regular exercise adds an average of seven extra years of life expectancy and increases the likelihood that people will be relatively trim and in good health.[635]

Many companies are improving productivity and lowering costs by providing financial incentives that encourage employees to lose weight, join a fitness program and/or get a medical exam. Obese employees often have higher rates of depression, absenteeism, low productivity and medical claims.[636] As a result, encouraging employees to adopt healthier lifestyles can substantially improve productivity and lower costs. One study found that employees who exercise more than three times per week have 44 percent lower medical costs than those who do not exercise.[637]

A Duke University study found that regular exercise was more effective at relieving depression than taking antidepressant drugs.[638] Exercise causes the brain to release serotonin, dopamine and other neurotransmitters. It often can regulate these substances more effectively than taking prescription drugs, while avoiding drug side effects.

Regular exercise is highly beneficial. But it sometimes is not enough to overcome a sedentary lifestyle. The average US adult spends about 50 to 70 percent of their time sitting. Even for people who regularly exercise, one study found that a sedentary lifestyle increases the risk of developing diabetes by 112 percent, heart disease by 147 percent and dying prematurely by 49 percent. Another study found that each hour of TV watching shortens life expectancy by 22 minutes. Therefore, in addition to regular exercise, it is important to periodically get up and move around, rather than sitting for extended periods.[639]

Stretching. Maintaining a flexible body minimizes injury and promotes optimal health. Cats and dogs frequently stretch throughout the day. They implicitly understand the benefits of regular stretching. Yoga is an excellent way to learn how to stretch and maintain flexibility. It also promotes increased strength, stress reduction, internal organ health, good posture and higher energy levels. Once people learn basic stretching exercises through yoga classes or other means, they can regularly stretch on their own. Even stretching for five to ten minutes per day, especially after exercising, can provide substantial health benefits.

Relaxation/Meditation. Many studies have shown that relaxation techniques such as meditation can significantly promote optimal health and healing. Meditation can substantially reduce stress, improve posture and provide many other physical benefits. In addition, as discussed below, meditation can provide immense psychological, emotional and spiritual benefits, such as increased ability to focus the mind, live in the present and access intuitive wisdom.

Be in Nature. Humans evolved in nature. It is our real home. We often instinctually or intuitively understand this when we are in nature. Regularly spending time in nature can provide immense physical, psychological, emotional and spiritual benefits.

Sleep with Windows Open. It generally is much healthier to breathe fresh, oxygen-rich air rather than stale, oxygen-depleted air while sleeping. If the air outside is cleaner than inside air and if windows can be opened without wasting energy (i.e. by turning off thermostats and closing well-sealed bedroom doors), it often is healthier to sleep with windows open.

Avoid Processed Foods. Processed foods are designed in part to facilitate centralized production and extended shelf lives. They often contain many harmful chemicals and other substances. Humans evolved to eat fresh, living foods. As a result, it can be highly beneficial to avoid dead processed foods to the greatest extent possible. In particular, it is beneficial to avoid processed foods that contain refined carbohydrates, high levels of fat, sugar and/or salt, preservatives and MSG in its many deceptively labeled forms.

MSG can remain in the body for several days. As a result, cravings for MSG-containing foods can continue even after people stop eating them for a few days. MSG strongly contributes to obesity and many severe neurological and other health problems. Most or nearly all restaurant and processed food contains MSG, including many organic processed foods. Conventional produce often is sprayed with products that contain MSG. One the best ways to avoid MSG is to eat organic produce and foods prepared at home with truly natural ingredients.

Avoid Animal Products. As discussed extensively, humans anatomically are raw food herbivores. In terms of the anatomical features that differentiate carnivores from herbivores, humans have virtually no similarities to carnivores and virtually no differences from herbivores. We did not evolve to eat meat or any other type of animal product, except for human milk when we are young. Many studies have shown that people who eat few or no animal products have low chronic disease rates. These diseases nearly always are substantially higher among those who eat larger amounts of animal products. People can survive by eating them. But they are not natural foods for humans. Therefore, avoiding animal products can substantially lower the risk of chronic disease and premature death.

Eat Whole Plant Foods. Also as discussed extensively, vegetables, fruits, whole grains and legumes are the optimal foods for humans. Consuming all or nearly all whole plant foods will maximize health, vitality and longevity. Vegetables in particular should comprise a large percentage by weight of daily diets. As noted, preparing and storing large chopped salads facilitates eating a large amount of raw vegetables on a daily basis.

Minimize Caffeine Intake. Coffee and black tea contain antioxidants that provide health benefits. Limited consumption of these beverages might have few negative health impact and some positive impacts. However, caffeine stimulates the adrenal glands to produce adrenaline. After this wears off, people can feel fatigue, irritability, headache or confusion. Excessive caffeine consumption can stress adrenal glands and cause other health problems.[640] As a result, finding alternatives to caffeinated beverages can promote improved health.

Ginger tea, for example, is an excellent, tasteful alternative. Natural ginger tea can be made by peeling and finely chopping ginger root, stirring it into hot water, and letting the tea brew for 10 minutes or longer. One half pound of ginger produces a gallon of inexpensive, tasty, very healthy tea that stays fresh for over a week when refrigerated. Ginger tea promotes improved digestion and blood circulation and provides many other health benefits.[641]

Eat Main Meal at Midday. Eating large amounts of food, especially unhealthy food, at night can promote obesity and other health problems. Eating the main or largest meal in the middle of the day whenever possible enables food to digest before going to bed. This can strongly promote weight loss, more rejuvenating sleep and improved health.

Eat at Structured Mealtimes. In the US, many people eat sugar, salt and fat-laden refined carbohydrates throughout the day. This strongly promotes the widespread obesity seen in the US. Obesity rates are lower in France, for example, in part because the French tend to eat at structured mealtimes.[642] Minimizing food grazing throughout the day can reduce obesity and make meals more enjoyable.

Eat Together. Eating throughout the day and several other factors contribute to many families frequently not eating meals together. In addition, as discussed in the Advertising, Media and Culture section, the television usually is on during mealtimes in 63 percent of US homes. As a result, even when families eat together there often is little communication because people are watching TV. Eating together and communicating without the television on strengthens families and teaches children social skills. As discussed by social scientist Janet Flammang, during family meals, children learn the art of conversation and acquire the habits of civility. These include sharing, listening, taking turns, navigating differences and arguing without offending.[643]

Minimize Television and other Cyberworld Activities. As discussed in the Real World vs. Cyberworld section of *Global System Change*, the greatest life success and satisfaction often results from face-to-face relationships in the real world. In the US, people watch about four hours of TV per day on average. In addition, they often spend hours on social media, playing video games, surfing the Internet or engaging in other cyberword activities. These activities can provide many benefits. But spending excessive time in the cyberworld can substantially degrade life satisfaction if it distracts people from the real world. Life satisfaction often can be enhanced by minimizing TV watching and other cyberworld activities, while engaging in more real world activities, such as being in nature, playing sports and spending time with family, friends and community members.

Support the Local Food Economy. As discussed in the Food Solutions section, if all real, relevant costs were included in prices, locally produced food often would be less expensive than industrial/conventional food. Supporting and consuming locally grown and produced food not only helps the local economy, it also strengthens communities and friendships. Food author Michael Pollan notes that there are over 5,000 farmers' markets in the US. Beyond selling food, these markets often provide a rich and appealing community experience. People frequently sell crafts, local performers play music and children often are playing throughout the market. One study found that people have about ten times as many conversations at a farmers' market as they do at a supermarket.[644] Supporting farmers' markets, food cooperatives, locally-owned restaurants and other locally-owned businesses protects and strengthens the local economy, community and environment (if food is produced sustainably).

Follow Your Heart. As discussed below, humbly making one's conscious mind the servant of deeper, wiser, intuitive guidance is critical to achieving a successful and satisfying life. Deep passion, bliss or excitement strongly indicates intuitive wisdom. From the available options, choosing and acting on the most exciting one with integrity in the present moment produces the most successful and satisfying life. While this might not always be the easiest path, it often leads people through a series of deeply fulfilling life experiences.

Practice Gratitude and Acceptance. People generally get more of what they focus on. If they focus on the negative, the negative will expand. If they focus on positive, it will expand. This is why practicing gratitude is a key component of a satisfying life. Being grateful for the good things in one's life tends to expand and bring more good things. Acceptance also is a key component of a satisfying life. People often cannot control others or external events. Focusing on things that one cannot control is a waste of time and energy. Through acceptance, people accept things that they cannot control and focus on those they can – their own thoughts and actions in the present moment.

Practice the Golden Rule. Treating other people the way one wishes to be treated probably is the most important action needed to have good relationships and a harmonious life. Treating other people with kindness, love and respect is the most important commandment or suggestion of virtually all of the world's great religions. This is the practical aspect of spirituality. Probably more than any other action, it will create Heaven on Earth (i.e. sustainability and real prosperity).

Whole Plant Food Benefits

Many benefits of switching to whole plant food diets have been discussed in previous sections. To bring them together into one place, this section summarizes previously discussed health benefits as well as a few others that were not mentioned earlier.

Prevent and Reverse Chronic Disease. Chronic diseases are by far the largest killer of humans in the developed world. More than 75 percent of people in the US die of heart disease, cancer or other chronic diseases. As discussed extensively in *The China Study* and *Prevent and Reverse Heart Disease*, groups of people who eat mainly plant-based diets nearly always have low chronic disease rates. As animal product consumption increases, chronic disease rates nearly always rise rapidly. As the main driver of many chronic diseases, eating animal products is the largest killer of humans in the developed world by far.

Overwhelming evidence from international and other studies shows that switching to whole plant food diets can substantially lower the risk of heart disease, breast cancer, prostate cancer, colorectal cancer, other cancers, diabetes, stroke, autoimmune diseases, osteoporosis, arthritis, Alzheimer's disease and many other chronic diseases. Whole food, plant-based diets also can reduce cholesterol and lower blood pressure as well as often reverse many chronic diseases.

Dr. Campbell notes that whole plant foods have many positive impacts on human health and no negative ones when adjustments are made for individual differences such as allergies. Whole plant foods positively impact virtually all chronic diseases. This strongly indicates that they are the optimal foods for humans. Animal products, on the other hand, strongly promote heart disease, cancer and many other chronic diseases. This strongly shows that they are suboptimal foods for humans.

Limit Harmful Gene Expression. As discussed in *The China Study*, genetics play a major role in cancer and many other chronic diseases. Nearly everyone has cancer-prone genes in their bodies, for example, due to genetic predisposition or exposure to carcinogenic chemicals or radiation. But cancer-prone genes and other potentially harmful genes generally will not grow or be expressed unless they have the proper environment. Nutrition is the main environmental factor that determines the activity of genes in the body. Extensive research by Dr. Campbell and many other experts shows that eating animal protein appears to create an ideal environment in the body for the initiation and promotion of cancer and other chronic diseases. Whole plant foods, on the other hand, create an environment that strongly suppresses these diseases.

Reduce Other Illnesses. In addition to reducing chronic disease risk, whole plant food diets can reduce the risk and occurrence of many other types of illnesses. This occurs for several reasons. Perhaps most importantly, whole plant food diets promote better health in general. Several studies have shown that eating whole plant foods strengthens the immune system.[645] This can reduce vulnerability to colds, influenza, allergies and other illnesses. In addition, eating whole plant food diets can greatly reduce the risk of urinary track infections (UTI's). As noted, E. coli causes about 90 percent of UTI's. People get E. coli mainly from eating contaminated meat and poultry.

Reduce COVID-19 Risk. By strengthening the immune system and promoting better health in general, whole plant food diets can substantially reduce COVID-19 risk. A study of healthcare workers found that those who consumed plant-based or plant and fish-based diets had 73 percent and 59 percent lower risk of contracting moderate or severe COVID-19, respectively. Those who consumed low carbohydrate, high protein diets (including animal products) had 48 percent higher risk of contracting moderate to severe COVID-19. The greatest COVID-19 risk reduction occurred with plant-based diets.[646]

Avoid Surgery and Prescription Drug Use. In many ways, food is the best medicine. As discussed in *Prevent and Reverse Heart Disease*, switching to a whole plant food diet can substantially reduce or eliminate heart disease, and thereby substantially reduce or eliminate the need for angioplasty, bypass surgery and other types of surgery.

In addition, switching to a whole plant food diet can substantially reduce or eliminate the need for prescription drugs. For example, as discussed in the Diabetes section, many people with type 2 diabetes were able to end insulin use by switching to whole plant food diets. Prescription drugs sometimes have severe side effects. Rather than eating foods that frequently raise blood pressure and cholesterol levels (i.e. animal products), for example, and then taking potentially harmful drugs, it often would be more effective and life-enhancing to eat foods that promote low cholesterol levels, optimal blood pressure and improved blood vessel health (i.e. whole plant foods).

Lose Weight and Maintain a Healthy Weight for Life. As discussed in the Diet section, plant-based diets are the only ones shown to consistently produce long-term weight loss. People can lose weight quickly by switching to whole food, plant-based diets and keep it off as long as they remain on them. Meat eaters are three times more likely to be obese than vegetarians and nine times more likely than vegans. Fat, sugar and salt-laden refined carbohydrates strongly promote obesity and poor health. However, whole plant foods strongly promote good health and long-term maintenance of a healthy weight.

Live Longer. Many studies have shown that whole plant foods slow the aging process and enable people to live longer. Animal products, on the other hand, can accelerate the aging process and shorten people's lives. Several studies of people who live longer than 100 years have found that vegetarianism is one of the most common and important characteristics promoting long lives.[647]

Whole plant foods slow the aging process through several mechanisms. For example, free radicals accelerate aging and promote heart disease, cancer, osteoporosis, Alzheimer's disease, and many other life restricting diseases and health problems. Fruits and vegetables contain antioxidants and other substances that suppress free radicals and slow the aging process. Animal products promote the expansion of free radicals. Through this mechanism, they can accelerate the aging process. Animal products also promote inflammation, which can accelerate aging. Fruits and vegetables have anti-inflammatory properties that slow the aging process.[648]

Several studies also have shown that reduced calorie intake can extend the life of normal human cells and inhibit the growth of precancerous cells.[649] Many animal studies have shown that calorie restriction without malnutrition (i.e. not excessive calorie restriction) improves age-related health and slows the aging process.[650] Whole plant foods often contain abundant fiber, which has virtually no calories. As a result, people frequently can eat more whole plant foods while consuming fewer calories. This healthy form of calorie restriction illustrates another mechanism by which whole plant foods potentially can slow the aging process and extend life.

Improve Cognitive Function and Brain Health. A study published in the British Medical Journal found that children who later became vegetarians by the age of 30 had an IQ that was five points above average.[651] The higher IQ might indicate a greater tendency to think about the health benefits of a vegetarian diet, and make the transition based on this rational assessment.

Whole plant foods promote improved mental acuity, cognitive function and brain health through many different mechanisms. As discussed in the Brain Diseases section, animal products promote cognitive impairment and dementia by increasing free radicals in the body. In addition, they often have high levels of cholesterol and saturated fat that clog blood vessels supplying the brain. Whole plant foods have high levels of antioxidants that suppress free radical damage. In addition, they help to keep blood vessels clear, flexible and healthy, which further supports optimal cognitive function and brain health.

As discussed in the Obesity section, obese people are nearly 300 percent more likely to develop dementia than people who are not overweight. Several mechanisms potentially help to explain this link. For example, a US study of over 700 adults found that people with more fat around the midsection had smaller brains, a factor that is linked to dementia. In addition, increased fat around the central organs is associated with increased blood pressure, cholesterol and diabetes rates, all of which are major risk factors for dementia.[652] A whole food, plant-based diet is the most effective way to avoid or end obesity and maintain a healthy weight over the long-term. Given the strong link between obesity and dementia, using a whole food, plant-based diet to maintain a healthy weight can support optimal cognitive function and brain health. US Founder and patriot Benjamin Franklin said, a vegetarian diet provides a "greater clearness of head and quicker comprehension".[653]

Maintain Good Vision. Animal products increase free radicals and restrict blood vessels. As discussed in the Vision section, this promotes macular degeneration, cataracts and other eye diseases and problems. Whole plant foods suppress free radical damage and protect blood vessels. This protects vision, especially in the later years of life.

Prevent and Reverse Impotence. As discussed in the Impotence section, the saturated fat, cholesterol and inflammatory properties of animal products can restrict blood vessels and contribute to erectile dysfunction. By maintaining the health of blood vessels and other body parts, whole plant foods can help to prevent and reverse ED.

Reduce High Blood Pressure. As discussed in the High Blood Pressure section, this condition is a main risk factor for heart disease, stroke and many other health problems. Diet usually is the main lifestyle factor causing high blood pressure. The saturated fat, cholesterol and inflammatory properties of animal products strongly promote high blood pressure. Salt, fat and sugar-laden refined carbohydrates also strongly promote it. Overeating these unhealthy foods is a main cause of obesity, which in turn is a main cause of high blood pressure. Eating whole plant foods strongly promotes long-term maintenance of healthy weight, healthy blood vessels, and reduced, healthy blood pressure levels.

Improve Attractiveness and Look Younger. Free radicals promoted by animal products accelerate aging of the skin and other body parts. The antioxidants in fruits, vegetables and other whole plant foods suppress free radical damage. This supports more youthful looking skin and a more youthful appearance in general.

A study published in the journal Evolution and Human Behavior found that eating fruits and vegetables made people look more attractive. Eating fruits and vegetables that contain carotenoids produces a healthy golden skin color. Carotenoids are natural pigments that are largely responsible for the red, yellow and orange colors of fruits and vegetables. They also are contained in many dark green vegetables. Most carotenoids are antioxidants.

As part of the attractiveness study, college students were asked to look at pictures of Caucasian faces with neutral skin tones, suntanned skin tones and skin tones produced by regularly eating fruits and vegetables. The students judged that people with skin tones caused by carotenoid-rich diets looked healthier and more attractive. This suggests that people who wish to improve their skin tone and look more attractive should eat more fruits and vegetables rather than lying in the sun or using tanning booths. Tanning can cause skin damage and accelerate skin aging, in part by producing free radicals. Fruits and vegetables suppress free radical damage and provide more youthful looking skin, while also providing a more attractive skin tone. Eating carotenoid-rich fruits and vegetables can produce a visibly improved skin tone within two months.[654]

Improving skin tone by eating fruits and vegetables instead of using tanning booths also can reduce melanoma (i.e. skin cancer) risk. A study published in the journal Mayo Clinic Proceedings found an eightfold increase in melanoma among young women and a fourfold increase among young men from 1970 to 2009. The increase among young women in particular is attributed largely to increased use of tanning booths. They are classified as a human carcinogen in the same category as smoking. Tanning booths can provide seven times as much UV radiation as the sun. Teenagers and young adults are more vulnerable to tanning booth damage.[655] By eating more fruits and vegetables, teenagers and adults can improve attractiveness, protect their skin and reduce cancer risk.

Keep Inside of Body Clean. Most people are diligent about keeping the outside of their bodies clean. But in many ways, it is more important to keep the inside clean. The human digestive system did not evolve to eat animal products, refined oils and fat-laden refined carbohydrates. These foods have little or no fiber. They often accumulate in the many turns and pouches of the relatively long human digestive tract, and thereby promote chronic diseases and other health problems.

Whole plant foods, on the other hand, often contain little fat and large amounts of fiber. These foods move easily through the digestive tract and often clean out toxins and other accumulated material along the way. Eating animal products and fat-laden refined carbohydrates is like rolling around in a mud puddle or walking into one's home with a bucket of dirt and throwing it on the living room floor. Regularly eating all or nearly all whole plant foods is like cleaning the inside of the body on a daily basis.

Prevent and Reverse ADHD. ADHD is a large and growing problem in the US and many other developed countries. As discussed in the Children's section, about 10 percent of children and teenagers in the US have been diagnosed with ADHD. Many children, teenagers and adults take Ritalin, Adderall or other stimulant drugs to treat ADHD symptoms. These drugs sometimes have severe side effects. The long-term cognitive and health impacts are unknown. Rather than taking potentially harmful, mind-altering drugs during critical childhood and teenage development years, ADHD often can be prevented or reversed by eating whole plant foods. Since the 1970s, many studies have shown that processed foods which contain chemical food dyes and other additives contribute to ADHD. In one study, two-thirds of children diagnosed with ADHD lost their symptoms when they were switched from processed foods to whole foods.

Teach Children Lifelong Healthy Eating Habits. As discussed in the Obesity section, feeding children animal products and sugar, fat and salt-laden refined carbohydrates often conditions them to a lifetime of over-eating, obesity and vastly increased chronic disease risk. Habits learned in childhood frequently last a lifetime. Feeding children all or nearly all whole plant foods teaches them to love these optimal foods. It conditions them to a lifetime of healthy eating, healthy weight, improved appearance, increased cognitive function and greatly reduced disease risk, all of which contribute to substantially improved life satisfaction.

Reduce Food Costs. Processed foods, especially when packaged as individual servings, and animal products often are more expensive than whole plant foods, especially when bought in bulk. The added chemicals and processing of processed foods frequently make them more expensive than whole plant foods, which have no chemicals and much less processing. Preparing whole plant food meals can be more time-consuming than buying processed or take-out foods. But it often is less expensive and nearly always is much healthier. By preparing large amounts of chopped salad, beans and rice, soups and other whole plant foods in advance, eating inexpensive, healthy meals can be quick and easy on most days of the week.

Feel Better and Have More Energy. Whole plant foods are the optimal foods for humans. As a result, it should not be surprising that eating all or nearly all whole plant foods causes people to feel better and have more energy. This occurs in part because they often have far fewer chronic diseases and other health problems. Fat and sugar-laden refined carbohydrates frequently cause blood sugar levels to rise and fall rapidly, which can cause people to feel energy-depleted. The complex carbohydrates in whole plant foods are absorbed more slowly into the bloodstream and have a more gradual effect on blood sugar levels. This enables higher and more consistent energy levels.

Athletic Performance

For more than 100 years, food companies, their allies and well-meaning researchers have convinced many people around the world that they must consume animal protein if they wish to grow big and strong. As discussed in the Plant Versus Animal Products section, some people in developing countries who eat mainly plant products do not grow as large as people in developed countries who eat animal products. But this largely is not caused by the failure to eat animal protein. It results primarily from not eating enough food in general, not eating well-balanced plant-based diets, illness and/or other factors.

In The China Study, Dr. Campbell found that greater protein intake was strongly linked to greater height and body weight. But as noted, 90 percent of the protein consumed in rural China is plant protein. Both plant and animal protein promote body growth.[656] The body does not utilize plant or animal protein directly. It breaks proteins down into constituent amino acids, and then reformulates them into human protein. The body must get eight essential amino acids from food. All vegetables, beans, grains, nuts and seeds contain protein and essential amino acids. Most whole plant foods contain all eight essential amino acids. Some plant products have high levels of all eight essential amino acids, such as soybeans, quinoa (a grain) and spinach. Other plant proteins have lower levels of one or two essential amino acids. However, by consuming a variety of plant products over one or two days, people can get all the essential amino acids and protein they need, provided that they are consuming enough calories. Meticulous meal planning or getting all eight essential amino acids in every meal is not necessary.

Regarding athletic performance, plant proteins and whole plant foods in general are far more likely to provide optimal performance for many reasons. Two important aspects of athletic performance are cardiovascular conditioning and strength. The cholesterol, saturated fat, inflammatory properties and free radical promotion of animal products often clog, harden and inflame blood vessels. This can severely restrict the ability to achieve optimal cardiovascular performance. Animal products also strongly promote heart disease, cancer and many other health problems. This can further restrict the ability to achieve optimal cardiovascular performance, especially as people get older. Whole plant foods, on the other hand, keep blood vessels clear, flexible and healthy, while also minimizing chronic diseases and other health problems. As a result, eating whole plant foods strongly supports achieving optimal cardiovascular performance.

Vegetarians tend to burn off more calories rather than store them as fat. As a result, people who eat whole plant foods generally have higher energy levels than those who eat animal products. As discussed in the Cancer section, rats fed low animal protein diets lived longer and were healthier on every measure than those that were fed high animal protein diets. In addition, rats on low protein diets voluntarily exercised twice as much. By providing increased energy levels, greatly reduced disease risk and vastly superior cardiovascular health, whole plant foods strongly support superior athletic performance, especially in sports that require excellent cardiovascular conditioning, such as running.

Regarding strength, the human body builds muscle from amino acids. They can be acquired from plant or animal protein. Some of the strongest animals in the world eat all or nearly all raw plants, such as elephants, rhinoceroses and gorillas. Humans anatomically are raw food herbivores. As a result, we can grow as big and strong by eating whole plant foods as we can by eating animal products. In some cases, animal products might promote faster muscle growth than plant products. This could be due in part to the added artificial hormones and natural hormones in meat, milk and other animal products.

Animals are higher on the food chain than plants. As a result, toxic chemicals tend to bioaccumulate in animal products. Meat, poultry, milk, eggs and fish nearly always have much higher chemical contamination than plant products. As noted, 80 to 90 percent of pesticide exposure results from eating animal products. Many of the chemical contaminants in animal products are actual or potential hormone disruptors. Chemicals that mimic hormones, along with the actual hormones in animal products, might promote faster muscle growth. In the same way that hormones are used to bulk up animals before slaughter, hormones and chemicals that mimic them in animal products also potentially can make humans larger. But there often is a big price to pay for promoting growth with these substances.

In addition to providing size and strength, animal products also greatly increase the risk of chronic disease, obesity and other health problems.

By eating whole plant foods, people can achieve their full genetic size and strength potential, while greatly reducing disease, obesity and other health risks. In addition, since whole plant foods support superior cardiovascular health, oxygen, energy and nutrients can be supplied to muscles more quickly, consistently and efficiently. This means that strength can be utilized more effectively during athletics and other physical activities.

As discussed in the Cancer section, people in the US usually eat far more protein than they need. Humans only need to consume about five to six percent protein as a percentage of calories. The recommended daily allowance is 10 percent of calories. This provides more than enough protein for most people, although athletes and bodybuilders might need to consume a little more. But they probably do not need to consume anywhere near 35 percent of calories as protein. As discussed in *The China Study*, consuming over 10 percent of calories as animal protein greatly increases the risk of heart disease, cancer, osteoporosis, Alzheimer's disease and many other health problems.[657] The 35 percent protein guideline established by the USDA strongly indicates inappropriate business influence of government. In this case, people literally are being killed to protect the shareholder returns of food companies.

Many bodybuilders and athletes consume protein powder supplements. But protein powder is a highly processed, unnatural food. As discussed in the MSG section, soy protein, whey protein, pea protein and virtually every other type of protein found in protein powder supplements contains MSG. This chemical promotes obesity, Alzheimer's disease, Parkinson's disease and many other health problems. Humans are not anatomically designed or evolved to eat animal protein or protein powder. Human health and athletic performance are maximized by eating the optimal foods for humans – whole plant foods.

As discussed in the Cancer section, increasing protein consumption above 10 percent of calories only causes cancer and other health problems when animal protein is consumed. Increasing plant protein above 10 percent of calories appears to have little or no health impact. As a result, bodybuilders and athletes can increase plant protein intake with little health risk. By eating whole plant foods, athletes and bodybuilders can improve cardiovascular health, have more energy and build strength, while greatly reducing obesity, chronic disease and other health risks. There is extensive information about effective and healthy vegan body building on the Internet.

Eating whole plant food is especially important for children. As discussed in the Heart Disease section, the animal product intensive US diet contributes to 70 percent of 12-year-old children in the US having fatty deposits in their arteries, a precursor to heart disease. By eating whole plant foods, children can reach their full genetic size and strength potential, while learning healthy lifetime eating habits and greatly lowering obesity and chronic disease risk.

Most professional athletes in the US eat animal products in part because of the animal product intensive US culture and the widespread misconception that eating them promotes optimal athletic performance. However, many leading athletes consume a vegetarian or vegan diet. Examples include Carl Lewis (Nine Olympic track and field gold medals), Desmond Howard (Heisman Trophy winner and Super Bowl MVP), Tony Gonzalez (leading NFL tight end), Robert Parish (leading NBA center), Bill Pearl (professional bodybuilder and four-time Mr. Universe), Mike Tyson (heavyweight boxing champion), Billie Jean King (tennis champion), Chris Evert (tennis champion), Martina Navratilova (tennis champion), Venus Williams (tennis champion), and Jack La Lanne (fitness movement founder). Carl Lewis said, "My best year of track competition was the first year I ate a vegan diet."[658]

Health Conclusion

Any part of the human body essentially is infinitely more sophisticated than the greatest human invention. In many ways, the body still is a mystery to us. For example, we do not know the causes or mechanisms of action of many diseases. Our heart, lungs and other internal organs function as silent friends giving us the gift of life. In return for this most precious gift, the least we can do is give our bodies what they want and need. They evolved in nature to eat whole plant foods. It may seem that we have separated ourselves from nature with our processed foods, homes and other creations. But we are no more separate than any other animal. Our minds make us different from other creatures. But our bodies are the same. They have not evolved in ways that make processed food the optimal food for humans.

Food is the most important factor affecting human health. This should not be surprising because our bodies are made of the food we eat. We evolved in tandem with whole plant foods. These are the optimal foods for us. As humans moved to colder regions, we ate animal products to survive. But our bodies did not evolve to become carnivores or omnivores. As noted, in terms of the anatomical features that differentiate carnivores from herbivores, we have virtually no similarities to carnivores and virtually no differences from herbivores. The only similarities we have to omnivores are to the parts that are adapted to eating plants, such as flat molars. Animal products are suboptimal foods for humans because we are anatomical herbivores.

Beyond animal products, we especially did not evolve to eat chemical-laden processed foods. Nature essentially is infinitely smarter than humans. We are not anywhere near smart enough to improve upon whole plant foods. Highly processed or genetically-engineered foods are vastly inferior to natural whole plant foods.

Eating animal products, processed foods and other unhealthy foods is by far the number one killer of humans in developed countries. As a result, switching to a whole plant food diet usually is by far the most important action that individuals can take to minimize chronic disease risk and maximize vitality, health and longevity. The cure to cancer, heart disease and other chronic diseases largely will not be treatment. It will be prevention. As discussed in *The China Study*, overwhelming scientific evidence shows that eating animal products and refined carbohydrates is the main driver of many chronic diseases. Rather than continuing to eat foods that cause chronic diseases and trying to develop drugs that treat (but often do not cure) these diseases, it would be far more logical, cost-effective and life-enhancing to stop eating disease-causing foods. It is like we are eating poison and searching for the antidote. The antidote is to stop eating the poison.

Eating tasteful foods is a major source of joy and comfort for many people. But there is much more to life than eating. It is hard to enjoy life when one has cancer, heart disease, dementia, vision loss, erectile dysfunction, amputated limbs or inability to engage in simple activities such as walking due to obesity. Once people reach these stages of poor health, they often wish they had changed their diets and implemented healthier lifestyles sooner. But it frequently is too late.

People do not have to wait until they suffer the consequences of eating animal products, refined carbohydrates and other unhealthy foods. They can switch to whole plant foods while they still are healthy. With two to three months of discipline and habit changing, people will discover that whole plant foods taste as good or better than animal products and processed foods. Ask an older person who quit smoking while they were young if they regret quitting. Probably to a person, they would say no. It is the same with whole plant foods. Once people switch and get used to well-balanced whole plant food diets and feel increased energy, health and well-being, they often will not turn back.

It can be difficult to switch to whole plant food diets. Animal products and processed foods in the US and many other developed countries are strongly promoted. They often are heavily subsidized and widely available. People are raised on animal products and misled into believing that they are healthy. This can make it more difficult to switch to whole plant foods. But millions of people have done it. The life-enhancing benefits are hugely worth it.

Changing culture and food production systems in ways that support healthy eating will greatly facilitate the transition to whole food, plant-based diets. These issues are addressed in the Food Deceptions and Food Solutions sections below. But first, Overeating, Hunger and Animal Welfare are discussed.

Overeating Causes and Solutions

Many aspects of diets and dieting have been discussed above. But people often find it difficult to change unhealthy eating habits or stop compulsive overeating. This section discusses the psychological causes of overeating, transitioning to healthy eating, and achieving life satisfaction.

Moderation

Some people believe that eating any food in moderation is safe. This is sometimes true and sometimes false. It is impossible to know in advance if a person can eat small amounts of unhealthy food, and still live a long, healthy life. There is overwhelming evidence that eating animal products and refined carbohydrates increases chronic disease risk. But not all people who eat these unhealthy foods get these diseases. It is better to eat smaller rather than larger amounts of unhealthy foods. This lowers disease risk. But the lowest risk strategy is to not eat any unhealthy food.

Moderation works for some people. Those who are not compulsive or addictive can eat small amounts of beef, ice cream, candy and other unhealthy foods without feeling compelled to eat more. But many people cannot do this. Moderation does not work for them. As noted, Dr. Kessler and other experts discuss how eating sugar, fat and salt-laden refined carbohydrates and other unhealthy foods leads to the formation of reward circuits in the brain, like the reward circuits that form in the brains of heroin addicts. Eating small amounts of unhealthy food can trigger these circuits and make it difficult to stop eating. The brain can develop new reward circuits, for example, related to delicious whole plant foods. But it takes some time to develop them. If people keep retriggering unhealthy food reward circuits, it will be more difficult to reprogram the brain.

In addition, it appears that addictive reward circuits might never fully disappear. This helps to explain why alcoholics can stop drinking for 30 years. Then after having a few drinks, they often quickly resume heavy, addictive drinking, as if they had never stopped. The same might be true with unhealthy foods. For people with addictive or compulsive traits, moderation frequently will not work.

Another problem with moderation is that people never lose their taste for unhealthy foods. Tastes, especially for unhealthy foods, partly are a function of habit. If people stop consuming unhealthy foods, their tastes or desire for these foods usually will go away, often within two to three months. However, the desire for highly unhealthy foods, such as ice cream, candy and other refined sugar products, can substantially decline in one to two weeks. But as soon as people eat these foods, reward circuits are retriggered and the desire reduction clock effectively is reset to zero.

Even if people successfully moderate their consumption of unhealthy foods, they often feel deprived. Their eating pleasure largely remains focused on unhealthy foods. This sense of deprivation can cause people to forgo moderation and overindulge.

If people stop eating unhealthy foods, it often is much easier to change tastes and find new favorite foods. If they largely shift their universe of food options to healthy whole plant foods, they give themselves the opportunity to realize the delicious nature of vegetables, fruits, whole grains and natural seasonings (i.e. truly natural spices and other seasonings, not 'natural flavors' which often contains MSG). As people find new favorite foods within the universe of healthy foods, there frequently is no sense of deprivation. Within the universe of healthy foods, there usually is no need to consciously moderate intake. The body naturally will moderate food intake by providing senses of fullness and satisfaction.

Dr. Esselstyn discusses additional problems with moderation in *Prevent and Reverse Heart Disease*. For example, moderating or reducing the consumption of animal products and added oils and fats slows the progression of heart disease, but does not stop it. In other words, moderation kills fewer people. But it still kills. Dr. Esselstyn advises people who wish to prevent and reverse heart disease to avoid all foods that are known to harm blood vessels, such as animal products and added fats. Eating even small amounts of oils and animal products can produce free radicals that damage blood vessels, the brain, eyes and other parts of the body.[659] Whole plant foods, on the other hand, restore and maintain the health of blood vessels and the rest of the body. Dr. Campbell points out that there are no negative impacts from eating a well-balanced whole food, plant-based diet that is adapted to individual characteristics, such as allergies.

Some doctors suggest moderating, rather than eliminating, the consumption of animal products, refined carbohydrates and other unhealthy foods. They often are concerned that people will not want to completely stop eating disease-promoting foods. But as Dr. Esselstyn says, this approach might not serve patients well. In effect, doctors are providing harmful information. Rather than leading patients to believe that eating some unhealthy food is healthy, doctors often might serve their patients better by advising them to eliminate unhealthy foods, and then provide assistance or guidance on how to do it.

Dr. Campbell notes that it often is difficult to avoid animal products in the US. He suggests that people not be too concerned about eating small amounts of them occasionally, for example, when eating at restaurants. Eating soup stock made with meat or some other animal product additive might be nutritionally irrelevant he suggests, although Dr. Esselstyn advises those trying to reverse heart disease to eat no animal products. Dr. Campbell points out that eating animal products occasionally might be more difficult than quitting completely. As discussed above, tastes for animal products often remain if they are eaten occasionally.

When people eat animal products, refined carbohydrates and other unhealthy foods, or feed them to their families, they literally are gambling with the health and lives of their loved ones and themselves. Perhaps they will be among the group of people who can eat unhealthy foods and nevertheless remain healthy. But perhaps they will not be in this group. The safest bet is to avoid unhealthy foods and learn to love healthy foods.

Believing that it is safe to eat any food in moderation often is not logical. One usually would not eat cyanide or other poisons in moderation. Animal products and refined carbohydrates effectively are slow acting poisons.

Even in small quantities, these foods will sicken and kill some people. Taking heroin or robbing banks in moderation would not be healthy or logical. Eating unhealthy foods in moderation also sometimes will be unhealthy, and therefore not logical.

Changing Habits

Previous sections summarized information from *The China Study*, *Prevent and Reverse Heart Disease* and many other sources. These showed that animal products and refined carbohydrates strongly promote obesity, heart disease, cancer, diabetes and other chronic diseases. Some of this information has been known for decades. Many obese and overweight people probably know that their eating habits are greatly increasing chronic disease and premature death risks, while lowering quality of life, for example, by restricting the ability to play with children, exercise, have an active sex life and engage in other life-enhancing activities.

This illustrates one of the most important aspects or problems of the human condition – the frequent inability to do what we want to do. For thousands of years, Buddhism and Hinduism have discussed how cravings for food, sex and other substances or activities essentially capture people and take away their freedom to do what they want. In discussing the human condition, the Bible says, "I do not understand what I do. For what I want to do I do not do, but what I hate I do" (Romans 7:15). Probably nearly everyone in the world at least sometimes does not do what they want to do. They are overcome by emotions or caught up in addictions, compulsive behavior or bad habits.

Once basic needs are met, one of the most important aspects of life satisfaction is learning to master or control one's mind. This gives people the freedom to do what they want in life. Most importantly, it gives them the freedom to choose to make the mind a servant of deeper wiser guidance. The mind is extremely complex. It is by far the least understood part of humans. As discussed in the Depression section, we do not even know if the mind is fully contained in the body. Many rigorous ESP and other experiments indicate that the mind extends beyond the body. The vast majority of people in the world believe that the mind or some non-physical part of humans continues in some form after physical death. It is impossible to prove that the mind does not extend beyond the body or continue after physical death. Therefore, anyone who states these positions as absolute facts is acting in an irrational and possibly fearful or egotistical manner (egotistical perhaps because they are unwilling to acknowledge that there are aspects of life which they cannot know or fully understand).

In one sense, the conscious mind is not the master of the individual. The mind frequently is receiving new information from outside and within, such as from intuitive inspirations and ideas. The conscious mind could be seen as a gatekeeper or mid-level manager. For those who wish to maximize life satisfaction, the primary responsibility of the conscious mind could be seen as accessing or perceiving deep intuitive wisdom. As discussed in the Raising Public Awareness section of *Global System Change*, this intuitive wisdom often is referred to as the wisdom of the heart or the inner word of God. Once the wisdom is brought to consciousness, the mind directs the individual to act and live their life based on it.

Referring to the conscious human mind as a mid-level manager obviously is a semantic or symbolic device. The mind also could be defined to include intuitive wisdom (i.e. all wisdom and knowledge on all levels everywhere). But nearly all of this wisdom is not conscious. Thinking of the mind as a mid-level manager promotes humility. This quality is critical to achieving life satisfaction. It places the conscious mind in a position of openness or receptivity to infinite wisdom. Each one of us is an infinitesimally small part of all that is or the cosmos. By humbly making our minds the servants of infinite wisdom, we open them to guidance that will place us in harmony with other people and nature and enable us to reach the highest possible levels of creativity, productivity and joy.

As discussed in the Advertising, Media and Culture section, the mind often is filled with other people's ideas and wisdom. Children frequently are not taught to seek, discern and apply the wisdom of their hearts. Instead, children and adults often are encouraged to blindly believe in myopic, unintentionally destructive religious, economic, political and social ideas.

Advertising and media convey ubiquitous, emotionally powerful, nonverbal messages that cause many people to feel inadequate and flawed. Abused or neglected children frequently believe on a deep, powerful, usually unconscious level that they are flawed and not worthy of having a good life.

These disruptive, often unconscious ideas produce inner turmoil or conflicts. As discussed in the Depression section, these conflicts could be thought of as conflicts between the head and the heart. Blind faith in myopic ideas and disempowering beliefs place people in conflict with their own inner wisdom. They frequently are not living authentic lives because they are guided by other people's well-intentioned, but harmful ideas. They are not being guided by the wisdom of their hearts.

The heart or intuitive wisdom is the master of one's life, whether one realizes it or not. People always will pay a price for failing to live an authentic, heart-led life. Head-heart conflicts and false ideas about life produce painful emotions, such as sadness, anger, loneliness, fear and boredom. Food or other addictive substances or activities often are used to quell or numb these painful emotions. This psychic pain or discomfort, and the head-heart conflicts that caused it, usually are the root causes of addictive or compulsive behavior.

Stressful situations and inner psychological conflicts possibly can effect brain chemistry and cause imbalances. In other words, brain chemical imbalances might be a symptom, rather than the root cause of addiction or compulsion. This probably is why taking psychiatric drugs often does not provide long-term relief from addictive or compulsive behavior. People probably will have little success in overcoming this behavior if they do not address inner conflicts and align their lives with the wisdom of their hearts.

Overeating and obesity sometimes result from bad habits or lack of information. There are no serious inner conflicts or addictive or compulsive behaviors. For these people, a cognitive approach to weight loss, such as that discussed below, can work. However, addictive or compulsive behaviors related to food are more than bad habits. Probably most obese people who are addictively or compulsively overeating know that their actions are harmful, risky and life-restricting. But they overeat anyway.

Many factors contribute to the high levels of addictive and compulsive overeating seen in developed countries. For example, two-thirds of the people around the world eat mainly plant-based diets, not by choice, but out of necessity. Plant-based foods usually are substantially less expensive and resource-intensive than animal products. As regions develop economically, people gain more food options. When incomes rise, they often eat more animal products in part because it is seen as a sign of prosperity and they have been misled into believing that animal products are healthy. Humans evolved in an environment of food scarcity. As a result, it frequently is difficult to resist the abundant food options available in developed countries. This contributes to compulsive or addictive overeating.

As noted, advertising and media strongly contribute to pervasive senses of emptiness in society. People often seek to fill this psychological or spiritual emptiness with food and other substances. This never works. People are constantly consuming and never satisfied. This also promotes addictive or compulsive overeating. In addition, as discussed in the Obesity section, reward circuits and brain chemistry triggered by unhealthy foods often compel people to overeat.

Addiction to food and other substances and activities is highly complex. The American Society of Addiction Medicine defines addiction as a specific biological phenomenon related to damaged reward circuits in the brain. However, the society also notes that addiction has psychological, social and spiritual components, in addition to biological components. Successful treatment often requires addressing all of these factors. Addressing only the potential biological aspects of addiction with prescription drugs rarely works.

Ultimately addiction or compulsive behavior is a psychological problem. People are not forced to overeat or engage in other addictions. Addiction related to damaged reward circuits is not a choice. But addictive behavior is. Damaged brain reward circuits and chemicals in food, such as MSG, can make it difficult to stop overeating. But addiction is tendency, not destiny. People can always choose to not overeat or engage in other addictive behaviors.

Ending addictive or compulsive behavior is an act of self-love. It often requires courage and a willingness to face the unknown. Overcoming addictive or compulsive behavior can be difficult, especially as people get older and more set in their ways. But it is not impossible. Millions of people have done it.

Overcoming addiction to alcohol, tobacco or drugs frequently is easier than overcoming addiction to food or sex. Humans do not need alcohol, tobacco or illegal drugs to survive. As a result, people can lose the desire to engage in these addictions. But the desire for food and sex is natural, normal and healthy. Without food, the individual dies. Without sex, humanity dies. Overcoming addictions to food or sex requires a sustained commitment and refocusing on healthier habits or activities.

The mind can make it difficult to overcome addictions. It often seeks the security of known habits or activities, even if they are destructive. It frequently tries to avoid the unknown future resulting from new behavior, such as ending addictions. The mind often rationalizes or creates many barriers to change, such as perfectionism (i.e. If I can't do it perfectly, I won't do it at all) or fear of success or failure.

Mastering or controlling the mind is one of the most important requirements for achieving life success and satisfaction. There are many techniques for mastering the mind and overcoming addictions. Options in the food and weight loss area include intuitive eating, cognitive-behavior therapy, strengthening healthy habits, Twelve Step programs and meditation. These are discussed in the following sections.

Intuitive Eating

An excellent article by psychotherapist Judith Matz, called *Why Diets Make You Fatter -- And What to Do About It*, discusses intuitive eating.[660] For over 25 years, Judith Matz has helped many clients achieve long-term weight loss with intuitive eating. But the goal of this type of eating is not weight loss. It is to develop a natural, anxiety-free relationship with food.

The process involves learning to identify natural, inner signals that tell when, what and how much to eat.

Children are born knowing how to eat. Infants cry when they are hungry and stop eating when they are full. But as children grow older, many factors restrict or suppress their ability to eat based on physical hunger signals. For example, scheduled meals in school and at home sometimes force children to eat when they are not hungry and prevent them from eating when they are hungry. Children sometimes are not allowed to eat food that they want. Food rules and structured mealtimes can separate people from their natural hunger cues.

Also, as people become more concerned about their appearance, they often begin dieting or restricting food intake. This inhibits the body's ability to self-regulate through natural hunger signals. In addition, people frequently use food to manage or suppress emotions. When this occurs, eating often is not tied to physical hunger or satiation. Emotional eating further distances people from their natural, intuitive hunger signals. Dieting or guilty feelings about food frequently produce anxiety, neediness and a sense of scarcity. This often leads to overeating and guilt, which leads to more overeating. If people feel that the next diet is coming soon, they frequently will overeat prior to the diet.

With intuitive eating, people learn to reconnect to their natural body signals. They learn to identify when they are hungry, what they want to eat and when they are full. They are encouraged to eat what they want when they want it based on their natural inner signals. The goal is to remove the sense of scarcity and deprivation that often leads to binging and overeating. This is replaced with a sense of abundance, which helps people to feel calm and satisfied. At first, people sometimes overeat when using this approach. But over time, as they listen to their inner signals, they are guided to eat the right amount of healthy food.

Once people improve their ability to eat based on inner signals, they are encouraged to address emotional eating. For example, people are encouraged to identify if they are eating when they are not physically hungry. They ask themselves, "what am I feeling? Why am I eating? Can I wait until I'm actually hungry?" If they cannot wait, people are encouraged to eat without any sense of guilt or self-judgment. Over time, they deal with the cause of their sadness, anger, loneliness or other unpleasant emotions, instead of overeating. Dealing with problems or situations that produce unpleasant emotions can resolve issues. This produces greater life satisfaction than temporarily numbing oneself with food.

A key aspect of intuitive eating is avoiding dieting because this produces the deprivation/binge/guilt cycle. Several studies have shown that intuitive eating is far more effective than dieting in achieving long-term weight loss. In one study, the dropout rate was 41 percent in the diet group compared to eight percent in the non-diet, intuitive eating group. Dieters achieved short-term weight loss and self-esteem improvement. But these results were not maintained after one year. The intuitive eating group largely was able to maintain weight loss and improved self-esteem over the long-term.

Judith Matz also discusses the advertising and media driven stigma attached to being obese or overweight. Unrealistic standards and expectations about appearance drive dieting, binging, guilt and obesity. The ideal size and appearance for each person varies based largely on genetics. Few people are meant to look like the overly thin and sometimes unhealthy models and actors frequently shown in advertising and media. As discussed in the Life Satisfaction section of *Global System Change*, acceptance of appearance and other personal characteristics is an important component of achieving life satisfaction. Lack of self-acceptance often produces negative emotions that lead to overeating. Self-acceptance makes it easier to lose weight.

Several studies have shown that regular exercise, lifestyle and eating healthy food are more important than being slightly overweight in terms of lowering chronic disease risk.[661] This indicates that being a few pounds overweight should not be a major concern as long as people are exercising regularly and living a healthy lifestyle. However, obesity often indicates unhealthy eating habits that substantially increase the risk of chronic disease and premature death. Extreme obesity is not natural. It indicates that people are disconnected from their natural hunger cues. Intuitive eating can help them reconnect to their natural hunger signals, lose weight, lower disease risk and improve life satisfaction.

Cognitive-Behavioral Therapy

An excellent article by Judith Beck, Ph.D., called *Five Steps to Developing a Healthy Relationship With Food*, discusses how Cognitive-Behavioral Therapy (CBT) can be used to achieve long-term weight loss and diet change.[662] CBT is based on the idea that thoughts cause feelings and behaviors, not external things like people, situations or events. As discussed in the Life Satisfaction section, life satisfaction results mainly from perceptions of past and present life circumstances, rather than life itself. To illustrate, some people face tremendous burdens, but nevertheless are happy. Other people seem to have everything, but are unhappy.

The fact that life satisfaction largely results from perceptions of reality, rather than reality itself, is highly empowering. People can change their thoughts and ideas about life circumstances, as well as actions that result from them. But they often cannot change external factors such as other people and past, present or future events.

CBT is based on the scientifically supported idea that most emotional and behavioral reactions are learned. Therefore, the goal of CBT is to help people unlearn unwanted or harmful reactions and learn new ways of thinking and reacting.[663] CBT is a shorter type of psychotherapy. The focus is not on resolving childhood issues or conflicts. Instead, it is on teaching clients new cognitive and behavioral skills over a limited time period. Working with a therapist can be highly beneficial. But people also can teach themselves new skills and ideas, such as those discussed below.

Dr. Beck explains that unsuccessful dieters usually have self-sabotaging thinking. Their negative thoughts might include, "This is too hard. What's the point. It's not fair. I want to eat now. I deserve a reward." These thoughts often create a sense of deprivation or entitlement that leads to overeating and diet failure. This frequently leads to disappointment or frustration, which causes further overeating.

Dr. Beck suggests that successful dieting and long-term weight loss require learning and practicing new skills, like the practice required to gain most other competencies. She suggests that people learn new behavioral and cognitive skills before they begin dieting. Then they will be prepared for the negative thoughts that frequently arise during diets.

Behavioral skills focus on how to diet. The skills might include learning how to schedule meals and snacks, arrange one's physical environment, set up reward systems, eat while traveling, eat during holidays, eat less junk food and more fruits and vegetables, and limit portion sizes while ensuring that one gets enough calories (because excessive calorie restriction does not work). These are important skills. But they often are not enough. Behavioral and nutritional counseling alone rarely produces long-term weight loss because people usually discontinue new dieting practices after a while.

In addition to behavioral skills, new cognitive skills often are needed to lose and maintain weight over the long-term. Cognitive skills include learning how to stay motivated over the longer-term, deal with hunger and cravings, and recover immediately from an eating mistake. The process often involves replacing negative thoughts with positive ones. This teaches people what to say to themselves when they are feeling deprived, unmotivated, discouraged, stressed or tired. Positive thoughts might include, "I can eat as much unhealthy food as I want or I can be a healthy weight. I cannot do both. Or, hunger and cravings will pass. They will go away faster if I focus on something else."

If someone is eating for emotional reasons instead of physical hunger, they learn to do something else, such as go for a walk, talk to a friend or address the cause of negative emotions, for example, by changing negative thoughts or making life changes. Several studies have shown that CBT is far more effective at achieving long-term weight loss than behavioral therapy alone.[664]

There are many approaches to dieting and weight loss. Probably none of them works for everyone. Having many different dieting approaches increases the chance that people will find the one that works best for them. To illustrate different approaches, intuitive eating teaches people to listen to inner hunger signals and eat when they are physically hungry. But some CBT approaches suggest that people only eat at scheduled meal or snack times. The goal of both approaches is to end uncontrolled overeating. But different processes are used to achieve it.

CBT could be thought of as an intellectual or knowledge-based approach to dieting. There are many positive ideas and thoughts that can be used to counteract negative thoughts and maintain long-term weight loss. Examples of positive, empowering concepts relate to enjoyment of life, tastes, taking health for granted, emotional eating, finance, sacrifice and planning, and rationalizations.

Regarding enjoyment of life, people often justify overeating by saying, I want to enjoy life by eating whatever I want. But eating animal products and refined carbohydrates greatly increases the risk of obesity, chronic disease and premature death. It is hard to enjoy life if one has heart disease, cancer, dementia, vision loss, erectile dysfunction, amputated limbs or inability to engage in normal activities such as walking due to obesity. There is more to life than eating. There also is no need to make compromises between eating and other aspects of life satisfaction. People can enjoy eating healthy foods as much as unhealthy foods if they take the time to change their tastes. Once this occurs, eating will enhance all other aspects of life satisfaction, rather than degrade them.

Regarding tastes, humans evolved to crave foods with high sugar and fat content. But tastes and cravings can be changed. Several studies have shown that people begin to crave whatever they eat in large quantities.[665] For example, if they regularly eat large salads and little candy, over time, they usually will strongly crave salads but not candy. Also, if people stop eating certain foods, especially unhealthy foods, their craving for them often will go away. Dr. Esselstyn points out that if people stop eating dairy products, other animal products and added oils, their craving for fat will go away in about 12 weeks if they are eating enough whole plant foods.[666] Nuts have high levels of protein, antioxidants and other important nutrients. However, they also have high levels of fat. As a result, Dr. Esselstyn suggests that people who wish to prevent or reverse heart disease minimize or avoid eating nuts. Eating them can make it more difficult to lose the craving or taste for fat.

Many times people eat unhealthy foods without enjoying them. Instead, they crave or are addicted to the fat, sugar, salt and MSG in unhealthy foods. If they stop eating these foods for a while, their tastes or craving for them often will be replaced by a taste for and appreciation of the natural flavors of vegetables, fruits, grains and legumes. If people eat healthy foods and avoid retriggering reward circuits for unhealthy foods, they will develop tastes and cravings for healthy foods.

Many people take their health for granted. They might eat unhealthy foods for years, continue to feel good and function well. But chronic diseases are insidious. They usually develop slowly and then last a long time, sometimes until they cause premature death. As discussed in previous sections, chronic diseases usually result from lifestyle factors, such is not exercising or eating animal products and refined carbohydrates. Once chronic diseases appear, it frequently is too late to avoid painful and expensive life-restricting treatments or premature death.

When people become seriously ill and realize that they might die prematurely, they often wish that they had eaten better, exercised more and maintained a healthier lifestyle. Awareness of the frequently devastating and sometimes life-ending consequences of eating animal products and refined carbohydrates can motivate people to change their diets before it is too late. Heightened awareness can cause them to not take their bodies and health for granted.

We literally are what we eat. If we eat chocolate doughnuts, our bodies literally will be made of the ingredients in chocolate doughnuts and probably be unhealthy. However, if we eat raw vegetables and other healthy foods, our bodies will be made of the strongest possible building blocks. We will be healthy, strong, vital and long-lived. The optimal fuel for most automobiles is gasoline. People do not occasionally put sugar, water or mustard in their gas tanks. They only use the optimal fuel. The human body has greater capacity to withstand suboptimal fuel than automobiles (because it is nearly infinitely more complex). But just because humans often can survive on suboptimal fuel does not mean that there are not optimal fuels for us. If we fill the human fuel tank only with optimal fuels (i.e. whole plant foods), we will maximize our chances of living long, healthy and vital lives.

Eating animal products causes blood vessels to become clogged, hardened and unhealthy. Eating whole plant products causes them to be clear, flexible and healthy. This strongly helps to prevent heart disease, cancer, diabetes, dementia, vision loss, erectile dysfunction and many other health problems.

Regarding emotional eating, this is one of the main causes of overeating, obesity and resulting chronic diseases. Our disempowering culture produces widespread negative emotions in society. Advertising and media often cause people to feel empty and inadequate. This can produce fear, isolation and anger. Also, people frequently are not taught to follow their hearts in the career area. As a result, many people do not like their jobs. They often feel bored or frustrated at work. In addition, our "Me first" advertising culture frequently causes people to focus on meeting their own needs. This produces selfishness, which often leads to frustration and lack of fulfillment in relationships.

Taken together, these and many other aspects of our disempowering, selfish, media and advertising driven culture produce widespread fear, loneliness, anger, sadness and boredom in society. People often overeat or engage in other addictive or compulsive behaviors to numb out and suppress these painful emotions. But as discussed, this never works. People are trying to fill a non-physical psychological or spiritual emptiness with food. It causes them to be constantly seeking and never satisfied. Emotional eating causes temporary numbness or distraction. As the this wears off, more overeating, numbing and avoiding problems occurs, which makes life worse.

The key is to recognize when one craves food to satisfy emotional not physical hunger, realize that food will not satisfy this hunger, and then take actions that actually do satisfy. Internal actions include replacing negative thoughts with positive ones. One of the most satisfying external actions is engaging in relationships. Humans are gregarious by nature. We are meant to be with other people through many types of relationships including friends, family, romance, coworkers and neighbors. But negative thoughts often fill people with fear and cause them to take actions that push other people away, such as overeating.

Being obese can protect people. Large size can intimidate others and push them away. For example, obesity can protect women from unwanted advances from men. But avoiding relationships or being unsatisfied in them is one of the largest causes of emptiness, sadness, loneliness and the ongoing overeating that often results from these emotions. By losing weight, people often take down psychological and physical barriers to relationships. Rather than suppressing emotions with food, they allow them and use negative emotions to motivate positive changes in thinking and behavior. They engage more with others through many types of relationships. And they frequently find real, enduring life satisfaction.

Finance or cost is another intellectual concept that can promote long-term weight loss. The healthiest foods often are the least expensive. For example, bean and whole rice combinations are highly nutritious. They provide all eight essential amino acids, high levels of fiber and many other nutrients, while also containing no cholesterol and very low-fat. In addition, they usually are far less expensive than animal products, especially when bought in bulk.

Producing animal products is highly inefficient compared to plant products. It often takes ten or more pounds of plant protein to produce one pound of animal protein.[667] Rather than essentially throwing away nine pounds of plant protein and feeding humans one pound of animal protein, it would be vastly more efficient to feed the ten pounds of plant protein directly to humans. The gross water and grain inefficiency of animal products often cause them to be more expensive than plant products, especially when animal products are not subsidized. By eating whole, unprocessed plant products, people frequently can greatly lower their food costs, while eating much healthier food.

Sacrifice and planning also are critical elements of successful long-term weight loss. Ending addictive, compulsive or habitual overeating can be difficult, especially at first. In the first few days, people can feel great emotional and even physical discomfort. These early days are critical. Once people make it through them, addictive brain chemistry and reward circuits begin to subside. The physical cravings of food addiction begin to weaken, provided that they are not retriggered by eating unhealthy foods. Making it through these first few days or weeks is greatly facilitated by having a well thought out, multi-faceted plan. Key components include planning diets and activities, getting support from other people, and learning how to deal with emotional triggers.

Beyond initial discomfort, ending food and other addictions can become difficult after a few months. Early success can build enthusiasm and momentum for ongoing healthy eating and weight loss. But if people do not deal with the underlying negative thoughts, emotions, conflicts and other psychological factors that drove overeating, they often will re-emerge and make long-term weight loss difficult. As a result, a long-term plan, in addition to a short-term plan, also is important for successful longer-term weight loss. The should include maintaining the healthy dieting and other practices implemented in the short-term. It also should emphasize transforming negative to positive thinking and engaging in truly satisfying activities.

Understanding the possible need for sacrifice is a critical component of successful long-term weight loss. Many people seem to be unwilling or unable to endure early discomfort when ending food and other addictions and habits. As a result, they continue to overeat and often suffer severely degraded health or premature death. By finding the courage and strength to endure a few days or weeks of high discomfort, and then a few months of lesser discomfort, they can free themselves from unhealthy, sometimes deadly addictions to food, tobacco and other substances. From an intellectual and logical perspective, it makes overwhelming good sense to endure a few weeks or months of discomfort in exchange for a lifetime of vastly greater health and satisfaction.

A highly empowering concept is the idea that success breeds more success and failure breeds more failure. Each healthy eating choice makes the next one easier. Each unhealthy eating choice makes those easier and more likely. As people maintain healthy eating, it becomes easier over time. After a while, it becomes automatic. Achieving this healthy transition is facilitated by taking the actions discussed above, such as transforming negative thoughts to positive and populating one's life with more fulfilling activities.

Rationalizations are one of the most important intellectual or psychological causes of diet failure, overeating and obesity. The mind often resists uncertainty and change. Harmful habits or addictions frequently produce senses of comfort and security. To protect them, the mind frequently sabotages efforts to end harmful activities. Rationalizations are a primary means of doing this. They often are irrational thoughts used to justify and perpetuate overeating and other harmful activities. Two of the most common and life-degrading rationalizations are, "I already overate, so I might as well continue overeating" and "I'll quit tomorrow".

Many times, dieters plan to avoid unhealthy food. Then if they eat some, they feel a sense of failure and rationalize, "I've already failed. So I might as well overeat for the rest of the day or week." This is highly irrational. It shows how the mind, perhaps driven by head-heart conflicts, achieves its objective of avoiding change and uncertainty. The mind essentially has given the person permission to overeat unhealthy food for the next day or week.

To illustrate the irrational nature of this type of thinking, a person might accidentally drive through a red light on the way to work in the morning. As a result, they say, "I already ran one red light today. I might as well continue running red lights for the rest of the day. Then I'll start driving safely tomorrow." One diet slip often would have little or no impact. But if people use it to justify or rationalize continued overeating, it could cause harm, especially when this rationalization is used repeatedly, as it often is.

Another version of this rationalization is the idea that servings or open containers of unhealthy food should be finished to avoid wasting food. For example, after opening a container of ice cream or box of cookies, someone might say, "I'll finish the container to avoid wasting food, and then quit once the unhealthy food is gone." Once again, the mind is giving the person permission to continue overeating unhealthy food. Obviously, wasting food should be avoided whenever possible. But if the choice is wearing the extra food as fat and increasing chronic disease risk or throwing it out, the healthier choice is throwing the unhealthy food away. The rationalization "I must finish every portion or open container" justifies continued overeating. With CBT, one learns to eat only what they need, rather than using their body as a garbage can.

One of the greatest enemies of life satisfaction is the rationalization "I'll do it tomorrow". This sometimes is cruelly referred to as the battle cry of the loser. In a sense, tomorrow does not exist. When it arrives, it is today. People only quit today or they do not quit it all. Obviously, this is semantics. Sometimes there are logical reasons for delaying an action until a future date. But the rationalization "I'll quit tomorrow" can be extremely destructive. It is widely used to delay ending harmful habits and addictions, sometimes for years, or even lifetimes.

The rationalization creates a sense of comfort because the mind feels that action will be taken. It just will be delayed for a day or two. The dieter might think, "one additional day of overeating will make no difference in the grand scheme of things." They are correct. It probably would not. The problem is that this rationalization frequently is used repeatedly, day after day. As a result, the harmful activity continues for years, or never ends.

This once again illustrates how the mind tricks the person into avoiding change and uncertainty. It often only cares about the present. In the heat of the moment, when emotions are overwhelming, the mind wants its comfort. And it gets it. It frequently says, "one day versus the rest of my life. Who cares. I'll overeat today, and then not do it for the rest of my life." But sadly, the one day of overeating or engaging in other addictions sometimes turns into the rest of their life.

While creating comfort on one level, the rationalization "I'll do it tomorrow" compounds the problem by also creating a sense of deprivation or scarcity. The dieter might think, "starting tomorrow, I'll never eat ice cream, candy, cheeseburgers or other unhealthy food ever again for the rest of my life. This is my last chance. I might as well enjoy it today." Then they often eat large amounts of unhealthy food. As the deadline for quitting keeps getting pushed into the future, the gorging continues. This type of irrational thinking is a major driver of obesity and addictions of all types. As discussed, an important aspect of CBT is teaching people to recover immediately from dieting mistakes. This frequently enables them to avoid becoming the victim of faulty thinking and destructive rationalizations.

While it may only be semantics, a useful intellectual tool is to assume that tomorrow does not exist. People never quit overeating or other addictions in the future. They quit today, or they do not quit it all. Rather than continuously extending the deadline to end overeating, it often is better to bite the bullet, quit now, deal with a few weeks of discomfort, and emerge at the other end into a vastly more satisfying and healthy life.

Everyone with a reasonably functioning mind can do this. No one is forced to overeat. Addiction is tendency, not destiny. People have the ability to end harmful behaviors instantly. They can choose to set down their fork and never take a bite of unhealthy food again. After a while, healthy eating will become as easy and automatic, if they take the actions discussed above and below.

Strengthening Healthy Habits

Strengthening healthy habits is a key aspect of making healthy eating easy and automatic. Simply ending a harmful habit often is difficult because it leaves a void. There frequently is a strong tendency to fill it with the old habit. A far more effective strategy is to develop and strengthen healthier, truly satisfying habits or behaviors. This fills the void and essentially pushes out the unhealthy habit.

An excellent article by Stephen Stosny, PhD, called *The Secret to Breaking Out of Our Most Destructive Habits*, discusses a highly effective means of replacing harmful or undesirable habits and behaviors, such as overeating unhealthy foods, with healthy behaviors.[668] Unhealthy habits are deeply ingrained, often unconscious behavior patterns. Many habits originate from and are triggered by negative emotions, such as fear, unworthiness, anxiety and anger. Senses of fear and unworthiness are common in our frequently fractured, angry and judgmental society. They can result from child abuse, omnipresent advertising and media, and many other factors. Unhealthy habits usually are ineffective or harmful ways of dealing with negative emotions.

To illustrate, Dr. Stosny explains that people often feel vulnerable, unworthy and powerless. They frequently respond to these feelings with anger and aggression, perhaps because they believe on an unconscious level that this increases power. But the key issue is not lack of power. It is lack of value. Anger and aggression usually do not relieve senses of unworthiness or low value. They often increase them by making people feel resentful or guilty. This harmful habit makes life worse for people who have it and those around them. It is the same with overeating. Dealing with fear, unworthiness or anxiety by overeating can cause more unworthiness and many other physical and psychological problems.

As responses to negative emotions and other triggers are repeated many times, neurological circuits are strengthened. Responses become automatic, unconscious and habituated. By adulthood, most emotional and behavioral responses are conditioned. People usually think, feel and act about the same in similar situations. Habits and other conditioned responses are easy. They require little mental energy or focus. Decisions are made almost instantaneously with little or no conscious awareness, especially when people are in familiar locations such as their homes. Conditioned or unconscious behaviors in familiar situations can flatten emotions. They can make unpleasant situations bearable (i.e. being in prison or having permanent disabilities), while making pleasant situations boring (i.e. marriages and other long-term relationships).[669]

Habits and other conditioned responses cause many people to live their lives mostly on autopilot. They frequently are not consciously choosing their behavior. This can make life suboptimal and create other problems. Even with healthy, positive conditioned responses, people often are not mentally present. As a result, they frequently miss the beauty or uniqueness of each moment.

The most destructive problems result from unhealthy or harmful conditioned responses and habits. In the above article, Dr. Stosny gives an example of a man who habitually responded to feelings of vulnerability and unworthiness with anger and aggression. As a result, he abused his wife and wound up in jail. People who habitually respond to negative emotions by overeating unhealthy foods often wind up with chronic diseases and severely degraded lives.

Changing unhealthy habits is possible. Millions of people have done it. But the process frequently requires hard work, motivation and commitment. Unhealthy habits become strengthened and automatic through repetition. Avoidance will weaken unhealthy habits, while increased repetition of healthy habits strengthens them and makes them easy and automatic.

Developing healthy habits can be difficult at first because it requires focused mental attention. People must consciously choose to act differently. This can be especially difficult when they are tired or feeling negative emotions. In these states, willpower often declines and habits take over.[670] Unhealthy habits frequently are the conditioned response to negative emotions. The habituated response, such as overeating, provides temporary relief from negative emotions. It is the easy and automatic action. It often overwhelms conscious efforts to respond differently to negative emotions and other triggers.

Strengthening healthy habits often involves replacing instant gratification with delayed gratification. People who are feeling fear, unworthiness, anxiety or anger frequently have a difficult time forgoing instant gratification and taking healthier actions. People with low self-esteem might believe on an unconscious level that they do not deserve a better life. As a result, delaying gratification for a better life down the road could be especially difficult.

Important aspects or phases of successfully changing habits include motivation, focus and practice. Regarding motivation, strengthening healthy habits requires repetition. Frequently repeating new thoughts and actions, when the strong tendency is to revert to old habits, can be tedious and difficult. High motivation and self-love can provide the energy and commitment needed to practice and strengthen healthy habits.

People can develop the motivation to change by focusing on positive attributes and a desired future. For example, they can write out and frequently review the type of person they would like to be, what they want to do with their lives, and how they would like to get along with family, coworkers and other people. To build self-esteem and hope that a better future is possible, people can focus on past successes and positive interactions. For example, they could write out and frequently review how they changed other unhealthy habits, achieved success in work and other areas, helped others, and felt love or strong connections to and from other people. They also can increase the motivation to change by honestly reviewing past actions and results. This often motivates change by showing how harmful habits degrade the most important things in life, such as health, relationships, career and happiness.

Changing unhealthy habits can be greatly facilitated by working with a psychotherapist or joining a self-help group, such as a Twelve Step program (discussed below). However, many people successfully change unhealthy habits on their own.

Regarding focus, mental attention is a precious resource. It not only is essential for changing unhealthy habits. It is needed to reach one's fullest potential and attain a successful and satisfying life. Many people fritter away or waste their lives by essentially living on autopilot. They engage in benign or harmful habits and allow their minds to wander much of the time. Most 'decisions' are unconscious. As discussed in the Life Satisfaction section, strengthening the ability to focus one's mind is essential for maximizing individual well-being.

Overcoming the inertia of overeating and other unhealthy habits requires focused mental attention. Two aspects of this include focusing on practice and repetition of healthy habits and focusing on the positive instead of the negative. As noted, psychotherapy can facilitate changing habits. Therapists can help clients to have epiphanies (heartfelt or powerful intellectual insights) and catharses (release of long-term, deeply held emotions). These insights and emotional releases can be uplifting and empowering. They can increase self-esteem and provide the motivation needed to change unhealthy habits.

But intellectual insight and emotional release often are not enough to cause long-term behavior change. The empowerment of epiphany and catharsis frequently produce positive changes, such as ending unhealthy habits, in the short-term. But the underlying neurological circuits and unconscious habituated responses have not been changed. Over time, these ingrained patterns often reassert themselves. As a result, unhealthy habits return. This illustrates why focusing on strengthening healthy habits through practice and repetition is essential. Unhealthy habits are formed through repetition. Therefore, repeating new thoughts and actions is necessary for replacing unhealthy habits with healthy ones.

Focusing on the positive is a critical aspect of changing habits. Behavior follows attention. Therefore, if people focus on the negative, they usually will think, feel and act negatively. In this sense, psychotherapy sometimes can become counterproductive. Understanding the causes of negative emotions, psychological problems and unhealthy habits can be very useful. But beyond a certain point, overemphasizing causes can expand unhealthy habits. For example, if people dwell on or overly analyze an abusive childhood or other harmful aspects of their past, it can create senses of unworthiness, anger or entitlement. This can expand or maintain negative emotions and unhealthy habits. Therapy often focuses on how people feel. But focusing on negative emotions can expand negative emotions.

As a result, Dr. Stosny suggests that people generally not focus on how they feel (i.e. the negative) but rather on how they *want* to feel, think and act (i.e. the positive). Focusing on the negative expands the negative. Focusing on the positive expands the positive. With diet, focusing on avoiding unhealthy eating can expand unhealthy eating. It usually is more effective to focus on healthy eating.

Focusing on the cause of negative emotions not only can be counterproductive. It also sometimes is irrelevant. For example, child abuse or growing up in the disempowering advertising and media culture can make people feel unworthy. This often triggers overeating. As the unworthiness-overeating cycle is repeated many times, the cause of unworthiness can become less relevant. Unworthiness caused by any factor triggers the unhealthy response.

A key aspect of changing unhealthy habits is developing new strategies for responding to unworthiness and other triggers. Recognizing harmful patterns can facilitate developing new responses. For example, people might recognize that overeating in response to unworthiness or other negative emotions does not work. It temporarily numbs feelings, and then produces more unworthiness. This can motivate people to develop new ways of responding to negative emotions. Instead of overeating, they focus on taking actions that actually increase value and self-worth, such as going for a walk, talking to a friend, completing a project or taking some other positive, productive action.

Reflecting the complexity of the human mind, focusing on causes sometimes is counterproductive, but it also can be highly beneficial. An article called *Can You Rewire Your Brain to Change Bad Habits, Thoughts, and Feelings?*, discusses how addressing the causes of negative emotions can help to change unhealthy habits.[671]

The article discusses a process called memory reconsolidation. It is based on the idea that painful or harmful beliefs and memories essentially are locked into the mind, possibly through reinforced neurological circuits. The theory holds that they can be 'unlocked' and dissolved or transformed. The process involves bringing painful memories or beliefs to consciousness. Then, while one is thinking about them, weakening or changing beliefs by repeatedly reviewing or emphasizing irrational or incorrect components of them.

The article illustrates how the process works by giving an example of a woman who frequently felt very uncomfortable in social situations. Her therapist helped her to identify the source or cause of this discomfort. As a child, the woman's mother was extremely critical when her daughter made the slightest mistake. The child developed the unconscious belief that the slightest imperfection made her unlovable. She believed that she would be rejected if she revealed any imperfection. Once this belief was made conscious, the therapist encouraged the woman to think of someone who loved her unconditionally and would not reject her for imperfection. This helped her to realize that it was irrational to believe that everyone was like her mother and would reject her for imperfection. She realized that the fault was with her mother, not herself. Changing the belief about the need for perfection greatly reduced the woman's discomfort in social situations.

A similar approach could be used to change beliefs and memories that cause overeating. For example, insecure, critical parents who frequently berate their children could cause children to believe on a deep, unconscious level that they have little value and do not deserve a good life. As the child grows up, this foundational belief could cause many problems, including depression and pervasive senses of unworthiness. Many people use overeating to suppress these and other negative emotions. Through inner exploration and self-honesty, possibly with the help of a therapist, people can bring to consciousness disempowering childhood beliefs. As they are made conscious, people can review their irrational nature. The review might show that all people are inherently valuable and worthy, as are all other creations of nature. All people deserve a good life. As disempowering beliefs are dissolved and replaced by empowering ones, unworthiness and other negative emotions decline. This often lowers the compulsion to overeat.

During the focus phase of changing habits, people might examine causes of negative emotions or simply develop new, healthier ways of responding to them. The key is focusing on the positive and developing new, more effective strategies for responding to old triggers.

Another critical aspect of changing habits involves controlling the contents of one's mind. People often cannot control what thoughts enter their minds. But once the thoughts are conscious, they can choose to dwell on them or focus on something else. This essentially pushes undesired thoughts out of consciousness. Failing to control thoughts in this way is a main reason why people often are unsuccessful at ending overeating and other harmful habits. As discussed in the Twelve Step section below, thought precedes action. The failure to end overeating or other unhealthy behaviors virtually always occurs in the mind before it occurs in reality.

For example, a person might begin to think about overeating, perhaps because an outer or inner factor, such as unworthiness, made them feel uncomfortable. If they dwell on thoughts about overeating, their minds probably will rationalize or justify it. Once the decision to overeat is made, overeating occurs. Ending overeating requires understanding that it starts in the mind. As people recognize that they are thinking about overeating, they can choose to change their mental focus. They can choose to focus instead on positive thoughts and behaviors.

Overeating and other unhealthy habits can seem unconscious and automatic. But if people honestly examine the contents of their minds, they virtually always will see that some thought about overeating, even a brief or nearly instantaneous thought, preceded the actual overeating. Therefore, learning to observe and manage the contents of one's mind greatly facilitates replacing unhealthy with healthy behavior and achieving a successful and satisfying life.

In the practice phase of changing habits, new strategies or responses are repeated and strengthened. Dr. Stosny suggests specific actions for developing and strengthening healthy habits. For example, people should frequently think about strategies for changing habits that were developed in the focus phase. What new actions will they take in response to old triggers? Instead of responding to negative emotions with overeating, what will they do instead? As discussed, perhaps they will eat a healthy amount of healthy food, go for a walk, talk to a friend, or engage in other pleasant, healthy activities.

People also should frequently think about how they will overcome barriers to change. These barriers might include thoughts and rationalizations that justify and perpetuate unhealthy habits. For example, people could say to themselves, "my mind might seek comfort by attempting to talk me into an old habit, such as overeating. If or when this occurs, I will lovingly listen without judgment to the part of me that seeks comfort and relief from negative emotions. I will thank it for trying to help. But like a wise and loving parent, I will say that the real peace I seek will come from new behaviors, not overeating."

Repetition of healthy habits is critical. Dr. Stosny suggests that people practice new habits in simulated and real life situations. Practice could occur internally or externally. For example, people might review in their minds several times per day how they will respond differently to old triggers. When one experiences negative emotions or other triggers, instead of automatically engaging in unhealthy habits, they pause, assess what they are experiencing, consider how to respond in a healthy manner, and then take the new actions. People also might intentionally bring up negative emotions or engage in activities that trigger them. This creates opportunities to practice new responses. If unhealthy habits such as overeating usually occur at certain times, people could practice new habits at these times.

Dr. Stosny suggests that if people practice new responses to old triggers about 12 times per day, they will form new habits in about six weeks. Only about one minute of practice is required in each practice 'session'.

He suggests that people make practicing new habits a part of their daily regime, for example, by practicing them at transition times, such as when they wake up, go to work, get home from work and go to bed. An important aspect of practice is being aware of positive emotions and responses that result from new positive behaviors. This helps to strengthen and accelerate the formation of healthy habits.

In the above article, Dr. Stosny emphasizes changing habits that cause problems in relationships. Relationship problems often create negative emotions. Many people deal with them by overeating. Therefore, resolving relationship problems often can help to reduce the desire or compulsion to overeat.

Dr. Stosny discusses his work with the man noted above who abused his wife. When she was critical or unhappy with him, he felt vulnerable, injured and powerless. He habitually responded with anger and aggression. The work involved changing this habituated response to one of compassion and problem solving. In exploring the cause of his feelings of vulnerability and powerlessness, the man recalled seeing his alcoholic father hit his mother when he was a child. His wife's unhappiness triggered unconscious beliefs and feelings of inadequacy related to his inability to protect his mother when he was a boy.

Dr. Stosny helped his client to build motivation to change his harmful behavior. The man was encouraged to focus on the type of husband and father he wanted to be. He also realized that he would lose the most important part in his life, his wife and marriage, if he did not change. Dr. Stosny then helped the man to develop new ways of responding to feelings of vulnerability, injury and powerlessness. The process involved noticing and assessing feelings, and then responding in a positive manner. For example, if his wife complained, he might notice that he felt ashamed and resentful. In assessing the situation, he could realize that the complaint does not lower his value. The shame he feels is not a punishment for failure. Rather it could be used as motivation to improve the situation. Then in response to the complaint, he might pay more attention to his wife and attempt to support or help her if possible.

Dr. Stosny also helped the man to build compassion and empathy by trying to see both perspectives. For example, if his wife criticized him, he might think, I'm hurt, but she is too. In seeking a positive interpretation of the situation, the husband might realize, my wife did not mean to hurt me. He then attempts to respond differently by treating his wife in a loving and compassionate manner.

Once motivation to change was increased and new strategies for responding to negative emotions were developed, practice was the key to achieving long-term behavior change. In this case, Dr. Stosny suggested that the wife send her husband texts to which he formally might have responded with anger. For example, she might announce her intention to buy something. This gives the husband an opportunity to practice responding with compassion, for example, by suggesting that they develop a budget and jointly decide what they can afford. Repeatedly practicing positive responses to negative emotions changed the man's harmful behavior. He became a compassionate and loving husband and father, and kept his family together.

In this case, a woman stayed with a husband who had hit her, and things worked out. But people often have difficulty changing harmful habits. Many women rightly tolerate no physical abuse. They leave their abusive husbands. No one is perfect. People often hurt each other emotionally in relationships. Physical abuse of course is completely unacceptable. But there is no single correct response for every situation. The optimal response generally varies according to the circumstances of each relationship.

Relationships frequently are the most important factor affecting life satisfaction. Therefore, changing harmful, habitual ways of dealing with other people can be highly beneficial. Our deeply divided and unsustainable society produces widespread senses of inadequacy, fear, vulnerability and powerlessness. Responding to these feelings with anger and aggression is a very large problem in society. It substantially expands division, fear and inadequacy. It would greatly benefit every person and society in general to practice the most important suggestion or commandment of nearly all religions – treating other people with kindness, love and respect. People can train themselves to respond in ways that benefit themselves and others. When they feel hurt or afraid, they can respond with compassion instead of aggression. Many wise spiritual leaders say that kindness is its own reward. Positive responses to negative emotions produce positive emotions and life results. They become self-reinforcing.

Long-term behavior changes that substantially improve one's life usually do not result from epiphanies and catharses. They mostly result from small changes practiced diligently and consistently. Many people live their lives mostly on autopilot. They might have pleasant lives. But they do not come close to reaching their fullest potential and joy. Novelty and learning are key aspects of maximizing life satisfaction. Consciously choosing to learn new habits and expand beneficial old ones can substantially increase novelty and improve life satisfaction.

An excellent article by Brent Atkinson, PhD, called *Why People Behave in Self-Defeating, Irrational Ways and How to Really Change*, further discusses strengthening healthy habits.[672] The article provides several important suggestions that support and enhance the effectiveness of the techniques discussed above. Dr. Atkinson discusses how the mind or brain can be retrained to respond differently to stressful situations and negative emotions that cause overeating and other problems.

In particular, Dr. Atkinson discusses the importance of learning to relax and soothe one's emotions. Before responding to stressful situations, for example by arguing or overeating, Dr. Atkinson suggests that people practice slowing their breathing and learning to calm or soothe themselves. Regularly practicing mindfulness meditation is an excellent way to gain this self-soothing ability. This type of meditation involves focusing on breathing and other physical sensations in the present moment. Regular meditation increases people's ability to relax, regulate emotions and reduce stress. Taking some time to relax before responding to stressful situations or emotions greatly increases the ability to respond positively, for example by speaking kindly or not overeating.

In addition to mindfulness meditation, Dr. Atkinson suggests that people practice compassion or loving-kindness meditation. This involves spending several minutes or extended periods of time focusing on and developing feelings of compassion and loving-kindness for other people. For example, one might visualize sending love and compassion to another person or group of people. Many studies have shown that this type of meditation causes people to feel more compassion and empathy in general, engage in more altruistic activities, and have a stronger desire to help others.[673] These feelings and actions substantially improve senses of individual well-being and happiness. Replacing negative with positive emotions greatly reduces the compulsion or inclination to engage in overeating and other destructive activities.

Benjamin Franklin said, "Eat to live, don't live to eat". This illustrates a major problem and solution related to unhealthy habits. Many people get much of their joy or comfort in life from overeating and other unhealthy habits. It often seems that ending these habits would make life boring, empty and even intolerable. But this is an illusion. Adopting healthy habits inevitably will make life more exciting and fulfilling. But as noted, the transition from unhealthy to healthy habits can be difficult. As discussed in the Twelve Step Programs section below, it requires faith and trust that a better life as possible. This is why self-love and motivation are so important for changing unhealthy habits. They give people the energy needed to delay gratification and improve their lives.

Many people frequently try but fail to end overeating and other unhealthy habits. This can be dispiriting. It can take away hope and make failure seem inevitable. But it definitely is not. People always have the power to change unhealthy habits. Successful change after frequent failure usually requires a different approach. For example, many people try but fail to limit or moderate the consumption of animal products, refined carbohydrates and other unhealthy foods. As discussed above, moderation often does not work. Most processed, packaged and restaurant food contains MSG. This essentially acts as a neurological drug that greatly increases the desire or compulsion to overeat. As a result, some people might only be able to stop overeating by ending the consumption of processed food, in the same way that people frequently must completely quit alcohol or tobacco to end overuse.

Overeating and other unhealthy habits might seem easy and automatic. But in reality, they usually are more difficult to maintain than healthy habits. Unhealthy habits degrade life. Maintaining them often requires tolerating a growing level of self-deception and injury. Healthy habits, on the other hand, improve health, happiness and other life factors. They are the truly easy habits. Once people make the transition to healthy eating and other habits, the new life becomes self-reinforcing, easy and automatic. The Twelve Step Programs section below provides greater detail about changing unhealthy habits.

Twelve Step Programs

Many people understand that overeating is a choice. No one forces them to overeat. They also often understand the grave health risks and life problems caused by overeating. In addition, they frequently understand the actions needed to end overeating and lose weight. Yet in spite of this knowledge, they continue to overeat or engage in other addictions. For people such as these, their problem is not lack of knowledge. It is lack of power.

In a sense, the conscious mind is not the master of one's life. If people do not align their lives with their inner wisdom (i.e. heart), they always will pay a price. Addiction is a common price paid for failing to live a heart-led life. Through addiction, people attempt to escape the painful emotions or boredom that inevitably result from failing to listen to one's heart.

Addictions cause pain and life problems. But they also provide temporary comfort and certainty. This often makes it difficult to change addictive, compulsive or habitual behavior. People frequently do not change until the pain of addiction becomes far greater than the comfort provided by it. The addiction causes people to hit bottom or reach some type of painful crisis. Life-changing crises might include failure of relationships, loss of jobs, loss of health or conviction for crimes. The great pain of addiction and resulting crises often provide the motivation needed to make difficult changes.

The Twelve Steps are one of the most successful programs for overcoming addiction in human history. The Twelve Steps of Alcoholics Anonymous (AA) have been used as the foundation for self-help programs related to nearly all addictions, including addiction to food. Twelve Step programs were briefly discussed in the Life Satisfaction section. However, a more detailed summary is provided here because the Twelve Steps often will provide the most effective strategy for ending overeating and achieving long-term weight loss. They also frequently are the most effective way to end many other types of harmful or undesirable behaviors.

The Twelve Steps and original instructions for using them are contained in the book *Alcoholics Anonymous* (also known as the Big Book). This section is based on these original instructions. Many people apply the Twelve Steps by participating in Twelve Step programs, such as Overeaters Anonymous. However, even for people who are not actively involved in these programs, understanding and applying the concepts of the Twelve Steps can be very helpful when seeking to end addictive, compulsive, habitual or otherwise undesirable behavior. Even for those not dealing with these behaviors, applying the Twelve Step concepts can improve quality of life. The Twelve Steps summarize the basic spiritual principles of the world's great religions into an easy-to-understand, nondogmatic form. These principles are universally applicable. They work for everyone who applies them.

Inability to end addictive or otherwise harmful behavior is a spiritual problem in the sense that it often appears to result from a lack of power to change. It is not spiritual in terms of dogma, religion or belief in God. It is spiritual as discussed in the Life Satisfaction section. Spirit refers to the unity of humanity and nature. It implies connection to intuitive wisdom (i.e. the heart or the inner word of God) and other people (i.e. community). Twelve Step programs are spiritual in the sense that they can greatly enhance one's connection to intuitive wisdom and other people.

A key element of Twelve Step programs is making the conscious mind the servant of a wiser source of guidance referred to as a higher power. People choose the version of a higher power that works best for them. At first, the higher power might be a group of people who have succeeded at ending addiction. But ultimately, the higher power is heard or perceived within as people access their own inner wisdom. The power to change what previously seemed unchangeable often results from a spiritual awakening. This also could be referred to as a renewal of the mind or discovery of inner resources that provide the motivation and determination needed to make difficult changes.

Life crises often drive spiritual awakenings or renewals of the mind by helping people to see the big picture more clearly. For example, after having a heart attack, parents might realize that watching and helping their children grow up is more important than continuing to eat animal products and other foods that clog arteries and cause heart attacks. Perhaps the most important aspect of spiritual awakenings or renewals of the mind is an increase in self-love. Ending harmful habits and addictions ultimately is an act of self-love. If people have low self-esteem or feel unworthy, it frequently is difficult to make life-enhancing, but difficult changes. They might unconsciously believe or feel that the effort is not worth it because they do not deserve a good life.

A belief in God often provides an increase in self-love. People sometimes experience a gradual or spontaneous awareness of an inner connection to a difficult to describe, but nevertheless real source of wise and loving guidance. Those who believe in God frequently perceive this inner connection as acceptance by a loving and powerful God. Belief that God loves them often increases self-worth (i.e. If God loves me, I must be okay). They also feel that they no longer are alone. They have a powerful ally. This heightened sense of self-love and connection to a loving, helpful God frequently provides the strength, power, courage and determination needed to overcome addiction to food or other substances.

However, a belief in God is not needed to have this empowering, life-transforming inner experience. Sometimes the inner experience can be more empowering without a belief in God. Intellectual concepts about God or religious dogma can block or limit the discernment and use of intuitive wisdom.

We all have access to infinite wisdom within. Allowing one's conscious mind to be guided by this inner resource provides the most successful and satisfying life. It also provides the sense of connection and love needed to make difficult life changes. The name of this inner resource ultimately is irrelevant. Many people call it God. Others call it intuitive wisdom or the wisdom of nature. As discussed in the Twelve Step programs, the key is finding a way of thinking about this inner resource that works for the individual. For many people, the most effective strategy is to think of this inner source of guidance and power as God. By far the most important issue is to discern the source of inner guidance, regardless of what it is called, and use it. It is there for everyone, regardless of religious or spiritual beliefs.

Step One

In *Step One* of the Twelve Steps, people admit that they are powerless over their addiction and that their lives have become unmanageable. A primary characteristic of addiction is the inability to end harmful behavior that is causing negative consequences. People engaging in harmful addictive, compulsive or habitual behavior often try to stop, but consistently fail. Even as life problems become larger and more obvious, they are unable to stop. In this sense, they are powerless and their lives are unmanageable. Admitting that they are powerless and that addiction has degraded their lives is the first step to change. It provides the humility and open-mindedness needed to try new approaches.

However, saying that people are powerless is a semantic device. Ultimately, people are not powerless. They always had the power to choose to stop addictive behavior. But they did not choose to quit and then maintain their decision. People also are not powerless in the sense that they always had the ability to access intuitive wisdom that would have guided them out of addiction. But once again, they did not choose to access this resource, perhaps because they did not know it was available.

Step Two

In *Step Two*, people believe or strive to believe that a power greater than themselves could restore them to sanity. The implied insanity involves continuing to take harmful actions in spite of negative consequences. Addicts and people in general often seem to act without thinking, as if they were on autopilot. The do not consider what their minds are directing them to do and whether there are alternate sources of guidance within or without.

The conscious mind or ego often does not like uncertainty. It frequently prefers to believe that it knows the answers. The ego often does not like to admit that it is powerless or does not know everything. But in Step One, people admitted that their egos or ways of thinking and acting were not working. In Step Two, they came to believe, or at least consider the idea, that there is an alternate, wiser and more effective source of guidance than their own egos. Addicts see that sober people have done what they were unable to do – stop addictive behavior. In this sense, sober people are a higher power that could provide more effective guidance about ending addictive behavior. People also can see the essentially infinitely greater implied intelligence in their own bodies and in nature. As a result, they often consider the possibility that they might be able to access this vastly greater source of wisdom, knowledge and power.

The Twelve Step programs focus on a higher power, not higher knowledge. Knowledge often is power. But knowledge frequently refers to intangible, abstract ideas. Power, on the other hand, refers to something tangible. The inner source of infinite power and wisdom is not an abstract idea. It is real. Millions of people can attest to this power through their own tangible inner experience. This experience never can be used to prove the existence of intuitive wisdom to another person. Each person must discover it on their own. However, just because it cannot be scientifically proven, does not mean it is not real.

As part of Step Two, people consider what type of higher power they could engage with and utilize most effectively. Many people think of their higher power as God. Atheists might conceive of it as the Twelve Step group, intuitive wisdom or the wisdom of nature.

Step Three

In *Step Three*, people decide to turn their will and lives over to the care of a higher power as they understand it. In Step Two, people came to believe that a higher power could guide them to do what previously seemed impossible. Step Three implements this belief by allowing a higher power to guide one's life. This involves making the conscious mind or ego the servant of something wiser. At first the higher power might be heard through the Twelve Step group or a more experienced person in the group, often referred to as a sponsor. But ultimately the higher power is heard within.

Once again, semantics are involved. From a broader perspective, if one hears a higher power within, it is not separate from the individual. From this higher perspective, the individual contains all knowledge, wisdom and power. This could be thought of as the larger self or higher self. However, infinite knowledge is not present in the conscious mind. In this sense, one's ego or smaller self is separate from the higher power or infinite wisdom. This view promotes the humility needed to make the ego a servant of something wiser, even if the wiser source is contained within oneself.

The concepts of higher self, smaller self, higher power, ego and powerlessness are complex and paradoxical. The individual is not powerless in the sense that they always choose to do or not do the will of their higher power or intuitive wisdom. However, they are powerless in the sense that if they choose incorrectly (i.e. choose not to do the will of their higher power), they inevitably will experience life problems such as addiction, unhappiness, failure, boredom or other negative consequences. Rather than getting caught up in semantics and paradoxes, it generally is easier to understand that choosing to do the will of the higher power or intuitive wisdom produces the most successful and satisfying life. One is not forced to be a servant. They choose to make their conscious mind a servant because this produces the best life.

The wording of the Third Step, turning one's will and life over to the care of a higher power, sometimes can seem confusing. The higher power cannot be seen if one chooses to make God or intuitive wisdom their higher power. As a result, the concept of turning one's will over or surrendering their will can seem abstract and difficult to understand and apply. The key is to realize that we always make choices because we have free will. It is impossible to give up free will and the ability to choose. Regardless of appearances or circumstances, we always are making conscious and unconscious choices.

Driving a car provides a good analogy for working with a higher power. In surrendering their will to a higher power, the person does not get out of the driver's seat and let the higher power (or God) drive. The person always is in the driver's seat and making decisions about where to turn. The key issue is where does the guidance come from. The higher power might say turn right, while the fear-filled ego says turn left. When following the will of the higher power, the driver *decides* to turn right.

To illustrate the application of Step Three, someone who is working the Twelve Steps might become emotionally upset and feel strongly tempted to return to addictive or harmful behavior, such as overeating. In the past, one often would follow their impulse, engage in the harmful behavior and degrade their life. But with the Third Step, one pauses and seeks the guidance of their higher power before acting. For most people, the higher power is God, intuitive wisdom or some other source of wise guidance heard within. As people practice discerning inner wisdom, they gain the ability to reliably 'hear' it. If ending addictive or harmful behavior is the most beneficial action, as it virtually always will be, the inner voice of wisdom will guide the person to not engage in harmful behavior.

Once higher power guidance becomes clear, the person has a choice. This is where the Third Step is applied. In the past, when not immediately acting on ego or other impulses, the person might have held an inner debate between what they want to do and what they feel they should do. But with the Third Step, the person simply chooses to do the will of their higher power. They end the inner debate and follow wise inner guidance.

It is like the old concept of having a good angel on one shoulder and a bad angel on the other. People know from experience that acting on the desire to engage in harmful behavior will make life worse. As they listen to and act on wise inner guidance, life gets better. Each time one chooses to do the will of the higher power, the next right choice becomes easier. After a while, doing the will of the higher power becomes the easy and automatic choice. But it always is a choice.

The Third Step suggests turning one's life over to a higher power. This relates to more than ending addictive or harmful behavior. It refers to every aspect of life. In all areas, one seeks to discern and do the will of their higher power or wise inner guidance. People in Twelve Step programs often wind up having better lives than they ever have imagined. This occurs in large part because consistently doing the will of one's higher power produces the most successful and satisfying life. This is the best, and probably only, way to reach one's fullest potential.

The original wording of the Third Step suggests turning one's will and life over to the care of God as one understands him. This reflects the Christian principles upon which the Twelve Steps are based. These principles essentially are the same as those in all the world's great religions. The Twelve Step programs are successful in large part because the religious dogma has been stripped away, leaving only pure spiritual principles. As noted, they are universally applicable. They work for everyone who applies them. In the Third Step, God refers to a higher power as people choose to define it.

As discussed in the Misleading the Public section, referring to God as him could be thought of as a symbolic device that facilitates holding a clearer mental image of God. But referring to God as male or female is humans creating God in man's image. Humans only are familiar with relating to conscious beings that are male or female. It often would be difficult to imagine communicating with something that was not one or the other. Therefore, believing that God is male or female helps the mind to focus on a comprehensible image or symbol of God and follow spiritual guidance. But this image can become a hindrance because God is not anything that the limited human mind can fully visualize or understand. Mental images of God can become barriers if they block access to intuitive wisdom (or God). People sometimes do not believe the inner word of God or intuitive wisdom if it differs from religious dogma.

Rational assessment shows that God probably is not male or female. (These ideas are relevant only for those who believe in God.) Many people see God as the creator of everything or the creation point. Creation emerges from this originating unity point. From this perspective, there is no duality, such as male-female. God does not need to have sex to create things, and therefore does not need to be male or female.

Continuing this hypothetical and unprovable discussion of God, at unity or the level of God, male and female could be seen as different but equal aspects of the same thing, as implied in the Yin-Yang symbol. As discussed in the Woman's section of *Global System Change*, feminine is associated with wisdom and masculine with power. In a sense, wisdom and power are different sides of the same coin. They are essential to each other. Wisdom can do nothing without power. And power can do nothing right without wisdom (because the focus of unguided, and therefore unbridled, power usually is domination, which is the opposite of wisdom).

At the level of unity, God has wisdom and power, and therefore would not be seen as masculine or feminine. At the physical level, humans split out as male or female. This makes life on Earth beautiful. As discussed in the Women's section, many studies show that women generally display greater cooperation, empathy, big picture thinking and other aspects of wisdom than men, while men generally display greater physical strength, aggressiveness and other aspects of power. But at the psychological level, we all contain power and wisdom, or masculine and feminine.

The dogma of several major religions, including Judaism, Christianity and Islam, states that God is male, men are made in the image of God, and women are not. For example, the Bible states, "For a man ought not to cover his head, since he is the image and glory of God, but woman is the glory of man. For man was not made from woman, but woman from man. Neither was man created for woman, but woman for man." (1 Corinthians 11:7-9)

As discussed under the Rule of Dumb deception technique in the Misleading the Public section, these irrational, unprovable, dogmatic ideas strongly promote the suppression of women. Claiming that only men are made in God's image implies that women have lower status or are subordinate to men. As discussed throughout *Global System Change*, one of the most important requirements for achieving sustainability and real prosperity is balancing power and wisdom. There is an abundance of power and lack of wisdom in human society, as shown by widespread environmental and social degradation. Every life support system is in rapid decline, with some regional exceptions, and there is extensive poverty, hunger, suffering, inequality and other problems in human society.

The abundance of power over wisdom is reflected in the status of men over women. Recognizing the critical importance of attaining greater wisdom in society naturally will elevate the status of women, because women innately manifest greater wisdom and cooperation than men. Elevating women to a position of true equality with men and promoting greater wisdom in society requires that we begin to use our perhaps God-given gifts of rational thought and intuitive wisdom more effectively. We must see beyond irrational religious and other ideas which imply that women are subordinate to men. The childish, irrational, unprovable idea that God is male is one of the most important factors promoting the suppression of women.

The idea of God being male is a myth. It has no more validity than a childhood fairytale. This myth was created by humans in part to help the conscious mind hold an image of something that ultimately is incomprehensible to the human mind. Humans can fully know or comprehend God (or intuitive wisdom) in the heart, but not in the finite conscious mind. This is one reason why it is so effective to see the conscious mind or ego as a servant to wise, deep inner guidance (or God).

Thought precedes action. The thinking of people who suffer from addiction, compulsion or harmful habits has degraded their lives. In Step Three, people commit to seeking a new form of thinking and guidance. The location of the source of guidance (i.e. Heaven, heart, Twelve Step group) and its name (i.e. God, intuitive wisdom, wisdom of nature) ultimately are irrelevant. The key is making the mind the servant of something wiser and turning one's will and life over to this wiser, loving, more powerful source of guidance. One does not become an unthinking automaton that blindly does what they are told. The mind ultimately is in charge because it always chooses to do or not do the will of the higher power.

Step Four

In *Step Four*, people make a searching and fearless moral inventory of themselves. This is one of the most important steps. Addiction mostly is a psychological or spiritual problem. The brain responds to thoughts, stresses and actions. If altered brain chemistry is related to addiction, it might be a symptom, not a cause, of psychological issues, stresses and problems. Addiction is spiritual in the sense that it often relates to psychological emptiness resulting from lack of connection to other people and intuitive wisdom. In other words, addiction frequently is a symptom of psychological or spiritual problems.

Step Four examines these root causes so that they can be brought to the surface (i.e. made conscious) and transformed. As the root drivers of addictive behavior are understood and eliminated, it becomes much easier to end the behavior. This type of self-honesty often produces a transformation of the mind that removes the desire or compulsion to engage in destructive, addictive behavior, such as overeating.

The Fourth Step inventory focuses mainly on character flaws that create problems for oneself and others. There are many interpretations and opinions about how to do a Fourth Step inventory. However, an original set of instructions for implementing the Twelve Steps were presented in the book *Alcoholics Anonymous* (i.e. the Big Book). This section is based on the original Fourth Step instructions. Chapter Five of the Big Book describes the three parts of the Fourth Step. These relate to resentments, fear and sex.

Resentments often result from selfishness. Selfishness and self-seeking are among the most important and problematic character defects. People engaged in addiction, compulsion or harmful habits often are obsessively focused on themselves, even when they appear to be kind and generous. As discussed in the Big Book, addicts frequently use kindness, manipulation, coercion and other means to try to get what they want. This often puts them in conflict with other people who resist covert or overt pressure to do something.

Addicts and other self-centered people frequently implicitly think, there are two ways to do things in life, "my way and the wrong way." They often think, "life would be good if other people did what I want them to do." But this frequently does not happen. People generally do what they want to do. As a result, addicts and other self-centered people do not get what they want. This can cause them to be filled with resentments. These resentments are poison. They often create the inner turmoil and suffering that drive people to overeat and engage in other addictive behaviors.

As discussed in the Big Book, a life based on deep resentment leads to futility and unhappiness. Holding resentments against another person gives that person power over oneself. Those holding resentments often think, "if the other person did what I thought they should do, I'd be happier." In other words, they allow their happiness to be based on the actions of other people. It usually is impossible to control another person. Therefore, resentful people are bound to be unhappy. Holding a resentment is like wanting to poison someone else, but drinking the poison oneself. It also is like hitting oneself over the head with a stick.

The Big Book provides a highly effective strategy for removing resentments, and thereby eliminating one of the root causes of overeating and other addictive behaviors. The process involves going back through one's life and writing down all lingering resentments at people, institutions (i.e. government, religion), and principles (i.e. honesty, fairness). People often have many resentments at those who are regularly in their lives, such as family members. The Big Book emphasizes the importance of thoroughness and honesty. As a result, each resentment is written down, along with the action that caused the resentment and what it affects (i.e. self-esteem, financial security, personal relations, fear).

Once this review of life and resentments is complete, the work of removing resentments begins. It first involves recognizing that every person has issues, problems and fears. No one is perfect. People are encouraged to see those who caused them real or perceived harm as being sick or not perfect. They strive to feel the same tolerance and patience that they might feel for a sick friend. With this more open-minded attitude, they begin the most important aspect of the resentment part of the Fourth Step, a process sometimes called the Turnarounds.

For each resentment, people focus on where they were at fault. Another person also might have been at fault. But that is irrelevant for the Fourth Step. People realize that both parties often make mistakes. But in this case, they only focus on their side of the street. For each resentment, they write down their own character flaws and mistakes. They identify where they were selfish, self-seeking, dishonest and fearful. (Selfishness generally relates to a desire, such as wanting something. Self-seeking usually refers to the action taken to fulfill the selfish desire.)

For example, a person doing the Fourth Step might have been selfish by wanting things their own way, not seeing the other person's point of view, or wanting more than their share. They might have been self-seeking by attempting to manipulate or control others, acting superior or insulting other people. They might have been dishonest by lying, cheating, blaming others for their problems, or not admitting that they have done the same thing in the past. And they might have been afraid of embarrassment, rejection loneliness or physical injury.

With some resentments, the person doing the Fourth Step is not at fault. For example, they might have been the victim of a crime or abused as a child. In these cases, the person identifies their harmful beliefs or behaviors related to the incident. For example, they might be holding on to anger, seeing themself as a victim, or blaming the incident for other problems. However, with the vast majority of resentments, as people get honest with themselves, they see that they played at least some role, often the major role, in causing friction with another person.

Doing the Turnarounds can be a highly enlightening and empowering exercise. It is like shining a light on one's personality and character defects. Addicts often think that their lives are bad because other people treated them poorly. But after writing out the Turnarounds for possibly hundreds of resentments, they begin to realize that they frequently were treating other people badly. Addicts often selfishly and dishonestly seek to get their own way. Other people frequently respond negatively. Then the addict becomes resentful at the negative response.

Through the Fourth Step, people realize that they often set the train of negative circumstances in motion through their own character defects and behavior. They realize that their lack of success and happiness results not so much from other people's actions, but from their own attitudes, character defects, thoughts and actions. This is empowering because people can change themselves, but not other people. As they focus more on their role in situations, while also taking a more tolerant view of others, resentments begin to disappear.

Writing the Turnarounds out many times teaches people how to avoid resentments going forward. As resentments arise, they pause before reacting and think, "why am I getting a resentment? Am I being selfish, self-seeking, dishonest or fearful?" Often resentments arise because someone else is not doing what one thinks they should. Honestly looking for the causes of resentments frequently helps people to see their own selfishness or fear. They realize that they often have no right to tell another person what to do. Instead, they might seek the guidance of their higher power or intuitive wisdom and ask how they can be more tolerant and helpful in a particular situation.

One of the most important lessons learned from the Fourth Step is to not take things personally. Addicts often have low self-esteem or a strong sense of inadequacy, which they sometimes hide with arrogance or grandiosity. People who do not like themselves frequently project that other people also do not like them. As a result, they often mistakenly believe that other people's actions are intentionally targeted against them. In other words, they take things personally, when they should not.

For example, if an insecure person is cut off by someone on the highway, they might take it personally and respond with anger or rage. But with Fourth Step training and awareness, they can rationally reflect on their developing resentment and realize that they should not take it personally because the other person does not know them. Instead, they can realize that they might be projecting their own insecurity or low self-esteem onto others and incorrectly assuming that other people want to hurt them or do not like them. With greater self-awareness and self-respect, people can take a more tolerant view and perhaps think that the person who cut them off might be late for an important appointment or distracted by major life problems. Regardless of the reason, a more self-aware person realizes that becoming resentful mainly is punishing themself rather than the other person.

When people do not like themselves, they often project this on to others. They develop unjustified resentments, wrongly thinking that others are trying to hurt them or put them down. Then they frequently wind up acting rudely or harming other people. In this way, low self-esteem degrades relationships. The solution to getting along better with others often is to first get along better with oneself. Building self-esteem and self-respect requires taking esteem-enhancing actions, such as helping others. That is a main reason why the Twelve Steps are so effective. They enable people to treat others well, even if they feel resentful. By taking esteemable actions, self-respect goes up, resentments go down, and treating others well becomes automatic. Treating other people with kindness, love and respect reflects the love that one has for themself.

Getting honest about one's character defects and then not acting on them is one of the most life-enhancing actions that anyone can take. This is one of the reasons why the Twelve Steps can be helpful to everyone, not just addicts. As noted, the Twelve Steps are based on spiritual principles contained in virtually all of the world's great religions. But they often provide more detailed and practical suggestions about how to implement the principles. For example, forgiveness is an important spiritual action. It helps to relieve resentments. Forgiveness, or being more tolerant, is a component of the Turnarounds discussed above. But the more important part is honestly acknowledging one's own faults and role in a particular situation.

The second part of the Fourth Step relates to fear. Fear is a major problem for addicts and often people in general. It is a common aspect of the human condition at our current level of development. As discussed in *Global System Change*, the limited conscious mind frequently misleads people into thinking that they are separate, and therefore ultimately alone in the world. This consciousness of separation often produces fear. People frequently are afraid of what might happen in the future or what other people might think or do. This sense of isolation and fear often causes inner discomfort and turmoil. This in turn frequently causes people to numb or suppress these feelings with overeating or other addictive behaviors. Fear also sometimes causes people to lash out inappropriately at other people. This can cause more unpleasant emotions that are suppressed with addiction or unhealthy habits.

The Big Book discusses the harmful nature of fear and provides a highly effective way of relieving it. As part of the Fourth Step inventory, one thoroughly reviews their fears and writes them down. People often have many fears. Common ones include fear of rejection, embarrassment, abandonment, financial insecurity, failure, success, loneliness, illness, death and public speaking.

After writing out fears, people write down the cause and solution to each fear. As the Big Book discusses, in virtually all cases, the root cause of fear is the failure of self-reliance. Fears nearly always relate to things that cannot be controlled, such as other people and the future. Through their own actions, people often try to limit fear and negative consequences. For example, one can limit the risk of being harmed by being a good person and treating other people well. Also, planning well, working hard and taking care of oneself can reduce the risk of financial and health problems. Self-reliant actions such as these are good for many reasons, including the reduction of fear. However, self-reliance often cannot eliminate the risk of negative outcomes or harm. As a result, it usually cannot fully eliminate fear of other people and the future. In other words, self-reliance can lower, but rarely, if ever, eliminate fear.

The Big Book suggests that the solution or means to eliminate fear is trusting and relying upon a higher power. Most people conceive of the higher power as a source of wisdom or force, such as God, the wisdom of nature or intuitive wisdom, that pervades and controls, or at least influences, everything. They also often believe that this force or higher power is benevolent and loving, and wants them to prosper at the highest possible level. By turning their will and lives over to a higher power, they no longer have to worry about other people or the future. Instead, they focus on what they can control – their own thoughts and actions in the present moment.

By striving to do the will of their higher power in the present moment and leaving things that they cannot control to the higher power, people come to believe that they are placing themselves in harmony with other people, the universe and the future. If problems arise, they deal with them in the moment. But they do not worry about possible negative outcomes before they happen. For most people, the vast majority of feared outcomes never occur. As a result, focusing on them is a waste of time and energy. People obviously should plan for the future as needed. But once they have done all that they reasonably can do, they let go of the outcome. They turn it over to their higher power and focus on what they can control.

Fear essentially is the expectation that an unpreferred outcome is most likely. Focusing on the negative increases the negative. Therefore, dwelling on fears increases the likelihood that negative outcomes will occur. Letting go of fears, focusing on one's thoughts and actions in the present moment, and expecting that one's higher power will bring about positive outcomes greatly increases life satisfaction and quality of life.

From a rational perspective, it makes good sense to not worry about things that one cannot control. However, for those who feel alone and isolated in the world, perhaps because they do not believe in a higher power, it often is difficult to stop worrying about external, uncontrollable factors. Believing in a benevolent, transcendent higher power greatly facilitates the alleviation of fear.

Some people say that believing in a benevolent higher power, such as God or intuitive wisdom, is a cowardly escape from reality. But there are many irrational, and paradoxically cowardly, components of this supposedly rational position. First, as discussed in the Raising Public Awareness section, it is impossible to know that God or intuitive wisdom does not exist. Therefore, stating this position as a fact or knowledge is irrational and ignorant. It also might be egotistical, arrogant and cowardly. Some people get their sense of self-worth from believing that their intellect can understand everything. Acknowledging that they did not know or understand something might cause uncertainty and discomfort. To avoid this intellectual discomfort, they irrationally and perhaps egotistically claim that the possible is impossible.

More importantly, in arguing that believing in a higher power is an escape from reality, they ignore reality. It is obvious that the implied intelligence and technology in the human body and nature essentially are infinitely greater than conscious human intelligence and technology. The instinctual or implied intelligence that guides components of nature produces nearly infinite sophistication, symmetry and coordination. In addition, millions, if not billions, of people claim that belief in a higher power or God has led them to a more successful and satisfying life. This strongly implies that there is some type of great wisdom available to individuals. If it is true that the implied wisdom of nature can be accessed and applied by individuals, the life benefits could be immense.

Some type of implied vast intelligence obviously is all around us. We are made of it. Millions or billions of people claim to have accessed and applied it successfully. It is highly unlikely that all of these people would

296

OVEREATING CAUSES AND SOLUTIONS

be mistaken about the existence of a real, tangible inner source of great wisdom and power. Therefore, it would be highly irrational to not at least try to access this potentially immense, life-enhancing resource, especially when there is no downside, except possibly acknowledging that the ego cannot understand everything. This unfortunately might be an insurmountable downside for some intellectually insecure people who do not feel comfortable acknowledging that they cannot understand everything.

Failing to at least try to take advantage of a higher power would be like being offered an opportunity to place a free bet at a horse race with a high chance of winning a large payout. But even though there is no cost to the wager, the person chooses not to bet because there is a small chance that they might lose. This essentially is what people are doing when they do not at least consider the possibility that there is a vast, life-enhancing resource available to them. Open-minded exploration of this concept will show that this resource is tangible, real and available. On this issue, there may be no proof outside of one's experience. But proof will manifest itself to individuals when they humbly seek guidance from the infinite wisdom that pervades everything.

Some people argue that it is not possible to know that a benevolent force guides everything, including humans who seek it. While it might not be possible to know this intellectually, there is strong evidence that such a force exists. As noted, the implied force guiding the components of nature produces nearly infinite sophistication, symmetry and cooperation. If this force were malevolent or nonexistent, the result probably would be chaos, instead of vast sophistication. Also, when people seek to discern and correctly apply intuitive wisdom, they invariably experience a more successful and satisfying life. Again, if this guiding force were malevolent or nonexistent, the results of seeking to apply it probably would be negative or nonexistent.

To summarize the fear component of Step Four, fear is a corrosive factor that severely degrades the human experience and produces negative outcomes such as overeating and addiction. Self-reliance never can completely alleviate fear. Probably the only way to fully alleviate fear of other people and the future is to trust and rely upon a higher power, and then focus on what one can control – their own thoughts and actions in the present moment.

In the second part of the Fourth Step, for each fear on the list of fears, people write out how self-reliance failed to alleviate the fear and how trusting and relying upon a higher power would have relieved it. This repetition reinforces the importance and benefit of trusting and relying upon a higher power. As people do this, many fears are reduced or eliminated. This in turn reduces or eliminates one of the main drivers of overeating and other harmful behaviors – fear.

The third part of the Fourth Step relates to sex. Sex is one of the most powerful forces in human society. It is normal, natural and essential for the survival of humanity. It often brings great joy. But it also frequently causes problems in relationships and other areas, especially when it is used selfishly. The Big Book notes that we all have sex problems or issues. We'd hardly be human if we didn't. It also suggests avoiding extreme advice on this issue. Some people call sex a base necessity of procreation and often speak of the evils of it. Others take sex too lightly and say that people don't have enough of it.

The Big Book suggests taking a rational approach to sex. Sex and relationships often cause problems and emotional discomfort. People frequently suppress these emotions with overeating and other addictive activities. As a result, reducing problems with sex can alleviate a frequent driver of addictive or harmful behavior.

As part of the Fourth Step inventory, people list their history of sexual situations, including relationships, encounters and categories of activity, such as pornography, masturbation or prostitution when relevant. Then for each situation or category, people write out: how they were selfish, dishonest or inconsiderate; who they hurt, including themselves; how they unjustifiably aroused jealousy, suspicion or bitterness; how they were at fault; and what they should have done differently.

This honest and thorough self-assessment helps people to see how selfishness and other character defects cause problems for themselves and others in the sex area. Becoming aware of selfish or harmful behavior is the first step toward changing it. After clarifying character defects in the sex area, the Big Book suggests that people develop a safe, sane and unselfish ideal for their future sex life. For each relationship, people are encouraged to ask, is it selfish or not? Going forward, they ask for guidance and support from their higher power on living up to their ideal.

As discussed in the Men's section, growth in the Internet and online pornography is driving increased sex addiction. This creates problems in relationships and other areas. Like overeating and alcohol abuse, excessive, uncontrolled sexual activity that causes problems in people's lives (i.e. sex addiction) often is a symptom of psychological or spiritual problems or emptiness. Sex addiction, like other addictions, temporarily suppresses painful or uncomfortable emotions, but frequently causes long-term pain and life problems. The Twelve Steps can be used to alleviate the root causes of sex addiction and provide the guidance, strength and power needed to live a healthy sex life and have fulfilling relationships.

Thoroughly and honestly writing out the Fourth Step inventory as it is described in the Big Book often is labor-intensive and time-consuming. It also frequently is emotionally disturbing because people are recalling past unpleasant events and getting honest with themselves, perhaps for the first time. Many people begin, but do not finish the Fourth Step for these reasons. As a result, some sponsors might suggest that those who are just ending addiction do a more simplified version of the Fourth Step at first, and then do the detailed version outlined in the Big Book when they are more stable. However, other people believe that those who have hit bottom and recently stopped addictive behavior are highly motivated to change. As a result, their sponsors or more experienced friends might advise them to do the Fourth Step as it was originally described in the Big Book.

To facilitate completing a labor-intensive Fourth Step, people often work with a sponsor in a Twelve Step group who already has done the Steps. They might commit to work on it three times per week for a minimum of two hours each time, for example. They also might commit to call their sponsor each time they begin working on the step and ask their higher power for guidance and support. These types of commitments and activities make it much more likely that people will complete the frequently difficult, but highly beneficial Fourth Step process.

Step Five

In *Step Five*, people admit their character flaws and specific wrongs to their higher power, themselves and another person. In practice, this often means reading the entire Fourth Step inventory, which frequently is long, to another person. That person might be a sponsor, religious leader, or other person who will not reveal confidences.

The Fifth Step is very important because people often feel ashamed of past actions that hurt themselves or others. They frequently wish to forget their mistakes. People often present a positive image to the world. But inside, they frequently feel ashamed and unworthy. Honesty and disclosure are critical. Everyone makes mistakes. Keeping them inside often poisons one's life. It frequently creates the shame and low self-esteem that drive overeating and other harmful behaviors. By disclosing or admitting flaws and mistakes, people often are freed of shame. As the Big Book says, they can look the world in the eye. They realize that their mistakes and flaws do not define them. They can change and become better, more productive persons.

It is particularly important to disclose things that cause shame, such as in the sex area (again, to a trustworthy person who will not reveal confidences). People often feel ashamed of thoughts and actions related to sex and other issues. But once they disclose this information, they learn that other people frequently think and do many of the same things. The person doing the Fifth Step often realizes that they are not as strange or unusual as they thought they were. Like nearly everyone else, they are a normal person doing their best to get by.

A common expression is that people are as sick as their secrets. Keeping things inside can severely degrade one's life. By disclosing this information to another person, people frequently feel peace and ease. They feel closer to their higher power and other people. They often begin to feel a tangible inner transformation that gives them the power to end overeating and other harmful behaviors.

Step Six

In *Step Six*, people become entirely ready to have their higher power remove their character defects. In the Fourth Step, they gained a clearer understanding of how they operate in the world. They saw how they use character defects, such as selfishness, self-seeking and dishonesty, to get what they want. These defects and behaviors caused many problems. But they also often provided some security and certainty. Letting go of defects and acting in new ways can create fear and uncertainty. People might worry that they will not get what they want if they do not lie or manipulate others. Becoming ready to let go of these defects is the focus of the Sixth Step. Even though they might provide some security, the Fourth Step showed how character defects cause pain and problems for oneself and others.

This is where faith in a higher power is helpful. Through the Twelve Steps, people are striving to move forward in ways that produce a more successful and satisfying life. By trusting that their higher power will take care of the future and coordinate other people, those doing the Twelve Steps do not have to worry about things they cannot control. Instead, they focus on being the best person they can be in the present moment.

Step Seven

In *Step Seven*, after becoming ready to have defects removed in Step Six, people humbly ask their higher power to remove their character defects. This involves humbly making one's conscious mind or ego the servant of something wiser. The person is seeking a new way of being in the world, led by a wiser source of guidance heard within.

Changing behavior can take time. In moments of fear, selfishness and dishonesty might arise. The point of the Twelve Steps is progress, not perfection. The Steps substantially increase awareness of character flaws and harmful behaviors. This greatly facilitates ending them. But the defects might still arise sometimes. If they do, the person asks their higher power to remove them, and then does the best they can going forward.

Doing the right thing produces life satisfaction. People often cheat, lie or act selfishly out of fear that they will not get what they want. But when they do the right thing, even if they do not get what they wanted, they frequently feel a much deeper level of satisfaction. They learn that doing the right thing produces a better life that continuing selfishness or other character defects. At first, it requires a leap of faith. People must trust that if they let go of character defects and try a new way of living, they will be much happier. After a while, doing the right thing, being honest and treating others well becomes easy and automatic.

Step Eight

In *Step Eight*, people make a list of all persons they had harmed and become willing to make amends to them all. Most of the Step Eight amends list usually is made in Step Four. In the resentment and sex parts of the Fourth Step inventory, people wrote down who they harmed and what they did to cause it. In the Eight Step, this list is expanded to include people and organizations that were harmed, but not included in the Fourth Step inventory.

Making amends often is difficult. People frequently are ashamed of past actions that hurt others. They often do not like to admit that they were wrong. The ego resists it. It is hard enough to admit faults and mistakes to a trusted person in Step Five. But admitting mistakes to people one has harmed can be much more difficult. Nevertheless, making amends is a critical part of achieving the spiritual awakening, renewal of the mind or inner transformation that enables people to end harmful behaviors, such as overeating. Shame or guilt for past actions is like a poison that drives inner turmoil and addictive behavior. Acknowledging faults and making amends often relieves shame, increases self-esteem and lowers the compulsion to overeat or engage in other harmful behaviors.

Making amends is like drawing a line in one's life. By rectifying damage done in the past to the greatest extent possible, people commit to end character defects and actions that harm themselves and others going forward. A major goal of making amends is to prepare oneself to be a more productive, effective and helpful member of society.

An important part of Step Eight is recognizing that the focus should be on one's own faults, not other people's. As shown in Step Four, people often hurt each other. One acts and the other reacts. At times, the other person might have caused more harm than the person making amends. As the Big Book says, it is harder to make amends to an enemy than to a friend. But it often is far more beneficial. A common mistake when making amends is to expect reciprocity or apologies from the other person, especially when the other person might be more at fault or have caused more harm. This expectation can sabotage the effort and make the situation worse.

The focus of amends is on rectifying one's own past. The other person might be at fault too. But that is irrelevant to the Eighth Step. People should focus only on their side of the street. In Step Four, they learned to take a more tolerant view of those who had harmed them. It often is helpful to see the other person as being sick or imperfect. During the Step Eight preparation for making amends, it is highly beneficial to adopt a tolerant attitude towards others and not expect reciprocity. One is asking for forgiveness. They should be willing to grant it to others, even if other people do not ask for it.

Step Nine

In *Step Nine*, people make direct amends to those they have harmed whenever possible, except when to do so would injure them or others. Remembering Step Eight preparation, when making amends, people never should criticize, argue or discuss the other person's faults or mistakes. The focus is completely on one's own faults and mistakes, regardless of what the other person has done. Most of the time, people respond favorably to amends. Sometimes they admit their own mistakes and long-standing feuds are ended.

However, there should be no expectations. Even if the other person responds negatively, it does not matter. The person making amends has done their best to make things right. The response from the other person is out of their hands. Of course, when making amends, one should not do anything to inflame other people. They should be tactful, considerate, sensible and humble, without being servile.

There are many types of amends. Apologizing for past harms and mistakes is important. But for people who are still in one's life, such as family members, the most important amend is to discontinue harmful behavior. Apologizing for past actions, and then doing the same thing again, will have little, if any, positive impact. As the Big Book discusses, before ending addictions and doing the Twelve Steps, people might have been selfish, dishonest and inconsiderate to spouses and other family members for many years. As a result, they should not expect instant change in others when they make amends and strive to be a better person. After years of selfishness, family members might be justifiably skeptical. The person doing the Twelve Steps should be patient. They might have to earn back the trust of others. Their actions will speak much louder than words.

The Ninth Step suggests that amends should be made, except when doing so injures others. People should not improve their lives at the expense of others. The decision to make amends should be based on what is best for everyone involved, not just the person making amends. In questionable cases, people often should seek guidance from their higher power, sponsor and other trusted advisors. For example, the Big Book discusses a situation where someone was unfaithful to their spouse. If the spouse does not know about the infidelity and the person does not intend to do it again, it might be best to not admit disloyalty in some cases. Admitting it might relieve guilt but bring heartache to one's spouse. However, many spouses would want to know about the infidelity. In cases such as these, people should seek guidance and strive to do what is best for everyone involved.

The Big Book also discusses making amends for or disclosing past criminal activity. Family members, business partners and other parties might be harmed by such disclosures. But guilt for past criminal actions could drive ongoing addictive behavior. The Big Book suggests seeking guidance and discussing disclosure with those involved before proceeding. When financial amends are owed, people should make them, possibly on a payment schedule if they cannot afford to pay immediately.

In some cases, it is not possible to make amends. The key issue is being willing to make them, and then doing so if one gets the opportunity. In other cases, there may be legitimate reasons for delaying amends. But they should not be unnecessarily delayed. It generally is better to make the amends as quickly as possible. Making amends often brings about an inner transformation. In Step One, people see that their egos and ways of thinking and acting caused problems for themselves and others. In a sense, the ego is the enemy. It does not want to give up power and control. But the purpose of the ego or conscious mind is not to be the leader. It is to be a follower or servant of something deeper and wiser. Admitting one's faults breaks down the ego. It promotes humility and a willingness to seek wiser guidance.

Through this process of making amends, people begin to see the full benefits of the Twelve Steps. As the Big Book describes, this is the point where people often begin to feel a new freedom and happiness. Feelings of uselessness and self-pity are replaced by serenity and peace. Fear of people and economic insecurity leaves. Selfishness and self-seeking are replaced with a desire to help others. People no longer regret their past. They see how their experience can be used to help others. They intuitively know how to handle situations that used to baffle them. They realize that their higher power is doing for them what they could not do for themselves.

By this time in the Twelve Steps, people often have lost their desire to overeat and engage in other harmful behaviors. The character defects and past mistakes that drove addiction have been addressed or resolved. However, in Chapter Six, the Big Book states that the relief of compulsion or addiction and the other benefits described above often are only temporary. Ongoing relief from addiction and achievement of a more successful and satisfying life require daily maintenance of one's new spiritual condition. As discussed, spiritual in this case does not refer to God or religion. It refers to continuing to do the will of one's higher power, as they define it, and maintaining more effective, cooperative and satisfying relationships.

That is the purpose of Steps Ten, Eleven and Twelve. The last three steps often are referred to as the maintenance steps. If people do a thorough job on Steps One through Nine, especially Steps Four and Nine, they might only do these steps once, although many people redo these steps periodically if they feel it would be helpful. However, Steps Ten, Eleven and Twelve should continue for one's lifetime. They maintain the more satisfying and effective way of living developed in Steps One through Nine.

Step Ten

In *Step Ten*, people continue to take personal inventory and promptly admit when they are wrong. Step Ten essentially is an extension of Steps Four through Nine. In Step Seven, people asked their higher power to remove character defects uncovered in Step Four. This process continues with Step Ten. People continue to watch for selfishness, dishonesty, resentment and fear. If these arise, they ask their higher power to remove them. These character defects once were the foundation of an unhappy and harmful life. If one is lax about maintaining their spiritual condition, these defects can return and poison one's life again. As this occurs, the desire or compulsion to engage in overeating or other harmful activities also can return.

In addition to limiting character defects, Step Ten also involves continuing Steps Eight and Nine. People monitor their interactions with others. If they cause harm, they quickly make amends. This activity often greatly improves quality of life. As discussed, addicts frequently are self-obsessed. They often have problems in relationships and do not know how to get along with others. They frequently feel that they are better or worse than other people. They often isolate and feed their loneliness with addiction. By working the Steps and getting involved in Twelve Step programs, people learn how to get along with others. Through self-love, they know that they are below no one. Through humility, they know that they are above no one. They become an equal among equals.

Knowing that one will have to make amends if they act inappropriately or cause harm helps to keep behavior in check. As discussed, the ego often does not like to make amends or admit fault. Going forward, if one feels resentment arising and a subsequent desire to lash out or act inappropriately, a person can say to themselves, "if I act inappropriately, I'll have to apologize to this person. I'd rather not do that. As a result, I'll avoid insulting or harming this person, and thereby avoid the need to make amends."

The desire to harm another person or treat them rudely usually results from fear, self-centeredness or resentment. As people consider the sources of these negative qualities, harmful desires often diminish. By not harming or treating others rudely, relationships improve and life becomes more satisfying.

Step Eleven

In *Step Eleven*, people seek through prayer and meditation to improve conscious contact with their higher power, asking only for knowledge of the higher power's will and the power to carry it out. This is one of the most important steps. It is the practical application of the most important concept in the Twelve Steps – making one's conscious mind or ego the servant of a deeper, wiser source of guidance.

This is not something that one does once or once in a while. Successful application of the Twelve Steps requires an ongoing reorientation of the mind toward seeking wiser guidance. Step Eleven continues the activities begun in Steps One through Three. Continuing to seek the guidance of a higher power makes people wise and effective in life. When they stop seeking wise guidance and revert to control by the ego, wisdom leaves and problems return.

The Big Book discusses prayer and meditation in Step Eleven. Prayer is more relevant for those who believe in God and make it their higher power. Those who see the higher power as intuitive wisdom or something other than God often would focus more on meditation. But even for people who believe in God, meditation is important. Prayer is useful for many reasons. It encourages the subjugation of the ego or will to the higher power. It attunes the mind to God or the higher power. And it makes one open and receptive to Divine or wiser guidance.

But prayer mostly is talking, not listening. Meditation often is listening. God does not need guidance, support, compliments or devotion from humans. The all-powerful God that many people believe in does not have low self-esteem. Its feelings will not be hurt by lack of attention from humans. These are human projections. It is God created in man's image with human frailties and foibles. However, humans do need to hear from God (or their higher power) if they wish to reach their highest potential and have a successful and satisfying life. Therefore, listening to their higher power, often through meditation, is critical.

The Big Book provides highly useful and practical guidance on this issue. Upon awakening, people are encouraged to begin their day with prayer and meditation. If they belong to a particular religion, they might say a few prayers from that religion. They ask their higher power to keep them free from selfishness, dishonesty, self-pity and fear throughout the day. They also ask that they be guided to be of maximum usefulness to others. They often spend time in quiet meditation waiting for guidance or input from their higher power on important issues. Some people pray or meditate with other people in the morning or attend religious services.

During the day, if people become agitated or doubtful, they pause and ask their higher power for guidance on the right thought or action. The Big Book suggests that people develop a new consciousness or orientation that says throughout the day, "Thy will not mine be done". This process of constantly seeking guidance from a higher power puts people in harmony with other people and life in general.

At first people might mistake their ego for their higher power and act on incorrect guidance. But over time, as they practice discernment, people learn to reliably discern the will of their higher power. One way to determine if guided thoughts, words or actions are from the higher power or ego is to consider if the guidance is kind and loving to all. If it is, the guidance probably is from the higher power. If it is not, the guidance almost certainly is a product of the fearful mind or ego. As people practice relying on intuitive guidance from their higher power, it becomes a functional, reliable part of the mind. They can turn to this source of wisdom and power at any time in any situation.

By frequently turning to their higher power for guidance throughout the day, people become much more efficient and effective. They no longer focus on things they cannot control, such as other people's actions and the future. Their higher power takes care of that. Instead, they focus on what they can control – themselves. By letting go of things they cannot control, they have more energy. Their relationships improve. They are more satisfied and effective at work, home and other places.

At the end of the day, before they retire at night, people review their day. The Big Book suggests that they consider if they were resentful, selfish, dishonest or fearful. Do they owe an apology to anyone? Have they kept something to themselves that should be discussed with another person? Were they kind and loving to all? What could they have done better? Were they thinking of themselves most of the time or of what they could do for others? Without drifting into worry or remorse, they ask their higher power what corrective actions are needed. Before retiring, they give thanks for all the good things in their lives, including relief from overeating and other harmful behaviors.

Step Twelve

In *Step Twelve*, having had a spiritual awakening as a result of the Twelve Steps, people try to carry this message to others who are engaged in addictive or harmful behavior, and practice the Twelve Step principles in all their affairs. By working the Steps, people often have a spiritual awakening or renewal of the mind that enables them to do what previously seemed impossible. But as noted, this relief from addiction or other harmful behavior usually is only temporary. It frequently will not last if people do not maintain their spiritual condition. Beyond doing the will of one's higher power, eliminating character defects and making amends, helping others is a critical component of maintaining one's spiritual condition.

As discussed in the Life Satisfaction section, spirit could be thought of as the interconnectedness of all things, or oneness. From this perspective, helping others is the same as helping oneself because we are all connected in ways that are real, but not always obvious to the five senses or myopic human mind. Perhaps the simplest and most practical definition of spirituality is love. Treating other people with kindness, love and respect is the most important commandment or suggestion of virtually all of the world's great religions. This is the practical aspect of spirituality. It is what loving God looks like in practice. It is the main commandment of nearly all religions because it works. It produces the most truly successful and satisfying life. The Twelve Steps are highly effective in large part because they are strongly focused on helping other people.

In addition to developing the Twelve Steps, AA developed the Twelve Traditions. These guide the structure and focus of Twelve Step groups. Many self-help groups are based on the Twelve Steps and Traditions. The Traditions state that the primary purpose of Twelve Step groups is to help people with similar problems. The only requirement for membership is a desire to stop addictive or harmful behavior. The groups are nonprofit and self-supporting. They usually only have small budgets for expenses, such as rent, literature and refreshments. To avoid controversy and distraction from their primary purpose, Twelve Step groups take no position on outside issues and do not endorse or affiliate with outside organizations.

To avoid linking Twelve Step groups to particular persons, members remain anonymous in the media and public forums. Twelve Step programs have helped millions of people to improve their lives by ending addictive or harmful behaviors. But the programs do not work for everyone. If a famous person was unsuccessful in a Twelve Step program and the media announced this, it might create the false public impression that the programs are ineffective. This could prevent people from seeking assistance. Placing principles above personalities in this and other ways promotes the humility and selfless service that make the Twelve Step programs so successful.

The Twelve Traditions also emphasize that the public relations policy of Twelve Step programs is based on attraction rather than promotion. The Big Book discusses how to work with alcoholics in Chapter Seven. But the principles and methods apply to all Twelve Step programs. The Big Book emphasizes that members should not promote or pressure anyone to join Twelve Step groups. Instead, they might share their experience with an interested person who is struggling with similar addictive or harmful behavior. This allows people to identify and feel that they would be understood. People always are free to come and go as they choose without pressure. However, Twelve Step groups have many different types of people. Sometimes members overzealously promote the program. Their intentions might be good. But they are not following the principles and traditions of the program.

Discussing spirituality with other people is another aspect of the attraction rather than promotion principle. The Big Book suggests that people never try to force their spiritual or religious views on others. These ideas often are unprovable or ultimately unknowable to the conscious human mind. For example, virtually all religious descriptions of God, creation stories and other dogma cannot be proven with logic, science or fact-based observations of reality. These concepts only can be believed through blind faith (i.e. believing something that cannot be proven or is logically incorrect, such as the economic concept of seeking infinite growth in a finite system).

People can have tangible inner experiences that convince them beyond a shadow of a doubt that some type of Divine, transcendent or all-powerful force exists and guides their lives. But this experience cannot be used to prove the existence of intuitive wisdom or God to anyone else. Also, the inner experience or experience of the heart often cannot be fully understood or articulated by the conscious mind because the mind cannot fully comprehend infinity or all that is on all levels of reality. Therefore, any mental or spoken concept of God only is a symbol. It points to something that is true and real. It is a mental device that gives the mind an image of something that ultimately is incomprehensible to the conscious mind.

This indicates why blind faith in religious dogma can be so harmful, destructive and unintentionally hateful. Religious dogma often demands that people blindly believe in a particular description of God and then seek to convert other people to this view. Various born again Christian sects encourage this among their followers. People in these groups usually are good and well-meaning. They treat others well and seek to have a positive impact in the world. But their dogma sometimes forces them to act in ways that other people justifiably find offensive and hateful. This is the great tragedy of religious dogma. Good, well-intentioned people are compelled to act in unintentionally harmful ways that create strife, division and suffering in the world. They mean well, but do bad.

When people loudly or assertively profess their religious beliefs, they often are implying that they have found the right path for everyone. Their dogma tells them that people only can get to God through the path of their religion. Therefore, they frequently believe that they are helping other people by showing them the one 'true' path to God. If blind faith people stopped to rationally consider their views, they would realize that their specific dogma or version of God is unknowable or unprovable. They may have had a powerful inner experience of the presence of God or intuitive wisdom. But this was an experience of the heart. The mind cannot fully comprehend it, although the mind might trick itself into thinking that it can fully understand.

When people realize that their inner experience is valid for themselves, but perhaps no one else, it may cause them to question their dogma. Some Christian, Muslim and other religious sects strongly discourage this. Dogma sometimes threatens people with eternal damnation for not believing in dogma. The Twelve Step programs encourage people to not promote their religious or spiritual views to those who are not interested in them. If someone is interested and asks about them, disclosing one's views is appropriate. But when someone publicly discusses their faith in a particular version of God, other people frequently and justifiably find this offensive.

Probably without intending to do so, the person professing their faith is implying that those holding different spiritual or religious views are misguided and making mistakes in their lives. They imply that they have found the path for everyone and that they know better than others what is best for other people. But they do not know this. They only have found their own path. It is not possible for them to see into the mind and heart of another person. They cannot know what is right for others. Each person must decide that for themself.

Advertising one's religious or spiritual views often is justifiably offensive. But those who quietly model how their views produce a good life are appealing. Others are drawn to them. They promote peace, brotherhood and respect for others. They truly benefit the world. By encouraging attraction rather than promotion, the Twelve Step programs once again show their great wisdom.

There are several ways to help others and be of service in Twelve Step groups. One of the most important is sponsorship. Sponsors usually have more experience successfully applying the Twelve Steps and ending addictive or harmful behavior. They often act as mentors, advisors, confidants and friends. Members also can help others by taking a service position in the group, such as coffeemaker, treasurer or chairperson. Simply attending meetings and sharing one's experience applying the Twelve Steps also is helpful. In general, members frequently spend substantial time and effort helping those who are trying to end addictive or harmful behavior. When people end their destructive self-obsession, they often find the help, happiness and relief from addiction that they fruitlessly sought for so long.

Twelve Step groups are fellowships of like-minded people who are helping each other to solve a common problem. No one it is looked down upon. Everyone is dealing with the same basic problem. In Twelve Step groups, people learn how to get along with others, honestly discuss important issues and make friends. Sometimes people ask why members continues to participate in Twelve Step groups after they end addictive or harmful behavior. This would be like asking someone why they continue to go to church after learning the basic lessons and practices of a particular religion. For many people, the Twelve Step group is a fellowship or spiritual community. By attending and helping the group and its members, people often get back friendship, sobriety, peace of mind and a far more satisfying life than they had before.

By continuing to implement the Twelve Steps and remain active in Twelve Step groups, people frequently not only achieve long-term relief from addictive and harmful behavior. They also receive help and support with life problems. Loss of loved ones, relationships, jobs and health are inevitable parts of life. The emotional stress of these situations often drives people to resume addictive or harmful behavior. Those who are active in Twelve Step groups and practicing the Twelve Steps are much more likely to avoid relapse and successfully navigate life's challenges.

In the second part of the Twelfth Step, people strive to practice the Twelve Step principles in all their affairs. This means that they seek to do the will of their higher power, eliminate character defects, make amends when necessary, and focus on helping others at home, work and all other areas of life. People engaged in addictive or harmful behavior often are self-centered. They frequently use manipulation, coercion or even kindness to get emotional security, complements or material things from other people. This selfishness often pushes people away and leaves addicts feeling frustrated and resentful. Through the Twelve Steps, members learn to focus on giving rather than getting. As people give without expectation, they usually get the support and friendship they fruitlessly sought for so long. As the old saying goes, love freely given brings a full return.

Addicts and other self-centered people often want to be the leader or center of attention. But few people want leaders who are egotistical, self-centered and pursuing leadership roles to further their own agendas. As people practice the Twelve Steps, they become more focused on cooperating and helping other people to succeed. When they stop wanting to be in charge, they become better leaders. Successful leaders frequently see themselves as servants. They focus on enhancing the well-being of others. Paradoxically, as people let go of wanting or needing to be leaders, they often get more leadership opportunities.

Many addicts and other self-centered people are filled with fear and insecurity. They frequently alternate between grandiosity and self-loathing. They have been described as egomaniacs with inferiority complexes. By working the Twelve Steps, people lose the fear that they are worse than other people and let go of the insecure need to be better than others. They humbly see all people as equal and important. They learn how to get along with others. As discussed in the AA book *Twelve Steps and Twelve Traditions*, they no longer are alone in a self-constructed prison of the mind.

People engaged in addictive or harmful behavior often tell tall tales and make many promises and commitments. But they frequently do not follow through. Perfectionism and other excuses are used to avoid action. As people practice the Twelve Steps, they become more reliable and trustworthy. They do not let perfectionism or any other excuse prevent them from living up to their responsibilities and commitments. They do not arrogantly believe that their work must be perfect. They humbly do the best they can, finish the task and move on to the next activity or commitment. They keep their word.

Through addictive or harmful behavior, people often try to meet higher-level spiritual, psychological or emotional needs with lower-level physical activities. For example, food meets a basic survival need – sustenance. But eating does not fulfill higher-level needs. These are met through things including love, relationships, being with friends and family, doing what one loves, and spiritual activities or experiences such as feeling a tangible connection to God or all that is.

When people try to meet higher-level needs with lower-level activities, such as overeating, sex or other addictions, they often block activities that actually could satisfy. Overeating and other addictions leave them feeling spiritually or psychologically empty. They seek life satisfaction through activities that never can provide it. Their lives often spiral downwards.

When the pain becomes great enough, people frequently realize that overeating or other addictions must end. But this can be difficult. It is like ending a relationship. The relationship/addiction provided comfort and certainty. In bad or uncomfortable times, the addiction could be counted on to provide temporary comfort or distraction. It was a friend. But the cost of the friendship/addiction became too high. There often is sadness, fear and uncertainty when ending harmful relationships or addictions. People frequently wonder if life will become boring or meaningless.

Ending overeating and other addictions requires courage. As people stop familiar but harmful behavior, uncomfortable emotions can arise. There often is a strong desire to rush back to the friend/addiction for comfort. People frequently give in to this desire. That is a main reason why change can be so difficult.

The Twelve Step programs greatly facilitate ending addictive or harmful behavior. People come to believe that they deserve a good life and will have it if they do the will of their higher power. In Twelve Step groups, they find like-minded friends who help them through the tough times of ending addiction. By working the Twelve Steps, people strive to eliminate the character defects and self-loathing that drove addiction.

Twelve Step programs help people to see their addictions or bad habits rationally. For example, they learn that love, connection and other higher-level needs never can be met with food. A few minutes of eating pleasure often is followed by hours of guilt and declining quality of life. Through overeating, people entertain themselves by abusing their bodies and degrading their health. Through Twelve Step awareness, people realize that they should not have to abuse and harm their bodies to be happy. Twelve Step programs provide the tools and support needed to attain true happiness and life satisfaction. As this is achieved, the desire to overeat declines and often ends.

With the growing use of antidepressants and other psychiatric drugs, more people are participating in Twelve Step programs while taking these drugs. This sometimes is beneficial. Depression and other psychological problems can make people unable to function at even the most basic levels. In these cases, psychiatric drugs might enable them to participate in Twelve Step programs and address the spiritual, psychological and emotional drivers of addiction. As these root causes are relieved, people often can end addiction and psychiatric drug use.

However, as discussed in the Depression and Psychiatric Drug sections of *Global System Change*, psychiatric drugs can be a problem in many cases. Psychological pain often is a gift because it signals that inner or outer changes are required. People might be depressed due to disempowering beliefs, character defects or being in the wrong jobs or relationships. Psychological pain frequently provides the motivation needed to make difficult inner or outer changes. Taking psychiatric drugs can numb this pain and thereby reduce the motivation to change. People might continue disempowering beliefs or remain in unfulfilling jobs or relationships. As the causes of psychological pain are ignored, pain continues and ongoing drug use might be required. Twelve Step programs can provide the support needed to face psychological pain and make it through the tough times of ending addiction without taking psychiatric drugs.

As discussed in the Psychiatric Drug section, antidepressants and other psychological drugs almost certainly are hugely overprescribed in the US and some other developed countries. Many people take these drugs because they feel uncomfortable. They are not immobilized by psychological problems. For those who are able to function without psychiatric drugs (i.e. go to work and meet their other obligations), it often might be better to avoid psychiatric drugs, allow emotional pain and use it to motivate necessary changes. Twelve Step groups provide safe vessels for allowing painful emotions, addressing the root causes of addiction, changing behavior, and emerging into a vastly more successful and satisfying life.

Ending addictive or harmful behavior often requires a leap of faith. This involves trusting that a better future is possible. Addiction frequently lowers self-worth and makes it difficult to believe this. In Twelve Step groups, people gain hope that a better future is possible because they see other people achieving it. By making amends and reducing character defects, they effectively address the causes of self-loathing. This improves self-esteem and helps people to believe that they deserve a good life.

People also learn to focus on the positive instead of the negative. For example, rather than focusing on giving up favorite foods, they focus on gaining a thinner, healthier body. But this can be difficult. The comfort of overeating occurs immediately. But losing weight takes some time and effort. This is why faith in a better future and self-love are so important. These qualities enable people to resist temptation, make it through the difficult times and achieve a satisfying life.

Trusting in a better future is a critical component of doing the will of one's higher power. People often live life based on self-will or ego. They might pursue wealth, power or popularity. Even when they achieve these goals, they frequently are not happy. In doing their higher power's will, people access a deeper, wiser source of guidance heard within. This could be called the authentic self, true self or higher self. Many people call it the voice of God. Whatever it is called, this is the voice that knows what is best for a person. Therefore, choosing to make the conscious mind the servant of this deeper, wiser source of guidance produces the most successful and satisfying life. In doing this, people replace ego goals for wealth, power and fame with the goal of doing their higher power's will on a daily basis. As they do this, people often wind up with more wealth and worldly success. But this was not the goal. It is a result of seeking and doing the higher power's will.

Following Your Bliss

Joseph Campbell was a leading expert on mythology and comparative religion. He spent his life studying the world's great religions. His television interviews with Bill Moyers, called *The Power of Myth*, helped many people to better understand the nature of life and success. The thesis of his life's work was "Follow your bliss". This is one of the most effective ways to do the will of one's higher power. This section discusses how to follow your bliss.

Doing the higher power's will produces true happiness and life satisfaction. It often is the most effective way to resolve the inner problems that drive overeating and other addictions. When the ego is in charge, people often pursue wealth, success and happiness, perhaps because family and society conditioned them to do so. But they frequently run into walls. The wiser part of them is trying to guide them onto the right path – the path of the heart.

As they consider life messages (i.e. the walls or problems facing them) and seek the guidance of their heart, they get on track. Synchronous events often occur that propel them forward. Unexpected resources or assistance frequently shows up. As Joseph Campbell says, we all have a unique path that we are meant to take in life. When we are off the path, life seeks to guide us back on, often with painful inner or outer events. When we are on the path, life flows more smoothly. People feel a closeness to life, other people and intuitive wisdom or God. They develop an inner strength and peace that is not shaken by outer circumstances.

Some people might ask, if we all have access to infinite wisdom, power, knowledge and intelligence through the intuitive function, why are people often not able to access winning lottery numbers or other desired information. This reflects the ego trying to control life, rather than trusting and relying upon a higher power. The ego frequently wants something. But inner wisdom knows that it would not serve them. As a result, they do not get conscious access to the information.

For example, some people might think that they would be happy if they had a lot of money. As a result, they play the lottery. But the chance of winning a large payout is extremely small. Without intending it, people essentially are affirming that their chance of having what they want and being abundant is very small. This unconscious expectation of scarcity is indicated by the fact that lotteries often are played by lower income people. Also, people might think that they want money, but a wiser part of them knows they really want happiness and life satisfaction. They believe money is the path to this. But if they do not perceive correct lottery numbers, perhaps something inside is telling them that there is a better, more effective way to achieve this goal. For example, real abundance and life satisfaction often result from love, friendship, doing fulfilling work and spiritual seeking, rather than having a lot of money, fame and power.

As Joseph Campbell discusses, probably the most effective way to identify the higher power's will is to discern one's excitement or bliss. We each have unique things that truly excite us on a deep level. This does not refer to comfortable or pleasant activities, such as watching TV or eating ice cream. It refers to the truly deep passions that we all have, but many are not aware of.

Following this excitement or passion might be very uncomfortable or difficult at times. But that often is the nature of life. Real, true, lasting joy frequently results from hard work done well. As Joseph Campbell discusses, by following one's excitement or bliss, people put themselves on a path that always has been there for them. Doors start to open, resources often arrive and life moves forward more quickly. As seen in nature, the higher power or wisdom of nature implicitly wants each individual to prosper and reach their fullest potential. This is why doing the will of one's higher power produces the most successful and satisfying life.

In nature, individual plants and animals often reach their fullest potential. They have no choice. They only can follow intuitive or instinctual guidance. Humans, however, do have a choice. We can choose to let our egos and fears lead our lives and not reach our fullest potential. Or we can choose to follow our intuitive guidance. When this occurs widely, humanity will be displaying the beauty, coordination and sophistication seen in nature. We will be reaching our fullest potential and creating Heaven on Earth.

Following one's true deep excitement with integrity is the same as doing the will of one's higher power. This deep excitement is one of the strongest indicators of the higher power's will. Integrity is a key part of following one's excitement. People always should live up to their commitments and obligations and ensure that their actions harm no one. For example, a parent might feel that they want to quit their unsatisfying job and pursue a different career. But if this would make them unable to support their child, following their heart would be out of integrity in this case.

Doing the will of one's higher power often requires faith and trusting in a better future because the conscious human mind cannot know the future. Life presents itself on daily basis. Not knowing the future can be exciting if people expect a positive one. They might wonder what gifts or new experiences will present themselves each day. On a deep level, we know everything. But the conscious mind only is aware of a tiny fraction of this, perhaps so that we can experience newness and learning. Life might be very boring if we knew in advance what would happen. Not knowing the future can make life wonderful. Each day is a party with new gifts awaiting.

However, not knowing the future can be frightening if one expects negative outcomes. People might worry about making the right choices. For example, in choosing one's academic or career path, there is no way to know in advance if the choice will be correct. Knowing the mechanics of following one's excitement can help people to make the best choices in this and other areas. As noted, one's true, deep excitement with integrity often is the best indicator of the higher power's will. For longer-term decisions, such as career choices, from the available options, people should choose the option that is most exciting. Pursuing money instead of excitement frequently leads to a less satisfying or unsatisfying life. On a shorter-term daily basis, again from the available options, people should choose the option that is most exciting with integrity (meaning living up to one's commitments and obligations).

Many times, as people are following their excitement, they discover an even more exciting option. But this often would not have been revealed if they had not pursued the first exciting option. Following one's excitement with integrity frequently is the fastest way to meet small and large goals, even if the excitement does not seem to be related to the goals. The higher power or intuitive wisdom sees everything. Therefore, it knows how certain actions can accelerate goal attainment, even when the conscious mind cannot see the connection. This is another reason why doing the higher power's will produces the most successful and satisfying life. For example, if someone is working on a project with a deadline, but their most exciting option is to take a walk, the walk often will accelerate meeting the deadline, perhaps by providing unexpected benefits such as intuitive, helpful, creative thoughts. Alternatively, the person with the deadline might meet someone while on their walk who becomes a friend and ally on the project.

When following one's excitement, a desired goal may not be an option at present. In these cases, people should focus on available options and choose the most exciting one. Focusing on options that are not available wastes time and energy, and distracts people from the path of their heart or higher power's will. One way to look at this situation is to assume that if a desired option is not available, it is not meant to be. It might appear to be the best option. But in reality, there are other options that would serve the person better. The higher power wants the person to focus on what is available. Many times, as people follow their hearts or higher power's will, they find that their goals change. They frequently realize that there are far more exciting goals than the ones they previously had.

However, if a desired option is not available in the present, people do not have to give up the goal. They can maintain it as a clear intention, but focus on what is available. If an option is not available in the present moment, it might mean that people are not ready for it. More preparation is needed. Choosing the most exciting available option is the fastest and most effective way to achieve the ultimate goal. It provides the preparation needed.

The conscious human mind cannot see and is not meant to see everything, including the future. It apparently is meant to focus primarily on experiencing life in the present. However, the human mind has access to intuitive wisdom. This wisdom sees and knows everything. It wants the individual to achieve their highest potential. This 'intention' of intuitive wisdom is strongly indicated by the beauty of nature. Letting go of future outcomes and relying upon higher power guidance enables individuals to focus on the present – the only place that life actually occurs.

When people make the commitment to follow their excitement, bliss or heart with integrity, no matter where it leads, they put themselves on a path that brings more and more fulfilling experiences. This is how human consciousness is meant to function. Following one's bliss helps people to reach their fullest potential and greatest joy. This is what doing the will of the higher power looks like in practice.

The Twelve Steps greatly facilitate this life-enhancing path. But there are many ways to get there. The key is following one's excitement with integrity on a daily basis. When people surrender to excitement or the will of their higher power, they are not powerless. In the human mind, there is an aspect that sits above all else. This could be called the chooser. It is the part of us that decides what to do and exercises our free will. The chooser decides our focus and actions. It chooses to do or not do the will of the higher power. We never are powerless because we always are choosing. But if one wants an amazing life, the best choice is to do the will of one's higher power.

Meditation and Metaphysics

Meditation can be a highly useful tool when seeking to end overeating and other harmful behaviors. General aspects and benefits of meditation were discussed in the Life Satisfaction section. An excellent book by Shaila Catherine, called *Wisdom Wide and Deep*, was recommended. The book provides detailed meditation instructions and a clear, comprehensive description of meditation concepts. This section discusses using meditation to help end overeating and other harmful behaviors. It also discusses other benefits of meditation that were not discussed in the Life Satisfaction section.

Sugar, fat, salt, MSG and other additives as well as emotional emptiness and other factors can create a desire or tendency to overeat. But overeating always is a choice. People never are forced to put food in their mouths. In this sense, overeating ultimately is a psychological problem.

Meditation could be thought of as the study or observation of the mind. One simultaneously is the observer and the observed. Meditation teaches people to observe without reacting. As noted in the Life Satisfaction section, cravings are temporary. If people physically crave or need food, they generally should eat it. However, obese and overweight people often eat due to non-physical cravings. The body does not need or want food, but the mind craves it anyway. These are spiritual, mental or emotional cravings. They all pass away. One does not have to respond to them.

Through meditation, people learn to observe their cravings and aversions, likes and dislikes, without reacting. Many people's lives are ruled by craving and aversion. They are not free to follow their hearts, intuitive wisdom or higher power's will. By learning to peacefully and equanimously observe without reacting, people see that all cravings and aversions pass away. As they gain this insight, they become free to do what they actually want in life. (Equanimity is a state of mental or emotional stability or composure arising from a deep awareness and acceptance of the present moment.)

Life only occurs in the present. But regrets about the past or fears of the future often pull people away from the present. This pulls them away from life. The Twelve Steps help people to let go of the past by rectifying past mistakes and let go of the future by trusting in a higher power. As a result, they are free to do the will of their higher power in the present moment.

Meditation facilitates this by training the mind to concentrate and focus better. One observes during meditation or at any time of the day when the mind is wandering in the past or the future or focusing on something other than what they can control in the present moment. Without condemnation, they choose to return their focus to the present moment. This training of the mind and greater ability to focus brings great power. The mind becomes a powerful ally, rather than a harmful distraction, in achieving one's fullest potential and joy.

Understanding the mechanics of the mind is important because the mind creates one's life. It often jumps from idea to idea, like a wild animal. Many people create their lives unconsciously. The mind switches between positive and negative ideas, and creates a sometimes positive, sometimes negative life. Conscious creation of a preferred, positive life requires learning to control the focus of one's mind. As this occurs, people gain the ability to think only about what they want. As they continuously focus on a positive, preferred existence, and act based on these ideas, they create a positive, highly satisfying life.

A basic meditation process involves sitting with the back straight and focusing on the breath. The focus could be on the skin between the nose and upper lip, sensing the breath entering and leaving. With new or inexperienced meditators, the mind often wanders. When it does, attention is gently returned to the breath, without criticism or judgment. As with most new behaviors and skills, practice is required. Over time, people gain the ability to maintain focus on the breath or other meditation object.

This process of deep concentration frequently produces a blissful state. But achieving this is not the goal. It is to observe whatever occurs without craving or aversion. Through deep concentration, wisdom arises. One can experience the interconnectedness or oneness of everything and understand the transitory nature of phenomena, such as feelings and sensations. The focus learned in meditation can be applied at all times. By focusing only on what one wants, they create a preferred life.

As discussed in the Life Satisfaction section, the mechanics of creating a preferred life essentially are making a decision, trusting it and acting on it. For example, an obese or overweight person might want to lose weight, resolve health problems, feel more comfortable physically and have more energy. They realize that ending overeating of unhealthy food will achieve these goals. As a result, they make a decision to be a healthy eater. They trust the decision in all situations and act on it.

If cravings to overeat unhealthy food arise, they might be tempted to lose faith in their decision and think, "apparently I am not a healthy eater because I have these cravings." But instead, they might trust their decision and think, "these cravings are a gift. They remind me of my decision to be a healthy eater. I trust that decision." Then they act like a healthy eater and do not overeat. If they succumb to the desire, they do not lose faith in their decision. For example, they do not say, "I overate. I guess I am not a healthy eater." Instead, they might say, "I am a healthy eater. I overate in the past. But that is over. I act like a healthy eater from this point on."

Through meditation, people strengthen their ability to make these observations and decisions. They gain the ability to observe and change harmful patterns. To illustrate, many people frequently overeat or engage in other harmful behaviors until they feel guilty or bad. Then they use the guilt or negative consequences to recommit themselves to stopping overeating or other addictions. With greater internal observational skills, people can look into the future, anticipate the consequences of their actions, and shortcut the process by avoiding the harmful action. For example, someone might say, "I know from extensive experience that if I overeat now, I will feel bad later and wish I had not overeaten. At that point, I might stop overeating. But I do not have to wait until then to stop overeating. I do not have to make myself feel bad or guilty before I stop. I can choose to not overeat now and skip the bad feeling."

Self-love and hope that a better future is possible are among the most important assets needed to end overeating and other harmful behaviors. They build upon themselves. Each positive, self-loving action, such as eating healthily, builds more self-love and hope. With repetition, positive actions become easier over time. Healthy eating becomes the new normal.

Through meditation, people gain the ability to more objectively discern reality. They realize that current conditions are the result of past actions. They are not the result of inherent unworthiness, for example. Through meditation-enhanced mental clarity, they see that their actions create their future. Therefore, they have the power to create a positive, desirable future. In meditation or at any other time, people can envision their preferred future, such as being a thinner, healthier person. Holding this image can build excitement and hope that a positive future is possible. Elevated mood helps people to make the positive short-term decisions, such as not overeating, that will bring them a positive long-term future.

Meditation also can help people to clarify what truly is intuitive wisdom or the will of their higher power versus what is social conditioning or blind faith. Once basic needs are met, one of the most important actions needed to have a successful and satisfying life is to gain control of the mind and make it the servant of deeper, wiser guidance. Meditation can be the laboratory where this discernment and exploration occurs.

The most important journey that people take in life often is the inner journey. The inner determines the outer. The quality of one's life is determined almost completely, if not completely, by one's inner experience, not outer experience. Overeating and other harmful behaviors are a reflection of the inner experience. The solution is to go within, or as said in the TV show *Star Trek*, to boldly go where no one has gone before. We each have our own private inner world. As people explore it through meditation, if they persevere, they realize that the inner world is infinite and not private. They discover and experience oneness. They are transformed. Overeating or any other pleasurable physical experience is nothing compared to the overwhelming, indescribable bliss that we all have access to within. This experience of oneness and bliss can happen any time, for example, when a parent first sees their newborn child. Meditation is not the only path to oneness and immense inner power. But it is a good way to get there.

People often use drugs, alcohol and other substances to achieve an altered state of consciousness. Frequently, they are trying to escape boredom and add some excitement to their lives. This is ironic. We are like blind people walking through a forest rich with every treasure one could imagine. But we cannot see them. People often feel empty, alone or unfulfilled. But if they open their inner eyes, they can see the immense beauty, treasure and excitement all around them. These inner eyes can be opened through meditation. People do not need to run from reality with drugs, food or alcohol. Rather than dulling their minds and perceptions, they can open and sharpen them.

As we open our inner eyes, we will see that we already are in Heaven. It has been here all the time. We just did not see it. We do not have to go anywhere or do anything to be in this Heaven. It all is here in the present moment. As people begin to see this, the need for overeating, drugs, alcohol or any other mind-altering substance or activity becomes unnecessary.

The realm of time and space that humans inhabit almost certainly is an infinitesimally small component of all that is. As indicated by many near-death, meditation and other experiences, beyond this version of time and space (i.e. this dimension), there apparently is an infinite realm. People have reported indescribable bliss when reaching it. Religions often call this realm

Heaven and say that we can go there when we die if we blindly believe religious dogma. But we do not have to wait for physical death to go to Heaven. As noted, it always has been here in the present moment. But most people did not see it. As we set aside irrational blind faith and open our minds, we can begin to manifest the wisdom of nature and experience Heaven now. *Global System Change* asserts that this is the destiny of humanity – to reach our fullest potential (i.e. create Heaven on Earth).

Heaven on Earth has physical and nonphysical components. The physical is humanity living in balance with nature, and thereby surviving and prospering over the very long-term. The nonphysical is each individual reaching their fullest potential on an inner and outer level. Achieving one's fullest potential on the inner level involves staying focused on the present moment, being free from craving and aversion, and freely choosing to follow one's heart.

We humans probably only have reached the tiniest fraction of our potential. The most amazing frontier for humanity almost certainly is the human mind. Human knowledge is bounded by the human perspective. We do not know how much we do not know. There may be an infinite number of parallel dimensions, including nonphysical dimensions. If other physical dimensions exist, they might have different natural laws and physical properties than our own.

Meditation potentially can be used to facilitate rapid expansion of human knowledge into the currently unknown realms. To illustrate, through Vipassana-like meditation, some practitioners discovered over 2,000 years ago that reality is comprised of tiny particles that appear to disappear and reappear. Quantum physics discovered this much more recently. The mind is an extremely fine instrument. Through meditation, it can be trained to sense or perceive interactions at the tiniest level.

Various spiritual traditions have suggested that everything is comprised of energy which vibrates at different frequencies and creates the illusion of solidness. Other spiritual traditions have said that parallel dimensions exist. More recently in physics, string theory postulates the existence of parallel dimensions and suggests that reality is comprised of tiny strings of energy.

In other words, some of the most advanced scientific concepts probably were discovered through meditation thousands of years ago.

Science usually validates only what can be proven. This could result in denying more than 99 percent of reality. Rather than beginning with a negative bias, an alternate approach is to assume that things which are not obviously impossible are possible. This idea could be applied to consciousness. Some people believe that consciousness is a function of matter (i.e. it would not exist without the brain). Spiritual traditions, on the other hand, sometimes say the opposite. Matter (or the illusion of matter) is a function of consciousness. They believe that a creative consciousness pervades everything.

It is impossible to prove that consciousness does not pervade everything and guide energy and the formation of our universe. Some people argue that our universe could have resulted from random action. In a nearly infinite number of interactions, it might be possible that life could have been spontaneously created. Once this occurred, the evolution of life could have been the ordering force on Earth, creating oxygen in the atmosphere and the web of life.

While this may be possible, it does not preclude the possibility that some type of consciousness formed our universe and operates in nature. The probability that our universe, or at least life, resulted from random action seems infinitesimally small. This implies that it is highly possible, and perhaps probable, that some form of consciousness drove the formation of our universe and life. When people allow their inner wisdom to guide their lives, it often produces positive results. Many people claim to have experienced oneness and connection to transcendent consciousness during meditation, near-death experiences and other events. This further indicates that the wisdom of nature or transcendent consciousness exists.

Some scientists are searching for a theory that explains everything. It seems unlikely that it will be found if the theory does not integrate consciousness. Rather than denying the existence of something that cannot be proven currently, scientists might adopt the hypothetical perspective that transcendent consciousness exists. This more open-minded perspective potentially could lead to new, provable insights about reality. By quieting, focusing and opening the mind, meditation might greatly facilitate this more advanced and productive scientific exploration.

This open-mindedness could be applied to extraterrestrials. Millions of people claim to have seen UFOs, including many credible witnesses, such as military and commercial aviation pilots. It is possible that many, perhaps the large majority, of people who say that they have seen UFOs are mistaken. But it seems unlikely that all of them, especially the highly credible and experienced witnesses, are wrong. The UK, Canada and several other national governments are releasing UFO files. The US government has said little about UFOs and extraterrestrials. If it felt that UFO or extraterrestrial technology had military applications, it might keep this information secret to protect national security.

Many people claim to have seen UFOs do things that are impossible with human technologies. According to these accounts, technology apparently exists to overcome gravity and provide large sources of energy. Taking the more open-minded position that these technologies might exist potentially could accelerate the advancement of science in many areas. For example, it might facilitate the development of inexpensive or free energy sources that enable humanity to reverse human-induced global warming and protect future generations.

The hypothetical examples of transcendent consciousness and extraterrestrials are used to illustrate the potentially infinite capabilities and resources available in the human mind. Meditation is one of the most important tools or vehicles for exploring this potential. The power of the mind can be harnessed through meditation to achieve many goals, including ending overeating and other harmful behaviors.

Another hypothetical example related to the mind, meditation, overeating and other harmful or addictive behaviors relates to the afterlife. It is impossible to prove that human consciousness does not continue after physical death. Therefore, stating this as a fact would be ignorant and possibly fearful. The large majority of people around the world believe that consciousness or the energetic essence of people continues in some form after death.

Some spiritual traditions say that people who are addicted to overeating or other activities remain addicted in the afterlife with little or no possibility of escaping from this form of hell. They continue to seek satisfaction in ways that never satisfy, possibly for eternity. According to this view, humans have the ability to make changes in beliefs and habits while in physical form. But this becomes much more difficult after physical death. This probably is unprovable with science. However, for people who believe that this scenario is possible, it could serve as a further incentive to end overeating or other addictions while they have the chance. If one felt interested or compelled, they could explore this concept of the afterlife in meditation and seek intuitive guidance.

Another concept related to meditation and exploration of the mind involves conscious knowledge. For example, it could be useful to assume that we always know what we need to know when we need to know it. Intuitive wisdom always delivers all the knowledge the conscious mind needs in the present moment. Using an earlier example, if one did not perceive winning lottery numbers, they could assume that a wiser part of them knew that they would receive more life-enhancing benefits by not winning the lottery. Perhaps they learned the lesson that playing the lottery indicates that they believe their chances of being abundant are very small. This awareness might compel them to seek abundance and life satisfaction in ways that have a much higher chance of achieving them.

Using the perspective that we always know what we need to know when we need to know it, a student might conclude that they were meant to fail a test if they did not intuitively perceive the answers. This probably is true. The lesson might be that studying and doing homework are important if one wants to pass tests. The perspective that we know all we need to know in the moment does not suggest that people should sit around, do nothing and wait to be inspired. In some cases, this might be the best option. But mental and physical work usually are needed to progress in life.

For example, a person might sit in meditation and try to ascertain the next major insight in quantum physics. However, if they have not studied the subject, their mind probably would not recognize the insight if it showed up. A field often requires plowing before the seed can be planted. Physicists understand the language and principles of physics. As a result, they are much more likely to recognize, understand and utilize intuitive insights that expand the boundaries of knowledge in their field. However, there are many cases where strong knowledge causes myopia or tunnel vision. This can block or inhibit intuitive wisdom. In some cases, having less knowledge produces an open mind and makes one more receptive to intuitive wisdom.

The idea that we know all we need to know in the moment is a tool that can help subjugate the ego to the will of the higher power. Rather than worrying about information that one does not know or cannot remember, they can let it go and focus on what they do know and what is happening in the moment. They can trust that if they are meant to know or remember something, it will come to consciousness at the right time. This enables people to be more effective and productive in the present moment.

As discussed in Step Eleven of the Twelve Step Programs section, through meditation people can develop a highly effective working relationship with their intuitive wisdom or higher power. This link to wise guidance can occur at all times. Meditation could be thought of as the exercise that strengthens this link.

Many of the concepts and techniques discussed in the Twelve Step Programs, Following Your Bliss and Meditation and Metaphysics sections probably cannot be proven intellectually or scientifically. However, they can be proven through the most powerful form of knowledge – one's inner and outer experience. There may be no proof outside of this. But one's own experience often is the strongest proof.

Hunger

Hunger is a major problem in the world, and the situation is poised to get much worse. More than one billion people are chronically hungry, mostly in Africa and South Asia.[674] About three-fourths of the global population lives on less than $2 per day. According to the World Bank, about 1.2 billion people live below the poverty level of $1.25 per day. The poorest people in the world spend 80 percent or more of their incomes on food. People in poorer countries often eat only once per day. Food prices have more than doubled over the past few years. As prices rise, poorer people frequently have less money available for healthcare, school and other necessities. In addition, they often are forced to cut back on the quantity and quality of food they eat.[675]

Rapidly growing food demand combined with growing food supply constraints will drive ongoing food price increases. This will increase hunger and push more people into poverty. Grain production is critical to addressing hunger. Grain represents a major component of the human diet, directly and indirectly (as livestock feed). Factors driving increased demand for grain include population growth (80 million people per year), increased consumption of grain-intensive animal products as income rises for about three billion people, and expanding conversion of grain to ethanol in the US.[676] Population is projected to increase from 7.9 billion to 9.7 billion by 2050, and then continue growing to 10.9 billion people by 2100. By 2050, it is projected that grain production must be increased by 70 percent to feed nearly 10 billion people eating more animal products.[677]

As food demand rises, many factors are constraining or lowering food supply. As discussed in the environmental sections of *Global System Change*, factors constraining the ability to increase grain production include expanding soil erosion, desertification, aquifer depletion, global warming and water shortages. Agriculture represents 70 percent of global freshwater use. Water demand is growing at about twice the population growth rate. By 2025, water demand is projected to exceed supply by 50 percent. These factors are strongly contributing to flat or declining crop yields in many regions. Declining environmental quality, reduced water availability and other factors will severely constrain the ability to increase grain production going forward.

As discussed in the Land section, meeting growing demand for animal products and grain with industrial agricultural approaches probably will require converting much of the Earth's remaining tropical forests and grasslands to agriculture. This is unsustainable and grossly irresponsible to future generations. Industrial agriculture well illustrates the frequently intense myopia of humanity. It often increases short-term food production at the expense of longer-term production. It frequently strongly drives soil erosion, aquifer depletion, water pollution, pesticide contamination, GE contamination and many other negative impacts. These often reduce the productive capacity of land or cause it to be abandoned. Clearing more natural areas and replacing them with industrial agriculture is a formula for disaster.

With rapidly growing food demand, constrained food supply and declining quality of agricultural land, hunger is poised to get much worse. Declining environmental conditions show that industrial agriculture cannot meet current food demand sustainably. It is an irrational, destructive, even suicidal fantasy to think that we can feed a growing amount of animal products produced with industrial agriculture to an expanding population. It will drive vast environmental degradation, and then probably become impossible. Using rational thought and a whole system perspective, it becomes clear that a different strategy is needed.

Vastly reducing the consumption of animal products probably is the most important action needed to relieve hunger now and in the future, meet growing food demand and restore the environmental life support systems that future generations will need to survive and prosper. As discussed, producing animal products is extremely inefficient compared to producing plant products. It takes over 100 times more water to produce one pound of beef than one pound of wheat. It takes 16 pounds of grain to produce one pound of beef. In general, it takes about six pounds of plant protein to produce one pound of animal protein. About 54 kcal of fossil fuel are needed to produce one kcal of beef protein. But only three kcal are required to produce one kcal of protein from grain.[678] One acre of land can produce 165 pounds of beef or 20,000 pounds of potatoes. And as noted, producing one pound of beef generates 53 pounds of animal urine and feces.

In a world without limits or environmental consequences, eating ever-increasing amounts of animal products might seem fine. But that world does not exist. It is a fantasy. In the real world, eating animal products and burning fossil fuels probably are the most environmentally destructive human activities by far. If we vastly reduce or nearly eliminate the consumption of animal products, there quickly could be a large surplus of food in the world. To illustrate, about 800 million tons of grain are fed to livestock globally each year. This is more than twice the amount needed to feed the 1.2 billion poorest people in the world.[679] In other words, if the grain currently fed to farm animals were delivered to humans instead, world hunger could be ended, and a large surplus of grain would be left over.

A University of Minnesota study analyzed global grain production and use. It found that calories available for human consumption would increase by up to 70 percent if grain used for animal feed and biofuels were instead used for direct human consumption. This would enable an additional four billion people to be fed with grain grown on existing farmland. It would be more than enough to feed the additional two billion people projected to be on Earth by 2050 without expanding farmland into natural areas.[680]

Greatly reducing the consumption of animal products would enable humanity to scale back industrial agriculture and farm the land sustainably. We probably could provide enough food for everyone now and in the future without eroding topsoil, depleting aquifers, causing chemical and GE contamination, and clearing our remaining precious, life-sustaining forests, grasslands and wetlands.

A report by the United Nations Environmental Programme said that rising incomes in China and other countries are causing a shift in diets to meat and dairy products. As a result, a growing percentage of the global grain harvest is being fed to livestock. The report found that rising animal product consumption and population growth would drive increased hunger and severe environmental degradation. It said, "A substantial reduction of [hunger and environmental degradation] would only be possible with a substantial worldwide diet change away from animal products."[681]

Humanity's unsustainability does not result from lack of knowledge. It mainly results from lack of public awareness and the will to change that would result from this awareness. There are many experts around the world who have extensive knowledge about sustainable agriculture and food production. For example, a study published in the journal Nature proposed a five-point plan for doubling food production while lowering the environmental impacts of agriculture.

The plan recommended: halting farmland expansion and land clearing for agricultural purposes, especially in tropical rainforests; improving agricultural yields in regions that are not reaching their full potential; reallocating water, nutrients and other resources from regions with excesses to those with shortages; dedicating cropland to producing food for direct human consumption rather than producing animal feeds and biofuels; and reducing waste. The report noted that one-third of food produced by farms is discarded, spoiled or eaten by pests. Eliminating this waste could increase food production by 50 percent. The report also noted that dedicating cropland to food for direct human consumption instead of animal feeds and biofuels could increase human food production by another 50 percent.[682]

The report suggested using agricultural chemicals and genetic engineering when necessary. However, these inputs cause extensive negative environmental and human health impacts. Many studies have shown that organic and other sustainable farming methods can increase yields more than industrial agriculture, produce healthier food and restore agricultural land.

Sustainable agriculture is particularly important in developing countries. The majority of the world's hungry are small plot farmers in developing countries who do not grow enough food to feed their families.[683] Often living on less than $1-2 per day, these farmers usually cannot afford GE seeds, chemical fertilizers, pesticides and other industrial agriculture inputs. From a global perspective, industrial agriculture probably can further increase short-term global grain production (usually at the expense of longer-term production). But this frequently will not help hungry people in developing countries because they cannot afford the food or it is not available in their regions. As a result, industrial agriculture in developed and developing countries often will not be the most effective way to relieve hunger in developing countries.

A comprehensive report sponsored by the UN and World Bank suggests a far more effective way to address hunger in developing countries. The report was issued by the International Assessment of Agricultural Knowledge, Science, and Technology for Development (IAASTD), an intergovernmental group comprised of 30 governments and involving over 400 scientists. The IAASTD report states, "To feed over nine billion people in 2050, we urgently need to adopt the most efficient farming techniques available."[684] The report strongly recommends an approach called agroecology, a form of sustainable agriculture.

Agroecology can increase yields in developing countries by more than twice as much as industrial agriculture approaches, while restoring previously degraded agricultural land. It involves saving seeds, fixing nitrogen in soil with cover crops instead of using nitrogen fertilizer, relying on beneficial insects and biodiversity to deal with pests instead of using pesticides, and fertilizing with manure and other natural materials. The approach is appropriate for developing countries because it requires few purchased inputs, optimizes long-term food production, and improves soil quality, carbon sequestration and biodiversity over time. It also helps to mitigate global warming and protect farmers from climate extremes.

Agroecology replaces chemical inputs with knowledge. It values traditional and indigenous farming techniques. Local farmers are seen as partners and experts, rather than as aid beneficiaries. The approach encourages the production of more fruits and vegetables to provide vitamins and other nutrients. Agroecology helps developing country farmers to increase yields, become self-sufficient, feed their families and generate income to buy other necessities. From a macro perspective, it helps developing countries to avoid trade deficits and protect environmental life support systems. Purchasing industrial agriculture inputs can create trade deficits. This increases pressure to exploit and export natural resources.

The IAASTD calls upon rich and poor nations to use sustainable agriculture to help build sustainable societies. To do this, agriculture must acknowledge and account for its true environmental and nonrenewable energy costs, seeds and livestock must be locally owned, food exports from rich countries must not be subsidized, and agricultural technologies must be chosen based on what is appropriate for the region, rather than what is profitable for private sector companies.[685]

The IAASTD report explained why industrial agriculture technologies, such as genetic engineering and nitrogen fertilizers, often are not appropriate for developing countries. Beyond the fact that subsistence farmers often cannot afford these and other industrial agricultural inputs, the report notes that genetic engineering frequently does not provide the claimed yield increases and pesticide use reductions. In addition, GE crops can contaminate non-GE crops and potentially cause human health problems, such as allergic reactions. Furthermore, genetic engineering concentrates seed ownership and can make developing country farmers dependent on or beholden to large companies. Regarding nitrogen fertilizers, the report notes that these contribute to greenhouse gas emissions and water pollution. Agroecology approaches such as using cover crops can outperform nitrogen fertilizers, while producing additional fodder for animals and vitamin-rich fruits, for example.[686]

The IAASTD report was strongly supported by nearly all developed and developing countries, in large part because agroecology has the potential to be superior to industrial agriculture in developing countries on nearly every measure, including cost, relieving hunger, applicability, self-sufficiency, strengthening local economies and communities, long-term food production, trade impacts and environmental protection. The US was one of only three countries that did not approve the IAASTD report (the other two were grain exporters Canada and Australia).

The US criticized the report for being protectionist and failing to promote genetic engineering as an important component of solving the world's hunger and agricultural problems. The US plays a major role in driving global warming, which has large and growing negative impacts on developing country farmers. The report discussed how agroecology could be used to mitigate climate change. This focus might have caused concerns among US politicians who accepted money from energy companies.

The US rejection of the IAASTD report illustrates economic and political system flaws and the greater influence of business on government. As discussed, businesses and their owners in the US are allowed to indirectly give unlimited amounts of money to politicians and inappropriately influence government in other ways. This causes the US government to largely become the agent or servant of business. Legally-corrupted government frequently focuses on doing what is best for the small group that gives the most money to politicians, rather than doing what is best for current and future society.

The industrial agriculture sector largely has not focused on agroecology in part because it usually cannot be patented and it generates few or no sales of seeds, pesticides and fertilizers. Also, banks and fossil fuels often are not required for agroecology. In addition, if developing country farmers use agroecology to feed their families and communities, it might reduce or eliminate markets for large agricultural companies.

The US did not support the IAASTD report, at least in part because agroecology could hurt the shareholder returns of companies that give money to politicians. US efforts to fight global hunger largely have focused on promoting industrial agriculture approaches, such as using genetic engineering and nitrogen fertilizers. In the food area, the US aggressively promotes public-private partnerships.[687] These often involve transferring taxpayer funds to corporations, which then provide inexpensive or free food to developing countries.

The US said the IAASTD report was against free trade. Since the 1980s, the US government usually supported free trade and opposed import tariffs. This illustrates how philosophies often are used to mislead the public and protect shareholder returns. The IAASTD report strongly criticized the subsidization of export crops in developed countries. When subsidized, inexpensive food commodities are exported to developing countries that have no import tariffs, local farmers frequently cannot compete on price. The inability of developing countries to protect their small farmers has been a major driver of massive rural poverty, rural flight and widespread hunger.[688]

When developing countries attempt to impose import tariffs to protect their farmers, the US often argues that this is restraint of trade. But the US position frequently is deceptive and dishonest. Subsidizing export crops is unfair competition. But when countries impose import tariffs to level the playing field against subsidized exports, the US often cries foul. If the US did not subsidize exports, import tariffs often would not be needed. This situation is like one person hitting another. Then, when the victim responds, the attacker gets mad. In other words, the US slaps a developing country and then expects the country to take no action in response.

Public deception occurs when businesses, politicians paid by them and other business allies suggest or imply that citizens should blindly believe in the philosophy of free trade. But free trade is not the priority. The well-being of society is. To see through vested interest deceptions, people must objectively analyze each situation to determine which approach most effectively benefits society. However, this logical thinking would show that free trade often is not the best approach. For example, prohibiting import tariffs that protect developing country farmers blocks self-sufficiency and strongly drives poverty and hunger. Rational thought shows that free trade obviously is not the best option in this case. It literally kills people through starvation and degrades society in many other ways.

In this and many other cases, rational thought would hurt shareholder returns. As a result, citizens implicitly are encouraged to not think rationally and instead blindly believe in the philosophy of free trade. As discussed in the Misleading the Public section, philosophies often inhibit rational, objective thinking. They frequently encourage people to blindly believe in economic and other dogma.

Unrestricted commodity speculation is another economic and political system flaw that causes food-related problems in developed and developing countries. Hedge funds, private equity companies and other speculators with no intention of using food commodities often essentially place financial bets about commodity prices. This frequently drives food prices up and hurts average citizens. As discussed in the Finance and Capital Markets section of *Global System Change*, wealthy speculators should be prohibited from using national and global economies like giant casinos. They should not be allowed to profit by degrading society. Creating liquidity or trades for those with legitimate interests in commodities might be acceptable. But benefiting society in this way is not the goal of hedge funds, private equity companies and other speculators. The primary focus is on maximizing investor returns.

US opposition to agroecology in developing countries illustrates another type of public deception. As discussed in the Misleading the Public section, businesses, politicians paid by them and other business allies often use whatever legal means are necessary to protect shareholder returns. This frequently includes misleading the public. Our flawed systems often compel dishonesty and public deception to ensure corporate survival. One of the most egregious public deceptions involves the misuse of religious ideas, proverbs and other wisdom teachings to protect shareholder returns. In this case, vested interests take advantage of citizens' desire to live good lives by following religious guidance or other wisdom teachings.

To illustrate, a famous Chinese proverb says, Give a man a fish and you feed him for a day. Teach a man to fish and you feed him for a lifetime. This saying sometimes is used to justify reducing or eliminating social welfare programs that might increase taxes and hurt shareholder returns. For example, a politician who accepted money from business might argue that it is better to help someone find a job than to give them food or other assistance. The politician might neglect to mention that, over the past 40 years, there often were far more people seeking jobs than there were available ones. As a result, many people did not find jobs, regardless of how hard they looked. This misuse of a wisdom teaching violates a much more important religious principle – help the needy. The deception is used to justify not helping citizens who are struggling because they cannot find jobs. By cutting social welfare programs, politicians who accept money from business can use more taxpayer dollars to expand corporate welfare and increase shareholder returns.

The proverb about teaching a man to fish is used when it helps shareholder returns, but often not when it hurts them. For example, it obviously is superior to help developing country farmers become self-sufficient through agroecology rather than give them food aid produced through industrial agriculture and funded with taxpayer dollars. But in this case, giving someone a fish (i.e. food aid) helps shareholder returns more than teaching them to fish (i.e. implement agroecology). As a result, the proverb about teaching someone to fish is not mentioned. (Food aid is a necessary humanitarian intervention during emergencies. But it generally should not be used as a long-term strategy for relieving hunger.)

Another economic and political system flaw that degrades developed and developing countries in food and other areas is the blind faith belief that private sector approaches benefit society more than public sector ones. Once again, this philosophy illustrates irrational thinking. In each situation, people should use objective, logical, fact-based reasoning to determine which approach maximizes the well-being of society. Sometimes private sector approaches will be most effective. At other times, the public sector will achieve better results.

However, inappropriate influence causes the US government to effectively be the agent of business. It often promotes private sector approaches, even when they objectively are not the best options for society. Promoting industrial agriculture and not supporting agroecology illustrates this flaw in the US government. Agroecology clearly often will be the best option in developing countries. As discussed in the IAASTD report, helping developing country farmers to implement agroecology largely would be done through the public sector. But large companies that give money to US politicians would not make money on this. As a result, a suboptimal private sector, industrial agriculture approach is advocated.

The private sector is systemically required to focus on maximizing profits and shareholder returns instead of social well-being. This often puts it in systemically mandated conflict with society. The public sector is systemically required to focus on maximizing social well-being (when it is not corrupted by vested interests). As a result, it often can provide higher quality, lower cost services.

Healthcare provides one of the best examples of this. As discussed in the Healthcare section, compared to other developed countries, the US for-profit, largely private healthcare system is the most expensive, provides the worst coverage and achieves mediocre healthcare results. The public healthcare systems of every other developed country provide vastly superior coverage, at far lower costs, often with superior outcomes. The goal of a national healthcare system should be to maximize public health. But the effectively measured and managed goal of the US for-profit healthcare system is maximizing shareholder returns.

In the same way, the goal of a nation's food production system should be to produce adequate, healthy food over the long-term in an environmentally and socially responsible manner. But the goal of large publicly traded food companies is not to ensure responsible long-term food production. It is to maximize short-term shareholder returns. The private sector can and should play an important role in food production. But the people's agent (government) must hold private sector companies fully responsible for all negative impacts. In this way, food companies maximize shareholder returns by maximizing the long-term well-being and food security of society.

This once again shows the importance of ending business domination of government in the US and returning control to the people, as the US Founders intended. When business controls government, it compels politicians to remove regulations that protect society but limit shareholder returns. This enables and drives the widespread negative environmental and social impacts of industrial agriculture.

Industrial agriculture has substantially degraded the long-term productive capacity of agricultural land in developed and developing countries. Sustainable agriculture, on the other hand, can restore this capacity. Vastly reducing animal product consumption and implementing sustainable agriculture will enable reliable and responsible long-term food production in developed and developing countries.

We have an obligation to protect our children and future generations. Their survival obviously is more important than our comfort or prosperity. We have no right to feed ourselves in ways that take away their ability to survive. If we have an option to feed ourselves sustainably, we must take it, regardless of cost, inconvenience or necessary dietary changes. The survival and prosperity of future generations is more important than eating animal products, the shareholder returns of food companies or anything else except our own survival (because future generations will not be here if we do not survive).

Switching to plant-based diets probably is the most important action that people can take to substantially lower environmental impacts, greatly reduce disease risk and significantly increase the chances of living long, healthy and vital lives. It also is one of the most important actions that they can take individually and collectively to relieve hunger in the world.

Animal Welfare

Eating animal products strongly drives several categories of major problems in the world, including environmental degradation, increased pandemic risk, human health degradation, global hunger and animal cruelty. The first four issues have been discussed. This section discusses the treatment of animals, rationalizations used to justify it and impacts on humanity.

Animal Cruelty

The existence of animal cruelty laws shows that humans understand that animals feel pain and suffer. If they did not, cruelty laws would not be needed. However, in the US, there are very few federal laws prohibiting cruelty to animals raised for food, such as cattle, pigs, sheep, poultry and fish. In addition, food animals are exempt from most state animal cruelty laws.[689] But farm animals such as cattle, pigs and sheep are similar to cats, dogs, horses and other animals that are protected by animal cruelty laws.

All mammals (including humans) share similar brain structures, such as the amygdala and other elements of the limbic system. These structures strongly influence emotions, behavior and memory. Many studies have shown that mammals, birds and even fish have cognitive abilities, feel emotions and experience suffering.[690] These creatures often understand cause-and-effect, such as pressing a button to release food. This indicates the presence of cognitive ability. Mammals and many other animals can feel emotions such as joy, empathy, grief, resentment, anger and fear.

Emotions probably evolved in animals in part for the same reasons they evolved in humans – to facilitate survival and well-being. Emotions regulate a wide variety of behaviors among friends and foes. They facilitate the formation of social networks that increase the chances of survival.[691] For example, empathy for offspring and other animals in a group facilitates survival. Joy encourages the continuation of positive actions that benefit the group. Anger, resentment and rejection discourage actions that might harm the group.

Many researchers used to believe that animals did not experience emotions. Instead they often attributed animal behavior to simple stimulus-response reactions. They sometimes argued that humans were projecting emotions onto animals and imagining humanlike behavior in them. Some researchers, possibly influenced by food companies, continue to take similar positions. Arguing that animals do not feel emotions or experience suffering can help to block the implementation of animal cruelty laws that might reduce the shareholder returns of food companies.

But these shareholder-friendly positions have been strongly refuted by many credible studies that provide extensive evidence of emotions, suffering and cognitive abilities in animals.[692] Speaking with pet owners can further refute them. Most pet owners probably would find it absurd to suggest that their cats, dogs, horses, birds and other higher pets do not experience suffering, feel emotions or have the cognitive ability to figure many things out.

In their natural environments, cattle, pigs, sheep, poultry and many other animals often form complex social networks. They frequently cooperate and help each other out. They often appear to love or show great affection for their offspring, other animals and humans who treat them kindly. They also obviously have memories and the ability to remember. As noted, animal cruelty laws imply that we understand these emotional and mental characteristics of animals, and therefore show compassion for them. But this compassion or humanity often is not extended to animals raised for food.

The requirement to provide ever-increasing shareholder returns is one of the main drivers of animal cruelty in the food sector. This requirement often creates ongoing pressure to reduce costs. This in turn drives industry consolidation and many efforts to improve production efficiency. Animals in the industrial food sector usually are not treated like living beings. Instead, they are treated like food inventory (i.e. livestock). As discussed in the Influenza Pandemic section, the industrial production of animal products frequently involves confining many animals in crowded, unsanitary conditions, preventing natural behavior, breeding for fast growth, and providing little or no access to sunlight and fresh air. These and many other practices often cause intense physical and emotional pain and suffering among animals raised for food.

Cattle

Each year in the US, about 35 million cattle are slaughtered for beef, two million calves are slaughtered for veal,[693] and nine million dairy cows are maintained for milk production.[694] Cattle have diverse personalities, like humans. Some cattle are bright, adventurous and bossy. Others are shy slow learners. Cattle form complex social relationships within their herds, including selecting leaders.[695] Most cattle raised for beef live their first six to twelve months on rangeland before being sent to feedlots.

Nearly all male calves are castrated, usually without anesthesia. Castration lowers testosterone levels, reduces aggressive behavior and produces a more tasteful, higher fat content meat. About 50 percent of calves are surgically castrated. The procedure involves cutting open the scrotum and extracting the testicles. For smaller calves, testicles normally are twisted off manually. For larger calves, an emasculator often is used. It crushes the vessels supplying the testicles to minimize bleeding, and then cuts the testicles off. About 45 percent of calves are castrated by placing a tight rubber ring around the scrotum. This cuts off blood flow and kills the testicles, which then fall off after about two to six weeks. At times, a Burdizzo clamp is applied to the scrotum to crush the vessels supplying the testicles. A rubber ring sometimes is applied after using a Burdizzo clamp. All of these procedures cause intense pain and suffering that can last for several days.[696]

More than 70 percent of male calves are bred to have no horns. For calves that have them, horns usually are cut off or horn buds are burned, cut or gouged out. Anesthesia rarely is used. Horns and horn buds contain nerves. As a result, these procedures cause intense pain and suffering. About 60 percent of cattle and calves are marked for identification. Nearly 50 percent of the markings occur through branding without anesthesia. The process usually involves heating a branding iron to about 1000°F and then pressing it to the skin for about five seconds. Branding causes third degree burns, leaves a permanent scar, and creates intense pain and suffering.[697]

After stressful transportation to feedlots, thousands of cattle are crammed together in feces-laden holding pens or lots. Cattle on feedlots are fed a highly unnatural diet to fatten them up. As noted, the feed often contains grain, feces and animal remains. It frequently causes bloating, high digestive acid levels and chronic digestive pain. The large amounts of feces on feedlots saturate the air with ammonia, methane and other noxious chemicals. This makes breathing painful and frequently causes chronic respiratory problems. In addition, being crammed together with thousands of unfamiliar animals often causes stress and fighting.

Beyond cruelty in industrial beef operations, extensive pain, suffering and animal cruelty occurs in industrial dairy operations in the US. Dairy cows are bred for increased milk production. On average, a US dairy cow produces over 20,000 pounds of milk per year, ten times more than she naturally would produce to feed her calf. Breeding for increased milk production can divert resources from other parts of the body. This can cause weaker hooves, legs and immune systems. This in turn can increase vulnerability to disease and other health problems, such as lameness (hoof and leg problems that can cause infertility and reduced milk production).[698]

Cows begin producing milk at about two years of age after their first pregnancy. As discussed in the Animal Feed section, calves are separated from mothers usually within one day so that milk can be sold for human consumption. This separation of mother and child causes great stress and suffering among calves and cows. Cows are artificially inseminated about four months after giving birth and are kept in a nearly constant state of pregnancy and lactation. They are milked several times per day. Producing unnaturally large amounts of milk requires high levels of metabolic energy. It is the equivalent of a human running for about six hours per day. In natural settings, cows can live as long as 25 years. But intensive milk production and confinement normally cause cows to become spent (i.e. inadequate milk production) within four to five years. At this point, cows are sent to slaughter.[699]

In industrial dairy operations, the vast majority of cows are not allowed to engage in natural behavior. In natural settings, cows graze on pasture-land throughout the day. But over 90 percent of cows are housed primarily indoors. Over 80 percent of US dairy cows rarely or never graze. Instead, they often are given one or two brief feedings per day. Inability to graze causes stress and suffering. In addition, as with beef cattle on feedlots, dairy cows often are given feed that contains grain, feces and animal remains. Being natural herbivores, this often causes bloating, high acid levels and chronic digestive pain.[700]

In natural settings, cows forms stable social relationships and rare-ly enter different herds willingly. However in industrial operations, cows frequently are grouped with unfamiliar animals. This increases stress and aggressive behavior. In addition, they often are tethered or kept in stalls, which limits interaction with other cows. This social isolation causes stress and suffering. Confining cows also makes them unable to exercise. This causes stress and contributes to lameness and other health problems. Cows often are forced to stand and sleep on concrete floors. The floors frequently are slick with urine. Cows hooves evolved to walk and stand on soft soil, not hard surfaces such as concrete. As a result, the animals sometimes slip, fall and hurt themselves on the hard surface. Standing and sleeping on concrete floors often causes foot lesions, lameness and other health problems.[701] In California and Southwest dairy operations, thousands of cows frequently are kept on CAFO-like dry lots, where they are packed into barren, fe-ces-laden pens.[702]

Mastitis is the most common health problem among US dairy cows and one of the most common causes of death. About 30 to 50 percent of cows suffer from mastitis.[703] It generally involves bacterial infection of the udder. Frequent milking, breeding for high milk production and unsanitary housing conditions contribute to widespread mastitis. As discussed in the Genetic Engineering section, bovine growth hormone (BGH) also increas-es the frequency of mastitis. About 40 percent of milk in the US is produced from cows that were given BGH. Various studies have shown that BGH in-creases the incidence of mastitis by about 25 percent, lameness by 50 percent, and hoof problems by 220 percent. All of these conditions cause pain and suffering in cows.[704] Milk from cows with mastitis often has lower quality protein and higher somatic cell counts (i.e. more pus in the milk).[705]

Between 50 percent and possibly more than 80 percent of US dairy cows have up to two-thirds of their tails docked (i.e. removed) without anesthesia. The tail either is cut off or a tight rubber ring is placed around it. This cuts off blood flow, kills the tail and causes it to fall off (in the same way that bulls frequently are converted to steers by placing a tight rubber ring around the scrotum and causing the testicles to die and fall off). Milk producers often argue that tail docking improves milking area cleanliness. But there is little or no scientific evidence to support these claims. Tail docking causes intense pain and suffering. It also can cause chronic pain, comparable to phantom pain in humans after limb amputation. Tail docking causes additional pain and suffering by leaving cows defenseless against biting flies.[706]

As noted, when milk production falls and cows are considered to be 'spent', they are sent to slaughter. One study estimated that, by the time dairy cows are killed, nearly 40 percent of them are lame due to a lifetime of intensive confinement in unsanitary conditions and the physical strain of nearly constant pregnancy and lactation. The US beef and dairy industries produce about 500,000 non-ambulatory or downed cattle per year (i.e. animals that fall and are too sick or weak to rise). Undercover videos showed downed cattle being beaten, dragged with chains, shocked with electric prods, and pushed by forklifts in efforts to move them at slaughter facilities. Dairy cows represent about 75 percent of downed cattle.[707]

Male calves born to dairy cows have little use in the dairy industry. They cannot produce milk and are different breeds than those typically raised for beef. The veal industry was developed to make use of unwanted male calves from the dairy industry. About 42 percent of male calves are sent to slaughter a few days after they are born to make low-grade "bob veal", which is used in hot dogs and dog food. More than half of male calves from dairy operations are sent to veal production. The remainder are kept for breeding or send to feedlots for beef production.[708]

In veal operations, calves often are kept in small dark veal crates that prevent them from exercising or turning around. Lack of exercise keeps their flesh tender. Veal calves are fed a mainly liquid diet that is low in iron and has poor nutritional value. Low iron diets produce the preferred white or light-colored veal meat. No exercise and poor nutrition often cause veal calves to suffer from anemia, diarrhea and pneumonia. After four to five months, veal calves are sent to slaughter.[709] Veal crates are being phased out in Europe. Some US states and companies also are phasing them out. But veal crates continue to be widely used in the US.

Nearly all beef cattle, spent dairy cows and veal calves are transported to slaughterhouses. Industry consolidation has greatly reduced the number of slaughterhouses. As a result, cattle often are transported long distances, sometimes up to 1,500 miles. As many as 45 cattle routinely are packed into tractor-trailers. The animals frequently are unfamiliar with each other. This often causes stress, exhaustion and fighting. Animals usually are given no food, water or rest during the journey, which can last 24 hours or longer.

Cattle are driven in open trailers at 60 mph or more. Summer temperatures as high as 100°F sometimes cause cattle to collapse. In the winter, windchill factors can lower temperatures on trailers to -50°F. Animals defecate and urinate on the trailer throughout the trip. Sometimes hooves freeze in place or cattle fall and freeze of the floor.[710] Unskilled drivers who brake hard or turn sharply often cause cattle to be thrown to the floor or into each other. The federal 28-Hour Law limits the time that farm animals (excluding poultry) can be transported without food, water and rest. This is the only federal law protecting animals prior to their arrival at a slaughterhouse. However, the maximum penalty under the law is $500 and the law apparently is never enforced. The last reported administrative decision involving USDA enforcement under the 28-Hour Law occurred in 1977, and no reported federal enforcement case has occurred since 1960.[711]

Transportation often produces downed cattle that are unable to walk off trailers once they arrive at slaughterhouses. In these cases, chains or ropes usually are tied around their legs so they can be dragged off trailers. Cattle frequently are afraid to exit trailers at slaughterhouses. These animals often are dragged off with chains or forced off with electric prods poked in their rectums or faces.[712]

The Humane Slaughter Act of 1958 requires that animals be quickly stunned into unconsciousness before they are hoisted, thrown or cut. As a result, slaughterhouse operations in the US attempt to minimize animal suffering by stunning animals before they are processed. However, ongoing pressure to reduce costs creates many problems. US slaughter operations process as many as 400 cattle per hour. This is up to twice as fast as anywhere else in the world.[713] Requiring rapid animal throughput often causes extensive animal cruelty and suffering. The Humane Slaughter Act was updated in 1978 in part by giving USDA inspectors the authority to stop slaughter lines when cruelty was observed. However, this authority was revoked mainly because stopping processing lines increases costs for companies that give money to politicians.

The slaughtering process commonly involves forcing cattle up ramps and through chutes, often by using electric prods. Floors frequently drop away and animals are suspended on conveyor belts against their undersides, which transport them to stunning stations. A captive bolt gun generally is placed against the animal's head. This fires a metal rod through the skull into the brain, which kills the animal or renders it unconscious. But the stunning process often fails to render cattle unconscious.

Slaughterhouses frequently are staffed by immigrants with inadequate training. Poor training combined with fast processing line speeds often make it difficult to effectively stun animals. If they remain conscious after the first stun, workers frequently attempt to shoot them again. However, subsequent stunning often is more difficult because animals are struggling frantically to stay alive. Slaughter lines rarely are stopped if stunning fails to render animals unconscious.[714]

After stunning, a chain frequently is attached to a rear leg. Then cattle are hoisted into the air and moved along suspended upside down on a conveyor. A cut is made in the throat area to drain blood and the esophagus often is bound to prevent stomach contents from contaminating the animal. Under common processing sequences, the head and legs are skinned, legs are removed, the head and hide are removed, the animal is cut open, organs are removed, the carcass is split in two and the meat is washed.

Undercover videos have shown and slaughterhouse workers have reported that animals sometimes are conscious after stunning for several minutes. Hoisting cattle into the air often breaks hip and other bones and causes extreme pain. Cattle sometimes struggle and experience intense suffering as they are hoisted into the air, cut and skinned.[715] If they are still conscious and struggling while their hides are being removed, the skinner sometimes inserts a knife into the back of an animal's head. This cuts the spinal cord, paralyzes the animal and stops it from struggling. But it does not stop cattle from feeling the pain of being skinned alive.[716]

Religious slaughter practices, such as Kosher (Jewish) and Halal (Muslim), are exempt under the Humane Slaughter Act. Kosher tradition requires that animals be healthy and moving when they are slaughtered. This usually is interpreted to mean that animals must be conscious when they are killed. In other words, they cannot be stunned before slaughter. Kosher tradition also requires that animals be killed by a single cut to the throat that severs the carotid arteries. When done properly, this process often causes rapid loss of blood and consciousness, which can minimize pain and suffering. However, as with stunning, problems often occur during kosher slaughter that cause intense pain and suffering among cattle.

For example, in many Latin American slaughterhouses and some US slaughterhouses, a chain is attached to a rear leg. Then cattle are hoisted into the air while still conscious. This often breaks animals' legs and hips. Cattle sometimes hang upside down twisting in pain and terror for two to five minutes before their throats are cut. Clamps sometimes are inserted into animals' noses to hold their heads steady while their throats are being cut. If cuts are off target, perhaps because animals are moving, cattle sometimes remain alive for several minutes while their hides and body parts are being cut off.

Most US kosher slaughterhouses no longer hoist cattle before cutting their throats. Instead, they usually are secured in a standing position while their throats are being cut. Through this process, animals can lose consciousness in as little as eight seconds. But they sometimes remain conscious for up to six minutes.[717] To keep the kosher slaughter line moving, conscious animals sometimes are hoisted and sent down the line for cutting and processing.

Kosher meat must have blood vessels removed, which usually is expensive. Blood vessel removal is inexpensive only for a few parts of cattle.

Generally, only these parts are sold as kosher. This results in abundant extra meat from kosher slaughtering that cannot be sold as kosher. As a result, while only about five percent of beef sold in the US is certified as kosher, a much greater percentage of cattle are slaughtered through the non-stunning, kosher method. Some surveys estimate that as many as 50 percent of US cattle are slaughtered in this manner.[718]

Pigs

Pigs and hogs (i.e. pigs weighing over 120 pounds) also experience extensive pain, suffering and cruelty in industrial pig production operations. More than 100 million pigs are slaughtered each year in the US. Pigs are highly social and intelligent animals, often more intelligent than dogs. In natural environments, pigs wander over a wide area and organize into small social groups. But about 99 percent of pigs in the US are raised in confined industrial operations that severely restrict their ability to engage in natural behavior. In natural settings, pigs live for about 10 to 15 years. But industrial pigs have been bred to grow faster, larger and leaner. Within about six months, pigs reached their slaughter weight of about 250 to 300 pounds.[719]

In nature, young pigs nurse for up to 22 weeks. But in industrial operations, piglets are taken from their mothers within two to four weeks. This causes great stress and suffering among sows (adult female pigs) and piglets. Within a few days or weeks of birth, piglets are altered in several ways, nearly always without anesthesia. For example, eight needle teeth usually are cut off or cut in half, often with wire cutters. The teeth contain nerves. As a result, this is extremely painful and sometimes causes infections. Notches often are cut in ears for identification. This also causes extreme pain. Tails are cut off, which causes additional extreme pain. Male piglets also are castrated. During the procedure, piglets usually are suspended upside down in a restraining device held between the pig handler's legs. The pig handler cuts open the scrotum with a scalpel and pushes the testicles through the incision. Then the testicles are cut or torn off. This causes intense pain and suffering that can last for several days.[720]

After eight to ten weeks, pigs are moved from nurseries to growing and finishing facilities. These often confine 1,000 or more pigs per shed. Pigs are crowded into pens that contain 30 to as many as 400 animals. Unfamiliar pigs are grouped together in ways that provide little room to move. As with cattle, grouping unfamiliar animals together often causes stress and fighting. Pigs are fed large or unlimited amounts of unnatural feed that is designed to make them grow faster. The low fiber feed often causes high acid levels, ulcers and other digestive problems. As noted, pigs are bred to grow unnaturally large. This frequently causes breathing difficulties, joint problems and other health problems.[721]

Pigs usually are forced to live on concrete or slatted floors with little or no bedding material. This often causes lameness and other foot problems. Large amounts of decomposing feces frequently saturate the air with ammonia, hydrogen sulfide, methane and other noxious gases. This causes many respiratory problems.[722] About 70 percent of pigs develop lesions caused by pneumonia.[723] The animals regularly are given antibiotics to help them stay alive in crowded, filthy conditions. Pigs in the US also regularly are given ractopamine to make them grow faster. As noted, ractopamine has been banned in 160 countries including China due to negative human and animal health impacts. Industrial pig operations often have mechanized feed, water and waste removal. As a result, pigs rarely see humans and get little or no individual attention.[724]

In addition to growing larger and faster, pigs also are bred to produce larger litters of leaner piglets. In nature, a sow normally would have one litter of five to seven piglets per year. But industrial sows are bred to produce 20 or more fast-growing, lean piglets annually. About 60 to 70 percent of pregnant sows in the US are confined to gestation crates for the length of their pregnancy (about 114 days). The crates are barely larger than the animal. They provide no room to turn around or lie down comfortably. Living in gestation crates causes skin lesions and many other health problems. In addition, the crates essentially drive pigs insane. Sows usually display extensive repetitive, abnormal behavior, such is chewing on the bars of their cages.

After giving birth, sows usually are confined to farrowing crates. The crates are slightly larger than gestation crates. They enable piglets to nurse, but do not allow sows to access their offspring. After piglets are removed, sows are artificially inseminated and placed back in gestation crates. When older sows become unable to profitably breed, they are sent to slaughter.[725] Like veal crates, gestation crates are being phased out in Europe and some US states. But they continue to be used widely in the US. Even without gestation crates, life for all pigs in industrial operations is extremely unpleasant. Pain, suffering and inability to engage in natural behavior are the norms.

When pigs reach slaughter weight and breeding sows no longer are productive, they are packed onto tractor-trailers with many unfamiliar animals and no room to move. Food and water often are limited or withheld for 16 to 24 hours before transportation to minimize vomiting. In addition, feed would not be converted to meat prior to slaughter, and therefore, from a profit maximization perspective, would be wasted.[726] Industry consolidation often requires long trips to slaughterhouses, during which animals received no food, water or rest. Pigs frequently face extremely hot or cold temperatures during transport. They sometimes freeze to the abundant urine and feces on trailer floors.[727] On some loads, as many as 10 percent of pigs are downed and unable to rise when they reach slaughter facilities. They must be pried loose if they are frozen, and then dragged off trucks, which sometimes pulls their legs off.

At slaughter facilities, pigs often are held in pens and then driven through a series of chutes, frequently with electric prods. At stunning stations, animals usually are stunned with captive bolt guns or tongs placed on either side of the head that pass electricity through their brains. After stunning, a chain is attached to a hind leg, pigs are hoisted into the air, a cut is made in the throat area to drain blood, and then animals are immersed in scalding water tanks to soften skin and remove hair prior to moving down the line for further processing.[728]

Pig slaughterhouses often have many of the same problems as cattle slaughterhouses. US pig slaughter operations frequently process up to 1,100 pigs per hour. Fast processing speeds, poor employee training and frantic, rapidly moving animals often result in pigs not being effectively stunned. As a result, they sometimes are hoisted, cut and immersed in scalding water tanks while still conscious. During inspections and audits of slaughterhouses, stunning frequently is shown to be effective most of the time. However, on several occasions, undercover videos have shown that many animals are hoisted, cut and scalded while still conscious. Ongoing pressure to maximize throughput apparently sometimes causes greatly increased animal cruelty when slaughter operators believe that they are not being observed by outsiders.[729]

Chicken

Chickens probably experience the highest level of pain, suffering and cruelty in US industrial food operations. About nine billion chickens are slaughtered each year in the US. This represents about 95 percent of all animals slaughtered for food (excluding fish). Many studies have shown the chickens have equivalent or superior cognitive abilities to cats, dogs and some primates. They form complex social structures and engage in a wide variety of natural behaviors.[730] However, about 99 percent of chickens in the US are raised in confined industrial facilities that severely restrict their ability to engage in natural behavior. The Humane Slaughter Act and 28-Hour Law noted above do not apply to chickens and other poultry.

The industrial production of broiler chickens (chickens raised for meat) and egg-laying hens was discussed in the Influenza Pandemic section. As noted, the H5N1 influenza virus and similar viruses pose some of the greatest threats to humanity. H5N1 almost certainly evolved in industrial chicken operations. In addition, these operations represent the most likely place where the virus would evolve into pandemic form. Outside of a laboratory, it would be difficult to develop a more perfect environment for promoting the evolution of H5N1 and other highly virulent diseases.

In addition to posing an extremely high risk to humanity, industrial chicken operations impose intense pain, suffering and cruelty on chickens. As discussed in the Influenza Pandemic section, up to 30,000 day-old chicks often are placed in a barren shed, sometimes on top of tons of feces from previous flocks. As chickens grow, they are crammed against each other and have little room to move. This causes high levels of stress and fighting. Beaks and toes frequently are cut off to prevent injury during fighting.

Chickens live on top of a growing amount of their own feces. Broiler chickens are bred to grow larger and faster. Their legs and hips often cannot support their unnaturally large bodies. As a result, chickens frequently spend three-quarters of their time lying in their own feces. Ammonia and other noxious chemicals from the feces burn their lungs, eyes and bodies. Broiler chickens are kept in near darkness and receive little sunshine or fresh air. Antibiotics are widely used to keep them alive in these filthy, disease-promoting environments. After about six weeks, industrial broiler chickens are sent to slaughter. The breeding chickens that produce broilers live for one to two years in similar filthy, intensively confined conditions.

Also as discussed in the Influenza Pandemic section, most egg-laying hens in the US are packed into battery cages that provide nearly no room to move. Dead birds often are left in cages. Hens frequently live on top of dead birds, develop bloody abscesses on their faces and egg vents, and are covered with feces. Natural hens lay about 25 eggs per year. But industrial hens are bred to lay about 250 eggs annually. After about two years of intensive egg production, egg-laying hens are sent to slaughter, usually to make cat or dog food. Male chicks born to egg-laying breeder hens have little use because they do not produce eggs and are not bred to produce excessive flesh for the meat industry. As a result, about 100 million male chicks are killed each year, usually by throwing them into grinders while still alive or placing them in plastic bags to suffocate.[731]

When broiler chickens reach slaughter weight and egg-laying hens are spent, they are packed into crates, stacked on trucks and sent to slaughter facilities. The journey often lasts many hours. Chickens receive no food and water and often face extreme hot or cold temperatures during transportation. At chicken slaughter facilities, animals are hung upside down by their legs. The terrified birds often scream, flap, vomit, defecate and urinate as they are being shackled. In many other countries, chickens are stunned or rendered unconscious before they are killed. However, this rarely occurs in the US because chickens are exempt from the Humane Slaughter Act. Instead, they usually are passed through an electrified water bath intended to paralyze them, but not render them unconscious. After the electric bath, chickens pass through automated throat cutting machines and then are submerged in scalding water to remove feathers. (Chickens are not rendered unconscious in the US in part because it is believed that they will bleed more effectively if they are conscious when their throats are cut.)[732]

Chickens that are paralyzed by the electric water bath usually have their throats cut while they are conscious. However, birds often miss the electric water bath because they are moving. As a result, they continue to move as they pass through the throat cutting machines and frequently do not have their throats cut. This results in many chickens being conscious when they are submerged in scalding water. Some industry trade associations have animal welfare programs. But these allow the inhumane confinement practices described above and apparently do little to curb inhumane transport and slaughter practices. In addition, there is little to no effective regulatory oversight that limits cruelty to chickens.[733]

Fish

Fish cruelty and suffering are more difficult to understand and empathize with because fish are so different from humans. They live in a different world. Humans and mammals suffocate when placed underwater. Fish suffocate when taken out of water. Humans and mammals often scream or make distorted facial expressions when they feel pain or are being tortured. But fish cannot scream because they do not have lungs and their faces express little or no emotion. However, this does not mean that fish cannot feel pain and suffer.

Some scientists formerly believed that fish could not feel pain because they lacked the anatomical features necessary to feel it. But many scientific studies have shown this position to be false. Fish have central nervous systems like mammals and birds. Painful stimuli are transmitted to and processed by the brains of fish. Some scientists argue that fish have no neocortex, the brain structure associated with consciousness and subjective experience in humans. Therefore, they contend that fish cannot experience pain or suffer as humans do.[734]

But this position is illogical for several reasons. It implies that the experience of pain is not relevant or worthy of compassion if it is not similar to the human experience. The position also is illogical because it assumes that the ability to experience pain is absent if the structure associated with that ability in humans is absent. But having different brains does not mean that the ability to feel pain is absent. Fish evolved in different environments to engage in different behaviors than humans. Therefore, it is highly possible that brain structures and the ability to feel pain also evolved differently.[735]

Rationally and objectively studying the behavior and anatomy of fish shows that they have high cognitive ability as well as strong ability to feel pain and suffer. Fish form complex social relationships and express affection for other fish, for example by rubbing up against them. They build nests, communicate with sound and sometimes use tools. Fish often have better long-term memories than non-human primates. They remember their environments and are able to orient themselves and navigate over wide areas. Fish often display strong cognitive ability. Some fish are able to gauge the fighting ability of potential rivals by observing earlier bouts. Humans cannot do this until they are four years old. Salmon can learn predator avoidance skills by observing more experienced fish. The grouper and moray eel cooperate in hunting prey. Aside from humans hunting with dogs, there are very few examples of two different species cooperating in a hunt. This requires intelligence, memory and planning.[736]

Scientists analyze pain and stress in fish by observing abnormal behavior in response to harmful stimuli and measuring changes in hormone levels, heart rates and other metabolic factors. Through this analysis, scientists have established that fish not only feel pain, but also can anticipate it and learn to avoid it. This implies a higher cognitive and emotional experience of pain, similar to humans. For example, after being hooked once, carp can learn to avoid bait for a year or more.[737] Having been shocked once, fish often grunt in anticipation of pain when they see an electrode being inserted in water. Fish produce neurotransmitters such as endorphins that relieve pain and suffering. If they did not feel pain, they apparently would not need these brain chemicals.[738]

Hundreds of studies have shown that fish have high cognitive ability and can feel pain. Given this overwhelming scientific evidence, taking the position that fish do not feel pain is not scientific or rational.[739] Instead, it is ignorant (i.e. lack of awareness of overwhelming scientific evidence) or obstinate (i.e. failure to acknowledge overwhelming evidence). The latter position might be embraced by researchers who receive money directly or indirectly from food companies.

As discussed in the Oceans section of *Global System Change*, the world's fish stocks are being rapidly depleted. About 90 percent of large fish populations, such as swordfish and tuna, are gone. At current overfishing rates, all fish and seafood species are projected to collapse (i.e. be more than 90 percent depleted) by 2048. Overfishing mainly is done by industrial scale fishing vessels, often the size of football fields. These vessels take billions of fish from the sea using long lines, gill nets, purse seines and bottom trawling. Fish frequently die long, slow painful deaths in these devices. If they are alive when pulled from the water, they often die slow painful deaths through suffocation.[740]

With ocean stocks being rapidly depleted, aquaculture (fish farming) is growing rapidly. About 40 percent of fish worldwide is provided through aquaculture. Like meat production, aquaculture often is highly inefficient. It takes about two to three pounds of wild fish input on average to produce one pound of carnivorous fish output. Salmon require five pounds of wild fish input to produce one pound of output. As a result, to lower pressure on wild fish stocks, some experts suggest that only herbivorous fish be produced with aquaculture.[741]

Aquaculture is very similar to the industrial production of food animals in confinement settings. It shares many of the same problems. For example, fish evolved to live, navigate and move in a vast three-dimensional world (as opposed to the two-dimensional movement world of humans). But in aquaculture operations, fish are packed into tanks, net pens and other confinement areas with little room to move. Inability to engage in natural behavior often causes great stress and injury to fish.

Like industrial animals, aquaculture fish frequently are bred to grow faster and larger. This often contributes to weak skeletons, blindness and other health problems. Fish also frequently are fed unnatural feed that is designed to make them grow faster and larger. This often weakens immune systems, increases vulnerability to disease and parasites, and causes other health problems. In aquaculture operations, fish frequently are confined in water that is highly contaminated with feces and other materials.[742] They regularly are given antibiotics to keep them alive in these filthy, disease-promoting conditions. Other substances also are put in fish feed and water. For example, the pink color of wild salmon often results from eating crustaceans. But farmed salmon are not fed crustaceans. As a result, dye frequently is put in aquaculture water to give farmed salmon the preferred pink color.[743]

Fish often are put through grates to sort them by size. This frequently removes scales and increases vulnerability to disease and parasites. Aquaculture fish often are contaminated with lice and other parasites. For example, lice frequently eat down to the skull of salmon and kill them. Up to 40 percent of fish raised in aquaculture settings die before being sent to slaughter. Prior to transport, fish often are starved for up to 10 days so that they will not defecate in transport water.[744]

At slaughter facilities, larger fish sometimes are stunned by hitting them on the head with a club (called a priest). But in the US, there are no regulations limiting cruelty to fish. As a result, nearly all fish are conscious when they are killed or processed. Many fish are killed by taking them out of water and allowing them to slowly suffocate or by cutting their gills and allowing them to bleed to death.[745] Alternatively, fish often are cut and processed while still alive. For example, fish sometimes are shackled into eviscerating machines and then sent down the processing line. They continue to struggle while machines cut them open and tear out internal organs.[746]

Organic, Free-Range and Cage-Free Animal Products

Growing consumer interest in food safety and animal well-being has driven rapid growth in markets for organic and free-range animal products. To avoid losing sales, many large food companies have entered these markets. Treating animals humanely, for example by avoiding the practices described above, often would severely restrict the ability to provide ever-increasing shareholder returns. As a result, businesses and their owners apparently have given money to politicians and inappropriately influenced government in other ways in an effort to weaken organic and free-range standards, or not implement strong standards in the first place. This enables food companies to continue producing animal products with industrial, intensive confinement practices, while also using organic, free-range, cage-free, humane, natural and other deceptive labels. Nearly all of the inhumane practices described above are used to produce organic, free-range and other supposedly healthier and more humane animal products.[747]

To illustrate, organic beef is not produced with antibiotics or hormones. But organic beef cattle usually are treated virtually the same as conventional beef cattle. They nearly always are castrated, dehorned and branded without anesthesia. They usually are fattened in feces-laden, crowded feedlots. They are transported with no food and water in extreme temperatures for many hours. And they often are hoisted, cut and skinned while still conscious.[748]

In the organic dairy area, the vast majority of organic milk and dairy products comes from industrial, intensive confinement operations. Cows producing organic milk are given organic feed and no BGH. But essentially every inhumane practice described above is used on dairy cows. They are kept in a nearly constant state of pregnancy and lactation, their calves are removed almost immediately after birth, they often are intensively confined and forced to stand and sleep on feces and urine covered concrete floors, and they usually are transported and slaughtered virtually the same as conventional dairy cows.[749]

Free-range and organic broiler chickens nearly always are intensively confined in the same type of feces-laden sheds described above and in the Influenza Pandemic section. Their free range often consists of a small, barren dirt lot accessed through a hole in a shed wall. However, like conventional chickens, organic chickens are bred to grow unnaturally large. As a result, they frequently are not able to walk out of the crowded shed into the small 'free-range' lot. Instead, organic chickens often spend most of their time lying in their own feces. They suffer the same painful debeaking and toe clipping as conventional chickens. They virtually always are killed while still conscious. And they often have higher disease rates because they usually live in filthy, crowded sheds, but are not given antibiotics.[750]

Cage-free egg-laying hens are not kept in battery cages. Instead, they nearly always are kept in crowded, feces-laden sheds, like broiler chickens. Aside from not living in battery cages, they usually suffer virtually all of the same abuses as conventional egg-laying hens, including debeaking without anesthesia and being slaughtered while conscious. USDA loopholes allow free-range and organic egg-laying hens to be "temporarily confined" for reasons such as health, safety, the animal's state of production, and protecting soil and water quality. Many free-range egg farms fully exploit this loophole by almost never letting 'free-range' chickens outside.[751]

In addition to cattle, pigs, chicken and fish, about 250 million turkeys, 24 million ducks and two million sheep and lambs are slaughtered each year in the US. Regardless of whether these animals are sold as conventional, organic or free-range, the large majority of them are subjected to similar types of inhumane confinement, transport and slaughter processes as those discussed above.[752]

Animal Cruelty Regulations

After several undercover videos raised public awareness about inhumane practices at US slaughter operations, the USDA issued a rule in 2011 intended to reduce the inhumane treatment of livestock. The rule requires USDA inspectors to ensure that animal pain and injury are minimized, disabled animals are not excessively beaten or prodded, and animals are stunned and unconscious before being cut and processed.[753] However, USDA inspectors were supposed to be doing much of this under the Humane Slaughter Act, but often failed to do so. It does not seem that the new rule is being vigorously enforced. Given the close relationship and inappropriate influence between food companies and the USDA, the rule might have been a cosmetic action intended to quell public outrage resulting from undercover videos.

Meaningful reductions of animal cruelty will require more significant legal and regulatory changes. For example, as discussed in the Antibiotics section, non-therapeutic use of antibiotics enables the intensive confinement of animals in their own feces and urine. Banning this practice would greatly reduce cruelty resulting from intensive confinement, as well as protect citizens from antibiotic-resistant bacteria. In addition, mandating slower processing line speeds would substantially lower cruelty by reducing the cutting and processing of conscious animals. Mandating minimum space requirements for each animal and prohibiting the use of battery cages, gestation crates and veal crates also would greatly reduce suffering.

Breeding animals for maximum egg and meat production often produces animals that are in pain, for example, because their bones and joints cannot support their unnaturally heavy bodies. It also frequently weakens immune systems, which increases health risks for animals and humans. Placing limits on breeding that weakens immune systems and causes chronic pain also would reduce animal suffering. However, all of these changes could substantially lower shareholder returns. As a result, it is unlikely that the business controlled US government will make them prior to the implementation of democracy.

Rationalizations

Cruelty is an inevitable part of killing and eating another creature. Killing is cruel, but sometimes necessary for survival. Limiting the ability of animals to engage in natural behavior also is cruel. Since animals were first domesticated about 10,000 years ago, they mostly were raised in ways that allowed them to engage in natural behaviors, such as grazing, forming social groups, breeding and raising offspring. The industrial production of animal products hugely increased animal cruelty, pain and suffering. In industrial operations, animals are not seen as living beings with basic rights. Instead, they are treated as units of production or inventory. The rise of industrial animal production coincides with the rise of large publicly traded companies that are structurally required to put shareholder returns before everything else, including the well-being of animals.

Industrial agriculture and the requirement to maximize shareholder returns are main drivers of animal cruelty. But the industrial production of animal products is driven by long-term, deeply held beliefs about eating animals. These beliefs drive demand for animal products, which in turn drove the establishment and expansion of industrial animal operations. Therefore, addressing fundamental beliefs about eating animals is a critical aspect of reducing animal cruelty.

Important beliefs driving the consumption of animal products include animals eat animals, humans traditionally ate animals, animal suffering is different than the human suffering, animal cruelty laws limit animal suffering, free range and organic production limit suffering, being a vegetarian limits animal suffering, and local, humane production limits suffering. Ideas such as these are used to justify or rationalize the ongoing consumption of animal products, and the cruelty that often goes along with it.

Many people say that, in nature, animals eat other animals. Therefore, eating animals is natural. In nature, carnivores and omnivores eat animals. Herbivores do not. As discussed in the Anatomy section, humans are anatomical herbivores. Therefore, eating animals is not natural for humans. Also, animals have few or no choices. They eat what their anatomy and instincts demand. Humans, on the other hand, do have choices. We can choose to eat animals, for example, to survive or because we like the taste of them. However, choosing to eat animals does not mean that they are the natural, optimal food for humans. Furthermore, animals kill in a cruel, vicious and painful way. Humans evolved to have empathy, hence the name humanity. As part of our humane nature, we can choose to show compassion for our fellow creatures on this planet by not eating them. The vicious behavior of animals it is not a good role model or rationalization for human behavior.

Many people also say that humans traditionally ate animals. They argue that this justifies the ongoing consumption of them. But culture and tradition are not good justifications for continuing actions that cause unnecessary suffering or some other type of harm. For example, slavery, torture and suppression of women once were traditional activities in human society (and unfortunately still are in some regions). But people did not choose to be enslaved, women did not choose patriarchy, and animals did not choose to be slaughtered.

In developed countries, most people do not need to eat animal products to survive. This means that the suffering of animals raised for food largely is unnecessary. In particular, the extensive cruelty and suffering in industrial animal operations is especially unnecessary. Like children, animals are vulnerable and defenseless against humans. As humane beings, we have an obligation to protect vulnerable creatures and avoid unnecessary suffering whenever possible. Traditions and values must evolve as societies become more aware and enlightened. The fact that humans traditionally killed and consumed animals is not a good rationalization for continuing to do so. This rationalization is no more valid than the idea that women should continue to be suppressed because they traditionally have been.

Some people argue that animals are not equal to humans and imply that animal suffering therefore is less relevant. They also sometimes argue that animals do not think about or experience suffering the same as humans. This further implies that animal suffering is less relevant. But the ability to anticipate or think about suffering should not be the basis for preventing it. If this were the case, causing suffering among infants and mentally disabled people might be considered acceptable. We can see that animals feel pain and suffer. They often can anticipate and remember it. Like humans, animals can be permanently altered or damaged by torture and suffering.

The fact that animals might not think about suffering like humans is irrelevant. When pets suffer, pet owners often feel like a family member is suffering. We are compassionate people. Nearly everyone agrees that animal suffering, including the suffering of food animals, should be minimized or avoided. But then people often buy animal products, which drives animal suffering. Part of this paradoxical behavior results from a lack of public awareness about the suffering of food animals.

Industrial food animals suffer for many reasons, including those described above. One of the most important drivers of suffering is breeding. In nature, animals usually evolve in ways that maximize their health and ability to prosper. Features such as the immune system, skeleton and body size are optimized to maximize animal well-being. This maximizes the chances of survival. But industrial food operations alter this natural balance. The goal of breeding is not to maximize the health and well-being of animals. It is to maximize food production and shareholder returns. As noted, animals are bred in unnatural ways that, for example, produce larger bodies and weaker immune systems and skeletons. As a result, they often live in chronic pain. It is as if they were bred or designed to suffer. Of course, suffering was not the goal of breeding. It is an unintended consequence of putting shareholder returns before all else. Raising public awareness about suffering will create pressure to end breeding that causes chronic pain and suffering in food animals.

Many people probably believe that animal cruelty laws minimize the suffering of food animals. But laws are products of society and political influence. As shown above, widespread animal product consumption combined with strong business influence of government cause animal cruelty laws to be woefully inadequate. Even in regions with more extensive and better enforced animal cruelty laws, such as Europe, widespread animal cruelty, pain and suffering occur in industrial animal operations.

Many people believe that buying cage-free, free-range and organic animal products minimizes animal suffering. But as discussed above, animals raised in these ways nearly always experience virtually the same high levels of cruelty, pain and suffering as animals raised under conventional methods.

People also often believe that being a vegetarian (i.e. eating dairy and eggs, but no meat, poultry or fish) minimizes animal suffering. In discussing animal cruelty, some people might say, at least no animals were killed to provide my eggs and dairy products. But this position is highly misleading.

As discussed above, virtually all dairy cows and egg-laying hens are slaughtered for meat when they no longer are productive. From birth to death, the lives of animals raised in industrial operations are filled with cruelty, pain and suffering. Therefore, the shorter the animals' lives, the lower the suffering.

Nearly all dairy and eggs in the US come from industrial operations. The lives of dairy cows and egg-laying hens, even in organic or cage-free environments, usually are extremely painful and cruel. Broiler chickens are slaughtered after about six weeks. But egg-laying hens live for up to two years. Beef cattle are slaughtered after about 12 to 18 months. But dairy cows can live for four to five years in industrial operations before being slaughtered. Therefore, based on the idea that long lives of torture are worse than short torturous lives, one could argue, if the goal were to minimize animal suffering, it would be better to eat only meat, poultry and fish, but avoid eggs and dairy products. However, the best way to minimize animal cruelty and suffering obviously is to eat no animal products. Being a vegetarian promotes extensive animal cruelty, pain and suffering. Being a vegan prevents it.

Some people argue that humanely raising animals, for example on small, local farms, minimizes animal suffering. This is true. It often does. Animals raised in these settings frequently are allowed to engage in natural behaviors and are fed more natural food. In addition, painful procedures often are minimized. However, while humane, locally-produced animal products usually are an improvement over industrial animal products, there still are several problems. For example, they often are expensive. Many people could not afford to buy them regularly. As a result, humane, local animal products sometimes could be seen as elitist.

In addition, local, humane production cannot come close to matching the output of industrial animal operations. Therefore, this type of production largely is not a substitute for industrial animal production. It cannot meet the currently high and growing demand for animal products. Furthermore, many of the inefficiencies and environmental degradations of industrial animal operations apply to humane, local production. In other words, producing local, humane animal products usually is highly inefficient and environmentally destructive compared to producing plant products.

From an animal cruelty perspective, local, humane animal production is less inhumane. But it still is inhumane in some ways. For example, some people argue that unnecessary suffering, but not unnecessary killing, is inhumane. Therefore, this type of meat is humane because local, humanely-raised animals largely do not suffer (until they are slaughtered). But unnecessary killing also is inhumane. As noted, most people in developed countries do not need to eat animal products to survive. Therefore, much of the animal killing is unnecessary. In addition, nearly all large animals in the US are sent to slaughterhouses. As a result, many local, humanely-raised animals are subjected to the same cruel and painful transport and slaughter procedures as those described above.

Humane meat is an oxymoron. Eating animals is not kind or humane. Animals are not happy to be killed and eaten. Raising food animals in humane local settings would be like inviting a guest to stay over, putting them up in a comfortable room and feeding them good food. But at some point, the host plans to kill and eat the guest. Most guests would not consider this to be humane treatment.

A Different Perspective

One of the most important rationalizations driving the consumption of animal products is the belief that we have a right to eat animals. This belief sometimes is justified by saying that we have greater intelligence and power than animals. This implicitly gives us the right to eat them. In other words, our power over animals and ability to eat them give us the right to eat them.

One of the most important justifications for the idea that we have a right to eat animals comes from religions. As discussed in the Well-Being of Society section, religious dogma often states that God put everything on Earth, including animals, for humans to use wisely. This dogma frequently sets humans above nature and animals. These ideas are unintentionally suicidal. In reality, humans are not above nature. We are part of it. We cannot survive without it. The implied intelligence of nature essentially is infinitely greater than human intelligence. We are not anywhere near being smart enough to be a wise steward or master of nature. We have proven this by rapidly degrading our life support systems. Flawed religious ideas that put us above nature (and the economic and political ideas that implicitly at least partly result from them) are causing us to kill ourselves.

These religious ideas also are being used to justify massive cruelty, pain and suffering among animals raised for food. If God exists, it speaks through humans. No one has a video or audio tape of God telling us that it created nature and animals for humans to use. Supposedly divine guidance or dogma always comes through humans. We have access to essentially infinite wisdom and intelligence through the intuitive function. This wisdom could be referred to as God. But ultimately, the name is irrelevant.

The key is that this divine or otherwise inspired guidance always comes through a human filter. All humans have biases and blind spots. Our conscious minds are not designed or evolved to know everything. Therefore, if people wish to communicate their divine or intuitive inspirations, they must put them into the limited language and perceptions of the human mind. This is how all religious books, including the Bible, were written. They were written by humans, often inspired or perhaps divinely guided humans.

Prior to the Agricultural Revolution, most religions saw humans as part of nature. Indigenous people often believed that we had no right to push other creatures aside or dominate nature. This would be like saying that the hand has more rights than the foot on the body. But humans began to violate old religions when we pushed nature aside to grow crops, domesticate animals and build cities. Around these times, new religions arose that said humans were above nature, not part of it. In effect, we pushed nature aside and made up religions that gave us permission to do so. We said that God said we could dominate animals and nature.

All religions come from or through humans. This means that humans said humans could dominate nature and use it as we see fit. It would be like a bank robber saying, God said I could rob the bank. We place a patina of divine justification over our domination of nature and cruel treatment of animals. It is like one group saying, God told us that we were the chosen people. If God told one group that a different group was the chosen people, it would be more believable. But when one group says that God told them they were the chosen people or gave them permission to dominate another group, it seems self-serving. It is equally questionable when humans say God said humans could dominate nature and animals. It would be less questionable if God told squirrels or some other non-human group that humans could dominate nature and animals. Then it would not seem self-serving.

Religious beliefs are deeply ingrained. Many people blindly believe that religious dogma is true without being able to logically prove or explain how or why it is true. This is fine when blind faith in religious dogma enhances society, for example, by promoting peace and brotherhood. But we must push back against dogma when it causes unnecessary pain and suffering. In several places, the Bible directs believers to kill or enslave other people. Our gifts of intuition and rational thought tell us that no loving God would direct its creations to do this. As a result, we correctly do not follow many of the barbaric teachings of the Bible and other religious books. We also should question religious dogma that causes unnecessary pain and suffering among animals.

God or intuitive wisdom did not die thousands of years ago. The primary guidance from God (or intuitive wisdom) does not come from old books with frequently barbaric instructions. The most important divine guidance for each person occurs in the present moment and is heard within. We should not allow the words of old books to dominate or suppress the living word of God (or intuitive wisdom) heard in the present moment. It was this wise inner guidance that told us to ignore religious dogma when it causes harm. Placing the inner word of God ahead of dogma caused us to end slavery and allow interracial marriages, for example.

However, letting go of religious dogma often causes fear. Dogma provides intellectual comfort and certainty. One simply and blindly accepts that things are as religious books say they are. We must find the courage to move beyond these childish, simple-minded ideas. God or nature gave us the gifts of rational thought and intuitive wisdom to use, not ignore. We must move beyond blind faith and use these gifts to correctly discern the appropriate treatment of animals. We do not need to eat them. Eating animals is the number one cause of death in the developed world. It is one of the two largest drivers of environmental destruction. And it is one of the largest causes of global hunger.

When considering new ideas, such as replacing religious dogma with rational thought and compassionate intuitive guidance, it often is useful to adopt a different perspective. As noted, humans eat animals when it is not necessary for survival in large part because we gave ourselves permission to eat them, and then attributed this permission to God. Putting ourselves in the position of animals, it would be terrifying to see a race with complete power over us using us only for food production with little or no regard for our pain and suffering. By empathizing with slaves and other abused or powerless people, we felt compassion for them and fought to end their suffering.

In the same way, if we empathize with animals and somehow try to see their point of view, we can feel compassion for them and fight to end their abuse and suffering. It probably is difficult for humans to place ourselves in the minds of animals. We can tell from their cognitive and memory abilities that they think in some way. But we largely do not know how animals think. This can make it more difficult to empathize with them. A more effective way to empathize and imagine animals' points of view might be to imagine how we would feel if a superior race treated us the way we treat animals.

To facilitate feeling empathy for animals, the following story illustrates how we might feel if humans were in the same position as animals raised for food. In this obviously fictional story, a group of beings from another part of the universe discovers Earth. The advanced technology and intelligence of these aliens enable them to completely dominate humans. All of our weapons and defense strategies are useless. They immediately subdue us. We are completely powerless against them (as food animals are powerless against humans). Unlike science fiction movies, there is no hope for us. No courageous group of human rebels will figure out how to beat the aliens. They use us as they see fit. We have no choices. Even the option of suicide is taken away. We will be used in whatever way they choose to use us (in the same way that humans use food animals however we choose).

In this thankfully fictitious scenario, aliens discover that they like the taste of humans. As a result, they convert the Earth into a large factory for producing human meat and dairy products, and then distribute the food to their home planet and other planets around the universe. Within a few decades, highly efficient industrial food production systems have been established on Earth. Humans raised for meat largely are confined to concentrated human feeding operations. Dairy humans are confined to large industrial human dairy operations. When meat humans are ready for slaughter and dairy humans are spent (i.e. no longer produce adequate milk), they are sent to large industrial human slaughter facilities.

The industrial production of humans on Earth is run by a large alien corporation (called Alien Corporation). Like human corporations, Alien Corporation is structurally required to provide ever-increasing financial returns to shareholders. If it does not do this, management will be fired, the company will be taken over or it will die. Alien Corporation rotates production workers on and off of the Earth colony in two-year cycles. But managers often remain for many years. In this story, an experienced manager of Alien Corporation (called EM) is training a new employee (called NE).

EM and NE are sitting in the cafeteria drinking a coffee-like beverage during a break. EM is explaining the industrial production of human food products on Earth. He asks if NE has any questions. NE says that he wondered why their civilization chose to consume humans instead of welcome them into the Association of Worlds, as was done with many other civilizations throughout the universe. EM said, I cannot answer that question. It is way over my head. Our Supreme Council made that decision. I can only speculate about their thought process.

Based on things I've heard from others, I assume that our leaders felt that human society had not reached a level of civilization that would warrant entry into the Association of Worlds. For example, humans were extremely cruel to animals raised for food on their planet. It's ironic given the name they chose for themselves. But their actions reflected a profound lack of humanity. NE said, but weren't there many humans on Earth who treated animals compassionately in part by not eating them? Yes, you're right, EM said. There were many like that. But again, the decision was way over my head. I suppose the Supreme Council felt that there were not enough humans acting this way to warrant equal, compassionate treatment.

As the old saying goes, what goes around comes around. Humans largely got what they gave. Prior to discovering Earth, our animal production operations on other planets integrated a high degree of care for food animals. We strove to minimize their suffering. But by studying how humans raised food animals, we discovered that we could greatly increase food production and profits if we eliminated concerns about the welfare of humans raised for food, in the same way that humans appeared to show little concern for the well-being of their animals raised for food.

NE said, but we are a compassionate race. How can we justify raising humans with little or no concern for their pain and suffering? EM said, you're right. We are compassionate. But my friend, it is important that you learn this lesson. We are running a business here. Humans are not the only food in the universe. If we do not keep production costs down, we will lose market share to less expensive food. Then you and I probably will lose our jobs. So while we try to minimize human suffering whenever possible, we must always keep the primary goal in mind – profit maximization. If minimizing the suffering of humans raised for food lowers profits, I'm afraid we won't be able to do it.

Then EM stood up and said, okay, break time is over. Let's get back to work. This afternoon, I'll be teaching you about humans raised for meat. At the birthing and weaning area, EM explained, human males formally grew to about 180 pounds in 18 years. But by using breeding techniques ironically learned from humans, we've developed humans that grow to about 300 pounds in seven years. We castrate more than 99 percent of the males because this makes them less aggressive and produces a more tasteful, higher fat content meat. NE watched a human handler securing a young human male upside down in a restraining device that held its legs apart. Then the handler cut open the scrotum, extracted the testicles, and tore them off (in the same way that humans often tear the testicles off of pigs and calves). NE said, humans sure make a lot of noise when their testicles are removed. Why don't we use anesthesia?

EM said, yes, again you're right. It obviously hurts them a lot. But we must keep costs down and throughput high. Anesthetizing humans would greatly slow production. So we simply cannot do it. As you can see, the human handlers usually wear headphones and listen to music while they're working. In this way, the screaming of humans during castration does not annoy or distract our workers.

Then EM pulled NE aside and said, I think it's time for you to learn another important lesson. As you know, our religion is the only true, correct religion in the universe. Our God said that everything in the universe was put here for us to use as we see fit. (This obviously excludes advanced civilizations like our own and other members of the Association of Worlds.) Humans are in the universe. Therefore, God put them here for us. The only purpose of humans is to serve us in whatever way we choose. If we decide that we like the taste of humans, we can eat them. Humans are God's gift to us.

NE said, but humans had religions too, didn't they? Didn't their religions say that God put everything on Earth for them? EM said, oh boy, you are new, aren't you. Okay, let me explain. Humans were heathens. Our God is the only true God. Humans were worshiping idols. If they were worshiping the real God, we wouldn't be eating them now. As you work on Earth for the next two years, it will help you a lot to remember that God put humans here to be our food. Yes, we should minimize their suffering whenever possible. But humans are animals. Their suffering is not the same as our suffering. God ordained that humans should be our food. It is inevitable that they will suffer in the process of becoming our food. I suppose that's just the way of the universe.

EM then took NE to the human feedlots. Humans were standing, sitting or lying in crowded, feces-laden pens. EM explained that crowding many humans into small spaces caused stress and fighting. To minimize injury during fighting, human front teeth and hands usually were removed without anesthesia. He also explained that the joints and bones of humans often could not support their unnaturally large bodies. As a result, they spent much of their time sitting or lying in their own feces.

NE asked, what do you feed the humans? EM explained that humans are anatomical herbivores. But to promote rapid growth, they are given hormones and fed human remains from slaughterhouses. They also are regularly given antibiotics to keep them alive in crowded conditions. NE asked, what do you do with all the feces? EM said, actually we learned a great strategy from humans about dealing with it. We feed feces back to humans. NE said, what?! Are you kidding?! That's disgusting! EM said, yes it is disgusting. That's one of the reasons why you were required to sign a non-disclosure agreement. If consumers in our world knew that we were feeding feces to humans, they wouldn't want to eat human meat or dairy products. That is why this practice never is disclosed.

But doesn't feeding feces to humans make them taste bad, NE asked? No, EM said. Believe it or not, feeding feces to humans actually makes them taste better. We ran taste panels and discovered that feeding feces to humans makes human meat taste more tender and juicy (in the same way that human taste panels found that feeding feces to their food animals made meat taste better). Feces has a lot of protein and other nutrients. More importantly, feeding feces to humans lowers feed and waste disposal costs. It's a huge benefit to our shareholders. So we basically are compelled to do it.

NE asked, how do you get humans to eat feces? EM said, once again we learned how to deal with this issue from humans. Humans normally would not eat feces, in the same way that their food animals would not eat it. But humans developed a chemical called MSG. It compelled humans to eat bland or poor tasting food that they normally would not eat. By adding chemicals like this and other ingredients to feces, humans made it more palatable for their food animals. In addition, hunger is a powerful motivator. If the only available food contains feces, food animals often would eat it when they got hungry enough. After a while, they got used to it. We use similar approaches with humans raised for food. As a result, humans regularly eat food that contains feces.

When NE went home after work, he felt sick to his stomach. He began to wonder if working on Earth for two years was a wise decision. But it was too late to turn back now.

At work the next morning, EM said, today I'll be showing you the human dairy operations. At a large industrial facility, thousands of dairy humans were crowded into feedlot-like, feces-laden pens. EM explained that human dairy females had been bred to produce ten times more milk than they normally would produce to feed their young. Dairy humans were kept in a nearly constant state of pregnancy and lactation. Offspring were removed from mothers immediately after birth so that human milk could be sent to market. Instead of milk, human infants were fed milk replacer that contained human blood from slaughterhouses.

NE asked why the newborn humans and mothers made so much noise when they were separated. EM said, I think the mother wants to take care of the child and the child wants to be taken care of by the mother. But that is irrelevant. The mother is our cash cow. We don't want her focusing on the baby she just had. Human milk is a valuable product. We can't waste it on human offspring. She'll forget about her baby and stop crying after a while.

EM explained that human male offspring born to dairy humans had little value because they could not produce milk and were not bred to grow large for meat production. As a result, most male offspring were thrown into meat grinders while still alive to produce food for other humans. Alternatively, they were placed in plastic bags and allowed to suffocate to death. Some male offspring of dairy humans were put into human veal operations. Under this production method, human males were placed in small cages that allowed virtually no movement, fed an anemic diet that produced light colored meat, and slaughtered after three or four months.

NE asked, how do the females get pregnant? Are they bred? EM laughed and said, very funny. Humans don't have sex anymore. As I mentioned, more than 99 percent of the males are castrated. The females are artificially inseminated. Life on Earth for humans is much worse than it was before we arrived. Humans used to communicate through language. But the males don't talk anymore. They just focus on survival. Females had superior communication skills. You sometimes see them talking in dairy herds. But mostly, they don't talk either.

A philosopher might say that this was a sad fate for humans. But we're not philosophers. We're business people. And we've got to take care of business. Then EM slapped NE on the back. In an upbeat tone, he said, don't look so glum. Let's head over to the human slaughterhouse. We'll finish your tour of human food production operations.

At the slaughterhouse, NE watched as spent dairy humans and slaughter-ready meat humans were unloaded from crowded transport vehicles.

Downer humans had to be dragged off with chains. Other humans seemed to be filled with fear. They refused to leave the vehicles. Electric prods and chains were used to force them out of the vehicles and into holding pens. After a while, humans were forced through chutes to stunning stations. A metal bolt was fired through their skulls to render them unconscious. But fast processing line speeds, poorly trained workers and frantically moving humans caused many of them to not be rendered unconscious. As a result, humans often were conscious as they were hoisted into the air upside down, had their throats cut to drain blood, and then had limbs and other body parts cut off. EM showed NE the entire slaughter facility. He explained how humans were killed, cut and processed, sometimes not in that order.

At the end of the day, NE looked at EM and said, how do you take it? EM said, it's tough. I fight with my wife all the time. As you now see, life here on Earth is no fun. But it's a job. All I can say is thank God for alcohol! Now let's go drink large quantities of it and try to forget everything we've seen in the past couple of days.

Many people might say that this story is disgusting and heartbreaking. It definitely is. The story is revolting and incredibly sad. But it is not a fantasy. This is reality for billions of our fellow creatures on Earth. As shown in the Animal Cruelty section, every cruel and painful procedure done to humans in the above story regularly is done to food animals in industrial operations. The Alien Corporation story is based on human ideas and actions. It is meant to serve as a mirror that reflects horrible human ideas and actions back to us. The story is meant to help humanity adopt a broader, whole system perspective. This will enable us to better understand how we cloak our evil actions in the supposed sanctity of religious and other myopic, dogmatic, irrational ideas.

Like EM and NE, we can distract ourselves and pretend that the cruelty done to animals is not happening all around us. But it is. Pretending will not make it go away. Ending the industrial production of animal products and greatly reducing or nearly eliminating the consumption of animals will end the suffering of our fellow creatures. We know that religious dogma is wrong about many things. It is not okay to kill or enslave people, even if the

Bible says it is. It also is not okay to unnecessarily torture, kill and consume our fellow creatures on this planet, even if religious dogma says that it is.

An important qualification should be made about the Alien Corporation story. The story necessarily casts extraterrestrials (ETs) in a very negative light (necessary because the story required that ETs treat humans the way humans treat animals). But if ETs exist, it seems highly likely that the opposite of the Alien Corporation story would be true. In other words, it appears much more likely that ETs would approach us in a benevolent and friendly, rather than harmful, manner.

As discussed in the Meditation and Metaphysics section, millions of people, including thousands of highly credible witnesses, claim to have seen UFOs. Many people also claim to have seen ETs. From a statistical perspective, it seems highly unlikely that all of these people would be wrong. It is highly possible that some people actually have seen UFOs or ETs. Yet in spite of millions of UFO and ET sightings, there are virtually no reports of harm to humans. (The few reports of harm usually come from people who claim to have been abducted by ETs and experienced psychological trauma, but little or no physical harm.) As a result, with millions of sightings and virtually no harm, one could speculate that if ETs have been here, it appears that their intention is not to harm us.

Further indicating that the intention of ETs is benevolent (again assuming they exist), it appears that technology and ethics evolve together. For example, human technology is at its highest level ever. At the same time, concern for human rights, environmental protection and other ethical issues also are near all-time highs. If ETs have been here, they clearly have vastly superior technology. If technology and ethics evolve together, as they apparently often do, this indicates that ETs might have advanced ethics that, for example, prohibit harming other societies.

Physics also potentially indicates the benevolent intention of ETs (if they exist). As discussed in the Meditation and Metaphysics section, some spiritual traditions have said for thousands of years that we are all one and everything is connected in ways that are not obvious to the five senses, but nevertheless are real. More recently, some physics theories indicate the reality of interconnectedness. Some spiritual traditions and physics theories, such as string theory, suggest that matter is an illusion. Everything is comprised of energy that is vibrating at different frequencies. Also as discussed, it is possible that consciousness plays a role in the direction of energy. Some physicists are searching for the theory of everything. This probably will not be discovered until consciousness or some plausible explanation for the movement and formations of energy is integrated into physics theories.

It might be the case that an understanding of the oneness of everything, the illusory nature of matter and the transcendence of consciousness are preconditions for the development of many advanced technologies. For example, traveling at the speed of light (a theoretical fastest possible speed), from a human time perspective, it appears that it might take too long for ETs to get here from anywhere but the nearest solar systems. As a result, one could speculate that if ETs exist and have been here, they might have traveled across time and space, rather than through it. If everything is energy vibrating at different frequencies and matter only is an illusion, then perhaps our location in time/space/dimension is based on a particular frequency. If this locational frequency is changed, we might instantly be elsewhere, including in a parallel or other dimension or universe if such other dimensions exist.

Of course, this is all extremely speculative. But following this line of speculative reasoning, the ability to travel across time/space/dimension (i.e. the ability to dematerialize and rematerialized somewhere else) might require an understanding of the reality of oneness. Assuming that this is true (of course, that is a very large assumption), it implies that, if ETs exist and have been here, they understand the reality of oneness. As a result, ETs would understand that hurting us ultimately is the same as hurting them. And helping us is the same as helping them. Assuming that one considers these speculative ideas to be possible, it provides another indication that ETs who have the technological ability to get here only would approach us in a friendly and benevolent manner.

If ETs have been here many times, one might ask, why have they not made their presence widely known? This is pure speculation, but one could assume that each society (assuming there are more societies than our own) in the universe (or multiverse if there are parallel dimensions) is autonomous. In other words, we must stand or fall on our own. If this were true, ETs might only approach us as equals. They would not come as saviors to rescue us from our problems.

Regardless of whether ETs exist, self-sufficiency is an important principle. As discussed at the beginning of *Global System Change*, we created nearly all of the problems in human society. And we must solve them on our own. If God exists, it works through human hands. God might inspire us. But we must do the work. It is a childish fantasy to think that God will come and save us from our folly, like children waiting for their parents. We must wake up, stand up and do what is right for our children. If we foolishly and childishly wait to be saved by God, ETs or anything/one else without taking the necessary difficult actions, we will continue to degrade life support systems and other aspects of society, and possibly perish.

The Alien Corporation story was used to illustrate the grossly inhumane way that we treat animals raised for food. Everything that was done to humans in the Alien Corporation story is done to animals in industrial food operations. The goal of the story is to show animals' points of view, and thereby build empathy for them. ETs necessarily were shown in a negative light. But if they exist, it seems much more likely that they would be our friends, rather than enemies. Once we use whole system thinking to solve our major problems, do the right thing for our children and treat our fellow creatures more humanely, perhaps ETs will approach us as friends and equals. It is impossible to prove that ETs do not exist. Numerous sightings indicate that it is highly possible that they do exist. Therefore, it is logical to remain open-minded about the existence of ETs and possible friendship with them.

Another goal of the Alien Corporation story is to show the extremely destructive influence of religious dogma and placing shareholder returns before all else. In effect, humans are saying to animals, we are eating you because God said we could eat you. We also effectively are saying, we are causing you to suffer because your suffering is less important than profits and shareholder returns. How would we like it if someone used these rationalizations to justify the torture and slaughter of humans? The Alien Corporation story attempts to show how we might feel in this situation.

We must base human society on the living word of God (or intuitive wisdom) heard now in the present moment. We should not run our society based on what someone else said God said thousands of years ago. Throughout history, we have seen millions of examples of how religious dogma can be horribly destructive, abusive and cruel. Religious ideas are well meaning. But they often are horribly myopic. This frequently makes them horribly abusive. We must wake up. We must use our full powers of comprehension and compassion. Compassion is a very strong power. Compassion and love probably are the strongest powers. As humans, we have these powers. If we want to reach our fullest potential and create Heaven on Earth, we must use our powers of love and compassion more extensively.

Impacts on Humanity

Consuming animals, especially those produced in industrial operations, not only is terrible for animals. It is extremely harmful to humans. Beyond the health impacts discussed above, the extensive violence and cruelty of industrial animal operations affects human society in ways that often are not obvious, but nevertheless are real. We literally are what we eat. From birth to death, the lives of industrial food animals are filled with pain, fear, cruelty and suffering. When we eat this meat or drink this milk, we take on these lifetimes of suffering. They literally become part of us. Perhaps science cannot measure the full physical, psychological and spiritual impact of eating tortured animals. But through intuition, we can sense that it has an impact.

In developed countries, many people were raised on animal products. As a result, eating them seems normal. People often remember family holidays and other great times eating turkey, ham, chicken, steak and hamburgers. They fondly remember ice cream sundaes and other childhood treats. Many people walk through supermarkets seeing cases full of meat and thinking about the delicious meals they could make. Meat and animal products in general are a major part of our culture. Parents, teachers and TV commercials often tell children that eating animal products makes people big, strong and healthy.

But we are not told about the lives of industrial food animals. Food companies frequently give money to politicians, who then sometimes make it illegal to educate citizens about how animal products are produced, for example, by showing videos of how animals are raised and slaughtered. As a result, we often live in a safe, comfortable cultural cocoon that tells us eating industrial food animals is okay. But it is not okay. Nearly anyone who witnessed the industrial production of food animals would be disgusted. The animals that we eat usually are treated in an extremely vile, heartless and filthy manner.

At many times in human history, people turned their backs on genocide, slavery and other abominable treatment of our fellow humans. Individuals often felt incapable of doing anything about it. As a result, they pretended that it was not happening and did their best to move on with life. But pretending that suffering is not happening does not mean that we are not affected by it. There is an energy to the suffering of food animals. It surrounds our world and fills our hearts in ways that we cannot see or perhaps sense consciously. But it poisons us.

The spiritual concept that the punishment is contained in the sin applies individually and collectively. In the US, we imposed the most unspeakable horrors on our fellow human beings through slavery. This poisoned all of us, whether we realized it or not. When we allowed slavery, we received the punishment for our sin. The widespread maiming and killing of the Civil War was only one form of this punishment. The people who argued that slavery was acceptable and should be continued were killing themselves spiritually, whether they realized it or not.

The same occurs with animals. We are all guilty, even if we do not eat them. The unbelievably horrible treatment of animals in the US and many other countries occurs because we allow it. Business only controls government in this supposed democracy because we have allowed vested interests to trick us, mainly by dividing us into liberals and conservatives, and causing us to often dislike or hate each other. But we do not have to remain deluded and divided any longer. We can take back control of our government and supposedly democratic society whenever we want. All we have to do is wake up and say enough is enough. The liberals or conservatives are not our enemies. We are fools to think this. We all mostly want the same things.

Once we take back control of our government, we can honestly assess what is happening. If business practices are acceptable, companies should not be afraid of showing them to the public. But if people saw what actually happened to industrial food animals, they would not tolerate it.

Vested interests have tricked us into thinking that eating meat is manly and cool. Vegans often are implicitly or explicitly criticized for not being manly, tough or socially acceptable. This idiotic, childish, ignorant and naïve behavior must end. It is not uncool to want to end the suffering of our fellow creatures. People who make fun of vegans are not bad people. They just want to fit in. They are following cultural norms. They are acting on beliefs such as, "everyone knows that real men eat meat". They do not understand that they are condoning the torture of animals. We must push back against these ignorant ideas. Would someone who insults vegans bend over, slap their knees and laugh out loud as they watched their family dog being lowered screaming into a tank of scalding water? If they drove by someone beating a horse, would they stop, clap and cheer the person on? Of course they wouldn't. Criticizing someone for not eating animal products is equally ignorant. It is similar to arguing that slavery or suppressing women should be continued.

Again, it is time to wake up. Billions of animals are being tortured all around us. It is foolish to think that this does not hugely degrade society. When we allow this, we are not living up to our name. We call ourselves humanity. But based on our actions, the more appropriate name is barbarity. We surround ourselves with cruelty, torture and suffering. We eat the victims of our torture. We act like barbarians. The violence and suffering that we create in the animal world infuses the human world because it is the same world. In spite of our progress, there still is tremendous violence and suffering in human society. One could ask, to what extent does heartlessly and unnecessarily torturing and killing billions of animals increase human violence and suffering? It seems inevitable that this would make society more violent and severely wound the human spirit.

There is much compassion in human society. We have come a long way. But we still have a long way to go. There still is much suffering in our world. We do not torture our fellow creatures out of malice. We do it out of ignorance. We have been tricked and deluded into thinking that nothing is seriously wrong. But torturing and killing animals is wrong, seriously wrong. If there is nothing wrong with industrial animal operations, we could install video cameras in feedlots, industrial dairy facilities and slaughterhouses, and then provide continuous broadcasts of these operations on cable TV channels. If what we are doing to animals is acceptable, we should not mind doing this.

Of course, many people know that something is wrong. But eating industrial food animals has been a part of our culture for so long that we often ignore the harm it causes. By ignoring it, we condone and enable the harm. After watching videos of industrial animal operations, probably nearly any child, except a budding psychopath, would not want to eat animal products. Torturing animals is widely seen as a sign of severe mental illness. What then does it say about our society when we allow the widespread torture of food animals? Unlike psychopaths, we do not lack compassion. Mostly, we have been deceived. Our government is supposed to protect citizens and prevent animal cruelty. But we allow businesses and their owners to give unlimited amounts of money to politicians. As a result, government does not do its job. Instead, it protects businesses and becomes a major driver of public deception.

Business control of government, especially in the US, is obvious. It can be observed in thousands of situations. Looking at the USDA website, for example, illustrates business domination of government. A fact sheet, called *Veal from Farm to Table*, describes how veal calves are raised in veal crates.[754] Someone who actually has seen veal being raised would think, what planet is the USDA on? The USDA description makes it sound like health experts and other caring people are huddled around each veal calf, making sure that it is comfortable, well fed and happy. One gets the picture of a smiling, happy calf moving freely and comfortably.

Of course, the reality for calves raised in veal crates is exactly the opposite. The calves are intentionally confined for their entire short lives in small spaces that severely restrict movement. This ensures that muscles do not develop and meat remains tender. It is astounding that the USDA would dare to put such a misleading description of veal production on its website. But if one remembers how food companies give money to the politicians who oversee the USDA and rotate their employees in and out of the agency, it does not seem astounding at all. Instead, it is the obvious and expected outcome. These types of deceptions and outright lies keep the public in the dark about industrial food operations.

People often feel that they can do nothing about horrible abuses occurring in society. But that is not the case in the food area. The whole cycle of animal torture and slaughter is driven by consumer demand. Government largely is controlled by business, not citizens. And publicly traded food companies are controlled by shareholders, not consumers. But citizens nevertheless have all the power in the food area. They can exercise that power by not buying animal products. Food company managers and slaughterhouse workers ultimately are not the main cause of animal torture. Consumers buying animal products at checkout counters ultimately are the responsible parties.

Attractively packaged meats and other animal products do not reflect the horrible torture and suffering that went into making these products. Consumers must be made aware of this. They must be given full information. Of course, food companies and their paid political servants will vehemently oppose this. They know that many customers would not buy animal products if they had full information about how the products were produced.

The meat in supermarkets frequently looks innocuous. But it usually comes from the most tortured and abused animals. By far the most humane way to eat meat is to hunt it oneself (buying and selling wild or game meat is illegal in the US). With hunting, animals live their whole lives free in their natural environments. They have no chemicals in their bodies, except what they pick up in the environment (which unfortunately might be a lot). And they die quick, relatively painless deaths (assuming that hunters know what they are doing).

As in every other part of this book, practicality is critical. The suggestion here is not that people should go hungry or die due to not eating animal products. Some people survive by eating animal products, such as those who feed their families with hunting and fishing. But the vast majority of people in developed countries do not need to eat animal products to survive. As noted, for people who are struggling to get by, plant products, such as beans and brown rice bought in bulk, usually are much cheaper than animal products. They also are vastly healthier.

As discussed above, spiritual teachings sometimes say that the punishment is contained in the sin. Consumers of animal products cause massive cruelty and suffering in animals raised for food. It probably is no coincidence that eating animals is by far the largest cause of death in developed countries. (As noted, chronic diseases kill about 75 percent of people in the US. These diseases are rare among populations that eat few or no animal products.) We drive the torture and killing of animals when we buy animal products. Then we are killed by eating them. The punishment is contained in the sin. We take many animal lives and then our lives appear to be taken prematurely as payment for the cruelty and suffering we caused.

We do not own the lives of animals. The life of an animal belongs to that animal, just as a human life belongs to that human. Taking an animal's life might be justified if it is done for survival. But other than that, we have no right to take an animal's life. Nearly all animal killing is not justified because humans are anatomical herbivores and we can feed nearly everyone with plants.

This idea will seem foreign to many people. Our cultures and religions often condone and encourage eating animals. But they used to condone killing and enslaving other people. We once thought the Sun revolved around the Earth. Those who said otherwise originally were seen as heretics. But after a while, we realized that the Sun does not revolve around the Earth and killing or enslaving other people is not okay.

Now we often think that humans are above nature and animals are here to serve us by being our food. But just because we think these ideas are true does not mean they are. Setting aside religious dogma and focusing instead on reality, it is obvious that we are not above nature. From a whole system perspective, rather than the myopic human perspective, it is obvious that humanity is no more important than any other part of nature. Nature would do fine without humanity. But humanity would not exist without nature. The idea that we are above nature came from humans. We made up this unrealistic, suicidal idea to justify our domination of nature. In the same way, we do not have a right to eat animals, unless it is necessary for survival. The idea that we can eat animals when it is not necessary for survival is another self-serving idea created by humans.

Animals such as cattle, pigs and chickens often show great affection for humans who treat them well. They are living, feeling, conscious, aware, social, cognitive beings. We co-inhabit this planet with them and other animals. But these particular food animals often have been bred away from their naturally balanced and healthy bodies. We alter their bodies so that they become better food for us. As a result, these unnatural food animals frequently experience pain. They are born to suffer. It is time for us to live up to our name and show more humanity. We should not be birthing animals that live in frequent pain.

The treatment of animals raised for food is similar to the former treatment of humans. During slavery, the Holocaust and other genocides, many people appeared to tolerate what is now seen as unbelievably horrible, abominable behavior. People in the Southern US before the Civil War and Germany during World War II often went about their lives as if the extreme evil happening around them was not occurring. We have evolved since then. Many people are disgusted by this former behavior of humanity. Unfortunately, slavery, severe suppression of women and genocides still occur in some parts of the world. But many people understand that this behavior is horribly wrong and we must do all we can to end it.

It is time for humanity to evolve again. The animals that we raise for food are conscious beings. They love their children and friends, as we do. They feel pain, as we do. They have memories and experience emotions, such as fear and sadness, just like we do. Our bodies are not designed or evolved to eat animals. We do not need to eat them to survive. We tolerate the lifelong torture and slaughter of innocent creatures, just like we used to tolerate the torture and slaughter of innocent humans. It is time for us to apply the compassion we have for humans to other conscious beings on this planet.

People in the future will look back on how we treat animals raised for food in the same way that we look back on past abominable treatment of humans. Some people might disagree and say that the treatment of animals is different than the treatment of humans. This belief or opinion perpetuates the widespread torture and slaughter of animals. Showing compassion for animals does not demean showing compassion for humans. Each human is precious. They should be treated with compassion and respect.

But this applies to all life, especially higher life forms such as mammals, birds and fish. We are part of one interconnected system. We are not separate from nature and its creatures. Whatever we do to animals, we ultimately do to ourselves. As wisdom and the awareness of interconnectedness expand in humanity, we will understand that showing compassion to animals is the same as showing compassion to humans. This is a major part of reaching our fullest potential and creating Heaven on Earth. Heaven on Earth will not include the torture and slaughter of our fellow conscious beings on this planet.

To justify eating animals, people sometimes argue that plants have a form of consciousness too. Therefore, eating plants is as immoral as eating animals, they irrationally imply. Perhaps plants do have a form of consciousness. But we should seek to be guided by the infinitely greater implied intelligence and wisdom of nature. Life requires sustenance. Rational analysis of human anatomy shows that nature designed or evolved humans to eat plants. We are not smart enough to second-guess nature. It would be foolish and suicidal to try. If there is a consciousness to plants, nature implicitly designed this consciousness, at least in part, to include sustaining human and other lives. The lives of plants are transferred to humans and other herbivores. The cycle of life continues, as nature intended.

As noted, defenders of eating animals also sometimes argue that cruelty and suffering exist in nature, such as when a lion eats a gazelle. Therefore, the suffering caused by eating animals is natural and moral. But carnivores have no choice. It is natural for them to eat as they do. However, humans do have a choice. In a sense, everything in the whole Earth system is connected. We are not separate from our food. The consciousness of humanity almost certainly is intended to evolve toward greater love, compassion and unity.

This higher consciousness will guide us to minimize unnecessary suffering and eat the food that nature designed for us – plants.

The title of this section is Impacts on Humanity. The impact of eating animals not only is that we die faster physically. We also die spiritually. When we fill our world with unnecessary violence toward animals, we fill our world with violence in general. The impact on humanity of killing animals is that we kill our humanity.

Food Deceptions

Public deception is one of the most important problems in the food area. The large majority of people in developed countries die of chronic diseases, such as heart disease, cancer and diabetes. As discussed in *The China Study*, *Prevent and Reverse Heart Disease* and previous sections, there is extensive scientific evidence showing that these diseases are caused primarily by poor nutrition (mainly eating animal products and refined carbohydrates). Yet the US government continues to publish food guidelines which imply that eating up to 35 percent of calories as protein (including animal protein) and 35 percent of calories as fat is healthy.

The food area illustrates the grossly flawed, suicidal nature of our myopic economic and political systems as well as any other area. Publicly traded food companies are structurally required to put shareholder returns before everything else. If they do not do this, they ultimately will die. Food companies often essentially are compelled by flawed systems to mislead the public when the negative impacts of eating animal products and refined carbohydrates are not immediate and obvious and they can avoid being held responsible, for example by strongly influencing all three branches of government in the US.

Politicians who accept money from food companies and the regulators they oversee frequently help food companies to convince the public that animal products and other unhealthy foods are healthy, for example, by publishing harmful food guidelines. In this case, millions of people literally are being sickened and killed to protect shareholder returns, while healthcare costs are being increased by literally trillions of dollars over many years. This perfectly illustrates how flawed systems frequently place shareholder returns ahead of the lives, health and prosperity of citizens and society.

To protect shareholder returns, food companies and their allies often must mislead the public into believing that their harmful products are not harmful. Probably the main concern of the US Founders about democracy was the ease with which non-expert citizens could be misled. Average citizens usually do not have time to study complex health and dietary issues in detail. This makes them highly vulnerable to the well-crafted, compelling deceptions promoted by food companies and their allies.

Many specific food deceptions have been discussed in previous sections. This section summarizes the main strategies used to mislead the public in the food area. These strategies relate to advertising and marketing, education, labeling, research, healthcare and influencing government.

Advertising and Marketing

Advertising and the broader category of marketing are important tools for increasing business sales. In the food area, companies often must continuously increase sales to provide ever-increasing shareholder returns. If markets are expanding slowly or not at all, this frequently means that companies must get existing customers to eat more food. As discussed, this often is done by adding sugar, fat, salt, MSG and other substances that inhibit people's ability to regulate food consumption. Advertising is another important strategy used to drive increased consumption.

Reversals in obesity trends strongly indicate the effectiveness of advertising. In the early 1900s, wealthier people were more likely to be obese because they could afford fattening foods. Lower income people were more likely to be thin. They often aspired to have the lifestyles and diets of wealthier people. As a result, as income increased, obesity also often rose. However, these trends largely have been reversed in the US and many other developed countries. In the US for example, as income declines, obesity tends to increase. Wealthier people are more likely to be thin, while low-income people are more likely to be overweight or obese.[755] The widespread availability of inexpensive, processed, subsidized, fattening foods it is a major driver of this trend. However, advertising also plays a major role in causing obesity among low and middle-income citizens.

As discussed in the Advertising, Media and Culture section, advertising is a strong driver of culture. Advertising and marketing professionals often are experts at taking advantage of people's emotional needs for self-worth and acceptance by peers. To increase sales, advertising frequently strongly promotes and deeply ingrains the idea that happiness results from buying the advertised products. It often is used to create strong cultural ideas about what it means to be a normal, average, acceptable citizen, or what it means to be a 'real' American. By consuming the advertised product, people can feel that they are accepted and normal in the American culture. They can feel that they fit in. (The term American is used because it is a common cultural reference for US citizens. It is not intended to offend citizens from other countries in North, South or Central America, all of whom could rightly be called Americans.)

The fast food and processed food industries have been highly effective at portraying their products as the normal, real American foods. They often do this with a "we're one of you" type of message.[756] They insinuate themselves into the American mind, and thereby become part of the culture. At the same time, through more subtle marketing efforts, healthier foods sometimes implicitly are portrayed as elitist. Encouraging people to eat organic, sustainable, locally-produced or other healthier foods sometimes is seen as an elitist or liberal agenda. This is tragic. Advertising and marketing have been used to trick millions of average citizens into thinking that real Americans eat fattening, unhealthy fast and processed foods.

This once again shows the extremely destructive nature of our flawed systems that place shareholder returns before all else. To protect food company shareholder returns, citizens often have been manipulated into believing that unhealthy foods are patriotic and healthy foods are un-American. As discussed, eating animal products, fast foods, processed foods and refined carbohydrates strongly drives obesity, chronic disease and premature death as well as severely degrades quality of life by causing dementia, amputations, erectile dysfunction and other health problems, including restriction of simple activities such as walking.

With nearly three-quarters of US citizens being overweight or obese, there appears to be more advertising and marketing efforts that attempt to portray obesity as a mainstream, acceptable lifestyle. For example, food ads sometimes use obese actors. This implies that becoming obese by eating fast and processed foods is acceptable.

Obviously, obese people should not be criticized or ostracized. People who compulsively overeat deserve honor and respect, as do all people who suffer from addiction to any other substance or activity. However, obesity strongly drives increased healthcare costs, chronic disease, premature death and reduced quality of life. It is a gross disservice to imply that extreme obesity is an acceptable lifestyle that requires no remedial action. It would be like condoning addiction to heroin or any other harmful substance. Of course, people are free to choose to overeat and become obese. Each person has a right to live their life as they choose. However, we should not be encouraging people en masse to become obese by portraying obesity as a normal, acceptable American lifestyle. This helps food company shareholder returns, but severely degrades society.

This is a difficult and sensitive issue. The suggestion here obviously is not that obese people should not be shown in advertising and media. They should be shown fully enjoying life and fully accepted by society. However, we have an obligation to protect society. Anti-smoking ads were highly effective because they criticized the harmful activity, not the person engaging in it. The same approach should be applied to harmful overeating.

To protect shareholder returns, companies selling unhealthy, obesity-promoting foods often appear to create the public impression that their products not only are acceptable, but preferable. Eating them indicates that one is a good American. Criticizing the products implies that one is un-American and perhaps should go live in another country. This public deception well illustrates the negative impacts of putting shareholder returns before everything else, including the well-being of society.

There are many other types of deceptive food advertisements. For example, ads for animal products often show happy, healthy animals. However, if consumers saw how food animals were raised and slaughtered, they frequently would be revolted. These animals are the opposite of happy.

Like advertising in general, food ads often strongly imply that emotional needs for happiness, self-worth and acceptance by peers can be met by consuming the advertised products. Food ads frequently show attractive people having fun with family and friends while consuming the advertised foods. They communicate highly effective, powerful emotional messages which imply that happiness comes from consumption. Some ads even state this directly. For example, in a commercial for a popular soda, the tagline was "open happiness". This ad is deceptive. Happiness mainly does not result from opening and drinking a can of carbonated water, sugar and chemicals. It often results from doing the things shown in ads, such as spending time with family and friends.

Food advertising to children also is highly effective at increasing food sales, shareholder returns and childhood obesity. As discussed in the Children's section, children see about 13,000 TV food ads on average per year, mostly for high calorie, low nutrition, fattening foods. TV ads often contain popular cartoon characters. These types of ads are highly effective at encouraging children to request and consume fast foods and other unhealthy, obesity-promoting foods. Indicating the effectiveness of fast food advertising, one study found that 84 percent of parents in the US take their children to a fast food restaurant at least once per week.[757]

Advertising and marketing also are used to create broad public ideas, myths and deceptions that increase shareholder returns by promoting the sale of unhealthy foods. Some of these myths were discussed in previous sections. Examples include carbohydrates are bad, people must consume animal products to get enough protein, heart-healthy oils are good, drinking milk prevents osteoporosis, and most cancer is caused by genetics. As discussed, all of these ideas are misleading or false. Refined carbohydrates are bad. But whole, complex carbohydrates are the healthiest foods that human can eat. Abundant protein is available from plant products. No human needs to eat animal products. All oils are heart unhealthy to varying degrees because humans did not evolve to eat refined oils. And as discussed in *The China Study*, milk promotes rather than prevents osteoporosis. Also as discussed in *The China Study*, the main driver of most cancers considered to be diseases of affluence, such as prostate, breast and colorectal cancer, is diet, not genetics.

Perhaps the most destructive general idea promoted by advertising and media in the food area is the widespread belief that industrial food is conventional and healthy. For nearly all of human history, food came from nature or farms. It only began to substantially come from factories in the past 70 to 100 years. This transition to industrial food facilitated centralized production and growth of large food companies. Industrial food might be conventional in the sense that it has become the primary means of feeding people in developed countries. But as discussed, the term conventional food is highly deceptive. Industrial food is not normal, natural or healthy food for humans. We did not evolve to eat it. That is why it so strongly drives chronic disease and premature death. As discussed in the Food Solutions sections below, it is imperative that we begin to use advertising and media in positive ways that correct widespread public misconceptions and deceptions about food.

Education

To maximize sales and develop lifelong customers, food companies often aggressively market their products to children and teenagers through school-based programs. In *The China Study*, Dr. Campbell describes how the dairy industry has been providing extensive nutrition 'education' (i.e. marketing) materials to schools for decades. The industry develops nutrition lesson plans and other so-called educational materials that portray dairy products as an important component of healthy diets.

Schools often have limited budgets. As a result, they frequently welcome these free teaching materials. For example, a set of kindergarten nutrition lesson plans developed by the dairy industry were placed in 76 percent of kindergarten sites in the US. A dairy industry report to Congress noted that two nutritional programs "targeted to second and fourth grades, reach over 12 million students with messages that milk and dairy products are a key part of a healthy diet." Another dairy industry report stated, "As the best avenue to increase fluid milk consumption long-term, children are without a doubt the future of dairy consumption." A dairy industry marketing plan stated, "As part of an effort to guide school-age children to become lifelong consumers of dairy products, [dairy marketing] activities will target students, parents, educators and school food-service professionals."[758]

As discussed in the Health sections, milk has been linked to type 1 diabetes, prostate cancer, osteoporosis, multiple sclerosis and other auto-immune diseases. In addition, casein, the main protein in dairy products, has been shown to promote cancer, increased blood cholesterol and plaque accumulation in blood vessels. But children, parents and teachers are not being made aware of this information by dairy industry funded 'educational' materials used in schools. Instead, by allowing the dairy industry to supply marketing materials to schools, under the guise of providing free education-al materials, children, parents and teachers are receiving inaccurate, biased information that will increase healthcare costs, obesity, chronic disease and premature death.

Labeling

Misleading labeling is one of the most important public deceptions in the food area. It is especially problematic in the US due to strong busi-ness influence of government. As discussed in previous sections, industrial food products often contain many harmful ingredients that are not shown on food labels. In addition, industrial food animals frequently are fed sub-stances or treated in ways that potentially affect food safety. But these feed additives and treatments often are not disclosed on labels.

For example, food animals in the US frequently are treated with hor-mones, antibiotics and drugs such as ractopine. These drugs sometimes re-main in the meat and milk of food animals. But customers would not know this because disclosure is not required. In addition, food animals often are fed feces, arsenic and other potentially harmful substances that also are not required to be disclosed on food labels. Meat and milk from cloned animals are not required to be labeled. Irradiated foods frequently are deceptively labeled or not labeled at all. And processed foods often contain pesticides, chemical residues and processing agents that are not required to be disclosed on food labels.

Publicly traded food companies are under nearly constant pressure to lower costs and increase sales. They frequently are able to compel government to implement misleading or fraudulent labeling requirements that facilitate profit growth because they are allowed to give money to politicians and inappropriately influence government in other ways. Business-influenced government allows many labeling loopholes that help shareholders but mislead consumers. MSG provides an important example of fraudulent labeling. As discussed, about 40 ingredients always or often contain MSG. But MSG and other potentially harmful chemicals are not required to be disclosed on food labels because companies frequently are not required to list the ingredients of ingredients.

One large and odious labeling deception in the US relates to the disconnect between ingredient listings and information on the rest of packages. Companies are required to list ingredients (subject to the many exceptions noted above). But other information on food packages is not required to reflect actual contents.[759] As a result, the fronts of food packages often contain highly deceptive information.

For example, the FDA does not define what constitutes "natural" or "all natural" processed food.[760] As a result, companies can state on the front of packages that products contain all natural ingredients. But they could contain many unnatural, processed or artificial ingredients, such as high fructose corn syrup and natural flavoring. As noted, natural flavoring is a highly deceptive term. The ingredient often contains off-gassing chemicals and MSG. Another misuse of the natural label occurs with vegetable oils. Some vegetable oils made from genetically modified plants are labeled "100 percent Natural".[761] But genetic engineering is one of the most unnatural food production processes. As a result, food produced with this technology is not natural and therefore should not be labeled natural.

Another labeling deception involves using the word "organic" in company and product line names. Through this approach, the word organic appears on the front of packages. Customers can be misled into believing that the product is certified organic, when it actually is not. USDA Organic certification only applies to crops, livestock and products derived from them. It does not apply to fish, nutritional supplements, pet food, cosmetics or personal care products.[762] As a result, use of the word organic on these products can deceptively imply a level of safety and oversight that does not exist.

There are many other ways to deceptively label food. For example, companies could trademark the term "no artificial anything" and put it on the front of food packages. But the product could contain many artificial ingredients because a trademark it is not a nutritional term.[763] Many food experts suggest that consumers ignore whatever is written on the front of packages and instead read ingredients labels. Ingredient listings can be misleading. But they generally are not as deceptive as other claims made on food packaging.

The food labeling requirements of the business dominated US government are so weak and deceptive that they could be called laughable, if they were not so harmful. As discussed in the Animal Feed section, labeling illustrates what happens when companies that are structurally required to always make more money are allowed to strongly influence government. When business controls the entity that regulates business, self-regulation or no regulation effectively exists. This creates a Lord of the Flies type situation were the most abominable practices, such as feeding feces to food animals, are allowed and not disclosed to consumers.

Citizens have an absolute right to decide what they will and will not feed to their children and themselves. Every potentially harmful ingredient, even if present in small quantities, and every abominable or potentially harmful practice used to raise animals should be disclosed on food labels. This disclosure would strongly encourage companies to remove harmful ingredients and end abominable, harmful practices. As noted, when labeling fails to disclose potentially harmful contents or production processes, citizens become like the farm animals that are forced to eat feces.

People have a right to avoid cloned, irradiated, genetically-engineered, hormone-treated, pesticide-contaminated, feces-fed and otherwise contaminated food. Business dominated government often relies on biased, untrustworthy company research to determine that these products are safe. Especially under these circumstances, citizens must be given the option to protect their families and themselves through honest, accurate labeling.

Research

Conducting and publishing biased research is a main public deception strategy in the food area. Dr. Campbell discusses this extensively in *The China Study*. He describes how food companies use various strategies to mislead the public about food research. For example, they often track research that shows animal products and other foods to be harmful. Then they frequently hire credible scientists to conduct studies that refute the harmful research. In addition, food companies sometimes engage in smear campaigns in an effort to discredit researchers who show their products to be harmful.[764] Researchers sometimes place their careers at risk by publishing studies that challenge the status quo, for example, by showing that animal products promote chronic diseases.

Dr. Campbell explains that the goal of food company research often appears to be creating controversy and confusion in the public mind. It frequently is difficult for average citizens to tell the difference between independent research and biased company research. By refuting studies that show animal products to be harmful and creating controversy and confusion, companies can diffuse or delay public demand for safer foods. If food company research finds that their products are harmful in ways that are not immediate and obvious, these studies rarely, if ever, are published. The goal of company funded or influenced research primarily is not to protect public health. It is to protect shareholder returns.

The business dominated US government often relies on company conducted, funded or influenced research to determine if food products and additives are safe. But this type of research is inherently biased, and therefore not trustworthy. If democracy existed and government were focused on protecting public health instead of shareholder returns, it would require independent research which proved that food products were safe before they were approved. In addition, a government that served and protected the people would not allow companies to publicize biased research that protects shareholder returns by refuting unbiased, independent research and creating confusion and controversy.

The Wrong Perspective and Wrong Reference Point deception techniques are used extensively to mislead the public in the food area. Food companies, politicians paid by them and other allies often argue that overwhelming evidence of harm should be provided before their products are restricted. But as discussed, this is the wrong perspective. Food products never should have been approved for human consumption until there was overwhelming independent proof that they were safe. The innocent until proven guilty approach to food safety advocated by food companies and politicians paid by them reflects wrong perspective logic.

The problem is compounded by using wrong reference point logic. Since independent evidence of safety often is not required before food products are approved, they should be restricted when new research shows a reasonable probability, perhaps in the 10 to 20 percent range, that they are harmful. But food companies and their allies often argue that very high levels of certainty, such as over 90 percent, should be required before potentially harmful products are restricted. Again, this wrong reference point logic would be like parents saying that they would not put seatbelts on their children unless the probability of having an accident were over 90 percent.

The type 1 diabetes studies discussed in the Autoimmune Diseases section reflect wrong reference point logic in the food area. Five of the ten studies found a significant link between cow's milk consumption and type 1 diabetes in children. Dairy companies and their allies argued that five studies not showing a link indicated considerable uncertainty and justified not taking action to restrict feeding cow's milk to infants. As noted, Dr. Campbell stated that there is less than a two percent chance that five studies would find a statistically significant link between type 1 diabetes and cow's milk by mistake. Therefore, food companies effectively were arguing that 98 percent certainty of harm did not justify taking action to protect children. Clearly, this was the wrong reference point.

Dr. Campbell also extensively discussed the problem of reductionism in food research. Rather than studying foods that people actually eat, food research often focuses on components of food, such as fat. This type of research helps companies to develop new products by mixing or varying certain ingredients. It also often protects shareholder returns by hiding links between animal products and chronic diseases. The Nurses' Health Study and Women's Health Initiative are good examples of reductionism. Focusing on one component of food, such as fat, often did not show links between animal products and chronic diseases such as cancer.

But as discussed in *The China Study* and *Prevent and Reverse Heart Disease*, saturated fat content is not the only aspect of animal products that promotes chronic diseases. Other factors include the cholesterol exclusively found in animal products, the inflammatory properties of animal protein and the promotion of free radicals. Accurately determining the relative benefits of consuming plant products versus animal products generally requires comparing groups of people who eat all or mainly plant products to those who eat animal products. As noted, the Nurses' Health Study and Women's Health Initiative did not do this. Nearly all of the people in the studies ate large amounts of animal products.

Illustrating another example of reductionism and public deception, dairy industry funded research showed that a component of milk, conjugated linoleic acid (CLA), lowered cancer risk in mice. The industry published this research and implied that drinking milk could lower cancer risk. But CLA is not the main ingredient of milk. From a cancer perspective, protein is. Many animal and human studies have shown that milk protein increases cancer risk. The CLA research creates public confusion, delays action to protect society and protects shareholder returns.[765]

Food companies and their allies engage in many other research-related deceptions. For example, food companies, trade groups and other allies sometimes form non-profit organizations with names that include deceptive terms such as consumer freedom and food facts. Then the organizations often publish research which shows that animal products are healthy. They also frequently do not disclose their membership and funding. Food companies and their allies also sometimes develop websites that are designed to show up in web searches about their products. The sites frequently display misleading information that, for example, says that mercury in fish is not a problem. In addition, food companies and their allies sometimes threaten to withhold research funding from universities that teach courses which show their products to be harmful or invite speakers who discuss the harmful nature of their products.[766]

Additional research related food deceptions include focusing on non-food causes of chronic diseases and emphasizing the nutrients provided by animal products. Food companies, trade groups and other food company allies sometimes conduct or fund research that highlights nonfood causes of chronic diseases. This can create public confusion and enable food companies to argue that more research is needed before taking action, such as restricting the consumption of animal products. But chronic diseases are complex. Many factors promote them. The fact that nonfood causes exist does not invalidate the extensive research that shows strong links between chronic diseases and the consumption of animal products. Studies that compare plant to animal eaters consistently find that people who eat fewer animal products have fewer chronic diseases.

Food companies and their allies also sometimes emphasize the protein and other important nutrients provided by animal products. The implication often appears to be that these nutrients are only available or best available from animal products. Animal products obviously provide some nutrients. But as discussed above, all nutrients, including protein, are better provided by plants. Along with nutrients, animal products also contain harmful substances, such as saturated fat and cholesterol. Plant products have few or none of these harmful materials. Instead, they have highly beneficial substances that are rarely or never found in animal products, such as antioxidants and fiber.

Healthcare

The healthcare sector is a major source of public confusion and deception about food. Extensive research indicates that chronic diseases mainly result from poor nutrition, not poor genes or bad luck.[767] As a result, they often are preventable, which essentially makes them voluntary. People give themselves chronic diseases, such as heart disease, cancer and diabetes, mainly by eating animal products, refined carbohydrates and other unhealthy foods. This is a highly empowering concept. It give people the power to control their own health, rather than having healthcare professionals or drug companies control it.

The largely for-profit US healthcare system is not focused on preventing disease, maximizing public health or minimizing healthcare costs. It is structurally focused on maximizing shareholder returns. Drug and other healthcare companies usually do not increase profits by preventing disease. They maximize them mainly by treating it. Partly as a result, citizens often receive inadequate information about the immense health and life-enhancing benefits of switching to whole plant food diets. This deception sickens and kills millions of citizens and raises healthcare costs by trillions of dollars. As a result, this may be the most important public deception in the US and many other developed countries.

As stated throughout *Global System Change*, there is no malice in these deceptions. Drug and other healthcare companies do not wish to harm society. The intention of business managers and politicians who take money from businesses is to help it. The purpose here, as everywhere else in this book, is not to criticize businesses, governments, or business and political leaders. It is to criticize and suggest improvements to our flawed economic and political systems that cause good, well-meaning leaders to take actions that degrade society. Many of the problems caused by business and business influence of government result from the extremely myopic, irrational and ultimately suicidal requirement to put shareholder returns before all else. This mechanism causes good people to do bad things.

Healthcare deceptions related to food probably are higher in the US than any other developed country. The US is the only developed country with a largely for-profit healthcare system. The main goal of the non-profit systems in every other developed country is to maximize the health of citizens. But this is not the effectively measured and managed goal of the US healthcare system. The main goal is to maximize the wealth of drug and healthcare company shareholders.

This focus on healthcare profits drives many mostly unintentional deceptions related to food and healthcare. For example, the vast majority of healthcare research funding is focused on developing new drugs and other disease treatments, rather than on disease prevention and nutrition. Drug companies are structurally required to always make more money. They do this mainly by developing new drugs, not by preventing diseases. The healthcare sector overall also is highly focused on disease treatment instead of prevention. This creates many tragic outcomes for citizens. People who get cancer, heart disease and other chronic diseases often are highly vulnerable. They frequently are willing to do anything or spend all their money to remain alive. The profit-focused US healthcare sector often recommends the most expensive and profitable treatment options.

Switching to a whole plant food diet frequently is the best way to prevent chronic disease. It also often is one of the best ways to treat them. But doctors frequently hesitate to suggest switching to whole plant food diets for several reasons. As noted, they usually receive little training about the links between chronic disease and diet in medical school. Doctors mainly are trained to treat, not prevent disease. Also, drug companies heavily influence medical education. Young doctors often learn that there is a pill to treat nearly every health problem.

Food companies also influence medical education. They frequently supply nutrition 'education' (i.e. marketing) materials to medical schools, in the same way that they widely supply biased nutrition education information to K-12 schools. This material almost certainly does not emphasize the strong links between animal products and chronic disease. Due to the heavy influence of drug and food companies on medical education and the strong focus of medical education on treatment rather than prevention, doctors often do not adequately promote diet solutions to health problems.

Doctors and researchers sometimes hesitate to discuss links between animal products and chronic disease because they do not want to disturb the public. But cancer, heart disease, diabetes and premature death will disturb citizens more than changing diets. Dr. Campbell notes that doctors sometimes hesitate to suggest switching to whole plant food diets because they are concerned that patients will not want to stop eating animal products. But this is not logical. It would be like a doctor not telling a lung cancer patient to stop smoking because the patient might not want to do so. Doctors should inform patients of the health benefits of whole plant food diets, and then possibly provide guidance and support on changing lifestyles. Doctors might make less money on disease treatments. But helping patients to change lifestyles could create new revenue opportunities.

The vulnerability of chronic disease patients often makes the marketing of for-profit healthcare services extremely tragic. To illustrate, a TV commercial for a cancer treatment center showed survivors discussing how the center cured their cancer. But small type at the bottom of the screen said, "No case is typical. You should not expect to receive these results." People with poor vision or those focusing on the main part of the ad, instead of the small print at the bottom of the screen, might not have seen this disclaimer.

The US for-profit healthcare system often forces citizens to use up their life savings, sell their homes or file for bankruptcy to pay for cancer and other treatments. As discussed in the Misleading the Public section, medical expenses are the largest cause of personal bankruptcies in the US. Chronic disease treatments often are expensive, painful, life restricting and ineffective over the longer-term. As Dr. Campbell and Dr. Esselstyn discuss, switching to a whole plant food diet frequently is the best way to prevent, treat and reverse heart disease, cancer and other chronic diseases. When citizens are not made aware of this option by doctors and the healthcare sector in general, extensive and tragic public deception occurs.

Influencing Government

Influencing government is an important public deception strategy in the food area. As discussed extensively throughout *Global System Change*, inappropriate business influence of government is one of the largest system flaws and problems in the US and many other countries. By allowing businesses and their owners to give money to politicians and inappropriately influence government in other ways, businesses are able to encourage or compel government to enact policies that protect shareholder returns, but mislead the public about food safety and other food related issues.

For example, large food companies and their allies have aggressively and often successfully lobbied to weaken organic food standards in the US.

This enables companies to increase profits by using industrial practices in organic food production. To illustrate, certified organic processed food must contain at least 95 percent organic ingredients. Synthetic ingredients originally were not allowed in the five percent non-organic portion. But business lobbying helped to reverse this requirement. Now synthetic and artificial ingredients are allowed in certified organic processed food.[768] Additional weakening of the original organic standards includes allowing the use of some synthetic pesticides on organic crops, allowing organic cattle to be fed non-organic fish meal that might contain PCBs, mercury and other toxic chemicals, and allowing the use of antibiotics in organic dairy cows provided that drug use ends at least 12 months before milk is sold.[769]

Other examples of food deceptions driven by government influence relate to children's food advertising, school lunch standards and salt content in processed foods. With rapidly growing childhood obesity, many citizens and organizations have said that advertising of obesity-promoting junk foods and fast foods to children should be limited or prohibited, in the same way that tobacco advertising to children is prohibited. However, by giving money to politicians and influencing government in other ways, food companies and their allies have been able to block restrictions on junk food advertising to children.

Many citizens also have argued that the national school lunch program in the US provides fattening, unhealthy food to children. To illustrate, the program defined French fries and pizza as vegetables. Updated guidelines were issued. But many food experts argue that food industry lobbying blocked the implementation of substantially healthier guidelines. For example, under the updated guidelines, French fries and pizza still are considered to be vegetables.[770] From a business perspective, promoting the sale of animal products, refined carbohydrates and other unhealthy foods in schools is important because it helps to develop lifelong customers for these foods.

Food companies and their allies also used lobbying and other influence activities to vigorously oppose restrictions on salt use in processed foods. With high blood pressure rising among adults and children, government health experts estimate that substantially reducing salt consumption could save 150,000 lives per year.[771] Processed and restaurant foods account for about 80 percent of the salt in the US diet. Like MSG, salt enhances the frequently bland or bitter taste of processed foods. If salt were restricted in processed foods, food companies often would have to use more expensive ingredients to make processed foods taste palatable. By using government influence to block salt restrictions, food companies protected shareholder returns, but increased illness and premature death in society.

In *The China Study*, Dr. Campbell discusses one of the most important ways that businesses influence government in the food area. Government scientists are not allowed to receive compensation from businesses. But food companies routinely hire scientists in academia as consultants. While employed by business, these scientists generally retain their academic roles and credibility. But they also often chair expert policy groups, assume leadership roles in science-based organizations, convene symposia and workshops, and write commissioned reports. Once in leadership roles, these business-controlled scientists can appoint other business-biased scientists to policy groups and science organizations. As discussed, members of the USDA's dietary guidelines committee often had ties to the food industry. Disclosure of financial and other ties to business is legally required. But committee members sometimes refused to disclose them. Lawsuits forced disclosure.[772]

Food companies can strongly influence academic research and government nutrition policies by employing academic scientists as consultants who then assume major roles on government policy boards and groups. As noted, two major studies, the Nurses' Health Study and Women's Health Initiative, were structured in ways that did not show links between animal products and chronic diseases, in part because groups of people who ate mainly or completely plant-based diets were not included in the studies. The studies protected the shareholder returns of food companies by refuting international studies that more correctly compared groups of people who ate animal products to those who ate plant-based diets. It is possible that scientists who received money from business played a role in structuring these and other studies that protect the shareholder returns of food companies.

The US dietary guidelines are based in part on a report by the Food and Nutrition Board (FNB). Dr. Campbell points out that the FNB also is heavily influenced by dairy and other food companies. These companies helped to fund FNB reports. By providing funding and controlling leadership positions on the FNB, food companies were able to drive the development of dietary guidelines that strongly benefit shareholders, at the expense of society. As noted, the 2020 guidelines imply that it is healthy and acceptable to eat up to 35 percent of calories as fat, 35 percent of calories as protein, and 50 percent of grains in refined form.

These guidelines strongly affect diets in the US. They guide food labels, school lunch programs, nutrition education programs from primary school to college, diets in hospitals and nursing homes that receive Medicare reimbursements, and the Women, Infants and Children Supplemental Feeding Program. Through the guidelines, large amounts of fattening, disease-promoting foods are being provided to the most vulnerable people in society, including the elderly, children and low-income women. Doctors and other experts are telling citizens that, based on the USDA guidelines, it is healthy to eat large amounts of animal protein, fat and refined carbohydrates.[773]

With obesity, diabetes and other diet-linked chronic diseases at historically high levels, these guidelines can seem difficult to understand. But once business influence of government is taken into account, the disease and obesity-promoting guidelines are seen as the obvious and expected outcome. In discussing the FNB report that drove earlier US dietary guidelines, Dr. Campbell said, this "FNB report, which represents the most sweeping, regressive nutrition policy statement I have ever seen, will either indirectly or directly promote sickness among Americans for many years to come."[774] Food companies continue to influence dietary guidelines. As a result, the guidelines protect food company shareholder returns, but strongly promote high levels of obesity, chronic disease and premature deaths, as well as greatly increase healthcare costs.

Another example of food company influence of dietary guidelines relates to the environment. As discussed in the Environmental Impacts section, the industrial production of animal products is one of the two most environmentally-destructive human activities on Earth, along with burning fossil fuels. Switching to plant-based diets would provide vast, possibly society-saving benefits to humanity. Acknowledging the link between animal product diets and environmental degradation, the 2015 dietary guidelines stated, "a diet higher in plant-based foods, such as vegetables, fruits, whole grains, legumes, nuts, and seeds, and lower in calories and animal-based foods is more health promoting and is associated with less environmental impact than is the current U.S. diet."[775]

Apparently to protect food company shareholder returns, some Republicans in Congress sought to limit discussion of animal product production and environmental degradation in the dietary guidelines. They argued that 'strong' evidence of this link must be required to warrant inclusion in the guidelines. But strong evidence is a difficult standard to achieve. It requires that a large number of studies reach near uniform conclusions.[776] Food companies can block this, create uncertainty and protect shareholder returns by conducting studies that find no link between animal product production and environmental degradation. As discussed in the Heart Disease section, food company influence succeeded in having discussion of climate change and environmental impacts removed from the 2020 guidelines.

Suggesting that 'strong' evidence be required reflects the hypocrisy of business-influenced politicians. They demand strong evidence for issues that threaten shareholder returns, but not for issues that protect them. Excluding biased food company-influenced research, there is no strong evidence that diets high in animal products and refined carbohydrates promote optimal health. Abundant independent research shows the opposite. Yet business-influenced-politicians allow dietary guidelines that promote high animal product and refined carbohydrate diets without strong evidence that these diets are healthy.

Further examples of government influence and public deception in the food area involve food libel laws and suppression of undercover videos. At least thirteen states have food libel laws that make it easier for food companies to sue citizens or organizations that criticize food products. Freedom of speech rights and traditional libel laws enabled citizens to freely and honesty discuss potentially unsafe or inhumane food production practices. But this free speech apparently threatened the ability of food companies to lower costs and continuously increase shareholder returns. As a result, it appears that inappropriate business influence of government was used to compel the implementation of unfair food libel laws.

Reflecting this influence, these laws often require a lower burden of proof than regular libel laws. In addition, they sometimes place the burden of proof on the party being sued to prove innocence, rather than on the plaintiff to prove guilt. This implied presumption of guilt violates the spirit of the US Constitution. The libel laws also sometimes include unfair provisions, such as allowing recovery of punitive damages and attorney's fees only for plaintiffs. This greatly reduces or eliminates the penalty for bringing frivolous lawsuits intended only to silence critics. In addition, the laws often require near scientific certainty from those criticizing food production practices.[777] But food companies and their allies directly or indirectly control, fund or influence extensive food research. They can conduct biased studies that refute studies which show harm, and thereby make it difficult for those being sued under food libel laws to reach the scientific certainty standard.

These unfair provisions combined with the ability of business to strongly influence the appointment of pro-business judges can make it difficult for citizens to defend themselves against frivolous, unfair food company lawsuits and freely express their concerns about food safety. Food libel laws apparently result from giving money to politicians, lobbying and other inappropriate business influence of government. The unfair and probably unconstitutional laws make it easier for food companies to harass and silence their critics. They also violate freedom of speech and put the public at risk by making it easier for companies to hide unsafe practices.

Perhaps most importantly, food libel laws set a dangerous precedent for other industries. It is extremely harmful that some states allowed food companies to unfairly intimidate, harass and silence critics. However, it would be much worse if many other industries were allowed to do this. Free speech and open public discourse are essential for effective democracy. Public scrutiny and criticism of potentially harmful practices put pressure on companies to operate safely and responsibly. If this public voice is suppressed or silenced, the requirement to put shareholder returns before all else often will compel companies to produce unsafe food and other products. This already occurs widely in the food area. Retaining existing food libel laws and implementing new ones, as many states are considering, will expand the production of unsafe food.

Implementing unfair libel laws, like the food libel laws, in other industries would gravely harm citizens and society. It would constitute one of the most severe suppressions of democracy ever implemented in the US. If companies are operating responsibly, they can defend themselves against unfair criticism by using the same libel laws that protect regular citizens. They also can defend themselves in the court of public opinion. Companies should not be allowed to give money to politicians and thereby compel the implementation of business-friendly libel laws that enable companies to unfairly silence critics. We should not be giving special protections to non-human entities that seek to silence citizens. Instead, we should protect average citizens from potential abuses by large and powerful corporations.

Darkness cannot survive in the light. Citizens often criticized food companies for raising animals in filthy, crowded, unsafe, inhumane conditions. Rather than ending the actions that brought justified criticism, companies apparently gave money to politicians and compelled government in other ways to silence critics. Citizens usually oppose food libel laws once they learn how the laws severely suppress free speech and greatly increase public health risks. One poll found that two-thirds of citizens believe that food libel laws are wrong and should be repealed.[778] Public awareness must be raised on this issue. It is imperative that unconstitutional, business-driven food libel laws be repealed as quickly as possible. This cancer must be removed before it can spread to other industries.

Several states also are considering laws that would make it illegal to photograph or film industrial animal operations, such as feedlots and slaughterhouses. As discussed above, industrial animal operations in the US cause widespread contamination of food with feces and harmful bacteria. They also cause widespread animal cruelty, pain and suffering. Business-influenced government often fails to limit food contamination and animal cruelty. In the absence of effective government regulation, undercover videos educated citizens about health risks and animal abuses occurring in industrial animal operations. These videos increased public and government pressure to limit food contamination and animal cruelty. However, they also can restrict the ability of food companies to cut costs and provide ever-increasing shareholder returns. By giving money to politicians, lobbying and influencing government in other ways, companies can encourage or compel politicians to make undercover videos illegal.

If government served the people, it would make food contamination and animal cruelty illegal. Instead, business controlled government sometimes makes exposing these actions illegal. This once again reflects the tragic nature of our flawed systems. Instead of protecting victims (i.e. sickened citizens and abused animals), government protects the abusers. This is not surprising given business control government. But it is tragic and wrong. And it is not democracy. If government does not do its job of protecting citizens and animals, it should not punish citizens who attempt to do what government should be doing.

If companies produce food safely and treat animals humanely, they should not fear public scrutiny of their operations. Food companies sometimes argue that undercover videos expose proprietary processes. But protecting the health and lives of citizens and preventing animal torture take priority over shareholder returns. Food libel laws and suppression of undercover videos protect the shareholder returns of companies that give money to politicians. These laws can deceive and threaten citizens by allowing companies to hide unsafe and inhumane practices. Once citizens take back control of government from business, the US government will criminalize unsafe and inhumane food production practices, rather than criminalizing the exposure of these practices.

Food Solutions

Many system changes and food solutions have been discussed or implied in the preceding food sections. For example, the Health section provided many suggestions about how individuals can protect and improve their health. Specific system changes related to lowering pandemic risks were discussed in the Influenza Pandemic section. This section summarizes broader system changes and solutions needed in the food area.

As discussed, the root causes of nearly all major problems facing humanity are our flawed ideas and systems. As a result, the foundational solution to these problems, including those related to food production and diet, is improving these ideas and systems. A whole system strategy that addresses essentially all major problems is needed. These problems are interconnected and therefore cannot be addressed effectively in isolation. The *Global System Change* books provide a detailed description of the whole system approach needed to evolve human society into sustainable form, and how to implement it.

The most important system changes required in the food area essentially are the same as those needed to resolve other major problems discussed throughout *Global System Change*. These changes include focusing on the well-being of society instead of the well-being of business, separating business and government, holding businesses fully responsible for all negative impacts, and charging accurate prices. These and other system changes required in the food area are summarized below.

Focus on the Well-Being of Society, Not the Well-Being of Business

Our flawed economic and political systems use economic growth (i.e. GDP) as the primary indicator of the well-being of society. But as discussed in the Economic Growth and Well-Being of Society sections of *Global Sys-*

tem Change, economic growth mostly is a measure of business success. It mainly measures growth of business sales. Most business assets are owned by a small group of wealthy citizens. As a result, economic growth mostly measures the financial well-being of this small group. Using economic growth and business success as the primary measures of the well-being of society causes many problems and unintended consequences. Economic growth is the means to the end of social well-being. But if we mostly measure the means, the means become the end.

Businesses and industry sectors have no inherent right to exist. Business is a tool meant to serve society. Companies and industries must evolve and adapt based completely on what is best for society, not on what is best for business. Publicly traded companies are man-made entities designed to always put their own well-being first. If they do not do this, they ultimately will die. This is why businesses must be constrained and prohibited from harming life support systems and society. Without these constraints, the structurally required mandate to grow forever will severely degrade and possibly destroy society.

For example, food companies often put MSG in processed foods. This causes people to overeat unhealthy foods. This in turn increases healthcare costs and food and drug sales. All of these often increase economic growth. When economic growth is used as the primary measure of social well-being, our flawed systems say that causing people to overeat unhealthy foods is good for society. But anyone with more than a room temperature IQ can see that greatly increasing obesity, chronic disease, premature death and healthcare costs is extremely bad for society. If we measured the ultimate goal (social well-being) instead of the means to the end (economic growth), we would not allow this destructive action.

Improving the way we measure the well-being of society is part of the high-level economic and political system changes discussed in *Global System Change*. However, it is noted here to illustrate how high-level system changes are needed to effectively resolve problems in the food production and diet areas.

Food demand is rapidly increasing while food supply constraints also are quickly expanding. We cannot feed a growing population increasing amounts of animal products. We also cannot afford to pay for the rapidly growing chronic diseases this will cause. A clear, rational, big picture assessment of reality shows that we must rapidly reduce our consumption of animal products.

But this will lower the shareholder returns of some food, drug and other healthcare companies because people often will be buying less expensive foods and getting sick much less frequently. Publicly traded food companies, like most other publicly traded companies, are structurally required to put shareholder returns before all else. As a result, their survival often will demand that they vigorously oppose the transition to plant-based diets. This perfectly reflects the suicidal nature of our grossly flawed systems. If greatly improving the health and longevity of citizens and substantially lowering healthcare costs reduces shareholder returns, food, drug and other companies essentially are required to oppose this vast improvement of society.

This is why it is absolutely essential that nonhuman entities (i.e. businesses) not be given a voice in the 'What' conversation. Only human citizens should decide what type of society we want. Once we make this decision, we will tell businesses what we need and want. Companies that can effectively meet these needs will prosper. Those that cannot will cease to exist.

We did not suppress the expansion of the automobile industry to protect the horse and buggy sector. In the same way, we should not suppress the development of sustainable food production processes and companies to protect harmful ones. When the measurement of society's success is focused on economic growth and business well-being, there often is strong pressure to protect and sustain existing companies, even if they are degrading society. Shifting the focus to the well-being of society will greatly facilitate the implementation of sustainable food production and diet.

Separate Business and Government

Only government has the effective power and expertise to constrain business and compel it to enhance rather than degrade society. Citizens ultimately have all power in a democracy through their votes and purchase decisions. However, non-expert citizens can be easily misled, as the US Founders well understood. Vested interests often protect shareholder returns by misleading citizens into focusing on false enemies (conservatives or liberals) and ignoring large problems, such as business control of government and degradation of the environment and society.

As the agent of the people with the ability to utilize leading experts, government can theoretically effectively constrain business. But this obviously cannot occur when businesses and their owners are allowed to indirectly give unlimited amounts of money to politicians, rotate employees in and out of regulatory roles, use former senior politicians to lobby current politicians, and inappropriately influence government in other ways. President Lincoln warned during the Civil War that once businesses got some influence of government, they would use it to get a lot more. This brought us to the current situation in the US and some other countries where business strongly influences and often controls government.

The simplistic, unilateral focus of publicly traded companies on shareholder returns prevents them from self-regulating. They often are not able to constrain themselves. If they voluntarily do this, they ultimately will die. As noted, when business controls the entity that regulates business (i.e. government), self-regulation or no regulation effectively exists. Unregulated businesses frequently cannot prevent themselves from degrading society. That is why it is essential that government be separated from business and returned to the control of the people.

Actions needed to do this in the US were discussed extensively throughout *Global System Change*. They include publicly funding political campaigns, imposing term limits on Congress and the Judicial branch, implementing popular election of the President, reversing the Supreme Court's Citizens United and McCutcheon decisions, and redefining corporations as artificial persons. Government will not be able to prevent companies from degrading society as long as it is under the strong influence of business.

Hold Businesses Fully Responsible

As discussed in the Pandemic Solutions section and throughout *Global System Change*, holding companies fully responsible for negative impacts is essential for achieving sustainability. Many economic and political system flaws compel companies to degrade the environment and society. They could be rolled up into one overarching system flaw – the failure to hold companies fully responsible for negative impacts. This is the general mechanism that makes it impossible for companies to act in a fully responsible manner and remain in business.

Generally speaking, companies can voluntarily mitigate about 20 percent of their short-term and long-term, tangible and intangible, negative environmental and social impacts in a profit-neutral or profit-enhancing manner. Beyond this point, costs usually go up and profits decline. If companies continue to voluntarily mitigate negative impacts, they will put themselves out of business long before reaching full impact mitigation. Beyond a certain point, voluntary corporate responsibility equals voluntary corporate suicide.

Holding companies fully responsible eliminates conflicts between business and society. When this occurs, businesses maximize profits by acting in a fully responsible manner (i.e. eliminating all negative impacts). Currently companies profit by hugely degrading the environment and society. When they are held fully responsible, this no longer is a viable option. Substantially harming life support systems and society will force companies to change or out of business, as must occur in civilized, sustainable society.

Many system flaws discussed in *Global System Change* compel companies to degrade the environment and society. These include externalities, limited liability, time value of money, focusing on economic growth instead of social well-being, and allowing regulated entities (businesses) to inappropriately influence regulators (government). Externalities are environmental and social costs that companies impose on society, instead of paying themselves. It creates the illusion that harmful products, such as industrial food, are cheap.

Limited liability intentionally does not hold investors and companies responsible for harm imposed on society, and by doing so compels companies to cause harm. The term is deceptive. Liability does not disappear. It is transferred, mostly to taxpayers. As a result, the more honest and accurate term is taxpayer liability or transferred liability. With limited liability, investors receive all of the financial upside. But if the harm their investments cause exceeds investment amounts, much of the downside is paid by citizens through higher taxes and reduced quality of life. Limited liability is socialism on the downside and capitalism on the upside because taxpayers are compelled to act as the owners of business on the downside (by paying for negative impacts), while receiving none of the upside. A limited liability corporation is not a private entity. It is a grossly unfair quasi-public structure.

Not holding companies responsible for negative impacts drives irresponsible and harmful corporate behavior. High-risk activities, such as using genetically engineered crops, synthetic pesticides and other industrial agriculture practices, often provide the highest financial returns. When the risks of these activities are transferred from investors to taxpayers, the requirement to maximize shareholder returns essentially compels companies to engage in them. This greatly increases total costs to society because citizens pay to clean up problems rather than prevent them. But this generally is not relevant to business because taxpayers are covering much of the downside.

Risky and harmful industrial agriculture practices often would not exist or would be used in much safer ways if companies were held fully responsible for all potential and actual negative impacts. Sustainability in any sector, including food, cannot be achieved unless companies and their investors are held fully responsible.

The survival and health of current and future generations take priority over everything else. There should be no trade-offs between these critical factors and economic growth or business well-being. If we require full corporate responsibility, businesses will figure out how to achieve it. If they cannot profit without degrading life support systems and society, they will cease to exist. As discussed, businesses have no inherent right to exist or earn a profit. Business existence is a privilege contingent on fully benefiting and not harming society. Businesses must not be allowed to earn a profit at the expense of society. Holding food and other companies fully responsible for all negative impacts will ensure that businesses profit only by benefiting society.

Implement Accurate Pricing

The industrial production of crops and animal products imposes (i.e. externalizes) many negative impacts on society. These externalities include environmental degradation, human health degradation, increased pandemic risks, animal cruelty and promotion of hunger in developing countries (i.e. by blocking self-sufficiency and sustainable agriculture). They are real, actual costs. They would not exist if industrial agriculture were not done. Not including these real costs in food prices creates the illusion that industrial food is cheap. But as discussed in the Pandemic Solutions section, this food is not cheap. In the case of industrial chicken (i.e. conventional and most organic and free range chicken), it probably is the most expensive product in human society on a real cost basis.

In addition to not including negative impacts in prices, many industrial agriculture inputs also are not priced accurately. As noted, animal products are far more grain and water inefficient than plant products. Grain and water often are heavily subsidized. This further enhances the illusion that industrial animal products are cheap.

Not including real, actual costs in prices greatly increases total costs to society. As noted, when food companies are not held responsible for the negative environmental, health and other impacts of their products, they often maximize profits and shareholder returns by degrading the environment and society. Citizens frequently pay for the negative impacts of industrial food through increased taxes, higher health insurance rates and lower quality of life. Holding companies fully responsible by including all real costs in prices would vastly lower total costs to society because citizens would be paying to prevent rather than remediate environmental, health and other problems.

Food prices might increase when real costs are included in prices. But taxes and other costs usually would decline by substantially more. Failing to include external costs in prices creates many distortions, inefficiencies and problems in society. It is imperative that we begin to use the market system accurately and effectively. When products and services are priced accurately, the market becomes a huge driver of social benefit. But when nearly all prices for industrial food and other industrial products are grossly inaccurate, as they are under current flawed systems, the market system becomes a major driver of environmental and social degradation. To rectify this problem, we must implement accurate pricing.

To illustrate, as discussed in the Health section, eating animal products and refined carbohydrates greatly increases chronic disease, premature death and healthcare costs. These are real, actual costs of these products. The costs would not exist if these products were not sold. But the costs do not show up in prices. Instead they are paid through higher taxes and healthcare costs and reduced quality of life. This creates the illusion that animal products, refined carbohydrates and other processed foods are cheap, while healthier foods often appear to be more expensive. Foods such as animal products and refined carbohydrates frequently cause obesity and make people sick. These real costs to society must be included in food prices. When this occurs, foods that do not make people sick, such as whole plant foods, nearly always will be the lowest cost foods.

Animal products used to be expensive foods that only wealthier people could afford. This often remains the case in developing countries. But industrial agriculture produces animal products that are sold cheaply. As a result, they are widely consumed in the US and other developed countries. The many costs of animal product production have been discussed. As noted, it causes vast environmental degradation. It is the largest land user on Earth. It is a major source of air and water pollution. Animal product production drives soil erosion and clearing of natural areas. Eating animal products probably is the largest cause of chronic disease and premature death in developed countries. Producing them uses vast amounts of water and grain.

A Union of Concerned Scientists report found that the US government spends about $100 million per year to clean up environmental damage caused by industrial animal operations.[779] These are real costs of producing animal products. But they do not show up in prices. Instead, consumers often pay to clean up these problems through higher income taxes. Food companies frequently are not held responsible for environmental damage. As a result, they often maximize profits by degrading the environment and letting taxpayers cover the remediation costs. If companies were held responsible for environmental, health and other problems by including the costs to address these problems in prices, they would maximize profits by acting responsibly and not degrading the environment and human health.

If we end our current fantasy pricing system and implement a reality-based system that includes all real costs in prices, animal products once again would be luxury foods. Few people could afford them. Achieving sustainable food production and diet requires that companies be held fully responsible for all negative impacts. Including all real, relevant costs in prices is one of the most important actions needed to achieve this.

Taxes represent one of the most important means of including real costs in prices, and thereby achieving accurate pricing. As noted, selling animal products, refined carbohydrates and other unhealthy foods increases total costs to society by creating environmental, health and other problems. Citizens often pay for these problems through higher income taxes. Instead of having citizens pay to remediate problems that they did not create, companies should pay for government services needed to resolve the problems they cause. Taxing unhealthy foods essentially is requiring companies to pay for public services rendered.

Businesses, politicians paid by them and other allies often try to mislead citizens into thinking that taxing companies in this way is placing a burden on business. But the reality is that businesses are being required to pay for the environmental, health and other burdens that they are placing on society. It is the same as taxing tobacco companies to pay for the healthcare costs of smoking. These costs would not exist without tobacco use. Therefore, the companies causing the costs should pay for them.

Taxing junk food (i.e. refined, processed sugar, fat and salt-laden carbohydrates), animal products and other unhealthy foods will make prices more accurate (by integrating real costs) and make healthier foods relatively less expensive. Several countries already tax junk foods, including France, Denmark, Finland and Hungary.[780] To minimize impacts on low-income people who currently buy inexpensive junk foods, the revenue from junk food taxes could be used to subsidize healthy foods, such as vegetables, fruits and whole grains.

Implement Effective Regulation

Implementing effective regulation is another critical aspect of holding companies fully responsible for all negative impacts. In the US, the FDA is responsible for ensuring the safety of about 80 percent of the food supply.[781] The USDA oversees safety regulation of meat, poultry, most eggs and most other animal products. But as discussed in previous sections, food regulations and oversight by the FDA and USDA often are woefully inadequate at protecting public safety and preventing food contamination. As discussed, one study found that nearly all chicken and over two-thirds of beef and pork have fecal contamination. Meat and poultry also frequently are contaminated with salmonella, campylobacter, E. coli and other pathogens.

Inappropriate business influence of government almost certainly is the main driver of weak, inadequate food safety regulations in the US. Holding companies responsible for contamination and other food safety problems could reduce shareholder returns. To protect shareholders, food companies often give money to politicians and inappropriately influence government in other ways. This frequently compels politicians and regulators to remove regulations, not implement new ones and not enforce existing regulations. It probably will be impossible to implement effective regulations that hold businesses fully responsible and protect society until businesses are separated from government. Public pressure can compel business-dominated government to protect society sometimes. But these protections often are weak and filled with loopholes, as one would expect of regulations made by politicians who accepted money from businesses.

For example, following several food recalls, the Food Safety Modernization Act (FSMA) was passed in 2010. The Act finally gave the FDA the power to recall contaminated food. (If government served people instead of business, the people's agent would have been empowered to order food recalls decades ago.) The Act requires that the FDA conduct more frequent inspections of domestic and foreign food production facilities that supply food to the US. While the Act improves food safety regulations, it still has several weaknesses. For example, the Act does not cover meat, poultry and other animal products overseen by the USDA. It increases inspections of domestic food production facilities from once every ten years to once every three years. Citizens often are required to get their automobiles inspected every year. Food production facilities potentially could have vastly greater negative impacts on public health and safety. As a result, inspections probably should occur more frequently than once every three years.

In addition, the Act provides no funding for implementation.[782] In addition to blocking the implementation of regulations, food companies can give money to politicians and encourage or compel them to block enforcement, for example, by requesting that little or no funding be provided to enforce regulations. In 2015, the FSMA had a $276 million funding gap. The law required implementation of several new food safety rules. But none of them were implemented.[783]

Aside from lack of funding and failure to implement food safety rules, the FSMA places an unfair and unnecessary burden on small farmers. The law was intended to prevent widespread food contamination, such as the large E. coli, Salmonella and other bacterial outbreaks regularly seen in the US. Tracing contamination that might result from small farms selling locally generally is not a major concern. But small farms nevertheless often are saddled with difficult, expensive filing requirements under FSMA. The law places a further burden on small and organic farmers by focusing mainly on biological contamination, rather than chemical contamination that results from the use of synthetic pesticides.[784] Not surprisingly, the big business-controlled US government implements food safety laws that do not hold large company/campaign donors responsible for negative impacts on society, inhibit competition from small companies and farmers, and fail to protect public health.

A Supreme Court decision further indicates the weakness of US food safety regulations. In 2012, the US Supreme Court struck down a California law which required that downed livestock be euthanized and not sold for human consumption. The California law resulted from an undercover video that showed downed cattle being abused at a California slaughterhouse. By unanimous decision, the Supreme Court found that the California law was preempted by federal meat safety laws.[785] The unanimous Supreme Court decision indicates that it was a valid legal decision, as opposed to the common political or business biased Supreme Court decisions that are split along party lines, such as Citizens United. There is a need for uniform food safety standards in the US, for example, to facilitate interstate commerce. But these federal standards should be adequate, not inadequate. One could argue that states should have the right to protect their citizens from inadequate federal food safety standards.

This illustrates an interesting point about states' rights and the US focus on protecting business instead of society. Meat companies opposed the California slaughter law, probably in part because it threatened shareholder returns. In this case, a state's right to protect its citizens threatened shareholder returns. As a result, businesses opposed states' rights. However, when federal regulations threaten shareholder returns, businesses and their allies often argue for increased states' rights. In virtually all business related areas, the main issue is protecting shareholder returns, not states' rights or any other factor.

Companies often are required by flawed systems to take whatever position helps their shareholders. The preference for state versus federal laws nearly always depends on which benefits shareholders, not on which maximizes the health and well-being of society. If increased states' rights help shareholders, companies strongly support them. If states' rights hurt shareholders, as with the California slaughter law, companies oppose them, usually in a quieter, less obvious manner. A similar situation occurs in families. If a child does not like the answer they get from their father, they often ask their mother.

The food inspection system in the US strongly indicates the US government's focus on protecting shareholder returns instead of public health.

The system is so poor that it could be called comical or ridiculous, if it were not so dangerous. About 20 percent of the $1.2 trillion of food sold in the US each year is imported. In 2011, the FDA inspected six percent of domestic food producers and 0.4 percent of importers.[786]

Since the 1980s, business-controlled-government has allowed for-profit, third-party auditors to take over much of food inspection in the US. Bloomberg Markets analyzed the US food inspection system and found many problems. Before and after the FSMA, private, for-profit auditors of domestic food production facilities were not required to receive federal certification, follow federal guidelines, report results to government or make results public.[787]

Instead, auditors often evaluate their client food companies based on standards selected by the companies or food industry organizations. The auditors sometimes have financial and other ties to the companies they audit. Private auditors frequently only review areas of production facilities that companies ask them to review. They also often are prohibited from searching for pathogens and other food contamination. For-profit, private sector auditors sometimes gave perfect safety scores to companies right before they produced contaminated food. Auditors also sometimes do not visit production facilities that they certify as safe.[788] Food inspection frequently is even worse at international farms and food production facilities exporting to the US. Bloomberg found unsanitary conditions at many developing country facilities providing produce and fish for the US market.[789]

The ridiculously unsafe food inspection system in the US illustrates the danger and tragedy of deregulation. Food safety and other regulations, like murder laws, are intended to protect society. But they often interfere with ever-increasing shareholder returns. To protect returns, large companies and their media and political allies often mislead the public into believing that regulations are bad, and therefore should be weakened or removed. By giving money to politicians and inappropriately influencing government in other ways, food companies can compel government to reduce regulations that protect society, but restrict shareholder returns. Once citizens stop allowing themselves to be misled and divided, they can demand that government implement a food safety system that is focused on protecting the health and lives of citizens, rather than the financial returns of wealthy campaign donors. This system would include using truly independent or government inspectors who are required to inspect all aspects of production.

Implementing effective regulation is critical to achieving sustainable food production and diet. Laws must give regulators the ability to shut down plants and processing lines, order food recalls, prevent animal cruelty, impose meaningful (rather than token) fines, and impose severe criminal penalties when public health is threatened or harmed. Adequate resources and authority must be provided so that regulators can effectively enforce these laws.

Require Adequate Safety Testing

Adequate safety testing is essential for achieving sustainable food production and diet. As discussed in the Chemicals section, safety testing in the US for many product categories, including food, often is based on Wrong Perspective and Wrong Reference Point logic. Many additives and other substances used in food products are assumed to be safe until overwhelming evidence shows them to be unsafe. This is the wrong perspective and the wrong reference point. Food obviously has a huge impact on human health and survival. Before food or anything else is placed in the human body, we must be nearly certain that it is safe (i.e. right perspective). Once foods and food additives are approved, if new evidence shows that they might be unsafe, we should not wait for overwhelming proof that they are unsafe before banning or restricting them (i.e. right reference point).

Safety testing by companies of their own products is inherently untrustworthy due to the financial bias. If there are no immediate and obvious negative impacts, no cost-effective alternatives available and little chance that they will be held responsible for negative impacts, companies have an extremely large incentive to show that their products are safe. In virtually every sector, company research of their own products shows them to be safe much more frequently than independent research. This occurs because companies are structurally required to put shareholder returns before everything else, including public health and survival. But these factors should take priority over everything else, including shareholder returns and economic growth.

As discussed in the Chemicals and Genetic Engineering sections, we probably should be over 99 percent certain that food and food additives are safe before allowing human consumption. This level of certainty and safety cannot be achieved with research that is directly or indirectly conducted, funded or influenced by companies. Achieving the 99 percent certainty and safety standards only can be achieved through truly independent research. This refers to research that is not influenced by business in hidden or intentionally deceptive ways, such as when companies fund academic research or set up and fund apparently independent organizations that conduct product safety research.

Companies should do their own internal research to ensure that they do not waste time and money by submitting unsafe products for independent research. However, research that is influenced by companies in any way must not be used to make decisions about public safety and product use. Also, company influenced research probably should be excluded from public conversations about food safety because it is so easy to mislead non-expert citizens.

Using genetically engineered crops provides a perfect example of inadequate safety testing and the US government's focus on protecting shareholder returns instead of public health and safety. As discussed in the Genetic Engineering section, life is dependent on genes. When they are altered, life often ends. Humans emerged from and are sustained by a web of life that is based on certain genetics. The genetics of this web of life essentially are infinitely complex. When GE companies alter crop genes to produce favorable characteristics, they rarely, if ever, can anticipate all the ways that these crops might affect human health and the web of life. It is virtually impossible to test the nearly infinite number of combinations and interactions that could occur in nature and the human body, especially over the long term. Even with truly independent research, it might be difficult, if not impossible, to prove at a 99 percent certainty level that GE crops do not harm human health or the environment.

But as discussed, little independent research has been done in the GE crop area, in large part because GE companies often use patents to restrict the ability of independent researchers to test GE crops. Using GE crops reflects massive myopia. The primary reason for using them is the same as the primary reason for virtually all other corporate actions – maximizing shareholder returns. The stated or marketing reason for using GE crops often is increasing yields, lowering pesticide use and other benefits. But these benefits frequently do not materialize. Myopia involves focusing on the narrow benefits and not adequately considering the vastly larger potential costs or risks. Again, we have virtually no idea how GE crops and seeds will impact nature. When there are problems, we often will not be able to remove GE contamination from nature. Problems already are occurring, such as the development of pesticide resistant superweeds. It is inevitable that more problems will emerge if GE crop use continues.

By using GE crops, we potentially are degrading the genetics of the web of life that sustains human life. We also potentially threaten human health. As noted, human health and survival take priority over all else. There never should be any trade-offs between these most important factors and anything else, including shareholder returns or using GE crops. If we cannot prove at a 99 percent level of certainty that GE crops are safe for the environment and human health, they should not be used.

This applies to every other activity, additive and substance used in industrial agriculture and food production in general. But we have failed to require this level of safety and public health protection in nearly all aspects of industrial agriculture. Many activities and ingredients that increase shareholder returns but potentially threaten public health were not proven to be safe at a 99 percent level of certainty before they were approved for use. In addition, once in use, extensive independent research often shows that these activities or ingredients potentially are unsafe. But their use continues because food companies, politicians paid by them and other allies frequently argue that greater certainty is needed before banning or restricting potentially harmful activities or ingredients.

Examples of processes and ingredients that were allowed without 99 percent certainty that they were safe, and continue to be used when extensive independent research shows them to be potentially unsafe, include GE crops, food animal cloning, food irradiation, livestock hormone use, non-therapeutic antibiotic use, feeding feces and animal remains to live-stock, and putting nanotechnology materials, MSG, synthetic chemicals and other potentially unsafe ingredients in food.

The negative impacts of these processes and ingredients often are not immediate and obvious. As a result, the business-focused US government allows them. Once the people regain control of government, we can demand that human health and survival be given priority over shareholder returns and everything else. This only can be achieved by requiring that every food production process and ingredient is shown to be safe through adequate, independent safety testing.

Reduce or Eliminate Subsidies for Unhealthy Foods and Exports

Agricultural subsidies cause many problems in the food production and diet areas. By artificially lowering the price of animal products, refined car-bohydrates and other unhealthy foods, subsidies strongly drive rapid growth in obesity, chronic disease, premature death and healthcare costs. In addi-tion, they greatly stifle innovation, efficiency, competition and production of healthier foods in the farm sector.

Three important survival requirements for humanity are air, water and food. Without these, we would be dead and everything else would be irrele-vant. Air currently is free. But if we continue to pollute the air, we may have to purchase sanitized air, as we often do with water, and wear breathing devices. (As discussed in the Externalities and Property Rights sections of *Global System Change*, air is not a free good, as economic theories sometimes incorrectly claim. The real cost of clean air is infinite because there is no hu-man life without it.) Water is nearly free to many people who live in or near nature. For those who buy water from utilities, prices usually are relatively low. With air prices being zero and water prices often being inexpensive, one could argue that the farm sector is the most important sector in society because it supplies our food.

Recognizing the importance of the farm sector, farm subsidies have been provided in the US in various forms since the 1860s.[790] They were expanded in the 1930s and essentially have remained high ever since. An effort to reform farm subsidies in 1996 mostly failed. Since then, new subsidy programs have been added and total subsidies have increased. An Environmental Working Group website (www.farm.EWG.org) details US farm subsidies.[791] From 1995 to 2010, US farm subsidies totaled $262 billion. Subsidy categories included commodities support ($167 billion), crop insurance ($39 billion), conservation ($35 billion) and disaster relief ($21 billion). Over 90 percent of subsidies are provided for five crops: corn ($77 billion), wheat ($32 billion), cotton ($31 billion), soybean ($24 billion) and rice ($13 billion). Total farm subsidies range between $15 billion and $35 billion per year.[792]

The US government supports prices in the farm sector more than in nearly all other sectors. This market support has been widely criticized for decades. The stated reason for continuing farm subsidies often is protecting small farmers. But this frequently appears to be a marketing or public deception statement rather than the actual reason. About 75 percent of farm subsidies go to the top 10 percent of recipients. This mostly includes large farms and corporations. Ironically, giving large taxpayer subsidies to large farms and corporations often enables them to buy up small farms. In these cases, farm subsidies do the opposite of protecting small farmers. They drive the elimination of small farms and consolidation of the farm sector.[793]

When politicians accept money from business, they effectively become the agents of business, not citizens in general. As business agents, the primary goal of politicians frequently becomes the same as the primary goal of business– maximizing shareholder returns. As is so often the case with corrupted government, the main reason for continuing agricultural subsidies frequently appears to be helping the wealthy individuals and companies that give large amounts of money to politicians.

Subsidy programs in the US include direct payments, marketing loans and countercyclical payments. Direct payments provide subsidies based on historical production. Marketing loans guarantee minimum prices for crops.

And countercyclical payments provide higher subsidies when crop prices fall. All of these programs disconnect farmers from market forces and encourage overproduction. This increases supply and drives prices down. This in turn increases pressure to provide more subsidies. By driving overproduction, subsidies often cause prices to fall below production costs. For example, from 1997 to 2005, corn prices were 23 percent below production costs on average and soy prices were 15 percent below cost.[794]

Subsidies cause prices for corn, soy, wheat and a few other commodities to be artificially low. Corn, soy and wheat are main ingredients in many unhealthy processed foods. Corn and soy also are main livestock feeds. With feed usually being the largest livestock production cost, artificially low feed costs drive artificially low animal product prices. Large subsidies for corn and soy effectively are large subsidies for animal products. As discussed, animal products and refined carbohydrates already are grossly underpriced because many of the real costs of these products are not included in prices. Subsidies further depress already artificially low prices for unhealthy foods.

From a whole system perspective, one sees that US agricultural subsidy programs are extremely illogical and expensive. In effect, taxpayers spend tens of billions of dollars per year to make unhealthy foods artificially inexpensive. Then we spend hundreds of billions of dollars per year, possibly over $1 trillion, to treat chronic diseases caused by these unhealthy foods. Agricultural subsidies are another form of corporate welfare. They help the wealthy farms and food companies that give large amounts of money to politicians. But the financial and quality of life costs to citizens of this form of corporate welfare are extremely high.

Agricultural subsidies and the failure to include real costs in food prices deceive citizens. The situation is similar to gasoline pricing. As discussed in the Externalities section, possibly more than 80 percent of the real cost of gasoline is hidden in higher taxes, other fees and reduced quality of life. Much of the real costs of industrial food also are hidden in higher taxes, healthcare costs and other fees, as well as in lower quality of life. The cheap animal products and processed foods that people buy in supermarkets are not cheap. Agricultural subsidies in the US and some other countries are used in a financially irrational manner. Rather than making unhealthy foods artificially inexpensive and raising healthcare costs, we should charge accurate prices for unhealthy foods and make healthy foods, such as fruits and vegetables, inexpensive. This would greatly lower healthcare costs.

Beyond substantially increasing taxes, obesity, chronic disease, premature death and healthcare costs, agricultural subsidies cause many other problems in society. For example, insulating farmers from market forces greatly reduces incentives for cost-cutting and innovation. As discussed in the Hunger section, subsidized exports often severely harm developing country farmers who cannot compete with artificially inexpensive imports. To illustrate, when the North American Free Trade Agreement took effect in 1994, corn exports to Mexico increased by about 400 percent. Subsidized corn exports drove corn prices in Mexico down by about two-thirds. This put many farmers out of work. Between 1993 and 2008, subsidized exports put an estimated 2.3 million people out of work in Mexico. Many of them sought work illegally in the US.[795] Export subsidies also restrict the sale of US crops that could compete without subsidies. This occurs because other countries often erect trade barriers in response to US export subsidies.

Subsidies also drive distortions in land use. For example, corn and soy represent over 50 percent of cropland use in the US. Wheat and hay represent another 36 percent. Vegetables and fruits, the healthiest foods that humans can eat, represent only three percent of cropland in the US.[796] Subsidizing healthy foods instead of unhealthy ones could substantially shift US food production and diets to healthier foods.

Other problems with US agricultural subsidy programs include corruption and mismanagement. A report by the Cato Institute details many of these problems.[797] For example, farmers sometimes create complex legal structures to get around subsidy limits. They often are experts at gaming the system. For example, farmers sometimes lock in high government subsidy payments when seasonal prices are low, and then sell crops when prices are high. They often default on government agricultural loans, which frequently are non-recourse (meaning that there is no personal liability). Conservation subsidies sometimes are paid to retired farmers for not farming. Subsidies also sometimes are paid on former agricultural land that is being used for residential and other nonfarm purposes.[798]

Disaster subsidy programs frequently are poorly managed. For example disaster payments sometimes go to farmers who do not need them or did not ask for them. In addition, farmers sometimes get paid twice for one disaster, once through government crop insurance and again through disaster subsidies.[799]

Agricultural subsidies also drive widespread environmental degradation. Subsidies cause extensive marginal land to be brought into production. Without subsidies, this land often would be left uncultivated, and possibly turned into parks or allowed to return to its natural state. Marginal, less productive land often requires more pesticides and fertilizers. This increases water pollution and other contamination. To illustrate, sugar subsidies and import barriers drove conversion of large areas of Florida wetlands to sugar production. Fertilizer runoff and other contamination have caused extensive environmental damage in the Florida Everglades.[800]

Beyond giving money to politicians, another factor that potentially explains the persistence of large agricultural subsidies is that many Congressmen are farmers or farmland owners. Some of them sit on agricultural committees. In effect, these congressmen are self-dealing. By continuing agricultural subsidies, they often are voting to use taxpayer funds to enrich themselves.[801]

Agricultural subsidies illustrate once again how citizens are misled through the use of free trade and other philosophies. As discussed in the Misleading the Public section, a virtually 100 percent accurate crystal ball can be used to predict and interpret corporate communications. In virtually every case, regardless of the words used or positions taken, the ultimate translation of corporate speech is, we want to maximize shareholder returns. Saying anything else ultimately would harm or kill the company. As a result, discussion of free trade and virtually all other issues often is deceptive.

For example, businesses, politicians paid by them and other business allies often support free trade because it opens markets, provides access to cheap labor and helps shareholders in other ways. However, when eliminating agricultural subsidies or promoting free trade in other ways hurts shareholders, companies often implicitly oppose free trade. The ultimate reason for virtually all corporate action is maximizing shareholder returns.

Essentially all other stated motivations, such as supporting free trade, ultimately are deceptive, unless companies also acknowledge that their underlying motivation is maximizing shareholder returns.

Ending or greatly reducing agricultural subsidies in the US would provide many benefits. Farmers would be highly motivated to cut costs, improve efficiency, innovate, and plant crops based on market demand, rather than government subsidy programs. New Zealand illustrates the benefits of ending agricultural subsidies. The country is four times more dependent on farming than the US. But in 1984, New Zealand ended farm subsidies. In spite of strong initial opposition, farm productivity, output and profits have risen substantially since then.[802]

Demand for food and farm products will exist as long as society exists. Ending subsidies will not end food demand or the farm sector. Some farm companies might disappear. But more efficient ones will take their place. In 2006, the US Congressional Budget Office reviewed major studies that examined the repeal of US and foreign agricultural subsidies and trade barriers. Every study reviewed found that repeal of subsidies and trade barriers would improve the US and global economies. Instead of subsidies, farmers could use hedging, insurance and other private-sector tools to protect against price fluctuations, weather damage and other factors.

Some continuing agricultural subsidies might be needed to protect smaller farms or provide weather or other types of insurance that is not available or less efficient from the private sector. But billions of taxpayer dollars should not be transferred to large farms and corporations. As discussed, agricultural subsidies for unhealthy foods substantially increase obesity, chronic disease, premature death and healthcare costs. The situation is like a person paying someone to damage their home, and then paying someone else a lot more to fix it. The obviously superior strategy is to not pay to cause problems that will cost much more to fix.

Only government can ensure that prices are accurate by requiring that all real costs be included in prices. Agricultural subsidies in the US currently do the opposite of this. They make already inaccurate prices even more inaccurate. Instead of using subsidies to lower the cost of already artificially inexpensive unhealthy foods, subsidies should be used to increase price accuracy. As discussed below, they should be used to ensure that healthy foods, the actual low cost foods in a reality-based pricing system, are the least expensive.

Ensure Accurate Labeling

Accurate labeling is critical to achieving sustainable food production and diet. Flawed systems compel companies to place shareholder returns before public health and all other factors. As a result, if industrial production processes or various ingredients increase profits and have no immediate and obvious negative impacts, businesses often will be compelled to use them. Extensive independent research indicates that many food production processes and ingredients potentially are harmful over the longer-term. The structurally required focus on short-term shareholder returns frequently makes companies unable to voluntarily avoid using these potentially harmful processes and ingredients. As a result, it is essential that businesses be constrained from using them.

Aside from holding companies fully responsible with effective regulations, requiring accurate labeling is one of the most effective ways to constrain food companies and protect public health. Probably the only time not disclosing a potentially harmful process or ingredient on labels would be acceptable is if independent research showed the process or ingredient to be safe, probably at a 99 percent certainty level. This level of certainty cannot be achieved with company research due to the financial bias. But the business dominated US government rarely requires 99 percent certainty of safety before allowing potentially harmful processes and ingredients in food. Instead, the government often relies heavily on company research.

This makes it even more critical that accurate labeling be required. Citizens have a right to decide what they will and will not feed their families and themselves. Failing to label potentially harmful processes and ingredients takes away this right. Citizens effectively are forced to eat foods that have not been shown to be safe at a high level of certainty.

To protect citizens' rights to decide what they will eat and feed their families, clear, honest labeling should be required for all food production processes and ingredients that lack overwhelming independent research which shows that they are safe. This includes cloning, irradiation, genetic engineering, and feeding feces, blood and slaughterhouse waste to animals. Also, hormones, antibiotics, veterinary drugs, arsenic and other substances used to promote growth should be disclosed. Furthermore, all ingredients, processing agents and residues remaining in food, such as ammonia in ground beef, should be disclosed.

All labeling loopholes should be removed, including those that allow MSG to be included in processed foods without disclosure. MSG in particular should be disclosed because it so strongly drives overeating, obesity, related chronic diseases and neurological problems. Given these health problems and the growing use of glutamate-blocking drugs, total glutamates probably should be disclosed on labels, in the same way that fats and other substances are disclosed.

Companies should not be allowed to hide ingredients in other ingredients, as occurs widely with MSG. As discussed, natural flavoring, artificial flavoring, spices and many other ingredients often are comprised of many different chemicals. All of these chemicals and other ingredients, processing residues and contaminants above a certain level should be disclosed on food labels. It might mean that the number of ingredients listed on food labels rises from 10 to 50, for example. Many of the ingredients would have long chemical names that consumers would not recognize. These chemicals in food help companies to maximize shareholder returns by enabling the use of lower quality ingredients and compelling citizens to overeat. Disclosing these ingredients will compel food companies to replace chemical ingredients with actual food ingredients, such as real spices.

Labeling effectively protects society and constrains companies because, once citizens see that products contain potentially harmful ingredients or were made with potentially harmful processes, they often will not buy them. To avoid losing sales, companies will be compelled to use safer production processes and ingredients. However, this frequently would reduce profits. As a result, food companies and politicians who accept money from them often will vigorously oppose honest, accurate labeling, as they have done successfully for many years in the US.

This is why control of government must be returned to the people and businesses must be prohibited from harming society in any way. Our flawed systems unintentionally require that companies sicken and kill citizens to protect shareholders. We must end these insanely suicidal systems. Companies must not be allowed to mislead the public with biased research or inappropriately influence government for the purpose of using potentially unsafe processes and ingredients in food.

Food companies and politicians who accept money from them often argue that disclosure would alarm or confuse citizens. But this is deceptive. Companies are not primarily concerned with alarming or confusing citizens. Any business leader who made this their primary concern probably should be fired according to current systems. The primary concern of publicly traded companies always ultimately is to protect shareholders. Concerns about alarming citizens are deceptions intended to protect shareholder returns. Many other developed countries require labeling of potentially harmful processes and ingredients, or ban them altogether. US citizens deserve the same protections.

Raise Public Awareness

Raising public awareness is one of the most important requirements for achieving sustainable food production and diet. Citizens collectively are the most powerful force in society. If the people understood their common best interests and worked together to achieve them, they could quickly change any government, business or economy. The main barrier to achieving public control of supposed democracies is the ease with which non-expert citizens can be misled and divided. Due to vested interest deceptions, citizens often do not understand their best interests or work together to achieve them.

In the food area, food companies, politicians who accept money from them and other business allies extensively mislead the public about food safety and the links between unhealthy foods and chronic diseases. To counteract this widespread public deception, extensive public awareness programs must be implemented. The primary responsibility for educating the public about food safety and health lies with the people's agent – government. But the US government is more the agent of business than the people. As a result, it often will be difficult to compel government to do its Constitutional duty of protecting the public welfare. Once the people regain control of government and establish democracy in the US, we can direct our servant government to implement effective public awareness programs in the food area. Important programs should include education, raising awareness about healthy foods and changing public perceptions.

Educating the public about food quality and safety is critical. People must be given full information about food content, quality and production processes. With full, accurate information, citizens can best protect their families and themselves. But food companies and their paid political servants often strongly oppose full disclosure because it would reduce sales. As a result, people frequently buy food products that they probably would not buy if they had full information. Citizens must be given full information about the potentially harmful nature of various ingredients in processed foods, such as MSG and preservatives. This awareness would change purchase patterns and compel companies to provide healthier foods.

For example, many years ago it seems that companies routinely added preservatives to processed foods. However, improved packaging, production processes and other factors enable many products to have long shelf lives without preservatives. There are many examples of products without preservatives that have the same or similar ingredients as products with preservatives, but nevertheless have the same or later expiration dates. In other words, preservatives frequently are not needed. But food companies probably often leave them in to avoid the expense of changing product formulas. However, if citizens better understood the potentially harmful nature of preservatives, they would buy fewer products that contain them. This would compel food companies to change product formulas. As noted, preservatives are chemicals that often are designed to kill living things. Many studies have shown that they frequently are harmful to human health.

Another example includes using titanium dioxide in dairy products. As discussed in the Food Additives section, skim milk usually is naturally light blue and cottage cheese usually is naturally light yellow. To produce a white color and make these products more appealing, titanium dioxide, possibly in nanoparticle form, often is added. Labeling loopholes allow dairy companies to avoid listing titanium dioxide as an ingredient on labels. As noted, the International Agency for Research on Cancer classifies nano titanium dioxide as a possible human carcinogen. People have a right to know that dairy products contain titanium dioxide, especially in nanoparticle form. This heightened public awareness probably would reduce sales and compel companies to make safer products.

People also should be given full information about animal products. If they were given this, it would drive widespread beneficial changes. To illustrate, people would not knowingly buy meat that was contaminated with HIV or hepatitis viruses. But as noted, one study showed that nearly all chicken and over two-thirds of beef and pork are contaminated with feces. A large percentage of meat and poultry also is contaminated with Salmonella, campylobacter, E. coli and other harmful pathogens. This is why people are strongly encouraged to cook meat thoroughly. If citizens better understood the widespread fecal and other contamination of animal products, it would put great pressure on companies to slow processing lines and reduce contamination in other ways.

People also should be given full information about how food animals are raised, transported and slaughtered. Animal products literally become the bodies of citizens who eat them. People have a right to know specifically how animal products are created. If they better understood how animals are raised and slaughtered, many people would be revolted. They probably would stop eating animal products. The solution is not to keep these disgusting, inhumane practices secret, as is currently often done. It is to end them. Raising public awareness will ensure that this happens.

In addition, citizens should be made aware of how employees in industrial animal and crop operations are treated. Slaughterhouse, farm and other industrial agriculture jobs often are highly risky and undesirable. That is one reason why many legal and illegal immigrants work in these operations. Raising public awareness about worker risks, abuses and lack of rights would compel positive changes in industrial agriculture labor practices. Farmworkers often wear protective clothing and breathing equipment while spraying highly toxic pesticides on crops. If citizens saw this, they would better understand the frequently toxic nature of produce and other foods produced with pesticides.

It is particularly important to teach children about healthy nutrition and the links between food and chronic disease. This honest education cannot occur if biased educational materials provided by dairy and other food companies are used to teach children. Food probably is the most important determinant of health and related quality of life issues. Therefore, children should understand where food comes from and how it is made. As part of K-12 education, children would greatly benefit by spending some time visiting and possibly working on farms during teenage years.

Raising public awareness about healthy foods also is critical. Like the human body, food is massively complex. We do not come close to understanding how the thousands of chemicals, genes and other components of food operate as one system and interact with humans in ways that produce optimal health over the long term. We have not figured out how to improve the human body. In the same way, we probably are not smart enough to improve the whole foods provided by nature. Processed and genetically engineered foods might seem to be an improvement. But this is an illusion. We did not evolve to eat these foods. Especially with genetically engineered foods, we have virtually no idea how genetic alteration will affect food, humans and nature over the long term.

Citizens should be made aware that, based on our anatomy, the optimal foods for humans are whole plant foods. The idea that some people are better off eating animal products while others are better off eating plant products is an illusion or deception. There are minor biochemical differences between individuals. But we all have virtually the same mouths, teeth and digestive systems. All humans are anatomically adapted to eat plants, not animals. As noted, it would be incorrect to say that some tigers should eat plants while other tigers should eat meat. All tigers are adapted to eat and thrive on meat. In the same way, all humans are adapted to eat and thrive on plants.

When people do not prosper on a plant-based diet, it is not because they were not eating animal products. It is because they were not eating the right type of plant products. As noted, all essential nutrients, including protein, are better provided by plants. Probably without exception, no human needs to eat animal products. Citizens should be made aware of the extensive chronic diseases that result from eating them and the extensive health benefits that result from eating whole plant foods. People also should be made aware that whole plant foods can taste as delicious or more delicious than animal products. Once people demand more delicious whole plant foods, restaurants and food companies will provide them.

As occurred with smoking public awareness campaigns, food awareness programs should educate citizens about how to transition from animal products to whole plant food diets. People should understand that a few weeks or months of persistence while changing habits and tastes will yield a longer, healthier and higher quality life. Citizens also should be made aware that nutrients are best obtained from whole plant foods, not supplements or vitamin pills. Widespread vitamin and supplement use mostly is a testament to the effectiveness of marketing. Much of this use is unnecessary. The vastly healthier option nearly always is to get nutrients from whole plant foods.

Also, in terms of raising awareness about healthy foods, citizens should be encouraged to buy organic or local foods whenever possible. If people want to continue eating animal products, local, humane animal products usually are better (for those who can afford them). However, as discussed, humane meat is an oxymoron. Taking an animal's life is not humane, unless one cannot survive without doing so.

Changing perceptions or images is another critical aspect of raising public awareness. As discussed in the Food Deception section, food company advertising and marketing have been highly effective at creating the widespread public perception that fast foods and processed foods are the 'real' American foods. But fattening fast food animal products and refined carbohydrate processed foods are highly unhealthy. These foods greatly increase obesity, chronic disease, premature death and healthcare costs. In other words, fast foods and processed foods often are harmful. They severely degrade society. Making citizens believe that these foods are the real American foods would be like socializing citizens to think that real, true Americans smoke cigarettes, use heroin or engage in other harmful activities. Being a real American should not involve becoming obese, getting sick, being unable to engage in sports and other normal activities, and dying prematurely.

We the people have the right to define and promote a healthy lifestyle. We should not let corporations implicitly convey the idea that being a real American means being overweight and unhealthy. Tobacco once was seen as cool and sophisticated. But extensive public awareness campaigns changed this image. Now smoking is widely seen as being unhealthy and uncool. We must achieve the same image change with foods that fatten, sicken and kill people. These foods are not cool. We should make healthy foods cool and change the image of what it means to be a real American. To encourage people to eat well and be healthy, public awareness campaigns should use upbeat, noncritical approaches which show real Americans to be strong, healthy and mentally sharp. Eating whole plant foods helps to produce these outcomes. Therefore, we should change images and perceptions so that whole plant foods are seen as the real American foods.

As discussed in the Animal Welfare section, mainstream media and culture sometimes implicitly or explicitly criticize or make fun of vegans, for example, by implying that they are not manly or cool. It is time to change this culture and perception. In one important aspect of manliness (sexual performance), vegans can have a significant advantage, especially as they get older. Being a vegan provides many benefits that are relevant to sexual performance. As discussed in the Whole Plant Food Benefits and Athletic Performance sections, eating whole plant foods often improves health, endurance, energy levels, mental clarity and attractiveness. Also as noted, eating animal products often clogs arteries and causes many problems, including obesity and erectile dysfunction. The cultural myth frequently is that meat-eaters are more manly than vegans. But at least in the area of sexual performance, the many benefits of whole plant foods frequently cause vegans to be more manly.

As shown with tobacco awareness efforts, public awareness campaigns can be highly effective at changing public perceptions and even culture. As the old saying goes, whole plant foods are on the side of the angels. Most people would prefer to be healthy, attractive and mentally sharp. Whole plant foods help to achieve this. As a result, there is a lot of good raw material to work with in food public awareness campaigns.

Changing the idea of food as entertainment is another important issue that should be addressed in public awareness campaigns. Food companies have been highly effective at promoting this idea. Unhealthy, fattening food is widely available and strongly promoted. In reality, the main purpose of food is sustaining life. Food also can be enjoyed. But there is far more to life than eating. As discussed in the Advertising, Media and Culture section, our advertising and media saturated culture drives vast emptiness and inadequacy in society. People often over-consume or overuse food and other substances in a fruitless effort to fill their spiritual or psychological emptiness. Food frequently implicitly is shown as the cure for uncomfortable emotions or a main source of happiness. But trying to make eating the main source of life satisfaction probably never will produce a happy life. Viewing food as entertainment or a main source of happiness drives overeating and obesity.

We must do a much better job of raising public awareness about the real sources of happiness in life, such as being with friends and family, doing fulfilling work or pursuing spiritual and personal growth. At the same time, we should reframe food as what it is or should be – sustenance mainly, and a source of joy minimally. Vastly greater true, lasting joy and fulfillment come from activities other than eating.

As discussed in the Food Deceptions section, raising public awareness about obesity is another important aspect of achieving sustainable food production and diet. With obesity rising rapidly in the US and many other developed countries, there sometimes appears to be more efforts to portray obesity as an acceptable lifestyle choice. As discussed in the Advertising, Media and Culture section, companies often use thin actors and models in ads to help sell products. One exception seems to be using more overweight or obese actors in some food commercials. The implication appears to be that becoming overweight or obese by eating the advertised products is acceptable, or even good.

As noted, this is a highly sensitive issue. Compared to other addictions, extreme overeating and resulting obesity are highly visible. There sometimes is a mistaken tendency to implicitly judge the person instead of the harmful activity. Most people do not consciously choose to be extremely obese. Instead they are engaged in addictive or compulsive behaviors. As with all humans, extremely obese people obviously deserve honor and respect. We the people have an obligation to protect our children and ourselves. Out of concern for all citizens, we must strive to limit harmful activities, as we do with smoking and excessive alcohol consumption.

Excessive overeating of unhealthy foods harms individuals and society. In a loving, kind, respectful and honorable manner, we must do all that we can to help our fellow citizens avoid this harmful activity. Public awareness campaigns that focus on harmful overeating, rather than the person engaging in it, are critical to this effort. A successful example of this approach already exists. Many of the same public awareness strategies used for tobacco can be used to change public perceptions about harmful overeating.

Limit Deceptive Corporate Communications

As discussed in the Misleading the Public section, publicly traded companies are structurally required to protect shareholder returns. If honestly acknowledging product risks that are not immediate and obvious threatens returns, companies often essentially are required to mislead the public about risks and negative impacts. If the choice is lie or die, flawed systems often compel companies to lie.

In terms of public health, safety and survival, food probably is the most important product category. Prescription drugs and automobiles present significant risks to society. But not everyone takes drugs or drives. Everyone eats, usually several times per day. Being the most important product affecting public health and safety, it is imperative that citizens receive clear, accurate, honest information about food quality, content and health risks.

Since corporations are structurally required to put shareholder returns before honest communications, it is absolutely essential, especially in the food area, that corporate communications to the public be restricted. As noted, corporations generally should be precluded from the "What" conversation. Only humans should decide what is best for society. We do not allow washing machines to have a voice in these conversations. It is not necessary. We know that washing machines always will want to wash clothes.

In the same way, we know that publicly traded corporations always will want to maximize shareholder returns. When corporate managers speak on behalf of their companies, they often must set aside their personal values or humanness. If they allow personal, human concerns to interfere with the systemic requirement to maximize shareholder returns, they might harm or kill their companies. As a result, if business managers or spokespeople do this, they probably deserve to be fired, according to current flawed systems.

During the What conversation, humans might decide that they are best served by reducing harmful sectors, such as fossil fuels and animal products, and replacing them with sustainable sectors, such as renewable energy and whole plant foods. The fact that society is best served by reducing fossil fuel use and animal product consumption often is irrelevant to fossil fuel and animal product companies. They are structurally required to provide ever-increasing shareholder returns, even if it degrades or destroys society.

It is not that corporations 'want' to destroy society. It is just that this essentially brainless, suicidally simplistic machine, the publicly traded corporation, is not designed to focus on the well-being of society. It often cannot voluntarily prevent itself from harming society. If it does, it frequently will kill itself. No one intended this outcome. It is the result of myopia and the failure to think systemically. These suicidally simplistic machines are designed to keep growing, even if they kill us. Of course, when we die, they die. But that is irrelevant to these nearly brainless machines. It is not on their radar screens. They are designed to keep growing no matter how much they damage society. This is why it is absolutely essential that corporations be constrained and compelled to focus primarily on the well-being of society. They of course can and should earn profits, but only by benefiting society.

Self-regulation of corporations is impossible under current systems and structures. It inevitably will degrade society. The idea that corporate self-regulation could work is one of the most suicidally stupid ideas being discussed in society. As discussed in the Business Responsibility section of *Global System Change*, it is vastly more important to hold companies rather than humans responsible. Individuals can and usually do act responsibly voluntarily. If murder laws were removed, for example, most people would not kill anyone. But companies often cannot do this. Flawed systems force them to degrade society. The equivalent situation would be, if murder laws were removed, every person would be compelled to kill other people.

As noted, publicly traded companies cannot mitigate roughly 80 percent of negative impacts without harming themselves. As companies reduce their harm to society, they often increase the harm to themselves. Society would be much better off if we removed laws that hold individuals responsible for murder, assault and robbery, than if we removed regulations that hold companies responsible. (As discussed, the suggestion here is not that individual laws should be removed. The purpose is to show the absolutely critical need to hold companies fully responsible.) We must end the idiotic conversation about corporate self-regulation. The logical conversation is, how to best regulate companies and hold them fully responsible for the harm they impose on society.

During the What conversation, publicly traded companies often would be compelled to block progress whenever it threatened shareholder returns. That is why these entities, washing machines and all other simplistic, non-human, nonliving human creations must be excluded from the What conversation. We know the ultimate translation of any corporate speech before it is given. Therefore, it is not needed. However, once the people decide "What" type of society they want, corporate input on the "How" to achieve what we want conversation is essential.

As discussed in the Misleading the Public section, average citizens are highly vulnerable to corporate deception. One of the most important and harmful deregulatory actions since the 1980s was the removal of the Fairness Doctrine. Implemented in 1949, the Fairness Doctrine required that broadcast companies present both sides of controversial issues. This strongly ensured that the public received clear, accurate information. It also strongly promoted mature, rational, logical, fair and balanced communication from media. The Fairness Doctrine prevented vested interests from making hysterical, wildly inaccurate, divisive claims. If someone tried to do this, the opposing commentator could make them look like a fool by exposing their irrational, hysterical positions. Knowing that the opposing side would rebut their position forced presenters to be rational, accurate and much more honest. It also often compelled people to speak in a mature and civilized manner.

However, requiring opposing rebuttal severely limited the ability of businesses and their allies to mislead the public by lying or distorting the truth about issues that threaten shareholder returns. As a result, as occurred widely over the past 40 years of deregulation, businesses gave money to politicians and inappropriately influenced government in other ways. Politicians in turn did what they were paid to do – remove impediments to shareholder returns, even if doing so degraded society. Removing the Fairness Doctrine in 1987 severely degraded society.

Possibly more than any other single action, this set the stage for and cultivated the extremely vitriolic, often hateful, divisive speech so often heard from radical media groups. Non-expert citizens are highly vulnerable to deception because they frequently do not have time to study complex issues. Without the Fairness Doctrine, radical media announcers can make wildly inaccurate or distorted claims. But average citizens often would not know that the claims are inaccurate because they lack full information.

As discussed in the Misleading the Public section, during the Constitutional Convention, Delegate Elbridge Gerry said, "The evils we experience flow from the excess of democracy. The people do not lack virtue but are the dupes of pretended patriots. In Massachusetts, it has been fully confirmed by experience that they are daily misled into the most baneful measures and opinions by the false rumors circulated by designing men and which no one on the spot can refute."[803] The key point related to the Fairness Doctrine is, "which no one on the spot can refute". Our Founders knew that it was easy to mislead non-expert citizens. This is why we must make sure that there is someone on the spot to refute the deceptive words of 'pretended patriots,' 'designing men' and other media commentators.

The most effective and widely used strategy for misleading the public probably is to divide citizens into debating, acrimonious factions. Eliminating the Fairness Doctrine vastly increased the ability of vested interests to mislead the public in this way. Radical media announcers often make idiotic, grossly irrational statements that blame society's problems on liberals or conservatives. President Washington warned in his Farewell Address that vested interests would divide, disempower and steal wealth from the public in this way. Reinstating the Fairness Doctrine would greatly reduce the ability of radical media announcers to divide and mislead the public for the purpose of putting shareholder returns before all else.

To illustrate, the Climate Change section of *Global System Change* described many strategies that energy companies, politicians paid by them and other business allies use to mislead the public about climate change. One of the main strategies is to split the public into liberal and conservative factions, and then call climate change a liberal conspiracy. Any rational person who thought about this position would quickly see its highly illogical nature. The implication is that liberals and scientists are making up a problem that does not exist for a vague purpose, sometimes implied as harming the economy. Rational reflection shows that virtually no one, liberal or conservative, would want to harm the economy. Also, while some scientists might distort results, the implication that thousands of the world's best climate scientists are intentionally lying and placing their careers and reputations at risk is highly irrational.

The vastly more logical assessment is that powerful energy companies and their allies are challenging and insulting scientists to protect shareholder returns. This group has the strongest possible motivation to mislead the public about climate change – survival and protecting shareholder returns. These points are obvious to any rational person. The key question is, why do so many citizens who label themselves as conservative not rationally consider the illogical nature of the liberal conspiracy theory about climate change. A main reason is that vitriolic media announcers can strongly promote tribalistic, my team versus your team thinking. In this way, it becomes more important to support one's team than think rationally. Questioning the liberal conspiracy theory could be seen as being unfaithful to the conservative dogma. Reinstating the Fairness Doctrine would make it much more difficult for radical media announcers to block rational thought and promote this type of divisive, tribalistic thinking.

For example, a radical media announcer might ignore the facts and call climate change a liberal conspiracy. On rebuttal, the opposing party could calmly and rationally state the facts and science of climate change or other issues that threaten shareholder returns. They would be able to portray the radical media announcer as irrational and hysterical. In this way, these types of radical, highly divisive media announcers would be driven out of media and replaced with rational people who fairly, accurately and maturely present information to citizens.

Re-establishing the Fairness Doctrine is one of the most important actions needed to end the poisonous, divisive, often hateful culture growing rapidly in the US. Of course, businesses, politicians who take money from them and radical news outlets that regularly deceive citizens often will strongly oppose reinstating the Fairness Doctrine. But by doing so, they will expose their true colors. They will be clearly showing that they wish to maintain their ability to deceive and divide the public. Some media companies might argue that the Fairness Doctrine limits their programming flexibility, advertising revenue or free speech. But the priority of broadcast companies should not be to maximize earnings. In a democracy, the priority should be maximizing the well-being of society.

In addition, free speech is not an unrestricted right, especially for nonliving, nonhuman entities. Democracy cannot exist if citizens do not have accurate information. Deceiving and dividing citizens enables vested interests to control government, the economy and society, as occurs in the US. Effective self-government takes priority over corporate free speech. Media companies should not be allowed to mislead the public about climate change and other issues for the purpose of maximizing shareholder returns.

Citizens should determine "What" type of broadcast environment maximizes the well-being of society, and then require that companies operate within these parameters. Businesses that cannot earn a profit within these constraints will cease to exist and more competent companies will take their place. The well-being of society demands that broadcast companies be prohibited from deceiving non-expert citizens by providing one-sided information that degrades society but protects shareholder returns. From a whole system perspective that is focused on the well-being of society, there is no logical way to argue that presenting non-expert citizens with both sides of important issues would harm or deceive citizens. Instead, it obviously will greatly limit public deception and thereby greatly enhance society. The people cannot exercise their leadership effectively in a democracy if they do not have accurate information. The Fairness Doctrine greatly enhances the accuracy of information provided to the people, and thereby greatly enhances democracy.

Beyond limiting public deception, reinstating the Fairness Doctrine will greatly benefit society in other ways. As discussed in the Advertising, Media and Culture section, radical media announcers often model childish, immature, irrational behavior to our children. These announcers teach children that it is acceptable to be rude to people with opposing views. In other words, these adults teach our children that it is acceptable for adults to act like children. Growing up is not necessary, these childish adults imply. Children and adults often admire and seek to emulate media figures. Radical, divisive media personalities are horrible role models for our children. If these announcers knew that a rational rebuttal would follow their childish, irrational outbursts, they would be strongly compelled to act in a more civilized, mature and rational manner.

One of the most important reasons for reinstating the Fairness Doctrine is that many citizens get news and information about society primarily from one source. If this source or media outlet is radical and highly partisan, citizens often will get biased, inaccurate information on many issues. Some broadcast companies present a nearly constant invective about how liberals or conservatives are destroying society. This information is worse that useless. It distracts citizens from logical, effective solutions to important problems. But these solutions often would restrict shareholder returns, for example, by saying that society should focus primarily on the well-being of society, rather than on the well-being of business.

Through ownership and influence of radical media outlets, for example with advertising expenditures, vested interests can create the vengeance, division and hatred in society that President Washington warned us about. This inaccurate, hateful speech fractures society and makes citizens unable to effectively address issues that degrade society but threaten shareholder returns (i.e. the perfect strategy for vested interests seeking to block change). Reinstating the Fairness Doctrine would greatly reduce the idiotic partisan invective in the US. This hateful speech from radical media causes many problems, including spurring mentally unbalanced citizens to murderous actions. The abundant mass shootings in the US probably were driven in large part by hateful, radical speech that pushed mentally ill people over the edge. Requiring balanced, fair information in media would help to heal the vast partisan divide in the US and enable citizens to work together to solve our common problems.

However, opposing reestablishment of the Fairness Doctrine is one of the most important business strategies for misleading the public. Since the US government largely is controlled by business, it might be difficult for citizens to compel government to reinstate this critical regulation. Once again, when the people regain control of government, we can demand that public deception be vastly reduced by reinstating the Fairness Doctrine.

Beyond reinstating this regulation, many other restrictions must be placed on corporate communications so that public deception in the food and other areas is minimized. For example, advertising high calorie, fattening, low nutritional value fast foods and junk foods to children should be severely restricted or prohibited. Unhealthy foods have a far greater negative impact on society than tobacco or any other product. Children are especially vulnerable to deception and manipulation. They can be tricked into requesting and consuming unhealthy foods by including popular cartoon characters in ads. This early nutritional training and conditioning greatly increases the risk that children will grow up to become obese, unhealthy adults.

In addition, corporations should be prohibited from providing 'educational' materials to schools. Schools might save some money by using them.

But these marketing materials are not free. By using deceptive, biased educational materials to teach children unhealthy eating habits, total costs to society are increased by orders of magnitude more than schools save.

Corporations also must be strongly precluded from misleading the public about food safety. As noted, they often conduct, fund or influence research which, not surprisingly, shows that their products are safe. But this research is not trustworthy. Therefore, corporations should not be allowed to present their biased research to citizens or government as being valid. If food or other products have negative impacts that are not immediate and obvious, it is highly unlikely that published corporate research would disclose this.

The survival and health of citizens take priority over everything else. No trade-offs with shareholder returns or anything else should be made with these most important factors. We must not allow biased corporate research intended to protect shareholder returns to be used to mislead the public about food safety. If government did its Constitutional duty of protecting the general welfare, it would not use corporate research to determine product safety and use. It also would not allow companies to present this information to the public.

As discussed in *The China Study*, food companies and their allies engage in many other strategies to mislead the public about food safety and protect shareholder returns. They often hire credible scientists, who then portray corporate products as safe. Food companies and their allies also sometimes seek to attack or discredit scientists or other experts who show their products to be unsafe. Industry trade groups also often engage in these deceptive activities. These and all other deceptive corporate communications and activities should be severely restricted or prohibited.

Restrict Unhealthy Foods

Citizens and their servant governments routinely restrict substances and activities that threaten public health and well-being. For example, tobacco, illegal drugs and drinking alcohol while driving are restricted or prohibited. In terms of the number of people killed, animal products and refined carbohydrates probably are the deadliest substances used in society. As noted, about 75 percent of people in the US die of chronic diseases. These diseases are rare among populations that eat few animal products, refined carbohydrates and processed foods. As the primary underlying cause of extensive chronic disease, eating animal products and refined carbohydrates potentially kills more people in the US and some other developed countries than all other causes of death combined.

The fact that animal products and refined carbohydrates are widely consumed and enjoyed is not a valid reason for failing to restrict them. Cocaine, opium and other harmful substances were unrestricted until society better understood their harmful nature. In the same way, as we better understand the harmful nature of animal products, refined carbohydrates and other unhealthy foods, we have an obligation to restrict them. These restrictions also should apply to potentially harmful ingredients, such as artificial food dyes and MSG, and potentially harmful production processes, such as cloning, irradiation, and genetic engineering.

Restrictions on unhealthy foods can take various forms. As noted above, marketing fattening, unhealthy foods to children should be restricted or prohibited. Also, many of the ingredients, processes and marketing strategies discussed in the Obesity section that are used to encourage or compel people to eat larger amounts of unhealthy food should be restricted.

As a starting point for restrictions, we potentially could emulate the practices of other developed countries that are more focused on maximizing the well-being of society than the US. For example, many European countries restrict potentially harmful food ingredients and production processes that are allowed in the US. Examples include prohibiting the use of artificial dyes in children's foods and bovine growth hormone in dairy cows. It is virtually impossible that European countries are unnecessarily restricting safe foods, ingredients and production processes. Instead, it is virtually guaranteed that the US is failing to restrict these unsafe items and processes. When democracy is established in the US and government is refocused on the well-being of society instead of the well-being of business, these foods, ingredients and production processes will be restricted.

Unhealthy foods also should be restricted in developing countries. Food companies often use advertising and marketing to promote the sale of unhealthy refined carbohydrates and other processed foods in these countries. As discussed in the Hunger section, the majority of the world's hungry are in developing countries. However, for citizens there who can produce or get enough food, diets frequently are healthy. For example, traditional diets in developing countries often are based on beans, vegetables, fruits, whole grains, local plants and sometimes animal products. These widespread, healthy, whole food, largely plant-based diets are a main reason why heart disease, cancer, diabetes and other chronic diseases frequently are rare in developing countries. However, in many urban and other densely populated areas of these countries, consumption of Western-style refined, processed foods often is high and growing. As a result, obesity and chronic disease frequently are increasing in these regions.

Colonization often produced the lingering idea in developing countries that Western ways are better. This frequently makes it easy to market Western, unhealthy processed foods in there. Advertising and marketing often are used to portray these foods as sophisticated and upscale. This frequently causes traditional whole food diets to be seen as lower class and less sophisticated. In many African and other developing regions, popular soda and US fast food brands often are widely available and widely seen as cool and sophisticated. But soda frequently is little more than a can of water, sugar and chemical flavors and preservatives. If everything unhealthy were removed from a can of soda, one often would be left only with a can of water. It would be much healthier and cheaper to simply drink clean water and get calories from traditional, local whole foods.

Allowing large international food companies to promote the sale of unhealthy processed and fast foods in developing countries often has a larger negative impact than in developed countries. This occurs because their already inadequate healthcare systems often are not able to treat rapidly growing chronic diseases.

Expanding the sale of Western processed foods in developing countries frequently increases Western-style malnutrition. As noted, in the US and many other developed countries, citizens often eat large amounts of high calorie, fattening processed foods that have little nutritional value. The lack of important nutrients, such as fiber, vitamins and minerals, frequently strongly promotes chronic diseases. Western-style malnutrition often involves being obese and malnourished (i.e. lacking essential nutrients). By promoting the sale of sodas, fast foods and other fattening, low nutrition foods in developing countries, food companies drive Western-style obese malnutrition in developing countries.

To illustrate, prior to the North American Free Trade Agreement, many people in Mexico ate traditional diets that often consisted of corn, beans, chili peppers, vegetables and wild plants. For people who had enough food, these whole food, plant-based diets were nearly perfect. They promoted optimal health and weight and minimized chronic diseases. However, following the passage of NAFTA in 1994, US companies heavily invested in the Mexican food processing industry. This greatly increased the availability of unhealthy, refined, processed foods in Mexico. Increased availability combined with heavy marketing drove processed food sales growth of five to ten percent per year from 1995 to 2003.[804] This contributed to rapid growth in obesity, diabetes and other chronic diseases in Mexico.

Excluding countries in Oceania, the US has nearly the highest obesity rate in the world (and the highest among developed countries).[805] As we export our food production systems and diets to Mexico, our next-door neighbor is gaining rapidly. Mexico also now has among the highest obesity rates in the world.[806] By promoting the sale of unhealthy processed foods, we effectively exported obesity to Mexico. A key component of achieving sustainable food production and diet is limiting the sale of unhealthy animal products and processed foods in developed and developing countries.

Eliminate Food Libel Laws

As discussed in the Food Deceptions section, at least 13 states in the US have food libel laws that make it much easier for food companies to harass, intimidate and silence critics. These laws illustrate the tragic and destructive nature of business-dominated government.

Food probably has a greater impact on public health and well-being than any other product category. Eating unhealthy food potentially kills more people than all other causes of death combined. Widespread public health risks exist in the US food sector. This is strongly indicated by the fact that many other countries prohibit ingredients and processes that are allowed in US food production. As noted, one study showed that nearly all chicken and over two-thirds of beef and pork were contaminated with feces. Experts might debate the percentages of contamination. But probably no credible, independent study would show that widespread fecal contamination of animal products does not exist.

Given all this, one could make a strong argument that a vigorous, honest public discussion is needed in the food sector more than in any other area. Ensuring that citizens are fully and accurately informed about safety risks is more important in this sector than any other. And yet, ironically and tragically, speech is suppressed probably to a greater degree than in any other sector.

Food libel laws are an immoral and dangerous concession to business. They almost certainly result from inappropriate business influence of government. They show as well as any other example how politicians who accept money from businesses often are compelled to put shareholder returns ahead of the safety, health and lives of citizens. By prohibiting people and organizations from informing fellow citizens about real, widespread food risks and dangers, these laws not only drive public deception. They probably also sicken and kill uninformed citizens who might have avoided harmful products if food companies had not unfairly silenced their critics.

As discussed, these laws are highly preferential to business. They often require a lower burden of proof than regular libel laws. The laws sometimes implicitly presume that critics of food companies are guilty until they prove themselves to be innocent. Food libel laws often give victims of frivolous food company lawsuits little or no recourse. And they frequently require a difficult or impossible scientific certainty standard that can make it nearly impossible for victims of unfair food company lawsuits to defend themselves.

The situation is similar to the Biblical David and Goliath story. Small David fights giant Goliath. But in this case, Goliath gives money to government, and then government requires David to fight with two hands and one leg tied behind his back. With Goliath (i.e. food companies) already being vastly larger and more powerful than David (i.e. average citizens), there is no hope for David. He will be smashed.

Food libel laws illustrate how strongly business controls government in the US. They also show how the emphasis on shareholder returns must eventually push everything else aside, including morality, fairness and honesty. These laws are an unbelievable giveaway to business. They are the types of laws that one would expect to see in the most corrupt dictatorships. They make a mockery of our supposedly impartial and fair judicial system.

Food companies and politicians who accept money from them might argue that business-friendly food libel laws are needed to protect jobs in their states. This is the type of deception that one would expect from businesses and politicians paid by them. The obvious primary reason for food libel laws is protecting shareholder returns, not jobs. As shown in many sectors, companies often quickly move jobs out of state or offshore when shareholder returns are threatened. Any business manager who puts jobs ahead of shareholder returns probably should be fired, according to current flawed systems. Also, any politician who put jobs ahead of shareholder returns probably would not get the business money needed to win elections and remain in office.

Saying that food libel laws are needed to protect jobs implies that the food industry cannot provide jobs unless it is allowed to produce harmful foods and silence critics who question food safety. This is ridiculous. Citizens will not stop demanding food (unless they die, for example from eating unsafe or unhealthy food). Allowing citizens to freely discuss food safety will not end the food sector. It will improve it. Companies that cannot transition from unsafe to safe foods might go out of business and some jobs might be lost. But better jobs will be created at more responsible and competent food companies.

Food companies, politicians paid by them and other allies might argue that citizens still can criticize food products and companies under food libel laws, provided that there is strong scientific evidence to support their position. But this argument is extremely harmful and irrational. The fact that companies could make it without being laughed at shows how easy it is to mislead non-expert citizens. An equivalent situation might be prohibiting teachers from telling parents about risks to children on class trips, unless there was at least a 90 percent certainty that risk of harm exists. In other words, if there were an 80 percent probability that a child would be killed on a class trip, the teacher would be prohibited from informing parents about the risk.

Food companies and their paid political servants should not be allowed to use grossly unfair food libel laws to stifle public discussion about food safety by requiring high levels of certainty that risk of harm exists. As noted, this reflects Wrong Reference Point logic. There should be no certainty limits or other limits placed on public discussions about food safety. Citizens should be allowed to publicly discuss any level of risk to their children and themselves, no matter how small or uncertain the risk may be. If citizens make invalid or inaccurate accusations, companies can rebut the claims and, if necessary, use the same libel laws that protect other citizens and companies.

Food libel laws set a dangerous precedent. When society allows shareholder returns and economic growth to take priority over everything else, it only is a matter of time before everything else is degraded or pushed aside. If we the people do not demand the immediate repeal of grossly unfair food libel laws, we probably will see this poison spread to other states and industry sectors. Several states already are considering similar business-biased libel laws. Politicians who take money from food companies and then implement food libel laws often have no choice. They must do their master's bidding by silencing their master's critics.

These laws are an outrage. They only can be sustained through public deception. Once citizens realize how their freedom to discuss critical food safety risks has been curtailed by corrupted government, they will not stand for it. As discussed in the Influencing the Supreme Court section of *Global System Change*, the Citizens United decision and other forms of inappropriate influence enable a small group of wealthy citizens and companies to largely control government. The decision is so outrageous and wrong that it makes business domination of government obvious. But darkness cannot survive in the light. As people clearly see the corrupt, business dominated nature of the US government, the flawed systems that allow this corruption soon will collapse.

Citizens United probably has a larger negative impact than business-biased food libel laws because the decision affects all sectors. But while the scale of food libel law harm might be lower, the laws are equally outrageous and unfair. When citizens expose unsafe food production practices that place public health at great risk, food companies should end the practices. They should not be allowed to intimidate and silence critics so that they can continue their harmful practices and protect shareholders. Food libel laws set an extremely dangerous precedent for other states, industries and possibly even the federal government.

As discussed in the Influencing the Supreme Court section, the Citizens United decision shows the great extent to which business has been able to influence the appointment of radical, pro-business justices to the Supreme Court, for example, by giving money to the politicians who appoint and approve justices. Given the obvious gross business bias of the Citizens United decision, one could expect that the business-dominated Supreme Court would uphold laws that place shareholder returns ahead of the well-being of society, such as food libel laws.

The outrageous and gross business bias of Citizens United shows that we have reached a stage where appearances no longer matter. We must expect that the business dominated and effectively appointed Supreme Court will put the well-being of business ahead of the well-being of society, even when it is obviously wrong to do so. In other words, people probably cannot trust that the Supreme Court will fulfill its Constitutional duty of promoting the general welfare whenever doing so threatens shareholder returns. They should not expect that the Supreme Court would reverse food libel laws, even though they obviously unfairly suppress free speech and place the public at great risk. As a result, citizens and organizations that wish to protect free speech, food safety and public health should take vigorous action to repeal food libel laws, rather than allowing them to work their way through the business-dominated US judicial system.

Implement Healthy Dietary Guidelines

Implementing healthy dietary guidelines is another important component of achieving sustainable food production and diet. As discussed in the Heart Disease, Diet and other sections, US dietary guidelines appear to be a compromise between protecting public health and protecting the shareholder returns of food companies. This is not surprising because the USDA is simultaneously tasked with protecting food safety and sales of food products. But the purpose of dietary guidelines solely should be to protect public health. The health and lives of citizens should not be traded off against the shareholder returns of food companies. Also, dietary guidelines probably should not be influenced by what citizens want to eat or what foods are popular. Speed limits are not influenced by what speeds people want to drive. They are based solely on safety.

Dietary guidelines should suggest that people only eat healthy foods that minimize disease and strongly promote optimal health. People are free to ignore the guidelines. But many will strive to maximize the health of their families and themselves by following them. Citizens should not be misled into believing that unhealthy foods are healthy.

Current guidelines promote high consumption of unhealthy foods. Eating up to 35 percent of calories as fat strongly drives heart disease, the number one killer in the US. Eating up to 35 percent of calories as animal protein strongly drives cancer, the number two killer in US. Eating 50 percent of grains in refined form strongly drives diabetes and obesity. Promoting the consumption of dairy products and other unhealthy foods also drives widespread obesity, chronic disease and other health problems. We should not be increasing healthcare costs by trillions of dollars over many years and massively degrading the quality of life of hundreds of millions of US citizens so that the shareholder returns of food companies can be protected. We should establish truly healthy dietary guidelines. This will strongly encourage food companies to adapt to the guidelines by providing healthier foods.

Dietary guidelines should be issued by an organization that is solely focused on maximizing public health, such as the HHS. Allowing an entity that is responsible for promoting the sale of animal products to issue dietary guidelines is absurd. This literally sickens and kills millions of US citizens.

Promote Healthy Foods

Promoting healthy foods is critical to achieving sustainable food production and diet. As discussed extensively, whole plant foods are the optimal, healthiest foods for humans. Our bodies evolved specifically to eat and thrive on them. A major component of promoting whole plant foods is changing systems and structures in ways that make them the least expensive, most convenient and most widely available.

Currently, processed foods, refined carbohydrates, animal products and fast foods often are the most widely available and inexpensive. This strongly reflects our flawed systems. As noted, much of the cost of these unhealthy foods is hidden in higher taxes, higher healthcare costs and reduced quality of life. In a reality-based economic system that included all real, relevant costs in prices, whole plant foods usually would be the least expensive foods by far, in large part because they strongly prevent instead of strongly promote chronic disease.

To accelerate the transition to reality-based pricing, subsidies should be switched from unhealthy to healthy foods. We should be subsidizing foods that lower healthcare costs and increase quality of life. As noted, the healthiest foods (fruits and vegetables) only comprise about three percent of US cropland. Corn and soy, the main feed crops or ingredients of the unhealthiest foods (animal products and refined carbohydrates), represent over 50 percent of cropland. Subsidizing healthy foods will increase their production and availability.

Public awareness components of promoting healthy foods include encouraging citizens to eat more family meals together and make more home-cooked meals. Even organic processed foods and animal products cause many health problems. Preparing home-cooked meals with whole plant food ingredients usually is the healthiest option.

Many people faithfully take vitamins or supplements on a daily basis, in part because it is easy and they sometimes believe taking them compensates for unhealthy diets. Another public awareness component of promoting healthy foods is encouraging people to eat abundant whole plant foods every day. They should be made aware that the healthiest part of food stores is the produce section, not the supplement or any other section.

Educating people about the delicious taste of whole plant foods is another important way to promote them. Whole plant foods can be made to taste as good as nearly all animal product meals. Encouraging restaurants, stores, schools and other venues to provide delicious whole plant foods will accelerate the transition to healthy eating. Citizens often have distorted impressions of whole plant foods. Some people might say, when we were children, our parents forced us to finish our vegetables before we were allowed to eat anything that tasted good. Developed country cultures frequently are focused on animal products and refined carbohydrates. These foods are made to taste delicious. But simple whole plant food meals, such as vegan lentil soup, can be made to taste incredibly good, while also being very healthy.

Focus on Preventing Disease

The US healthcare system is strongly focused on treating rather than preventing chronic diseases and other health problems. US healthcare costs on a total and per capita basis already are much higher than any other country. As a percentage of GDP, healthcare costs are projected to rise from 16 percent to 33 percent in 2035. Type 2 diabetes is projected to increase from 10 percent of adults to 33 percent by 2050. Obesity is projected to increase from over one-third of adults to as much as one-half by 2030. Annual diabetes and obesity related healthcare costs currently are about $175 billion and $190 billion, respectively.

The US cannot afford to pay rapidly rising, world's highest healthcare costs. Obviously, a different approach is needed. Doctors, drug companies and healthcare companies usually maximize profits by treating rather than preventing disease. Food companies are not held fully responsible for negative impacts. As a result, they often maximize profits by selling unhealthy foods.

Every other developed country has a not-for-profit, government-owned or government-managed healthcare system. Compared to the US, these systems always achieve far lower costs, always provide vastly better coverage and frequently achieve superior healthcare results. Widespread public deception and inappropriate government influence have prevented the US from implementing what every other developed country has proven to be the obviously superior healthcare strategy.

As discussed in the Healthcare Costs section, several actions are needed to bring US healthcare costs, coverage and results in line with other developed countries. One of the most important actions is switching to a not-for-profit, government-owned or government-managed healthcare system. The goal of a not-for-profit healthcare system is to maximize the health of society. But the primary measured and managed goal of a for-profit system is to maximize the wealth of shareholders. A for-profit healthcare system is incompatible with maximizing the health of society. It prospers by treating rather than preventing illness. This severely degrades society. A not-for-profit healthcare system is structurally focused on preventing illness. This minimizes healthcare costs while maximizing the health and quality of life of citizens.

Another critical aspect of disease prevention is shifting the focus of healthcare research from developing drugs to nutrition and preventing disease. Taxpayers fund extensive drug research, and then drug companies often are allowed to license drugs developed with taxpayer funding and charge very high patent-protected prices. This is grossly unfair to taxpayers and grossly fiscally imprudent.

One of the most important aspects of disease prevention is switching to whole plant food diets. A key element of this is better educating doctors and other health care professionals about the benefits of whole plant foods, and then encouraging them to tell their patients about these benefits. Doctors often receive biased information about the risks and benefits of drugs. This frequently encourages them to over-prescribe or over-rely on drug treatments. As noted, about 65 percent of people in the US are taking prescription drugs. Doctors often quickly prescribe drugs to lower blood pressure or cholesterol, for example. But the less expensive, more effective, higher quality of life approach often is to encourage patients to stop eating the foods that raise blood pressure and cholesterol.

Dr. Campbell and Dr. Esselstyn explain that patients frequently are not adequately informed about dietary solutions to health problems. Instead they often are encouraged to undergo expensive, risky, painful and life-restricting surgeries or other mechanical interventions. When surgery is not immediately required, Dr. Esselstyn encourages heart disease patients to undergo eight to twelve weeks of arrest and reverse nutrition therapy. As discussed in *Prevent and Reverse Heart Disease*, this approach often is highly effective at lowering costs and risks, while improving quality of life.

Heart disease and other chronic diseases are biological problems. They often cannot be solved with drug, surgical or other mechanical interventions. Drugs and surgery frequently treat symptoms, but do not cure chronic diseases. The implied intelligence in the human body is essentially infinitely greater than conscious human intelligence. We do not know the cure to cancer and many other chronic diseases. However, the far more intelligent human body often can cure these diseases under the right conditions. Diet usually is the most important factor for preventing, treating and reversing chronic diseases.

The most important strategy in the war on cancer and other chronic diseases is to prevent them in the first place. For example, many people wear pink ribbons to show their support for finding a cure for breast cancer. But we already know the most effective cure for the breast cancer epidemic. The best 'cure' is to prevent breast cancer in the first place. As discussed in the Breast Cancer section, eating animal products greatly increases the risk of breast cancer. They usually have much higher levels of carcinogens. They create an environment in the body that is conducive to the initiation and promotion of cancer. As a result, ending the consumption of animal products can greatly lower breast cancer risks.

Educating citizens about the benefits of whole plant foods empowers them to take control of their health. Doctors and drug companies can treat diseases. But citizens often can prevent them by eating whole plant foods. Empowering citizens to take control of their health and prevent chronic diseases by eating whole plant foods frequently will reduce the sales of drug, healthcare and food companies. Shrinking the healthcare sector by focusing on preventing rather than treating diseases will greatly benefit society.

However, publicly traded drug and healthcare companies are structurally required to grow, not shrink. As a result, to protect shareholder returns, they often will oppose what clearly is the best option for society. This once again shows why it is imperative that the people regain control of government, hold companies fully responsible for all negative impacts, and determine "What" type of society they want without interference from nonhuman entities that are required to grow even when it degrades society.

Improve Industrial Agriculture

A whole system perspective shows industrial agriculture to be extremely counterproductive. The industrial production of crops and animal products often severely degrades environmental life support systems. To feed ourselves in the short term, we are degrading the life support systems needed for survival and future food production. The industrial production of animal products also often causes widespread food contamination and other food safety risks. As a result, improving industrial agriculture is one of the most important requirements for achieving sustainable food production and diet.

Many improvements were discussed in previous sections. Examples include implementing laws that reduce slaughterhouse processing speeds, require adequate space per animal, ban non-therapeutic antibiotic use, and ban abusive confinement rearing (i.e. veal crates, gestation crates and battery cages). In addition, food irradiation, animal cloning, genetically engineered food and nanotechnology food ingredients should be prohibited until overwhelming independent research shows them to be safe. Hormones, ractopine, arsenic and other substances used to promote animal growth also should be banned. And breeding that causes animal suffering and weakens immune systems should be prohibited.

Slaughterhouses and other industrial agriculture operations often are staffed by legal and illegal immigrants. About one quarter of slaughterhouse workers are estimated to be illegal immigrants.[807] They often do not complain about labor abuses, unsafe working conditions and food safety risks due to fear of deportation. Industrial crop and animal product production frequently involves working for low pay in unsafe and unhealthy conditions. Food companies often aggressively block unionization efforts. A key element of improving industrial agriculture involves ensuring that working conditions are safe, employees are treated fairly and unionization is allowed.

Undercover videos showed that food companies frequently abuse animals and allow unsanitary, unsafe food production when they believe they are not being monitored. To ensure the safety of consumers and employees and humane treatment of animals, video cameras probably should be installed at slaughterhouses, feedlots, dairy facilities and other industrial animal operations. The cameras probably should be monitored by independent third parties, rather than business-influenced regulators.

In the industrial crop area, environmentally-destructive substances and processes should be banned or severely restricted. This includes limiting or banning the use of synthetic pesticides, genetically-engineered crops, unsustainable irrigation and agricultural methods that promote soil erosion. Neonicotinoid pesticides that harm bees also should be prohibited. Holding companies fully responsible for all negative impacts will greatly accelerate the improvement of industrial agriculture. When this occurs, companies will maximize profits by acting in a fully responsible manner.

Improve Aquaculture and Ocean Fishing

As discussed in the Oceans and Animal Welfare sections, aquaculture and industrial harvesting of ocean fish cause many problems. About 80 percent of the world's seafood stocks are significantly or fully exploited. At current overfishing rates, all seafood species are projected to collapse by 2048.

Industrial ocean fishing causes vast destruction of target and non-target fish (through bycatch). Aquaculture of carnivorous fish, such as salmon, depletes ocean stocks. Aquaculture also causes widespread environmental degradation, including destruction of 38 percent of the world's mangrove wetlands due to shrimp aquaculture.

Future generations have as much right to ocean fish as we do. Our generation has no right to take more fish than the oceans can sustainably provide. We should vastly scale back ocean fishing to allow ocean stocks to replenish, and then only take sustainable amounts of fish after that. Also, industrial fishing methods should be modified in ways that greatly reduce or eliminate bycatch and environmental degradation. Bottom trawling in particular causes extensive bycatch and environmental destruction. Therefore, it should be prohibited. Aquaculture also should be restricted in ways that minimize the depletion of ocean stocks and environmental damage. To protect ocean stocks, aquaculture of carnivorous fish should be restricted or prohibited.

The need to scale back ocean fishing and aquaculture further reflects the importance of switching to whole plant food diets. Fish production is highly inefficient compared to the production of plant products. In addition, ocean and aquaculture fish often are highly contaminated with mercury, PCBs and other toxins. Fish is healthier than some other animal products. But whole plant foods are vastly healthier than fish because humans did not evolve to eat it.

Expand Sustainable/Organic Agriculture

Expanding the use of organic and other types of sustainable agriculture in developed and developing countries obviously is a key component of achieving sustainable food production and diet. With industrial agriculture, we essentially are mining the land. It regularly converts fertile, productive land to unproductive, degraded land. This is grossly irresponsible to future generations, increasingly counterproductive and ultimately suicidal. We say that we care about our children and future generations. But with industrial agriculture, we act as if we do not care about them. But the issue is not lack of concern. It is lack of awareness and big picture thinking.

GE crops reflect the myopia and destructiveness of industrial agriculture. Humans probably are not smart enough to anticipate the nearly infinite number of interactions in nature and impacts of GMOs on human health and the environment. But the business-influenced US government allowed them to be used with little or no restrictions. GE contamination cannot be recalled when problems occur, as they do frequently. GE crops give a few large companies extensive control over farmers and the seeds needed for human survival and prosperity. The crops are designed to perpetuate industrial agriculture (instead of implement sustainable agriculture) by reducing the use of pesticides or using proprietary pesticides. GMOs provide no benefits to consumers. Many independent studies show that they pose human health risks. Given a choice, most people probably would not buy GE foods, especially if they had full, accurate information about the risks and benefits.

Agriculture in the US and some other developed countries largely has been taken over by a small group of large companies that are structurally required to put their own well-being ahead of the well-being of society. This illustrates once again why it is absolutely critical that real democracy be established in the US (i.e. control of government by the people) and business be placed in service of society. We should not allow large companies to perpetuate industrial agriculture by inappropriately influencing government and misleading the public. We must do what is best for society, not what is best for shareholders. Paradoxically doing what is best for society ultimately is what is best for shareholders. But companies often cannot admit this under our flawed systems. Putting shareholders ahead of society will degrade and ultimately destroy society. Clearly this will be bad for shareholders.

The Hunger section described a form of sustainable agriculture (agroecology) that has been highly successful in developing countries. On virtually every measure, sustainable agriculture is the superior approach in these regions. A review of nearly 300 published studies on organic yields found that organic farming could increase yields by nearly three times more than industrial agriculture in developing countries.[808]

The study also found that organic farming could increase yields in developed countries by nearly as much as industrial agriculture. But yield is not the only factor, or even most important factor, to consider when comparing industrial to sustainable agriculture. As always, the most important factor is survival (because everything else is irrelevant without it). Industrial agriculture takes away the ability of future generations to survive and feed themselves. Therefore, even if industrial agriculture was superior on every other measure, we should not use it because we have an obligation to protect our children and future generations.

However, industrial agriculture does not come close to being superior on every measure. Instead it is inferior on many key metrics. For example, sustainable agriculture protects and retains topsoil, and thereby protects long-term food production. By using cover crops or multi-cropping (i.e. planting more than one crop per year), sustainable agriculture often improves carbon sequestration and climate change mitigation. It also maintains healthier soil that produces healthier foods, which have more vitamins and minerals, for example. Organic and sustainable agriculture currently can nearly match the yields of industrial agriculture. But as industrial production continues to degrade land, yields will fall. Then sustainable agriculture will outperform on yields as well.

A critical aspect of sustainable agriculture is reducing the consumption of animal products. As noted, it takes far more grain and water to produce animal products than plant products. As a result, cutting back animal product consumption will significantly lower demand for grain and freshwater. This will allow more marginal land to be left uncultivated and productive land to be farmed less intensively and more sustainably.

Probably the main barrier to switching food production from industrial to sustainable agriculture is large companies trying to protect shareholder returns. These companies face strong systemic pressure to oppose sustainable agriculture if it lowers shareholder returns. Once citizens regain control of government in the US, we will manage the economy for the good of society, not the good of business. Industry sectors will expand or contract based solely on what maximizes the well-being of society.

Protect Natural Areas and Restore Degraded Ones

The degradation and conversion of the Earth's natural areas to human use shows the destructive, ultimately suicidal nature of religious dogma and intensely myopic human economic, political and social ideas. We act as if we have the right to push nature aside and use it as we see fit. We act as if it is acceptable to clear natural areas and convert Earth to a large colony for raising humans and our food. This is irrational and destructive. Nature is essentially infinitely smarter than humans. We emerged from and are sustained by nature as it existed before the Agricultural Revolution. Some people believe that God created humans. But the actual creator was nature. If God exists, it created us through nature. We effectively are saying to the creator. Thanks for creating us. But we don't need you anymore. You can go away now.

No one intends this. But actions speak louder than words. This is what our actions say. The failure to think systemically produces suicidal action among humanity. We act like a cancer on this planet by rapidly killing that which created and sustains us. We myopically see the narrow benefits of clearing natural areas. But we often do not see how these actions multiplied many of times over severely degrade humanity.

Reality always wins. Our religious, economic and other myopic ideas that justify clearing natural areas are irrelevant to nature. It holds the power of life and death over us. The technology of nature essentially is infinitely more sophisticated than human technology. In this sense, nature is the master and we are the servant. The idea that we are the master of nature is unintentionally suicidal. We absolutely will abide by the laws of nature, or we will not be here. This is a non-debatable fact of reality.

Human destruction of nature will end. The key question is, will we end it voluntarily or will nature bring the hammer down on us? Our only options are voluntary or involuntary compliance with the laws of nature. Non-compliance definitely is not an option over the long-term. It also probably is not an option for much longer in the shorter-term. It is a suicidal fantasy to think that we can continue to degrade or destroy forests, grasslands, wetlands and other life support systems.

Rapidly expanding diseases represents one of the most likely ways that nature could force compliance with its laws. As discussed in the Pandemic section, humanity is driving the third era of epidemic diseases – the age of emerging plagues or zoonotic diseases (i.e. infectious diseases from animals). Since the 1970s, more new diseases have emerged in a shorter period of time than any other period in human history. The main factor driving them is environmental degradation, such as forest clearing. The vast majority of viruses that could infect humans are unknown. As we continue to intrude into natural areas, especially tropical forests, we will expose ourselves to potentially tens of thousands of new diseases.

We do not have the right to push nature and other creatures aside. The idea that we do is a self-serving (although ultimately suicidal) concept that was created by humans, and often attributed to God. No loving God would instruct its creations to kill themselves. The idea that we are above nature did not come from God because it is suicidal. It is perhaps a myopic misinterpretation of Divine guidance. Even if we had a right to push nature aside, it would be irrational to do so. Emerging plagues or other natural factors would stop the cancerous human expansion into nature and restore balance on Earth.

Consuming animal products is the largest driver of forest clearing in many areas. As noted, since 1970, livestock production has driven 90 percent of forest degradation in the Amazon. About 70 percent of previously forested land is used for livestock grazing. A large portion of the remainder is used to grow feed crops. Similar destruction is occurring and poised to rapidly expand in Africa. As discussed, Saudi Arabia, other Middle Eastern countries, some European countries, China and India are buying or leasing vast areas of forests and grasslands in Africa. Corruption, financial stress and/or lack of democracy often cause this land to be sold or leased at hugely discounted prices. Purchasing countries usually plan to convert African natural areas to industrial agriculture. This is causing many problems in Africa, including increasing hunger as indigenous people are forced off of their illegally or immorally sold land.

We as a global people must find ways to end the conversion and destruction of our remaining natural areas and rapidly restore degraded areas to their natural states. Forests in particular are a major part of the lungs of our planet. They absorb our waste air and give us life-sustaining oxygen-rich air. Clearing forests is like giving our planet lung cancer.

Probably the most important action needed to end the clearing of natural areas and restore degraded areas is to vastly reduce the consumption of animal products. In addition, implementing sustainable agriculture in developing countries will greatly increase yields and reduce pressure to clear forests, grasslands and wetlands. As noted, reducing animal product consumption and implementing sustainable agriculture in developed countries will reduce pressure on agricultural land and allow marginal areas to be returned to their natural states. As discussed in the Land section of *Global System Change*, the US, China, India and some other countries are aggressively replanting trees and expanding forests. This activity should be expanded to many other countries, especially developing countries with tropical forests.

It often is difficult for humans to see the big picture. We cannot see the whole planet at once. We usually only see the relatively small part nearby. But individual actions collectively have broad impacts. The failure to think and act sustainably is causing us to rapidly degrade our ability to survive on Earth. We have a sacred obligation to protect our children and future generations. This takes priority over everything else, except our own survival. It definitely takes priority over our preference for eating animal products. We must find the courage and wisdom to think and act from a whole system perspective. This will compel us to protect and restore our natural areas, and thereby protect future generations.

Protect Seeds

Protecting seeds is a critical aspect of achieving sustainable food production and diet. Simple plants like algae reproduce through cell division. Other plants reproduce from spores, bulbs or roots. But many of the most important plants for humanity are grown from seeds. Seeds are nearly as important to human survival as air, water and soil. All oxygen and food ultimately come from plants. Even fossil fuels come from them. Seeds sustain the beauty, vitality and diversity of life on Earth.

But the diversity and integrity of wild and cultivated seeds are threatened by several factors, including industrial agriculture, environmental degradation, and patents and corporate ownership. Concerns about seed risks drove the construction of a global seed vault on a Norwegian island near the North Pole.[809] Millions of seeds are stored there. In the event of a massive ecological or other type of crisis, the seeds could be used to reconstruct the Earth's agricultural systems.

There are over 50,000 edible plants on Earth. Only about 150 have been commercialized. About 40 are cultivated regularly. Rice, corn and wheat provide most of humanity's food. Other important crops include soy, cotton, canola, potatoes, casava, taro, barley, sorghum, sugar, coffee, fruits and vegetables.[810]

Seeds are essential for human survival. Patents and corporate ownership are substantial threats to seeds. As discussed in the Property Rights and Genetic Engineering sections of *Global System Change*, patents should not be allowed on the creations of nature. Seeds and all other natural creations are the common wealth or common property of humanity. They belong to current and future generations. (As discussed in the Property Rights section, this position is based on the conventional idea that humanity owns nature. As we becomes more enlightened, we probably will develop more realistic, accurate and sustainable ideas about the ownership of nature.)

Many of the most important seeds for human food and industrial production are patented and owned by genetic engineering companies. But these companies did not create GE seeds. Virtually all of the intelligence used to develop the seeds were provided by nature. GE companies make small modifications to nature's creations without knowing or being able to predict the long-term impacts on human health and life support systems. Allowing companies to patent and exclusively use a slightly modified creation of nature would be like putting an artificial or altered fingernail on a human, and then being allowed to patent and exclusively use the whole slightly altered human body.

Seeds should not be patented because human survival is so heavily dependent on them. As noted, publicly traded companies are structurally required to put the financial well-being of shareholders ahead of all other factors, including the survival of humanity. It is insane and suicidal to place the keys to humanity's survival in the hands of organizations that are structurally required to focus on something often is in conflict with our survival (shareholder returns).

The human food supply should be controlled by all humans through democratically elected governments. There is a place for profit-seeking organizations. But activities should not be delegated to business when doing so severely degrades society. Healthcare provides a perfect example of this. As discussed, the profit motive is not compatible with maximizing public health. Every other developed country proves this by providing much lower cost healthcare with far better coverage often with superior results by using a non-profit government-based system. In the same way, the profit motive is not compatible with business ownership of seeds. When businesses own seeds needed for human survival, the seeds are used to maximize the well-being of business, even if it degrades humanity.

This situation shows the extremely destructive and illogical nature of over-relying on philosophies. Many people have a philosophical bias or preference for private sector activities. But this often blocks rational, objective assessment of which option actually produces the best outcome in reality. For example, the blind faith or philosophical preference for private sector activities frequently prevents people from realizing that what they think is a private sector entity is not private in reality. As noted, limited liability companies are not private entities because taxpayers and government are compelled to act as the owners of business on the downside.

In the case of seeds, the survival and well-being of humanity demand that we place simple-minded, rational thought-blocking philosophies where they belong – in the garbage can. Instead, we must use our gifts of rational thought and objectivity to determine how to best protect resources that are vital for the survival and well-being of humanity, such as seeds. Genetic alteration of life-sustaining seeds should not be allowed unless independent research shows it to be safe at over a 99 percent level of certainty. In addition, corporations or individuals should not be allowed to own seeds or other creations of nature. Nature's creations must only be owned collectively by current and future generations.

Beyond corporate seed ownership, industrial agriculture threatens seeds through monoculture production. This makes our food supply more vulnerable to pests and other problems. To minimize risks to the food supply, greater efforts should be made to protect seed diversity. Shifting from industrial agriculture to sustainable, local food production will facilitate this.

Implement Safe New Technologies

Developing and implementing new technologies also is an important component of achieving sustainable food production and diet. Technology already has played a large role in increasing food production and minimizing or remediating environmental damage. Feeding a growing population while restoring life support systems probably will require new technologies. Fortunately, many are being developed and implemented.

The most important aspect of technology is safety. Human myopia often causes us to develop new technologies that provide narrow benefits, but cause larger potential or actual problems. Genetic engineering provides the perfect example of this. GE provides some benefits, especially to GE company shareholders. But GE is an unnatural process that would not occur in nature. It is impossible to anticipate all of the negative impacts of releasing new unnatural lifeforms into nature that cannot be recalled. In the case of GE, the potential negative impacts vastly outweigh the benefits. Therefore, GE is one type of technology that probably should not be used in the agricultural area, unless independent research shows it to be safe at a very high level of certainty.

However, developing new types of crops probably is critical to meeting food demand. Society would greatly benefit from crops that resist droughts, insects, flooding, salt and plant diseases. These types of crops often can be developed safely with conventional breeding technologies. These technologies emulate natural processes. It is much safer because the breeding essentially is done by the far more intelligent wisdom of nature. To illustrate the potential of conventional crop breeding, a type of "green super rice" was developed in China using conventional crop breeding. The rice is more resistant to droughts, floods, salty water, insects and diseases.[811]

New technologies also are being developed to make greater use of algae. Algae are at the base of the food chain and often are highly nutritious. They are widely consumed in China and Japan in the form of seaweeds. Algae also are used as fertilizer and animal feed. They can play a much larger role in human food production, for example, by providing fats, oils and sugars. Algae can grow in polluted water and other areas that cannot produce crops. Technology is being developed to produce oil from algae. It is estimated that algae farms could produce 5,000 to 10,000 gallons of oil per acre, compared to 350 gallons of ethanol per acre of corn. Replacing ethanol production with algae would free up extensive land and water for human food production.[812]

New technologies that can grow food in deserts or dry areas also will greatly benefit humanity and reduce pressure to convert forests and grasslands to agriculture. Many new technologies are being created in this area. For example, coastal desert greenhouses are being developed that convert seawater to freshwater for growing crops while also producing energy.[813] These and other new technologies will be an important component of achieving sustainable food production and diet, provided that independent research shows them to be safe at a high level of certainty.

Increase Halophyte Crop Production

Increasing halophyte crop production represents a major opportunity for humanity. Plants can be segmented into glycophyte (salt-intolerant) and halophyte (salt-tolerant). There are about 10,000 varieties of halophyte plants. About 250 of these could be used as staple crops to produce food, animal feed, edible oils, fiber, biofuels and chemical feedstocks. The crops can be grown in deserts and irrigated with brackish water or seawater. Halophyte crop production takes advantage of abundant, vastly underutilized resources on Earth – deserts (33 percent of Earth's land surface), seawater (97 percent of Earth's water), sunlight, and 10,000 varieties of halophyte plants.[814]

Growing halophyte crops could provide very large environmental and social benefits. As discussed in the Freshwater section, agriculture represents about 70 percent of human freshwater use. Water shortages will be one of the greatest challenges facing humanity in the 21st Century. Halophyte crop production could greatly alleviate freshwater shortages by using seawater and saline aquifer water for irrigation. Growing crops in deserts would substantially reduce pressure to convert the Earth's remaining forests and grasslands to agriculture. Burning halophyte biofuels instead of fossil fuels could significantly reduce global warming because halophyte crops sequester carbon dioxide.

In addition to deserts, halophyte crops can be grown on wasteland and in marshes and coastal areas. This can take pressure off of fertile lands and provide coastal protection. Halophyte algae biofuel production can be combined with aquaculture. This increases efficiency and reduces waste because algae feeds on fish waste.

Humans have been using halophyte plants as food and animal feed for thousands of years. Hybridized halophyte crops have been developed that can serve as substitutes for wheat, soy, alfalfa and edible oils. Research is continuing on developing more efficient halophyte biofuel crops.[815]

Dr. Dennis Bushnell, a leading authority on halophyte crop production, said, "a goodly portion of the Sahara is capable of providing (using halophytes and seawater irrigation) sufficient biomass to replace ALL of the fossil carbon, provide requisite food, replace petrochemical feedstock, whilst returning 68 percent of the freshwater now used for conventional (glycophyte) agriculture to human use. This addresses our overall crises of overuse of land, water, needs for food, energy and stabilizing climate – since halophytes are great storers of carbon and soil enrichers."[816]

In summary, halophyte crop production could greatly alleviate food and water shortages, substantially reduce pressure to clear forests and grasslands, and significantly alleviate global warming. Given these and other large environmental and social benefits, the development and use of halophyte crops should be rapidly expanded.

Expand Seaweed Production

Seaweed represents a huge, sustainable food production opportunity. There are over 10,000 types of seaweed, or marine macroalgae. Seaweed is widely consumed in Asia. Many companies are developing delicious food products based on seaweed, such as snacks and meat substitutes. Seaweed could be a major source of food, biofuel and animal feed.[817]

It has the potential to become one of the world's most sustainable, nutritious and cost-effective crops. Seaweed production can help to restore threatened ocean ecosystems. It absorbs nitrogen and phosphorus runoff into the oceans, and thereby helps to prevent algae blooms. It also absorbs carbon dioxide and helps to mitigate global climate change. As ocean fish stocks have fallen, many coastal communities in the US and other countries have declined. A growing number of fishermen are turning to cultivating seaweed. This could help to restore coastal communities.[818]

Oceans cover about 70 percent of the Earth's surface, but produce less than two percent of our food. The rest is produced by using nearly 40 percent of the Earth's land and about 70 percent of our freshwater. Seaweed production has the potential to replace nearly all of the world's agriculture with less than one percent of the oceans' surface area. Seaweed grows quickly. It requires no fertilizer or freshwater. It could be used to supplement corn, soy and other crops. Seaweed could become the Earth's cheapest and most sustainable food.[819] Therefore, seaweed production and development of sea-weed-based food products should be rapidly expanded.

Reduce Food Waste

Reducing food waste is a critically important component of achieving sustainable food production and diet. As discussed in the Hunger section, about one-third of food produced by farms worldwide is discarded, spoiled or eaten by pests. A UN report found that over half of food overall world-wide is lost, wasted or discarded. About one-third of the food bought in the US and UK is discarded.[820] About 40 to 50 percent of fruits and vegetables ready for harvest are not eaten in the US. And about 30 million tons of fish are discarded at sea annually, for example as bycatch.

The above UN report estimated that using food more efficiently could feed the entire new population projected to arrive by 2050. Wasting food wastes the water and other resources used to produce it. It also often unnecessarily degrades the land used to produce it. Wasting vast amounts of food while more than one billion people around the world suffer from hunger and malnutrition is tragic, immoral and wrong.

Extensive food waste results from centralized, industrial food production and food subsidization. When much of the cost of industrial processed foods and animal products is hidden in higher taxes and health insurance rates, people often do not value food adequately. They therefore are more inclined to waste it. Many actions are needed to lower food waste, such as reducing food subsidization (except for low-income people), improving agricultural planning so that far fewer crops are left unharvested, and improving industrial fishing practices by greatly reducing bycatch and other waste. Rebuilding local economies and food production also will minimize waste, in part because there will be much less distance between producers and consumers.

Improve Organic Certification

Improving organic certification is another important component of achieving sustainable food production and diet. Organic certification in the US once again reflects inappropriate business influence of government. Many people increased their consumption of organic foods as they became more aware of the health and safety risks of industrial produce, processed foods and animal products. Organic food sales have grown substantially faster than conventional food sales for more many years. They grew from $11 billion in 2001 to over $62 billion in 2020.[821]

To avoid losing sales, many large food companies entered the organic market. They often aggressively lobbied for weaker organic food standards. This frequently enabled them to use similar industrial production processes as those used for conventional food. Organic food often was sold originally by smaller companies and farms. However, it appears that inappropriate government influence was used to make it relatively more difficult for these groups to get organic certification. This enables large companies to capture a larger share of the organic market.

To illustrate, the USDA administers the organic certification program through a network of private certifying organizations. Farmers and food companies must pay for certification. While certification fees usually vary based on size, getting and maintaining organic certification still can be a significant barrier for small farms and food companies. The cost of certification for large farms and food companies often is insignificant. This structure of paying for certification can make it easier for larger companies to take market share from smaller companies.

The organic certification fee structure strongly indicates business influence of government. As discussed, the USDA provides on-site, often daily inspections at many meat production facilities. It frequently pays the full cost for these inspections. The cost of on-site inspections often is much higher than organic certification. This certification improves the safety and quality of the US food supply, for example, by reducing pesticide contamination. As discussed, pesticides usually are highly toxic chemicals. Many studies have shown that regularly eating conventional pesticide-treated produce and other foods causes neurological problems, endocrine disruption and many other health problems. In addition, conventional produce often has fewer vitamins, minerals and other important nutrients than organic produce.

Given these health and safety benefits, the US should be strongly promoting the rapid expansion of organic produce. As discussed, organic animal products and processed foods often strongly promote chronic disease. But these foods usually are at least marginally healthy than conventional ones. Therefore, all organic certification probably should be free. But instead of promoting the sale of organic foods, the business dominated US government essentially erects barriers that often keep small farms and companies out of the organic market.

Organic certification provides a perfect example of subsidizing unhealthy foods instead of healthy ones. This should be reversed. Providing free inspections for animal products subsidizes the cost of these products. This real cost of animal product production is hidden in higher income taxes. This makes unhealthy food artificially inexpensive, which in turn increases healthcare costs, chronic disease and premature death. Rather than subsidizing animal products with free inspections and charging for organic certification, we should do the opposite. Organic produce and food substantially benefit society. Providing healthier food lowers healthcare costs. Therefore, promoting these foods by providing free organic certification is a wise use of taxpayer funds.

The USDA is overseen by politicians who take money from food companies, As a result, USDA inspectors often are under great pressure to not take actions that might hurt shareholder returns, such as shutting down processing lines due to contamination or inhumane treatment of animals. Meat with fecal and bacterial contamination routinely is produced at USDA inspected facilities. In other words, even though taxpayers pay for meat inspection, they often do not get safe meat. A less expensive and potentially more effective approach might be to install video cameras at animal product production facilities and have them monitored by independent third parties. Less frequent on-site inspections still would occur, for example, when video evidence indicated contamination or cruelty. Given the business bias of the USDA, it probably would not be effective to have the agency monitor cameras. USDA inspectors often fail to prevent contamination even when they are on-site.

Third parties are not required to protect shareholder returns, as the USDA implicitly is. The bias of third parties should be on protecting public health. As a result, they probably would be more effective at noticing and reporting contamination and inhumane animal treatment. Also, third-party monitoring could create a public record. This would help to ensure that the USDA follows up and effectively ends contamination and inhumane treatment. Third-party monitoring should be paid out of taxes or through other means that prevent companies from inappropriately influencing monitoring organizations. Requiring companies to pay could give them inappropriate influence, unless the payment goes into a blind fund, for example. This system probably would be much less expensive than having on-site inspectors. The savings could be used to fund free organic certification.

Another major problem with the USDA organic certification program is requiring companies and farms to pay private inspectors. As discussed in the Finance and Capital Markets section, allowing bond and other financial security rating agencies to be paid by the organizations issuing the securities creates a conflict of interest. It is the same as allowing companies to pay auditors. Allowing the revenues and even survival of auditors and rating agencies to be dependent on receiving money from the companies that they audit or rate can create bias and many other problems. As discussed, many high-risk securities were rated as low risk. This strongly contributed to the financial crash of 2008.

Allowing private organic certifiers to earn money directly from the companies that they certify can create similar bias and other problems. On many occasions, organic certifiers have been sanctioned for failing to report problems.[822] Certification potentially could be done by third parties, as with camera monitoring. But third-party certifiers should be paid by government or through other means that prevent farms and companies from inappropriately influencing them.

Beyond promoting organic foods by providing free certification, the weakening of the organic label, driven in large part by food company lobbying, should be reversed. As discussed, organic certification used to prohibit synthetic and artificial ingredients in the five percent non-organic portion of certified organic foods. This prohibition should be re-established. The sole purpose of organic certification should be to provide safe, healthy food. There should be no trade-offs that facilitate industrial food production and increase shareholder returns.

People often buy organic food to avoid GE ingredients. But the five percent non-organic provision allows GE contamination of certified organic foods. This also should be reversed. GE companies should be held fully responsible for the inevitable contamination that results from the use of their products. The business dominated US government sometimes allows GE companies to sue farmers whose fields get contaminated by GE pollen and seeds blowing in from GE crops. GE companies sometimes argue that farmers are using their seeds illegally, rather than paying farmers for contaminating their fields. This absurd and unfair giveaway to large companies must be reversed. As noted, GE contamination has become so widespread that it already may be impossible to get truly GE free organic or other food. Nevertheless, holding GE companies responsible and reducing allowed GE contamination of organic food would compel GE companies to limit further contamination.

In summary, organic certification greatly benefits society by providing safer, healthier foods. Therefore, organic foods, or at least organic produce, are the appropriate foods to subsidize. Organic certification should be free and provided by government or third parties that cannot be influenced by the farms and companies being certified.

Protect Smaller Farmers and Strengthen Local Economies

As discussed in the Environmental Sustainability Principles section of *Global System Change*, achieving sustainability and real prosperity requires emulating the nearly infinitely greater intelligence of nature. Nature largely is comprised of local, self-sustaining communities. Food mostly is produced and consumed locally. As discussed in the Trade, Scale and Competitive Advantage section, it may appear that centralized production and global distribution of food and other products is more efficient. But this often is an illusion. Industrial production of food and other products frequently imposes many negative environmental, economic and social impacts on society that are not included in prices. As a result, the idea that centralized production of food is more efficient and cost-effective often is false. In reality, local food production frequently is the lowest cost, most beneficial option.

Centralized production by large companies has severely degraded local economies. This has created an unstable and fragile economic system. Local communities often have lost their self-sufficiency. As a result, society is strongly dependent on a relatively small number of large companies. If these companies have problems, much of society suffers. If supply lines are shut down, local communities frequently will become destitute.

Therefore, it is important that local farms and economies be quickly revitalized. Strong local economies provide the most resilient overall economy. Problems in one area or company often have little or no impact on other areas. The decimation of local farms and economies largely has been driven by inappropriate government influence. This drove policies that favored large companies at the expense of small ones. This must be reversed. One of the most important ways to do this is to hold large companies fully responsible for negative impacts. This will naturally expand local farms and food production because large companies no longer will have unfair advantages.

Other policies should be implemented to expand and strengthen local food production and economies. Making organic certification free helps to level the playing field between large and small companies. As discussed, 75 percent of farm subsidies in the US go to the top 10 percent of recipients, which mostly include large farms and corporations. This should be reversed. Large companies should not be coddled with subsidies. They should be held responsible. Local production keeps profits in the community, creates more jobs, and makes the economy more resilient and stable. Therefore, when subsidies are used, they mostly should go to smaller local farms.

Replace Investor Safety Net with Social Safety Net

Implementing a strong social safety net is critical to achieving sustainable food production and diet as well as achieving sustainability and real prosperity overall. As discussed in the Misleading the Public section, true capitalism probably is not possible without a strong social safety net. In spite of the name, the purpose of capitalism is to enhance society, not capital (i.e. business owners). If the purpose of capitalism were not to enhance society, citizens would not implement it in a democracy (unless they were misled).

Effective capitalism requires that industry sectors expand and contract based solely on what maximizes the well-being of society. As discussed extensively, reducing the production of animal products and refined carbohydrates while increasing the production of whole plant foods would vastly lower obesity, chronic disease, premature death and healthcare costs. We must not allow large companies that are structurally required to grow forever to block the transition to healthy eating through inappropriate government influence and misleading the public. But this is what is happening in the US.

As discussed in the Pandemic Solutions section, over the past 40 years of deregulation, the social safety net in the US has been greatly weakened while an extremely strong investor safety net has been put in place. Literally trillions of dollars of taxpayer and public wealth are used every year through many forms of corporate welfare to ensure that a small group of wealthy people continuously gets wealthier. At the same time, we removed many of the protections which ensure that the basic needs of citizens are met. People have been misled into using trillions of taxpayer dollars to essentially expand billionaires' fleets of mansions, yachts and luxury cars. But we appear to be unwilling to help parents who are struggling to stay in their homes, feed their children or send children to college.

Through public deception, US citizens have allowed themselves to become overly dependent on corporations. For example, virtually all other developed countries provide full healthcare and a secure retirement to all citizens through government programs. But in the business dominated US, we have allowed businesses to provide these necessities to most. This gives business great power over individuals and society. It creates strong pressure to use taxpayer funds to bail out and subsidize businesses when they are not able to achieve ever-increasing profits. In many other developed countries, a strong social safety net ensures that citizens do not become destitute when companies shrink or go out of business. But in the US, citizens often lose healthcare and pensions when companies get into trouble.

Healthcare and a secure retirement are seen as basic rights in nearly all other developed countries. US citizens are as worthy of having these basic rights and needs met as citizens of other countries. The US is a wealthy country. If we end corporate welfare, we could use our wealth to ensure that every citizen has healthcare, affordable college and a secure retirement. As discussed in the Taxes section, we probably could provide these basic needs while greatly lowering or eliminating individual income taxes on all but the wealthiest citizens.

Having a strong social safety net will make it much easier to downsize the production of products that degrade society (animal products and refined carbohydrates) and expand the production of those that enhance it (whole plant foods). With a strong social safety net, there is much less pressure for taxpayers to perpetuate animal product and refined carbohydrate companies so that employees do not lose healthcare, retirement and other benefits. When citizens are not dependent on companies for these critical services, it is much easier to downsize harmful companies and transition workers to sustainable ones. The lack of a strong social safety net often compels taxpayers and government to cover the downside of business. In effect, taxpayers are compelled to act as the owners of business on the downside. As noted, this is socialism not capitalism.

A strong social safety net greatly reduces the need for taxpayers to cover the downside of business. This means that companies truly would be privately owned (i.e. investors would own the upside and downside, rather than transferring the downside to taxpayers). This is capitalism. Implementing a strong social safety net would enable the great reduction or elimination of corporate welfare. The savings resulting from this would be much more than the cost of implementing a strong social safety net. In other words, implementing a strong social safety net could substantially lower individual income taxes while greatly enhancing the well-being of society. It also would greatly facilitate the rapid transition from unhealthy to healthy diets in the US.

Prevent Influenza Pandemic

As discussed in the Influenza Pandemic section, an H5N1 or similar pandemic probably represents the greatest threat to humanity. H5N1 is the most lethal form of influenza ever. It kills about 60 percent of victims. Many experts believe that H5N1 is only a few mutations away from gaining easy transmissibility between humans. If this occurs, half of the world could be infected with a 60 percent lethal disease. It would be the greatest disaster in human history by far.

As discussed extensively, industrial production of chicken is the main driver of H5N1 risk. Many experts believe that H5N1 evolved in industrial chicken operations. They also believe that H5N1 and similar viruses are most likely to evolve into pandemic (i.e. easily transmissible) form in these operations. The Influenza Pandemic section discussed the many reasons why industrial chicken operations provide nearly perfect environments for the evolution of pandemic H5N1 and other highly lethal viruses.

The potentially grave consequences of an H5N1 pandemic (i.e. billions dead, shutdown of human society for years) mean that we must have zero tolerance for such an event. As discussed, the first priority is the survival of current generations. The second is the survival of future generations. The third priority is the well-being of future generations. And finally, the lowest priority is our own comfort and well-being. The Founders of the US risked and sometimes gave their lives to protect future generations. The least we can do is give up eating a favorite food to greatly reduce potentially the largest threat facing humanity. Children and mentally handicapped people are highly vulnerable. They are not responsible for the high risk of an H5N1 or similar pandemic. But they could be killed by it. This would be tragic. We have an obligation to protect vulnerable people by doing all that we can to lower the risk of a severe pandemics.

As described in detail, industrial animal operations often are filthy, crowded, ideal breeding grounds for diseases that can infect or, in the case of H5N1, decimate humanity. There are many reasons for vastly improving or eliminating these operations. Reducing pandemic risk may be the most important one. As discussed, no business or industry sector has a right to exist. When sectors or companies place society at great risk, they must be reduced, changed or eliminated. Industrial chicken operations (as well as pig and other poultry operations to a lesser degree) present such a risk. Therefore, these operations must be greatly improved or eliminated.

Citizens often cannot trust business dominated governments in the US and some other countries to put the survival of humanity ahead of the financial returns of chicken and other companies that give money to politicians. Once an H5N1-like pandemic strikes, it probably will be too late to avoid unprecedented death and the collapse of society. Therefore, prevention of these types industrial animal operation spawned pandemics is critical. Business dominated government cannot be trusted to take the actions needed to protect society. As a result, people may have to prevent or greatly reduce the risk of a pandemic themselves by not buying chicken meat or eggs. Large sales reductions will compel industrial chicken operations to make major (not token or cosmetic) changes that greatly reduce pandemic risks.

Conclusion

Extensive details about sustainable food production and diet are provided in the Influenza Pandemic, Environmental Impacts, Contamination and Production, Health, Overeating Causes and Solutions, Hunger, Animal Welfare, Food Deceptions and Food Solutions sections. The most important overall suggestion of this book is to greatly reduce or nearly eliminate the consumption of animal products.

Eating them is the main driver of one of the most severe threats facing humanity, an H5N1 or similar pandemic. Along with burning fossil fuels, producing animal products drives greater destruction of environmental life support systems than any other activity in human society. Eating animal products is by far the largest killer of humans in developed countries. Eating them and refined carbohydrates probably kills more people than all other causes of death combined. Producing animal products is vastly less efficient than producing plant products. It drives extensive waste of grain and water. As a result, eating animal products probably is the largest driver of growing food shortages and hunger in the world.

The industrial production of animal products causes billions of our fellow creatures on this planet to live lives of intense pain and suffering. Consuming these tortured animals kills us physically more than any other factor. But it also probably severely wounds the spirit of humanity in ways that often are not obvious. Killing animals to survive can be justified. But humans are anatomical herbivores and we can feed nearly everyone with plants. Therefore, the vast majority of animal torture and killing is unnecessary and not justified.

A whole system perspective shows that eating animal products probably is the most destructive activity in human society. Given this and the readily available alternative (eating plants), the logic of nearly ending the consumption of animal products is overwhelmingly strong.

But eating them is a deeply ingrained part of culture in the US and many other countries. Some people would say that nearly ending animal product consumption is too extreme. But human society has made many large changes that did not seem practical or even possible before they occurred. For example, many people felt that completely ending slavery was too extreme. Much of the US economy was based on it. It seemed that society might collapse, especially in the South, if slavery were ended. But society did not collapse. Instead, it became vastly better when we ended this barbaric, evil, indescribably horrible treatment of our fellow human beings.

Ending animal product consumption usually is the single most powerful action people can take to protect the life support systems that will sustain our children, vastly reduce the risk of chronic disease and premature death, reduce severe pandemic risks, alleviate world hunger, and end the evil, horrible treatment of animals on this planet.

Ending the consumption of animal products probably will be difficult for many people. But we should not hesitate to take actions that greatly benefit humanity because they might be inconvenient, require different eating habits, or hurt business sectors. Business is a servant of society and humanity. Businesses and business sectors only should exist if they benefit and do not harm us. If reducing or ending the consumption of animal products, especially chicken, benefits society, we must make it happen. Business and the economy should be constantly evolving and adapting based solely on what maximizes the well-being of society. We must exert control over myopic, suicidal, non-human entities that are structurally required to put their own well-being ahead of the survival and well-being of humanity.

When people learn of the frequently filthy, disgusting, disease-promoting nature of industrial animal operations, they often might feel betrayed by business and government. How could our servant government allow such filthy, inhumane operations to exist, they might ask. Many people might get angry when they learn how the food they fed their children was produced. But anger or blame largely is counterproductive.

Food companies do not intend to harm anyone. Their goal is not to sicken and kill people. These are unintended consequences of our suicidally myopic systems that compel business leaders and politicians who take money from them to put shareholder returns before all else. In other words, the enemy is not people. All business and political leaders intend to benefit, or at least not harm society. The enemies are our flawed ideas and systems that compel good people to do bad things.

These flawed systems will end, probably soon. No system that massively violates the laws of nature survives. Humanity has greater awareness and intelligence than at any other time in human history. We definitely have the ability to evolve our food, economic, political and other systems into sustainable forms. More importantly, we have the core desire to do this. No one but the insane thinks that humanity should sicken and kill itself. We all want future generations to prosper. We all want sustainability. We have the ability to change and the core desire to do so. The only thing lacking is greater public awareness. But that is manifesting rapidly.

Darkness cannot survive in the light. We are in the midst of unprecedented change. The flaws of our ideas and systems are becoming obvious to many people. System change is inevitable. The key is to manage the process in ways that minimize disruption. *Global System Change* extensively describes how to achieve practical, minimally-disruptive change of economic, political and social systems.

In the food area, probably the most important system change needed in developed countries is transitioning away from promoting animal products and refined carbohydrates to promoting the foods that we were designed or evolved to eat – whole plant foods. Another critical system change involves removing the investor safety net and strengthening the social safety net. Investors in food companies should have no expectation of being bailed out or having their downsides covered by taxpayers. If people invest in companies that produce harmful products, there is a good chance they will lose their investments. If we end socialistic investing in the US by eliminating limited liability, investors in companies that make harmful products not only might lose their investments. They also could lose their other assets.

There would be no harmful corporate activities without investors because there would be no corporations without them. Therefore, investors ultimately are responsible for all corporate harm done to society. Holding investors fully responsible will greatly reduce or end the sale of harmful products because companies that make these products will be unable to attract investment. It does not matter if a non-living entity, such as a food company, disappears. But all people associated with companies do matter. A strong social safety net will ensure that the basic needs of all citizens are met when harmful sectors decline.

In conclusion, humans are part of nature. We have access to the nearly infinite wisdom and intelligence displayed there. It might seem that improving society by nearly ending the consumption of animal products would be difficult. But this belief results from a limited perspective. Flying once seemed impossible. Now millions of people do it daily.

Humans only have reached the tiniest fraction of our potential. We can be nearly infinitely more sustainable and prosperous than we are now. As we manifest the infinite wisdom of nature, already present within us, we will live in harmony with nature and each other. And we will eat the perfect foods made for us by nature—whole plant foods.

About the Author

For Speaking Engagements:

Please email me at:
info@FrankDixon.com

Or contact me via my website at:
FrankDixon.com

Frank Dixon is a sustainability and system change visionary, pioneer, innovator and leader. He saw 20 years ago that system change was the most important sustainability issue. As a result, he established Global System Change and developed the System Change Investing (SCI) approach. It provided the first model for rating companies on system change performance and integrating system change into corporate sustainability strategies. He also developed a true whole system approach to sustainability, described in the Global System Change books. It provides systemic solutions for all major areas of society. In the financial and corporate sectors, SCI offers the most advanced and effective sustainability strategies.

Before writing the GSC books, Frank Dixon was the Managing Director of Research for the largest corporate sustainability research firm in the world (Innovest/MSCI). He developed ESG rating models and research processes that consistently provided superior investment returns. He advises companies, investors and governments, including Walmart and the US Environmental Protection Agency, on sustainability and system change. He has presented at many corporate and financial sector conferences around the world, and spoken at leading universities, including Harvard, Yale, Stanford, MIT and Cambridge.

Frank Dixon has an MBA from the Harvard Business School and is a Fellow of the World Academy of Art and Science.

Endnotes

1   Kathy Freston, Flu Season: Factory Farming Could Cause A Catastrophic Pandemic, The Huffington Post, January 5, 2010.

2   Michael Greger, M.D., Bird Flu: A Virus of Our Own Hatching, Lantern Books, 2006, IV.3.b.

3   Bird Flu: A Virus of Our Own Hatching, II.3.a.

4   six more bird flu cases in China reported, one of them fatal, www.CNN.com, February 1, 2014.

5   Michael Greger, M.D., Bird Flu: A Virus of Our Own Hatching, Lantern Books, 2006.

6   Bird Flu: A Virus of Our Own Hatching, I.1.c.

7   Bird Flu: A Virus of Our Own Hatching, II.5.d.

8   Bird Flu: A Virus of Our Own Hatching, I.1.b.

9   Bird Flu: A Virus of Our Own Hatching, I.1.c.

10 Bird Flu: A Virus of Our Own Hatching, I.1.d.

11 Bird Flu: A Virus of Our Own Hatching, II.1.c.

12 Same as above.

13 Bird Flu: A Virus of Our Own Hatching, II.1.e.

14 Same as above.

15 Bird Flu: A Virus of Our Own Hatching, II.2.a.

16 Bird Flu: A Virus of Our Own Hatching, II.1.b.

17 Bird Flu: A Virus of Our Own Hatching, II.5.a.

18 Bird Flu: A Virus of Our Own Hatching, II.5.c.

19 Bird Flu: A Virus of Our Own Hatching, I.2.c.

20 Bird Flu: A Virus of Our Own Hatching, I.2.g.

21 Bird Flu: A Virus of Our Own Hatching, I.3.b.

22 Maggie Fox, Bird Flu Spreading as Scientists Look Everywhere for Clues, www.NBCnews.com, May 24, 2015.

23 Bird Flu: A Virus of Our Own Hatching, I.3.d.

24 Bird Flu: A Virus of Our Own Hatching, I.3.e.

25 Bird Flu: A Virus of Our Own Hatching, I.4.a.

26 Bird Flu: A Virus of Our Own Hatching, Introduction.

27 Bird Flu: A Virus of Our Own Hatching, I.3.e.

28 Bird Flu: A Virus of Our Own Hatching, I.3.f.

29 Bird Flu: A Virus of Our Own Hatching, I.5.a.

30 Kathy Freston, Flu Season: Factory Farming Could Cause A Catastrophic Pandemic, The Huffington Post, January 5, 2010.

31 Same as above.

32 Bird Flu: A Virus of Our Own Hatching, I.6.b.

33 Same as above.

34 Bird Flu: A Virus of Our Own Hatching, II.5.b.

35 Same as above.

36 Bird Flu: A Virus of Our Own Hatching, II.6.b.

37 Bird Flu: A Virus of Our Own Hatching, II.6.a.

38 Bird Flu: A Virus of Our Own Hatching, II.6.c.

39 Same as above.

40 Same as above.

41 Same as above.

42 Bird Flu: A Virus of Our Own Hatching, II.6.f.

43 Bird Flu: A Virus of Our Own Hatching, II.6.g.

44 Bird Flu: A Virus of Our Own Hatching, II.5.b.

45 Bird Flu: A Virus of Our Own Hatching, II.5.f.

46 Bird Flu: A Virus of Our Own Hatching, V.1.d.

47 Bird Flu: A Virus of Our Own Hatching, II.7.a.

48 Same as above.

49 Bird Flu: A Virus of Our Own Hatching, II.7.b.

50 Bird Flu: A Virus of Our Own Hatching, V.1.b.

51 Same as above.

52 Bird Flu: A Virus of Our Own Hatching, V.1.b.

53 Bird Flu: A Virus of Our Own Hatching, V.1.d.

54 Bird Flu: A Virus of Our Own Hatching, V.1.c.

55 Bird Flu: A Virus of Our Own Hatching, I.6.a.

56 Bird Flu: A Virus of Our Own Hatching, I.6.b.

57 Bird Flu: A Virus of Our Own Hatching, I.6.a.

58 Bird Flu: A Virus of Our Own Hatching, I.5.c.

59 Bird Flu: A Virus of Our Own Hatching, III.2.c.

60 Congressional Budget Office, Stockpiling Vaccines, www.cbo.gov/ftp-docs/95xx/doc9573/Chapter4.8.1.shtml, Accessed April 15, 2011.

61 Same as above.

62 Susan Blumenthal, M.D., Flu in the 21st Century, The Huffington Post, March 19, 2011.

63 Bird Flu: A Virus of Our Own Hatching, IV.1.c.

64 US Centers for Disease

Control and Prevention, Avian Influenza: Current H5N1 Situation, http://www.cdc.gov/flu/avian/outbreaks/current.htm, October 2008.

65 Beat Bird Flu, Tamiflu – Pros and Cons, http://www.beat-bird-flu.com/articles/tamiflu_review.htm, Accessed May 11, 2011.

66 Bird Flu: A Virus of Our Own Hatching, I.5.d.

67 Same as above.

68 Bird Flu: A Virus of Our Own Hatching, III.3.b.

69 Bird Flu: A Virus of Our Own Hatching, III.3.c.

70 Bird Flu: A Virus of Our Own Hatching, III.3.d.

71 Bird Flu: A Virus of Our Own Hatching, III.2.b.

72 Bird Flu: A Virus of Our Own Hatching, III.1.c.

73 Bird Flu: A Virus of Our Own Hatching, I.6.c.

74 Bird Flu: A Virus of Our Own Hatching, I.6.d.

75 Bird Flu: A Virus of Our Own Hatching, I.6.e.

76 Bird Flu: A Virus of Our Own Hatching, I.5.e.

77 Same as above.

78 Same as above.

79 Same as above.

80 Bird Flu: A Virus of Our Own Hatching, I.6.e.

81 Bird Flu: A Virus of Our Own Hatching, IV.2.a.

82 Bird Flu: A Virus of Our Own Hatching, IV.3.b.

83 Same as above.

84 Same as above.

85 Bird Flu: A Virus of Our Own Hatching, IV.3.e.

86 Bird Flu: A Virus of Our Own Hatching, IV.3.c.

87 Bird Flu: A Virus of Our Own Hatching, IV.3.e.

88 Same as above.

89 Bird Flu: A Virus of Our Own Hatching, IV.2.a.

90 Bird Flu: A Virus of Our Own Hatching, IV.3.e.

91 Bird Flu: A Virus of Our Own Hatching, III.2.a.

92 Bird Flu: A Virus of Our Own Hatching, IV.3.b.

93 Bird Flu: A Virus of Our Own Hatching, IV.2.e.

94 Bird Flu: A Virus of Our Own Hatching, I.4.a.

95 Bird Flu: A Virus of Our Own Hatching, IV.2.a.

96 Bird Flu: A Virus of Our Own Hatching, IV.2.e.

97 Bird Flu: A Virus of Our Own Hatching, IV.2.b.

98 Bird Flu: A Virus of Our Own Hatching, IV.2.d.

99 Bird Flu: A Virus of Our Own Hatching, IV.2.b.

100 Bird Flu: A Virus of Our Own Hatching, IV.1.c.

101 Bird Flu: A Virus of Our Own Hatching, IV.1.d.

102 Bird Flu: A Virus of Our Own Hatching, IV.1.c.

103 Bird Flu: A Virus of Our Own Hatching, IV.3.f.

104 Bird Flu: A Virus of Our Own Hatching, II.5.f.

105 Bird Flu: A Virus of Our Own Hatching, II.7.a.

106 Bird Flu: A Virus of Our Own Hatching, II.5.f.

107 Bird Flu: A Virus of Our Own Hatching, V.2.a.

108 Same as above.

109 Virgina Hughes, Transgenic chickens curb bird flu transmission, Nature, January 13, 2011.

110 Bird Flu: A Virus of Our Own Hatching, V.2.b.

111 Bird Flu: A Virus of Our Own Hatching, III.2.b.

112 Bird Flu: A Virus of Our Own Hatching, I.4.e.

113 Bird Flu: A Virus of Our Own Hatching, V.2.a.

114 The Great Pandemic, www.1918.PandemicFlu.gov, Accessed May 7, 2011.

115 Bird Flu: A Virus of Our Own Hatching, V.2.b.

116 Bird Flu: A Virus of Our Own Hatching, II.3.e.

117 Bird Flu: A Virus of Our Own Hatching, III.1.b.

118 Bird Flu: A Virus of Our Own Hatching, V.2.b.

119 Same as above.

120 Same as above.

121 Same as above.

122 Same as above.

123 Same as above.

124 Livestock and Climate Change, World Watch Institute, November/December 2009.

125 Bryan Walsh, Meat: Making Global Warming Worse, www.Time.com, September 10, 2008.

126 Reynard Loki, The three Most Environmentally Damaging Habits You Might Be Able to Change, www.AlterNet.org, April 13, 2016.

127 Kathy Freston, 13 Breathtaking Effects of Cutting Back on Meat, www.AlterNet.org, April 22, 2009.

128 Charles Duhigg, Debating How Much Weed Killer Is Safe in Your Water Glass, New York Times, August 23, 2009.

129 Randy Dotinga, Organic Food Fends Off Pesticides, HealthDay Reporter, February 20, 2010.

130 Emily Elert, Food in the

U.S. Is Still Tainted with Chemicals That Were Banned Decades Ago, Environmental Health News, April 22, 2010.

131 Dioxin Homepage, www. ejnet.org/dioxin/, Accessed January 27, 2011.

132 Dioxins and their effects on human health, Fact Sheet No. 225, World Health Organization, May 2010.

133 Dioxin Homepage, www. ejnet.org/dioxin/, Accessed January 27, 2011.

134 Dioxins and their effects on human health, Fact Sheet No. 225, World Health Organization, May 2010.

135 Dioxin Homepage, www. ejnet.org/dioxin/, Accessed January 27, 2011.

136 Meat Contamination, www.PETA.org, Accessed February 19, 2011.

137 GMO Crops, Animal Food and Beyond, US Food and Drug Administration, www.FDA.gov, Accessed July 24, 2021.

138 Tom Laskawy, Canola gone wild! Uh-oh, transgenic plants are escaping and interbreeding, www. Grist.org, August 6, 2010.

139 US Consumers Have Been Given a False Sense of Security About the Safety of Our Food Supply, www. SeedsOfDeception.com, September 2010.

140 Ken Roseboro, Scientist: GM Food Safety Testing Is "Woefully Inadequate", The Organic and Non-GMO Report, www.OrganicConsumers.org, Dec/Jan 2009.

141 US Consumers Have Been Given a False Sense of Security About the Safety of Our Food Supply, www. SeedsOfDeception.com, September 2010.

142 Monsanto and Genetic Engineering: Risks for Investors, Innovest Strategic Value Advisors, January 2005.

143 Failure to Yield: Evaluating the Performance of Genetically Engineered Crops, Union of Concerned Scientists, April 2009.

144 William Neuman et al, Farmers Cope with Roundup-Resistant Weeds, New York Times, May 2, 2010.

145 By 2048 all current fish, seafood species projected to collapse, Science, November 3, 2006.

146 Jill Richardson, Shrimp's Dirty Secrets: Why America's Favorite Seafood Is a Health and Environmental Nightmare, www.AlterNet. org, January 25, 2010.

147 Tara Lohan, Our Drinkable Water Supply Is Vanishing, www.AlterNet.org, October 11, 2007.

148 World heads for 'water bankruptcy', says Davos report, Agence France-Presse, January 29, 2009.

149 Jaymi Heimbuch, World's Water Supply: Here Are the Haves and Have Nots, www.AlterNet.org, June 29, 2010.

150 U.S. could feed 800 million people with grain that livestock eat, Science News, Cornell University, August 7, 1997.

151 Kathy Freston, 13 Breathtaking Effects of Cutting Back on Meat, www.AlterNet.org, April 22, 2009.

152 John Robbins, Diet for a New America, Stillpoint Publishing, 1987.

153 Kathy Freston, 13 Breathtaking Effects of Cutting Back on Meat, www.AlterNet.org, April 22, 2009.

154 Same as above.

155 Same as above.

156 Kali Holloway, America's Pill Popping Is Making Our Fish Anxious and Possibly Getting Into Our Vegetables, www.AlterNet. org, May 3, 2016.

157 Lower IQs in mercury-exposed children cost U.S. billions, study says, www. Grist.org, March 1, 2005.

158 Half of All Freshwater Fish in U.S. High in Mercury, www.Grist.org, August 4, 2004.

159 One in five U.S. women have high mercury levels, suggests new report, www. Grist.org, February 9, 2006.

160 Lower IQs in mercury-exposed children cost U.S. billions, study says, www. Grist.org, March 1, 2005.

161 Kathy Freston, 13 Breathtaking Effects of Cutting Back on Meat, www.AlterNet.org, April 22, 2009.

162 Lester Brown, Rethinking food production for a world of eight billion, www.Grist. org, July 7, 2009.

163 Agriculture: major impacts on species and places, www.WWF.Panda.org, 2010.

164 Agriculture: major impacts on species and places, www.WWF.Panda.org, 2010.

165 Tom Paulson, The lowdown on topsoil: It's disappearing, www.SeattlePI. com, January 22, 2008.

166 Deborah Rich, Organic fruits and vegetables work harder for their nutrients – Produce has been losing vitamins and minerals over the past half-century,

www.SFGate.com, March 25, 2006.

167 Lester Brown, Peak soil is no joke: Civilization's foundation is eroding, www.Grist.org, September 29, 2010.

168 Agriculture: major impacts on species and places, www.WWF.Panda.org, 2010.

169 Wetlands Decline, Vital Signs 2001, Worldwatch Institute, 2002.

170 Ron Nielsen, The Little Green Handbook: Seven Trends Shaping the Future of Our Planet, Picador, 2006.

171 Kathy Freston, 13 Breathtaking Effects of Cutting Back on Meat, www.AlterNet.org, April 22, 2009.

172 Population boom will pressure forests: reports, www.Reuters.com, July 14, 2008.

173 John Vidal, Billionaires and Mega-Corporations Behind Immense Land Grab in Africa, www.AlterNet.org, March 10, 2010.

174 Kathy Freston, 13 Breathtaking Effects of Cutting Back on Meat, www.AlterNet.org, April 22, 2009.

175 Brian Halweil, Grain Harvest Sets Record, But Supplies Still Tight, Worldwatch Institute, December 12, 2007.

176 Kathy Freston, 13 Breathtaking Effects of Cutting Back on Meat, www.AlterNet.org, April 22, 2009.

177 Matters of Scale - Visible vs. Invisible Waste, www.WorldWatch.org, Accessed December 4, 2010.

178 Andrew Revkin, Tossed Food Is Also Lost Water, New York Times, August 22, 2008.

179 Half of US food goes to waste, www.FoodProductionDaily.com, November 25, 2004.

180 Kathy Freston, 13 Breathtaking Effects of Cutting Back on Meat, www.AlterNet.org, April 22, 2009.

181 Same as above.

182 Kathy Freston, How Factory Farms Are Pumping Americans Full of Deadly Bacteria and Pathogens, www.AlterNet.org, January 18, 2010.

183 Meat: Not Suitable for Children, www.PETA.org, Accessed February 19, 2011.

184 Kathy Freston, How Factory Farms Are Pumping Americans Full of Deadly Bacteria and Pathogens, www.AlterNet.org, January 18, 2010.

185 Jill Richardson, Factory Farms Produce 100 Times More Waste Than All People Combined and It's Killing Our Drinking Water, www.AlterNet.org, May 23, 2011.

186 Food – How Safe?, National Geographic Magazine, May 2002.

187 Food, Inc., Documentary film by Magnolia Pictures, 2009.

188 Michael Moss, Trail of E. Coli Shows Flaws in Inspection of Ground Beef, New York Times, October 4, 2009.

189 Same as above.

190 Kathy Freston, How Factory Farms Are Pumping Americans Full of Deadly Bacteria and Pathogens, www.AlterNet.org, January 18, 2010.

191 Matthew Scully, Dominion: The Power of Man, the Suffering of Animals, and the Call to Mercy, St. Martin's Griffin, Page 29, 2003.

192 Slaughterhouses and Processing, www.SustainableTable.org, Accessed March 7, 2011.

193 Food, Inc., Documentary film by Magnolia Pictures, 2009.

194 Rick Weiss, Report Targets Costs of Factory Farming, Washington Post, April 30, 2008.

195 Tom Philpott, Big Poultry ramps up its assault on the Chesapeake, www.Grist.org, December 2, 2010.

196 Tom Philpott, Risk, bacteria, and the tragedy of food-safety reform, www.Grist.org, November 23, 2010.

197 Kathy Freston, How Factory Farms Are Pumping Americans Full of Deadly Bacteria and Pathogens, www.AlterNet.org, January 18, 2010.

198 Richard Arsenault, Corn Fed Cattle: Bigger Cows, Bigger E. coli Threat, More Foodborne Illness, www.NBAFoodAdvocate.com, July 27, 2009.

199 Kathy Freston, How Factory Farms Are Pumping Americans Full of Deadly Bacteria and Pathogens, www.AlterNet.org, January 18, 2010.

200 Michael Greger, M.D., Superbugs: Chicken Out of Urinary Tract Infections, www.All-Creatures.org, Accessed March 6, 2011.

201 Kenneth Todar, PhD, Pathogenic E. Coli, Online Textbook of Bacteriology, University of Wisconsin—Madison Department of Bacteriology, Accessed November 30, 2007.

202 Michael Greger, M.D., Superbugs: Chicken Out

of Urinary Tract Infections, www.All-Creatures.org, Accessed March 6, 2011.

203 Michael Moss, Trail of E. Coli Shows Flaws in Inspection of Ground Beef, New York Times, October 4, 2009.

204 Slaughterhouses and Processing, www.SustainableTable.org, Accessed March 7, 2011.

205 Michael Moss, Trail of E. Coli Shows Flaws in Inspection of Ground Beef, New York Times, October 4, 2009.

206 Tom Philpott, Lessons on the food system from the ammonia-hamburger fiasco, www.Grist.org, January 5, 2010.

207 Michael Moss, Safety of Beef Processing Method is Questioned, New York Times, December 31, 2009.

208 Same as above

209 Bill Tomson et al, 'Pink slime' returns to school lunches in four more states, www.Politico.com, September 9, 2013.

210 Safe and Suitable Ingredients Used in the Production of Meat, Poultry, and Egg Products, United States Department of Agriculture, January 4, 2012.

211 Tom Laskawy, 'Pink slime' is the tip of the iceberg: Look what else is in industrial meat, www.Grist.org, March 19, 2012.

212 Michael Moss, Trail of E. Coli Shows Flaws in Inspection of Ground Beef, New York Times, October 4, 2009.

213 Same as above.

214 Same as above.

215 Kathy Freston, How Factory Farms Are Pumping Americans Full of Deadly

Bacteria and Pathogens, www.AlterNet.org, January 18, 2010.

216 Bird Flu: A Virus of Our Own Hatching, I.4.c.

217 Kathy Freston, How Factory Farms Are Pumping Americans Full of Deadly Bacteria and Pathogens, www.AlterNet.org, January 18, 2010.

218 Same as above.

219 Bird Flu: A Virus of Our Own Hatching, I.4.b.

220 Kathy Freston, How Factory Farms Are Pumping Americans Full of Deadly Bacteria and Pathogens, www.AlterNet.org, January 18, 2010.

221 Bird Flu: A Virus of Our Own Hatching, II.2.d.

222 Same as above.

223 Michael Moss, Safety of Beef Processing Method is Questioned, New York Times, December 31, 2009.

224 Kathy Freston, How Factory Farms Are Pumping Americans Full of Deadly Bacteria and Pathogens, www.AlterNet.org, January 18, 2010.

225 Carol Rados, Listeria Monocytogenes Comtamination in Foods, FDA Consumer magazine, Jan-Feb 2004.

226 Warrell et al, Oxford Textbook of Medicine, Oxford University Press, 2003.

227 Food Poisoning Bacteria - Salmonella, Listeria, E.coli O157, Campylobacter, www.Accepta.com, Accessed March 10, 2011.

228 David E. Gumpert, How the Federal Government Manufactured 21 Actual Raw Milk Illnesses into a Much Scarier 20,000, www.AlterNet.org, January 7, 2014.

229 Prevalence and incidence statistics for food poisoning, www.WrongDiagnosis.com, Accessed March 11, 2011.

230 How safe is that chicken?, Consumer Reports, January 2010.

231 Bird Flu: A Virus of Our Own Hatching, II.3.d.

232 Same as above.

233 Same as above.

234 David Kirby, You Want Chicken Poop With That Steak? Why FDA Should Ban Feces From Feed, The Huffington Post, April 9, 2010.

235 Same as above.

236 M. Thornle, Mad Cow Disease in the USA: Profits Take Priority, Part I, www.NaturalNews.com, June 9, 2010.

237 Shannon Pettypiece, Mad-Cow Feed Rules Should Ban Poultry Feces, U.S. Senator Says, www.Bloomberg.com, March 14, 2006.

238 Bird Flu: A Virus of Our Own Hatching, II.3.d.

239 Manure, Animal Feed Resources Information System, www.FAO.org, Accessed March 22, 2011.

240 Same as above.

241 Tom Philpott, More biofuel waste for cows, www.Grist.org, February 16, 2010.

242 Same as above.

243 Bird Flu: A Virus of Our Own Hatching, II.3.d.

244 Same as above.

245 Same as above.

246 Bird Flu: A Virus of Our Own Hatching, II.3.f.

247 Tom Philpott, The FDA finally reveals how many antibiotics factory farms

use, www.Grist.org, December 10, 2010.

248 Ralph Loglisci, Will the U.S. hog industry ever kick its reliance on low-dose antibiotics?, www.Grist.org, April 5, 2011.

249 Bird Flu: A Virus of Our Own Hatching, II.3.f.

250 Tom Philpott, Flies and cockroaches carry antibiotic-resistant bacteria from factory farms, study finds, www.Grist.org, February 25, 2011.

251 Bird Flu: A Virus of Our Own Hatching, II.3.f.

252 Same as above.

253 Eric Eckholm, U.S. Meat Farmers Brace for Limits on Antibiotics, New York Times, September 14, 2010.

254 Same as above.

255 Bird Flu: A Virus of Our Own Hatching, II.3.f.

256 Amanda Gardner, Bacteria seen in nearly half of U.S. meat, www.CNN.com, April 15, 2011.

257 MRSA and Animal Agriculture: A Need to Understand the Public Health Impact, www.keepantibioticsworking.com, Accessed May 15, 2011.

258 Same as above.

259 Bird Flu: A Virus of Our Own Hatching, II.3.f.

260 Kate Kelland, Scientists find superbugs in Delhi drinking water, www.Reuters.com, April 7, 2011.

261 Liz Szabo, Woman found to harbor infection resistant to antibiotic of last resort, USA Today, May 26, 2016.

262 Bird Flu: A Virus of Our Own Hatching, II.3.f.

263 Liz Szabo, Woman found to harbor infection resistant to antibiotic of last resort, USA Today, May 26, 2016.

264 Eric Eckholm, U.S. Meat Farmers Brace for Limits on Antibiotics, New York Times, September 14, 2010.

265 Ralph Loglisci, Will the U.S. hog industry ever kick its reliance on low-dose antibiotics?, www.Grist.org, April 5, 2011.

266 Tom Philpott, Think tainted Chinese pork is scary? Check out the nearest supermarket meat case, www.Grist.org, March 19, 2011.

267 Eric Eckholm, U.S. Meat Farmers Brace for Limits on Antibiotics, New York Times, September 14, 2010.

268 Ralph Loglisci, Will the U.S. hog industry ever kick its reliance on low-dose antibiotics?, www.Grist.org, April 5, 2011.

269 Same as above.

270 Artificial Hormones, www.SustainableTable.org, Accessed February 19, 2011.

271 Samuel Epstein, Hormonal Milk and Meat: A Dangerous Public Health Risk, The Huffington Post, April 13, 2010.

272 Hormones, www.SustainableTable.org, Accessed February 19, 2011.

273 Meat Contamination, www.PETA.org, Accessed February 19, 2011.

274 Samuel Epstein, Hormonal Milk and Meat: A Dangerous Public Health Risk, The Huffington Post, April 13, 2010.

275 Same as above.

276 None of Us Should Eat Extra Estrogen, Los Angeles Times, March 24, 1997.

277 Samuel Epstein, Hormonal Milk and Meat: A Dangerous Public Health Risk, The Huffington Post, April 13, 2010.

278 Same as above.

279 Ari LeVaux, American Meat Is Even Grosser Than You Thought, www.AlterNet.org, May 1, 2010.

280 Same as above.

281 Martha Rosenberg, Why Has the FDA Allowed a Drug Marked 'Not Safe for Use in Humans' to Be Fed to Livestock Right Before Slaughter?, www.AlterNet.org, February 2, 2010.

282 Same as above.

283 Ari LeVaux, American Meat Is Even Grosser Than You Thought, www.AlterNet.org, May 1, 2010.

284 Center for Food Safety and Institute for Agriculture and Trade Policy Petition FDA to Remove Arsenic from Animal Feeds, Center for Food Safety, December 8, 2009.

285 Tom Philpott, Time to end the insane practice of lacing chicken feed with arsenic, www.Grist.org, March 3, 2011.

286 Meat Contamination, www.PETA.org, Accessed February 19, 2011.

287 Tom Philpott, Time to end the insane practice of lacing chicken feed with arsenic, www.Grist.org, March 3, 2011.

288 Ari LeVaux, American Meat Is Even Grosser Than You Thought, www.AlterNet.org, May 1, 2010.

289 Tom Philpott, Time to end the insane practice of lacing chicken feed with arsenic, www.Grist.org, March 3, 2011.

290 Ari LeVaux, American Meat Is Even Grosser Than You Thought, www.Alter-

Net.org, May 1, 2010.

291 Pascale Santi, Study maps chemical residues in European children's diets, www.Guardian.co.uk, December 28, 2010.

292 Brad Jacobson, Why Is the FDA Saying It's OK to Eat Seafood 10,000 Times Over the Safe Limit for Dangerous Carcinogens?, www.AlterNet.com, December 18, 2011.

293 Martha Rosenberg, Cloned Meat May Already Have Invaded Our Food Supply, Posing Alarming Health Risks, www.AlterNet.org, August 20, 2010.

294 Cloned Animals, www.CenterForFoodSafety.org, January 2008.

295 Martha Rosenberg, Cloned Meat May Already Have Invaded Our Food Supply, Posing Alarming Health Risks, www.AlterNet.org, August 20, 2010.

296 Same as above.

297 Cloned Animals, www.CenterForFoodSafety.org, January 2008.

298 Same as above.

299 Barbara Casassus, Europe fails to reach deal on cloned meat, www.Nature.com, March 29, 2011.

300 Patricia Whisnant, DVM, Clean Beef or Irradiated Dirty Beef? A Veterinarian's Perspective, www.AmericanGrassFedBeef.com, Accessed May 25, 2011.

301 What's Wrong with Food Irradiation, www.OrganicConsumers.org, February 2001.

302 History, Background and Status of Labeling of Irradiated Foods, www.OrganicConsumers.org, August 25, 2008.

303 Patricia Whisnant, DVM, Clean Beef or Irradiated Dirty Beef? A Veterinarian's Perspective, www.AmericanGrassFedBeef.com, Accessed May 25, 2011.

304 What's Wrong with Food Irradiation, www.OrganicConsumers.org, February 2001.

305 Top 10 Reasons for Opposing Food Irradiation, www.Mercola.com, Accessed January 9, 2011.

306 What's Wrong with Food Irradiation, www.OrganicConsumers.org, February 2001.

307 Same as above.

308 Patricia Whisnant, DVM, Clean Beef or Irradiated Dirty Beef? A Veterinarian's Perspective, www.AmericanGrassFedBeef.com, Accessed May 25, 2011.

309 Top 10 Reasons for Opposing Food Irradiation, www.Mercola.com, Accessed January 9, 2011.

310 Laura Weldon, Common Additives in Your Food Contain Shocking Dangers, Part I, www.NaturalNews.com, February 18, 2010.

311 Food Safety: FDA Should Strengthen Its Oversight of Food Ingredients Determined to Be Generally Recognized as Safe (GRAS), U.S. Government Accountability Office, February 2010.

312 Same as above.

313 Kristen Wartman, Are you Enjoying your daily chemical cocktail?, www.Grist.org, April 27, 2011.

314 Mark Gold, Aspartame... the BAD news!, www.Dorway.com, October 2003.

315 Dr. Joseph Mercola, America's Deadliest Sweetener Betrays Millions, Then Hoodwinks You with Name Change, www.AlterNet.org, July 8, 2010.

316 Same as above.

317 Dr. Leo Rebollo, Buy Your Poison – Aspartame, Diet Soda, Splenda, www.NaturalNews.com, September 24, 2008.

318 Dr. Joseph Mercola, America's Deadliest Sweetener Betrays Millions, Then Hoodwinks You with Name Change, www.AlterNet.org, July 8, 2010.

319 Vanessa Barrington, High Fructose Corn Syrup Proven to Cause Human Obesity, www.AlterNet.org, December 30, 2009.

320 Tom Philpott, Some heavy metal with that sweet roll?, www.Grist.org, January 26, 2009.

321 Tom Laskawy, What a 'Sweet surprise'! HFCS contains more fructose than believed, www.Grist.org, October 26, 2010.

322 Vanessa Barrington, High Fructose Corn Syrup Proven to Cause Human Obesity, www.AlterNet.org, December 30, 2009.

323 Mike Adams, Food manufacturers hide dangerous ingredients in everyday foods by using confusing terms on the label, www.NaturalNews.com, July 27, 2004.

324 Laura Weldon, Common Additives in Your Food Contain Shocking Dangers, Part I, www.NaturalNews.com, February 18, 2010.

325 Dr. Joseph Mercola, What's In That? How Food Affects Your Behavior, www.Mercola.com, July 29, 2008.

326 Titanium Dioxide: A Paint & Food Additive That Makes Things White, www.Food.TheFunTimes-Guide.com, Accessed December 15, 2011.

327 80 percent of Pre-Packaged Foods in America Are Banned in Other Countries, www.Yahoo.com, June 24, 2013.

328 Same as above.

329 Same as above.

330 Barbara Minton, Consuming Common Food Additive MSG Increases Risk of Weight Gain, www.NaturalNews.com, January 9, 2009.

331 Dr. Joseph Mercola, MSG: Is This Silent Killer Lurking in Your Kitchen Cabinets?, www.OrganicConsumers.org, April 21, 2009.

332 What is MSG?, www.MSGmyth.com, May 2011.

333 Same as above.

334 How are monosodium glutamate and the other ingredients that contain MSG manufactured?, www.TruthInLabeleing.org, Accessed June 23, 2011.

335 Names of ingredients that contain processed free glutamic acid (MSG), www.TruthInLabeling.org/HiddenSources.html, March 2014.

336 Barbara Minton, Consuming Common Food Additive MSG Increases Risk of Weight Gain, www.NaturalNews.com, January 9, 2009.

337 Dr. Joseph Mercola, What's In That? How Food Affects Your Behavior, www.Mercola.com, July 29, 2008.

338 Same as above.

339 Dr. Joseph Mercola, MSG: Is This Silent Killer Lurking in Your Kitchen Cabinets?, www.OrganicConsumers.org, April 21, 2009.

340 Worst Food Additives, www.GreenDragonSuperFoods.com, July 1, 2010.

341 George, Schwartz, M.D., In Bad Taste: The MSG Symptom Complex, Health Press, 1999.

342 Dr. Joseph Mercola, MSG: Is This Silent Killer Lurking in Your Kitchen Cabinets?, www.OrganicConsumers.org, April 21, 2009.

343 Worst Food Additives, www.GreenDragonSuperFoods.com, July 1, 2010.

344 The Hidden Food Additive That Eats Your Brain, www.HealthBeyondHype.com, September 25, 2008.

345 Same as above.

346 Dr. Joseph Mercola, What's In That? How Food Affects Your Behavior, www.Mercola.com, July 29, 2008.

347 George, Schwartz, M.D., In Bad Taste: The MSG Symptom Complex, Health Press, 1999.

348 Dr. Joseph Mercola, What's In That? How Food Affects Your Behavior, www.Mercola.com, July 29, 2008.

349 The Hidden Food Additive That Eats Your Brain, www.HealthBeyondHype.com, September 25, 2008.

350 Worst Food Additives, www.GreenDragonSuperFoods.com, July 1, 2010.

351 The Hidden Food Additive That Eats Your Brain, www.HealthBeyondHype.com, September 25, 2008.

352 Barbara Minton, Consuming Common Food Additive MSG Increases Risk of Weight Gain, www.NaturalNews.com, January 9, 2009.

353 Aleisha Fetters, 11 Foods That Make You Hungrier, ABC News, July 29, 2014.

354 Barbara Minton, Consuming Common Food Additive MSG Increases Risk of Weight Gain, www.NaturalNews.com, January 9, 2009.

355 Dr. Joseph Mercola, New Chemical Alternative to MSG That is Coming Soon, www.Mercola.com, January 15, 2009.

356 The China Study (see below), Page 76.

357 T. Colin Campbell, Ph.D. and Thomas M. Campbell II, The China Study: The Most Comprehensive Study of Nutrition Ever Conducted And Startling Implications for Diet, Weight Loss and Long-Term Health, Benbella Books, 2005.

358 Douglas J. Lisle, Ph.D., Praise for the China Study, www.TheChinaStudy.com, Accessed September 27, 2011.

359 The China Study, Page 7.

360 Same as above.

361 The China Study, Page 274.

362 How Many Adults Are Vegan in the U.S.?, The Vegetarian Resource Group, December 5, 2011.

363 The China Study, Page 92.

364 The China Study, Page 230.

365 Dr. Joseph Mercola, New US Guidelines Will Lift Limits on Dietary Cholesterol, www.Mercola.com, March 2, 2015.

366 The China Study, Page 231.

367 The China Study, Page 31.

368 The China Study, Page

230.

369 Milton R. Mills, M.D., The Comparative Anatomy of Eating, www.VegSource. com, November 21, 2009.

370 Gorillas, Diet and Eating Habits, www.SeaWorld. org, Accessed July 28, 2011.

371 Ker Than, First Proof Gorillas Eat Monkeys?, National Geographic News, March 5, 2010.

372 John Coleman, Comparative Anatomy & Taxonomy, www.tierversuchsgegner. org, Accessed July 28, 2011.

373 The China Study, Page 111.

374 Deaths and Mortality, US Centers for Disease Control and Prevention, 2009.

375 The China Study, Page 111.

376 Walter Willett et. al., Dietary fat and heart disease study is seriously misleading, The Nutrition Source, Harvard University, March 19, 2019.

377 T. Colin Campbell, A plant-based diet and animal protein: questioning dietary fat and considering animal protein as the main cause of heart disease, Journal of Geriatric Cardiology, May 2017.

378 Fats and Cholesterol: Out with the Bad, In with the Good, The Nutrition Source, Harvard School of Public Health, www.hsph. Harvard.edu, Accessed July 14, 2011.

379 Caldwell B. Esselstyn, Jr., M.D., Prevent and Reverse Heart Disease, Penguin Group, 2007, Page 10.

380 The China Study, Page 116.

381 Prevent and Reverse Heart Disease, Page 17.

382 Prevent and Reverse Heart Disease, Page 92.

383 The China Study, Page 112.

384 The China Study, Page 124.

385 Prevent and Reverse Heart Disease, Page 104.

386 Same as above.

387 The China Study, Page 123.

388 Prevent and Reverse Heart Disease, Page 8.

389 The China Study, Page 123.

390 The China Study, Page 125.

391 Caldwell B. Esselstyn, Jr., M.D., Prevent and Reverse Heart Disease, Penguin Group, 2007.

392 Prevent and Reverse Heart Disease, Page 20.

393 Prevent and Reverse Heart Disease, Page 36.

394 The China Study, Page 128.

395 The China Study, Page 130.

396 The China Study, Page 78.

397 The China Study, Page 79.

398 The China Study, Page 132.

399 Prevent and Reverse Heart Disease, Page 58.

400 Prevent and Reverse Heart Disease, Page 33.

401 Prevent and Reverse Heart Disease, Page 40.

402 Prevent and Reverse Heart Disease, Page 42.

403 Prevent and Reverse Heart Disease, Page 82.

404 Prevent and Reverse Heart Disease, Page 85.

405 Dietary Guidelines for Americans 2020 – 2025, US Dept. of Agriculture and US Dept. of Health and Human Services, December 2020, Page 133.

406 Andrew Jacobs, Scientific Panel on New Dietary Guidelines Draws Criticism From Health Advocates, New York Times, June 17, 2020.

407 Same as above.

408 Dietary Guidelines for Americans 2020 – 2025, US Dept. of Agriculture and US Dept. of Health and Human Services, December 2020, Page 44.

409 Prevent and Reverse Heart Disease, Page 78.

410 Low-Fat Diet Not a Cure-All, The Nutrition Source, Harvard School of Public Health, www.hsph.Harvard.edu, Accessed July 29, 2011.

411 The China Study, Page 225.

412 The China Study, Page 272.

413 The China Study, Page 285.

414 Michael Greger, M.D., Dietary Cholesterol Affects Blood Cholesterol Levels, www.NutritionFacts.org, August 18, 2015.

415 Maggie Fox, Most teens well down road to heart disease, study finds, NBC News, April 1, 2013

416 The China Study, Page 12.

417 Deaths and Mortality, US Centers for Disease Control and Prevention, 2009.

418 Gina Kolata et al., Weighing Hope and Reality in Kennedy's Cancer Battle, New York Times, August 28, 2009

419 The China Study, Page 12.

420 Maggie Fox, Do I Have to Stop Eating Meat? Key Questions About WHO Group Report, www. NBCnews.com, October 26, 2015.

421 The China Study, Page 79.

422 The China Study, Page 85.

423 The China Study, Page 65.

424 The China Study, Page 62.

425 The China Study, Page 53.

426 The China Study, Page 352.

427 The China Study, Page 63.

428 The China Study, Page 65.

429 The China Study, Page 66.

430 The China Study, Page 235.

431 The China Study, Page 50.

432 The China Study, Page 71.

433 The China Study, Page 104.

434 Josh Harkinson, Turns Out Your "Hormone-Free" Milk Is Full of Sex Hormones, www.MotherJones. com, April 10, 2014.

435 Same as above.

436 The China Study, Page 165.

437 The China Study, Page 308.

438 The China Study, Page 182.

439 The China Study, Page 159.

440 The China Study, Page 87.

441 Same as above.

442 Martha Rosenberg, Early Puberty in Girls Is Becoming Epidemic and Getting Worse, www.AlterNet.org, June 11, 2016.

443 The China Study, Page 161.

444 Same as above.

445 Josh Harkinson, Turns Out Your "Hormone-Free" Milk Is Full of Sex Hormones, www.MotherJones. com, April 10, 2014.

446 The China Study, Page 87.

447 The China Study, Page 88.

448 The China Study, Page 162.

449 Florence Williams, The wonder of breasts, The Guardian, June 15, 2012.

450 Same as above.

451 The China Study, Page 167.

452 The China Study, Page 164.

453 The China Study, Page 89.

454 The China Study, Page 164.

455 Prostate Cancer, www. Cancer.org, November 22, 2010.

456 The China Study, Page 178.

457 Same as above.

458 The China Study, Page 179.

459 The China Study, Page 180.

460 Josh Harkinson, Turns Out Your "Hormone-Free" Milk Is Full of Sex Hormones, www.MotherJones. com, April 10, 2014.

461 Colorectal Cancer, www. Cancer.org, March 2, 2011.

462 The China Study, Page 172.

463 Maggie Fox, Do I Have to Stop Eating Meat? Key Questions About WHO Group Report, www. NBCnews.com, October 26, 2015.

464 The China Study, Page 172.

465 The China Study, Page 174.

466 The China Study, Page 176.

467 Joel Fuhrman, M.D., By 2050, diabetes prevalence will double or even triple, www.DiseaseProof.com, November 12, 2010.

468 Diabetes Overview, U.S. Department of Health and Human Services, www.diabetes.niddk.nih.gov, retieved August 10, 2010.

469 Same as above.

470 Joel Fuhrman, M.D., By 2050, diabetes prevalence will double or even triple, www.DiseaseProof.com, November 12, 2010.

471 Diabetes Overview, U.S. Department of Health and Human Services, www.diabetes.niddk.nih.gov, retieved August 10, 2010.

472 The China Study, Page 147.

473 Diabetes Overview, U.S. Department of Health and Human Services, www.diabetes.niddk.nih.gov, retieved August 10, 2010.

474 The China Study, Page 150.

475 Tom Philpott, Why Eating Meat Could Give You Diabetes, www.AlterNet. org, July 6, 2011.

476 The China Study, Page 152.

477 The China Study, Page 153.

478 Rachael Rettner, Diabetes Reversed in Patients on Extreme Diet, www.LiveScience.com, June 28, 2011.

479 Jennifer Warner, Refined Carbohydrates Up Diabetes Risk, WebMD Health News, November 26, 2007.

480 Joel Fuhrman, M.D., By 2050, diabetes prevalence will double or even triple, www.DiseaseProof.com, November 12, 2010.

481 The China Study, Page 74.

482 The China Study, Page 183.

483 The China Study, Page 188.

484 The China Study, Page 190.

485 The China Study, Page 191.

486 The China Study, Page 190.

487 The China Study, Page 152.

488 The China Study, Page 197.

489 The China Study, Page 196.

490 The China Study, Page 198.

491 The China Study, Page 200.

492 The China Study, Page 193.

493 The China Study, Page 193.

494 The China Study, Page 194.

495 James Gallagher, Salt linked to immune rebellion in study, BBC News, March 6, 2013.

496 Calcium and Milk: What's Best for Your Bones and Health, The Nutrition Source, www.hsph.Harvard.edu, Accessed August 8, 2011

497 The China Study, Page 206.

498 The China Study, Page 204.

499 The China Study, Page 205.

500 The China Study, Page 207.

501 The China Study, Page 208.

502 Same as above.

503 The China Study, Page 215.

504 Same as above.

505 The China Study, Page 216.

506 The China Study, Page 217.

507 Prevent and Reverse Heart Disease, Page 98.

508 Marshall Brain et al., How Viagra Works, www.science.howstuffworks.com, Accessed August 14, 2011.

509 Side Effects of Viagra, www.Drugs.com, Accessed August 15, 2011.

510 Oral Medications (PDE5 Inhibitors), www.Health.NYTimes.com, Accessed August 15, 2011.

511 The China Study, Page 218.

512 Same as above.

513 Same as above.

514 The China Study, Page 221.

515 The China Study, Page 220.

516 Same as above.

517 Prevent and Reverse Heart Disease, Page 97.

518 The China Study, Page 218.

519 What is High Blood Pressure?, www.Heart.org, June 6, 2012.

520 Nanci Hellmich, Millions don't have their blood pressure under control, www.USAtoday.com, September 4, 2012.

521 High blood pressure dangers: Hypertension's effects on your body, www.MayoClinic.com, Retrieved September 5, 2012.

522 Nanci Hellmich, Heart disease in men can be fought head-on, www.USAtoday.com, July 9, 2012.

523 Nanci Hellmich, Millions don't have their blood pressure under control, www.USAtoday.com, September 4, 2012.

524 Side Effects of High Blood Pressure Medications, www.WebMD.com, Accessed September 5, 2012.

525 Obesity and Overweight, US Centers for Disease Control and Prevention, Accessed September 12, 2021.

526 Nick Triggle, Global governments 'must get tough on obesity', BBC News, August 25, 2011.

527 Obesity and Overweight, US Centers for Disease Control and Prevention, Accessed September 12, 2021.

528 Zachary J. Ward, M.P.H. et. al., Projected U.S. State-Level Prevalence of Adult Obesity and Severe Obesity, New England Journal of Medicine, December 19, 2019.

529 Overweight and Obesity Statistics, National Institutes of Health, www.win.niddk.nih.gov, Accessed August 29, 2011.

530 Lindsey Tanner, Autism may be linked to obesity during pregnancy, USA Today, April 9, 2012.

531 James Gallagher, Being overweight 'linked to dementia', BBC News, May 3, 2011.

532 Overweight and Obesity Statistics, National Institutes of Health, www.win.niddk.nih.gov, Accessed August 29, 2011.

533 The China Study, Page 137.

534 Study: Obesity adds $190 billion in health costs, Reuters, April 30, 2012

535 Obesity Accounts for 21 Percent of U.S. Health Care Costs, Study Finds, www.ScienceDaily.com, Apr. 9, 2012.

http://

536 Same as above.

537 Overweight and Obesity Statistics, National Institutes of Health, www.win.niddk.nih.gov, Accessed August 29, 2011.

538 The China Study, Page 140.

539 Vongsvat Kosulwat, The Nutrition and Health

Transition in Thailand, Public Health Nutrition, December 22, 2006.

540 The China Study, Page 95.

541 Anneli Rufus, Is Eating Sugar Really That Bad for Us?, www.AlterNet.org, January 27, 2010.

542 The China Study, Page 98.

543 Anneli Rufus, Is Eating Sugar Really That Bad for Us?, www.AlterNet.org, January 27, 2010.

544 Greta Christina, Why Is It So Hard To Lose Weight?, www.AlterNet.org, January 25, 2011.

545 Amy Goodman, "When in Doubt, Add Bacon and Cheese": How the Food Industry Hijacked out Brains and Made Us Fat, www.AlterNet.org, August 10, 2009.

546 Laura Sanders, Junk Food Turns Rats Into Addicts, www.ScienceNews.org, October 21, 2009.

547 Tom Laskawy, High-fat diet may damage the brain, study finds, www.Grist.org, June 10, 2011.

548 Jennifer Matesa et al., A Radical New Definition of Addiction Creates a Big Storm, www.AlterNet.org, August 18, 2011.

549 Greta Christina, Why Is It So Hard To Lose Weight?, www.AlterNet.org, January 25, 2011.

550 Same as above.

551 The China Study, Page 310.

552 Sugar Linked To $1 Trillion In U.S. Healthcare Spending, Forbes, October 27, 2013.

553 Alan Farago, Killer Fact: 30-40 Percent of Health Care Spending in the U.S. Is Tied to Excess Sugar Consumption, www.Alter-

Net.org, January 10, 2014

554 Amy Goodman, "When in Doubt, Add Bacon and Cheese": How the Food Industry Hijacked out Brains and Made Us Fat, www.AlterNet.org, August 10, 2009.

555 Overweight in Children, American Heart Association, March 29, 2011.

556 The China Study, Page 137.

557 Same as above.

558 Sara Ellison et al., Panel Faults Food Packaging for Kid Obesity, The Wall Street Journal, December 7, 2005.

559 University of Michigan Health System, Children and TV, www.med.umich.edu/yourchild/topics/tv.htm, July 2009.

560 The Y Urges Healthier Habits for Kids during Childhood Obesity Awareness Month, Saratoga YMCA Newsletter, September 2011.

561 Same as above.

562 Overweight in Children, American Heart Association, March 29, 2011.

563 Maggie Fox, Most teens well down road to heart disease, study finds, NBC News, April 1, 2013

564 Leslie Orr, Eating Beef While Pregnant Could Lower Sperm Counts, University of Rochester Medical Center, www.AlterNet.org, June 28, 2007.

565 Cow's Milk: A Cruel and Unhealthy Product, www.PETA.org, Accessed September 4, 2011.

566 Processed food linked to lower kids' IQs, www.CNN.com, February 7, 2011.

567 Kristin Wartman, ADHD: It's the food, stupid, www.

Grist.org, March 28, 2011.

568 Tom Laskawy, Study links 'Western diet' with ADHD in kids, www.Grist.org, July 30, 2010.

569 Kristin Wartman, ADHD: It's the food, stupid, www.Grist.org, March 28, 2011.

570 David Gutierrez, Artificial food colors cause hyperactivity in children, www.NaturalNews.com, April 4, 2011.

571 Alan Schwarz et. al., A.D.H.D. Seen in 11 percent of U.S. Children as Diagnoses Rise, New York Times, March 31, 2013.

572 Martha Rosenberg, Nation of Pill Poppers: 19 Potentially Dangerous Drugs Pushed By Big Pharma, www.AlterNet.org, December 5, 2010.

573 Martha Rosenberg, Nation of Pill Poppers: 19 Potentially Dangerous Drugs Pushed By Big Pharma, www.AlterNet.org, December 5, 2010.

574 Kristin Wartman, ADHD: It's the food, stupid, www.Grist.org, March 28, 2011.

575 Same as above.

576 Jeremiah Smith, New Study supports link between diet and ADHD, www.NaturalNews.com, March 30, 2011.

577 Overweight in Children, American Heart Association, March 29, 2011.

578 Prevent and Reverse Heart Disease, Page 92.

579 National Health and Expenditure Data, www.CMS.gov, Accessed June 11, 2016.

580 Michael Pollan, The Mighty Rise of the Food Revolution, www.AlterNet.org, July 29, 2010.

581 Maggie Fox, New Diet

Proposals: Eat Your Veggies, Have Some Coffee, www.NBCnews.com, February 19, 2015.

582 T. Colin Campbell, PhD, USDA Adds to Your Confusion About What to Eat, www.NutritionStudies.org, July 17, 2015.

583 The China Study, Page 334.

584 The China Study, Page 333.

585 The China Study, Page 334.

586 The China Study, Page 333.

587 Daniela Perdomo, 100,000 Americans Die Each Year from Prescription Drugs, While Pharma Companies Get Rich, www.AlterNet.org, June 25, 2010.

588 The China Study, Page 334.

589 The China Study, Page 327.

590 The China Study, Page 328.

591 Kaki Holloway, America's Pill Popping Is Making Our Fish Anxious and Possibly Getting Into Our Vegetables, www.AlterNet.org, May 3, 2016.

592 Daniela Perdomo, 100,000 Americans Die Each Year from Prescription Drugs, While Pharma Companies Get Rich, www.AlterNet.org, June 25, 2010.

593 Same as above.

594 Same as above.

595 The China Study, Page 16.

596 Prevent and Reverse Heart Disease, Page 32.

597 Prevent and Reverse Heart Disease, Page 109.

598 The China Study, Page 131.

599 U.S. Weight Loss Market Worth $60.9 Billion, Marketdata Enterprises, Inc., May 09, 2011.

600 Dr. Deborah Wilson, Maintaining a Healthy Weight, www.peta.org, Accessed August 28, 2011.

601 Judith Matz, Why Diets Make You Fatter -- And What to Do About It, Psychotherapy Networker, January 29, 2011.

602 Martha Rosenberg, Can Drugs Make Americans Less Fat? Not Likely, www.AlterNet.com, July 26, 2010.

603 Judith Matz, Why Diets Make You Fatter -- And What to Do About It, Psychotherapy Networker, January 29, 2011.

604 Dr. Deborah Wilson, Maintaining a Healthy Weight, www.peta.org, Accessed August 28, 2011.

605 The China Study, Page 95.

606 Judith Matz, Why Diets Make You Fatter -- And What to Do About It, Psychotherapy Networker, January 29, 2011.

607 Same as above.

608 Same as above.

609 The China Study, Page 139.

610 Dr. Deborah Wilson, Maintaining a Healthy Weight, www.peta.org, Accessed August 28, 2011.

611 The China Study, Page 98.

612 Carla K. Johnson, Study: Eating more fiber could mean longer life, www.CBSnews.com, February 15, 2011.

613 Kathleen M. Zelman, MPH, Fiber: How Much Do You Need?, www.wedMD.com, Accessed August 28, 2013.

614 The China Study, Page 141.

615 The China Study, Page 138.

616 Judith Matz, Why Diets Make You Fatter -- And What to Do About It, Psychotherapy Networker, January 29, 2011.

617 The China Study, Page 101.

618 The China Study, Page 140.

619 Prevent and Reverse Heart Disease, Page 30.

620 The China Study, Page 141.

621 The China Study, Page 229.

622 Louise Atkinson, Ignore all that hype about anti-oxidant supplements: Why daily vitamin pills can INCREASE your risk of disease, www.DailyMail.co.uk, May 21, 2012.

623 Same as above.

624 The China Study, Page 228.

625 The China Study, Page 232.

626 Chris Shugart, Poison Protein, Kaayla T. Daniel, Ph.D. Exposes the Whole Soy Story, www.T-Mag.com, February 27, 2004.

627 Same as above.

628 Tara Lohan, The War on Soy: Why the 'Miracle Food' May Be a Health Risk and Environmental Nightmare, www.AlterNet.com, November 21, 2009.

629 Chris Shugart, Poison Protein, Kaayla T. Daniel, Ph.D. Exposes the Whole Soy Story, www.T-Mag.com, February 27, 2004.

630 Tara Lohan, The War on Soy: Why the 'Miracle Food' May Be a Health Risk and Environmental Nightmare, www.AlterNet.com, November 21, 2009.

631 Chris Shugart, Poison Protein, Kaayla T. Daniel,

Ph.D. Exposes the Whole Soy Story, www.T-Mag.com, February 27, 2004.

632 Same as above.

633 Same as above.

634 Prevent and Reverse Heart Disease, Page 61.

635 Katherine Harmon, Ultra Marathons Might Be Ultra Bad for your Heart, Scientific American, June 4, 2012.

636 Kelly Kennedy, More companies using incentives to prod employees to fitness, USA Today, November 24, 2011.

637 Same as above.

638 Study: Exercise Has Long-Lasting Effect on Depression, Duke Today, September 22, 2000.

639 Mary Elizabeth Williams, Is Sitting Worse Than Smoking?, www.AlterNet.org, January 10, 2013.

640 Dani Veracity, The hidden dangers of caffeine: How coffee causes exhaustion, fatigue and addiction, www.NaturalNews.com, October 11, 2005.

641 Health Benefits of Ginger Tea and Side Effects, www.HealthBuzzOnline.com, March 2011.

642 Amy Goodman, "When in Doubt, Add Bacon and Cheese": How the Food Industry Hijacked out Brains and Made Us Fat, www.AlterNet.org, August 10, 2009.

643 Michael Pollan, The Mighty Rise of the Food Revolution, www.AlterNet.org, July 29, 2010.

644 Same as above.

645 Bernhard Waltzl et al., Modulation of human T–lymphocyte functions by the consumption of carotenoid–rich vegetables,

British Journal of Nutrition, 82: 383-389, 1999.

646 Hyunju Kim et. al., Plant-based diets, pescatarian diets and COVID-19 severity: a population-based case–control study in six countries, BMJ Nutrition, Prevention & Health, June 7, 2021.

647 Brian Merchant, Scientists Crack Code of How to Live Past 100: Vegetarianism, Religion, Good Genes, www.AlterNet.org, July 2, 2010.

648 Kathleen M. Zelman, The Anti-Aging Diet, www.WebMD.com, Accessed January 6, 2012.

649 Scientists take important step toward the proverbial fountain of youth, www.physorg.com, December 22, 2009.

650 Rozalyn M. Anderson et al, Calorie Restriction and Aging: Studies in Mice and Monkeys, Toxicologic Pathology, 37: 47-51, 2009.

651 Vegetarians soy much smarter, www.DailyTelegraph.com.au, January 22, 2007.

652 'Beer belly' link to Alzheimer's, BBC News, May 20, 2010.

653 Vegetarians soy much smarter, www.DailyTelegraph.com.au, January 22, 2007.

654 Eating Vegetables Gives Skin a More Healthy Glow Than the Sun, Study Shows, www.ScienceDaily.com, January 11, 2011.

655 Alexandra Sifferlin, Study Finds Dramatic Rise in Skin Cancer Among Young Adults, www.Heartland.Time.com, April 2, 2012.

656 The China Study, Page 103.

657 The China Study, Page 308.

658 Kathy Freston, You Call Yourself a Progressive -- But You Still Eat Meat?, www.AlterNet.org, March 14, 2007.

659 Prevent and Reverse Heart Disease, Page 38.

660 Judith Matz, Why Diets Make You Fatter -- And What to Do About It, Psychotherapy Networker, January 29, 2011.

661 Salynn Boyles, Study: Overweight People Live Longer, WebMD Health News, June 25, 2009.

662 Judith Beck, Ph.D., Five Steps to Developing a Healthy Relationship With Food, Psychotherapy Networker, January 27, 2011.

663 Cognitive-Behavior Therapy, National Association of Cognitive-Behavioral Therapists, www.nacbt.org, Accessed November 19, 2011.

664 Judith Beck, Ph.D., Five Steps to Developing a Healthy Relationship With Food, Psychotherapy Networker, January 27, 2011.

665 Elizabeth Cohen, Train your brain to crave healthy foods, www.CNN.com, August 4, 2011.

666 Prevent and Reverse Heart Disease, Page 76.

667 Jess McNally, Can Vegetarianism Save the World? Nitty-gritty, Stanford Magazine, January/February 2010.

668 Steven Stosny, PhD, The Secret to Breaking Out of Our Most Destructive Habits, www.AlterNet.org, November 7, 2013.

669 Same as above.

670 Same as above.

671 Bruce Ecker et al, Can You Rewire Your Brain to Change Bad Habits, Thoughts, and Feelings?, www.AlterNet.org, July 10, 2013.

672 Brent Atkinson, PhD, Why People Behave in Self-Defeating, Irrational Ways and How to Really Change, www.AlterNet.org, February 27, 2014.

673 Same as above.

674 Richard Black, Food push urged to avoid hunger, BBC News, March 25, 2010.

675 Stephan A. Schwartz, The Coming Food Crisis—The Social Tsunami Headed Our Way, Explore: The Journal of Science and Healing, September 2011.

676 Lester Brown, Why world food prices may keep climbing, www.Grist.org, March 10, 2011.

677 John Feffer, seven Billion People By October: How Are We Going to Feed Ourselves?, www.AlterNet.org, September 1, 2011.

678 U.S. could feed 800 million people with grain that livestock eat, Cornell ecologist advises animal scientists, Cornell University Science News, August 7, 1997.

679 Kathy Freston, The Startling Effects of Going Vegetarian for Just One Day, Huffington Post, April 2, 2009.

680 John Roach, To feed four billion more, skip meat, milk and eggs, study says, NBC News, August 5, 2013.

http://www.nbcnews.com

681 Felicity Carus, UN urges global move to meat and dairy-free diet, www. Guardian.co.uk, June 2, 2010.

682 Feeding the World While Protecting the Planet: Global Plan for Sustainable Agriculture, www.ScienceDaily.com, October 12, 2011.

683 Jill Richardson, Groundbreaking New UN Report on How to Feed the World's Hungry: Ditch Corporate-Controlled Agriculture, www.AlterNet.org, March 8, 2011.

684 Same as above

685 Jill Richardson, Is Obama's Plan for Tackling Hunger Just Another Chance for Big Ag and Biotech to Cash In?, www.AlterNet.org, August 10, 2009.

686 Jill Richardson, Groundbreaking New UN Report on How to Feed the World's Hungry: Ditch Corporate-Controlled Agriculture, www.AlterNet.org, March 8, 2011.

687 Same as above.

688 Same as above.

689 An HSUS Report: The Welfare of Animals In the Meat, Egg, and Dairy Industries, The Humane Society of the United States, www.HumaneSociety.org, Accessed January 21, 2012.

690 Marc Bekoff, Ph.D., Do Animals Have Emotions?, The Bark, Issue #42, May/Jun 2007.

691 Same as above.

692 Same as above.

693 Tara Lohan, Got Milk? A Disturbing Look at the Dairy Industry, www.AlterNet.org, January 26, 2010.

694 An HSUS Report: The Welfare of Animals In the Meat, Egg, and Dairy Industries, The Humane Society of the United States, www.HumaneSociety.org, Accessed January 21, 2012.

695 Factory Farming: Cruelty to Animals, People for the Ethical Treatment of Animals, www.PETA.org, Accessed January 24, 2012.

696 An HSUS Report: The Welfare of Calves in the Beef Industry, The Humane Society of the United States, www.HumaneSociety.org, Accessed January 21, 2012.

697 Same as above.

698 An HSUS Report: The Welfare of Cows in the Dairy Industry, The Humane Society of the United States, www.HumaneSociety.org, Accessed January 21, 2012.

699 Same as above.

700 Same as above.

701 Same as above.

702 Tara Lohan, Got Milk? A Disturbing Look at the Dairy Industry, www.AlterNet.org, January 26, 2010.

703 Factory Farming: Cruelty to Animals, People for the Ethical Treatment of Animals, www.PETA.org, Accessed January 24, 2012.

704 An HSUS Report: The Welfare of Cows in the Dairy Industry, The Humane Society of the United States, www.HumaneSociety.org, Accessed January 21, 2012.

705 Understanding the Basics of Mastitis, Virginia Cooperative Extension, www.pubs.vt.edu, Accessed January 26, 2012.

706 An HSUS Report: The Welfare of Cows in the Dairy Industry, The Humane Society of the United States, www.HumaneSo-

ciety.org, Accessed January 21, 2012.

707 Same as above.

708 Tara Lohan, Got Milk? A Disturbing Look at the Dairy Industry, www.AlterNet.org, January 26, 2010.

709 Factory Farming: Cruelty to Animals, People for the Ethical Treatment of Animals, www.PETA.org, Accessed January 24, 2012.

710 Same as above.

711 An HSUS Report: The Welfare of Calves in the Beef Industry, The Humane Society of the United States, www.HumaneSociety.org, Accessed January 21, 2012.

712 Factory Farming: Cruelty to Animals, People for the Ethical Treatment of Animals, www.PETA.org, Accessed January 24, 2012.

713 Inside the Slaughterhouse, www.PBS.org/Frontline/, Accessed January 27, 2012.

714 Factory Farming: Cruelty to Animals, People for the Ethical Treatment of Animals, www.PETA.org, Accessed January 24, 2012.

715 Same as above.

716 Gail A. Eisnitz, Slaughterhouse, Prometheus Books, Page 310, 1997.

717 Temple Grandin, Welfare During Slaughter without stunning (Kosher or Halal) differences between Sheep and Cattle, www.Grandin.com, Accessed December 21, 2010.

718 John Robbins, Diet for a New America, Stillpoint Publishing, 1987.

719 An HSUS Report: The Welfare of Animals in the Pig Industry, The Humane Society of the United States, www.HumaneSo-

ciety.org, Accessed January 21, 2012.

720 An HSUS Report: The Welfare of Piglets in the Pig Industry, The Humane Society of the United States, www.HumaneSociety.org, Accessed January 21, 2012.

721 An HSUS Report: The Welfare of Animals in the Pig Industry, The Humane Society of the United States, www.HumaneSociety.org, Accessed January 21, 2012.

722 Same as above.

723 Factory Farming: Cruelty to Animals, People for the Ethical Treatment of Animals, www.PETA.org, Accessed January 24, 2012.

724 An HSUS Report: The Welfare of Animals in the Pig Industry, The Humane Society of the United States, www.HumaneSociety.org, Accessed January 21, 2012.

725 An HSUS Report: The Welfare of Sows Used for Breeding in the Pig Industry, The Humane Society of the United States, www. HumaneSociety.org, Accessed January 21, 2012.

726 An HSUS Report: The Welfare of Animals in the Pig Industry, The Humane Society of the United States, www.HumaneSociety.org, Accessed January 21, 2012.

727 Factory Farming: Cruelty to Animals, People for the Ethical Treatment of Animals, www.PETA.org, Accessed January 24, 2012.

728 An HSUS Report: The Welfare of Animals in the Pig Industry, The Humane Society of the United States, www.HumaneSociety.org, Accessed January 21, 2012.

729 Factory Farming: Cruelty to Animals, People for the Ethical Treatment of Animals, www.PETA.org, Accessed January 24, 2012.

730 Same as above.

731 Same as above.

732 Same as above.

733 Same as above.

734 An HSUS Report: The Welfare of Animals in the Aquaculture Industry, The Humane Society of the United States, www.HumaneSociety.org, Accessed January 21, 2012.

735 Same as above.

736 Michael Hanlon, Do fish have feelings too? It's a slippery question for science, www.DailyMail.co.uk, March 8, 2021.

737 An HSUS Report: The Welfare of Animals in the Aquaculture Industry, The Humane Society of the United States, www.HumaneSociety.org, Accessed January 21, 2012.

738 Factory Farming: Cruelty to Animals, People for the Ethical Treatment of Animals, www.PETA.org, Accessed January 24, 2012.

739 An HSUS Report: The Welfare of Animals in the Aquaculture Industry, The Humane Society of the United States, www.HumaneSociety.org, Accessed January 21, 2012.

740 Factory Farming: Cruelty to Animals, People for the Ethical Treatment of Animals, www.PETA.org, Accessed January 24, 2012.

741 An HSUS Report: The Welfare of Animals in the Aquaculture Industry, The Humane Society of the United States, www.HumaneSociety.org, Accessed January 21, 2012.

742 Same as above.

743 Chloe J., Are Chicken And Fish as Unhealthy as Red Meat?, www.AlterNet. org, September 23, 2009.

744 Factory Farming: Cruelty to Animals, People for the Ethical Treatment of Animals, www.PETA.org, Accessed January 24, 2012.

745 An HSUS Report: The Welfare of Animals in the Aquaculture Industry, The Humane Society of the United States, www.HumaneSociety.org, Accessed January 21, 2012.

746 Chloe J., Are Chicken And Fish as Unhealthy as Red Meat?, www.AlterNet. org, September 23, 2009.

747 The Organic and Free-Range Myth, People for the Ethical Treatment of Animals, www.PETA.org, Accessed January 24, 2012.

748 Same as above.

749 Same as above.

750 Same as above.

751 Same as above.

752 Factory Farming: Cruelty to Animals, People for the Ethical Treatment of Animals, www.PETA.org, Accessed January 24, 2012.

753 Tom Laskawy, Baby steps: USDA tiptoes toward fighting animal cruelty, www.Grist.org, August 17, 2011.

754 Veal from Farm to Table, United States Department of Agriculture, https://www.fsis.usda.gov/food-safety/safe-food-handling-and-preparation/meat/veal-farm-table,

Accessed December 27, 2021.

755 Kristin Wartman, The hatin' spoonful: Big Food refuses to swallow guidelines, www.Grist.org, August 1, 2011.

756 Kristin Wartman, Life, liberty and the pursuit of fatness, www.Grist.org, January 14, 2011.

757 Tom Philpott, The fast-food industry's $4.2 billion marketing blitz, www.Grist.org, November 10, 2010.

758 The China Study, Page 293.

759 How to Read Food Labels, www.ScientificPsychic.com, Accessed February 16, 2012.

760 Sarah Parsons, Many "All Natural" Foods Are Actually Heavily Processed, www.Change.org, September 29, 2010.

761 "Natural" Label on Genetically Engineered Products, Center for Food Safety, July 19, 2011.

762 Amanda Griscom, Organics Program Weakened Under Bush Administration Changes, Activists say, www.Grist.org, May 19, 2004.

763 How to Read Food Labels, www.ScientificPsychic.com, Accessed February 16, 2012.

764 Jill Richardson, Meet the Food Industry Front Groups That Push for Carcinogens in Your Food, www.AlterNet .org, July 6, 2010.

765 The China Study, Page 297.

766 Jill Richardson, Meet the Food Industry Front Groups That Push for Carcinogens in Your Food, www.AlterNet .org, July 6, 2010.

767 The China Study, Page 321.

768 Fighting for a strong "organic" label, Consumer Reports, February 2006.

769 Jennifer Lance, Bush Administration Actions that Weakened USDA Organic Label, Food and Cuisine, July 12, 2009.

770 Michele Simon, How did pizza become a vegetable? Blame lobbyists, www.Grist.org, November 18, 2011.

771 Michael Moss, The Hard Sell on Salt, New York Times, May 29, 2010.

772 The China Study, Page 312.

773 The China Study, Page 313.

774 The China Study, Page 314.

775 Lindsay Abrams, The Republican War on Vegetables, www.AlterNet.org, June 26, 2015.

776 Same as above.

777 Ronald K.L. Collins et. al., "Veggie-Libel" Law Still Poses a Threat, Center for Science in the Public Interest, Accessed February 17, 2012.

778 Same as above.

779 Rick Weiss, Report Targets Costs Of Factory Farming, Washington Post, April 30, 2008.

780 Jill Richardson, How America Is Making the Whole World Fat and Unhealthy, www.AlterNet. org, March 7, 2012.

781 Reynard Loki, People Are Dying from Contaminated Food, but Obama and Congress Don't Seem to Care, www.AlterNet.org, August 2, 2015.

782 Bryan Walsh, The Food Safety Bill Finally Passes, But It's Just the First Step, www.Time.com, December 22, 2010.

783 Reynard Loki, People Are Dying from Contaminated Food, but Obama and Congress Don't Seem to

Care, www.AlterNet.org, August 2, 2015.

784 Same as above.

785 James Vicini, Supreme Court overturns California slaughterhouse law, www.Reuters.com, January 23, 2012.

786 Stephanie Armour et al, Food Sickens Millions as Company-Paid Checks Find It Safe, Bloomberg Markets Magazine, October 11, 2012.

787 Same as above.

788 Same as above.

789 Same as above.

790 Chris Edwards, Agricultural Subsidies, The Cato Institute, June 2009.

791 2011 Farm Subsidy Database, Environmental Working Group, www.farm.EWG.org, Accessed March 1, 2012.

792 Chris Edwards, Agricultural Subsidies, The Cato Institute, June 2009.

793 Same as above.

794 Tim Wise, The Only Real Way to Fix Immigration, www.AlterNet.org, May 22, 2010.

795 Same as above.

796 Jill Richardson, Salmonella in Peanut Butter, Melamine in Milk -- How Do We Know What's Safe to Eat?, www.AlterNet.org, February 24, 2009.

797 Chris Edwards, Agricultural Subsidies, The Cato Institute, June 2009.

798 Same as above.

799 Same as above.

800 Same as above.

801 Same as above.

802 Same as above.

803 William Peters, A More Perfect Union: The Making of the United States Constitution, Page 43, Crown Publishers, 1987.

804 Jill Richardson, How America Is Making the Whole World Fat and Unhealthy, www.AlterNet.org, March 7, 2012.

805 Country Comparison: Obesity - Adult Prevalence Rate, Central Intelligence Agency, www.CIA.gov, Assessed April 2, 2013.

806 Same as above.

807 Tim Wise, The Only Real Way to Fix Immigration, www.AlterNet.org, May 22, 2010

808 Organic farming can yield more than conventional ag, says analysis, www.Grist.org, July 12, 2007

809 Claire Hope Cummings, Artificial Foods and Corporate Crops: Can We Escape the 'Frankenstate'?, Beacon Press, May 2, 2008.

810 Same as above.

811 John Vidal, The future of food, The Observer, January 21, 2012.

812 Same as above.

813 Same as above.

814 Hazel Henderson, Desert-Greening: The Next Big Thing for Green Investors, www.GreenMoney-Journal.com, August 2014.

815 Same as above.

816 Same as above.

817 Dana Goodyear, A New Leaf, The New Yorker, November 2, 2015.

818 Same as above.

819 Same as above.

820 UN unveils ambitious 'green' food programme, www.Grist.org, February 18, 2009.

821 Russell Redman, Organic food sales jump nearly 13% to record high in 2020, SuperMarketNews.com, May 25, 2021.

822 Kim Severson et al, It's Organic, but Does That Mean It's Safer?, New York Times, March 4, 2009.

INDEX

Index

CPSIA information can be obtained
at www.ICGtesting.com
Printed in the USA
BVHW081129200722
642493BV00015B/764